Resource Guide
to Accompany
Assessment of Children
Cognitive Foundations
Fifth Edition

Jerome M. Sattler
San Diego State University

Jerome M. Sattler, Publisher, Inc.
San Diego

Editorial Services: Sally Lifland and Quica Ostrander, Lifland et al., Bookmakers
Interior Design: Jerome M. Sattler and Sally Lifland
Proofreaders: Sheryl Avruch, Jeanne Yost, Gail Magin, and David N. Sattler
Production Coordinators: Sally Lifland and Jerome M. Sattler
Compositor: Omegatype Typography, Inc.
Cover Printer: Edwards Brothers Malloy
Printer and Binder: Edwards Brothers Malloy

This text was set in Times Roman and Helvetica, printed on 45# Utopia Filmcote, Perfect bind.

Assessment of Children: Cognitive Foundations, Fifth Edition: ISBN: 978-0-9702671-4-6
Resource Guide to Accompany Assessment of Children: Cognitive Foundations, Fifth Edition:
   ISBN: 978-0-9702671-5-3
Combined *Assessment of Children: Cognitive Foundations, Fifth Edition* and *Resource Guide to Accompany
   Assessment of Children: Cognitive Foundations, Fifth Edition:* ISBN: 978-0-9702671-6-0

16   15   14   13   12   11   10   9   8   7
Printed in the United States of America

CONTENTS

APPENDIX A

TABLES FOR THE WISC–IV

Table A-1
Confidence Intervals for WISC–IV Full Scale IQs and Composite Scores Based on Obtained Score Only

Age	Index or Full Scale	Confidence level				
		68%	85%	90%	95%	99%
6 (6-0-0 through 6-11-30)	Verbal Comprehension	±5	±7	±8	±9	±12
	Perceptual Reasoning	±5	±7	±8	±9	±12
	Working Memory	±5	±7	±7	±9	±11
	Processing Speed	±7	±9	±11	±13	±16
	Full Scale	±3	±5	±5	±6	±8
7 (7-0-0 through 7-11-30)	Verbal Comprehension	±5	±7	±7	±9	±11
	Perceptual Reasoning	±5	±7	±7	±9	±11
	Working Memory	±5	±7	±8	±10	±13
	Processing Speed	±7	±10	±11	±13	±17
	Full Scale	±3	±5	±5	±6	±8
8 (8-0-0 through 8-11-30)	Verbal Comprehension	±5	±7	±7	±9	±11
	Perceptual Reasoning	±4	±6	±7	±8	±11
	Working Memory	±5	±7	±8	±9	±12
	Processing Speed	±6	±8	±9	±11	±14
	Full Scale	±3	±4	±5	±6	±7
9 (9-0-0 through 9-11-30)	Verbal Comprehension	±4	±6	±7	±8	±10
	Perceptual Reasoning	±4	±6	±7	±8	±11
	Working Memory	±5	±7	±7	±9	±11
	Processing Speed	±5	±8	±9	±10	±13
	Full Scale	±3	±4	±5	±6	±7
10 (10-0-0 through 10-11-30)	Verbal Comprehension	±4	±6	±7	±8	±10
	Perceptual Reasoning	±4	±6	±7	±8	±11
	Working Memory	±5	±7	±7	±9	±11
	Processing Speed	±5	±7	±8	±10	±13
	Full Scale	±3	±4	±5	±6	±7
11 (11-0-0 through 11-11-30)	Verbal Comprehension	±4	±6	±7	±8	±11
	Perceptual Reasoning	±4	±6	±7	±8	±11
	Working Memory	±5	±7	±7	±9	±11
	Processing Speed	±5	±7	±8	±10	±13
	Full Scale	±3	±4	±5	±6	±7
12 (12-0-0 through 12-11-30)	Verbal Comprehension	±4	±5	±6	±7	±9
	Perceptual Reasoning	±4	±6	±7	±8	±11
	Working Memory	±4	±6	±7	±8	±11
	Processing Speed	±5	±8	±9	±10	±13
	Full Scale	±3	±4	±5	±6	±7
13 (13-0-0 through 13-11-30)	Verbal Comprehension	±4	±6	±7	±8	±10
	Perceptual Reasoning	±4	±6	±7	±8	±11
	Working Memory	±5	±7	±8	±9	±12
	Processing Speed	±5	±8	±9	±10	±13
	Full Scale	±3	±4	±5	±6	±7

(*Continued*)

Table A-1 (Continued)

Age	Index or Full Scale	Confidence level				
		68%	85%	90%	95%	99%
14	Verbal Comprehension	±4	±5	±6	±7	±9
(14-0-0 through 14-11-30)	Perceptual Reasoning	±5	±7	±7	±9	±11
	Working Memory	±4	±6	±7	±8	±11
	Processing Speed	±5	±8	±9	±10	±13
	Full Scale	±3	±4	±5	±6	±7
15	Verbal Comprehension	±4	±5	±6	±7	±9
(15-0-0 through 15-11-30)	Perceptual Reasoning	±5	±7	±7	±9	±11
	Working Memory	±5	±7	±7	±9	±11
	Processing Speed	±5	±7	±8	±10	±13
	Full Scale	±3	±4	±5	±6	±7
16	Verbal Comprehension	±4	±5	±6	±7	±9
(16-0-0 through 16-11-30)	Perceptual Reasoning	±5	±7	±8	±9	±12
	Working Memory	±4	±6	±7	±8	±11
	Processing Speed	±5	±8	±9	±10	±13
	Full Scale	±3	±4	±5	±6	±7
Average	Verbal Comprehension	±4	±6	±7	±8	±10
	Perceptual Reasoning	±5	±6	±7	±9	±11
	Working Memory	±5	±7	±8	±9	±12
	Processing Speed	±6	±8	±9	±11	±14
	Full Scale	±3	±4	±5	±6	±7

Note. Chapter 4 describes the procedure for computing confidence intervals. For example, for the WISC–IV Verbal Comprehension Index, the confidence intervals are obtained using the following procedure: The appropriate SEM for the child's age is located in Table 4.3 of the Technical Manual. For a 6-year-old child, the SEM = 4.50 for the Verbal Comprehension Index. This SEM is multiplied by the respective z values in order to obtain the confidence interval for the desired level. At the 68% confidence level, the SEM is multiplied by ±1 (±1 × 4.50 = ±5). At the 85% level, the SEM is multiplied by ±1.44 (±1.44 × 4.50 = ±7). At the 90% level, the SEM is multiplied by ±1.65 (±1.65 × 4.50 = ±8). At the 95% level, the SEM is multiplied by ±1.96 (±1.96 × 4.50 = ±9). At the 99% level, the SEM is multiplied by ±2.58 (±2.58 × 4.50 = ±12).

Table A-2
Differences Between WISC–IV Subtest Scaled Scores and Between Index Scores Required for Statistical Significance at the .05 and .01 Levels of Significance for the 11 Age Groups and the Total Group
(.05 significance level above diagonal, .01 significance level below diagonal)

Age 6

Subtest	BD	SI	DS	PCn	CD	VC	LN	MR	CO	SS	PCm	CA	IN	AR	WR	VCI	PRI	WMI	PSI
BD	—	4	4	4	4	4	3	4	4	4	4	4	4	4	4	—	—	—	—
SI	5	—	4	4	4	4	3	4	4	4	4	4	4	4	4	—	—	—	—
DS	5	5	—	4	4	4	3	3	4	4	4	4	4	4	4	—	—	—	—
PCn	5	5	5	—	4	4	3	4	4	4	4	4	4	4	4	—	—	—	—
CD	6	6	6	6	—	4	4	4	5	5	4	4	4	4	5	—	—	—	—
VC	5	5	5	5	6	—	3	4	4	4	4	4	4	4	4	—	—	—	—
LN	4	4	4	4	5	4	—	3	4	4	3	3	3	3	4	—	—	—	—
MR	5	5	4	5	5	5	4	—	4	4	4	4	4	3	4	—	—	—	—
CO	5	5	5	5	6	5	5	5	—	4	4	4	4	4	4	—	—	—	—
SS	5	5	5	5	6	5	5	5	5	—	4	4	4	4	4	—	—	—	—
PCm	5	5	5	5	6	5	4	5	5	5	—	4	4	4	4	—	—	—	—
CA	5	5	5	5	6	5	4	5	5	5	5	—	4	4	4	—	—	—	—
IN	5	5	5	5	6	5	4	5	5	5	5	5	—	4	4	—	—	—	—
AR	5	5	5	5	6	5	4	4	5	5	5	5	5	—	4	—	—	—	—
WR	5	5	5	5	6	5	5	5	5	6	5	5	5	5	—	—	—	—	—
VCI	—	—	—	—	—	—	—	—	—	—	—	—	—	—	—	—	13	13	15
PRI	—	—	—	—	—	—	—	—	—	—	—	—	—	—	—	17	—	13	15
WMI	—	—	—	—	—	—	—	—	—	—	—	—	—	—	—	16	16	—	15
PSI	—	—	—	—	—	—	—	—	—	—	—	—	—	—	—	20	20	20	—

Age 7

Subtest	BD	SI	DS	PCn	CD	VC	LN	MR	CO	SS	PCm	CA	IN	AR	WR	VCI	PRI	WMI	PSI
BD	—	4	4	4	4	4	3	4	4	4	4	4	4	3	4	—	—	—	—
SI	5	—	4	4	4	4	3	4	4	4	4	4	4	3	4	—	—	—	—
DS	5	5	—	4	5	4	4	4	4	4	4	4	4	4	4	—	—	—	—
PCn	5	5	5	—	4	4	3	4	4	4	4	4	4	3	4	—	—	—	—
CD	6	6	6	6	—	4	4	4	5	5	4	4	5	4	5	—	—	—	—
VC	5	5	5	5	6	—	3	4	4	4	4	4	4	3	4	—	—	—	—
LN	4	4	5	4	5	4	—	3	4	4	3	3	4	3	4	—	—	—	—
MR	5	5	5	5	5	5	4	—	4	4	4	4	4	3	4	—	—	—	—
CO	6	6	6	5	6	5	5	5	—	5	4	4	5	4	4	—	—	—	—
SS	5	5	5	5	6	5	5	5	6	—	4	4	4	4	4	—	—	—	—
PCm	5	5	5	5	6	5	4	5	5	5	—	4	4	3	4	—	—	—	—
CA	5	5	5	5	6	5	4	5	6	5	5	—	4	4	4	—	—	—	—
IN	5	5	5	5	6	5	5	5	6	6	5	5	—	4	4	—	—	—	—
AR	4	4	5	4	5	4	4	4	5	5	4	5	5	—	4	—	—	—	—
WR	5	5	5	5	6	5	5	5	6	5	5	5	5	5	—	—	—	—	—
VCI	—	—	—	—	—	—	—	—	—	—	—	—	—	—	—	—	12	13	16
PRI	—	—	—	—	—	—	—	—	—	—	—	—	—	—	—	16	—	13	16
WMI	—	—	—	—	—	—	—	—	—	—	—	—	—	—	—	17	17	—	16
PSI	—	—	—	—	—	—	—	—	—	—	—	—	—	—	—	21	21	21	—

(Continued)

Table A-2 (Continued)

Age 8

Subtest	BD	SI	DS	PCn	CD	VC	LN	MR	CO	SS	PCm	CA	IN	AR	WR	VCI	PRI	WMI	PSI
BD	—	4	4	4	4	4	3	3	4	4	4	4	4	4	4	—	—	—	—
SI	5	—	4	4	4	4	3	3	4	4	4	4	4	4	4	—	—	—	—
DS	5	5	—	4	4	4	3	3	4	4	4	4	4	4	4	—	—	—	—
PCn	5	5	5	—	4	4	4	4	4	4	4	4	4	4	4	—	—	—	—
CD	5	5	5	5	—	4	4	3	4	4	4	4	4	4	4	—	—	—	—
VC	5	5	5	5	5	—	3	3	4	4	4	4	4	4	4	—	—	—	—
LN	4	4	4	5	5	4	—	3	4	4	3	4	4	3	4	—	—	—	—
MR	4	4	4	5	4	4	4	—	4	3	3	4	3	3	3	—	—	—	—
CO	5	5	5	5	5	5	5	5	—	4	4	5	4	4	4	—	—	—	—
SS	5	5	5	5	5	5	5	4	5	—	4	4	4	4	4	—	—	—	—
PCm	5	5	5	5	5	5	4	4	5	5	—	4	4	4	4	—	—	—	—
CA	5	5	6	6	6	5	5	5	6	6	6	—	4	4	4	—	—	—	—
IN	5	5	5	5	5	5	5	4	5	5	5	6	—	4	4	—	—	—	—
AR	5	5	5	5	5	5	4	4	5	5	5	6	5	—	4	—	—	—	—
WR	5	5	5	5	5	5	5	4	5	5	5	6	5	5	—	—	—	—	—
VCI	—	—	—	—	—	—	—	—	—	—	—	—	—	—	—	—	12	13	14
PRI	—	—	—	—	—	—	—	—	—	—	—	—	—	—	—	15	—	12	13
WMI	—	—	—	—	—	—	—	—	—	—	—	—	—	—	—	16	16	—	14
PSI	—	—	—	—	—	—	—	—	—	—	—	—	—	—	—	18	17	18	—

Age 9

Subtest	BD	SI	DS	PCn	CD	VC	LN	MR	CO	SS	PCm	CA	IN	AR	WR	VCI	PRI	WMI	PSI
BD	—	4	4	4	4	4	3	3	4	4	4	4	4	3	4	—	—	—	—
SI	5	—	3	4	4	3	3	3	4	4	4	4	4	3	4	—	—	—	—
DS	5	4	—	4	4	3	3	3	4	4	4	4	4	3	4	—	—	—	—
PCn	5	5	5	—	4	4	3	3	4	4	4	4	4	4	4	—	—	—	—
CD	5	5	5	5	—	4	3	3	4	4	4	4	4	4	4	—	—	—	—
VC	5	4	4	5	5	—	3	3	4	4	4	4	4	3	4	—	—	—	—
LN	4	4	4	4	4	4	—	3	4	3	4	4	3	3	4	—	—	—	—
MR	4	4	4	4	4	4	4	—	4	3	4	4	3	3	4	—	—	—	—
CO	5	5	5	5	5	5	5	5	—	4	4	4	4	4	4	—	—	—	—
SS	5	5	5	5	5	5	4	4	5	—	4	4	4	4	4	—	—	—	—
PCm	5	5	5	5	5	5	5	5	5	5	—	4	4	4	4	—	—	—	—
CA	6	5	5	6	6	5	5	5	6	6	6	—	4	4	5	—	—	—	—
IN	5	5	5	5	5	5	4	4	5	5	5	6	—	3	4	—	—	—	—
AR	4	4	4	5	5	4	4	4	5	5	5	5	4	—	4	—	—	—	—
WR	5	5	5	5	5	5	5	5	5	5	5	6	5	5	—	—	—	—	—
VCI	—	—	—	—	—	—	—	—	—	—	—	—	—	—	—	—	11	12	13
PRI	—	—	—	—	—	—	—	—	—	—	—	—	—	—	—	14	—	12	13
WMI	—	—	—	—	—	—	—	—	—	—	—	—	—	—	—	15	15	—	13
PSI	—	—	—	—	—	—	—	—	—	—	—	—	—	—	—	16	17	17	—

(Continued)

Table A-2 (Continued)

Age 10

Subtest	BD	SI	DS	PCn	CD	VC	LN	MR	CO	SS	PCm	CA	IN	AR	WR		VCI	PRI	WMI	PSI
BD	—	4	4	4	4	3	4	4	4	4	4	4	4	3	4		—	—	—	—
SI	5	—	3	4	3	3	3	3	4	4	4	4	4	3	4		—	—	—	—
DS	5	4	—	4	3	3	3	3	4	4	3	4	4	3	4		—	—	—	—
PCn	5	5	5	—	4	3	4	4	4	4	4	4	4	3	4		—	—	—	—
CD	5	4	4	5	—	3	3	3	4	4	3	4	4	3	4		—	—	—	—
VC	4	4	4	4	4	—	3	3	4	4	3	3	4	3	4		—	—	—	—
LN	5	4	4	5	4	4	—	3	4	4	3	4	4	3	4		—	—	—	—
MR	5	4	4	5	4	4	4	—	4	4	3	4	4	3	4		—	—	—	—
CO	5	5	5	5	5	5	5	5	—	4	4	4	4	4	4		—	—	—	—
SS	5	5	5	5	5	5	5	5	5	—	4	4	4	4	4		—	—	—	—
PCm	5	5	4	5	4	4	4	4	5	5	—	4	4	3	4		—	—	—	—
CA	5	5	5	5	5	4	5	5	5	5	5	—	4	3	4		—	—	—	—
IN	5	5	5	5	5	5	5	5	5	5	5	5	—	3	4		—	—	—	—
AR	4	4	4	4	4	4	4	4	5	5	4	4	4	—	4		—	—	—	—
WR	5	5	5	5	5	5	5	5	5	5	5	5	5	5	—		—	—	—	—
VCI	—	—	—	—	—	—	—	—	—	—	—	—	—	—	—		—	11	12	12
PRI	—	—	—	—	—	—	—	—	—	—	—	—	—	—	—		14	—	12	13
WMI	—	—	—	—	—	—	—	—	—	—	—	—	—	—	—		15	15	—	13
PSI	—	—	—	—	—	—	—	—	—	—	—	—	—	—	—		16	16	17	—

Age 11

Subtest	BD	SI	DS	PCn	CD	VC	LN	MR	CO	SS	PCm	CA	IN	AR	WR		VCI	PRI	WMI	PSI
BD	—	4	4	4	3	3	3	3	4	4	3	4	4	4	4		—	—	—	—
SI	5	—	4	4	4	4	3	4	4	4	4	4	4	4	4		—	—	—	—
DS	5	5	—	4	3	4	3	3	4	4	4	4	4	4	4		—	—	—	—
PCn	5	5	5	—	4	4	3	4	4	4	4	4	4	4	4		—	—	—	—
CD	4	5	4	5	—	3	3	3	4	4	3	4	4	4	4		—	—	—	—
VC	4	5	5	5	4	—	3	3	4	4	3	4	4	4	4		—	—	—	—
LN	4	4	4	4	4	4	—	3	4	4	3	3	3	3	4		—	—	—	—
MR	4	5	4	5	4	4	4	—	4	4	3	4	4	4	4		—	—	—	—
CO	5	5	5	5	5	5	5	5	—	4	4	4	4	4	4		—	—	—	—
SS	5	5	5	5	5	5	5	5	5	—	4	4	4	4	4		—	—	—	—
PCm	4	5	5	5	4	4	4	4	5	5	—	4	4	4	4		—	—	—	—
CA	5	5	5	5	5	5	4	5	5	5	5	—	4	4	4		—	—	—	—
IN	5	5	5	5	5	5	4	5	5	5	5	5	—	4	4		—	—	—	—
AR	5	5	5	5	5	5	4	5	5	5	5	5	5	—	4		—	—	—	—
WR	5	5	5	5	5	5	5	5	5	6	5	5	5	5	—		—	—	—	—
VCI	—	—	—	—	—	—	—	—	—	—	—	—	—	—	—		—	12	12	13
PRI	—	—	—	—	—	—	—	—	—	—	—	—	—	—	—		15	—	12	13
WMI	—	—	—	—	—	—	—	—	—	—	—	—	—	—	—		15	15	—	13
PSI	—	—	—	—	—	—	—	—	—	—	—	—	—	—	—		16	16	17	—

(Continued)

Table A-2 (Continued)

Age 12

Subtest	BD	SI	DS	PCn	CD	VC	LN	MR	CO	SS	PCm	CA	IN	AR	WR	VCI	PRI	WMI	PSI
BD	—	3	3	4	3	3	3	3	4	4	4	4	3	3	4	—	—	—	—
SI	4	—	3	4	3	3	3	3	4	4	4	4	3	4	4	—	—	—	—
DS	4	4	—	4	3	3	3	3	3	4	4	4	3	3	4	—	—	—	—
PCn	5	5	5	—	4	4	4	4	4	4	4	4	4	4	4	—	—	—	—
CD	4	4	4	5	—	3	3	3	4	4	4	4	3	4	4	—	—	—	—
VC	4	4	4	5	4	—	3	3	3	4	3	4	3	3	4	—	—	—	—
LN	4	4	4	5	4	4	—	3	3	4	3	4	3	3	4	—	—	—	—
MR	4	4	4	5	4	4	4	—	3	4	3	4	3	3	4	—	—	—	—
CO	5	5	4	5	5	4	4	4	—	4	4	4	4	4	4	—	—	—	—
SS	5	5	5	5	5	5	5	5	5	—	4	4	4	4	4	—	—	—	—
PCm	5	5	5	5	5	4	4	4	5	5	—	4	4	4	4	—	—	—	—
CA	5	5	5	6	5	5	5	5	5	6	5	—	4	4	5	—	—	—	—
IN	4	4	4	5	4	4	4	4	5	5	5	5	—	4	4	—	—	—	—
AR	4	5	4	5	5	4	4	4	5	5	5	5	5	—	4	—	—	—	—
WR	5	5	5	6	5	5	5	5	5	6	5	6	5	5	—	—	—	—	—
VCI	—	—	—	—	—	—	—	—	—	—	—	—	—	—	—	—	11	11	12
PRI	—	—	—	—	—	—	—	—	—	—	—	—	—	—	—	14	—	12	13
WMI	—	—	—	—	—	—	—	—	—	—	—	—	—	—	—	14	15	—	13
PSI	—	—	—	—	—	—	—	—	—	—	—	—	—	—	—	16	17	17	—

Age 13

Subtest	BD	SI	DS	PCn	CD	VC	LN	MR	CO	SS	PCm	CA	IN	AR	WR	VCI	PRI	WMI	PSI
BD	—	4	3	4	3	3	4	3	4	4	4	4	3	4	4	—	—	—	—
SI	5	—	4	4	4	3	4	4	4	4	4	4	4	4	4	—	—	—	—
DS	4	5	—	4	3	3	4	3	4	4	4	4	3	4	4	—	—	—	—
PCn	5	5	5	—	4	4	4	4	4	4	4	4	4	4	4	—	—	—	—
CD	4	5	4	5	—	3	4	3	4	4	4	4	3	4	4	—	—	—	—
VC	4	4	4	5	4	—	3	3	4	4	4	4	3	3	4	—	—	—	—
LN	5	5	5	5	5	4	—	3	4	4	4	4	4	4	4	—	—	—	—
MR	4	5	4	5	4	4	4	—	4	4	4	4	3	3	4	—	—	—	—
CO	5	5	5	5	5	5	5	5	—	4	4	4	4	4	4	—	—	—	—
SS	5	5	5	5	5	5	5	5	5	—	4	4	4	4	4	—	—	—	—
PCm	5	5	5	5	5	5	5	5	5	5	—	4	4	4	4	—	—	—	—
CA	5	5	5	6	5	5	5	5	6	6	6	—	4	4	4	—	—	—	—
IN	4	5	4	5	4	4	5	4	5	5	5	5	—	4	4	—	—	—	—
AR	5	5	5	5	5	4	5	4	5	5	5	5	5	—	4	—	—	—	—
WR	5	5	5	5	5	5	5	5	5	5	5	6	5	5	—	—	—	—	—
VCI	—	—	—	—	—	—	—	—	—	—	—	—	—	—	—	—	11	12	13
PRI	—	—	—	—	—	—	—	—	—	—	—	—	—	—	—	14	—	12	13
WMI	—	—	—	—	—	—	—	—	—	—	—	—	—	—	—	15	16	—	14
PSI	—	—	—	—	—	—	—	—	—	—	—	—	—	—	—	16	17	18	—

(Continued)

Table A-2 (*Continued*)

Age 14

Subtest	BD	SI	DS	PCn	CD	VC	LN	MR	CO	SS	PCm	CA	IN	AR	WR	VCI	PRI	WMI	PSI
BD	—	3	3	4	4	3	3	4	4	4	4	4	4	4	4	—	—	—	—
SI	4	—	3	4	3	3	3	3	3	4	4	4	3	3	4	—	—	—	—
DS	4	4	—	4	3	3	3	3	3	4	4	4	3	3	4	—	—	—	—
PCn	5	5	5	—	4	3	3	4	4	4	4	4	4	4	4	—	—	—	—
CD	5	4	4	5	—	3	3	3	4	4	4	4	3	4	4	—	—	—	—
VC	4	4	4	4	4	—	3	3	3	4	4	4	3	3	3	—	—	—	—
LN	4	4	4	4	4	4	—	3	3	4	4	4	3	3	4	—	—	—	—
MR	5	4	4	5	4	4	4	—	4	4	4	4	3	4	4	—	—	—	—
CO	5	4	4	5	5	4	4	5	—	4	4	4	4	4	4	—	—	—	—
SS	5	5	5	5	5	5	5	5	5	—	4	4	4	4	4	—	—	—	—
PCm	5	5	5	5	5	5	5	5	5	5	—	4	4	4	4	—	—	—	—
CA	5	5	5	5	5	5	5	5	5	6	5	—	4	4	4	—	—	—	—
IN	5	4	4	5	4	4	4	4	5	5	5	5	—	4	4	—	—	—	—
AR	5	4	4	5	5	4	4	5	5	5	5	5	5	—	4	—	—	—	—
WR	5	5	5	5	5	4	5	5	5	5	5	5	5	5	—	—	—	—	—
VCI	—	—	—	—	—	—	—	—	—	—	—	—	—	—	—	—	11	11	12
PRI	—	—	—	—	—	—	—	—	—	—	—	—	—	—	—	14	—	12	13
WMI	—	—	—	—	—	—	—	—	—	—	—	—	—	—	—	14	15	—	13
PSI	—	—	—	—	—	—	—	—	—	—	—	—	—	—	—	16	17	17	—

Age 15

Subtest	BD	SI	DS	PCn	CD	VC	LN	MR	CO	SS	PCm	CA	IN	AR	WR	VCI	PRI	WMI	PSI
BD	—	3	3	4	3	3	3	3	4	4	4	4	3	3	4	—	—	—	—
SI	4	—	3	4	3	3	3	3	4	4	4	4	3	3	4	—	—	—	—
DS	4	4	—	4	3	3	3	3	4	4	4	4	3	3	4	—	—	—	—
PCn	5	5	5	—	4	4	4	4	4	4	4	4	4	4	4	—	—	—	—
CD	4	4	4	5	—	3	3	4	4	4	4	4	3	3	4	—	—	—	—
VC	4	4	4	5	4	—	3	3	3	4	3	4	3	3	3	—	—	—	—
LN	4	4	4	5	4	4	—	4	4	4	4	4	3	3	4	—	—	—	—
MR	4	4	4	5	5	4	5	—	4	4	4	4	3	3	4	—	—	—	—
CO	5	5	5	6	5	4	5	5	—	4	4	4	4	4	4	—	—	—	—
SS	5	5	5	6	5	5	5	5	6	—	4	4	4	4	4	—	—	—	—
PCm	5	5	5	5	5	4	5	5	5	5	—	4	3	3	4	—	—	—	—
CA	5	5	5	6	5	5	5	5	5	6	5	—	4	4	4	—	—	—	—
IN	4	4	4	5	4	3	4	4	5	5	4	5	—	3	3	—	—	—	—
AR	4	4	4	5	4	3	4	4	5	5	4	5	4	—	3	—	—	—	—
WR	5	5	5	5	5	4	5	5	5	5	5	5	4	4	—	—	—	—	—
VCI	—	—	—	—	—	—	—	—	—	—	—	—	—	—	—	—	11	11	12
PRI	—	—	—	—	—	—	—	—	—	—	—	—	—	—	—	14	—	12	13
WMI	—	—	—	—	—	—	—	—	—	—	—	—	—	—	—	14	16	—	13
PSI	—	—	—	—	—	—	—	—	—	—	—	—	—	—	—	15	17	17	—

(*Continued*)

Table A-2 (*Continued*)

Age 16

Subtest	BD	SI	DS	PCn	CD	VC	LN	MR	CO	SS	PCm	CA	IN	AR	WR	VCI	PRI	WMI	PSI
BD	—	4	3	4	3	3	3	3	4	4	4	4	3	3	4	—	—	—	—
SI	5	—	3	4	4	3	4	4	4	4	4	4	3	3	4	—	—	—	—
DS	4	4	—	4	3	3	3	3	3	4	3	4	3	3	4	—	—	—	—
PCn	5	5	5	—	4	4	4	4	4	4	4	4	4	4	5	—	—	—	—
CD	4	5	4	5	—	3	3	3	4	4	4	4	3	3	4	—	—	—	—
VC	4	4	4	5	4	—	3	3	3	4	3	4	3	3	4	—	—	—	—
LN	4	5	4	5	4	4	—	3	4	4	4	4	3	3	4	—	—	—	—
MR	4	5	4	5	4	4	4	—	4	4	4	4	3	3	4	—	—	—	—
CO	5	5	4	5	5	4	5	5	—	4	4	4	3	3	4	—	—	—	—
SS	5	5	5	6	5	5	5	5	5	—	4	4	4	4	4	—	—	—	—
PCm	5	5	4	5	5	4	5	5	5	5	—	4	3	3	4	—	—	—	—
CA	5	5	5	6	5	5	5	5	5	6	5	—	4	4	4	—	—	—	—
IN	4	4	4	5	4	4	4	4	4	5	4	5	—	3	4	—	—	—	—
AR	4	4	4	5	4	4	4	4	4	5	4	5	4	—	4	—	—	—	—
WR	5	5	5	6	5	5	5	5	5	6	5	6	5	5	—	—	—	—	—
VCI	—	—	—	—	—	—	—	—	—	—	—	—	—	—	—	—	12	11	12
PRI	—	—	—	—	—	—	—	—	—	—	—	—	—	—	—	15	—	12	14
WMI	—	—	—	—	—	—	—	—	—	—	—	—	—	—	—	14	16	—	13
PSI	—	—	—	—	—	—	—	—	—	—	—	—	—	—	—	16	18	17	—

Total Group

Subtest	BD	SI	DS	PCn	CD	VC	LN	MR	CO	SS	PCm	CA	IN	AR	WR	VCI	PRI	WMI	PSI
BD	—	4	4	4	4	3	3	3	4	4	4	4	4	3	4	—	—	—	—
SI	5	—	4	4	4	3	3	3	4	4	4	4	4	3	4	—	—	—	—
DS	5	5	—	4	4	3	3	3	4	4	4	4	4	3	4	—	—	—	—
PCn	5	5	5	—	4	4	4	4	4	4	4	4	4	4	4	—	—	—	—
CD	5	5	5	5	—	3	3	3	4	4	4	4	4	4	4	—	—	—	—
VC	4	4	4	5	4	—	3	3	4	4	4	4	3	3	4	—	—	—	—
LN	4	4	4	5	4	4	—	3	4	4	3	4	3	3	4	—	—	—	—
MR	4	4	4	5	4	4	4	—	4	4	4	4	3	3	4	—	—	—	—
CO	5	5	5	5	5	5	5	5	—	4	4	4	4	4	4	—	—	—	—
SS	5	5	5	5	5	5	5	5	5	—	4	4	4	4	4	—	—	—	—
PCm	5	5	5	5	5	5	4	5	5	5	—	4	4	4	4	—	—	—	—
CA	5	5	5	5	5	5	5	5	5	6	5	—	4	4	4	—	—	—	—
IN	5	5	5	5	5	4	4	4	5	5	5	5	—	3	4	—	—	—	—
AR	4	4	4	5	5	4	4	4	5	5	5	5	4	—	4	—	—	—	—
WR	5	5	5	5	5	5	5	5	5	5	5	5	5	5	—	—	—	—	—
VCI	—	—	—	—	—	—	—	—	—	—	—	—	—	—	—	—	12	12	13
PRI	—	—	—	—	—	—	—	—	—	—	—	—	—	—	—	15	—	12	14
WMI	—	—	—	—	—	—	—	—	—	—	—	—	—	—	—	15	16	—	14
PSI	—	—	—	—	—	—	—	—	—	—	—	—	—	—	—	17	18	18	—

(*Continued*)

Table A-2 (*Continued*)

Note. Abbreviations: BD = Block Design, SI = Similarities, DS = Digit Span, PCn = Picture Concepts, CD = Coding, VC = Vocabulary, LN = Letter–Number Sequencing, MR = Matrix Reasoning, CO = Comprehension, SS = Symbol Search, PCm = Picture Completion, CA = Cancellation, IN = Information, AR = Arithmetic, WR = Word Reasoning, VCI = Verbal Comprehension Index, PRI = Perceptual Reasoning Index, WMI = Working Memory Index, PSI = Processing Speed Index.

The critical values at the .05 level appear *above* the diagonal in the *shaded* area; the critical values for the .01 level appear *below* the diagonal in the *unshaded* area.

Sample reading: At age 6 (6-0 to 6-11), a difference of 4 points between scaled scores on the Block Design and Similarities subtests is significant at the 5% level and a difference of 5 points is significant at the 1% level. Similarly, a difference of 13 points between the Verbal Comprehension Index and the Perceptual Reasoning Index is significant at the 5% level and a difference of 17 points is significant at the 1% level.

The values in this table for subtest comparisons are overly liberal when more than one comparison is made for a subtest. They are more accurate when a priori planned comparisons are made, such as Similarities vs. Vocabulary or Block Design vs. Matrix Reasoning.

See Exhibit 11-1 in Chapter 11 for the procedure used to arrive at magnitudes of differences.

A. B. Silverstein (personal communication, February 1990) suggests that the following formula be used to obtain a value for the significant difference (at the .05 level) that must exist between the highest and lowest subtest scores on a profile before individual subtest comparisons can be made:

$$D = q \sqrt{\frac{\Sigma \, \mathrm{SEM}^2}{k}}$$

where

D = significant difference
q = critical value of the Studentized range statistic
SEM = standard error of measurement of a particular subtest
k = number of subtests

For the WISC–IV, the q value is 4.47 at the .05 level for $k = 10$ (10 subtests) and ∞ degrees of freedom. The sum of the SEM^2 for the 10 subtests is $1.13 + 1.13 + 1.07 + 1.29 + 1.20 + 1.00 + 0.97 + 0.99 + 1.31 + 1.36 = 11.45$. Thus,

$$D = 4.47 \times \sqrt{\frac{11.45}{10}} = 4.47 \times \sqrt{1.145} = 4.47 \times 1.0700 = 4.78$$

Thus, a difference of 5 points between the highest and lowest subtest scaled scores represents a significant difference at the .05 level.

Table A-3
Estimates of the Probability of Obtaining Designated Differences Between WISC–IV Composite Scores by Chance

Verbal Comprehension and Perceptual Reasoning

Probability of obtaining given or greater discrepancy by chance	Age (in years)											Total
	6	7	8	9	10	11	12	13	14	15	16	
.50	4.30	4.05	3.92	3.65	3.65	3.79	3.51	3.65	3.65	3.65	3.79	3.79
.25	7.32	6.90	6.68	6.22	6.22	6.46	5.97	6.22	6.21	6.21	6.45	6.46
.20	8.16	7.69	7.45	6.93	6.93	7.20	6.66	6.93	6.93	6.93	7.19	7.20
.10	10.47	9.86	9.55	8.89	8.89	9.24	8.55	8.89	8.89	8.89	9.23	9.23
.05	12.47	11.75	11.38	10.60	10.60	11.00	10.18	10.60	10.59	10.59	11.00	11.00
.02	14.81	13.95	13.52	12.58	12.58	13.06	12.09	12.58	12.57	12.57	13.05	13.06
.01	16.39	15.44	14.96	13.92	13.92	14.46	13.38	13.92	13.91	13.91	14.45	14.45
.001	21.00	19.79	19.17	17.84	17.84	18.53	17.14	17.84	17.83	17.83	18.51	18.52

Verbal Comprehension and Working Memory

Probability of obtaining given or greater discrepancy by chance	Age (in years)											Total
	6	7	8	9	10	11	12	13	14	15	16	
.50	4.17	4.29	4.17	3.79	3.79	3.92	3.51	3.92	3.51	3.65	3.51	3.85
.25	7.11	7.31	7.11	6.45	6.45	6.68	5.97	6.68	5.97	6.21	5.97	6.56
.20	7.93	8.15	7.93	7.19	7.19	7.45	6.66	7.44	6.66	6.93	6.66	7.31
.10	10.17	10.46	10.17	9.22	9.22	9.55	8.55	9.55	8.55	8.89	8.55	9.38
.05	12.12	12.46	12.12	10.99	10.99	11.38	10.18	11.38	10.18	10.59	10.18	11.18
.02	14.39	14.80	14.39	13.05	13.05	13.52	12.09	13.51	12.09	12.57	12.09	13.27
.01	15.92	16.38	15.92	14.44	14.44	14.96	13.38	14.95	13.38	13.91	13.38	14.68
.001	20.40	20.99	20.40	18.51	18.51	19.17	17.14	19.16	17.14	17.83	17.14	18.82

Verbal Comprehension and Processing Speed

Probability of obtaining given or greater discrepancy by chance	Age (in years)											Total
	6	7	8	9	10	11	12	13	14	15	16	
.50	5.16	5.26	4.53	4.17	4.05	4.17	4.05	4.17	4.05	3.92	4.05	4.34
.25	8.79	8.96	7.72	7.10	6.89	7.11	6.89	7.10	6.89	6.67	6.89	7.40
.20	9.80	9.99	8.60	7.92	7.69	7.93	7.68	7.92	7.68	7.44	7.68	8.25
.10	12.58	12.82	11.04	10.16	9.86	10.17	9.86	10.16	9.86	9.55	9.86	10.59
.05	14.98	15.28	13.15	12.11	11.75	12.12	11.75	12.11	11.75	11.38	11.75	12.62
.02	17.79	18.14	15.61	14.38	13.95	14.39	13.95	14.38	13.95	13.51	13.95	14.98
.01	19.69	20.07	17.28	15.91	15.44	15.92	15.43	15.91	15.43	14.95	15.43	16.57
.001	25.23	25.72	22.14	20.39	19.78	20.40	19.78	20.39	19.78	19.15	19.78	21.24

(Continued)

Table A-3 (*Continued*)

Perceptual Reasoning and Working Memory

Probability of obtaining given or greater discrepancy by chance	Age (in years)											
	6	7	8	9	10	11	12	13	14	15	16	Total
.50	4.17	4.29	4.05	3.92	3.92	3.92	3.79	4.05	3.92	4.05	4.05	4.02
.25	7.11	7.31	6.90	6.68	6.68	6.68	6.46	6.90	6.68	6.90	6.90	6.85
.20	7.93	8.15	7.69	7.45	7.45	7.45	7.20	7.69	7.45	7.69	7.69	7.63
.10	10.17	10.46	9.87	9.55	9.55	9.55	9.24	9.87	9.55	9.86	9.87	9.80
.05	12.12	12.46	11.76	11.38	11.38	11.38	11.00	11.76	11.38	11.75	11.76	11.67
.02	14.39	14.80	13.96	13.52	13.52	13.52	13.06	13.96	13.52	13.95	13.96	13.86
.01	15.92	16.38	15.45	14.96	14.96	14.96	14.46	15.45	14.96	15.44	15.45	15.33
.001	20.40	20.99	19.80	19.17	19.17	19.17	18.53	19.80	19.17	19.79	19.80	19.65

Perceptual Reasoning and Processing Speed

Probability of obtaining given or greater discrepancy by chance	Age (in years)											
	6	7	8	9	10	11	12	13	14	15	16	Total
.50	5.16	5.26	4.42	4.29	4.17	4.17	4.29	4.29	4.41	4.29	4.53	4.50
.25	8.79	8.96	7.52	7.32	7.11	7.11	7.32	7.32	7.51	7.31	7.71	7.66
.20	9.80	9.99	8.39	8.15	7.93	7.93	8.15	8.15	8.38	8.15	8.60	8.54
.10	12.58	12.82	10.76	10.46	10.17	10.17	10.46	10.46	10.75	10.46	11.03	10.96
.05	14.98	15.28	12.82	12.47	12.12	12.12	12.47	12.47	12.80	12.46	13.14	13.06
.02	17.79	18.14	15.22	14.80	14.39	14.39	14.80	14.80	15.20	14.80	15.60	15.50
.01	19.69	20.07	16.85	16.38	15.92	15.92	16.38	16.38	16.82	16.38	17.26	17.15
.001	25.23	25.72	21.59	20.99	20.40	20.40	20.99	20.99	21.56	20.99	22.12	21.98

Working Memory and Processing Speed

Probability of obtaining given or greater discrepancy by chance	Age (in years)											
	6	7	8	9	10	11	12	13	14	15	16	Total
.50	5.06	5.45	4.64	4.41	4.29	4.29	4.29	4.53	4.29	4.29	4.29	4.55
.25	8.62	9.29	7.91	7.51	7.31	7.31	7.32	7.71	7.32	7.31	7.32	7.75
.20	9.61	10.35	8.82	8.38	8.15	8.15	8.15	8.60	8.15	8.15	8.15	8.64
.10	12.33	13.29	11.31	10.75	10.46	10.46	10.46	11.03	10.46	10.46	10.46	11.08
.05	14.69	15.83	13.48	12.80	12.46	12.46	12.47	13.14	12.47	12.46	12.47	13.20
.02	17.44	18.80	16.00	15.20	14.80	14.80	14.80	15.60	14.80	14.80	14.80	15.68
.01	19.30	20.80	17.71	16.82	16.38	16.38	16.38	17.26	16.38	16.38	16.38	17.35
.001	24.73	26.65	22.69	21.56	20.99	20.99	20.99	22.12	20.99	20.99	20.99	22.23

Note. To use the table, find the column appropriate to the child's age. Locate the discrepancy that is just *less than* the discrepancy obtained by the child. The entry in the first column in that same row gives the probability of obtaining a given or greater discrepancy by chance. For example, the hypothesis that a 6-year-old child obtained a Verbal Comprehension–Perceptual Reasoning discrepancy of 17 by chance can be rejected at the .01 level of significance. The table is two-tailed.

See Exhibit 11-1 in Chapter 11 for an explanation of the method used to arrive at magnitudes of differences.

The following z values were used for the eight probability levels: $z = .675$ for .50, $z = 1.15$ for .25, $z = 1.282$ for .20, $z = 1.645$ for .10, $z = 1.96$ for .05, $z = 2.327$ for .02, $z = 2.575$ for .01, and $z = 3.30$ for .001.

Differences Required for Significance When Each WISC–IV Subtest Scaled Score Is Compared to the Mean Subtest Scaled Score for Any Individual Child for the 11 Age Groups and the Total Group

Age 6-0-0 through 6-11-30

Subtest	Mean of 2 subtests for WMI		Mean of 2 subtests for PSI		Mean of 3 subtests for VCI		Mean of 3 subtests for PRI	
	.05	.01	.05	.01	.05	.01	.05	.01
Block Design	—	—	—	—	—	—	2.33	2.86
Similarities	—	—	—	—	2.50	3.07	—	—
Digit Span	1.38	1.81	—	—	—	—	—	—
Picture Concepts	—	—	—	—	—	—	2.29	2.81
Coding	—	—	2.06	2.71	—	—	—	—
Vocabulary	—	—	—	—	2.50	3.07	—	—
Letter–Number Sequencing	1.38	1.81	—	—	—	—	—	—
Matrix Reasoning	—	—	—	—	—	—	2.09	2.57
Comprehension	—	—	—	—	2.57	3.15	—	—
Symbol Search	—	—	2.06	2.71	—	—	—	—
Picture Completion	—	—	—	—	—	—	—	—
Cancellation	—	—	—	—	—	—	—	—
Information	—	—	—	—	—	—	—	—
Arithmetic	—	—	—	—	—	—	—	—
Word Reasoning	—	—	—	—	—	—	—	—

Subtest	Mean of 3 subtests for WMI		Mean of 3 subtests for PSI		Mean of 4 subtests for VCI		Mean of 4 subtests for VCI	
	.05	.01	.05	.01	.05	.01	.05	.01
Block Design	—	—	—	—	—	—	—	—
Similarities	—	—	—	—	2.76	3.33	2.78	3.36
Digit Span	2.11	2.58	—	—	—	—	—	—
Picture Concepts	—	—	—	—	—	—	—	—
Coding	—	—	2.93	3.59	—	—	—	—
Vocabulary	—	—	—	—	2.76	3.33	2.78	3.36
Letter–Number Sequencing	1.85	2.27	—	—	—	—	—	—
Matrix Reasoning	—	—	—	—	—	—	—	—
Comprehension	—	—	—	—	2.86	3.45	2.88	3.48
Symbol Search	—	—	2.71	3.32	—	—	—	—
Picture Completion	—	—	—	—	—	—	—	—
Cancellation	—	—	2.59	3.17	—	—	—	—
Information	—	—	—	—	2.71	3.28	—	—
Arithmetic	2.11	2.58	—	—	—	—	—	—
Word Reasoning	—	—	—	—	—	—	2.93	3.53

Subtest	Mean of 4 subtests for PRI		Mean of 5 subtests for VCI		Mean of 10 subtests for FS		Mean of 15 subtests	
	.05	.01	.05	.01	.05	.01	.05	.01
Block Design	2.63	3.18	—	—	3.31	3.88	3.52	4.04
Similarities	—	—	2.95	3.54	3.38	3.97	3.60	4.13
Digit Span	—	—	—	—	3.02	3.55	3.21	3.68
Picture Concepts	2.57	3.11	—	—	3.21	3.77	3.42	3.92
Coding	—	—	—	—	4.15	4.87	4.45	5.10
Vocabulary	—	—	2.95	3.54	3.38	3.97	3.60	4.13
Letter–Number Sequencing	—	—	—	—	2.40	2.82	2.51	2.88
Matrix Reasoning	2.27	2.75	—	—	2.72	3.20	2.87	3.29
Comprehension	—	—	3.07	3.69	3.54	4.16	3.79	4.34
Symbol Search	—	—	—	—	3.62	4.25	3.87	4.43
Picture Completion	2.57	3.11	—	—	—	—	3.42	3.92
Cancellation	—	—	—	—	—	—	3.52	4.04
Information	—	—	2.90	3.48	—	—	3.52	4.04
Arithmetic	—	—	—	—	—	—	3.21	3.68
Word Reasoning	—	—	3.12	3.75	—	—	3.87	4.43

(Continued)

Table A-4 (Continued)

Age 7-0-0 through 7-11-30

Subtest	Mean of 2 subtests for WMI		Mean of 2 subtests for PSI		Mean of 3 subtests for VCI		Mean of 3 subtests for PRI	
	.05	.01	.05	.01	.05	.01	.05	.01
Block Design	—	—	—	—	—	—	2.28	2.79
Similarities	—	—	—	—	2.45	3.00	—	—
Digit Span	1.56	2.05	—	—	—	—	—	—
Picture Concepts	—	—	—	—	—	—	2.24	2.75
Coding	—	—	2.06	2.71	—	—	—	—
Vocabulary	—	—	—	—	2.41	2.96	—	—
Letter–Number Sequencing	1.56	2.05	—	—	—	—	—	—
Matrix Reasoning	—	—	—	—	—	—	2.12	2.60
Comprehension	—	—	—	—	2.78	3.40	—	—
Symbol Search	—	—	2.06	2.71	—	—	—	—
Picture Completion	—	—	—	—	—	—	—	—
Cancellation	—	—	—	—	—	—	—	—
Information	—	—	—	—	—	—	—	—
Arithmetic	—	—	—	—	—	—	—	—
Word Reasoning	—	—	—	—	—	—	—	—

Subtest	Mean of 3 subtests for WMI		Mean of 3 subtests for PSI		Mean of 4 subtests for VCI		Mean of 4 subtests for VCI	
	.05	.01	.05	.01	.05	.01	.05	.01
Block Design	—	—	—	—	—	—	—	—
Similarities	—	—	—	—	2.70	3.26	2.68	3.24
Digit Span	2.33	2.86	—	—	—	—	—	—
Picture Concepts	—	—	—	—	—	—	—	—
Coding	—	—	2.93	3.59	—	—	—	—
Vocabulary	—	—	—	—	2.64	3.19	2.62	3.17
Letter–Number Sequencing	1.93	2.36	—	—	—	—	—	—
Matrix Reasoning	—	—	—	—	—	—	—	—
Comprehension	—	—	—	—	3.18	3.84	3.16	3.82
Symbol Search	—	—	2.71	3.32	—	—	—	—
Picture Completion	—	—	—	—	—	—	—	—
Cancellation	—	—	2.59	3.17	—	—	—	—
Information	—	—	—	—	3.00	3.62	—	—
Arithmetic	1.97	2.42	—	—	—	—	—	—
Word Reasoning	—	—	—	—	—	—	2.83	3.42

Subtest	Mean of 4 subtests for PRI		Mean of 5 subtests for VCI		Mean of 10 subtests for FS		Mean of 15 subtests	
	.05	.01	.05	.01	.05	.01	.05	.01
Block Design	2.56	3.09	—	—	3.22	3.78	3.38	3.87
Similarities	—	—	2.85	3.42	3.22	3.78	3.38	3.87
Digit Span	—	—	—	—	3.48	4.08	3.67	4.21
Picture Concepts	2.50	3.02	—	—	3.12	3.67	3.27	3.75
Coding	—	—	—	—	4.15	4.87	4.42	5.07
Vocabulary	—	—	2.78	3.34	3.12	3.67	3.27	3.75
Letter–Number Sequencing	—	—	—	—	2.52	2.96	2.58	2.96
Matrix Reasoning	2.33	2.81	—	—	2.84	3.34	2.95	3.38
Comprehension	—	—	3.42	4.11	3.93	4.61	4.26	4.88
Symbol Search	—	—	—	—	3.62	4.25	3.83	4.39
Picture Completion	2.50	3.02	—	—	—	—	3.27	3.75
Cancellation	—	—	—	—	—	—	3.48	3.99
Information	—	—	3.21	3.85	—	—	3.94	4.51
Arithmetic	—	—	—	—	—	—	2.72	3.11
Word Reasoning	—	—	3.03	3.65	—	—	3.67	4.21

(Continued)

Age 8-0-0 through 8-11-30

Subtest	Mean of 2 subtests for WMI		Mean of 2 subtests for PSI		Mean of 3 subtests for VCI		Mean of 3 subtests for PRI	
	.05	.01	.05	.01	.05	.01	.05	.01
Block Design	—	—	—	—	—	—	2.18	2.67
Similarities	—	—	—	—	2.29	2.81	—	—
Digit Span	1.50	1.97	—	—	—	—	—	—
Picture Concepts	—	—	—	—	—	—	2.37	2.90
Coding	—	—	1.74	2.29	—	—	—	—
Vocabulary	—	—	—	—	2.29	2.81	—	—
Letter–Number Sequencing	1.50	1.97	—	—	—	—	—	—
Matrix Reasoning	—	—	—	—	—	—	1.93	2.36
Comprehension	—	—	—	—	2.58	3.16	—	—
Symbol Search	—	—	1.74	2.29	—	—	—	—
Picture Completion	—	—	—	—	—	—	—	—
Cancellation	—	—	—	—	—	—	—	—
Information	—	—	—	—	—	—	—	—
Arithmetic	—	—	—	—	—	—	—	—
Word Reasoning	—	—	—	—	—	—	—	—

Subtest	Mean of 3 subtests for WMI		Mean of 3 subtests for PSI		Mean of 4 subtests for VCI		Mean of 4 subtests for VCI	
	.05	.01	.05	.01	.05	.01	.05	.01
Block Design	—	—	—	—	—	—	—	—
Similarities	—	—	—	—	2.51	3.03	2.51	3.03
Digit Span	2.25	2.76	—	—	—	—	—	—
Picture Concepts	—	—	—	—	—	—	—	—
Coding	—	—	2.54	3.12	—	—	—	—
Vocabulary	—	—	—	—	2.51	3.03	2.51	3.03
Letter–Number Sequencing	2.01	2.47	—	—	—	—	—	—
Matrix Reasoning	—	—	—	—	—	—	—	—
Comprehension	—	—	—	—	2.93	3.54	2.93	3.54
Symbol Search	—	—	2.57	3.15	—	—	—	—
Picture Completion	—	—	—	—	—	—	—	—
Cancellation	—	—	2.86	3.51	—	—	—	—
Information	—	—	—	—	2.68	3.23	—	—
Arithmetic	2.21	2.71	—	—	—	—	—	—
Word Reasoning	—	—	—	—	—	—	2.68	3.23

Subtest	Mean of 4 subtests for PRI		Mean of 5 subtests for VCI		Mean of 10 subtests for FS		Mean of 15 subtests	
	.05	.01	.05	.01	.05	.01	.05	.01
Block Design	2.43	2.94	—	—	3.00	3.52	3.20	3.67
Similarities	—	—	2.65	3.18	3.00	3.52	3.20	3.67
Digit Span	—	—	—	—	3.19	3.75	3.41	3.91
Picture Concepts	2.71	3.28	—	—	3.45	4.05	3.70	4.24
Coding	—	—	—	—	3.29	3.86	3.52	4.03
Vocabulary	—	—	2.65	3.18	3.00	3.52	3.20	3.67
Letter–Number Sequencing	—	—	—	—	2.60	3.06	2.76	3.16
Matrix Reasoning	2.06	2.49	—	—	2.38	2.79	2.50	2.87
Comprehension	—	—	3.16	3.79	3.69	4.34	3.97	4.55
Symbol Search	—	—	—	—	3.36	3.94	3.60	4.12
Picture Completion	2.55	3.08	—	—	—	—	3.41	3.91
Cancellation	—	—	—	—	—	—	4.37	5.01
Information	—	—	2.86	3.43	—	—	3.52	4.03
Arithmetic	—	—	—	—	—	—	3.31	3.79
Word Reasoning	—	—	2.86	3.43	—	—	3.52	4.03

(Continued)

Table A-4 (Continued)

Age 9-0-0 through 9-11-30

Subtest	Mean of 2 subtests for WMI		Mean of 2 subtests for PSI		Mean of 3 subtests for VCI		Mean of 3 subtests for PRI	
	.05	.01	.05	.01	.05	.01	.05	.01
Block Design	—	—	—	—	—	—	2.26	2.77
Similarities	—	—	—	—	2.11	2.59	—	—
Digit Span	1.35	1.77	—	—	—	—	—	—
Picture Concepts	—	—	—	—	—	—	2.30	2.82
Coding	—	—	1.74	2.29	—	—	—	—
Vocabulary	—	—	—	—	2.06	2.53	—	—
Letter–Number Sequencing	1.35	1.77	—	—	—	—	—	—
Matrix Reasoning	—	—	—	—	—	—	1.93	2.37
Comprehension	—	—	—	—	2.38	2.92	—	—
Symbol Search	—	—	1.74	2.29	—	—	—	—
Picture Completion	—	—	—	—	—	—	—	—
Cancellation	—	—	—	—	—	—	—	—
Information	—	—	—	—	—	—	—	—
Arithmetic	—	—	—	—	—	—	—	—
Word Reasoning	—	—	—	—	—	—	—	—

Subtest	Mean of 3 subtests for WMI		Mean of 3 subtests for PSI		Mean of 4 subtests for VCI		Mean of 4 subtests for VCI	
	.05	.01	.05	.01	.05	.01	.05	.01
Block Design	—	—	—	—	—	—	—	—
Similarities	—	—	—	—	2.33	2.81	2.36	2.85
Digit Span	2.00	2.45	—	—	—	—	—	—
Picture Concepts	—	—	—	—	—	—	—	—
Coding	—	—	2.54	3.12	—	—	—	—
Vocabulary	—	—	—	—	2.26	2.73	2.29	2.77
Letter–Number Sequencing	1.77	2.17	—	—	—	—	—	—
Matrix Reasoning	—	—	—	—	—	—	—	—
Comprehension	—	—	—	—	2.72	3.29	2.75	3.32
Symbol Search	—	—	2.57	3.15	—	—	—	—
Picture Completion	—	—	—	—	—	—	—	—
Cancellation	—	—	2.86	3.51	—	—	—	—
Information	—	—	—	—	2.56	3.09	—	—
Arithmetic	1.87	2.29	—	—	—	—	—	—
Word Reasoning	—	—	—	—	—	—	2.79	3.37

Subtest	Mean of 4 subtests for PRI		Mean of 5 subtests for VCI		Mean of 10 subtests for FS		Mean of 15 subtests	
	.05	.01	.05	.01	.05	.01	.05	.01
Block Design	2.57	3.11	—	—	3.18	3.73	3.40	3.90
Similarities	—	—	2.49	2.99	2.80	3.28	2.98	3.42
Digit Span	—	—	—	—	2.89	3.39	3.09	3.54
Picture Concepts	2.63	3.18	—	—	3.27	3.84	3.51	4.02
Coding	—	—	—	—	3.27	3.84	3.51	4.02
Vocabulary	—	—	2.40	2.89	2.68	3.15	2.85	3.27
Letter–Number Sequencing	—	—	—	—	2.36	2.77	2.49	2.86
Matrix Reasoning	2.09	2.53	—	—	2.36	2.77	2.49	2.86
Comprehension	—	—	2.95	3.55	3.37	3.96	3.70	4.24
Symbol Search	—	—	—	—	3.34	3.93	3.59	4.11
Picture Completion	2.73	3.30	—	—	—	—	3.70	4.24
Cancellation	—	—	—	—	—	—	4.36	5.00
Information	—	—	2.76	3.32	—	—	3.40	3.90
Arithmetic	—	—	—	—	—	—	2.75	3.15
Word Reasoning	—	—	3.01	3.61	—	—	3.77	4.33

16

(Continued)

Table A-4 (*Continued*)

Age 10-0-0 through 10-11-30

Subtest	Mean of 2 subtests for WMI		Mean of 2 subtests for PSI		Mean of 3 subtests for VCI		Mean of 3 subtests for PRI	
	.05	.01	.05	.01	.05	.01	.05	.01
Block Design	—	—	—	—	—	—	2.28	2.79
Similarities	—	—	—	—	2.21	2.71	—	—
Digit Span	1.37	1.81	—	—	—	—	—	—
Picture Concepts	—	—	—	—	—	—	2.28	2.79
Coding	—	—	1.63	2.15	—	—	—	—
Vocabulary	—	—	—	—	2.06	2.52	—	—
Letter–Number Sequencing	1.37	1.81	—	—	—	—	—	—
Matrix Reasoning	—	—	—	—	—	—	2.08	2.55
Comprehension	—	—	—	—	2.43	2.98	—	—
Symbol Search	—	—	1.63	2.15	—	—	—	—
Picture Completion	—	—	—	—	—	—	—	—
Cancellation	—	—	—	—	—	—	—	—
Information	—	—	—	—	—	—	—	—
Arithmetic	—	—	—	—	—	—	—	—
Word Reasoning	—	—	—	—	—	—	—	—

Subtest	Mean of 3 subtests for WMI		Mean of 3 subtests for PSI		Mean of 4 subtests for VCI		Mean of 4 subtests for VCI	
	.05	.01	.05	.01	.05	.01	.05	.01
Block Design	—	—	—	—	—	—	—	—
Similarities	—	—	—	—	2.46	2.97	2.49	3.01
Digit Span	1.90	2.33	—	—	—	—	—	—
Picture Concepts	—	—	—	—	—	—	—	—
Coding	—	—	2.13	2.61	—	—	—	—
Vocabulary	—	—	—	—	2.23	2.69	2.26	2.73
Letter–Number Sequencing	1.90	2.33	—	—	—	—	—	—
Matrix Reasoning	—	—	—	—	—	—	—	—
Comprehension	—	—	—	—	2.78	3.36	2.81	3.39
Symbol Search	—	—	2.47	3.03	—	—	—	—
Picture Completion	—	—	—	—	—	—	—	—
Cancellation	—	—	2.33	2.85	—	—	—	—
Information	—	—	—	—	2.64	3.18	—	—
Arithmetic	1.82	2.23	—	—	—	—	—	—
Word Reasoning	—	—	—	—	—	—	2.85	3.45

Subtest	Mean of 4 subtests for PRI		Mean of 5 subtests for VCI		Mean of 10 subtests for FS		Mean of 15 subtests	
	.05	.01	.05	.01	.05	.01	.05	.01
Block Design	2.56	3.09	—	—	3.18	3.73	3.40	3.89
Similarities	—	—	2.64	3.17	2.99	3.51	3.19	3.65
Digit Span	—	—	—	—	2.68	3.15	2.84	3.26
Picture Concepts	2.56	3.09	—	—	3.18	3.73	3.40	3.89
Coding	—	—	—	—	2.68	3.15	2.84	3.26
Vocabulary	—	—	2.36	2.83	2.59	3.04	2.74	3.14
Letter–Number Sequencing	—	—	—	—	2.68	3.15	2.84	3.26
Matrix Reasoning	2.26	2.73	—	—	2.68	3.15	2.84	3.26
Comprehension	—	—	3.02	3.63	3.51	4.12	3.77	4.32
Symbol Search	—	—	—	—	3.51	4.12	3.77	4.32
Picture Completion	2.50	3.02	—	—	—	—	3.29	3.77
Cancellation	—	—	—	—	—	—	3.40	3.89
Information	—	—	2.85	3.42	—	—	3.50	4.02
Arithmetic	—	—	—	—	—	—	2.61	2.99
Word Reasoning	—	—	3.08	3.70	—	—	3.85	4.41

(*Continued*)

Table A-4 (Continued)

Age 11-0-0 through 11-11-30

Subtest	Mean of 2 subtests for WMI		Mean of 2 subtests for PSI		Mean of 3 subtests for VCI		Mean of 3 subtests for PRI	
	.05	.01	.05	.01	.05	.01	.05	.01
Block Design	—	—	—	—	—	—	2.14	2.62
Similarities	—	—	—	—	2.39	2.94	—	—
Digit Span	1.41	1.85	—	—	—	—	—	—
Picture Concepts	—	—	—	—	—	—	2.29	2.81
Coding	—	—	1.63	2.15	—	—	—	—
Vocabulary	—	—	—	—	2.24	2.75	—	—
Letter–Number Sequencing	1.41	1.85	—	—	—	—	—	—
Matrix Reasoning	—	—	—	—	—	—	2.05	2.51
Comprehension	—	—	—	—	2.46	3.02	—	—
Symbol Search	—	—	1.63	2.15	—	—	—	—
Picture Completion	—	—	—	—	—	—	—	—
Cancellation	—	—	—	—	—	—	—	—
Information	—	—	—	—	—	—	—	—
Arithmetic	—	—	—	—	—	—	—	—
Word Reasoning	—	—	—	—	—	—	—	—

Subtest	Mean of 3 subtests for WMI		Mean of 3 subtests for PSI		Mean of 4 subtests for VCI		Mean of 4 subtests for VCI	
	.05	.01	.05	.01	.05	.01	.05	.01
Block Design	—	—	—	—	—	—	—	—
Similarities	—	—	—	—	2.66	3.22	2.70	3.27
Digit Span	2.15	2.63	—	—	—	—	—	—
Picture Concepts	—	—	—	—	—	—	—	—
Coding	—	—	2.13	2.61	—	—	—	—
Vocabulary	—	—	—	—	2.44	2.94	2.48	3.00
Letter–Number Sequencing	1.94	2.38	—	—	—	—	—	—
Matrix Reasoning	—	—	—	—	—	—	—	—
Comprehension	—	—	—	—	2.77	3.34	2.80	3.39
Symbol Search	—	—	2.47	3.03	—	—	—	—
Pictur e Completion	—	—	—	—	—	—	—	—
Cancellation	—	—	3.03	2.85	—	—	—	—
Information	—	—	—	—	2.61	3.15	—	—
Arithmetic	2.23	2.73	—	—	—	—	—	—
Word Reasoning	—	—	—	—	—	—	2.95	3.57

Subtest	Mean of 4 subtests for PRI		Mean of 5 subtests for VCI		Mean of 10 subtests for FS		Mean of 15 subtests	
	.05	.01	.05	.01	.05	.01	.05	.01
Block Design	2.35	2.84	—	—	2.90	3.40	3.09	3.54
Similarities	—	—	2.87	3.45	3.28	3.85	3.51	4.02
Digit Span	—	—	—	—	2.99	3.51	3.19	3.66
Picture Concepts	2.59	3.13	—	—	3.28	3.85	3.51	4.02
Coding	—	—	—	—	2.69	3.15	2.85	3.27
Vocabulary	—	—	2.60	3.12	2.90	3.40	3.09	3.54
Letter–Number Sequencing	—	—	—	—	2.48	2.91	2.62	3.00
Matrix Reasoning	2.23	2.69	—	—	2.69	3.15	2.85	3.27
Comprehension	—	—	2.99	3.59	3.44	4.04	3.69	4.23
Symbol Search	—	—	—	—	3.52	4.13	3.77	4.32
Picture Completion	2.35	2.84	—	—	—	—	3.09	3.54
Cancellation	—	—	—	—	—	—	3.40	3.90
Information	—	—	2.80	3.36	—	—	3.40	3.90
Arithmetic	—	—	—	—	—	—	3.40	3.90
Word Reasoning	—	—	3.17	3.81	—	—	3.96	4.54

(Continued)

Table A-4 (*Continued*)

Age 12-0-0 through 12-11-30

Subtest	Mean of 2 subtests for WMI		Mean of 2 subtests for PSI		Mean of 3 subtests for VCI		Mean of 3 subtests for PRI	
	.05	.01	.05	.01	.05	.01	.05	.01
Block Design	—	—	—	—	—	—	2.08	2.56
Similarities	—	—	—	—	2.08	2.55	—	—
Digit Span	1.34	1.77	—	—	—	—	—	—
Picture Concepts	—	—	—	—	—	—	2.39	2.93
Coding	—	—	1.71	2.25	—	—	—	—
Vocabulary	—	—	—	—	1.91	2.34	—	—
Letter–Number Sequencing	1.63	2.15	—	—	—	—	—	—
Matrix Reasoning	—	—	—	—	—	—	1.91	2.35
Comprehension	—	—	—	—	2.16	2.65	—	—
Symbol Search	—	—	1.71	2.25	—	—	—	—
Picture Completion	—	—	—	—	—	—	—	—
Cancellation	—	—	—	—	—	—	—	—
Information	—	—	—	—	—	—	—	—
Arithmetic	—	—	—	—	—	—	—	—
Word Reasoning	—	—	—	—	—	—	—	—

Subtest	Mean of 3 subtests for WMI		Mean of 3 subtests for PSI		Mean of 4 subtests for VCI		Mean of 4 subtests for VCI	
	.05	.01	.05	.01	.05	.01	.05	.01
Block Design	—	—	—	—	—	—	—	—
Similarities	—	—	—	—	2.32	2.81	2.40	2.90
Digit Span	1.96	2.41	—	—	—	—	—	—
Picture Concepts	—	—	—	—	—	—	—	—
Coding	—	—	2.36	2.90	—	—	—	—
Vocabulary	—	—	—	—	2.07	2.50	2.15	2.60
Letter–Number Sequencing	1.93	2.36	—	—	—	—	—	—
Matrix Reasoning	—	—	—	—	—	—	—	—
Comprehension	—	—	—	—	2.44	2.95	2.51	3.04
Symbol Search	—	—	2.63	3.23	—	—	—	—
Picture Completion	—	—	—	—	—	—	—	—
Cancellation	—	—	2.76	3.39	—	—	—	—
Information	—	—	—	—	2.32	2.81	—	—
Arithmetic	2.09	2.57	—	—	—	—	—	—
Word Reasoning	—	—	—	—	—	—	2.93	3.54

Subtest	Mean of 4 subtests for PRI		Mean of 5 subtests for VCI		Mean of 10 subtests for FS		Mean of 15 subtests	
	.05	.01	.05	.01	.05	.01	.05	.01
Block Design	2.31	2.79	—	—	2.90	3.40	2.93	3.36
Similarities	—	—	2.53	3.04	3.28	3.85	3.04	3.49
Digit Span	—	—	—	—	2.99	3.51	2.80	3.21
Picture Concepts	2.75	3.33	—	—	3.28	3.85	3.74	4.28
Coding	—	—	—	—	2.69	3.15	3.04	3.49
Vocabulary	—	—	2.23	2.68	2.90	3.40	2.56	2.94
Letter–Number Sequencing	—	—	—	—	2.48	2.91	2.70	3.09
Matrix Reasoning	2.06	2.48	—	—	2.69	3.15	2.43	2.79
Comprehension	—	—	2.67	3.21	3.44	4.04	3.25	3.73
Symbol Search	—	—	—	—	3.52	4.13	3.82	4.38
Picture Completion	2.54	3.07	—	—	—	—	3.36	3.85
Cancellation	—	—	—	—	—	—	4.17	4.78
Information	—	—	2.53	3.04	—	—	3.04	3.49
Arithmetic	—	—	—	—	—	—	3.15	3.61
Word Reasoning	—	—	3.17	3.81	—	—	4.01	4.59

19

(*Continued*)

Age 13-0-0 through 13-11-30

Subtest	Mean of 2 subtests for WMI		Mean of 2 subtests for PSI		Mean of 3 subtests for VCI		Mean of 3 subtests for PRI	
	.05	.01	.05	.01	.05	.01	.05	.01
Block Design	—	—	—	—	—	—	2.12	2.60
Similarities	—	—	—	—	2.31	2.83	—	—
Digit Span	1.55	2.04	—	—	—	—	—	—
Picture Concepts	—	—	—	—	—	—	2.42	2.97
Coding	—	—	1.71	2.25	—	—	—	—
Vocabulary	—	—	—	—	2.07	2.54	—	—
Letter–Number Sequencing	1.55	2.04	—	—	—	—	—	—
Matrix Reasoning	—	—	—	—	—	—	2.08	2.55
Comprehension	—	—	—	—	2.42	2.96	—	—
Symbol Search	—	—	1.71	2.25	—	—	—	—
Picture Completion	—	—	—	—	—	—	—	—
Cancellation	—	—	—	—	—	—	—	—
Information	—	—	—	—	—	—	—	—
Arithmetic	—	—	—	—	—	—	—	—
Word Reasoning	—	—	—	—	—	—	—	—

Subtest	Mean of 3 subtests for WMI		Mean of 3 subtests for PSI		Mean of 4 subtests for VCI		Mean of 4 subtests for VCI	
	.05	.01	.05	.01	.05	.01	.05	.01
Block Design	—	—	—	—	—	—	—	—
Similarities	—	—	—	—	2.56	3.09	2.61	3.15
Digit Span	2.16	2.65	—	—	—	—	—	—
Picture Concepts	—	—	—	—	—	—	—	—
Coding	—	—	2.36	2.90	—	—	—	—
Vocabulary	—	—	—	—	2.20	2.66	2.26	2.73
Letter–Number Sequencing	2.24	2.74	—	—	—	—	—	—
Matrix Reasoning	—	—	—	—	—	—	—	—
Comprehension	—	—	—	—	2.72	3.29	2.77	3.34
Symbol Search	—	—	2.63	3.23	—	—	—	—
Picture Completion	—	—	—	—	—	—	—	—
Cancellation	—	—	2.76	3.39	—	—	—	—
Information	—	—	—	—	2.38	2.88	—	—
Arithmetic	2.24	2.74	—	—	—	—	—	—
Word Reasoning	—	—	—	—	—	—	2.81	3.39

Subtest	Mean of 4 subtests for PRI		Mean of 5 subtests for VCI		Mean of 10 subtests for FS		Mean of 15 subtests	
	.05	.01	.05	.01	.05	.01	.05	.01
Block Design	2.34	2.83	—	—	2.90	3.40	2.99	3.43
Similarities	—	—	2.76	3.32	3.28	3.85	3.41	3.91
Digit Span	—	—	—	—	2.99	3.51	3.09	3.55
Picture Concepts	2.78	3.36	—	—	3.28	3.85	3.78	4.33
Coding	—	—	—	—	2.69	3.15	3.09	3.55
Vocabulary	—	—	2.34	2.81	2.90	3.40	2.75	3.16
Letter–Number Sequencing	—	—	—	—	2.48	2.91	3.30	3.79
Matrix Reasoning	2.27	2.75	—	—	2.69	3.15	2.86	3.28
Comprehension	—	—	2.95	3.55	3.44	4.04	3.70	4.24
Symbol Search	—	—	—	—	3.52	4.13	3.86	4.42
Picture Completion	2.63	3.18	—	—	—	—	3.51	4.03
Cancellation	—	—	—	—	—	—	4.21	4.82
Information	—	—	2.55	3.07	—	—	3.09	3.55
Arithmetic	—	—	—	—	—	—	3.30	3.79
Word Reasoning	—	—	3.01	3.61	—	—	3.78	4.33

(Continued)

Age 14-0-0 through 14-11-30

Subtest	Mean of 2 subtests for WMI		Mean of 2 subtests for PSI		Mean of 3 subtests for VCI		Mean of 3 subtests for PRI	
	.05	.01	.05	.01	.05	.01	.05	.01
Block Design	—	—	—	—	—	—	2.25	2.76
Similarities	—	—	—	—	1.96	2.41	—	—
Digit Span	1.34	1.77	—	—	—	—	—	—
Picture Concepts	—	—	—	—	—	—	2.29	2.81
Coding	—	—	1.74	2.29	—	—	—	—
Vocabulary	—	—	—	—	1.88	2.30	—	—
Letter–Number Sequencing	1.34	1.77	—	—	—	—	—	—
Matrix Reasoning	—	—	—	—	—	—	2.17	2.67
Comprehension	—	—	—	—	2.13	2.62	—	—
Symbol Search	—	—	1.74	2.29	—	—	—	—
Picture Completion	—	—	—	—	—	—	—	—
Cancellation	—	—	—	—	—	—	—	—
Information	—	—	—	—	—	—	—	—
Arithmetic	—	—	—	—	—	—	—	—
Word Reasoning	—	—	—	—	—	—	—	—

Subtest	Mean of 3 subtests for WMI		Mean of 3 subtests for PSI		Mean of 4 subtests for VCI		Mean of 4 subtests for VCI	
	.05	.01	.05	.01	.05	.01	.05	.01
Block Design	—	—	—	—	—	—	—	—
Similarities	—	—	—	—	2.18	2.63	2.21	2.67
Digit Span	1.96	2.41	—	—	—	—	—	—
Picture Concepts	—	—	—	—	—	—	—	—
Coding	—	—	2.33	2.85	—	—	—	—
Vocabulary	—	—	—	—	2.05	2.48	2.09	2.52
Letter–Number Sequencing	1.93	2.36	—	—	—	—	—	—
Matrix Reasoning	—	—	—	—	—	—	—	—
Comprehension	—	—	—	—	2.43	2.93	2.46	2.97
Symbol Search	—	—	2.64	3.24	—	—	—	—
Picture Completion	—	—	—	—	—	—	—	—
Cancellation	—	—	2.60	3.19	—	—	—	—
Information	—	—	—	—	2.31	2.79	—	—
Arithmetic	2.09	2.57	—	—	—	—	—	—
Word Reasoning	—	—	—	—	—	—	2.57	3.11

Subtest	Mean of 4 subtests for PRI		Mean of 5 subtests for VCI		Mean of 10 subtests for FS		Mean of 15 subtests	
	.05	.01	.05	.01	.05	.01	.05	.01
Block Design	2.53	3.05	—	—	2.90	3.40	3.29	3.77
Similarities	—	—	2.34	2.81	3.28	3.85	2.84	3.26
Digit Span	—	—	—	—	2.99	3.51	2.84	3.26
Picture Concepts	2.58	3.12	—	—	3.28	3.85	3.40	3.89
Coding	—	—	—	—	2.69	3.15	3.08	3.53
Vocabulary	—	—	2.19	2.63	2.90	3.40	2.61	2.99
Letter–Number Sequencing	—	—	—	—	2.48	2.91	2.74	3.14
Matrix Reasoning	2.41	2.91	—	—	2.69	3.15	3.08	3.53
Comprehension	—	—	2.63	3.16	3.44	4.04	3.29	3.77
Symbol Search	—	—	—	—	3.52	4.13	3.96	4.53
Picture Completion	2.69	3.24	—	—	—	—	3.58	4.11
Cancellation	—	—	—	—	—	—	3.85	4.41
Information	—	—	2.49	3.00	—	—	3.08	3.53
Arithmetic	—	—	—	—	—	—	3.19	3.65
Word Reasoning	—	—	2.77	3.33	—	—	3.50	4.02

21

(*Continued*)

Table A-4 (Continued)

Age 15-0-0 through 15-11-30

Subtest	Mean of 2 subtests for WMI		Mean of 2 subtests for PSI		Mean of 3 subtests for VCI		Mean of 3 subtests for PRI	
	.05	.01	.05	.01	.05	.01	.05	.01
Block Design	—	—	—	—	—	—	2.20	2.70
Similarities	—	—	—	—	1.99	2.44	—	—
Digit Span	1.44	1.89	—	—	—	—	—	—
Picture Concepts	—	—	—	—	—	—	2.60	3.18
Coding	—	—	1.74	2.29	—	—	—	—
Vocabulary	—	—	—	—	1.76	2.16	—	—
Letter–Number Sequencing	1.44	1.89	—	—	—	—	—	—
Matrix Reasoning	—	—	—	—	—	—	2.28	2.79
Comprehension	—	—	—	—	2.35	2.88	—	—
Symbol Search	—	—	1.74	2.29	—	—	—	—
Picture Completion	—	—	—	—	—	—	—	—
Cancellation	—	—	—	—	—	—	—	—
Information	—	—	—	—	—	—	—	—
Arithmetic	—	—	—	—	—	—	—	—
Word Reasoning	—	—	—	—	—	—	—	—

Subtest	Mean of 3 subtests for WMI		Mean of 3 subtests for PSI		Mean of 4 subtests for VCI		Mean of 4 subtests for VCI	
	.05	.01	.05	.01	.05	.01	.05	.01
Block Design	—	—	—	—	—	—	—	—
Similarities	—	—	—	—	2.16	2.61	2.22	2.68
Digit Span	1.93	2.37	—	—	—	—	—	—
Picture Concepts	—	—	—	—	—	—	—	—
Coding	—	—	2.33	2.85	—	—	—	—
Vocabulary	—	—	—	—	1.81	2.19	1.88	2.27
Letter–Number Sequencing	2.02	2.48	—	—	—	—	—	—
Matrix Reasoning	—	—	—	—	—	—	—	—
Comprehension	—	—	—	—	2.69	3.25	2.73	3.30
Symbol Search	—	—	2.64	3.24	—	—	—	—
Picture Completion	—	—	—	—	—	—	—	—
Cancellation	—	—	2.60	3.19	—	—	—	—
Information	—	—	—	—	2.03	2.46	—	—
Arithmetic	1.85	2.27	—	—	—	—	—	—
Word Reasoning	—	—	—	—	—	—	2.52	3.05

Subtest	Mean of 4 subtests for PRI		Mean of 5 subtests for VCI		Mean of 10 subtests for FS		Mean of 15 subtests	
	.05	.01	.05	.01	.05	.01	.05	.01
Block Design	2.38	2.88	—	—	2.90	3.40	2.97	3.41
Similarities	—	—	2.32	2.79	3.28	3.85	2.84	3.26
Digit Span	—	—	—	—	2.99	3.51	2.84	3.26
Picture Concepts	2.96	3.58	—	—	3.28	3.85	4.03	4.62
Coding	—	—	—	—	2.69	3.15	3.08	3.53
Vocabulary	—	—	1.90	2.28	2.90	3.40	2.18	2.49
Letter–Number Sequencing	—	—	—	—	2.48	2.91	3.08	3.53
Matrix Reasoning	2.49	3.01	—	—	2.69	3.15	3.18	3.65
Comprehension	—	—	2.94	3.53	3.44	4.04	3.77	4.32
Symbol Search	—	—	—	—	3.52	4.13	3.95	4.53
Picture Completion	2.60	3.15	—	—	—	—	3.40	3.89
Cancellation	—	—	—	—	—	—	3.85	4.41
Information	—	—	2.17	2.61	—	—	2.61	2.99
Arithmetic	—	—	—	—	—	—	2.61	2.99
Word Reasoning	—	—	2.69	3.23	—	—	3.40	3.89

(Continued)

Table A-4 (*Continued*)

Age 16-0-0 through 16-11-30

Subtest	Mean of 2 subtests for WMI		Mean of 2 subtests for PSI		Mean of 3 subtests for VCI		Mean of 3 subtests for PRI	
	.05	.01	.05	.01	.05	.01	.05	.01
Block Design	—	—	—	—	—	—	2.25	2.76
Similarities	—	—	—	—	2.16	2.65	—	—
Digit Span	1.35	1.77	—	—	—	—	—	—
Picture Concepts	—	—	—	—	—	—	2.64	3.24
Coding	—	—	1.74	2.29	—	—	—	—
Vocabulary	—	—	—	—	1.87	2.29	—	—
Letter–Number Sequencing	1.35	1.77	—	—	—	—	—	—
Matrix Reasoning	—	—	—	—	—	—	2.25	2.76
Comprehension	—	—	—	—	2.12	2.60	—	—
Symbol Search	—	—	1.74	2.29	—	—	—	—
Picture Completion	—	—	—	—	—	—	—	—
Cancellation	—	—	—	—	—	—	—	—
Information	—	—	—	—	—	—	—	—
Arithmetic	—	—	—	—	—	—	—	—
Word Reasoning	—	—	—	—	—	—	—	—

Subtest	Mean of 3 subtests for WMI		Mean of 3 subtests for PSI		Mean of 4 subtests for VCI		Mean of 4 subtests for VCI	
	.05	.01	.05	.01	.05	.01	.05	.01
Block Design	—	—	—	—	—	—	—	—
Similarities	—	—	—	—	2.42	2.92	2.51	3.04
Digit Span	1.76	2.15	—	—	—	—	—	—
Picture Concepts	—	—	—	—	—	—	—	—
Coding	—	—	2.33	2.85	—	—	—	—
Vocabulary	—	—	—	—	1.98	2.39	2.09	2.52
Letter–Number Sequencing	1.98	2.43	—	—	—	—	—	—
Matrix Reasoning	—	—	—	—	—	—	—	—
Comprehension	—	—	—	—	2.36	2.85	2.46	2.97
Symbol Search	—	—	2.64	3.24	—	—	—	—
Picture Completion	—	—	—	—	—	—	—	—
Cancellation	—	—	2.60	3.19	—	—	—	—
Information	—	—	—	—	2.11	2.55	—	—
Arithmetic	1.80	2.21	—	—	—	—	—	—
Word Reasoning	—	—	—	—	—	—	2.93	3.54

Subtest	Mean of 4 subtests for PRI		Mean of 5 subtests for VCI		Mean of 10 subtests for FS		Mean of 15 subtests	
	.05	.01	.05	.01	.05	.01	.05	.01
Block Design	2.43	2.93	—	—	2.90	3.40	3.08	3.53
Similarities	—	—	2.66	3.19	3.28	3.85	3.29	3.77
Digit Span	—	—	—	—	2.99	3.51	2.48	2.85
Picture Concepts	3.00	3.62	—	—	3.28	3.85	4.12	4.72
Coding	—	—	—	—	2.69	3.15	3.08	3.53
Vocabulary	—	—	2.14	2.57	2.90	3.40	2.48	2.85
Letter–Number Sequencing	—	—	—	—	2.48	2.91	3.08	3.53
Matrix Reasoning	2.43	2.93	—	—	2.69	3.15	3.08	3.53
Comprehension	—	—	2.59	3.11	3.44	4.04	3.19	3.65
Symbol Search	—	—	—	—	3.52	4.13	3.96	4.54
Picture Completion	2.48	3.00	—	—	—	—	3.19	3.65
Cancellation	—	—	—	—	—	—	3.85	4.41
Information	—	—	2.30	2.76	—	—	2.74	3.14
Arithmetic	—	—	—	—	—	—	2.61	3.00
Word Reasoning	—	—	3.16	3.79	—	—	4.04	4.63

(*Continued*)

Table A-4 (Continued)

Total Group

Subtest	Mean of 2 subtests for WMI		Mean of 2 subtests for PSI		Mean of 3 subtests for VCI		Mean of 3 subtests for PRI	
	.05	.01	.05	.01	.05	.01	.05	.01
Block Design	—	—	—	—	—	—	2.22	2.72
Similarities	—	—	—	—	2.23	2.73	—	—
Digit Span	1.42	1.86	—	—	—	—	—	—
Picture Concepts	—	—	—	—	—	—	2.38	2.92
Coding	—	—	1.78	2.34	—	—	—	—
Vocabulary	—	—	—	—	2.11	2.58	—	—
Letter–Number Sequencing	1.42	1.86	—	—	—	—	—	—
Matrix Reasoning	—	—	—	—	—	—	2.09	2.56
Comprehension	—	—	—	—	2.41	2.95	—	—
Symbol Search	—	—	1.78	2.34	—	—	—	—
Picture Completion	—	—	—	—	—	—	—	—
Cancellation	—	—	—	—	—	—	—	—
Information	—	—	—	—	—	—	—	—
Arithmetic	—	—	—	—	—	—	—	—
Word Reasoning	—	—	—	—	—	—	—	—

Subtest	Mean of 3 subtests for WMI		Mean of 3 subtests for PSI		Mean of 4 subtests for VCI		Mean of 4 subtests for VCI	
	.05	.01	.05	.01	.05	.01	.05	.01
Block Design	—	—	—	—	—	—	—	—
Similarities	—	—	—	—	2.46	2.98	2.50	3.02
Digit Span	2.05	2.51	—	—	—	—	—	—
Picture Concepts	—	—	—	—	—	—	—	—
Coding	—	—	2.46	3.01	—	—	—	—
Vocabulary	—	—	—	—	2.28	2.76	2.32	2.80
Letter–Number Sequencing	1.95	2.39	—	—	—	—	—	—
Matrix Reasoning	—	—	—	—	—	—	—	—
Comprehension	—	—	—	—	2.73	3.30	2.76	3.34
Symbol Search	—	—	2.61	3.20	—	—	—	—
Picture Completion	—	—	—	—	—	—	—	—
Cancellation	—	—	2.63	3.23	—	—	—	—
Information	—	—	—	—	2.51	3.03	—	—
Arithmetic	2.03	2.49	—	—	—	—	—	—
Word Reasoning	—	—	—	—	—	—	2.81	3.39

Subtest	Mean of 4 subtests for PRI		Mean of 5 subtests for VCI		Mean of 10 subtests for FS		Mean of 15 subtests	
	.05	.01	.05	.01	.05	.01	.05	.01
Block Design	2.47	2.98	—	—	2.90	3.40	3.22	3.69
Similarities	—	—	2.65	3.18	3.28	3.85	3.22	3.69
Digit Span	—	—	—	—	2.99	3.51	3.06	3.51
Picture Concepts	2.70	3.26	—	—	3.28	3.85	3.64	4.18
Coding	—	—	—	—	2.69	3.15	3.40	3.60
Vocabulary	—	—	2.43	2.92	2.90	3.40	2.88	3.30
Letter–Number Sequencing	—	—	—	—	2.48	2.91	2.80	3.21
Matrix Reasoning	2.27	2.74	—	—	2.69	3.15	2.85	3.27
Comprehension	—	—	2.96	3.55	3.44	4.04	3.70	4.24
Symbol Search	—	—	—	—	3.52	4.13	3.83	4.39
Picture Completion	2.57	3.10	—	—	—	—	3.40	3.90
Cancellation	—	—	—	—	—	—	3.88	4.45
Information	—	—	2.70	3.24	—	—	3.30	3.78
Arithmetic	—	—	—	—	—	—	3.01	3.45
Word Reasoning	—	—	3.01	3.62	—	—	3.78	4.33

(Continued)

Table A-4 (*Continued*)

Note. Abbreviations: VCI = Verbal Comprehension Index, PRI = Perceptual Reasoning Index, WMI = Working Memory Index, PSI = Processing Speed Index, FS = Full Scale.

The table shows the minimum deviations from a child's average subtest scaled score that are significant at the .05 and .01 levels.

The following formula, obtained from Davis (1959), was used to compute the deviations from average that are significant at the desired significance level:

$$D = \text{CR} \times \text{SEM}_{((T/m)-Z_I)}$$

where

D = deviation from average
CR = critical ratio desired
$\text{SEM}_{((T/m)-Z_I)}$ = standard error of measurement of the difference between an average subtest scaled score and any one of the subtest scaled scores that entered into the average

The standard error of measurement can be obtained from the following formula:

$$\text{SEM}_{((T/m)-Z_I)} = \sqrt{\frac{\text{SEM}_T^2}{m^2} + \left(\frac{m-2}{m}\right)\text{SEM}_{Z_I}^2}$$

where

SEM_T^2 = sum of the squared standard errors of measurement of the m subtests
m = number of subtests included in the average
T/m = average of the subtest scaled scores
$\text{SEM}_{Z_I}^2$ = squared standard error of measurement of any one of the subtest scaled scores

The critical ratios used were based on the Bonferroni inequality, which controls the family-wise error rate at .05 (or .01) by setting the error rate per comparison at .05/m (or .01/m). The critical ratios at the .05 level are 2.39 for 3 subtests, 2.50 for 4 subtests, 2.58 for 5 subtests, 2.81 for 10 subtests, and 2.94 for 15 subtests. The critical ratios at the .01 level are 2.93 for 3 subtests, 3.02 for 4 subtests, 3.10 for 5 subtests, 3.30 for 10 subtests, and 3.37 for 15 subtests. For 6 and 7 subtests, the Bonferroni inequality critical ratios would be 2.64 and 2.69, respectively, at the .05 level and 3.14 and 3.19, respectively, at the .01 level.

The following example illustrates the procedure. We will determine the minimum deviation required for a 6-year-old child's score on the WISC–IV Similarities subtest to be significantly different from his or her average score on the three standard Verbal Comprehension subtests (Similarities, Vocabulary, and Comprehension) at the 95% level of confidence. We calculate SEM_T^2 by first squaring the appropriate average standard error of measurement for each of the three subtests and then summing the squares. These standard errors of measurement are in Table 4.3 (p. 38) in the Technical Manual.

$$\text{SEM}_T^2 = (1.27)^2 + (1.27)^2 + (1.34)^2 = 5.02$$

We determine $\text{SEM}_{Z_I}^2$ by squaring the average standard error of measurement of the subtest of interest, the Similarities subtest:

$$\text{SEM}_{Z_I}^2 = (1.27)^2 = 1.6129$$

The number of subtests, m, equals 3. Substituting these values into the formula yields the following:

$$\text{SEM}_{((T/m)-Z_I)} = \sqrt{\frac{5.02}{(3)^2} + \left(\frac{3-2}{3}\right)1.6129} = 1.046$$

The value, 1.046, is then multiplied by the appropriate z value for the 95% confidence level to obtain the minimum significant deviation (D). Using the Bonferroni correction (.05/3 = .0167), we have a z value of 2.39.

$$D = 2.39 \times 1.046 = 2.499$$

The Bonferonni correction was not applied to the two-subtest mean comparisons.

Table A-5
Differences Between WISC–IV Process Scaled Scores Required for Statistical Significance at the .05 and .01 Levels of Significance for the 11 Age Groups and the Total Group

Comparison	Level	Age (in years)											Total
		6	7	8	9	10	11	12	13	14	15	16	
BD vs. BDN	.05	4	4	4	4	4	4	3	4	4	3	4	4
	.01	5	5	5	5	5	5	4	5	5	4	5	5
DSF vs. DSB	.05	4	5	5	4	4	4	4	4	4	4	4	4
	.01	5	6	6	5	5	5	5	5	5	5	5	5
CAR vs. CAS	.05	5	5	5	5	5	5	5	5	5	5	5	5
	.01	6	6	6	6	6	6	6	6	6	6	6	6

Note. Abbreviations: BD = Block Design, BDN = Block Design No Time Bonus, DSF = Digit Span Forward, DSB = Digit Span Backward, CAR = Cancellation Random, CAS = Cancellation Structured.

Sample reading: At age 6 (6-0 to 6-11), a difference of 4 points between scaled scores on the Block Design and Block Design No Time Bonus is significant at the 5% level and a difference of 5 points is significant at the 1% level.

All values in this table have been rounded up to the next higher number.

See Exhibit 11-1 in Chapter 11 for the procedure used to arrive at magnitudes of differences.

Table A-6
Estimates of the Differences Obtained by Various Percentages of the WISC–IV Standardization Sample When Each WISC–IV Subtest Scaled Score Is Compared to the Mean Scaled Score for Any Individual Child

| | Verbal Comprehension | | | | | | | | Perceptual Reasoning | | | |
| | Core subtests | | | | Core subtests plus Information | | | | Core subtests | | | |
Subtest	10%	5%	2%	1%	10%	5%	2%	1%	10%	5%	2%	1%
Block Design	—	—	—	—	—	—	—	—	2.90	3.45	4.11	4.53
Similarities	2.28	2.72	3.24	3.57	2.39	2.84	3.39	3.73	—	—	—	—
Digit Span	—	—	—	—	—	—	—	—	—	—	—	—
Picture Concepts	—	—	—	—	—	—	—	—	3.11	3.71	4.42	4.87
Coding	—	—	—	—	—	—	—	—	—	—	—	—
Vocabulary	2.05	2.45	2.92	3.22	2.09	2.49	2.96	3.27	—	—	—	—
Letter–Number Sequencing	—	—	—	—	—	—	—	—	—	—	—	—
Matrix Reasoning	—	—	—	—	—	—	—	—	2.72	3.24	3.87	4.26
Comprehension	2.48	2.96	3.53	3.89	2.72	3.24	3.86	4.26	—	—	—	—
Symbol Search	—	—	—	—	—	—	—	—	—	—	—	—
Picture Completion	—	—	—	—	—	—	—	—	—	—	—	—
Cancellation	—	—	—	—	—	—	—	—	—	—	—	—
Information	—	—	—	—	2.36	2.81	3.35	3.69	—	—	—	—
Arithmetic	—	—	—	—	—	—	—	—	—	—	—	—
Word Reasoning	—	—	—	—	—	—	—	—	—	—	—	—

| | Verbal Comprehension | | | | | | | | Perceptual Reasoning | | | |
| | Core subtests plus Word Reasoning | | | | Core subtests plus Information and Word Reasoning | | | | Core subtests plus Picture Completion | | | |
Subtest	10%	5%	2%	1%	10%	5%	2%	1%	10%	5%	2%	1%
Block Design	—	—	—	—	—	—	—	—	2.93	3.49	4.16	4.59
Similarities	2.46	2.93	3.49	3.84	2.49	2.97	3.54	3.90	—	—	—	—
Digit Span	—	—	—	—	—	—	—	—	—	—	—	—
Picture Concepts	—	—	—	—	—	—	—	—	3.37	4.02	4.79	5.28
Coding	—	—	—	—	—	—	—	—	—	—	—	—
Vocabulary	2.19	2.61	3.12	3.43	2.18	2.60	3.10	3.41	—	—	—	—
Letter–Number Sequencing	—	—	—	—	—	—	—	—	—	—	—	—
Matrix Reasoning	—	—	—	—	—	—	—	—	2.97	3.54	4.22	4.65
Comprehension	2.69	3.21	3.82	4.21	2.82	3.36	4.01	4.42	—	—	—	—
Symbol Search	—	—	—	—	—	—	—	—	—	—	—	—
Picture Completion	—	—	—	—	—	—	—	—	3.15	3.75	4.48	4.93
Cancellation	—	—	—	—	—	—	—	—	—	—	—	—
Information	—	—	—	—	2.47	2.95	3.51	3.87	—	—	—	—
Arithmetic	—	—	—	—	—	—	—	—	—	—	—	—
Word Reasoning	2.74	3.26	3.89	4.28	2.86	3.40	4.06	4.47	—	—	—	—

(Continued)

Table A-6 (*Continued*)

Subtest	Working Memory								Full Scale			
	Core subtests				Core subtests plus Arithmetic				Core subtests			
	10%	5%	2%	1%	10%	5%	2%	1%	10%	5%	2%	1%
Block Design	—	—	—	—	—	—	—	—	3.52	4.20	5.00	5.51
Similarities	—	—	—	—	—	—	—	—	3.15	3.75	4.47	4.93
Digit Span	2.49	2.97	3.54	3.90	2.93	3.50	4.17	4.59	3.92	4.66	5.56	6.13
Picture Concepts	—	—	—	—	—	—	—	—	3.78	4.50	5.36	5.91
Coding	—	—	—	—	—	—	—	—	4.10	4.88	5.82	6.41
Vocabulary	—	—	—	—	—	—	—	—	3.08	3.67	4.37	4.82
Letter–Number Sequencing	2.49	2.97	3.54	3.90	2.82	3.36	4.01	4.42	3.57	4.25	5.07	5.59
Matrix Reasoning	—	—	—	—	—	—	—	—	3.41	4.06	4.84	5.34
Comprehension	—	—	—	—	—	—	—	—	3.46	4.12	4.91	5.42
Symbol Search	—	—	—	—	—	—	—	—	3.70	4.41	5.26	5.80
Picture Completion	—	—	—	—	—	—	—	—	—	—	—	—
Cancellation	—	—	—	—	—	—	—	—	—	—	—	—
Information	—	—	—	—	—	—	—	—	—	—	—	—
Arithmetic	—	—	—	—	2.88	3.43	4.09	4.50	—	—	—	—
Word Reasoning	—	—	—	—	—	—	—	—	—	—	—	—

Subtest	Processing Speed								Full Scale			
	Core subtests				Core subtests plus Cancellation				Core subtests plus Information, Word Reasoning, Picture Completion, Arithmetic, and Cancellation			
	10%	5%	2%	1%	10%	5%	2%	1%	10%	5%	2%	1%
Block Design	—	—	—	—	—	—	—	—	3.52	4.20	5.01	5.52
Similarities	—	—	—	—	—	—	—	—	3.11	3.70	4.42	4.87
Digit Span	—	—	—	—	—	—	—	—	4.05	4.82	5.75	6.34
Picture Concepts	—	—	—	—	—	—	—	—	3.88	4.63	5.52	6.08
Coding	2.39	2.85	3.40	3.74	2.81	3.35	3.99	4.40	4.15	4.95	5.90	6.50
Vocabulary	—	—	—	—	—	—	—	—	3.00	3.58	4.27	4.70
Letter–Number Sequencing	—	—	—	—	—	—	—	—	3.71	4.42	5.27	5.81
Matrix Reasoning	—	—	—	—	—	—	—	—	3.52	4.19	5.00	5.51
Comprehension	—	—	—	—	—	—	—	—	3.45	4.11	4.90	5.40
Symbol Search	2.39	2.85	3.40	3.74	3.03	3.61	4.31	4.75	3.80	4.53	5.40	5.95
Picture Completion	—	—	—	—	—	—	—	—	3.70	4.41	5.26	5.80
Cancellation	—	—	—	—	3.36	4.01	4.78	5.26	4.93	5.87	7.00	7.72
Information	—	—	—	—	—	—	—	—	3.11	3.70	4.42	4.87
Arithmetic	—	—	—	—	—	—	—	—	3.23	3.85	4.59	5.06
Word Reasoning	—	—	—	—	—	—	—	—	3.45	4.11	4.89	5.39

Note. The formula used to obtain the values in this table was obtained from Silverstein (1984):

$$SD_{Da} = 3\sqrt{1 + \bar{G} - 2\bar{T_a}}$$

where

SD_{Da} = standard deviation of the difference for subtest a

3 = standard deviation of the scaled scores on each of the subtests

$\bar{G}$ = mean of all the elements in the matrix (including 1s in the diagonal)

$\bar{T_a}$ = mean of the elements in row or column a of the matrix (again including 1s in the diagonal)

Table A-7
Reliability and Validity Coefficients of WISC–IV Short Forms for 2-, 3-, 4-, and 5-Subtest Combinations

Two subtests			Three subtests			Four subtests			Five subtests		
Short form	r_{ss}	r	Short form	r_{ss}	r	Short form	r_{ss}	r	Short form	r_{ss}	r
VC AR	.928	.879	VC SS AR	.924	.911	SI VC SS AR	.943	.933	SI CD MR AR WR	.955	.949
BD VC	.916	.874	VC MR AR	.946	.908	VC SS AR WR	.945	.932	CD VC MR AR WR	.957	.949
SI AR	.917	.874	BD VC AR	.941	.907	SI CD VC AR	.946	.931	VC MR SS AR WR	.955	.949
VC MR	.926	.873	VC PCm AR	.935	.906	SI CD AR WR	.944	.931	SI CD VC MR AR	.956	.948
VC SS	.884	.863	BD VC LN	.939	.905	SI VC MR SS	.942	.931	SI VC MR SS AR	.954	.948
BD IN	.905	.861	SI SS AR	.918	.905	SI CD VC MR	.945	.930	BD SI CD VC LN	.953	.947
SI MR	.916	.860	SI VC SS	.924	.904	SI SS AR WR	.941	.930	SI MR SS AR WR	.953	.947
AR WR	.926	.860	VC MR SS	.923	.904	VC MR SS IN	.942	.930	BD SI CD VC AR	.954	.946
IN AR	.920	.858	VC SS IN	.924	.904	VC MR SS AR	.943	.930	BD CD VC AR WR	.955	.946
MR IN	.917	.857	BD VC IN	.939	.903	VC MR SS WR	.944	.930	SI CD VC PCm AR	.952	.946
LN AR[a]	.927	.818	SI VC IN	.947	.874	BD SI DS CD[h]	.932	.909	SI VC CO IN WR[l]	.963	.891
DS AR[a]	.915	.779	SI VC WR[d]	.950	.870	SI VC CO IN[i]	.953	.882			
SS CA[b,c]	.841	.583	SI CO IN[d]	.932	.867	SI VC CO WR[i]	.954	.878			
CD CA[b,c]	.871	.517	VC CO IN[d]	.938	.863	BD PCn MR PCm[c,j]	.939	.858			
			SI CO WR[d]	.935	.858	DS LN CD SS[k]	.931	.826			
			VC CO WR[d]	.942	.854						
			BD MR PCm[e]	.933	.831						
			PCn MR PCm[c,e]	.920	.828						
			BD PCn PCm[e]	.915	.823						
			DS LN AR[f]	.941	.819						
			CD SS CA[c, g]	.896	.636						

Note. Abbreviations: BD = Block Design, SI = Similarities, DS = Digit Span, PCn = Picture Concepts, CD = Coding, VC = Vocabulary, LN = Letter–Number Sequencing, MR = Matrix Reasoning, CO = Comprehension, SS = Symbol Search, PCm = Picture Completion, CA = Cancellation, IN = Information, AR = Arithmetic, WR = Word Reasoning.

The estimated Full Scale IQs associated with each short form are shown in Tables A-9 to A-12.

The first 10 combinations in each list represent the best ones, based on validity. See Table D-11 in Appendix D for formulas used to obtain reliability and validity coefficients.

[a]This combination represents the subtests in the Working Memory Composite with the substitution of Arithmetic.
[b]This combination represents the subtests in the Processing Speed Composite with the substitution of Cancellation.
[c]This combination is useful for children who are hearing impaired.
[d]This combination represents the subtests in the Verbal Comprehension Composite with the substitution of a supplemental subtest.

[e]This combination represents the subtests in the Perceptual Reasoning Composite with the substitution of a supplemental subtest.
[f]This combination represents all core and supplemental subtests in the Working Memory Composite.
[g]This combination represents all core and supplemental subtests in the Processing Speed Composite.
[h]This combination represents one core subtest from each Composite.
[i]This combination represents three core subtests and one supplemental subtest (all with high *g* loadings) in the Verbal Comprehension Composite.
[j]This combination represents all core and supplemental subtests in the Perceptual Reasoning Composite.
[k]This combination represents all core subtests in both Working Memory and Processing Speed Composites.
[l]This combination represents all core and supplemental subtests in the Verbal Comprehension Composite.

Table A-8
Reliable and Unusual Scaled-Score Ranges for Selected WISC–IV Subtest Combinations

Composite or short form				Reliable scaled-score range	Unusual scaled-score range
Two subtests					
DS	LN			3	5
CD	SS			4	5
VC	AR			3	5
BD	VC			3	6
SI	AR			4	5
VC	MR			3	5
VC	SS			4	6
BD	IN			4	6
SI	MR			3	5
AR	WR			4	6
IN	AR			4	5
MR	IN			3	5
LN	AR			3	5
DS	AR			3	6
SS	CA			4	6
CD	CA			4	6
Three subtests					
SI	VC	CO		4	5
BD	PCn	MR		4	7
DS	LN	AR		4	7
CD	SS	CA		5	7
VC	SS	AR		4	7
VC	MR	AR		4	6
BD	VC	AR		4	6
VC	PCm	AR		4	7
BD	VC	LN		4	7
SI	SS	AR		4	7
SI	VC	SS		4	7
VC	MR	SS		4	7
VC	SS	IN		4	7
BD	VC	IN		4	6
SI	VC	IN		4	5
SI	VC	WR		4	5
SI	CO	IN		4	6
VC	CO	IN		4	5
SI	CO	WR		5	6
VC	CO	WR		5	6
BD	MR	PCm		4	7
PCn	MR	PCm		4	7
BD	PCn	PCm		4	7

Composite or short form					Reliable scaled-score range	Unusual scaled-score range
Four subtests						
SI	VC	CO	IN		5	6
SI	VC	CO	WR		5	6
BD	PCn	MR	PCm		5	8
SI	VC	SS	AR		5	7
VC	SS	AR	WR		5	8
SI	CD	VC	AR		5	8
SI	CD	AR	WR		5	8
SI	VC	MR	SS		5	7
SI	CD	VC	MR		4	8
SI	SS	AR	WR		5	8
VC	MR	SS	IN		5	7
VC	MR	SS	AR		4	7
VC	MR	SS	WR		5	8
BD	SI	DS	CD		5	8
DS	CD	LN	SS		5	8
Five subtests						
SI	VC	CO	IN	WR	6	7
SI	CD	MR	AR	WR	6	8
CD	VC	MR	AR	WR	5	8
VC	MR	SS	AR	WR	6	8
SI	CD	VC	MR	AR	5	8
SI	VC	MR	SS	AR	5	8
BD	SI	CD	VC	LN	5	8
SI	MR	SS	AR	WR	6	8
BD	SI	CD	VC	AR	5	8
BD	CD	VC	AR	WR	6	8
SI	CD	VC	PCm	AR	5	8
Six subtests						
BD	SI	PCn	VC	MR	CO	5	8
10 subtests (core only)						
10 subtests					6	10
15 subtests (core plus supplemental)						
15 subtests					6	12

(Continued)

Table A-8 (*Continued*)

Note. Abbreviations: BD = Block Design, SI = Similarities, DS = Digit Span, PCn = Picture Concepts, CD = Coding, VC = Vocabulary, LN = Letter–Number Sequencing, MR = Matrix Reasoning, CO = Comprehension, SS = Symbol Search, PCm = Picture Completion, CA = Cancellation, IN = Information, AR = Arithmetic, WR = Word Reasoning.

The formula used to obtain the reliable scaled-score range is as follows (Silverstein, 1989):

$$R = q\sqrt{\frac{\Sigma \mathrm{SEM}_i^2}{k}}$$

where

q = critical value (n/v) of the Studentized range for a specified probability level (.05 in this case)

SEM_i = standard error of measurement of the scores on subtest i

k = number of subtests in the short form

The formula used to obtain the unusual scaled-score range is as follows (Silverstein, 1989):

$$R = q \times \sigma\sqrt{1 - \frac{2\Sigma r_{ij}}{k(k-1)}}$$

where

q = critical value (n/v) of the Studentized range for a specified probability level (.10 in this case)

σ = standard deviation of the subtest scores

r_{ij} = correlation between subtests i and j

k = number of subtests in the short form

The following are the appropriate q values to use in the two formulas for sample sizes of from 2 to 10 and of 15, with v (degrees of freedom) = ∞, at the .10 probability level and at the .05 probability level (.10 or .05): for 2, 2.33 or 2.77; for 3, 2.90 or 3.31; for 4, 3.24 or 3.63; for 5, 3.48 or 3.86; for 6, 3.66 or 4.03; for 7, 3.81 or 4.17; for 8, 3.93 or 4.29; for 9, 4.04 or 4.39; for 10, 4.13 or 4.47; and for 15, 4.47 or 4.80.

The table is read as follows: In the two-subtest short form composed of Digit Span and Letter–Number Sequencing, a range of 3 points between the two scores indicates a nonchance difference at the .05 level. A range of 5 occurs in less than 10% of the population and should be considered unusual, as should all ranges higher than 5 points. Less credence can be placed in a Composite score or short-form IQ when the scatter is larger than expected.

Table A-9
Estimated WISC–IV Full Scale IQs for Sum of Scaled Scores
for 10 Best 2-Subtest Short Forms and Other Combinations

Sum of scaled scores	Combination										
	C2	C3	C4	C5	C6	C7	C8	C9	C10	C11	C12
2	45	46	48	48	48	48	48	49	50	50	54
3	48	49	50	51	51	51	51	52	52	53	56
4	51	52	53	54	54	54	54	55	55	56	59
5	54	55	56	56	57	57	57	58	58	58	61
6	57	58	59	59	59	60	60	60	61	61	64
7	60	61	62	62	62	62	63	63	64	64	66
8	63	64	65	65	65	65	65	66	66	67	69
9	66	67	68	68	68	68	68	69	69	69	72
10	69	70	71	71	71	71	71	72	72	72	74
11	72	73	74	74	74	74	74	75	75	75	77
12	75	76	77	77	77	77	77	77	78	78	79
13	78	79	80	80	80	80	80	80	80	81	82
14	82	82	83	83	83	83	83	83	83	83	85
15	85	85	85	85	86	86	86	86	86	86	87
16	88	88	88	88	88	88	88	89	89	89	90
17	91	91	91	91	91	91	91	92	92	92	92
18	94	94	94	94	94	94	94	94	94	94	95
19	97	97	97	97	97	97	97	97	97	97	97
20	100	100	100	100	100	100	100	100	100	100	100
21	103	103	103	103	103	103	103	103	103	103	103
22	106	106	106	106	106	106	106	106	106	106	105
23	109	109	109	109	109	109	109	108	108	108	108
24	112	112	112	112	112	112	112	111	111	111	110
25	115	115	115	115	114	114	114	114	114	114	113
26	118	118	117	117	117	117	117	117	117	117	115
27	122	121	120	120	120	120	120	120	120	119	118
28	125	124	123	123	123	123	123	123	122	122	121
29	128	127	126	126	126	126	126	125	125	125	123
30	131	130	129	129	129	129	129	128	128	128	126
31	134	133	132	132	132	132	132	131	131	131	128
32	137	136	135	135	135	135	135	134	134	133	131
33	140	139	138	138	138	138	137	137	136	136	134
34	143	142	141	141	141	140	140	140	139	139	136
35	146	145	144	144	143	143	143	142	142	142	139
36	149	148	147	146	146	146	146	145	145	144	141
37	152	151	150	149	149	149	149	148	148	147	144
38	155	154	152	152	152	152	152	151	150	150	146

Note. The subtest combinations are as follows:

C2 = SS + CA[a,b]
C3 = VC + SS[c]
    CD + CA[a, b]
C4 = DS + AR[d]

C5 = BD + IN[c]
    BD + VC[c]
C6 = SI + MR[c]
    VC + MR[c]

C7 = MR + IN[c]
C8 = LN + AR[d]
C9 = SI + AR[c]

C10 = VC + AR[c]
C11 = IN + AR[c]
C12 = AR + WR[c]

Abbreviations: BD = Block Design, SI = Similarities, DS = Digit Span, PCn = Picture Concepts, CD = Coding, VC = Vocabulary, LN = Letter–Number Sequencing, MR = Matrix Reasoning, CO = Comprehension, SS = Symbol Search, PCm = Picture Completion, CA = Cancellation, IN = Information, AR = Arithmetic, WR = Word Reasoning.

Reliability and validity coefficients associated with each short-form combination are shown in Table A-7. See Table D-11 in Appendix D for an explanation of the procedure used to obtain the estimated IQs.

[a]This combination represents the subtests in the Processing Speed Composite with the substitution of Cancellation.

[b]This combination is useful for children who are hearing impaired.

[c]This combination is one of the 10 best 2-subtest short forms.

[d]This combination represents the subtests in the Working Memory Composite with the substitution of Arithmetic.

32

Table A-10
Estimated WISC–IV Full Scale IQs for Sum of Scaled Scores
for 10 Best 3-Subtest Short Forms and Other Combinations

Sum of scaled scores	Combination																
	C2	C3	C4	C5	C6	C7	C8	C9	C10	C11	C12	C13	C14	C15	C16	C17	C18
3	42	43	43	44	44	44	45	45	45	46	47	47	47	48	49	49	50
4	45	45	45	46	46	46	47	47	47	48	49	49	49	50	50	51	52
5	47	48	47	48	48	48	49	49	49	50	51	51	51	52	52	53	54
6	49	50	49	50	50	50	51	51	51	52	53	53	53	54	54	55	56
7	51	52	51	52	52	52	53	53	53	54	55	55	55	56	56	57	58
8	53	54	53	54	54	54	55	55	55	56	57	57	57	58	58	59	60
9	55	56	56	56	56	56	57	57	57	58	58	59	59	60	60	61	61
10	57	58	58	58	58	58	59	59	60	60	60	61	61	62	62	62	63
11	59	60	60	60	60	61	61	61	62	62	62	63	63	64	64	64	65
12	62	62	62	62	62	63	63	63	64	64	64	64	65	65	66	66	67
13	64	64	64	64	65	65	65	65	66	66	66	66	67	67	68	68	69
14	66	66	66	67	67	67	67	67	68	68	68	68	69	69	70	70	71
15	68	69	68	69	69	69	69	69	70	70	70	70	71	71	71	72	72
16	70	71	70	71	71	71	71	71	72	72	72	72	73	73	73	74	74
17	72	73	72	73	73	73	73	74	74	74	74	74	75	75	75	76	76
18	74	75	75	75	75	75	75	76	76	76	76	76	77	77	77	77	78
19	77	77	77	77	77	77	77	78	78	78	78	78	79	79	79	79	80
20	79	79	79	79	79	79	79	80	80	80	80	80	81	81	81	81	82
21	81	81	81	81	81	81	82	82	82	82	82	82	82	83	83	83	83
22	83	83	83	83	83	83	84	84	84	84	84	84	84	85	85	85	85
23	85	85	85	85	85	85	86	86	86	86	86	86	86	87	87	87	87
24	87	87	87	87	88	88	88	88	88	88	88	88	88	88	89	89	89
25	89	90	89	90	90	90	90	90	90	90	90	90	90	90	90	91	91
26	91	92	92	92	92	92	92	92	92	92	92	92	92	92	92	92	93
27	94	94	94	94	94	94	94	94	94	94	94	94	94	94	94	94	94
28	96	96	96	96	96	96	96	96	96	96	96	96	96	96	96	96	96
29	98	98	98	98	98	98	98	98	98	98	98	98	98	98	98	98	98
30	100	100	100	100	100	100	100	100	100	100	100	100	100	100	100	100	100
31	102	102	102	102	102	102	102	102	102	102	102	102	102	102	102	102	102
32	104	104	104	104	104	104	104	104	104	104	104	104	104	104	104	104	104
33	106	106	106	106	106	106	106	106	106	106	106	106	106	106	106	106	106
34	109	108	108	108	108	108	108	108	108	108	108	108	108	108	108	108	107
35	111	110	111	110	110	110	110	110	110	110	110	110	110	110	110	109	109
36	113	113	113	113	113	112	112	112	112	112	112	112	112	112	111	111	111
37	115	115	115	115	115	115	114	114	114	114	114	114	114	113	113	113	113
38	117	117	117	117	117	117	116	116	116	116	116	116	116	115	115	115	115
39	119	119	119	119	119	119	118	118	118	118	118	118	118	117	117	117	117
40	121	121	121	121	121	121	121	120	120	120	120	120	119	119	119	119	118
41	123	123	123	123	123	123	123	122	122	122	122	122	121	121	121	121	120
42	126	125	125	125	125	125	125	124	124	124	124	124	123	123	123	123	122
43	128	127	128	127	127	127	127	126	126	126	126	126	125	125	125	124	124
44	130	129	130	129	129	129	129	129	128	128	128	128	127	127	127	126	126
45	132	131	132	131	131	131	131	131	130	130	130	130	129	129	129	128	128
46	134	134	134	133	133	133	133	133	132	132	132	132	131	131	130	130	129
47	136	136	136	136	135	135	135	135	134	134	134	134	133	133	132	132	131
48	138	138	138	138	138	137	137	137	136	136	136	136	135	135	134	134	133
49	141	140	140	140	140	139	139	139	138	138	138	137	137	136	136	136	135

(Continued)

Table A-10 (*Continued*)

Sum of scaled scores	Combination																
	C2	C3	C4	C5	C6	C7	C8	C9	C10	C11	C12	C13	C14	C15	C16	C17	C18
50	143	142	142	142	142	142	141	141	140	140	140	139	139	138	138	138	137
51	145	144	144	144	144	144	143	143	143	142	142	141	141	140	140	139	139
52	147	146	147	146	146	146	145	145	145	144	143	143	143	142	142	141	140
53	149	148	149	148	148	148	147	147	147	146	145	145	145	144	144	143	142
54	151	150	151	150	150	150	149	149	149	148	147	147	147	146	146	145	144
55	153	152	153	152	152	152	151	151	151	150	149	149	149	148	148	147	146
56	155	155	155	154	154	154	153	153	153	152	151	151	151	150	150	149	148
57	158	157	157	156	156	156	155	155	155	154	153	153	153	152	151	151	150

Note. The subtest combinations are as follows:

C2 = CD + SS + CA[a, b]
C3 = BD + PCn + PCm[c]
    PCn + MR + PCm[c]
    BD + VC + AR[d]
C4 = VC + MR + SS[d]
C5 = BD + VC + LN[d]
C6 = SI + SS + AR[d]
C7 = VC + SS + AR[d]
C8 = DS + LN + AR[e]
C9 = VC + PCm + AR[d]
    SI + VC + SS[d]
    VC + SS + IN[d]

C10 = BD + MR + PCm[a, c]
C11 = VC + MR + AR[d]
    BD + VC + AR[d]
C12 = SI + CO + WR[f]
C13 = BD + VC + IN[d]
C14 = VC + CO + WR[f]
C15 = SI + VC + WR[f]
C16 = SI + CO + IN[f]
C17 = VC + CO + IN[f]
C18 = SI + VC + IN[f]

Abbreviations: BD = Block Design, SI = Similarities, DS = Digit Span, PCn = Picture Concepts, CD = Coding, VC = Vocabulary, LN = Letter–Number Sequencing, MR = Matrix Reasoning, CO = Comprehension, SS = Symbol Search, PCm = Picture Completion, CA = Cancellation, IN = Information, AR = Arithmetic, WR = Word Reasoning.

Reliability and validity coefficients associated with each short-form combination are shown in Table A-7. See Table D-11 in Appendix D for an explanation of the procedure used to obtain the estimated IQs.
[a]This combination is useful for children who are hearing impaired.
[b]This combination represents all core and supplemental subtests in the Processing Speed Composite.
[c]This combination represents the subtests in the Perceptual Reasoning Composite with the substitution of a supplemental subtest.
[d]This combination is one of the 10 best 3-subtest short forms.
[e]This combination represents all core and supplemental subtests in the Working Memory Composite.
[f]This combination represents the subtests in the Verbal Comprehension Composite with the substitution of a supplemental subtest.

Table A-11
Estimated WISC–IV Full Scale IQs for Sum of Scaled Scores
for 10 Best 4-Subtest Short Forms and Other Combinations

Sum of scaled scores	Combination												
	C2	C3	C4	C5	C6	C7	C8	C9	C10	C11	C12	C13	C14
4	37	38	41	42	42	43	43	43	44	44	45	47	49
5	39	40	43	44	44	44	44	45	45	46	46	48	50
6	41	42	44	45	45	46	46	46	47	48	48	50	51
7	42	43	46	47	47	47	47	48	48	49	49	51	53
8	44	45	48	48	49	49	49	49	50	51	51	53	54
9	46	47	49	50	50	51	51	51	51	52	52	54	56
10	48	49	51	52	52	52	52	53	53	54	54	56	57
11	49	50	52	53	53	54	54	54	55	55	55	57	59
12	51	52	54	55	55	55	55	56	56	57	57	59	60
13	53	54	56	57	57	57	57	57	58	58	59	60	61
14	55	55	57	58	58	59	59	59	59	60	60	62	63
15	56	57	59	60	60	60	60	60	61	61	62	63	64
16	58	59	61	61	61	62	62	62	62	63	63	64	66
17	60	61	62	63	63	63	63	64	64	65	65	66	67
18	62	62	64	65	65	65	65	65	66	66	66	67	69
19	63	64	66	66	66	66	67	67	67	68	68	69	70
20	65	66	67	68	68	68	68	68	69	69	69	70	71
21	67	67	69	69	69	70	70	70	70	71	71	72	73
22	69	69	70	71	71	71	71	72	72	72	72	73	74
23	70	71	72	73	73	73	73	73	73	74	74	75	76
24	72	73	74	74	74	74	74	75	75	75	75	76	77
25	74	74	75	76	76	76	76	76	76	77	77	78	79
26	76	76	77	77	78	78	78	78	78	78	78	79	80
27	77	78	79	79	79	79	79	79	80	80	80	81	81
28	79	79	80	81	81	81	81	81	81	81	82	82	83
29	81	81	82	82	82	82	82	83	83	83	83	84	84
30	83	83	84	84	84	84	84	84	84	85	85	85	86
31	84	85	85	86	86	86	86	86	86	86	86	87	87
32	86	86	87	87	87	87	87	87	87	88	88	88	89
33	88	88	89	89	89	89	89	89	89	89	89	90	90
34	90	90	90	90	90	90	90	91	91	91	91	91	91
35	91	91	92	92	92	92	92	92	92	92	92	93	93
36	93	93	93	94	94	94	94	94	94	94	94	94	94
37	95	95	95	95	95	95	95	95	95	95	95	96	96
38	97	97	97	97	97	97	97	97	97	97	97	97	97
39	98	98	98	98	98	98	98	98	98	98	98	99	99
40	100	100	100	100	100	100	100	100	100	100	100	100	100
41	102	102	102	102	102	102	102	102	102	102	102	101	101
42	103	103	103	103	103	103	103	103	103	103	103	103	103
43	105	105	105	105	105	105	105	105	105	105	105	104	104
44	107	107	107	106	106	106	106	106	106	106	106	106	106
45	109	109	108	108	108	108	108	108	108	108	108	107	107
46	110	110	110	110	110	110	110	109	109	109	109	109	109
47	112	112	111	111	111	111	111	111	111	111	111	110	110
48	114	114	113	113	113	113	113	113	113	112	112	112	111
49	116	115	115	114	114	114	114	114	114	114	114	113	113

(Continued)

Table A-11 (*Continued*)

Sum of scaled scores	Combination												
	C2	C3	C4	C5	C6	C7	C8	C9	C10	C11	C12	C13	C14
50	117	117	116	116	116	116	116	116	116	115	115	114	114
51	119	119	118	118	118	118	118	117	117	117	117	116	116
52	121	121	120	119	119	119	119	119	119	119	118	117	117
53	123	122	121	121	121	121	121	121	120	120	120	119	119
54	124	124	123	123	122	122	122	122	122	122	122	120	120
55	126	126	125	124	124	124	124	124	124	123	123	121	121
56	128	127	126	126	126	126	126	125	125	125	125	123	123
57	130	129	128	127	127	127	127	127	127	126	126	124	124
58	131	131	130	129	129	129	129	128	128	128	128	126	126
59	133	133	131	131	131	130	130	130	130	129	129	127	127
60	135	134	133	132	132	132	132	132	131	131	131	129	129
61	137	136	134	134	134	134	133	133	133	132	132	130	130
62	138	138	136	135	135	135	135	135	134	134	134	131	131
63	140	139	138	137	137	137	137	136	136	135	135	133	133
64	142	141	139	139	139	138	138	138	138	137	137	134	134
65	144	143	141	140	140	140	140	140	139	139	138	136	136
66	145	145	143	142	142	141	141	141	141	140	140	137	137
67	147	146	144	143	143	143	143	143	142	142	141	139	139
68	149	148	146	145	145	145	145	144	144	143	143	140	140
69	151	150	148	147	147	146	146	146	145	145	145	141	141
70	152	151	149	148	148	148	148	147	147	146	146	143	143
71	154	153	151	150	150	149	149	149	149	148	148	144	144
72	156	155	152	152	151	151	151	151	150	149	149	146	146
73	158	157	154	153	153	153	153	152	152	151	151	147	147
74	159	158	156	155	155	154	154	154	153	152	152	149	149
75	161	160	157	156	156	156	156	155	155	154	154	150	150
76	163	162	159	158	158	157	157	157	156	156	155	151	151

Note. The subtest combinations are as follows:

C2 = BD + SI + DS + CD[a]
C3 = DS + LN + CD + SS[b]
C4 = SI + CD + VC + MR[c]
C5 = BD + PCn + MR + PCm[d,e]

C6 = VC + MR + SS + WR[c]
    SI + CD + VC + AR[c]
    VC + MR + SS + AR[c]
C7 = SI + VC + MR + SS[c]
C8 = VC + MR + SS + IN[c]

C9 = SI + CD + AR + WR[c]
C10 = SI + VC + SS + AR[c]
C11 = SI + SS + AR + WR[c]
C12 = VC + SS + AR + WR[c]
C13 = SI + VC + CO + WR[f]
C14 = SI + VC + CO + IN[f]

Abbreviations: BD = Block Design, SI = Similarities, DS = Digit Span, PCn = Picture Concepts, CD = Coding, VC = Vocabulary, LN = Letter–Number Sequencing, MR = Matrix Reasoning, CO = Comprehension, SS = Symbol Search, PCm = Picture Completion, CA = Cancellation, IN = Information, AR = Arithmetic, WR = Word Reasoning.

Reliability and validity coefficients associated with each short-form combination are shown in Table A-7. See Table D-11 in Appendix D for an explanation of the procedure used to obtain the estimated IQs.

[a]This combination represents one core subtest from each Composite.
[b]This combination represents the core subtests in both Working Memory and Processing Speed Composites.
[c]This combination is one of the 10 best 4-subtest short forms.
[d]This combination is useful for children who are hearing impaired.
[e]This combination represents all core and supplemental subtests in the Perceptual Reasoning Composite.
[f]This combination represents three core subtests and one supplemental subtest in the Verbal Comprehension Composite.

Table A-12
Estimated WISC–IV Full Scale IQs for Sum of Scaled Scores
for 10 Best 5-Subtest Short Forms and Other Combinations

Sum of scaled scores	Combination									
	C2	C3	C4	C5	C6	C7	C8	C9	C10	C11
5	39	40	41	42	42	42	42	43	43	47
6	40	41	42	43	43	43	43	44	44	48
7	42	43	43	44	44	45	45	45	46	49
8	43	44	45	45	46	46	46	47	47	50
9	44	45	46	47	47	47	47	48	48	51
10	46	47	47	48	48	48	48	49	49	53
11	47	48	49	49	50	50	50	50	51	54
12	48	49	50	51	51	51	51	52	52	55
13	50	51	51	52	52	52	52	53	53	56
14	51	52	53	53	54	54	54	54	54	57
15	53	53	54	55	55	55	55	56	56	59
16	54	55	55	56	56	56	56	57	57	60
17	55	56	57	57	57	57	57	58	58	61
18	57	57	58	58	59	59	59	59	59	62
19	58	59	59	60	60	60	60	61	61	63
20	59	60	60	61	61	61	61	62	62	64
21	61	61	62	62	63	63	63	63	63	66
22	62	63	63	64	64	64	64	64	65	67
23	63	64	64	65	65	65	65	66	66	68
24	65	65	66	66	66	66	67	67	67	69
25	66	67	67	68	68	68	68	68	68	70
26	67	68	68	69	69	69	69	70	70	72
27	69	69	70	70	70	70	70	71	71	73
28	70	71	71	71	72	72	72	72	72	74
29	72	72	72	73	73	73	73	73	73	75
30	73	73	74	74	74	74	74	75	75	76
31	74	75	75	75	75	75	76	76	76	77
32	76	76	76	77	77	77	77	77	77	79
33	77	77	78	78	78	78	78	78	78	80
34	78	79	79	79	79	79	79	80	80	81
35	80	80	80	81	81	81	81	81	81	82
36	81	81	82	82	82	82	82	82	82	83
37	82	83	83	83	83	83	83	83	84	85
38	84	84	84	84	85	85	85	85	85	86
39	85	85	86	86	86	86	86	86	86	87
40	86	87	87	87	87	87	87	87	87	88
41	88	88	88	88	88	88	88	89	89	89
42	89	89	89	90	90	90	90	90	90	91
43	91	91	91	91	91	91	91	91	91	92
44	92	92	92	92	92	92	92	92	92	93
45	93	93	93	94	94	94	94	94	94	94
46	95	95	95	95	95	95	95	95	95	95
47	96	96	96	96	96	96	96	96	96	96
48	97	97	97	97	97	97	97	97	97	98
49	99	99	99	99	99	99	99	99	99	99
50	100	100	100	100	100	100	100	100	100	100
51	101	101	101	101	101	101	101	101	101	101
52	103	103	103	103	103	103	103	103	103	102
53	104	104	104	104	104	104	104	104	104	104
54	105	105	105	105	105	105	105	105	105	105

(*Continued*)

Table A-12 (*Continued*)

Sum of scaled scores	Combination									
	C2	C3	C4	C5	C6	C7	C8	C9	C10	C11
55	107	107	107	106	106	106	106	106	106	106
56	108	108	108	108	108	108	108	108	108	107
57	109	109	109	109	109	109	109	109	109	108
58	111	111	111	110	110	110	110	110	110	109
59	112	112	112	112	112	112	112	111	111	111
60	114	113	113	113	113	113	113	113	113	112
61	115	115	114	114	114	114	114	114	114	113
62	116	116	116	116	115	115	115	115	115	114
63	118	117	117	117	117	117	117	117	116	115
64	119	119	118	118	118	118	118	118	118	117
65	120	120	120	119	119	119	119	119	119	118
66	122	121	121	121	121	121	121	120	120	119
67	123	123	122	122	122	122	122	122	122	120
68	124	124	124	123	123	123	123	123	123	121
69	126	125	125	125	125	125	124	124	124	123
70	127	127	126	126	126	126	126	125	125	124
71	128	128	128	127	127	127	127	127	127	125
72	130	129	129	129	128	128	128	128	128	126
73	131	131	130	130	130	130	130	129	129	127
74	133	132	132	131	131	131	131	130	130	128
75	134	133	133	132	132	132	132	132	132	130
76	135	135	134	134	134	134	133	133	133	131
77	137	136	136	135	135	135	135	134	134	132
78	138	137	137	136	136	136	136	136	135	133
79	139	139	138	138	137	137	137	137	137	134
80	141	140	140	139	139	139	139	138	138	136
81	142	141	141	140	140	140	140	139	139	137
82	143	143	142	142	141	141	141	141	141	138
83	145	144	143	143	143	143	143	142	142	139
84	146	145	145	144	144	144	144	143	143	140
85	147	147	146	145	145	145	145	144	144	141
86	149	148	147	147	146	146	146	146	146	143
87	150	149	149	148	148	148	148	147	147	144
88	152	151	150	149	149	149	149	148	148	145
89	153	152	151	151	150	150	150	150	149	146
90	154	153	153	152	152	152	152	151	151	147
91	156	155	154	153	153	153	153	152	152	149
92	157	156	155	155	154	154	154	153	153	150
93	158	157	157	156	156	155	155	155	154	151
94	160	159	158	157	157	157	157	156	156	152

Note. The subtest combinations are as follows:

C2 = BD + SI + CD + VC + LN[a]   C5 = SI + CD + MR + AR + WR[a]   C9 = SI + MR + SS + AR + WR[a]
C3 = SI + CD + VC + PCm + AR[a]   C6 = CD + VC + MR + AR + WR[a]   C10 = VC + MR + SS + AR + WR[a]
C4 = BD + SI + CD + VC + AR[a]   C7 = BD + CD + VC + AR + WR[a]   C11 = SI + VC + CO + IN + WR[b]
   SI + CD + VC + MR + AR[a]   C8 = SI + VC + MR + SS + AR[a]

Abbreviations: BD = Block Design, SI = Similarities, DS = Digit Span, PCn = Picture Concepts, CD = Coding, VC = Vocabulary, LN = Letter–Number Sequencing, MR = Matrix Reasoning, CO = Comprehension, SS = Symbol Search, PCm = Picture Completion, CA = Cancellation, IN = Information, AR = Arithmetic, WR = Word Reasoning.

Reliability and validity coefficients associated with each short-form combination are shown in Table A-7. See Table D-11 in Appendix D for an explanation of the procedure used to obtain the estimated IQs.
[a]This combination is one of the 10 best 5-subtest short forms.
[b]This combination represents all core and supplemental subtests in the Verbal Comprehension Composite.

Table A-13
General Ability Index (GAI) Equivalents for Sum of Scaled Scores on the Block Design, Similarities, Picture Concepts, Vocabulary, Matrix Reasoning, and Comprehension Subtests

Sum of scaled scores	GAI	Sum of scaled scores	GAI	Sum of scaled scores	GAI
6	40	46	86	86	130
7	40	47	87	87	132
8	40	48	88	88	133
9	40	49	89	89	135
10	40	50	90	90	136
11	40	51	91	91	138
12	41	52	92	92	139
13	42	53	93	93	140
14	43	54	94	94	142
15	44	55	95	95	143
16	45	56	96	96	144
17	46	57	97	97	146
18	47	58	98	98	147
19	49	59	99	99	148
20	51	60	100	100	150
21	52	61	101	101	151
22	53	62	102	102	153
23	55	63	103	103	154
24	57	64	104	104	155
25	58	65	105	105	156
26	59	66	106	106	157
27	61	67	107	107	158
28	63	68	108	108	159
29	64	69	110	109	160
30	65	70	111	110	160
31	67	71	112	111	160
32	69	72	113	112	160
33	70	73	115	113	160
34	71	74	116	114	160
35	73	75	117		
36	74	76	119		
37	75	77	120		
38	77	78	121		
39	78	79	122		
40	79	80	123		
41	81	81	124		
42	82	82	126		
43	83	83	127		
44	84	84	128		
45	85	85	129		

Note. Average reliability for ages 6 through 11 is r_{xx} = .95 and average reliability for ages 12 through 16 is r_{xx} = .96.
Source: Adapted from Saklofske, Prifitera, Weiss, Rolfhus, & Zhu (2005). Permission to adapt this table was given by Elsevier Academic Press.

Table A-14
Estimated WISC–IV Full Scale IQs for Sum of Scaled Scores for Three Combinations Proposed by Keith, Fine, Taub, Reynolds, and Kranzler (2006)

Sum of scaled scores	Combination			Sum of scaled scores	Combination		
	C2	C3	C4		C2	C3	C4
2	49	48	42	30	128	129	100
3	52	50	44	31	131	132	102
4	54	53	46	32	134	135	104
5	57	56	48	33	137	138	106
6	60	59	50	34	140	141	108
7	63	62	52	35	143	144	110
8	66	65	55	36	146	147	112
9	69	68	57	37	148	150	114
10	72	71	59	38	151	152	117
11	74	74	61	39	154	155	119
12	77	77	63	40	157	158	121
13	80	80	65	41			123
14	83	83	67	42			125
15	86	85	69	43			127
16	89	88	71	44			129
17	91	91	73	45			131
18	94	94	75	46			133
19	97	97	77	47			135
20	100	100	79	48			137
21	103	103	81	49			139
22	106	106	83	50			141
23	109	109	86	51			143
24	111	112	88	52			145
25	114	115	90	53			148
26	117	117	92	54			150
27	120	120	94	55			152
28	123	123	96	56			154
29	126	126	98	57			156

Note. The subtest combinations are as follows:

C2 = BD + PCm[a]
C3 = PCn + MR[b]
C4 = PCn + MR + AR[c]

Abbreviations: BD = Block Design, PCm = Picture Completion, PCn = Picture Concepts, MR = Matrix Reasoning, AR = Arithmetic.

The reliability and validity coefficients for C2 are r_{ss} = .903 and r = .770; for C3, r_{ss} = .901 and r = .765; and for C4, r_{ss} = .930 and r = .856.

[a] This combination represents a measure of visual processing.
[b] This combination represents a measure of fluid reasoning.
[c] This combination represents a measure of fluid reasoning, with increased emphasis on novel tasks.

Table A-15
Administrative Checklist for the WISC–IV

ADMINISTRATIVE CHECKLIST FOR THE WISC–IV

Name of examiner: _____   Date: _____

Name of child: _____   Name of observer: _____

(Note: If an item is not applicable, mark NA to the left of the number.)

Before Beginning	Circle One	
1. Room is well lit	Yes	No
2. Furniture is comfortable and size is appropriate for child	Yes	No
3. Room is free of distractions	Yes	No
4. Asks parent, if present, to remain in background and observe quietly	Yes	No
5. Positions child correctly	Yes	No
6. Sits directly across from child	Yes	No
7. Establishes rapport	Yes	No
8. Tells child that breaks are OK and asks child to let examiner know when he or she needs a break	Yes	No
9. Does not prolong getting-acquainted period	Yes	No
10. Does not overstimulate child or entertain child excessively before starting test	Yes	No
11. Avoids use of term *intelligence* when introducing test	Yes	No
12. Responds truthfully to any questions child has about purpose of testing	Yes	No
13. Keeps test materials in order	Yes	No
14. Keeps test kit out of child's view	Yes	No
15. Begins test after establishing rapport	Yes	No
16. Positions Record Form and Administration Manual so that child cannot read questions or answers	Yes	No
17. Introduces test by reading directions in Administration Manual verbatim	Yes	No

Comments

_____

_____

_____

Block Design
(See pp. 318–320 in text for detailed information.)

Background Considerations

	Circle One	
1. Clears table	Yes	No
2. Seats child directly in front of table	Yes	No
3. Reads directions verbatim	Yes	No
4. Reads directions clearly	Yes	No
5. Uses stopwatch	Yes	No
6. Places stopwatch correctly	Yes	No
7. Repeats directions correctly	Yes	No

Block Design (*Continued*)	Circle One	
8. For items 5 to 10, shortens directions correctly	Yes	No
9. Clarifies directions correctly	Yes	No
10. Shows different sides of block correctly while reading directions	Yes	No
11. Gives child number of blocks needed for each item	Yes	No
12. Disassembles models correctly	Yes	No
13. Places intact model or Stimulus Book and blocks properly	Yes	No
14. Turns pages of Stimulus Book correctly	Yes	No
15. Use blocks and pictures as models correctly	Yes	No
16. Leaves model intact for items 1 and 2	Yes	No
17. Gives appropriate caution if child attempts to duplicate sides of model for items 1 and 2	Yes	No
18. Follows appropriate procedure for item 3	Yes	No
19. Scrambles blocks between designs	Yes	No
20. Removes all unnecessary blocks from child's view	Yes	No
21. For items 13 and 14, does not permit child to rotate Stimulus Book	Yes	No
22. Times correctly	Yes	No
23. Gives appropriate prompts	Yes	No
24. Administers trials correctly	Yes	No

Starting Considerations

25. Starts with appropriate item	Yes	No

Reverse Sequence

26. Administers items in reverse sequence correctly	Yes	No

Discontinue Considerations

27. Counts items administered in reverse sequence toward discontinue criterion	Yes	No
28. Discontinues subtest correctly	Yes	No
29. Removes Stimulus Book and blocks from child's view once subtest is completed	Yes	No

Scoring Guidelines

30. Scores items correctly	Yes	No

Record Form

31. Records completion time correctly	Yes	No
32. Completes Correct Design column correctly	Yes	No
33. Adds check marks in Constructed Design column correctly	Yes	No

(*Continued*)

Table A-15 (*Continued*)

Block Design (*Continued*)	Circle One	
34. Notes or sketches incorrect designs in Constructed Design column correctly	Yes	No
35. Notes rotations in Constructed Design column correctly	Yes	No
36. Circles 0, 1, 2, 4, 5, 6, or 7 in Score column correctly	Yes	No
37. Notes additional points correctly	Yes	No
38. Adds points correctly	Yes	No
39. Enters Total Raw Score in shaded box correctly	Yes	No
40. Enters Block Design No Time-Bonus Total Raw Score in shaded box correctly	Yes	No

Comments

_____

_____

_____

Similarities
(See pp. 323–324 in text for detailed information.)

Background Considerations	Circle One	
1. Reads directions verbatim	Yes	No
2. Reads directions clearly	Yes	No
3. Reads items verbatim	Yes	No
4. Reads items clearly	Yes	No
5. Repeats directions correctly	Yes	No
6. Repeats items correctly	Yes	No
7. Queries correctly	Yes	No
8. For sample and items 1 and 2, gives child correct answers, if needed	Yes	No
9. For items 3 to 23, does not give child correct answers	Yes	No
10. Grants additional time appropriately	Yes	No

Starting Considerations

11. Starts with appropriate item	Yes	No

Reverse Sequence

12. Administers items in reverse sequence correctly	Yes	No

Discontinue Considerations

13. Counts items administered in reverse sequence toward discontinue criterion	Yes	No
14. Discontinues subtest correctly	Yes	No

Scoring Guidelines

15. Scores responses correctly	Yes	No

Record Form

16. Records child's responses correctly	Yes	No
17. Circles 0, 1, or 2 in Score column correctly	Yes	No
18. Notes additional points correctly	Yes	No
19. Adds points correctly	Yes	No
20. Enters Total Raw Score in shaded box correctly	Yes	No

Similarities (*Continued*)   Circle One

Comments

_____

_____

_____

Digit Span
(See pp. 326–327 in text for detailed information.)

Background Considerations	Circle One	
1. Reads directions verbatim	Yes	No
2. Reads directions clearly	Yes	No
3. Repeats directions correctly	Yes	No
4. Shields digits in Record Form and Administration Manual from child's view	Yes	No
5. Reads digits clearly, at rate of one digit per second and without chunking, and drops voice slightly on last digit	Yes	No
6. Administers items correctly	Yes	No
7. Does not repeat trials	Yes	No

Starting Considerations

8. Starts with appropriate item	Yes	No

Discontinue Considerations

9. Discontinues subtest correctly	Yes	No

Scoring Guidelines

10. Scores items correctly	Yes	No

Record Form

11. Records child's responses correctly	Yes	No
12. Circles 0 or 1 in Trial Score column correctly	Yes	No
13. Circles 0, 1, or 2 in Item Score column correctly	Yes	No
14. Enters Total Raw Scores correctly	Yes	No
15. Enters Longest Digit Span Forward score correctly	Yes	No
16. Enters Longest Digit Span Backward score correctly	Yes	No

Comments

_____

_____

_____

Picture Concepts
(See pp. 329–330 in text for detailed information.)

Background Considerations	Circle One	
1. Reads directions verbatim	Yes	No
2. Reads directions clearly	Yes	No
3. Repeats directions correctly	Yes	No
4. Places Stimulus Book correctly	Yes	No
5. Positions Stimulus Book correctly	Yes	No

(*Continued*)

Table A-15 (*Continued*)

Picture Concepts (*Continued*)	Circle One	
6. Points across rows correctly while reading directions	Yes	No
7. Turns pages of Stimulus Book correctly	Yes	No
8. For items 2 to 12 and 14 to 28, shortens or eliminates directions correctly	Yes	No
9. Gives appropriate prompts	Yes	No
10. If asked, tells child name of picture	Yes	No
11. If response is not clear, asks child to point to picture	Yes	No
12. If child gives correct answer to sample A or B, asks appropriate question	Yes	No
13. Gives reason for correct answer to sample A or sample B, if appropriate	Yes	No
14. If child does not give correct answer to either sample A or B, gives correct answer, points to correct object, and gives reasons for correct answer	Yes	No
15. For test items, does not give correct answers or reasons for correct answers	Yes	No
16. Grants additional time appropriately	Yes	No

Starting Considerations

17. Starts with appropriate item	Yes	No

Reverse Sequence

18. Administers items in reverse sequence correctly	Yes	No

Discontinue Considerations

19. Counts items administered in reverse sequence toward discontinue criterion	Yes	No
20. Discontinues subtest correctly	Yes	No
21. Removes Stimulus Book from child's view once subtest is completed	Yes	No

Scoring Guidelines

22. Scores items correctly	Yes	No

Record Form

23. Circles response number or DK correctly	Yes	No
24. Circles 0 or 1 in Score column correctly	Yes	No
25. Notes additional points correctly	Yes	No
26. Adds points correctly	Yes	No
27. Enters Total Raw Score in shaded box correctly	Yes	No

Comments

_____

_____

_____

Coding

(See pp. 331–333 in text for detailed information.)

Background Considerations

1. Provides smooth working surface	Yes	No
2. Reads directions verbatim	Yes	No
3. Reads directions clearly	Yes	No

Coding (*Continued*)	Circle One	
4. Repeats directions correctly	Yes	No
5. Points to key while reading directions	Yes	No
6. Waits until child understands task before proceeding with items	Yes	No
7. Uses stopwatch	Yes	No
8. Places stopwatch correctly	Yes	No
9. Times correctly	Yes	No
10. Notes child's handedness on Record Form	Yes	No
11. Positions Response Booklet properly for left-handed child	Yes	No
12. Demonstrates sample correctly	Yes	No
13. Gives child number 2 pencil without eraser	Yes	No
14. Does not provide or allow child to use eraser	Yes	No
15. Gives appropriate responses to inquiries and appropriate prompts	Yes	No
16. Counts time for prompts as part of 120-second time limit	Yes	No
17. Allows spontaneous corrections, unless corrections impede performance	Yes	No

Starting Considerations

18. Starts with appropriate item	Yes	No

Discontinue Considerations

19. Discontinues subtest correctly	Yes	No
20. Stops timing if child finishes before 120 seconds	Yes	No
21. Says "Stop" after 120 seconds and discontinues subtest	Yes	No
22. Closes Response Booklet and removes it from child's view once subtest is completed	Yes	No

Scoring Guidelines

23. Scores subtest correctly	Yes	No

Response Booklet

24. Enters identifying data on Response Booklet 1 correctly	Yes	No

Record Form

25. Records completion time correctly	Yes	No
26. For Coding A, circles appropriate time-bonus points correctly	Yes	No
27. Adds points correctly	Yes	No
28. Enters Total Raw Score in shaded box correctly	Yes	No

Comments

_____

_____

_____

Table A-15 (*Continued*)

Vocabulary	Circle One		Letter–Number Sequencing	Circle One	
(See pp. 334–336 in text for detailed information.)			(See pp. 338–339 in text for detailed information.)		

Vocabulary

(See pp. 334–336 in text for detailed information.)

Background Considerations

	Circle One	
1. Reads directions verbatim	Yes	No
2. Reads directions clearly	Yes	No
3. Pronounces words clearly	Yes	No
4. Repeats directions correctly	Yes	No
5. Repeats items correctly	Yes	No
6. In cases of suspected hearing deficit, queries appropriately	Yes	No
7. Places closed Stimulus Book properly and opens it to appropriate page	Yes	No
8. On items 1 to 4, points to the picture	Yes	No
9. On items 5 to 36, points to each word in Stimulus Book while pronouncing it	Yes	No
10. Turns pages of Stimulus Book toward child	Yes	No
11. Queries correctly	Yes	No
12. If child gives 0- or 1-point response to item 5 or 6, tells child correct 2-point answer	Yes	No
13. For items 1 to 4 and items 7 to 36, does not tell child correct answers	Yes	No
14. Grants additional time appropriately	Yes	No

Starting Considerations

	Circle One	
15. Starts with appropriate item	Yes	No

Reverse Sequence

	Circle One	
16. Administers items in reverse sequence correctly	Yes	No

Discontinue Considerations

	Circle One	
17. Counts items administered in reverse sequence toward discontinue criterion	Yes	No
18. Discontinues subtest correctly	Yes	No
19. Removes Stimulus Book from child's view once subtest is completed	Yes	No

Scoring Guidelines

	Circle One	
20. Scores responses correctly	Yes	No

Record Form

	Circle One	
21. Records child's responses correctly	Yes	No
22. Circles 0, 1, or 2 in Score column correctly	Yes	No
23. Notes additional points correctly	Yes	No
24. Adds points correctly	Yes	No
25. Enters Total Raw Score in shaded box correctly	Yes	No

Comments

_____

_____

_____

Letter–Number Sequencing

(See pp. 338–339 in text for detailed information.)

Background Considerations

	Circle One	
1. Reads directions verbatim	Yes	No
2. Reads directions clearly	Yes	No
3. Repeats directions correctly	Yes	No
4. Shields digits and letters in Administration Manual and on Record Form from child's view	Yes	No
5. Reads digits and letters clearly, at rate of one digit or letter per second and without chunking	Yes	No
6. Drops voice slightly on last digit or letter in sequence	Yes	No
7. Gives all three trials of each item	Yes	No
8. Pauses after each sequence to allow child to respond	Yes	No
9. Does not repeat any digits or letters during subtest proper	Yes	No
10. If asked to repeat a trial of an item, gives appropriate response	Yes	No
11. Uses appropriate wording to correct child, as needed	Yes	No
12. Says nothing if child makes a mistake on certain items	Yes	No

Starting Considerations

	Circle One	
13. Starts with appropriate item	Yes	No

Discontinue Considerations

	Circle One	
14. Discontinues subtest correctly	Yes	No

Scoring Guidelines

	Circle One	
15. Scores items correctly	Yes	No

Record Form

	Circle One	
16. Circles Y or N correctly	Yes	No
17. Records responses in Verbatim Response column correctly	Yes	No
18. Circles 0 or 1 in Trial Score column correctly	Yes	No
19. Circles 0, 1, 2, or 3 in Item Score column correctly	Yes	No
20. Adds points correctly	Yes	No
21. Enters Total Raw Score in shaded box correctly	Yes	No

Comments

_____

_____

_____

(*Continued*)

Table A-15 (Continued)

Matrix Reasoning	Circle One	

(See pp. 340–341 in text for detailed information.)

Background Considerations

1.	Reads directions verbatim	Yes	No
2.	Reads directions clearly	Yes	No
3.	Places Stimulus Book properly	Yes	No
4.	Positions Stimulus Book correctly	Yes	No
5.	Clarifies directions correctly	Yes	No
6.	If child fails any sample, demonstrates correct way to solve problem	Yes	No
7.	Repeats directions correctly	Yes	No
8.	Gives appropriate prompts	Yes	No
9.	Provides feedback only on three samples	Yes	No
10.	Grants additional time appropriately	Yes	No

Starting Considerations

11.	Starts with appropriate item	Yes	No

Reverse Sequence

12.	Administers items in reverse sequence correctly	Yes	No

Discontinue Considerations

13.	Counts items administered in reverse sequence toward discontinue criterion	Yes	No
14.	Discontinues subtest correctly	Yes	No
15.	Removes Stimulus Book from child's view once subtest is completed	Yes	No

Scoring Guidelines

16.	Scores items correctly	Yes	No

Record Form

17.	Circles response number or DK correctly	Yes	No
18.	Circles 0 or 1 in Score column correctly	Yes	No
19.	Notes additional points correctly	Yes	No
20.	Adds points correctly	Yes	No
21.	Enters Total Raw Score in shaded box correctly	Yes	No

Comments

_____

_____

_____

Comprehension

(See pp. 342–343 in text for detailed information.)

Background Considerations

1.	Reads directions verbatim	Yes	No
2.	Reads directions clearly	Yes	No
3.	Reads items verbatim	Yes	No
4.	Reads items clearly	Yes	No
5.	Repeats questions correctly	Yes	No
6.	Repeats items correctly	Yes	No
7.	If child is hesitant, gives appropriate prompts	Yes	No

Comprehension (*Continued*)	Circle One	

8.	If child gives 0- or 1-point response to item 1, tells child correct 2-point answer	Yes	No
9.	For items 2 to 21, does not tell child correct answers	Yes	No
10.	Queries correctly	Yes	No
11.	Grants additional time appropriately	Yes	No

Starting Considerations

12.	Starts with appropriate item	Yes	No

Reverse Sequence

13.	Administers items in reverse sequence correctly	Yes	No

Discontinue Considerations

14.	Counts items administered in reverse sequence toward discontinue criterion	Yes	No
15.	Discontinues subtest correctly	Yes	No

Scoring Guidelines

16.	Scores items correctly	Yes	No

Record Form

17.	Records responses in Response column correctly	Yes	No
18.	Circles 0, 1, or 2 in Score column correctly	Yes	No
19.	Notes additional points correctly	Yes	No
20.	Adds points correctly	Yes	No
21.	Enters Total Raw Score in shaded box correctly	Yes	No

Comments

_____

_____

_____

Symbol Search

(See pp. 345–346 in text for detailed information.)

Background Considerations

1.	Provides smooth working surface	Yes	No
2.	Reads directions verbatim	Yes	No
3.	Reads directions clearly	Yes	No
4.	Repeats directions correctly	Yes	No
5.	Uses stopwatch	Yes	No
6.	Places stopwatch correctly	Yes	No
7.	During sample and practice items, makes sure that child sees only sample page of Response Booklet 1	Yes	No
8.	Gives child number 2 pencil without eraser	Yes	No
9.	Opens Response Booklet 1 to appropriate page	Yes	No
10.	For samples, points to target symbol and array	Yes	No

(Continued)

Table A-15 (*Continued*)

Symbol Search (*Continued*)	Circle One	
11. For samples, draws diagonal line through correct box (YES or NO)	Yes	No
12. For practice items, points to target symbol and array and gives appropriate directions	Yes	No
13. Gives appropriate feedback	Yes	No
14. If child makes an error on practice items, follows correct procedure	Yes	No
15. Explains directions using practice items, if needed	Yes	No
16. Does not proceed to test items unless child understands task	Yes	No
17. Opens Response Booklet 1 to page 4 or 8, as appropriate	Yes	No
18. Reads directions verbatim, including word "Go," even if explanations are not necessary	Yes	No
19. Before saying "Go," gives further explanations, if necessary	Yes	No
20. Begins timing correctly	Yes	No
21. Turns pages of Response Booklet 1, if needed	Yes	No
22. Gives appropriate prompts	Yes	No
23. Counts time for prompts as part of 120-second time limit	Yes	No
24. Does not discourage child from making spontaneous corrections, unless corrections impede performance	Yes	No

Starting Considerations

25. Starts with appropriate item	Yes	No

Discontinue Considerations

26. Discontinues subtest correctly	Yes	No
27. Stops timing if child finishes before 120 seconds	Yes	No
28. Says "Stop" after 120 seconds and discontinues subtest	Yes	No
29. Closes Response Booklet 1 and removes it from child's view once subtest is completed	Yes	No

Scoring Guidelines

30. Scores subtest correctly	Yes	No

Response Booklet

31. If needed, enters identifying data on Response Booklet 1	Yes	No
32. Enters number of correct responses correctly	Yes	No
33. Enters number of incorrect responses correctly	Yes	No

Record Form

34. Records completion time correctly	Yes	No
35. Enters total number of correct items in Number Correct box correctly	Yes	No
36. Enters total number of incorrect items in Number Incorrect box correctly	Yes	No

Symbol Search (*Continued*)	Circle One	
37. Enters Total Raw Score in shaded box correctly	Yes	No
38. Enters 0 if Total Raw Score is equal to or less than 0	Yes	No

Comments

_____

_____

_____

Picture Completion
(See pp. 348–349 in text for detailed information.)

Background Considerations

1. Reads directions verbatim	Yes	No
2. Reads directions clearly	Yes	No
3. Reads items verbatim	Yes	No
4. Reads items clearly	Yes	No
5. Repeats directions correctly	Yes	No
6. Places Stimulus Book properly	Yes	No
7. Turns pages of Stimulus Book correctly	Yes	No
8. Allows 20 seconds for each item	Yes	No
9. For items 3 to 38, shortens or eliminates directions correctly	Yes	No
10. Begins timing correctly	Yes	No
11. Stops timing correctly	Yes	No
12. On sample, repeats child's correct answer	Yes	No
13. For sample and items 1 and 2, gives child correct answers, if needed	Yes	No
14. For items 3 to 38, does not give child correct answers	Yes	No
15. Prompts or queries specific responses only once during subtest	Yes	No
16. Queries ambiguous or incomplete responses correctly	Yes	No
17. Queries responses noted in right-hand column of pages 166 to 169 in Administration Manual correctly	Yes	No

Starting Considerations

18. Starts with appropriate item	Yes	No

Reverse Sequence

19. Administers items in reverse sequence correctly	Yes	No

Discontinue Considerations

20. Counts items administered in reverse sequence toward discontinue criterion	Yes	No
21. Discontinues subtest correctly	Yes	No
22. Removes Stimulus Book from child's view once subtest is completed	Yes	No

Scoring Guidelines

23. Scores items correctly	Yes	No

(*Continued*)

Table A-15 (*Continued*)

Picture Completion (*Continued*)

	Circle One

Record Form

24. Records child's responses in Response column correctly — Yes No
25. Records PC for correct pointing responses — Yes No
26. Records PX for incorrect pointing responses — Yes No
27. Circles 0 or 1 in Score column correctly — Yes No
28. Notes additional points correctly — Yes No
29. Adds points correctly — Yes No
30. Enters Total Raw Score in shaded box correctly — Yes No

Comments

_____

_____

_____

Cancellation

(See pp. 351–352 in text for detailed information.)

Background Considerations

1. Reads directions verbatim — Yes No
2. Reads directions clearly — Yes No
3. Repeats directions correctly — Yes No
4. Provides smooth working surface — Yes No
5. At beginning, shows only cover page of Response Booklet 2 to child — Yes No
6. Provides red pencil without eraser — Yes No
7. Uses stopwatch — Yes No
8. Places stopwatch correctly — Yes No
9. When administering sample, directs child's attention to animals at top of page — Yes No
10. Points to row of animals in sweeping motion, left to right from child's perspective — Yes No
11. Draws line through two animal pictures of samples — Yes No
12. Points to practice items while reading directions — Yes No
13. Gives appropriate feedback — Yes No
14. If child makes an error on practice items, follows correct procedure — Yes No
15. Gives appropriate prompts — Yes No
16. Counts time for prompts as part of 45-second time limit — Yes No
17. Allows spontaneous corrections, unless corrections impede performance — Yes No
18. Proceeds to item 1 when child understands task — Yes No
19. Opens Response Booklet 2 to appropriate page for item 1 when appropriate — Yes No
20. Gives directions verbatim for item 1, including word "Go," even if explanations are not necessary — Yes No

Cancellation (*Continued*)

	Circle One

21. Before saying "Go," gives further explanations for item 1, if necessary — Yes No
22. Begins timing item 1 correctly — Yes No
23. Administers item 2 if child finishes item 1 early — Yes No
24. Says "Stop" after 45 seconds on item 1 and administers item 2 — Yes No
25. After item 1 is completed, opens Response Booklet 2 to appropriate page for item 2 — Yes No
26. Gives directions verbatim for item 2, including word "Go," even if explanations are not necessary — Yes No
27. Before saying "Go," gives further explanations for item 2, if necessary — Yes No
28. Begins timing item 2 correctly — Yes No

Starting Considerations

29. Starts with appropriate item — Yes No

Discontinue Considerations

30. Discontinues subtest correctly — Yes No
31. Records time and discontinues subtest if child completes item 2 early — Yes No
32. Says "Stop" after 45 seconds on item 2 and discontinues subtest — Yes No
33. Closes Response Booklet 2 and removes it from child's view once subtest is completed — Yes No

Scoring Guidelines

34. Scores subtest correctly — Yes No

Response Booklet

35. Enters identifying data on Response Booklet 2 correctly — Yes No

Record Form

36. Enters completion time correctly — Yes No
37. Enters total number of correct objects marked in Number Correct column — Yes No
38. Enters total number of incorrect objects marked in Number Incorrect column — Yes No
39. For each item, subtracts Number Incorrect from Number Correct and records result in Difference column correctly — Yes No
40. Enters time-bonus points for each item correctly — Yes No
41. For items 1 and 2, enters sum of Difference *plus* Bonus Points (if any) in Total Raw Score column correctly — Yes No
42. Enters Total Raw Score for item 1 *plus* item 2 in shaded box correctly — Yes No

Comments

_____

_____

_____

(Continued)

Table A-15 (*Continued*)		

Information
(See pp. 354–355 in text for detailed information.)

	Circle One	
Background Considerations		
1. Reads directions verbatim	Yes	No
2. Reads directions clearly	Yes	No
3. Reads items verbatim	Yes	No
4. Reads items clearly	Yes	No
5. Repeats items correctly	Yes	No
6. Repeats directions correctly	Yes	No
7. Queries and prompts correctly	Yes	No
8. For items 1 and 2, gives child correct answers, if needed	Yes	No
9. For items 3 to 33, does not give child correct answers	Yes	No
10. Grants additional time appropriately	Yes	No
Starting Considerations		
11. Starts with appropriate item	Yes	No
Reverse Sequence		
12. Administers items in reverse sequence correctly	Yes	No
Discontinue Considerations		
13. Counts items administered in reverse sequence toward discontinue criterion	Yes	No
14. Discontinues subtest correctly	Yes	No
Scoring Guidelines		
15. Scores items correctly	Yes	No
Record Form		
16. Records child's responses correctly	Yes	No
17. Circles 0 or 1 in Score column correctly	Yes	No
18. Notes additional points correctly	Yes	No
19. Adds points correctly	Yes	No
20. Enters Total Raw Score in shaded box correctly	Yes	No

Comments

_____

_____

_____

Arithmetic
(See pp. 357–358 in text for detailed information.)

	Circle One	
Background Considerations		
1. Reads directions verbatim	Yes	No
2. Reads directions clearly	Yes	No
3. Repeats directions correctly	Yes	No
4. Repeats items correctly	Yes	No
5. Places closed Stimulus Book properly and then opens it to correct page	Yes	No
6. Turns pages of Stimulus Book toward child during subtest administration	Yes	No

Arithmetic (*Continued*)

	Circle One	
7. Times correctly	Yes	No
8. For items 1, 2, and 3, provides appropriate feedback for incorrect responses	Yes	No
9. For items 4 to 34, does not give child correct answers	Yes	No
10. Does not allow child to use pencil and paper	Yes	No
11. Allows child to use finger to "write" on table	Yes	No
12. When it is not clear which of two responses is final choice, gives appropriate prompt	Yes	No
Starting Considerations		
13. Starts with appropriate item	Yes	No
Reverse Sequence		
14. Administers items in reverse sequence correctly	Yes	No
Discontinue Considerations		
15. Counts items administered in reverse sequence toward discontinue criterion	Yes	No
16. Discontinues subtest correctly	Yes	No
17. Removes Stimulus Book from child's view once subtest is completed	Yes	No
Scoring Guidelines		
18. Scores items correctly	Yes	No
Record Form		
19. Records child's responses in Response column correctly	Yes	No
20. Circles 0 or 1 in Score column correctly	Yes	No
21. Notes additional points correctly	Yes	No
22. Adds points correctly	Yes	No
23. Enters Total Raw Score in shaded box correctly	Yes	No

Comments

_____

_____

Word Reasoning
(See pp. 359–360 in text for detailed information.)

	Circle One	
Background Considerations		
1. Reads items verbatim	Yes	No
2. Reads items clearly	Yes	No
3. Introduces each item correctly	Yes	No
4. After giving each clue, allows child about 5 seconds to answer	Yes	No
5. Repeats each clue correctly and notes R on Record Form if clue is repeated	Yes	No
6. Allows child additional time after repeating a clue	Yes	No
7. Restates previous clues correctly	Yes	No

(*Continued*)

Table A-15 (*Continued*)

Word Reasoning (*Continued*)	Circle One	
8. Administers next item if child gets previous item correct before all clues are presented	Yes	No
9. Grants additional time appropriately	Yes	No

Starting Considerations

10. Starts with appropriate item	Yes	No

Reverse Sequence

11. Administers items in reverse sequence correctly	Yes	No

Discontinue Considerations

12. Counts items administered in reverse sequence toward discontinue criterion	Yes	No
13. Discontinues subtest correctly	Yes	No

Scoring Guidelines

14. Scores responses correctly	Yes	No

Record Form

15. Records responses verbatim in Response column	Yes	No
16. Circles Y or N for each clue administered	Yes	No
17. Circles 0 or 1 for each item administered	Yes	No
18. Notes additional points correctly	Yes	No
19. Adds points correctly	Yes	No
20. Enters Total Raw Score in shaded box correctly	Yes	No

Comments

_____

_____

_____

Front Page of Record Form

	Circle One	
1. Enters child's full name and examiner's full name correctly	Yes	No

Calculation of Child's Age

2. Records date of testing correctly (Y, M, D)	Yes	No
3. Records child's date of birth correctly (Y, M, D)	Yes	No
4. Computes child's age at testing correctly (Y, M, D)	Yes	No

Total Raw Score to Scaled Score Conversions

5. For each subtest administered, transfers Total Raw Score to front of Record Form correctly	Yes	No
6. Enters correct scaled score in appropriate unshaded box	Yes	No
7. For Verbal Comprehension Index, sums three scaled scores correctly and enters sum in appropriate shaded box	Yes	No
8. For Perceptual Reasoning Index, sums three scaled scores correctly and enters sum in appropriate shaded box	Yes	No

Front Page of Record Form (*Continued*)	Circle One	
9. For Working Memory Index, sums two scaled scores correctly and enters sum in appropriate shaded box	Yes	No
10. For Processing Speed Index, sums two scaled scores correctly and enters sum in appropriate shaded box	Yes	No
11. For Full Scale IQ, sums 10 scaled scores correctly and enters sum in appropriate shaded box	Yes	No

Sum of Scaled Scores to Composite Score Conversions

12. Transfers sums of scaled scores to appropriate shaded boxes	Yes	No
13. Enters correct Verbal Comprehension Index	Yes	No
14. Enters correct Perceptual Reasoning Index	Yes	No
15. Enters correct Working Memory Index	Yes	No
16. Enters correct Processing Speed Index	Yes	No
17. Enters correct Full Scale IQ	Yes	No
18. Enters correct Verbal Comprehension Index percentile rank	Yes	No
19. Enters correct Perceptual Reasoning Index percentile rank	Yes	No
20. Enters correct Working Memory Index percentile rank	Yes	No
21. Enters correct Processing Speed Index percentile rank	Yes	No
22. Enters correct Full Scale IQ percentile rank	Yes	No
23. Enters selected confidence interval	Yes	No
24. Enters correct Verbal Comprehension Index confidence interval	Yes	No
25. Enters correct Perceptual Reasoning Index confidence interval	Yes	No
26. Enters correct Working Memory Index confidence interval	Yes	No
27. Enters correct Processing Speed Index confidence interval	Yes	No
28. Enters correct Full Scale IQ confidence interval	Yes	No

Subtest Scaled Score Profile

29. Completes Subtest Scaled Score Profile correctly (optional)	Yes	No

Composite Score Profile

30. Completes Composite Score Profile correctly (optional)	Yes	No
31. Notes on Record Form order of administering subtests, if different from standard order	Yes	No

Comments

_____

_____

_____

(*Continued*)

Table A-15 (Continued)

Analysis Page	Circle One	
Discrepancy Comparisons		
1. Enters scaled scores in Scaled Score 1 and Scaled Score 2 columns correctly	Yes	No
2. Calculates difference scores correctly	Yes	No
3. Enters critical values correctly	Yes	No
4. Enters significant differences (Y or N) correctly	Yes	No
5. Enters base rate in standardization sample correctly	Yes	No
6. Checks one of two basis-for-comparison boxes	Yes	No
7. Checks one of two basis-for-statistical-significance boxes	Yes	No
Determining Strengths and Weaknesses		
8. Enters subtest scaled scores correctly	Yes	No
9. Enters mean scaled scores correctly	Yes	No
10. Calculates differences from mean scaled scores correctly	Yes	No
11. Enters critical values correctly	Yes	No
12. Enters significant strengths or weaknesses (S or W) correctly, if needed	Yes	No
13. Enters base rate in standardization sample for strengths and weaknesses correctly, if needed	Yes	No
14. Checks one of two basis-for-comparison boxes	Yes	No
15. Checks one of two basis-for-statistical-significance boxes	Yes	No
16. Enters sums of scaled scores for 10 subtests, 3 Verbal Comprehension subtests, and 3 Perceptual Reasoning subtests correctly	Yes	No
Process Analysis		
17. Enters raw scores for Process scores correctly	Yes	No
18. Enters scaled scores for Process scores correctly	Yes	No
19. Enters raw scores for Longest Digit Span Forward (LDSF) and Longest Digit Span Backward (LDSB) correctly	Yes	No
20. Enters base rates for LDSF and LDSB correctly	Yes	No
21. Enters raw score 1 and raw score 2 for LDSF–LDSB discrepancy comparison correctly	Yes	No
22. Computes difference score for LDSF–LDSB discrepancy comparison correctly	Yes	No
23. Enters base rate for LDSF–LDSB discrepancy comparison correctly	Yes	No
24. Enters scaled score 1 and scaled score 2 for three subtest/Process score discrepancy comparisons correctly	Yes	No
25. Computes difference scores for three subtest/Process score discrepancy comparisons correctly	Yes	No

Analysis Page (Continued)	Circle One	
26. Enters critical values for three subtest/Process score discrepancy comparisons correctly	Yes	No
27. Enters base rates for three subtest/Process score discrepancy comparisons correctly, if needed	Yes	No
28. Checks one of two statistical significance levels for three subtest/Process score discrepancy comparisons	Yes	No

Comments

_____

_____

_____

General Evaluation

Rapport	Circle One	
1. Maintains rapport throughout testing	Yes	No
2. Is alert to child's moods	Yes	No
3. Does not become impatient or frustrated with child	Yes	No
4. Does not badger child	Yes	No
5. Handles behavior problems correctly	Yes	No
6. Makes accommodations for any physical impairments child has that may affect assessment (e.g., hearing or visual loss)	Yes	No
7. Does not take break in middle of a subtest	Yes	No
8. Allows child to walk around room, if needed	Yes	No
9. Encourages child to perform a task, if needed	Yes	No
10. Praises child's effort	Yes	No
11. Does not say "Good" or "Right" after a correct response	Yes	No
12. Shows empathy if child is concerned about poor performance	Yes	No
Administering Test Items		
13. Administers test in professional, unhurried manner	Yes	No
14. Speaks clearly throughout testing	Yes	No
15. Is well organized and has all needed materials nearby	Yes	No
16. Administers subtests in order noted on page 25 of Administration Manual, altering order based on clinical need	Yes	No
17. Maintains steady pace	Yes	No
18. Makes a smooth transition from one subtest to the next	Yes	No
19. Repeats directions on request when appropriate	Yes	No
20. Repeats items when appropriate	Yes	No
21. Uses good judgment in deciding how much time to give child to solve each item on untimed subtests	Yes	No
22. Begins timing correctly	Yes	No

(Continued)

Table A-15 (*Continued*)

General Evaluation (*Continued*)	Circle One	
23. Adheres to time limits	Yes	No
24. Stops timing when child has obviously finished	Yes	No
25. Stops timing when time limit is reached	Yes	No
26. Does not stop timing prematurely	Yes	No
27. Places test materials not currently in use out of child's sight	Yes	No
28. Clears table of unessential materials	Yes	No
29. Positions Record Form so that child cannot see correct answers	Yes	No
30. Positions Administration Manual so that child cannot see correct answers	Yes	No
31. Makes appropriate eye contact with child	Yes	No
32. Reads directions exactly as written in Administration Manual	Yes	No
33. Reads items exactly as written in Administration Manual	Yes	No
34. Takes short break, as needed, at end of a subtest	Yes	No
35. Does not give additional items for practice	Yes	No
36. Does not ask leading questions	Yes	No
37. Does not spell words on any subtest	Yes	No
38. Does not define words	Yes	No
39. Does not use Vocabulary words in a sentence	Yes	No
40. Queries correctly	Yes	No
41. Records Q for queried responses	Yes	No
42. Prompts correctly	Yes	No
43. Records P for prompted responses	Yes	No
44. Gives second trials correctly	Yes	No
45. Follows start item with appropriate item	Yes	No
46. Administers reverse sequence correctly	Yes	No
47. Shows child how to solve problems when appropriate	Yes	No
48. Permits child to use scrap paper to write on, if appropriate	Yes	No
49. Conducts testing-of-limits after all subtests have been administered, if desired	Yes	No
50. Makes every effort to administer entire test in one session	Yes	No

Scoring Test Items

	Circle One	
51. Scores each item after child answers	Yes	No
52. Gives credit for correct responses given at any time during test, when appropriate	Yes	No
53. Does not give credit for correct answers given after time limit	Yes	No
54. Makes entry in Record Form for every item administered	Yes	No
55. Awards full credit for all items preceding first two items with perfect scores, regardless of child's performance on preceding items, by putting slash mark in Score column through the possible scores for the item preceding the two items with perfect scores and writing the numerals for these points	Yes	No

General Evaluation (*Continued*)	Circle One	
56. Does not give credit for any items beyond last score of 0 required for discontinue criterion, regardless of child's performance on these items if they have been administered	Yes	No
57. Does not count a supplemental subtest in computing Full Scale IQ, unless it is substituted for one of the 10 core subtests	Yes	No
58. Uses good judgment overall in scoring responses	Yes	No
59. Rechecks scoring after test is administered	Yes	No

Completing Record Form

	Circle One	
60. Records any deviation from procedure on Record Form	Yes	No
61. Completes Front Page of Record Form correctly	Yes	No
62. Completes Analysis Page of Record Form correctly	Yes	No

Qualitative Feedback

_____
_____
_____

Overall Strengths

_____
_____
_____

Areas Needing Improvement

_____
_____
_____

Other Comments

_____
_____
_____

Overall Evaluation

Circle One: Excellent Good Average Below Average Poor

APPENDIX B

TABLES FOR THE WPPSI–III

Table B-1
Confidence Intervals for WPPSI–III Individual Composite Scores and Full Scale IQs Based on Obtained Score Only

Age level	Individual Composite or Full Scale	Confidence level				
		68%	85%	90%	95%	99%
2½ (2-6-0 through 2-11-30)	Verbal	±4	±5	±6	±7	±9
	Performance	±5	±7	±8	±10	±13
	Full Scale	±4	±5	±6	±7	±9
3 (3-0-0 through 3-5-30)	Verbal	±4	±5	±6	±7	±9
	Performance	±5	±8	±9	±10	±13
	Full Scale	±4	±5	±6	±7	±9
3½ (3-6-0 through 3-11-30)	Verbal	±4	±5	±6	±7	±9
	Performance	±5	±7	±8	±9	±12
	Full Scale	±3	±5	±5	±6	±8
Average (2-6-0 through 3-11-30)	Verbal	±4	±5	±6	±7	±9
	Performance	±5	±7	±8	±10	±13
	Full Scale	±4	±5	±6	±7	±9
4 (4-0-0 through 4-5-30)	Verbal	±4	±5	±6	±7	±9
	Performance	±5	±7	±8	±9	±12
	Processing Speed	±5	±7	±7	±9	±11
	Full Scale	±3	±5	±5	±6	±8
4½ (4-6-0 through 4-11-30)	Verbal	±4	±5	±6	±7	±9
	Performance	±4	±6	±7	±8	±10
	Processing Speed	±5	±7	±8	±9	±12
	Full Scale	±3	±4	±5	±6	±7
5 (5-0-0 through 5-5-30)	Verbal	±3	±5	±5	±6	±8
	Performance	±4	±6	±7	±8	±10
	Processing Speed	±5	±7	±7	±9	±11
	Full Scale	±3	±4	±5	±6	±7
5½ (5-6-0 through 5-11-30)	Verbal	±4	±5	±6	±7	±9
	Performance	±4	±6	±7	±8	±10
	Processing Speed	±6	±8	±9	±11	±14
	Full Scale	±3	±4	±5	±6	±7
6 (6-0-0 through 6-11-30)	Verbal	±4	±6	±7	±8	±10
	Performance	±4	±6	±7	±8	±10
	Processing Speed	±6	±8	±9	±11	±14
	Full Scale	±3	±5	±5	±6	±8
7 (7-0-0 through 7-3-30)	Verbal	±4	±5	±6	±7	±9
	Performance	±4	±5	±6	±7	±9
	Processing Speed	±6	±9	±10	±11	±15
	Full Scale	±3	±4	±5	±6	±7
Average (4-0-0 through 7-3-30)	Verbal	±4	±5	±6	±7	±9
	Performance	±4	±6	±7	±8	±10
	Processing Speed	±5	±8	±9	±10	±13
	Full Scale	±3	±4	±5	±6	±8

Note. Chapter 4 describes the procedure for computing confidence intervals. For the WPPSI–III Verbal Composite, the confidence intervals are obtained by the following procedure: The appropriate SEM for the child's age is located in Table 4.3 of the Technical Manual. For example, for a child who is 2 years, 6 months old, the SEM = 3.35 for the Verbal Composite. This SEM is multiplied by the respective z values in order to obtain the confidence interval for the desired level. At the 68% confidence level, the SEM is multiplied by ±1 (±1 x 3.35 = ±4). At the 85% level, the SEM is multiplied by ±1.44 (±1.44 x 3.35 = ±5). At the 90% level, the SEM is multiplied by ±1.65 (±1.65 x 3.35 = ±6). At the 95% level, the SEM is multiplied by ±1.96 (±1.96 x 3.35 = ±7). At the 99% level, the SEM is multiplied by ±2.58 (±2.58 x 3.35 = ±9).

Table B-2
Differences Between WPPSI–III Subtest Scaled Scores and Between Composite Scores Required for Statistical Significance at the .05 and .01 Levels of Significance for Ages 2-6 to 3-11 and Combined Ages (.05 significance level above diagonal, .01 significance level below diagonal)

Age 2-6 to 2-11

Subtest	RV	BD	IN	OA	PN	VIQ	PIQ
Receptive Vocabulary	—	3	3	3	3	—	—
Block Design	4	—	4	4	4	—	—
Information	4	3	—	3	3	—	—
Object Assembly	4	5	4	—	4	—	—
Picture Naming	4	5	4	5	—	—	—
Verbal IQ	—	—	—	—	—	—	12
Performance IQ	—	—	—	—	—	16	—

Age 3-0 to 3-5

Subtest	RV	BD	IN	OA	PN	VIQ	PIQ
Receptive Vocabulary	—	3	3	3	3	—	—
Block Design	4	—	4	4	3	—	—
Information	4	3	—	3	3	—	—
Object Assembly	4	5	4	—	3	—	—
Picture Naming	4	4	4	4	—	—	—
Verbal IQ	—	—	—	—	—	—	12
Performance IQ	—	—	—	—	—	16	—

Age 3-6 to 3-11

Subtest	RV	BD	IN	OA	PN	VIQ	PIQ
Receptive Vocabulary	—	3	3	3	3	—	—
Block Design	4	—	4	3	3	—	—
Information	4	3	—	3	3	—	—
Object Assembly	4	4	4	—	3	—	—
Picture Naming	4	4	4	4	—	—	—
Verbal IQ	—	—	—	—	—	—	11
Performance IQ	—	—	—	—	—	15	—

Average

Subtest	RV	BD	IN	OA	PN	VIQ	PIQ
Receptive Vocabulary	—	3	3	3	3	—	—
Block Design	4	—	4	3	3	—	—
Information	4	3	—	3	3	—	—
Object Assembly	4	4	4	—	3	—	—
Picture Naming	4	4	4	4	—	—	—
Verbal IQ	—	—	—	—	—	—	12
Performance IQ	—	—	—	—	—	15	—

(*Continued*)

Table B-2 (*Continued*)

Note. Abbreviations: RV = Receptive Vocabulary, BD = Block Design, IN = Information, OA = Object Assembly, PN = Picture Naming, VIQ = Verbal IQ, PIQ = Performance IQ.

The critical values at the .05 level appear *above* the diagonal in the *shaded area*; the critical values for the .01 level appear *below* the diagonal in the *unshaded area*.

Sample reading: At age 2-6 to 2-11, a difference of 3 points between scaled scores on the Information and Receptive Vocabulary subtests is significant at the 5% level and a difference of 4 points is significant at the 1% level. Similarly, a difference of 12 points between the Verbal IQ and the Performance IQ is significant at the 5% level and a difference of 16 points is significant at the 1% level.

The values in this table for subtest comparisons are overly liberal when more than one comparison is made for a subtest. They are more accurate when a priori planned comparisons are made, such as Receptive Vocabulary vs. Information or Block Design vs. Object Assembly.

See Exhibit 11-1 in Chapter 11 for an explanation of the method used to arrive at magnitudes of differences.

A. B. Silverstein (personal communication, February 1990) suggests that the following formula be used to obtain a value for the significant difference (at the .05 level) that must exist between the highest and lowest subtest scores on a profile before individual subtest comparisons can be made:

$$D = q \sqrt{\frac{\Sigma\, \mathrm{SEM}^2}{k}}$$

where

D = significant difference
q = critical value of the Studentized range statistic
SEM = standard error of measurement of a particular subtest
k = number of subtests

For the WPPSI–III, the q value is 3.86 at the .05 level for $k = 5$ (5 subtests) and ∞ degrees of freedom. The sum of the SEM^2 for the 5 subtests at age 2-6 to 2-11 is $1.44 + 0.72 + 0.81 + 1.44 + 1.17 = 5.58$. Thus,

$$D = 3.86 \times \sqrt{\frac{5.58}{5}} = 3.86 \times \sqrt{1.116} = 3.86 \times 1.0564 = 4.08$$

Thus, a difference of 4 points between the highest and lowest subtest scaled scores represents a significant difference at the .05 level.

Table B-3
Differences Between WPPSI–III Subtest Scaled Scores, IQs, and Composite Scores for Ages 4-0 to 7-3
(.05 significance level above diagonal, .01 significance level below diagonal)

Age 4-0 to 4-5

Subtest	BD	IN	MR	VC	PCn	SS	WR	CD	CO	PCm	SI	RV	OA	PN	VIQ	PIQ	PSQ
Block Design	—	4	4	4	4	4	4	4	4	4	4	4	4	4	—	—	—
Information	5	—	3	3	3	4	3	3	4	3	3	3	3	3	—	—	—
Matrix Reasoning	5	4	—	3	3	3	3	3	3	3	3	3	3	3	—	—	—
Vocabulary	5	4	4	—	3	3	3	3	3	3	3	3	3	3	—	—	—
Picture Concepts	5	4	4	4	—	3	3	3	3	3	3	3	3	3	—	—	—
Symbol Search	5	5	4	4	4	—	3	3	4	3	3	3	3	3	—	—	—
Word Reasoning	5	4	4	4	4	4	—	3	3	3	3	3	3	3	—	—	—
Coding	5	4	4	4	4	4	4	—	3	3	3	3	3	3	—	—	—
Comprehension	5	5	4	4	4	5	4	4	—	3	3	3	3	3	—	—	—
Picture Completion	5	4	4	4	4	4	4	4	4	—	3	3	3	3	—	—	—
Similarities	5	5	4	4	4	5	4	4	5	4	—	3	3	3	—	—	—
Receptive Vocabulary	5	4	4	4	4	4	4	4	4	4	3	—	3	3	—	—	—
Object Assembly	5	4	4	4	4	4	4	4	4	4	4	4	—	3	—	—	—
Picture Naming	5	4	4	4	4	4	4	4	4	4	3	4	4	—	—	—	—
Verbal IQ	—	—	—	—	—	—	—	—	—	—	—	—	—	—	—	11	11
Performance IQ	—	—	—	—	—	—	—	—	—	—	—	—	—	—	15	—	15
Processing Speed Q	—	—	—	—	—	—	—	—	—	—	—	—	—	—	14	16	—

Age 4-6 to 4-11

Subtest	BD	IN	MR	VC	PCn	SS	WR	CD	CO	PCm	SI	RV	OA	PN	VIQ	PIQ	PSQ
Block Design	—	4	4	4	3	4	3	4	3	3	3	4	4	4	—	—	—
Information	5	—	4	4	3	4	3	4	3	3	3	4	4	4	—	—	—
Matrix Reasoning	5	5	—	3	3	3	3	3	3	3	3	3	3	3	—	—	—
Vocabulary	5	5	4	—	3	3	3	3	3	3	3	3	3	3	—	—	—
Picture Concepts	4	4	4	4	—	3	3	3	3	3	3	3	3	3	—	—	—
Symbol Search	5	5	4	4	4	—	3	3	3	3	3	4	4	3	—	—	—
Word Reasoning	4	4	4	4	4	4	—	3	3	3	2	3	3	3	—	—	—
Coding	5	5	4	4	4	4	4	—	3	3	3	3	3	3	—	—	—
Comprehension	4	4	4	4	4	4	4	4	—	3	3	3	3	3	—	—	—
Picture Completion	4	4	4	4	4	4	3	4	4	—	3	3	3	3	—	—	—
Similarities	4	4	3	4	3	4	3	4	3	3	—	3	3	3	—	—	—
Receptive Vocabulary	5	5	4	4	4	5	4	4	4	4	4	—	4	3	—	—	—
Object Assembly	5	5	4	4	4	5	4	4	4	4	4	5	—	3	—	—	—
Picture Naming	5	5	4	4	4	4	4	4	4	4	4	4	4	—	—	—	—
Verbal IQ	—	—	—	—	—	—	—	—	—	—	—	—	—	—	—	10	11
Performance IQ	—	—	—	—	—	—	—	—	—	—	—	—	—	—	13	—	12
Processing Speed Q	—	—	—	—	—	—	—	—	—	—	—	—	—	—	15	15	—

(*Continued*)

Table B-3 (*Continued*)

Age 5-0 to 5-5

Subtest	BD	IN	MR	VC	PCn	SS	WR	CD	CO	PCm	SI	RV	OA	PN	VIQ	PIQ	PSQ
Block Design	—	4	4	4	3	4	3	4	4	4	3	4	4	4	—	—	—
Information	5	—	3	3	3	3	3	3	3	3	3	3	3	3	—	—	—
Matrix Reasoning	5	4	—	3	3	3	3	3	3	3	3	3	3	3	—	—	—
Vocabulary	5	4	4	—	3	3	3	3	3	3	3	3	3	3	—	—	—
Picture Concepts	4	4	4	4	—	3	3	3	3	3	3	3	3	3	—	—	—
Symbol Search	5	4	4	4	4	—	3	3	3	3	3	3	4	4	—	—	—
Word Reasoning	4	4	4	4	3	4	—	3	3	3	3	3	3	3	—	—	—
Coding	5	4	4	4	4	4	4	—	3	3	3	3	4	3	—	—	—
Comprehension	5	4	4	4	4	4	4	4	—	3	3	3	3	3	—	—	—
Picture Completion	5	4	4	4	4	4	4	4	4	—	3	3	3	3	—	—	—
Similarities	4	3	3	4	3	4	3	4	4	3	—	3	3	3	—	—	—
Receptive Vocabulary	5	4	4	4	4	4	4	4	4	4	4	—	3	3	—	—	—
Object Assembly	5	4	4	4	4	5	4	5	4	4	4	4	—	4	—	—	—
Picture Naming	5	4	4	4	4	5	4	4	4	4	4	4	5	—	—	—	—
Verbal IQ	—	—	—	—	—	—	—	—	—	—	—	—	—	—	—	10	11
Performance IQ	—	—	—	—	—	—	—	—	—	—	—	—	—	—	13	—	11
Processing Speed Q	—	—	—	—	—	—	—	—	—	—	—	—	—	—	14	15	—

Age 5-6 to 5-11

Subtest	BD	IN	MR	VC	PCn	SS	WR	CD	CO	PCm	SI	RV	OA	PN	VIQ	PIQ	PSQ
Block Design	—	4	3	4	3	4	3	4	4	4	3	4	4	4	—	—	—
Information	5	—	3	3	3	4	3	4	3	3	3	3	4	3	—	—	—
Matrix Reasoning	4	4	—	3	3	4	3	4	3	3	3	3	4	3	—	—	—
Vocabulary	5	4	4	—	3	4	3	4	3	3	3	4	4	3	—	—	—
Picture Concepts	4	4	4	4	—	4	3	4	3	3	3	3	3	3	—	—	—
Symbol Search	5	5	5	5	5	—	4	4	4	4	3	4	4	4	—	—	—
Word Reasoning	4	4	4	4	4	5	—	4	3	3	3	3	4	3	—	—	—
Coding	5	5	5	5	5	5	5	—	4	4	3	4	4	4	—	—	—
Comprehension	5	4	4	4	4	5	4	5	—	3	3	3	4	3	—	—	—
Picture Completion	5	4	4	4	4	5	4	5	4	—	3	3	4	3	—	—	—
Similarities	4	4	3	4	3	4	3	4	3	4	—	3	3	3	—	—	—
Receptive Vocabulary	5	4	4	5	4	5	4	5	4	4	4	—	4	3	—	—	—
Object Assembly	5	5	5	5	4	5	5	5	5	5	4	5	—	4	—	—	—
Picture Naming	5	4	4	4	4	5	4	5	4	4	3	4	5	—	—	—	—
Verbal IQ	—	—	—	—	—	—	—	—	—	—	—	—	—	—	—	10	13
Performance IQ	—	—	—	—	—	—	—	—	—	—	—	—	—	—	13	—	13
Processing Speed Q	—	—	—	—	—	—	—	—	—	—	—	—	—	—	17	17	—

(*Continued*)

Table B-3 (*Continued*)

Age 6-0 to 6-11

Subtest	BD	IN	MR	VC	PCn	SS	WR	CD	CO	PCm	SI	RV	OA	PN	VIQ	PIQ	PSQ
Block Design	—	4	3	3	3	4	3	4	4	3	3	4	4	4	—	—	—
Information	5	—	4	4	4	4	4	4	4	4	3	4	4	4	—	—	—
Matrix Reasoning	4	5	—	3	3	4	3	4	3	3	3	4	4	3	—	—	—
Vocabulary	4	5	4	—	3	4	3	4	3	3	3	4	4	4	—	—	—
Picture Concepts	4	5	4	4	—	4	3	4	3	3	3	4	4	4	—	—	—
Symbol Search	5	5	5	5	5	—	4	4	4	4	4	4	4	4	—	—	—
Word Reasoning	4	5	4	4	4	5	—	4	3	3	3	4	4	4	—	—	—
Coding	5	5	5	5	5	5	5	—	4	4	4	4	4	4	—	—	—
Comprehension	5	5	4	4	4	5	4	5	—	3	3	4	4	4	—	—	—
Picture Completion	4	5	4	4	4	5	4	5	4	—	3	4	4	4	—	—	—
Similarities	4	4	4	4	4	5	4	5	4	4	—	4	4	3	—	—	—
Receptive Vocabulary	5	5	5	5	5	5	5	5	5	5	5	—	4	4	—	—	—
Object Assembly	5	5	5	5	5	6	5	6	5	5	5	5	—	4	—	—	—
Picture Naming	5	5	4	5	5	5	5	5	5	5	4	5	5	—	—	—	—
Verbal IQ	—	—	—	—	—	—	—	—	—	—	—	—	—	—	—	11	13
Performance IQ	—	—	—	—	—	—	—	—	—	—	—	—	—	—	14	—	13
Processing Speed Q	—	—	—	—	—	—	—	—	—	—	—	—	—	—	17	17	—

Age 7-0 to 7-3

Subtest	BD	IN	MR	VC	PCn	SS	WR	CD	CO	PCm	SI	RV	OA	PN	VIQ	PIQ	PSQ
Block Design	—	3	3	3	3	4	3	4	3	3	3	3	4	3	—	—	—
Information	4	—	4	3	3	4	3	4	4	4	3	4	4	4	—	—	—
Matrix Reasoning	4	5	—	3	3	4	3	4	3	3	3	3	4	4	—	—	—
Vocabulary	4	4	4	—	3	4	3	4	3	3	3	3	4	3	—	—	—
Picture Concepts	4	4	4	4	—	4	3	4	3	3	3	3	4	3	—	—	—
Symbol Search	5	5	5	5	5	—	4	4	4	4	3	4	4	4	—	—	—
Word Reasoning	4	4	4	4	4	5	—	4	3	3	3	3	4	3	—	—	—
Coding	5	5	5	5	5	5	5	—	4	4	3	4	4	4	—	—	—
Comprehension	4	5	4	4	4	5	4	5	—	3	3	3	4	4	—	—	—
Picture Completion	4	5	4	4	4	5	4	5	4	—	3	4	4	4	—	—	—
Similarities	3	4	4	3	3	4	3	4	4	4	—	3	3	3	—	—	—
Receptive Vocabulary	4	5	4	4	4	5	4	5	4	5	4	—	4	4	—	—	—
Object Assembly	5	5	5	5	5	5	5	6	5	5	4	5	—	4	—	—	—
Picture Naming	4	5	5	4	4	5	4	5	5	5	4	5	5	—	—	—	—
Verbal IQ	—	—	—	—	—	—	—	—	—	—	—	—	—	—	—	10	13
Performance IQ	—	—	—	—	—	—	—	—	—	—	—	—	—	—	13	—	13
Processing Speed Q	—	—	—	—	—	—	—	—	—	—	—	—	—	—	17	17	—

(*Continued*)

Table B-3 (*Continued*)

| | | | | | | | Average | | | | | | | | | | |
Subtest	BD	IN	MR	VC	PCn	SS	WR	CD	CO	PCm	SI	RV	OA	PN	VIQ	PIQ	PSQ
Block Design	—	4	3	4	3	4	3	4	4	3	3	4	4	4	—	—	—
Information	5	—	3	3	3	4	3	4	3	3	3	4	4	4	—	—	—
Matrix Reasoning	4	4	—	3	3	4	3	3	3	3	3	3	3	3	—	—	—
Vocabulary	5	4	4	—	3	4	3	4	3	3	3	3	4	3	—	—	—
Picture Concepts	4	4	4	4	—	3	3	3	3	3	3	3	3	3	—	—	—
Symbol Search	5	5	5	5	4	—	3	4	4	4	3	4	4	4	—	—	—
Word Reasoning	4	4	4	4	4	4	—	3	3	3	3	3	3	3	—	—	—
Coding	5	5	4	5	4	5	4	—	4	3	3	4	4	4	—	—	—
Comprehension	5	4	4	4	4	5	4	5	—	3	3	3	4	3	—	—	—
Picture Completion	4	4	4	4	4	5	4	4	4	—	3	3	3	3	—	—	—
Similarities	4	4	3	4	3	4	3	4	4	3	—	3	3	3	—	—	—
Receptive Vocabulary	5	5	4	4	4	5	4	5	4	4	4	—	4	3	—	—	—
Object Assembly	5	5	4	5	4	5	4	5	5	4	4	5	—	4	—	—	—
Picture Naming	5	5	4	4	4	5	4	5	4	4	4	4	5	—	—	—	—
Verbal IQ	—	—	—	—	—	—	—	—	—	—	—	—	—	—	—	10	12
Performance IQ	—	—	—	—	—	—	—	—	—	—	—	—	—	—	13	—	13
Processing Speed Q	—	—	—	—	—	—	—	—	—	—	—	—	—	—	16	16	—

Note. Abbreviations: BD = Block Design, IN = Information, MR = Matrix Reasoning, VC = Vocabulary, PCn = Picture Concepts, SS = Symbol Search, WR = Word Reasoning, CD = Coding, CO = Comprehension, PCm = Picture Completion, SI = Similarities, RV = Receptive Vocabulary, OA = Object Assembly, PN = Picture Naming, VIQ = Verbal IQ, PIQ = Performance IQ, PSQ = Performance Speed IQ.

The critical values at the .05 level appear *above* the diagonal in the *shaded* area; the critical values for the .01 level appear *below* the diagonal in the *unshaded* area.

Sample reading: At age 4-0 to 4-5, a difference of 3 points between scaled scores on the Information and Vocabulary subtests is significant at the 5% level and a difference of 4 points is significant at the 1% level. Similarly, a difference of 11 points between the Verbal IQ and the Performance IQ is significant at the 5% level and a difference of 15 points is significant at the 1% level.

The values in this table for subtest comparisons are overly liberal when more than one comparison is made for a subtest. They are more accurate when a priori planned comparisons are made, such as Information vs. Vocabulary or Block Design vs. Object Assembly.

See Exhibit 11-1 in Chapter 11 for the procedure used to arrive at magnitudes of differences.

A. B. Silverstein (personal communication, February 1990) suggests that the following formula be used to obtain a value for the significant difference (at the .05 level) that must exist between the highest and lowest subtest scores on a profile before individual subtest comparisons can be made:

$$D = q \sqrt{\frac{\Sigma \, \text{SEM}^2}{k}}$$

where

D = significant difference
q = critical value of the Studentized range statistic
SEM = standard error of measurement of a particular subtest
k = number of subtests

For the WPPSI–III, the q value is 4.62 at the .05 level for k = 12 (12 subtests) and ∞ degrees of freedom. The sum of the SEM^2 for the 12 subtests is 1.30 + 1.02 + 0.77 + 1.46 + 0.192 + 0.83 + 1.49 + 1.51 + 1.06 + 0.92 + 0.48 + 1.49 = 13.26. Thus,

$$D = 4.62 \times \sqrt{\frac{13.26}{12}} = 4.62 \times \sqrt{1.10} = 4.62 \times 1.0488 = 4.85$$

Thus, at ages 4-0 to 7-3 a difference of 5 points between the highest and lowest subtest scaled scores represents a significant difference at the .05 level.

Table B-4
Estimates of the Probability of Obtaining Designated Differences Between WPPSI–III Composite Scores by Chance

Verbal and Performance

Probability of obtaining given or greater discrepancy by chance	Age											
	2-6	3-0	3-6	Total[a]	4-0	4-6	5-0	5-6	6-0	7-0	Total[b]	Ov.[c]
.50	4.05	4.05	3.79	3.96	3.79	3.35	3.20	3.35	3.50	3.20	3.40	3.60
.25	6.89	6.89	6.45	6.75	6.45	5.71	5.45	5.71	5.97	5.45	5.80	6.13
.20	7.68	7.68	7.19	7.53	7.19	6.37	6.08	6.37	6.65	6.07	6.47	6.84
.10	9.86	9.86	9.23	9.66	9.23	8.17	7.80	8.17	8.54	7.79	8.30	8.77
.05	11.75	11.75	11.00	11.50	11.00	9.74	9.29	9.74	10.17	9.29	9.88	10.45
.02	13.95	13.95	13.05	13.66	13.05	11.56	11.03	11.56	12.08	11.02	11.74	12.41
.01	15.43	15.43	14.45	15.11	14.45	12.80	12.21	12.80	13.36	12.20	12.99	13.73
.001	19.78	19.78	18.51	19.37	18.51	16.40	15.64	16.40	17.13	15.63	16.64	17.60

Verbal and Processing Speed

Probability of obtaining given or greater discrepancy by chance	Age											
	2-6	3-0	3-6	Total[a]	4-0	4-6	5-0	5-6	6-0	7-0	Total[b]	Ov.[d]
.50	—	—	—	—	3.65	3.79	3.51	4.37	4.41	4.41	4.03	4.03
.25	—	—	—	—	6.21	6.45	5.97	7.45	7.52	7.51	6.86	6.86
.20	—	—	—	—	6.93	7.19	6.66	8.30	8.38	8.38	7.65	7.65
.10	—	—	—	—	8.89	9.23	8.54	10.65	10.75	10.75	9.82	9.82
.05	—	—	—	—	10.59	11.00	10.18	12.69	12.81	12.81	11.70	11.70
.02	—	—	—	—	12.57	13.05	12.09	15.07	15.21	15.20	13.89	13.89
.01	—	—	—	—	13.91	14.45	13.37	16.67	16.83	16.83	15.37	15.37
.001	—	—	—	—	17.83	18.51	17.14	21.36	21.57	21.56	19.70	19.70

Performance and Processing Speed

Probability of obtaining given or greater discrepancy by chance	Age											
	2-6	3-0	3-6	Total[a]	4-0	4-6	5-0	5-6	6-0	7-0	Total[b]	Ov.[d]
.50	—	—	—	—	4.17	3.92	3.79	4.49	4.41	4.41	4.19	4.35
.25	—	—	—	—	7.11	6.68	6.45	7.64	7.52	7.51	7.15	7.42
.20	—	—	—	—	7.93	7.44	7.19	8.52	8.38	8.38	7.97	8.27
.10	—	—	—	—	10.17	9.55	9.22	10.93	10.75	10.75	10.22	10.61
.05	—	—	—	—	12.12	11.38	10.99	13.02	12.81	12.81	12.18	12.65
.02	—	—	—	—	14.39	13.51	13.05	15.46	15.21	15.20	14.46	15.01
.01	—	—	—	—	15.92	14.95	14.44	17.11	16.83	16.83	16.00	16.61
.001	—	—	—	—	20.40	19.16	18.51	21.93	21.57	21.56	20.51	21.29

Note. To use the table, find the column appropriate to the child's age. Locate the discrepancy that is just *less than* the discrepancy obtained by the child. The entry in the first column in that same row gives the probability of obtaining a given or greater discrepancy by chance. For example, the hypothesis that a 6-year-old child obtained a Verbal–Performance discrepancy of 17 by chance can be rejected at the .01 level of significance. The table is two-tailed.

See Exhibit 11-1 in Chapter 11 for an explanation of the method used to arrive at magnitudes of differences.

The following z values were used for the eight probability levels: $z = .675$ for .50, $z = 1.15$ for .25, $z = 1.282$ for .20, $z = 1.645$ for .10, $z = 1.96$ for .05, $z = 2.327$ for .02, $z = 2.575$ for .01, and $z = 3.30$ for .001.
[a]Total = Total for ages 2-6 to 3-11.
[b]Total = Total for ages 4-0 to 7-3.
[c]Ov. = Overall for ages 2-6 to 7-3.
[d]Ov. = Overall for ages 4-0 to 7-3.

Table B-5
Differences Required for Significance When Each WPPSI–III Subtest Scaled Score Is Compared to the Mean Subtest Scaled Score for Any Individual Child

Age 2-6 to 2-11

Subtest	Mean of 2 subtests[a]		Mean of 2 subtests		Mean of 3 subtests		Mean of 4 subtests		Mean of 5 subtests	
	.05	.01	.05	.01	.05	.01	.05	.01	.05	.01
Block Design	1.66	2.19	—	—	—	—	2.49	3.01	2.69	3.44
Information	1.21	1.60	—	—	1.76	2.15	2.00	2.41	2.09	2.67
Receptive Vocabulary	1.21	1.60	1.38	1.81	1.80	2.21	2.06	2.49	2.17	2.78
Object Assembly	1.66	2.19	—	—	—	—	2.49	3.01	2.69	3.44
Picture Naming	—	—	1.38	1.81	1.98	2.43	—	—	2.48	3.17

Age 3-0 to 3-5

Subtest	Mean of 2 subtests[a]		Mean of 2 subtests		Mean of 3 subtests		Mean of 4 subtests		Mean of 5 subtests	
	.05	.01	.05	.01	.05	.01	.05	.01	.05	.01
Block Design	1.58	2.08	—	—	—	—	2.42	2.92	2.60	3.32
Information	1.25	1.64	—	—	1.77	2.17	2.04	2.47	2.14	2.74
Receptive Vocabulary	1.25	1.64	1.28	1.69	1.77	2.17	2.04	2.47	2.14	2.74
Object Assembly	1.58	2.08	—	—	—	—	2.36	2.85	2.52	3.23
Picture Naming	—	—	1.28	1.69	1.82	2.23	—	—	2.23	2.85

Age 3-6 to 3-11

Subtest	Mean of 2 subtests[a]		Mean of 2 subtests		Mean of 3 subtests		Mean of 4 subtests		Mean of 5 subtests	
	.05	.01	.05	.01	.05	.01	.05	.01	.05	.01
Block Design	1.47	1.93	—	—	—	—	2.38	2.88	2.57	3.29
Information	1.21	1.59	—	—	1.65	2.03	1.85	2.24	1.93	2.47
Receptive Vocabulary	1.21	1.59	1.32	1.73	1.81	2.21	2.07	2.50	2.20	2.82
Object Assembly	1.47	1.93	—	—	—	—	2.07	2.50	2.20	2.82
Picture Naming	—	—	1.32	1.73	1.81	2.21	—	—	2.20	2.82

Average for Ages 2-6 to 3-11

Subtest	Mean of 2 subtests[a]		Mean of 2 subtests		Mean of 3 subtests		Mean of 4 subtests		Mean of 5 subtests	
	.05	.01	.05	.01	.05	.01	.05	.01	.05	.01
Block Design	1.57	2.06	—	—	—	—	2.43	2.93	2.61	3.34
Information	1.23	1.62	—	—	1.73	2.13	1.97	2.38	2.06	2.64
Receptive Vocabulary	1.23	1.62	1.33	1.75	1.80	2.21	2.06	2.49	2.18	2.79
Object Assembly	1.57	2.06	—	—	—	—	2.31	2.79	2.47	3.16
Picture Naming	—	—	1.33	1.75	1.88	2.30	—	—	2.31	2.96

(Continued)

Table B-5 (Continued)

Age 4-0 to 4-5

Subtest	Mean of 2 subtests[b] .05	.01	Mean of 3 subtests[c] .05	.01	Mean of 4 subtests .05	.01	Mean of 4 subtests .05	.01	Mean of 4 subtests .05	.01
Block Design	—	—	2.63	3.22	3.00	3.63	2.99	3.61	—	—
Information	—	—	2.07	2.53	—	—	—	—	2.29	2.77
Matrix Reasoning	—	—	2.08	2.55	2.19	2.65	2.17	2.62	—	—
Vocabulary	—	—	1.93	2.37	—	—	—	—	2.10	2.53
Picture Concepts	—	—	2.12	2.60	2.25	2.72	2.23	2.69	—	—
Symbol Search	1.50	1.97	—	—	—	—	—	—	—	—
Word Reasoning	—	—	1.80	2.21	—	—	—	—	1.89	2.29
Coding	1.50	1.97	—	—	—	—	—	—	—	—
Comprehension	—	—	—	—	—	—	—	—	—	—
Picture Completion	—	—	—	—	—	—	2.04	2.46	—	—
Similarities	—	—	—	—	—	—	—	—	1.65	2.00
Receptive Vocabulary	1.32	1.73	—	—	—	—	—	—	—	—
Object Assembly	—	—	—	—	2.25	2.72	—	—	—	—
Picture Naming	1.32	1.73	—	—	—	—	—	—	—	—

Subtest	Mean of 4 subtests .05	.01	Mean of 5 subtests .05	.01	Mean of 5 subtests .05	.01	Mean of 7 subtests .05	.01	Mean of 12 subtests .05	.01
Block Design	—	—	3.25	4.15	—	—	3.58	4.25	4.02	4.69
Information	2.35	2.84	—	—	2.50	3.19	2.77	3.29	3.06	3.57
Matrix Reasoning	—	—	2.27	2.90	—	—	2.42	2.87	2.63	3.07
Vocabulary	2.16	2.61	—	—	2.27	2.90	2.50	2.97	2.73	3.19
Picture Concepts	—	—	2.34	2.99	—	—	2.50	2.97	2.73	3.19
Symbol Search	—	—	—	—	—	—	—	—	3.06	3.57
Word Reasoning	1.97	2.38	—	—	2.03	2.59	2.22	2.64	2.39	2.78
Coding	—	—	—	—	—	—	2.61	3.09	2.86	3.33
Comprehension	2.29	2.77	—	—	2.42	3.10	—	—	2.96	3.45
Picture Completion	—	—	2.11	2.69	—	—	—	—	2.39	2.78
Similarities	—	—	—	—	1.74	2.22	—	—	1.95	2.28
Receptive Vocabulary	—	—	—	—	—	—	—	—	—	—
Object Assembly	—	—	2.34	2.99	—	—	—	—	2.73	3.19
Picture Naming	—	—	—	—	—	—	—	—	—	—

(Continued)

Table B-5 (Continued)

Age 4-6 to 4-11

Subtest	Mean of 2 subtests[b]		Mean of 3 subtests[c]		Mean of 4 subtests		Mean of 4 subtests		Mean of 4 subtests	
	.05	.01	.05	.01	.05	.01	.05	.01	.05	.01
Block Design	—	—	2.20	2.70	2.50	3.02	2.47	2.98	—	—
Information	—	—	2.18	2.67	—	—	—	—	2.42	2.93
Matrix Reasoning	—	—	1.99	2.44	2.19	2.65	2.15	2.60	—	—
Vocabulary	—	—	2.01	2.47	—	—	—	—	2.18	2.63
Picture Concepts	—	—	1.96	2.40	2.14	2.58	2.10	2.53	—	—
Symbol Search	1.50	1.97	—	—	—	—	—	—	—	—
Word Reasoning	—	—	1.78	2.19	—	—	—	—	1.82	2.20
Coding	1.50	1.97	—	—	—	—	—	—	—	—
Comprehension	—	—	—	—	—	—	—	—	—	—
Picture Completion	—	—	—	—	—	—	1.96	2.37	—	—
Similarities	—	—	—	—	—	—	—	—	1.58	1.91
Receptive Vocabulary	1.50	1.97	—	—	—	—	—	—	—	—
Object Assembly	—	—	—	—	2.32	2.81	—	—	—	—
Picture Naming	1.50	1.97	—	—	—	—	—	—	—	—

Subtest	Mean of 4 subtests		Mean of 5 subtests		Mean of 5 subtests		Mean of 7 subtests		Mean of 12 subtests	
	.05	.01	.05	.01	.05	.01	.05	.01	.05	.01
Block Design	—	—	2.67	3.42	—	—	2.93	3.47	3.25	3.79
Information	2.47	2.98	—	—	2.63	3.37	2.93	3.47	3.25	3.79
Matrix Reasoning	—	—	2.30	2.95	—	—	2.49	2.95	2.72	3.18
Vocabulary	2.23	2.69	—	—	3.34	3.00	2.59	3.07	2.85	3.32
Picture Concepts	—	—	2.23	2.86	—	—	2.40	2.85	2.62	3.06
Symbol Search	—	—	—	—	—	—	—	—	3.05	3.56
Word Reasoning	1.88	2.27	—	—	1.91	2.45	2.08	2.47	2.23	2.60
Coding	—	—	—	—	—	—	2.59	3.07	2.85	3.32
Comprehension	2.10	2.53	—	—	2.19	2.80	—	—	2.62	3.06
Picture Completion	—	—	2.07	2.64	—	—	—	—	2.38	2.77
Similarities	—	—	—	—	1.62	2.07	—	—	1.78	2.07
Receptive Vocabulary	—	—	—	—	—	—	—	—	—	—
Object Assembly	—	—	2.46	3.15	—	—	—	—	2.95	3.44
Picture Naming	—	—	—	—	—	—	—	—	—	—

(Continued)

Table B-5 (*Continued*)

Age 5-0 to 5-5

Subtest	Mean of 2 subtests[b]		Mean of 3 subtests[c]		Mean of 4 subtests		Mean of 4 subtests		Mean of 4 subtests	
	.05	.01	.05	.01	.05	.01	.05	.01	.05	.01
Block Design	—	—	2.24	2.74	2.60	3.14	2.56	3.09	—	—
Information	—	—	1.82	2.23	—	—	—	—	1.99	2.41
Matrix Reasoning	—	—	1.86	2.29	2.06	2.49	2.01	2.43	—	—
Vocabulary	—	—	1.86	2.28	—	—	—	—	2.05	2.48
Picture Concepts	—	—	1.77	2.17	1.91	2.31	1.86	2.25	—	—
Symbol Search	1.50	1.97	—	—	—	—	—	—	—	—
Word Reasoning	—	—	1.67	2.04	—	—	—	—	1.76	2.13
Coding	1.50	1.97	—	—	—	—	—	—	—	—
Comprehension	—	—	—	—	—	—	—	—	—	—
Picture Completion	—	—	—	—	—	—	2.01	2.43	—	—
Similarities	—	—	—	—	—	—	—	—	1.60	1.93
Receptive Vocabulary	1.44	1.89	—	—	—	—	—	—	—	—
Object Assembly	—	—	—	—	2.43	2.94	—	—	—	—
Picture Naming	1.44	1.89	—	—	—	—	—	—	—	—

Subtest	Mean of 4 subtests		Mean of 5 subtests		Mean of 5 subtests		Mean of 7 subtests		Mean of 12 subtests	
	.05	.01	.05	.01	.05	.01	.05	.01	.05	.01
Block Design	—	—	2.80	3.58	—	—	3.05	3.62	3.42	4.00
Information	2.05	2.47	—	—	2.16	2.76	2.38	2.82	2.62	3.06
Matrix Reasoning	—	—	2.15	2.75	—	—	2.27	2.70	2.49	2.91
Vocabulary	2.10	2.54	—	—	2.23	2.85	2.46	2.92	2.72	3.17
Picture Concepts	—	—	1.97	2.52	—	—	2.05	2.43	2.22	2.59
Symbol Search	—	—	—	—	—	—	—	—	3.04	3.55
Word Reasoning	1.82	2.20	—	—	1.88	2.41	2.05	2.43	2.22	2.59
Coding	2.10	2.54	—	—	—	—	2.56	3.04	2.84	3.32
Comprehension	—	—	—	—	2.23	2.85	—	—	2.72	3.17
Picture Completion	—	—	2.15	2.75	—	—	—	—	2.49	2.91
Similarities	—	—	—	—	1.69	2.16	—	—	1.93	2.26
Receptive Vocabulary	—	—	—	—	—	—	—	—	—	—
Object Assembly	—	—	2.60	3.33	—	—	—	—	3.15	3.67
Picture Naming	—	—	—	—	—	—	—	—	—	—

(*Continued*)

Table B-5 (*Continued*)

Age 5-6 to 5-11

Subtest	Mean of 2 subtests[b]		Mean of 3 subtests[c]		Mean of 4 subtests		Mean of 4 subtests		Mean of 4 subtests	
	.05	.01	.05	.01	.05	.01	.05	.01	.05	.01
Block Design	—	—	2.16	2.65	2.51	3.03	2.47	2.99	—	—
Information	—	—	2.03	2.49	2.15	2.60	—	—	2.19	2.64
Matrix Reasoning	—	—	1.91	2.35	—	—	2.11	2.55	—	—
Vocabulary	—	—	2.11	2.58	—	—	—	—	2.31	2.79
Picture Concepts	—	—	1.82	2.23	2.01	2.43	1.97	2.38	—	—
Symbol Search	1.88	2.47	—	—	—	—	—	—	—	—
Word Reasoning	—	—	1.94	2.38	—	—	—	—	2.06	2.48
Coding	1.88	2.47	—	—	—	—	—	—	—	—
Comprehension	—	—	—	—	—	—	—	—	—	—
Picture Completion	—	—	—	—	—	—	2.24	2.70	—	—
Similarities	—	—	—	—	—	—	—	—	1.59	1.92
Receptive Vocabulary	1.44	1.89	—	—	—	—	—	—	—	—
Object Assembly	—	—	—	—	2.57	3.10	—	—	—	—
Picture Naming	1.44	1.89	—	—	—	—	—	—	—	—

Subtest	Mean of 4 subtests		Mean of 5 subtests		Mean of 5 subtests		Mean of 7 subtests		Mean of 12 subtests	
	.05	.01	.05	.01	.05	.01	.05	.01	.05	.01
Block Design	—	—	2.70	3.45	—	—	2.94	3.49	3.27	3.81
Information	2.24	2.71	—	—	2.35	3.01	2.61	3.09	2.87	3.35
Matrix Reasoning	—	—	2.26	2.89	—	—	2.42	2.87	2.64	3.09
Vocabulary	2.36	2.85	—	—	2.50	3.19	2.77	3.29	3.07	3.58
Picture Concepts	—	—	2.10	2.68	—	—	2.22	2.64	2.40	2.80
Symbol Search	—	—	—	—	—	—	—	—	3.62	4.23
Word Reasoning	2.11	2.55	—	—	2.20	2.81	2.42	2.87	2.64	3.09
Coding	—	—	—	—	—	—	3.30	3.92	3.70	4.32
Comprehension	2.17	2.62	—	—	2.27	2.90	—	—	2.74	3.20
Picture Completion	—	—	2.42	3.09	—	—	—	—	2.87	3.35
Similarities	—	—	—	—	1.63	2.08	—	—	1.81	2.11
Receptive Vocabulary	—	—	—	—	—	—	—	—	—	—
Object Assembly	—	—	2.77	3.54	—	—	—	—	3.37	3.93
Picture Naming	—	—	—	—	—	—	—	—	—	—

(Continued)

Table B-5 (Continued)

Age 6-0 to 6-11

Subtest	Mean of 2 subtests[b]		Mean of 3 subtests[c]		Mean of 4 subtests		Mean of 4 subtests		Mean of 4 subtests	
	.05	.01	.05	.01	.05	.01	.05	.01	.05	.01
Block Design	—	—	2.09	2.57	2.43	2.94	2.36	2.85	—	—
Information	—	—	2.28	2.80	—	—	—	—	2.55	3.09
Matrix Reasoning	—	—	1.93	2.36	2.20	2.65	2.11	2.55	—	—
Vocabulary	—	—	2.08	2.56	—	—	—	—	2.26	2.73
Picture Concepts	—	—	1.96	2.41	2.25	2.72	2.17	2.62	—	—
Symbol Search	1.88	2.47	—	—	—	—	—	—	—	—
Word Reasoning	—	—	2.04	2.50	—	—	—	—	2.19	2.64
Coding	1.88	2.47	—	—	—	—	—	—	—	—
Comprehension	—	—	—	—	—	—	—	—	—	—
Picture Completion	—	—	—	—	—	—	2.24	2.71	—	—
Similarities	—	—	—	—	—	—	—	—	2.06	2.49
Receptive Vocabulary	1.71	2.25	—	—	—	—	—	—	—	—
Object Assembly	—	—	—	—	2.87	3.46	—	—	—	—
Picture Naming	1.71	2.25	—	—	—	—	—	—	—	—

Subtest	Mean of 4 subtests		Mean of 5 subtests		Mean of 5 subtests		Mean of 7 subtests		Mean of 12 subtests	
	.05	.01	.05	.01	.05	.01	.05	.01	.05	.01
Block Design	—	—	2.58	3.30	—	—	2.78	3.30	3.08	3.60
Information	2.59	3.13	—	—	2.77	3.54	3.04	3.60	3.38	3.95
Matrix Reasoning	—	—	2.29	2.93	—	—	2.44	2.89	2.66	3.11
Vocabulary	2.30	2.77	—	—	2.41	3.09	2.62	3.11	2.88	3.37
Picture Concepts	—	—	2.36	3.02	—	—	2.52	2.99	2.76	3.22
Symbol Search	—	—	—	—	—	—	—	—	3.64	4.24
Word Reasoning	2.23	2.69	—	—	2.33	2.98	2.52	2.99	2.76	3.22
Coding	—	—	—	—	—	—	3.31	3.93	3.71	4.33
Comprehension	2.41	2.91	—	—	2.55	3.27	—	—	3.08	3.60
Picture Completion	—	—	2.44	3.13	—	—	—	—	2.88	3.37
Similarities	—	—	—	—	2.18	2.79	—	—	2.54	2.96
Receptive Vocabulary	—	—	—	—	—	—	—	—	—	—
Object Assembly	—	—	3.10	3.96	—	—	—	—	3.81	4.45
Picture Naming	—	—	—	—	—	—	—	—	—	—

Table B-5 (Continued)

Age 7-0 to 7-3

Subtest	Mean of 2 subtests[b]		Mean of 3 subtests[c]		Mean of 4 subtests		Mean of 4 subtests		Mean of 4 subtests	
	.05	.01	.05	.01	.05	.01	.05	.01	.05	.01
Block Design	—	—	1.80	2.21	2.08	2.51	2.01	2.43	—	—
Information	—	—	2.21	2.71	—	—	—	—	2.49	3.00
Matrix Reasoning	—	—	1.94	2.38	2.27	2.75	2.21	2.67	1.91	2.30
Vocabulary	—	—	1.82	2.24	—	—	—	—	—	—
Picture Concepts	—	—	1.80	2.21	2.08	2.51	2.01	2.43	—	—
Symbol Search	1.88	2.47	—	—	—	—	—	—	—	—
Word Reasoning	—	—	1.87	2.29	—	—	—	—	1.98	2.39
Coding	1.88	2.47	—	—	—	—	—	—	—	—
Comprehension	—	—	—	—	—	—	—	—	—	—
Picture Completion	—	—	—	—	—	—	2.27	2.74	—	—
Similarities	—	—	—	—	—	—	—	—	1.67	2.01
Receptive Vocabulary	1.58	2.08	—	—	—	—	—	—	—	—
Object Assembly	—	—	—	—	2.77	3.34	—	—	—	—
Picture Naming	1.58	2.08	—	—	—	—	—	—	—	—

Subtest	Mean of 4 subtests		Mean of 5 subtests		Mean of 5 subtests		Mean of 7 subtests		Mean of 12 subtests	
	.05	.01	.05	.01	.05	.01	.05	.01	.05	.01
Block Design	—	—	2.18	2.79	—	—	2.31	2.73	2.52	2.94
Information	2.54	3.06	—	—	2.71	3.47	3.01	3.57	3.37	3.93
Matrix Reasoning	—	—	2.42	3.09	—	—	2.59	3.07	2.87	3.35
Vocabulary	1.97	2.38	—	—	2.03	2.59	2.21	2.62	2.40	2.80
Picture Concepts	—	—	2.18	2.79	—	—	2.31	2.73	2.52	2.94
Symbol Search	—	—	—	—	—	—	—	—	3.62	4.23
Word Reasoning	2.04	2.46	—	—	2.11	2.70	2.31	2.73	2.52	2.94
Coding	—	—	—	—	—	—	3.29	3.90	3.70	4.32
Comprehension	2.24	2.70	—	—	2.35	3.01	—	—	2.87	3.35
Picture Completion	—	—	2.49	3.18	—	—	—	—	2.97	3.46
Similarities	—	—	—	—	1.74	2.22	—	—	1.97	2.30
Receptive Vocabulary	—	—	—	—	—	—	—	—	—	—
Object Assembly	—	—	3.00	3.84	—	—	—	—	3.70	4.32
Picture Naming	—	—	—	—	—	—	—	—	—	—

(Continued)

Table B-5 (*Continued*)

Average for Ages 4-0 to 7-3

Subtest	Mean of 2 subtests[b]		Mean of 3 subtests[c]		Mean of 4 subtests		Mean of 4 subtests		Mean of 4 subtests	
	.05	.01	.05	.01	.05	.01	.05	.01	.05	.01
Block Design	—	—	2.20	2.69	2.53	3.06	2.49	3.01	—	—
Information	—	—	2.11	2.58	—	—	—	—	2.34	2.82
Matrix Reasoning	—	—	1.95	2.39	2.17	2.62	2.12	2.56	—	—
Vocabulary	—	—	1.98	2.42	—	—	—	—	2.14	2.59
Picture Concepts	—	—	1.90	2.33	2.10	2.54	2.05	2.48	—	—
Symbol Search	1.70	2.23	—	—	—	—	—	—	—	—
Word Reasoning	—	—	1.85	2.27	—	—	—	—	1.95	2.36
Coding	1.70	2.23	—	—	—	—	—	—	—	—
Comprehension	—	—	—	—	—	—	—	—	—	—
Picture Completion	—	—	—	—	—	—	2.12	2.56	—	—
Similarities	—	—	—	—	—	—	—	—	1.70	2.05
Receptive Vocabulary	1.50	1.97	—	—	—	—	—	—	—	—
Object Assembly	—	—	—	—	2.55	3.08	—	—	—	—
Picture Naming	1.50	1.97	—	—	—	—	—	—	—	—

Subtest	Mean of 4 subtests		Mean of 5 subtests		Mean of 5 subtests		Mean of 7 subtests		Mean of 12 subtests	
	.05	.01	.05	.01	.05	.01	.05	.01	.05	.01
Block Design	—	—	2.71	3.47	—	—	2.95	3.50	3.29	3.84
Information	2.38	2.88	—	—	2.53	3.24	2.81	3.33	3.11	3.63
Matrix Reasoning	—	—	2.28	2.91	—	—	2.43	2.88	2.66	3.11
Vocabulary	2.19	2.65	—	—	2.30	2.95	2.53	3.01	2.79	3.25
Picture Concepts	—	—	2.19	2.80	—	—	2.33	2.76	2.54	2.96
Symbol Search	—	—	—	—	—	—	—	—	3.34	3.90
Word Reasoning	2.01	2.43	—	—	2.08	2.66	2.27	2.69	2.46	2.88
Coding	—	—	—	—	—	—	2.97	3.53	3.31	3.87
Comprehension	2.22	2.68	—	—	2.34	2.99	—	—	2.84	3.31
Picture Completion	—	—	2.28	2.91	—	—	—	—	2.66	3.11
Similarities	—	—	—	—	1.77	2.26	—	—	2.01	2.34
Receptive Vocabulary	—	—	—	—	—	—	—	—	—	—
Object Assembly	—	—	2.73	3.49	—	—	—	—	3.31	3.87
Picture Naming	—	—	—	—	—	—	—	—	—	—

(*Continued*)

Table B-5 (*Continued*)

Note. The table shows the minimum deviations from a child's average subtest scaled score that are significant at the .05 and .01 levels.

The following formula, obtained from Davis (1959), was used to compute the deviations from average that are significant at the desired significance level:

$$D = CR \times SEM_{((T/m) - z_I)}$$

where

D = deviation from average

CR = critical ratio desired

$SEM_{((T/m) - z_I)}$ = standard error of measurement of the difference between an average subtest scaled score and any one of the subtest scaled scores that entered into the average

The standard error of measurement can be obtained from the following formula:

$$SEM_{((T/m) - z_I)} = \sqrt{\frac{SEM_T^2}{m^2} + \left(\frac{m-2}{m}\right) SEM_{z_I}^2}$$

where

SEM_T^2 = sum of the squared standard errors of measurement of the m subtests

m = number of subtests included in the average

T/m = average of the subtest scaled scores

$SEM_{z_I}^2$ = squared standard error of measurement of any one of the subtest scaled scores

The critical ratios used were based on the Bonferroni inequality, which controls the family-wise error rate at .05 (or .01) by setting the error rate per comparison at .05/m (or .01/m). The critical ratios at the .05 level are 2.39 for 3 subtests, 2.50 for 4 subtests, 2.58 for 5 subtests, 2.81 for 10 subtests, and 2.87 for 12 subtests. The critical ratios at the .01 level are 2.93 for 3 subtests, 3.02 for 4 subtests, 3.10 for 5 subtests, 3.30 for 10 subtests, and 3.35 for 12 subtests. For 6 and 7 subtests, the Bonferroni inequality critical ratios would be 2.64 and 2.69, respectively, at the .05 level and 3.14 and 3.19, respectively, at the .01 level.

The following example illustrates the procedure. We will determine the minimum deviation required for a 6-year-old child's score on the WPPSI–III Information subtest to be significantly different from his or her average score on the three standard Verbal subtests (Information, Vocabulary, and Word Reasoning) at the 95% level of confidence. We calculate SEM_T^2 by first squaring the appropriate average standard error of measurement for each of the three subtests and then summing the squares. These standard errors of measurement are in Table 4.3 (p. 57) in the Technical Manual.

$$SEM_T^2 = (1.24)^2 + (1.04)^2 + (.99)^2 = 3.599$$

We determine $SEM_{z_I}^2$ by squaring the average standard error of measurement of the subtest of interest, the Information subtest:

$$SEM_{z_I}^2 = (1.24)^2 = 1.53$$

The number of subtests, m, equals 3. Substituting these values into the formula yields the following:

$$SEM_{((T/m) - z_I)} = \sqrt{\frac{3.599}{(3)^2} + \left(\frac{3-2}{3}\right) 1.53} = .953$$

The value, .953, is then multiplied by the appropriate z value for the 95% confidence level to obtain the minimum significant deviation (D). Using the Bonferroni correction (.05/3 = .0167), we have a z value of 2.39.

$$D = 2.39 \times .953 = 2.28$$

The Bonferonni correction was not applied to the two-subtest mean comparisons.

[a]In this column, the entries for Block Design and Object Assembly are compared to the mean of these two subtests. Similarly, the entries for Information and Receptive Vocabulary are compared to the mean of these two subtests.

[b]In this column, the entries for Symbol Search and Coding are compared to the mean of these two subtests. Similarly, the entries for Receptive Vocabulary and Picture Naming are compared to the mean of these two subtests.

[c]In this column, the entries for Block Design, Matrix Reasoning, and Picture Concepts are compared to the mean of these three subtests. Similarly, the entries for Information, Vocabulary, and Word Reasoning are compared to the mean of these three subtests.

Table B-6
Estimates of the Differences Obtained by Various Percentages of the WPPSI–III Standardization Sample When Each WPPSI–III Subtest Scaled Score Is Compared to the Mean Scaled Score for Any Individual Child

Ages 2-6 to 3-11

Subtest	Verbal (core subtests)				Performance (core subtests)				General Language (core plus supplemental subtests)			
	10%	5%	2%	1%	10%	5%	2%	1%	10%	5%	2%	1%
Block Design	—	—	—	—	2.68	3.19	3.81	4.20	—	—	—	—
Information	1.88	2.24	2.67	2.94	—	—	—	—	—	—	—	—
Receptive Vocabulary	1.88	2.24	2.67	2.94	—	—	—	—	1.88	2.24	2.67	2.94
Object Assembly	—	—	—	—	2.68	3.19	3.81	4.20	—	—	—	—
Picture Naming	—	—	—	—	—	—	—	—	1.88	2.24	2.67	2.94

Subtest	Verbal (core plus supplemental subtests)				Full Scale (core subtests)				Full Scale (core plus supplemental subtests)			
	10%	5%	2%	1%	10%	5%	2%	1%	10%	5%	2%	1%
Block Design	—	—	—	—	3.49	4.15	4.95	5.46	3.75	4.47	5.33	5.87
Information	2.09	2.49	2.97	3.28	2.74	3.27	3.90	4.29	2.60	3.10	3.69	4.07
Receptive Vocabulary	2.21	2.63	3.14	3.45	2.94	3.50	4.17	4.59	2.82	3.36	4.00	4.41
Object Assembly	—	—	—	—	3.36	4.00	4.77	5.26	3.55	4.23	5.04	5.56
Picture Naming	2.09	2.49	2.97	3.28	—	—	—	—	2.67	3.19	3.80	4.19

Ages 4-0 to 7-3

Subtest	Processing Speed (core plus supplemental subtests)				General Language (optional subtests)				Verbal (core subtests)			
	10%	5%	2%	1%	10%	5%	2%	1%	10%	5%	2%	1%
Block Design	—	—	—	—	—	—	—	—	—	—	—	—
Information	—	—	—	—	—	—	—	—	2.14	2.56	3.05	3.36
Matrix Reasoning	—	—	—	—	—	—	—	—	—	—	—	—
Vocabulary	—	—	—	—	—	—	—	—	2.26	2.69	3.20	3.53
Picture Concepts	—	—	—	—	—	—	—	—	—	—	—	—
Symbol Search	2.23	2.66	3.17	3.50	—	—	—	—	—	—	—	—
Word Reasoning	—	—	—	—	—	—	—	—	2.07	2.46	2.94	3.24
Coding	2.23	2.66	3.17	3.50	—	—	—	—	—	—	—	—
Comprehension	—	—	—	—	—	—	—	—	—	—	—	—
Picture Completion	—	—	—	—	—	—	—	—	—	—	—	—
Similarities	—	—	—	—	—	—	—	—	—	—	—	—
Receptive Vocabulary	—	—	—	—	2.00	2.39	2.85	3.14	—	—	—	—
Object Assembly	—	—	—	—	—	—	—	—	—	—	—	—
Picture Naming	—	—	—	—	2.00	2.39	2.85	3.14	—	—	—	—

Subtest	Performance (core subtests)				Verbal (core subtests plus Comprehension)				Verbal (core subtests plus Similarities)			
	10%	5%	2%	1%	10%	5%	2%	1%	10%	5%	2%	1%
Block Design	2.98	3.55	4.23	4.66	—	—	—	—	—	—	—	—
Information	—	—	—	—	2.37	2.82	3.36	3.70	2.32	2.77	3.30	3.63
Matrix Reasoning	2.78	3.31	3.95	4.35	—	—	—	—	—	—	—	—
Vocabulary	—	—	—	—	2.34	2.79	3.33	3.66	2.35	2.80	3.33	3.67
Picture Concepts	3.06	3.65	4.35	4.79	—	—	—	—	—	—	—	—

(Continued)

Subtest	Performance (core subtests)				Verbal (core subtests plus Comprehension)				Verbal (core subtests plus Similarities)			
	10%	5%	2%	1%	10%	5%	2%	1%	10%	5%	2%	1%
Symbol Search	—	—	—	—	—	—	—	—	—	—	—	—
Word Reasoning	—	—	—	—	2.21	2.63	3.14	3.45	2.27	2.70	3.22	3.55
Coding	—	—	—	—	—	—	—	—	—	—	—	—
Comprehension	—	—	—	—	2.44	2.91	3.47	3.82	—	—	—	—
Picture Completion	—	—	—	—	—	—	—	—	—	—	—	—
Similarities	—	—	—	—	—	—	—	—	2.50	2.98	3.55	3.91
Receptive Vocabulary	—	—	—	—	—	—	—	—	—	—	—	—
Object Assembly	—	—	—	—	—	—	—	—	—	—	—	—
Picture Naming	—	—	—	—	—	—	—	—	—	—	—	—

Subtest	Performance (core subtests plus Object Assembly)				Performance (core subtests plus Picture Completion)				Verbal (core plus supplemental subtests)			
	10%	5%	2%	1%	10%	5%	2%	1%	10%	5%	2%	1%
Block Design	3.00	3.58	4.26	4.70	3.10	3.69	4.40	4.85	—	—	—	—
Information	—	—	—	—	—	—	—	—	2.43	2.90	3.46	3.81
Matrix Reasoning	3.04	3.62	4.32	4.76	3.02	3.59	4.29	4.72	—	—	—	—
Vocabulary	—	—	—	—	—	—	—	—	2.37	2.83	3.37	3.71
Picture Concepts	3.33	3.97	4.73	5.21	3.23	3.85	4.59	5.06	—	—	—	—
Symbol Search	—	—	—	—	—	—	—	—	—	—	—	—
Word Reasoning	—	—	—	—	—	—	—	—	2.31	2.75	3.28	3.62
Coding	—	—	—	—	—	—	—	—	2.61	3.11	3.70	4.08
Comprehension	—	—	—	—	—	—	—	—	—	—	—	—
Picture Completion	—	—	—	—	3.08	3.67	4.37	4.82	—	—	—	—
Similarities	—	—	—	—	—	—	—	—	2.66	3.17	3.78	4.17
Receptive Vocabulary	—	—	—	—	—	—	—	—	—	—	—	—
Object Assembly	3.18	3.79	4.52	4.98	—	—	—	—	—	—	—	—
Picture Naming	—	—	—	—	—	—	—	—	—	—	—	—

Subtest	Performance (core plus supplemental subtests)				Full scale (core subtests)				Full scale (core plus supplemental subtests)			
	10%	5%	2%	1%	10%	5%	2%	1%	10%	5%	2%	1%
Block Design	3.10	3.69	4.40	4.85	3.44	4.10	4.88	5.38	3.50	4.17	4.97	5.47
Information	—	—	—	—	2.84	3.38	4.03	4.44	2.96	3.53	4.21	4.64
Matrix Reasoning	3.17	3.78	4.51	3.97	3.32	3.96	4.72	5.20	3.45	4.11	4.90	5.40
Vocabulary	—	—	—	—	3.06	3.65	4.35	4.80	3.12	3.72	4.44	4.89
Picture Concepts	3.41	4.06	4.85	5.34	3.48	4.14	4.94	5.44	3.58	4.26	5.08	5.60
Symbol Search	—	—	—	—	—	—	—	—	3.58	4.27	5.09	5.61
Word Reasoning	—	—	—	—	2.89	3.44	4.10	4.52	2.96	3.52	4.20	4.63
Coding	—	—	—	—	4.09	4.88	5.82	6.41	4.14	4.93	5.88	6.48
Comprehension	—	—	—	—	—	—	—	—	3.26	3.88	4.63	5.10
Picture Completion	3.16	3.76	4.49	4.94	—	—	—	—	3.39	4.04	4.82	5.31
Similarities	—	—	—	—	—	—	—	—	3.17	3.78	4.51	4.97
Receptive Vocabulary	—	—	—	—	—	—	—	—	—	—	—	—
Object Assembly	3.26	3.89	4.64	5.11	—	—	—	—	3.86	4.59	5.48	6.03
Picture Naming	—	—	—	—	—	—	—	—	—	—	—	—

Note. The formula used to obtain the values in this table was obtained from Silverstein (1984):

$$SD_{Da} = 3\sqrt{1 + \bar{G} - 2\bar{T_a}}$$

where

SD_{Da} = standard deviation of the difference for subtest a

3 = standard deviation of the scaled scores on each of the subtests

$\bar{G}$ = mean of all the elements in the matrix (including 1s in the diagonal)

$\bar{T_a}$ = mean of the elements in row or column a of the matrix (again including 1s in the diagonal)

Table B-7
Reliability and Validity Coefficients of WPPSI–III Short Forms
for 2-, 3-, and 4-Subtest Combinations for Ages 2-6 to 3-11

Two subtests				Three subtests					Four subtests					
Short form		r_{ss}	r	Short form			r_{ss}	r	Short form				r_{ss}	r
IN	PN[a]	.945	.730	IN	RV	OA	.951	.767	BD	RV	OA	PN	.949	.781
IN	RV[b]	.950	.729	IN	OA	PN	.949	.764	BD	IN	OA	PN	.951	.780
IN	OA	.927	.729	BD	RV	PN	.940	.762	BD	IN	RV	PN	.960	.778
RV	PN[b]	.942	.721	BD	IN	RV	.946	.761	IN	RV	OA	PN	.962	.778
RV	OA	.922	.720	BD	IN	PN	.944	.761						
OA	PN	.917	.718	RV	OA	PN	.946	.760						
BD	PN	.905	.717	IN	RV	PN[b]	.962	.747						
BD	IN	.919	.713	BD	IN	OA	.935	.744						
BD	RV	.912	.712	BD	RV	OA	.931	.744						
BD	OA[c]	.901	.633	BD	OA	PN	.929	.743						

Note. Abbreviations: BD = Block Design, IN = Information, RV = Receptive Vocabulary, OA = Object Assembly, PN = Picture Naming. The estimated Full Scale IQs associated with each short form are shown in Tables B-11, B-12, and B-13.
[a]This combination is useful for a rapid screening; it also has the highest *g* loadings.
[b]This combination is useful for a rapid screening.
[c]This combination is useful for children who are hearing impaired.

Table B-8
Reliability and Validity Coefficients of WPPSI–III Short Forms for 2-, 3-, 4-, and 5-Subtest Combinations for Ages 4-0 to 7-3

Two subtests				Three subtests			
Short form		r_{xx}	r	Short form			r_{xx}	r

Short form		r_{xx}	r	Short form			r_{xx}	r
SS	WR	.908	.869	IN	SS	WR	.935	.909
IN	SS	.890	.868	SS	WR	SI	.949	.907
MR	WR	.936	.868	IN	SS	SI	.940	.906
PCm	SI	.949	.864	IN	VC	SS	.930	.905
IN	MR[a]	.921	.858	VC	SS	WR	.939	.903
WR	PCm	.939	.858	SS	WR	PCm	.938	.903
VC	PCm	.930	.857	SS	PCm	SI	.943	.903
MR	VC	.929	.856	BD	MR	VC	.942	.902
BD	VC	.906	.855	IN	SS	PCm[a]	.929	.902
IN	PCm	.923	.854	MR	VC	PCm	.947	.902
IN	CD[a]	.866	.822	IN	MR	SS[a]	.930	.896
BD	MR[b]	.914	.771	IN	MR	CD[a]	.926	.879
BD	PCn[b]	.911	.789	IN	MR	PCm[a]	.944	.896
BD	SS[b]	.890	.753	IN	CD	PCm[a]	.927	.876
BD	CD[b]	.886	.707	BD	MR	CD[a]	.924	.802
MR	PCn[b]	.936	.804	BD	SS	CD[b]	.918	.757
MR	SS[b]	.909	.795	BD	CD	PCm[a]	.924	.807
PCn	CD[b]	.905	.755	BD	SS	PCm[b]	.927	.833
IN	WR[c]	.934	.849	BD	PCm	OA[b]	.930	.800
				BD	PCn	SS[a, b]	.927	.828
				BD	PCn	CD[a, b]	.922	.812
				BD	PCn	PCm[a, b]	.939	.848
				BD	PCn	OA[a, b]	.928	.810
				MR	CD	PCm[a, b]	.933	.846
				PCn	SS	CD[a, b]	.927	.791
				PCn	SS	PCm[a, b]	.937	.863
				PCn	PCm	OA[a, b]	.938	.843
				BD	MR	PCm[d]	.940	.842
				MR	PCn	PCm[e]	.950	.870
				VC	WR	SI[f]	.965	.868

(Continued)

Table B-8 (*Continued*)

Four subtests				r_{xx}	r	Five subtests					r_{xx}	r
Short form						Short form						
SS	WR	PCm	SI	.959	.934	MR	SS	WR	PCm	SI	.966	.947
IN	SS	PCm	SI	.954	.932	MR	VC	SS	WR	PCm	.962	.945
IN	MR	SS	WR	.951	.929	IN	MR	VC	SS	PCm	.958	.944
IN	VC	SS	PCm	.948	.929	IN	MR	SS	PCm	SI	.962	.944
VC	SS	WR	PCm	.953	.929	MR	WR	CD	PCm	SI	.964	.944
BD	VC	SS	WR	.946	.928	BD	VC	PCn	SS	WR	.957	.943
IN	VC	SS	OA	.938	.928	BD	VC	SS	WR	PCm	.957	.943
IN	SS	WR	PCm	.951	.928	IN	MR	SS	WR	PCm	.960	.943
MR	VC	SS	WR	.953	.928	IN	SS	CO	SI	OA	.955	.943
MR	WR	PCm	SI	.967	.928	MR	VC	SS	PCm	SI	.964	.943
IN	MR	SS	PCm[a]	.948	.921	IN	MR	SS	CD	PCm[a]	.952	.914
IN	MR	SS	CD[a]	.939	.885	BD	MR	PCn	SS	CD[b]	.952	.863
IN	MR	CD	PCm[a]	.955	.919	BD	MR	PCn	SS	PCm[b]	.957	.896
BD	MR	SS	CD[b]	.939	.821	BD	MR	PCn	CD	PCm[b]	.955	.891
BD	MR	SS	PCm[b]	.946	.869	BD	MR	SS	CD	PCm[b]	.952	.866
BD	MR	PCn	SS[b]	.946	.863	MR	PCn	SS	CD	PCm[b]	.960	.931
BD	MR	CD	PCm[b]	.944	.857	BD	PCn	SS	CD	PCm[a, b]	.951	.871
BD	PCn	SS	CD[b]	.938	.827	IN	VC	WR	CO	SI[h]	.973	.890
BD	MR	PCn	CD[a, b]	.943	.857							
BD	PCn	CD	PCm[a, b]	.943	.863							
MR	PCn	CD	PCm[a, b]	.950	.886							
IN	VC	WR	SI[g]	.968	.885							

Note. Abbreviations: BD = Block Design, IN = Information, MR = Matrix Reasoning, VC = Vocabulary, PCn = Picture Concepts, SS = Symbol Search, WR = Word Reasoning, CD = Coding, CO = Comprehension, PCm = Picture Completion, SI = Similarities, OA = Object Assembly. The estimated Full Scale IQs associated with each short form are shown in Tables B-14, B-15, B-16, and B-17.

The highest *g* loadings on three Verbal subtests are for Word Reasoning, Information, and Vocabulary—the three subtests that form the Verbal IQ.

[a]This combination is useful for a rapid screening.
[b]This combination is useful for children who are hearing impaired.
[c]Highest *g* loadings on two Verbal subtests.
[d]Highest *g* loadings on three Performance subtests.
[e]Highest reliability on three Performance subtests.
[f]Highest reliability on three Verbal subtests.
[g]Highest *g* loadings on four subtests.
[h]Highest *g* loadings on five subtests.

Table B-9
Reliable and Unusual Scaled-Score Ranges for Selected WPPSI–III Subtest Combinations for Ages 2-6 to 3-11

Composite or short form				Reliable scaled-score range	Unusual scaled-score range
Two subtests					
IN	PN			3	4
IN	RV			3	4
IN	OA			3	6
RV	PN			3	4
RV	OA			3	6
OA	PN			3	6
BD	PN			3	6
BD	IN			3	6
BD	RV			3	6
BD	OA			4	6
Three subtests					
IN	RV	OA		4	7
IN	OA	PN		4	6
BD	RV	PN		4	7
BD	IN	RV		4	7
BD	IN	PN		4	7
RV	OA	PN		4	7
IN	RV	PN		4	5
BD	IN	OA		4	7
BD	RV	OA		4	7
BD	OA	PN		4	7
Four subtests					
BD	RV	OA	PN	4	8
BD	IN	OA	PN	4	8
BD	IN	RV	PN	4	7
IN	RV	OA	PN	4	7

Note. Abbreviations: BD = Block Design, IN = Information, RV = Receptive Vocabulary, OA = Object Assembly, PN = Picture Naming.

The formula used to obtain the reliable scaled-score range is as follows (Silverstein, 1989):

$$R = q \sqrt{\frac{\sum \mathrm{SEM}_i^2}{k}}$$

where

q = critical value (n/v) of the Studentized range for a specified probability level (.05 in this case)

SEM_i = standard error of measurement of the scores on subtest i

k = number of subtests in the short form

The formula used to obtain the unusual scaled-score range is as follows (Silverstein, 1989):

$$R = q \times \sigma \sqrt{1 - \frac{2\sum r_{ij}}{k(k-1)}}$$

where

q = critical value (n/v) of the Studentized range for a specified probability level (.10 in this case)

σ = standard deviation of the subtest scores

r_{ij} = correlation between subtests i and j

k = number of subtests in the short form

The following are the appropriate q values to use in the two formulas for sample sizes of from 2 to 10 and of 12, with v (degrees of freedom) = ∞, at the .10 probability level and at the .05 probability level (.10 or .05): for 2, 2.33 or 2.77; for 3, 2.90 or 3.31; for 4, 3.24 or 3.63; for 5, 3.48 or 3.86; for 6, 3.66 or 4.03; for 7, 3.81 or 4.17; for 8, 3.93 or 4.29; for 9, 4.04 or 4.39; for 10, 4.13 or 4.47; and for 12, 4.28 or 4.62.

The table is read as follows: In the two-subtest short form composed of Information and Receptive Vocabulary, a range of 3 points between the two scores indicates a nonchance difference at the .05 level. A range of 4 occurs in less than 10% of the population and should be considered unusual, as should all ranges higher than 4 points. Less credence can be placed in a Composite score or short-form IQ when the scatter is larger than expected.

Table B-10
Reliable and Unusual Scaled-Score Ranges for Selected WPPSI–III Subtest Combinations for Ages 4-0 to 7-3

Composite or short form			Reliable scaled-score range	Unusual scaled-score range	Composite or short form			Reliable scaled-score range	Unusual scaled-score range
Two subtests					**Three subtests (Continued)**				
SS	WR		3	6	BD	SS	PCm	4	7
IN	SS		4	6	BD	PCm	OA	4	7
MR	WR		3	5	BD	PCn	SS	4	7
PCm	SI		3	6	BD	PCn	CD	4	7
IN	MR		3	5	BD	PCn	PCm	4	7
WR	PCm		3	5	BD	PCn	OA	4	7
VC	PCm		3	5	MR	CD	PCm	4	7
MR	VC		3	6	PCn	SS	CD	4	7
BD	VC		4	6	PCn	SS	PCm	4	7
IN	PCm		3	5	PCn	PCm	OA	4	7
IN	CD		4	6	BD	MR	PCm	4	7
BD	MR		4	5	MR	PCn	PCm	4	7
BD	PCn		3	6	VC	WR	SI	3	5
BD	SS		4	5	**Four subtests**				
BD	CD		4	6	SS	WR	PCm	SI	4	7
MR	PCn		3	6	IN	SS	PCm	SI	4	7
MR	SS		4	5	IN	MR	SS	WR	4	7
PCn	CD		3	6	IN	VC	SS	PCm	4	7
IN	WR		3	4	VC	SS	WR	PCm	4	7
Three subtests					BD	VC	SS	WR	5	7
IN	SS	WR	4	7	IN	VC	SS	OA	5	8
SS	WR	SI	4	7	IN	SS	WR	PCm	4	7
IN	SS	SI	4	7	MR	VC	SS	WR	4	7
IN	VC	SS	4	7	MR	WR	PCm	SI	4	7
VC	SS	WR	4	7	IN	MR	SS	PCm	4	8
SS	WR	PCm	4	7	IN	MR	SS	CD	5	8
SS	PCm	SI	4	7	IN	MR	CD	PCm	4	8
BD	MR	VC	4	7	BD	MR	SS	CD	5	8
IN	SS	PCm	4	7	BD	MR	SS	PCm	4	7
MR	VC	PCm	4	7	BD	MR	PCn	SS	4	8
IN	MR	SS	4	7	BD	MR	CD	PCm	4	8
IN	MR	CD	4	7	BD	PCn	SS	CD	5	8
IN	MR	PCm	4	7	BD	MR	PCn	CD	4	8
IN	CD	PCm	4	7	BD	PCn	CD	PCm	4	8
BD	MR	CD	4	7	MR	PCn	CD	PCm	4	8
BD	SS	CD	5	7	IN	VC	WR	SI	4	6
BD	CD	PCm	4	7					

(Continued)

Table B-10 (Continued)

Composite or short form					Reliable scaled-score range	Unusual scaled-score range
Five subtests						
MR	SS	WR	PCm	SI	4	8
MR	VC	SS	WR	PCm	4	8
IN	MR	VC	SS	PCm	5	8
IN	MR	SS	PCm	SI	4	8
MR	WR	CD	PCm	SI	4	8
BD	VC	PCn	SS	WR	5	8
BD	VC	SS	WR	PCm	5	8
IN	MR	SS	WR	PCm	5	8
IN	SS	CO	SI	OA	5	8
MR	VC	SS	PCm	SI	4	8
IN	MR	SS	CD	PCm	5	8
BD	MR	PCn	SS	CD	5	8
BD	MR	PCn	SS	PCm	5	8
BD	MR	PCn	CD	PCm	5	8
BD	MR	SS	CD	PCm	5	8
MR	PCn	SS	CD	PCm	5	8
BD	PCn	SS	CD	PCm	5	8
IN	VC	WR	CO	SI	4	6
Six subtests						
MR	VC	PCn	WR	PCm	SI	4	8
BD	IN	MR	VC	PCn	WR	5	8
BD	IN	MR	VC	WR	PCm	4	8
Seven subtests						
MR	VC	PCn	WR	CD	PCm	SI	4	9
BD	IN	MR	VC	PCn	SS	WR	5	9
BD	IN	MR	VC	SS	WR	Cm	5	8

Note. Abbreviations: BD = Block Design, IN = Information, MR = Matrix Reasoning, VC = Vocabulary, PCn = Picture Concepts, SS = Symbol Search, WR = Word Reasoning, CD = Coding, CO = Comprehension, PCm = Picture Completion, SI = Similarities, OA = Object Assembly.

The formula used to obtain the reliable scaled-score range is as follows (Silverstein, 1989):

$$R = q \sqrt{\frac{\Sigma \, \text{SEM}_i^2}{k}}$$

where

q = critical value (n/v) of the Studentized range for a specified probability level (.05 in this case)

SEM_i = standard error of measurement of the scores on subtest i

k = number of subtests in the short form

The formula used to obtain the unusual scaled-score range is as follows (Silverstein, 1989):

$$R = q \times \sigma \sqrt{1 - \frac{2\Sigma r_{ij}}{k(k-1)}}$$

where

q = critical value (n/v) of the Studentized range for a specified probability level (.10 in this case)

σ = standard deviation of the subtest scores

r_{ij} = correlation between subtests i and j

k = number of subtests in the short form

The following are the appropriate q values to use in the two formulas for sample sizes of from 2 to 10 and of 12, with v (degrees of freedom) = ∞, at the .10 probability level and at the .05 probability level (.10 or .05): for 2, 2.33 or 2.77; for 3, 2.90 or 3.31; for 4, 3.24 or 3.63; for 5, 3.48 or 3.86; for 6, 3.66 or 4.03; for 7, 3.81 or 4.17; for 8, 3.93 or 4.29; for 9, 4.04 or 4.39; for 10, 4.13 or 4.47; and for 12, 4.28 or 4.62.

The table is read as follows: In the two-subtest short form composed of Information and Receptive Vocabulary, a range of 3 points between the two scores indicates a nonchance difference at the .05 level. A range of 4 occurs in less than 10% of the population and should be considered unusual, as should all ranges higher than 4 points. Less credence can be placed in a Composite score or short-form IQ when the scatter is larger than expected.

Table B-11
Estimated WPPSI–III Full Scale IQs for Sum of Scaled Scores for 10 Best 2-Subtest Short Forms for Ages 2-6 to 3-11

Sum of scaled scores	Combination						
	C2	C3	C4	C5	C6	C7	C8
2	45	46	47	47	47	51	52
3	48	49	50	50	50	54	54
4	51	52	53	53	53	57	57
5	55	55	55	56	56	59	60
6	58	58	58	59	59	62	62
7	61	61	61	62	62	65	65
8	64	64	64	65	65	68	68
9	67	67	67	68	68	70	71
10	70	70	70	71	71	73	73
11	73	73	73	73	74	76	76
12	76	76	76	76	77	78	79
13	79	79	79	79	79	81	81
14	82	82	82	82	82	84	84
15	85	85	85	85	85	86	87
16	88	88	88	88	88	89	89
17	91	91	91	91	91	92	92
18	94	94	94	94	94	95	95
19	97	97	97	97	97	97	97
20	100	100	100	100	100	100	100
21	103	103	103	103	103	103	103
22	106	106	106	106	106	105	105
23	109	109	109	109	109	108	108
24	112	112	112	112	112	111	111
25	115	115	115	115	115	114	113
26	118	118	118	118	118	116	116
27	121	121	121	121	121	119	119
28	124	124	124	124	123	122	121
29	127	127	127	127	126	124	124
30	130	130	130	129	129	127	127
31	133	133	133	132	132	130	129
32	136	136	136	135	135	132	132
33	139	139	139	138	138	135	135
34	142	142	142	141	141	138	138
35	145	145	145	144	144	141	140
36	149	148	147	147	147	143	143
37	152	151	150	150	150	146	146
38	155	154	153	153	153	149	148

Note. The subtest combinations are as follows:

C2 = BD + RV	C4 = BD + IN	C7 = RV + PN[b]
C3 = RV + OA	C5 = IN + OA	IN + RV[b]
BD + PN	C6 = OA + PN	C8 = IN + PN[b]
BD + OA[a]		

Abbreviations: BD = Block Design, IN = Information, RV = Receptive Vocabulary, OA = Object Assembly, PN = Picture Naming.

Reliability and validity coefficients associated with each short-form combination are shown in Table B-7. See Table D-11 in Appendix D for an explanation of the procedure used to obtain the estimated IQs.

[a]This combination is useful for children who are hearing impaired.
[b]This combination is useful for a rapid screening.

Table B-12
Estimated WPPSI–III Full Scale IQs for Sum of Scaled Scores for 10 Best 3-Subtest Short Forms for Ages 2-6 to 3-11

Sum of scaled scores	Combination								
	C2	C3	C4	C5	C6	C7	C8	C9	C10
3	42	42	43	44	45	45	45	46	50
4	44	44	45	46	47	47	47	48	52
5	46	47	47	48	49	49	49	50	54
6	48	49	49	51	51	51	51	52	56
7	50	51	51	53	53	53	54	54	57
8	52	53	53	55	55	55	56	56	59
9	55	55	55	57	57	57	58	58	61
10	57	57	58	59	59	59	60	60	63
11	59	59	60	61	61	61	62	62	65
12	61	61	62	63	63	63	64	64	67
13	63	64	64	65	65	65	66	66	69
14	65	66	66	67	67	68	68	68	70
15	68	68	68	69	69	70	70	70	72
16	70	70	70	71	71	72	72	72	74
17	72	72	72	73	73	74	74	74	76
18	74	74	75	75	75	76	76	76	78
19	76	76	77	77	78	78	78	78	80
20	78	79	79	79	80	80	80	80	82
21	81	81	81	81	82	82	82	82	83
22	83	83	83	84	84	84	84	84	85
23	85	85	85	86	86	86	86	86	87
24	87	87	87	88	88	88	88	88	89
25	89	89	89	90	90	90	90	90	91
26	91	91	92	92	92	92	92	92	93
27	94	94	94	94	94	94	94	94	94
28	96	96	96	96	96	96	96	96	96
29	98	98	98	98	98	98	98	98	98
30	100	100	100	100	100	100	100	100	100
31	102	102	102	102	102	102	102	102	102
32	104	104	104	104	104	104	104	104	104
33	106	106	106	106	106	106	106	106	106
34	109	109	108	108	108	108	108	108	107
35	111	111	111	110	110	110	110	110	109
36	113	113	113	112	112	112	112	112	111
37	115	115	115	114	114	114	114	114	113
38	117	117	117	116	116	116	116	116	115
39	119	119	119	119	118	118	118	118	117
40	122	121	121	121	120	120	120	120	118
41	124	124	123	123	122	122	122	122	120
42	126	126	125	125	125	124	124	124	122
43	128	128	128	127	127	126	126	126	124
44	130	130	130	129	129	128	128	128	126
45	132	132	132	131	131	130	130	130	128
46	135	134	134	133	133	132	132	132	130
47	137	136	136	135	135	135	134	134	131
48	139	139	138	137	137	137	136	136	133
49	141	141	140	139	139	139	138	138	135

(Continued)

Table B-12 (*Continued*)

Sum of scaled scores	Combination								
	C2	C3	C4	C5	C6	C7	C8	C9	C10
50	143	143	142	141	141	141	140	140	137
51	145	145	145	143	143	143	142	142	139
52	148	147	147	145	145	145	144	144	141
53	150	149	149	147	147	147	146	146	143
54	152	151	151	149	149	149	149	148	144
55	154	153	153	152	151	151	151	150	146
56	156	156	155	154	153	153	153	152	148
57	158	158	157	156	155	155	155	154	150

Note. The subtest combinations are as follows:

C2 = BD + RV + OA   C7 = BD + IN + PN
C3 = BD + OA + PN   C8 = IN + RV + OA
C4 = BD + IN + OA   C9 = IN + OA + PN
C5 = BD + RV + PN   RV + OA + PN
C6 = BD + IN + RV   C10 = IN + RV + PN[a]

Abbreviations: BD = Block Design, IN = Information, RV = Receptive Vocabulary, OA = Object Assembly, PN = Picture Naming.

Reliability and validity coefficients associated with each short-form combination are shown in Table B-7. See Table D-11 in Appendix D for an explanation of the procedure used to obtain the estimated IQs.
[a]This combination is useful for a rapid screening.

Table B-13
Estimated WPPSI–III Full Scale IQs for Sum of Scaled Scores for 4-Subtest Short Forms for Ages 2-6 to 3-11

Sum of scaled scores	Combination				Sum of scaled scores	Combination			
	C2	C3	C4	C5		C2	C3	C4	C5
4	41	42	45	46	43	105	105	105	105
5	43	44	46	47	44	107	106	106	106
6	45	45	48	49	45	108	108	108	108
7	46	47	49	50	46	110	110	109	109
8	48	49	51	52	47	111	111	111	111
9	49	50	52	53	48	113	113	112	112
10	51	52	54	55	49	115	114	114	114
11	53	53	56	56	50	116	116	115	115
12	54	55	57	58	51	118	118	117	117
13	56	57	59	59	52	120	119	118	118
14	58	58	60	61	53	121	121	120	120
15	59	60	62	62	54	123	123	121	121
16	61	61	63	64	55	124	124	123	123
17	63	63	65	65	56	126	126	125	124
18	64	65	66	67	57	128	127	126	126
19	66	66	68	68	58	129	129	128	127
20	67	68	69	70	59	131	131	129	129
21	69	69	71	71	60	133	132	131	130
22	71	71	72	73	61	134	134	132	132
23	72	73	74	74	62	136	135	134	133
24	74	74	75	76	63	137	137	135	135
25	76	76	77	77	64	139	139	137	136
26	77	77	79	79	65	141	140	138	138
27	79	79	80	80	66	142	142	140	139
28	80	81	82	82	67	144	143	141	141
29	82	82	83	83	68	146	145	143	142
30	84	84	85	85	69	147	147	144	144
31	85	86	86	86	70	149	148	146	145
32	87	87	88	88	71	151	150	148	147
33	89	89	89	89	72	152	151	149	148
34	90	90	91	91	73	154	153	151	150
35	92	92	92	92	74	155	155	152	151
36	93	94	94	94	75	157	156	154	153
37	95	95	95	95	76	159	158	155	154
38	97	97	97	97					
39	98	98	98	98					
40	100	100	100	100					
41	102	102	102	102					
42	103	103	103	103					

Note. The subtest combinations are as follows:

C2 = BD + RV + OA + PN   C4 = BD + IN + RV + PN
C3 = BD + IN + PN + OA   C5 = IN + RV + OA + PN

Abbreviations: BD = Block Design, IN = Information, RV = Receptive Vocabulary, OA = Object Assembly, PN = Picture Naming.

Reliability and validity coefficients associated with each short-form combination are shown in Table B-7. See Table D-11 in Appendix D for an explanation of the procedure used to obtain the estimated IQs.

Table B-14
Estimated WPPSI–III Full Scale IQs for Sum of Scaled Scores
for 10 Best 2-Subtest Short Forms and Other Combinations for Ages 4-0 to 7-3

Sum of scaled scores	Combination										
	C2	C3	C4	C5	C6	C7	C8	C9	C10	C11	C12
2	45	46	47	47	47	48	48	48	48	49	52
3	48	49	50	50	50	50	51	51	51	52	54
4	51	52	53	53	53	53	54	54	54	55	57
5	54	55	55	56	56	56	56	57	57	57	60
6	57	58	58	59	59	59	59	59	60	60	62
7	60	61	61	62	62	62	62	62	63	63	65
8	63	64	64	65	65	65	65	65	65	66	68
9	66	67	67	68	68	68	68	68	68	69	71
10	69	70	70	71	71	71	71	71	71	72	73
11	72	73	73	74	73	74	74	74	74	74	76
12	75	76	76	77	76	77	77	77	77	77	79
13	78	79	79	80	79	80	80	80	80	80	81
14	82	82	82	82	82	83	83	83	83	83	84
15	85	85	85	85	85	85	85	86	86	86	87
16	88	88	88	88	88	88	88	88	88	89	89
17	91	91	91	91	91	91	91	91	91	91	92
18	94	94	94	94	94	94	94	94	94	94	95
19	97	97	97	97	97	97	97	97	97	97	97
20	100	100	100	100	100	100	100	100	100	100	100
21	103	103	103	103	103	103	103	103	103	103	103
22	106	106	106	106	106	106	106	106	106	106	105
23	109	109	109	109	109	109	109	109	109	109	108
24	112	112	112	112	112	112	112	112	112	111	111
25	115	115	115	115	115	115	115	114	114	114	113
26	118	118	118	118	118	117	117	117	117	117	116
27	122	121	121	120	121	120	120	120	120	120	119
28	125	124	124	123	124	123	123	123	123	123	121
29	128	127	127	126	127	126	126	126	126	126	124
30	131	130	130	129	129	129	129	129	129	128	127
31	134	133	133	132	132	132	132	132	132	131	129
32	137	136	136	135	135	135	135	135	135	134	132
33	140	139	139	138	138	138	138	138	137	137	135
34	143	142	142	141	141	141	141	141	140	140	138
35	146	145	145	144	144	144	144	143	143	143	140
36	149	148	147	147	147	147	146	146	146	145	143
37	152	151	150	150	150	150	149	149	149	148	146
38	155	154	153	153	153	152	152	152	152	151	148

Note. The subtest combinations are as follows:

C2 = IN + CD[a]	C4 = SS + WR[c]	C8 = MR + PCn[b]	C10 = IN + MR[a, c]
PCn + CD[b]	C5 = PCm + SI[c]	C9 = MR + WR[c]	BD + MR[b]
C3 = IN + SS[c]	C6 = BD + VC[c]	VC + PCm[c]	C11 = WR + PCm[c]
BD + PCn[b]	C7 = MR + VC[c]	BD + SS[b]	IN + PCm[c]
BD + CD[b]		MR + SS[b]	C12 = IN + WR[d]

Abbreviations: BD = Block Design, IN = Information, MR = Matrix Reasoning, VC = Vocabulary, PCn = Picture Concepts, SS = Symbol Search, WR = Word Reasoning, CD = Coding, CO = Comprehension, PCm = Picture Completion, SI = Similarities, OA = Object Assembly.

Reliability and validity coefficients associated with each short-form combination are shown in Table B-8. See Table D-11 in Appendix D for an explanation of the procedure used to obtain the estimated IQs.
[a]This combination is useful for a rapid screening.
[b]This combination is useful for children who are hearing impaired.
[c]This combination is one of the 10 best 2-subtest short forms.
[d]Highest *g* loadings on two subtests.

Table B-15
Estimated WPPSI–III Full Scale IQs for Sum of Scaled Scores for 10 Best 3-Subtest Short Forms and Other Combinations for Ages 4-0 to 7-3

Sum of scaled scores	Combination																					
	C2	C3	C4	C5	C6	C7	C8	C9	C10	C11	C12	C13	C14	C15	C16	C17	C18	C19	C20	C21	C22	C23
3	41	42	42	42	43	43	43	44	44	44	44	44	44	44	45	45	45	45	45	45	46	49
4	43	44	44	44	45	45	45	46	46	46	46	46	46	46	47	47	47	47	47	47	48	51
5	45	46	46	47	47	47	47	48	48	48	48	48	48	48	49	49	49	49	49	49	50	53
6	48	48	48	49	49	49	50	50	50	50	50	50	50	51	51	51	51	51	51	51	52	55
7	50	50	51	51	51	52	52	52	52	52	52	52	52	53	53	53	53	53	53	53	54	57
8	52	53	53	53	53	54	54	54	54	54	54	54	55	55	55	55	55	55	55	55	56	59
9	54	55	55	55	55	56	56	56	56	56	56	57	57	57	57	57	57	57	57	57	58	61
10	56	57	57	57	58	58	58	58	58	58	59	59	59	59	59	59	59	59	59	59	60	63
11	59	59	59	59	60	60	60	60	60	61	61	61	61	61	61	61	61	61	61	61	62	64
12	61	61	61	62	62	62	62	62	62	63	63	63	63	63	63	63	63	63	64	63	64	66
13	63	63	63	64	64	64	64	64	65	65	65	65	65	65	65	65	65	65	66	65	66	68
14	65	66	66	66	66	66	66	67	67	67	67	67	67	67	67	67	67	68	68	67	68	70
15	67	68	68	68	68	68	68	69	69	69	69	69	69	69	69	69	69	70	70	69	70	72
16	69	70	70	70	70	71	71	71	71	71	71	71	71	71	71	71	71	72	72	71	72	74
17	72	72	72	72	72	73	73	73	73	73	73	73	73	73	73	73	73	74	74	74	74	76
18	74	74	74	74	75	75	75	75	75	75	75	75	75	75	75	75	76	76	76	76	76	78
19	76	76	76	77	77	77	77	77	77	77	77	77	77	77	77	78	78	78	78	78	78	79
20	78	78	78	79	79	79	79	79	79	79	79	79	79	79	80	80	80	80	80	80	80	81
21	80	81	81	81	81	81	81	81	81	81	81	81	81	81	82	82	82	82	82	82	82	83
22	83	83	83	83	83	83	83	83	83	83	83	83	83	84	84	84	84	84	84	84	84	85
23	85	85	85	85	85	85	85	85	85	85	85	86	86	86	86	86	86	86	86	86	86	87
24	87	87	87	87	87	87	87	87	87	88	88	88	88	88	88	88	88	88	88	88	88	89
25	89	89	89	89	89	89	89	90	90	90	90	90	90	90	90	90	90	90	90	90	90	91
26	91	91	91	91	92	92	92	92	92	92	92	92	92	92	92	92	92	92	92	92	92	93
27	93	94	94	94	94	94	94	94	94	94	94	94	94	94	94	94	94	94	94	94	94	94
28	96	96	96	96	96	96	96	96	96	96	96	96	96	96	96	96	96	96	96	96	96	96
29	98	98	98	98	98	98	98	98	98	98	98	98	98	98	98	98	98	98	98	98	98	98
30	100	100	100	100	100	100	100	100	100	100	100	100	100	100	100	100	100	100	100	100	100	100
31	102	102	102	102	102	102	102	102	102	102	102	102	102	102	102	102	102	102	102	102	102	102
32	104	104	104	104	104	104	104	104	104	104	104	104	104	104	104	104	104	104	104	104	104	104
33	107	106	106	106	106	106	106	106	106	106	106	106	106	106	106	106	106	106	106	106	106	106
34	109	109	109	109	108	108	108	108	108	108	108	108	108	108	108	108	108	108	108	108	108	107

(Continued)

Table B-15 (Continued)

	Combination																					
Sum of scaled scores	C2	C3	C4	C5	C6	C7	C8	C9	C10	C11	C12	C13	C14	C15	C16	C17	C18	C19	C20	C21	C22	C23
35	111	111	111	111	111	111	111	110	110	110	110	110	110	110	110	110	110	110	110	110	110	109
36	113	113	113	113	113	113	113	113	113	112	112	112	112	112	112	112	112	112	112	112	112	111
37	115	115	115	115	115	115	115	115	115	115	115	114	114	114	114	114	114	114	114	114	114	113
38	117	117	117	117	117	117	117	117	117	117	117	117	117	116	116	116	116	116	116	116	116	115
39	120	119	119	119	119	119	119	119	119	119	119	119	119	119	118	118	118	118	118	118	118	117
40	122	122	122	121	121	121	121	121	121	121	121	121	121	121	120	120	120	120	120	120	120	119
41	124	124	124	123	123	123	123	123	123	123	123	123	123	123	123	122	122	122	122	122	122	121
42	126	126	126	126	125	125	125	125	125	125	125	125	125	125	125	125	124	124	124	124	124	122
43	128	128	128	128	128	127	127	127	127	127	127	127	127	127	127	127	127	126	126	126	126	124
44	131	130	130	130	130	129	129	129	129	129	129	129	129	129	129	129	129	128	128	128	128	126
45	133	132	132	132	132	132	132	131	131	131	131	131	131	131	131	131	131	130	130	130	130	128
46	135	134	134	134	134	134	134	133	133	133	133	133	133	133	133	133	133	132	132	132	132	130
47	137	137	137	136	136	136	136	136	135	135	135	135	135	135	135	135	135	135	134	135	134	132
48	139	139	139	138	138	138	138	138	138	137	137	137	137	137	137	137	137	137	136	137	136	134
49	141	141	141	141	140	140	140	140	140	139	139	139	139	139	139	139	139	139	139	139	138	136
50	144	143	143	143	142	142	142	142	142	142	141	141	141	141	141	141	141	141	141	141	140	137
51	146	145	145	145	145	144	144	144	144	144	144	143	143	143	143	143	143	143	143	143	142	139
52	148	147	147	147	147	146	146	146	146	146	146	146	145	145	145	145	145	145	145	145	144	141
53	150	150	149	149	149	148	148	148	148	148	148	148	148	147	147	147	147	147	147	147	146	143
54	152	152	152	151	151	151	150	150	150	150	150	150	150	149	149	149	149	149	149	149	148	145
55	155	154	154	153	153	153	153	152	152	152	152	152	152	152	151	151	151	151	151	151	150	147
56	157	156	156	156	155	155	155	154	154	154	154	154	154	154	153	153	153	153	153	153	152	149
57	159	158	158	158	157	157	157	156	156	156	156	156	156	156	155	155	155	155	155	155	154	151

(Continued)

Table B-15 (Continued)

Note. The subtest combinations are as follows:

C2 = BD + PCn + CD[a, b]
C3 = IN + MR + CD[a]
C4 = MR + CD + PCm[a, b]
C5 = IN + CD + PCm[a]
C6 = BD + MR + CD[a]
    BD + CD + PCm[a]
C7 = SS + PCm + SI[c]
C8 = BD + PCn + OA[a, b]
    PCn + PCm + OA[a, b]
C9 = PCn + SS + PCm[a, b]
C10 = BD + PCn + SS[b]
    BD + PCn + PCm[a, b]
    PCn + SS + CD[a, b]
C11 = IN + SS + PCm[a, c]
C12 = SS + WR + PCm[c]
    IN + MR + SS[a]
    MR + PCn + PCm[d]

C13 = BD + MR + VC[c]
C14 = MR + VC + PCm[c]
C15 = BD + SS + PCm[b]
C16 = BD + MR + PCm[e]
C17 = BD + SS + CD[b]
C18 = IN + SS + SI[c]
C19 = IN + MR + PCm[a]
C20 = VC + SS + WR[c]
C21 = SS + WR + SI[c]
    IN + VC + SS[c]
    BD + PCm + OA[b]
C22 = IN + SS + WR[c]
C23 = VC + WR + SI[f]

Abbreviations: BD = Block Design, IN = Information, MR = Matrix Reasoning, VC = Vocabulary, PCn = Picture Concepts, SS = Symbol Search, WR = Word Reasoning, CD = Coding, CO = Comprehension, PCm = Picture Completion, SI = Similarities, OA = Object Assembly.

Reliability and validity coefficients associated with each short-form combination are shown in Table B-8. See Table D-11 in Appendix D for an explanation of the procedure used to obtain the estimated IQs.

The three Verbal subtests with the highest *g* loadings are the core Verbal subtests—Information, Vocabulary, and Word Reasoning.

[a]This combination is useful for a rapid screening.
[b]This combination is useful for children who are hearing impaired.
[c]This combination is one of the 10 best 3-subtest short forms.
[d]Highest reliability on three Performance subtests.
[e]Highest *g* loadings on three Performance subtests.
[f]Highest reliability on three Verbal subtests.

Table B-16
Estimated WPPSI–III Full Scale IQs for Sum of Scaled Scores
for 10 Best 4-Subtest Short Forms and Other Combinations for Ages 4-0 to 7-3

Sum of scaled scores	Combination																	
	C2	C3	C4	C5	C6	C7	C8	C9	C10	C11	C12	C13	C14	C15	C16	C17	C18
4	40	40	41	41	41	41	42	42	43	43	43	43	43	43	44	44	49
5	41	42	42	42	43	43	44	44	44	44	44	45	45	45	45	45	50
6	43	43	44	44	44	44	45	46	46	46	46	46	46	47	47	47	52
7	45	45	45	46	46	46	47	47	47	47	48	48	48	48	48	49	53
8	46	47	47	47	48	48	49	49	49	49	49	49	50	50	50	50	54
9	48	48	49	49	49	49	50	50	51	51	51	51	51	51	52	52	56
10	50	50	50	51	51	51	52	52	52	52	52	53	53	53	53	53	57
11	51	52	52	52	53	53	53	54	54	54	54	54	54	54	55	55	59
12	53	53	54	54	54	54	55	55	55	55	56	56	56	56	56	56	60
13	55	55	55	56	56	56	57	57	57	57	57	57	57	58	58	58	62
14	56	57	57	57	57	58	58	58	59	59	59	59	59	59	59	59	63
15	58	58	59	59	59	59	60	60	60	60	60	60	61	61	61	61	64
16	60	60	60	60	61	61	61	62	62	62	62	62	62	62	62	63	66
17	61	62	62	62	62	62	63	63	63	63	63	64	64	64	64	64	67
18	63	63	64	64	64	64	65	65	65	65	65	65	65	65	66	66	69
19	65	65	65	65	66	66	66	66	67	66	67	67	67	67	67	67	70
20	67	67	67	67	67	67	68	68	68	68	68	68	68	69	69	69	72
21	68	68	69	69	69	69	69	70	70	70	70	70	70	70	70	70	73
22	70	70	70	70	71	71	71	71	71	71	71	72	72	72	72	72	74
23	72	72	72	72	72	72	73	73	73	73	73	73	73	73	73	73	76
24	73	73	74	74	74	74	74	74	75	74	75	75	75	75	75	75	77
25	75	75	75	75	75	75	76	76	76	76	76	76	76	76	77	77	79
26	77	77	77	77	77	77	78	78	78	78	78	78	78	78	78	78	80
27	78	78	79	79	79	79	79	79	79	79	79	79	79	80	80	80	81
28	80	80	80	80	80	80	81	81	81	81	81	81	81	81	81	81	83
29	82	82	82	82	82	82	82	82	82	82	83	83	83	83	83	83	84
30	83	83	83	84	84	84	84	84	84	84	84	84	84	84	84	84	86
31	85	85	85	85	85	85	86	86	86	86	86	86	86	86	86	86	87
32	87	87	87	87	87	87	87	87	87	87	87	87	87	87	87	88	89
33	88	88	88	88	89	89	89	89	89	89	89	89	89	89	89	89	90
34	90	90	90	90	90	90	90	90	90	90	90	91	91	91	91	91	91
35	92	92	92	92	92	92	92	92	92	92	92	92	92	92	92	92	93
36	93	93	93	93	93	93	94	94	94	94	94	94	94	94	94	94	94
37	95	95	95	95	95	95	95	95	95	95	95	95	95	95	95	95	96
38	97	97	97	97	97	97	97	97	97	97	97	97	97	97	97	97	97
39	98	98	98	98	98	98	98	98	98	98	98	98	98	98	98	98	99
40	100	100	100	100	100	100	100	100	100	100	100	100	100	100	100	100	100
41	102	102	102	102	102	102	102	102	102	102	102	102	102	102	102	102	101
42	103	103	103	103	103	103	103	103	103	103	103	103	103	103	103	103	103
43	105	105	105	105	105	105	105	105	105	105	105	105	105	105	105	105	104
44	107	107	107	107	107	107	106	106	106	106	106	106	106	106	106	106	106
45	108	108	108	108	108	108	108	108	108	108	108	108	108	108	108	108	107
46	110	110	110	110	110	110	110	110	110	110	110	109	109	109	109	109	109
47	112	112	112	112	111	111	111	111	111	111	111	111	111	111	111	111	110
48	113	113	113	113	113	113	113	113	113	113	113	113	113	113	113	112	111
49	115	115	115	115	115	115	114	114	114	114	114	114	114	114	114	114	113

(Continued)

Table B-16 (*Continued*)

Sum of scaled scores	Combination																
	C2	C3	C4	C5	C6	C7	C8	C9	C10	C11	C12	C13	C14	C15	C16	C17	C18
50	117	117	117	116	116	116	116	116	116	116	116	116	116	116	116	116	114
51	118	118	118	118	118	118	118	118	118	118	117	117	117	117	117	117	116
52	120	120	120	120	120	120	119	119	119	119	119	119	119	119	119	119	117
53	122	122	121	121	121	121	121	121	121	121	121	121	121	120	120	120	119
54	123	123	123	123	123	123	122	122	122	122	122	122	122	122	122	122	120
55	125	125	125	125	125	125	124	124	124	124	124	124	124	124	123	123	121
56	127	127	126	126	126	126	126	126	125	126	125	125	125	125	125	125	123
57	128	128	128	128	128	128	127	127	127	127	127	127	127	127	127	127	124
58	130	130	130	130	129	129	129	129	129	129	129	128	128	128	128	128	126
59	132	132	131	131	131	131	131	130	130	130	130	130	130	130	130	130	127
60	133	133	133	133	133	133	132	132	132	132	132	132	132	131	131	131	128
61	135	135	135	135	134	134	134	134	133	134	133	133	133	133	133	133	130
62	137	137	136	136	136	136	135	135	135	135	135	135	135	135	134	134	131
63	139	138	138	138	138	138	137	137	137	137	137	136	136	136	136	136	133
64	140	140	140	140	139	139	139	138	138	138	138	138	138	138	138	137	134
65	142	142	141	141	141	141	140	140	140	140	140	140	139	139	139	139	136
66	144	143	143	143	143	142	142	142	141	141	141	141	141	141	141	141	137
67	145	145	145	144	144	144	143	143	143	143	143	143	143	142	142	142	138
68	147	147	146	146	146	146	145	145	145	145	144	144	144	144	144	144	140
69	149	148	148	148	147	147	147	146	146	146	146	146	146	146	145	145	141
70	150	150	150	149	149	149	148	148	148	148	148	147	147	147	147	147	143
71	152	152	151	151	151	151	150	150	149	149	149	149	149	149	148	148	144
72	154	153	153	153	152	152	151	151	151	151	151	151	150	150	150	150	146
73	155	155	155	154	154	154	153	153	153	153	152	152	152	152	152	151	147
74	157	157	156	156	156	156	155	154	154	154	154	154	154	153	153	153	148
75	159	158	158	158	157	157	156	156	156	156	156	155	155	155	155	155	150
76	160	160	159	159	159	159	158	158	157	157	157	157	157	157	156	156	151

Note. The subtest combinations are as follows:

C2 = BD + PCn + CD + PCm[a, b]
      MR + PCn + CD + PCm[a, b]
C3 = BD + MR + PCn + CD[a, b]
C4 = IN + MR + CD + PCm[a]
C5 = BD + MR + CD + PCm[b]
C6 = IN + VC + SS + OA[c]
C7 = IN + MR + SS + CD[a]
      BD + PCn + SS + CD[b]
C8 = BD + MR + SS + CD[b]
      BD + MR + PCn + SS[b]
C9 = IN + MR + SS + PCm[a]

C10 = BD + VC + SS + WR[c]
C11 = BD + MR + SS + PCm[b]
C12 = SS + WR + PCm + SI[c]
      IN + SS + PCm + SI[c]
C13 = IN + VC + SS + PCm[c]
      MR + VC + SS + WR[c]
C14 = VC + SS + WR + PCm[c]
C15 = IN + MR + SS + WR[c]
C16 = IN + SS + WR + PCm[c]
C17 = MR + WR + PCm + SI[c]
C18 = IN + VC + WR + SI[d]

Abbreviations: BD = Block Design, IN = Information, MR = Matrix Reasoning, VC = Vocabulary, PCn = Picture Concepts, SS = Symbol Search, WR = Word Reasoning, CD = Coding, CO = Comprehension, PCm = Picture Completion, SI = Similarities, OA = Object Assembly.

Reliability and validity coefficients associated with each short-form combination are shown in Table B-9. See Table D-11 in Appendix D for an explanation of the procedure used to obtain the estimated IQs.
[a]This combination is useful for a rapid screening.
[b]This combination is useful for children who are hearing impaired.
[c]This combination is one of the 10 best 4-subtest short forms.
[d]Highest *g* loadings on four subtests.

**Estimated WPPSI–III Full Scale IQs for Sum of Scaled Scores
for 10 Best 5-Subtest Short Forms and Other Combinations for Ages 4-0 to 7-3**

Sum of scaled scores	Combination													
	C2	C3	C4	C5	C6	C7	C8	C9	C10	C11	C12	Cl3	C14	C15
5	39	40	40	40	40	41	41	41	41	42	42	42	42	48
6	40	41	41	41	42	42	42	42	43	43	43	43	43	49
7	42	42	42	43	43	43	43	44	44	44	44	44	45	50
8	43	44	44	44	44	45	45	45	45	45	46	46	46	51
9	44	45	45	45	46	46	46	46	46	47	47	47	47	53
10	46	46	46	47	47	47	47	48	48	48	48	48	49	54
11	47	48	48	48	48	48	49	49	49	49	49	49	50	55
12	48	49	49	49	50	50	50	50	50	51	51	51	51	56
13	50	50	50	51	51	51	51	51	52	52	52	52	52	57
14	51	52	52	52	52	52	53	53	53	53	53	53	54	58
15	52	53	53	53	54	54	54	54	54	55	55	55	55	60
16	54	54	54	55	55	55	55	55	56	56	56	56	56	61
17	55	56	56	56	56	56	57	57	57	57	57	57	58	62
18	57	57	57	57	58	58	58	58	58	58	58	59	59	63
19	58	58	58	59	59	59	59	59	60	60	60	60	60	64
20	59	60	60	60	60	60	61	61	61	61	61	61	61	65
21	61	61	61	61	62	62	62	62	62	62	62	62	63	66
22	62	62	62	63	63	63	63	63	63	64	64	64	64	68
23	63	64	64	64	64	64	64	65	65	65	65	65	65	69
24	65	65	65	65	66	66	66	66	66	66	66	66	67	70
25	66	66	66	67	67	67	67	67	67	68	68	68	68	71
26	67	68	68	68	68	68	68	69	69	69	69	69	69	72
27	69	69	69	69	70	70	70	70	70	70	70	70	70	73
28	70	70	71	71	71	71	71	71	71	71	71	71	72	75
29	71	72	72	72	72	72	72	72	73	73	73	73	73	76
30	73	73	73	73	74	74	74	74	74	74	74	74	74	77
31	74	75	75	75	75	75	75	75	75	75	75	75	76	78
32	76	76	76	76	76	76	76	76	77	77	77	77	77	79
33	77	77	77	77	77	78	78	78	78	78	78	78	78	80
34	78	79	79	79	79	79	79	79	79	79	79	79	79	81
35	80	80	80	80	80	80	80	80	80	81	81	81	81	83
36	81	81	81	81	81	82	82	82	82	82	82	82	82	84
37	82	83	83	83	83	83	83	83	83	83	83	83	83	85
38	84	84	84	84	84	84	84	84	84	84	84	84	85	86
39	85	85	85	85	85	85	86	86	86	86	86	86	86	87
40	86	87	87	87	87	87	87	87	87	87	87	87	87	88
41	88	88	88	88	88	88	88	88	88	88	88	88	88	90
42	89	89	89	89	89	89	89	90	90	90	90	90	90	91
43	90	91	91	91	91	91	91	91	91	91	91	91	91	92
44	92	92	92	92	92	92	92	92	92	92	92	92	92	93
45	93	93	93	93	93	93	93	93	93	94	94	94	94	94
46	95	95	95	95	95	95	95	95	95	95	95	95	95	95
47	96	96	96	96	96	96	96	96	96	96	96	96	96	97
48	97	97	97	97	97	97	97	97	97	97	97	97	97	98
49	99	99	99	99	99	99	99	99	99	99	99	99	99	99
50	100	100	100	100	100	100	100	100	100	100	100	100	100	100
51	101	101	101	101	101	101	101	101	101	101	101	101	101	101
52	103	103	103	103	103	103	103	103	103	103	103	103	103	102
53	104	104	104	104	104	104	104	104	104	104	104	104	104	103
54	105	105	105	105	105	105	105	105	105	105	105	105	105	105

(Continued)

Table B-17 (Continued)

Sum of scaled scores	Combination													
	C2	C3	C4	C5	C6	C7	C8	C9	C10	C11	C12	CI3	C14	C15
55	107	107	107	107	107	107	107	107	107	106	106	106	106	106
56	108	108	108	108	108	108	108	108	108	108	108	108	108	107
57	110	109	109	109	109	109	109	109	109	109	109	109	109	108
58	111	111	111	111	111	111	111	110	110	110	110	110	110	109
59	112	112	112	112	112	112	112	112	112	112	112	112	112	110
60	114	113	113	113	113	113	113	113	113	113	113	113	113	112
61	115	115	115	115	115	115	114	114	114	114	114	114	114	113
62	116	116	116	116	116	116	116	116	116	116	116	116	115	114
63	118	117	117	117	117	117	117	117	117	117	117	117	117	115
64	119	119	119	119	119	118	118	118	118	118	118	118	118	116
65	120	120	120	120	120	120	120	120	120	119	119	119	119	117
66	122	121	121	121	121	121	121	121	121	121	121	121	121	119
67	123	123	123	123	123	122	122	122	122	122	122	122	122	120
68	124	124	124	124	124	124	124	124	123	123	123	123	123	121
69	126	125	125	125	125	125	125	125	125	125	125	125	124	122
70	127	127	127	127	126	126	126	126	126	126	126	126	126	123
71	129	128	128	128	128	128	128	128	127	127	127	127	127	124
72	130	130	129	129	129	129	129	129	129	129	129	129	128	125
73	131	131	131	131	130	130	130	130	130	130	130	130	130	127
74	133	132	132	132	132	132	132	131	131	131	131	131	131	128
75	134	134	134	133	133	133	133	133	133	132	132	132	132	129
76	135	135	135	135	134	134	134	134	134	134	134	134	133	130
77	137	136	136	136	136	136	136	135	135	135	135	135	135	131
78	138	138	138	137	137	137	137	137	137	136	136	136	136	132
79	139	139	139	139	138	138	138	138	138	138	138	138	137	134
80	141	140	140	140	140	140	139	139	139	139	139	139	139	135
81	142	142	142	141	141	141	141	141	140	140	140	140	140	136
82	143	143	143	143	142	142	142	142	142	142	142	141	141	137
83	145	144	144	144	144	144	143	143	143	143	143	143	142	138
84	146	146	146	145	145	145	145	145	144	144	144	144	144	139
85	148	147	147	147	146	146	146	146	146	145	145	145	145	140
86	149	148	148	148	148	148	147	147	147	147	147	147	146	142
87	150	150	150	149	149	149	149	149	148	148	148	148	148	143
88	152	151	151	151	150	150	150	150	150	149	149	149	149	144
89	153	152	152	152	152	152	151	151	151	151	151	151	150	145

(Continued)

Table B-17 (*Continued*)

Sum of scaled scores	Combination													
	C2	C3	C4	C5	C6	C7	C8	C9	C10	C11	C12	Cl3	C14	C15
90	154	154	154	153	153	153	153	152	152	152	152	152	151	146
91	156	155	155	155	154	154	154	154	154	153	153	153	153	147
92	157	156	156	156	156	155	155	155	155	155	154	154	154	149
93	158	158	158	157	157	157	157	156	156	156	156	156	155	150
94	160	159	159	159	158	158	158	158	157	157	157	157	157	151
95	161	160	160	160	160	159	159	159	159	158	158	158	158	152

Note. The subtest combinations are as follows:

C2 = BD + MR + PCn + CD + PCm[a]
C3 = MR + PCn + SS + CD + PCm[a]
    BD + PCn + SS + CD + PCm[a, b]
C4 = MR + WR + CD + PCm + SI[c]
C5 = IN + MR + SS + CD + PCm[b]
    BD + MR + PCn + SS + CD[a]
C6 = BD + MR + SS + CD + PCm[b]
C7 = IN + SS + CO + SI + OA[c]
C8 = BD + MR + PCn + SS + PCm[a]
C9 = BD + VC + PCn + SS + WR[c]
C10 = MR + VC + SS + PCm + SI[c]
C11 = MR + SS + WR + PCm + SI[c]
    IN + MR + SS + PCm + SI[c]
    BD + VC + SS + WR + PCm[c]
C12 = IN + MR + VC + SS + PCm[c]
C13 = MR + VC + SS + WR + PCm[c]
C14 = IN + MR + SS + WR + PCm[c]
C15 = IN + VC + WR + CO + SI[d]

Abbreviations: BD = Block Design, IN = Information, MR = Matrix Reasoning, VC = Vocabulary, PCn = Picture Concepts, SS = Symbol Search, WR = Word Reasoning, CD = Coding, CO = Comprehension, PCm = Picture Completion, SI = Similarities, OA = Object Assembly.

Reliability and validity coefficients associated with each short-form combination are shown in Table B-9. See Table D-11 in Appendix D for an explanation of the procedure used to obtain the estimated IQs.

[a]This combination is useful for children who are hearing impaired.
[b]This combination is useful for a rapid screening.
[c]This combination is one of the 10 best 5-subtest short forms.
[d]Highest *g* loadings on five subtests.

Table B-18
Estimated WPPSI–III Full Scale IQs for Sum of Scaled Scores
for Three 6-Subtest Short-Form Combinations for Ages 4-0 to 7-3

Sum of scaled scores	Combination C2	C3	C4	Sum of scaled scores	Combination C2	C3	C4	Sum of scaled scores	Combination C2	C3	C4	Sum of scaled scores	Combination C2	C3	C4
6	42	42	43	36	74	74	74	66	106	106	106	96	139	139	138
7	43	43	44	37	75	75	76	67	107	108	107	97	140	140	139
8	44	44	45	38	76	76	77	68	109	109	109	98	141	141	140
9	45	45	46	39	78	77	78	69	110	110	110	99	142	142	141
10	47	46	47	40	79	79	79	70	111	111	111	100	143	143	143
11	48	47	48	41	80	80	80	71	112	112	112	101	144	144	144
12	49	49	49	42	81	81	81	72	113	113	113	102	145	145	145
13	50	50	50	43	82	82	82	73	114	114	114	103	146	146	146
14	51	51	51	44	83	83	83	74	115	115	115	104	147	147	147
15	52	52	52	45	84	84	84	75	116	116	116	105	148	148	148
16	53	53	53	46	85	85	85	76	117	117	117	106	149	149	149
17	54	54	54	47	86	86	86	77	118	118	118	107	150	150	150
18	55	55	55	48	87	87	87	78	119	119	119	108	151	151	151
19	56	56	56	49	88	88	88	79	120	120	120	109	152	153	152
20	57	57	57	50	89	89	89	80	121	121	121	110	153	154	153
21	58	58	59	51	90	90	90	81	122	123	122	111	155	155	154
22	59	59	60	52	91	91	91	82	124	124	123	112	156	156	155
23	60	60	61	53	93	92	93	83	125	125	124	113	157	157	156
24	61	61	62	54	94	94	94	84	126	126	126	114	158	158	157
25	63	62	63	55	95	95	95	85	127	127	127	115	159	159	158
26	64	64	64	56	96	96	96	86	128	128	128				
27	65	65	65	57	97	97	97	87	129	129	129				
28	66	66	66	58	98	98	98	88	130	130	130				
29	67	67	67	59	99	99	99	89	131	131	131				
30	68	68	68	60	100	100	100	90	132	132	132				
31	69	69	69	61	101	101	101	91	133	133	133				
32	70	70	70	62	102	102	102	92	134	134	134				
33	71	71	71	63	103	103	103	93	135	135	135				
34	72	72	72	64	104	104	104	94	136	136	136				
35	73	73	73	65	105	105	105	95	137	138	137				

Note. The subtest combinations are as follows:

C2 = MR + VC + PCn + WR + PCm + SI[a]
C3 = BD + IN + MR + VC + PCn + WR[b]
C4 = BD + IN + MR + VC + WR + PCm[c]

Abbreviations: BD = Block Design, IN = Information, MR = Matrix Reasoning, VC = Vocabulary, PCn = Picture Concepts, SS = Symbol Search, WR = Word Reasoning, CD = Coding, CO = Comprehension, PCm = Picture Completion, SI = Similarities, OA = Object Assembly.

See Table D-11 in Appendix D for an explanation of the procedure used to obtain the estimated IQs.
[a]The reliability and validity of this combination are $r_{ss} = .975$ and $r = .945$, respectively.
[b]The reliability and validity of this combination are $r_{ss} = .968$ and $r = .948$, respectively.
[c]The reliability and validity of this combination are $r_{ss} = .968$ and $r = .946$, respectively.

Table B-19
Estimated WPPSI–III Full Scale IQs for Sum of Scaled Scores for Three 7-Subtest Short-Form Combinations for Ages 4-0 to 7-3

Sum of scaled scores	C2	C3	C4	Sum of scaled scores	C2	C3	C4	Sum of scaled scores	C2	C3	C4	Sum of scaled scores	C2	C3	C4
6	38	40	40	41	72	73	73	76	106	106	106	111	140	139	138
7	39	41	41	42	73	74	74	77	107	107	107	112	141	140	139
8	40	42	42	43	74	75	75	78	108	108	107	113	142	141	140
9	41	42	43	44	75	75	76	79	109	108	108	114	143	142	141
10	42	43	44	45	76	76	77	80	110	109	109	115	144	142	142
11	43	44	45	46	77	77	78	81	111	110	110	116	145	143	143
12	44	45	46	47	78	78	78	82	112	111	111	117	145	144	144
13	45	46	47	48	79	79	79	83	113	112	112	118	146	145	145
14	46	47	48	49	80	80	80	84	114	113	113	119	147	146	146
15	47	48	48	50	81	81	81	85	115	114	114	120	148	147	147
16	48	49	49	51	82	82	82	86	115	115	115	121	149	148	148
17	49	50	50	52	83	83	83	87	116	116	116	122	150	149	149
18	50	51	51	53	84	84	84	88	117	117	117	123	151	150	150
19	51	52	52	54	85	85	85	89	118	118	118	124	152	151	151
20	52	53	53	55	85	86	86	90	119	119	119	125	153	152	152
21	53	54	54	56	86	87	87	91	120	120	120	126	154	153	152
22	54	55	55	57	87	88	88	92	121	121	121	127	155	154	153
23	55	56	56	58	88	89	89	93	122	122	122	128	156	155	154
24	55	57	57	59	89	90	90	94	123	123	122	129	157	156	155
25	56	58	58	60	90	91	91	95	124	124	123	130	158	157	156
26	57	58	59	61	91	92	92	96	125	125	124	131	159	158	157
27	58	59	60	62	92	92	93	97	126	125	125	132	160	158	158
28	59	60	61	63	93	93	93	98	127	126	126	133	161	159	159
29	60	61	62	64	94	94	94	99	128	127	127				
30	61	62	63	65	95	95	95	100	129	128	128				
31	62	63	63	66	96	96	96	101	130	129	129				
32	63	64	64	67	97	97	97	102	131	130	130				
33	64	65	65	68	98	98	98	103	132	131	131				
34	65	66	66	69	99	99	99	104	133	132	132				
35	66	67	67	70	100	100	100	105	134	133	133				
36	67	68	68	71	101	101	101	106	135	134	134				
37	68	69	69	72	102	102	102	107	136	135	135				
38	69	70	70	73	103	103	103	108	137	136	136				
39	70	71	71	74	104	104	104	109	138	137	137				
40	71	72	72	75	105	105	105	110	139	138	137				

Note. The subtest combinations are as follows:

C2 = MR + VC + PCn + WR + CD + PCm + SI[a]
C3 = BD + IN + MR + VC + PCn + SS + WR[b]
C4 = BD + IN + MR + VC + SS + WR + PCm[c]

Abbreviations: BD = Block Design, IN = Information, MR = Matrix Reasoning, VC = Vocabulary, PCn = Picture Concepts, SS = Symbol Search, WR = Word Reasoning, CD = Coding, CO = Comprehension, PCm = Picture Completion, SI = Similarities, OA = Object Assembly.

See Table D-11 in Appendix D for an explanation of the procedure used to obtain the estimated IQs.
[a]The reliability and validity of this combination are r_{ss} = .974 and r = .955, respectively.
[b]The reliability and validity of this combination are r_{ss} = .969 and r = .953, respectively.
[c]The reliability and validity of this combination are r_{ss} = .969 and r = .953, respectively.

Table B-20
Administrative Checklist for the WPPSI–III

ADMINISTRATIVE CHECKLIST FOR THE WPPSI–III

Name of examiner: _____   Date: _____

Name of child: _____   Name of observer: _____

(Note: If an item is not applicable, mark NA to the left of the number.)

Before Beginning	Circle One	
1. Room is well lit	Yes	No
2. Furniture is comfortable and size is appropriate for child	Yes	No
3. Room is free of distractions	Yes	No
4. Asks parent, if present, to remain in background and sit quietly out of child's view	Yes	No
5. Positions child correctly	Yes	No
6. Sits directly across from child	Yes	No
7. Attempts to establish rapport	Yes	No
8. Tells child that breaks are OK and to let examiner know when he or she needs a break	Yes	No
9. Does not prolong getting-acquainted period	Yes	No
10. Does not overstimulate child or entertain child excessively before administering test	Yes	No
11. Avoids use of term *test* when introducing test	Yes	No
12. Responds in truthful manner to child's questions (if any) about purpose of testing	Yes	No
13. Keeps test materials in order	Yes	No
14. Keeps test kit out of child's view	Yes	No
15. Begins test when rapport has been established	Yes	No
16. Positions Record Form and Administration Manual so that child cannot read questions or answers	Yes	No
17. Introduces test by reading directions in Administration Manual verbatim	Yes	No

Comments

_____

_____

_____

Block Design

(See pp. 442–445 in text for detailed information.)

Background Considerations

	Circle One	
1. Clears table	Yes	No
2. Seats child directly in front of table	Yes	No
3. Reads directions verbatim	Yes	No
4. Reads directions clearly	Yes	No
5. Uses stopwatch	Yes	No
6. Places stopwatch correctly	Yes	No
7. Repeats directions correctly	Yes	No
8. Clarifies directions appropriately	Yes	No

Block Design (*Continued*)	Circle One	
9. Uses appropriate directions for item 6	Yes	No
10. Shows different sides of block correctly while reading directions for Part B	Yes	No
11. Gives child number of blocks needed for each item	Yes	No
12. Disassembles models correctly	Yes	No
13. Places intact model or Stimulus Book 1 and blocks properly	Yes	No
14. Turns pages of Stimulus Book 1 correctly	Yes	No
15. Uses blocks and pictures as models correctly	Yes	No
16. Leaves model intact for items 1 to 12	Yes	No
17. Follows appropriate procedure for item 13	Yes	No
18. Scrambles blocks between designs	Yes	No
19. Removes all unnecessary blocks from child's view	Yes	No
20. Does not permit child to rotate Stimulus Book 1	Yes	No
21. Times correctly	Yes	No
22. Gives appropriate prompts	Yes	No
23. Administers trials correctly	Yes	No

Starting Considerations

	Circle One	
24. Starts with appropriate item	Yes	No

Reverse Sequence

25. Administers items in reverse sequence correctly	Yes	No

Discontinue Considerations

26. Counts items administered in reverse sequence toward discontinue criterion	Yes	No
27. Discontinues subtest correctly	Yes	No
28. Removes Stimulus Book 1 and blocks from child's view once subtest is completed	Yes	No

Scoring Guidelines

29. Scores items correctly	Yes	No

Record Form

30. Records completion time correctly	Yes	No
31. Adds check marks in Incorrect Design column correctly	Yes	No
32. Notes or sketches incorrect designs in Incorrect Design column correctly	Yes	No
33. Notes rotations in Incorrect Design column correctly	Yes	No
34. Circles Y or N in Correct Design column correctly	Yes	No

(*Continued*)

Table B-20 (*Continued*)

Block Design (*Continued*)	Circle One	
35. Circles 0, 1, or 2 in Score column correctly	Yes	No
36. Notes additional points correctly	Yes	No
37. Adds points correctly	Yes	No
38. Enters Total Raw Score in shaded box correctly	Yes	No

Comments

_____

_____

_____

Information

(See pp. 448–449 in text for detailed information.)

Background Considerations

	Circle One	
1. Reads directions verbatim	Yes	No
2. Reads directions clearly	Yes	No
3. Reads items verbatim	Yes	No
4. Reads items clearly	Yes	No
5. Places Stimulus Book 1 properly and then opens it to correct page	Yes	No
6. Removes Stimulus Book 1 from child's view after item 6	Yes	No
7. Repeats items correctly	Yes	No
8. Queries and prompts correctly	Yes	No
9. For item 1, gives correct answer, if needed	Yes	No
10. For items 2 to 34, does not give child correct answers	Yes	No
11. Grants additional time appropriately	Yes	No

Starting Considerations

12. Starts with appropriate item	Yes	No

Reverse Sequence

13. Administers items in reverse sequence correctly	Yes	No

Discontinue Considerations

14. Counts items administered in reverse sequence toward discontinue criterion	Yes	No
15. Discontinues subtest correctly	Yes	No

Scoring Guidelines

16. Scores items correctly	Yes	No

Record Form

17. For items 1 to 6, circles response number or DK in Response column correctly	Yes	No
18. For items 7 to 17, records child's responses in Response column correctly	Yes	No
19. Circles 0 or 1 in Score column correctly	Yes	No
20. Notes additional points correctly	Yes	No
21. Adds points correctly	Yes	No
22. Enters Total Raw Score in shaded box correctly	Yes	No

Information (*Continued*)   Circle One

Comments

_____

_____

_____

Matrix Reasoning

(See pp. 450–451 in text for detailed information.)

Background Considerations

	Circle One	
1. Reads directions verbatim	Yes	No
2. Reads directions clearly	Yes	No
3. Places Stimulus Book 1 properly	Yes	No
4. Positions Stimulus Book 1 correctly	Yes	No
5. Clarifies directions correctly	Yes	No
6. If child fails any sample, demonstrates correct way to solve problem	Yes	No
7. Repeats directions correctly	Yes	No
8. For items 1 to 29, shortens or eliminates directions appropriately	Yes	No
9. Gives appropriate prompts	Yes	No
10. Provides feedback only on three samples	Yes	No
11. Grants additional time appropriately	Yes	No

Starting Considerations

12. Starts with appropriate item	Yes	No

Reverse Sequence

13. Administers items in reverse sequence correctly	Yes	No

Discontinue Considerations

14. Counts items administered in reverse sequence toward discontinue criterion	Yes	No
15. Discontinues subtest correctly	Yes	No
16. Removes Stimulus Book 1 from child's view once subtest is completed	Yes	No

Scoring Guidelines

17. Scores items correctly	Yes	No

Record Form

18. Circles response number or DK in Response column correctly	Yes	No
19. Circles 0 or 1 in Score column correctly	Yes	No
20. Notes additional points correctly	Yes	No
21. Adds points correctly	Yes	No
22. Enters Total Raw Score in shaded box correctly	Yes	No

Comments

_____

_____

_____

(*Continued*)

Table B-20 (*Continued*)

Vocabulary	Circle One

(See pp. 452–454 in text for detailed information.)

Background Considerations

1. Reads directions verbatim	Yes	No
2. Reads directions clearly	Yes	No
3. Pronounces words clearly	Yes	No
4. Repeats directions correctly	Yes	No
5. Repeats items correctly	Yes	No
6. In cases of suspected hearing deficit, queries appropriately	Yes	No
7. Places closed Stimulus Book 1 properly and then opens it to correct page	Yes	No
8. On items 1 to 5, points to the picture	Yes	No
9. Turns pages of Stimulus Book 1 toward child	Yes	No
10. Queries correctly	Yes	No
11. If child gives 0-point response to item 1, 6, or 7, tells child correct 1-point answer	Yes	No
12. For items 2 to 5 and items 8 to 25, does not tell correct answers	Yes	No
13. Grants additional time appropriately	Yes	No

Starting Considerations

14. Starts with appropriate item	Yes	No

Reverse Sequence

15. Administers items in reverse sequence correctly	Yes	No

Discontinue Considerations

16. Counts items administered in reverse sequence toward discontinue criterion	Yes	No
17. Discontinues subtest correctly	Yes	No
18. Removes Stimulus Book 1 from child's view once subtest is completed	Yes	No

Scoring Guidelines

19. Scores responses correctly	Yes	No

Record Form

20. Records child's responses in Response column correctly	Yes	No
21. Circles 0, 1, or 2 in Score column correctly	Yes	No
22. Notes additional points correctly	Yes	No
23. Adds points correctly	Yes	No
24. Enters Total Raw Score in shaded box correctly	Yes	No

Comments

_____

_____

_____

Picture Concepts

(See pp. 456–457 in text for detailed information.)

Background Considerations

1. Reads directions verbatim	Yes	No
2. Reads directions clearly	Yes	No

Picture Concepts (*Continued*)	Circle One

3. Repeats directions correctly	Yes	No
4. Places Stimulus Book 1 correctly	Yes	No
5. Positions Stimulus Book 1 correctly	Yes	No
6. Points across rows correctly while reading directions	Yes	No
7. Turns pages of Stimulus Book 1 correctly	Yes	No
8. For items 1 to 26, shortens or eliminates directions correctly	Yes	No
9. Gives appropriate prompts	Yes	No
10. If asked, tells child name of picture	Yes	No
11. If response is not clear, asks child to point to picture	Yes	No
12. If child does not give correct answer to sample A or B, gives correct answer and reason for correct answer	Yes	No
13. For test items, does not give correct answers or reasons for correct answers	Yes	No
14. Grants additional time appropriately	Yes	No

Starting Considerations

15. Starts with appropriate item	Yes	No

Reverse Sequence

16. Administers items in reverse sequence correctly	Yes	No

Discontinue Considerations

17. Counts items administered in reverse sequence toward discontinue criterion	Yes	No
18. Discontinues subtest correctly	Yes	No
19. Removes Stimulus Book 1 from child's view once subtest is completed	Yes	No

Scoring Guidelines

20. Scores items correctly	Yes	No

Record Form

21. Circles response number or DK in Response Column correctly	Yes	No
22. Circles 0 or 1 in Score column correctly	Yes	No
23. Notes additional points correctly	Yes	No
24. Adds points correctly	Yes	No
25. Enters Total Raw Score in shaded box correctly	Yes	No

Comments

_____

_____

_____

Symbol Search

(See pp. 458–459 in text for detailed information.)

Background Considerations

1. Provides smooth working surface	Yes	No
2. Reads directions verbatim	Yes	No

(*Continued*)

Table B-20 (*Continued*)

Symbol Search (*Continued*)	Circle One	
3. Reads directions clearly	Yes	No
4. Repeats directions correctly	Yes	No
5. Uses stopwatch	Yes	No
6. Places stopwatch appropriately	Yes	No
7. During sample and practice items, makes sure that child sees only sample page of Response Booklet	Yes	No
8. Gives child number 2 pencil without eraser	Yes	No
9. For samples, points to target symbol and array	Yes	No
10. For samples, draws diagonal line through matching symbol	Yes	No
11. For practice items, points to target symbol and array and gives appropriate directions	Yes	No
12. Gives appropriate feedback	Yes	No
13. If child makes an error on practice items, follows correct procedure	Yes	No
14. Explains directions using sample items, if needed	Yes	No
15. Does not proceed to test items unless child understands task	Yes	No
16. Opens Response Booklet to page 2, as appropriate	Yes	No
17. Reads directions verbatim, including word "Go," even if explanations are not necessary	Yes	No
18. Before saying "Go," gives further explanations, if necessary	Yes	No
19. Begins timing correctly	Yes	No
20. Turns pages of Response Booklet, if needed	Yes	No
21. Gives appropriate prompts	Yes	No
22. Counts time for prompts as part of 120-second time limit	Yes	No
23. Does not discourage child from making spontaneous corrections, unless corrections impede performance	Yes	No

Starting Considerations

24. Starts with appropriate item	Yes	No

Discontinue Considerations

25. Discontinues subtest correctly	Yes	No
26. Stops timing if child finishes before 120 seconds	Yes	No
27. Says "Stop" after 120 seconds and discontinues subtest	Yes	No
28. Closes Response Booklet and removes it from child's view once subtest is completed	Yes	No

Scoring Guidelines

29. Scores subtest correctly	Yes	No

Response Booklet

30. Enters identifying data on Response Booklet	Yes	No
31. Enters number of correct responses correctly	Yes	No
32. Enters number of incorrect responses correctly	Yes	No

Symbol Search (*Continued*)	Circle One	
Record Form		
33. Records completion time correctly	Yes	No
34. Enters total number of correct items in Number Correct box correctly	Yes	No
35. Enters total number of incorrect items in Number Incorrect box correctly	Yes	No
36. Enters Total Raw Score in shaded box correctly	Yes	No
37. Enters a 0 if Total Raw Score is equal to or less than 0	Yes	No

Comments

_____

_____

_____

Word Reasoning

(See pp. 461–462 in text for detailed information.)

Background Considerations

1. Reads items verbatim	Yes	No
2. Reads items clearly	Yes	No
3. Introduces each item correctly	Yes	No
4. After giving each clue, allows child about 5 seconds to answer	Yes	No
5. Repeats each clue correctly and notes R on Record Form if clue is repeated	Yes	No
6. Allows child additional time after repeating a clue	Yes	No
7. Restates previous clues correctly	Yes	No
8. Administers next item if child gets previous item correct before all clues are presented	Yes	No
9. Grants additional time appropriately	Yes	No

Starting Considerations

10. Starts with appropriate item	Yes	No

Reverse Sequence

11. Administers items in reverse sequence correctly	Yes	No

Discontinue Considerations

12. Counts items administered in reverse sequence toward discontinue criterion	Yes	No
13. Discontinues subtest correctly	Yes	No

Scoring Guidelines

14. Scores responses correctly	Yes	No

Record Form

15. Records responses verbatim in Response column	Yes	No
16. Circles Y or N for each clue administered	Yes	No
17. Circles 0 or 1 for each item administered	Yes	No
18. Notes additional points correctly	Yes	No
19. Adds points correctly	Yes	No

(*Continued*)

Table B-20 (Continued)

Word Reasoning (Continued)	Circle One	
20. Enters Total Raw Score in shaded box correctly	Yes	No

Comments

_____

_____

_____

Coding

(See pp. 463–464 in text for detailed information.)

Background Considerations

		Circle One	
1.	Provides smooth working surface	Yes	No
2.	Reads directions verbatim	Yes	No
3.	Reads directions clearly	Yes	No
4.	Repeats directions correctly	Yes	No
5.	Points to key while reading directions	Yes	No
6.	Waits until child understands task before proceeding with items	Yes	No
7.	Uses stopwatch	Yes	No
8.	Places stopwatch correctly	Yes	No
9.	Times correctly	Yes	No
10.	Notes child's handedness on Record Form	Yes	No
11.	Positions Response Booklet properly for left-handed child	Yes	No
12.	Demonstrates sample correctly	Yes	No
13.	Gives child a pencil without eraser	Yes	No
14.	Does not provide or allow child to use eraser	Yes	No
15.	Gives appropriate responses to inquiries and appropriate prompts	Yes	No
16.	Counts time for prompts as part of 120-second time limit	Yes	No
17.	Allows spontaneous corrections, unless corrections impede performance	Yes	No

Starting Considerations

18.	Starts with appropriate item	Yes	No

Discontinue Considerations

19.	Discontinues subtest correctly	Yes	No
20.	Stops timing if child finishes before 120 seconds	Yes	No
21.	Says "Stop" after 120 seconds and discontinues subtest	Yes	No
22.	Closes Response Booklet and removes it from child's view once subtest is completed	Yes	No

Scoring Guidelines

23.	Scores subtest correctly	Yes	No

Response Booklet

24.	Enters identifying data on Response Booklet, if needed	Yes	No

Record Form

25.	Records completion time correctly	Yes	No

Coding (Continued)	Circle One	
26. Circles appropriate time-bonus points	Yes	No
27. Adds points correctly	Yes	No
28. Enters Total Raw Score in shaded box correctly	Yes	No

Comments

_____

_____

_____

Comprehension

(See pp. 466–467 in text for detailed information.)

Background Considerations

		Circle One	
1.	Reads directions verbatim	Yes	No
2.	Reads directions clearly	Yes	No
3.	Reads items verbatim	Yes	No
4.	Reads items clearly	Yes	No
5.	Repeats directions correctly	Yes	No
6.	Repeats items correctly	Yes	No
7.	If child is hesitant, gives appropriate prompts	Yes	No
8.	If child gives 0-point responses to items 1 and 2, tells child correct 1-point answers	Yes	No
9.	For items 3 to 20, does not tell child correct answers	Yes	No
10.	Queries correctly	Yes	No
11.	Grants additional time appropriately	Yes	No

Starting Considerations

12.	Starts with appropriate item	Yes	No

Reverse Sequence

13.	Administers items in reverse sequence correctly	Yes	No

Discontinue Considerations

14.	Counts items administered in reverse sequence toward discontinue criterion	Yes	No
15.	Discontinues subtest correctly	Yes	No

Scoring Guidelines

16.	Scores items correctly	Yes	No

Record Form

17.	Records responses in Response column correctly	Yes	No
18.	Circles 0, 1, or 2 in Score column correctly	Yes	No
19.	Notes additional points correctly	Yes	No
20.	Adds points correctly	Yes	No
21.	Enters Total Raw Score in shaded box correctly	Yes	No

Comments

_____

_____

_____

(Continued)

Table B-20 (*Continued*)

Picture Completion	Circle One	
(See pp. 468–469 in text for detailed information.)		

Background Considerations

1. Reads directions verbatim	Yes	No
2. Reads directions clearly	Yes	No
3. Reads items verbatim	Yes	No
4. Reads items clearly	Yes	No
5. Repeats directions correctly	Yes	No
6. Places Stimulus Book 2 properly	Yes	No
7. Turns pages of Stimulus Book 2 correctly	Yes	No
8. Allows 20 seconds for each item	Yes	No
9. For items 3 to 32, shortens or eliminates directions correctly	Yes	No
10. Begins timing correctly	Yes	No
11. Stops timing correctly	Yes	No
12. On sample, repeats child's correct answer	Yes	No
13. For sample and items 1 and 2, gives child correct answers, if needed	Yes	No
14. For items 3 to 32, does not give child correct answers	Yes	No
15. Queries correctly	Yes	No
16. Queries responses noted in right-hand column of pages 153 to 156 in Administration Manual correctly	Yes	No

Starting Considerations

17. Starts with appropriate item	Yes	No

Reverse Sequence

18. Administers items in reverse sequence correctly	Yes	No

Discontinue Considerations

19. Counts items administered in reverse sequence toward discontinue criterion	Yes	No
20. Discontinues subtest correctly	Yes	No
21. Removes Stimulus Book 2 from child's view once subtest is completed	Yes	No

Scoring Guidelines

22. Scores items correctly	Yes	No

Record Form

23. Records child's responses in Response Column correctly	Yes	No
24. Records PC for correct pointing responses	Yes	No
25. Records PX for incorrect pointing responses	Yes	No
26. Circles 0 or 1 in Score column correctly	Yes	No
27. Records completion time correctly	Yes	No
28. Notes additional points correctly	Yes	No
29. Adds points correctly	Yes	No
30. Enters Total Raw Score in shaded box correctly	Yes	No

Comments

_____

_____

_____

Similarities	Circle One	
(See pp. 471–472 in text for detailed information.)		

Background Considerations

1. Reads directions verbatim	Yes	No
2. Reads directions clearly	Yes	No
3. Read items verbatim	Yes	No
4. Read items clearly	Yes	No
5. Repeats directions correctly	Yes	No
6. Repeats items correctly	Yes	No
7. Emphasizes word *both* in reading each item	Yes	No
8. Queries correctly	Yes	No
9. For trials 1 and 2 of items 1 and 2, gives child correct answers, if needed	Yes	No
10. For items 3 to 24, does not give child correct answers	Yes	No
11. Grants additional time appropriately	Yes	No

Starting Considerations

12. Starts with appropriate item	Yes	No

Discontinue Considerations

13. Discontinues subtest correctly	Yes	No

Scoring Guidelines

14. Scores responses correctly	Yes	No

Record Form

15. Records child's responses correctly	Yes	No
16. Circles 0, 1, or 2 in Score column correctly	Yes	No
17. Adds points correctly	Yes	No
18. Enters Total Raw Score in shaded box correctly	Yes	No

Comments

_____

_____

_____

Receptive Vocabulary

(See pp. 473–474 in text for detailed information.)

Background Considerations

1. Reads items verbatim	Yes	No
2. Reads items clearly	Yes	No
3. Positions Stimulus Book 1 correctly	Yes	No
4. Turns pages of Stimulus Book 1 correctly	Yes	No
5. Repeats items correctly	Yes	No
6. For item 1, gives child correct answer, if needed	Yes	No
7. For items 2 to 38, does not give child correct answers	Yes	No

Starting Considerations

8. Starts with appropriate item	Yes	No

Reverse Sequence

9. Administers items in reverse sequence correctly	Yes	No

(*Continued*)

Table B-20 (*Continued*)

Receptive Vocabulary (*Continued*)	Circle One	

Discontinue Considerations

10. Counts items administered in reverse sequence toward discontinue criterion — Yes   No
11. Discontinues subtest correctly — Yes   No
12. Removes Stimulus Book 1 from child's view once subtest is completed — Yes   No

Scoring Guidelines

13. Scores items correctly — Yes   No

Record Form

14. For items 1 to 22 and for items 24 to 38, circles response number or DK in Response column correctly — Yes   No
15. For item 23, circles one of four colors or DK in Response column correctly — Yes   No
16. Circles 0 or 1 in Score column correctly — Yes   No
17. Notes additional points correctly — Yes   No
18. Adds points correctly — Yes   No
19. Enters Total Raw Score in shaded box correctly — Yes   No

Comments

_____

_____

_____

Object Assembly

(See pp. 475–477 in text for detailed information.)

Background Considerations

1. Seats child correctly — Yes   No
2. Has puzzle pieces stacked correctly before administering each item — Yes   No
3. Places puzzle pieces on table correctly — Yes   No
4. Reads directions verbatim — Yes   No
5. Reads directions clearly — Yes   No
6. Times correctly — Yes   No
7. Gives appropriate prompts if child is hesitant or seems merely to be playing with puzzles — Yes   No
8. For trials 1 and 2 of items 1 and 2, allows child to look at assembled puzzle for about 3 seconds — Yes   No
9. For items 3 to 14, introduces items correctly — Yes   No

Starting Considerations

10. Starts with appropriate item — Yes   No

Reverse Sequence

11. Administers items in reverse sequence correctly — Yes   No

Discontinue Considerations

12. Counts items administered in reverse sequence toward discontinue criterion — Yes   No

Object Assembly (*Continued*)	Circle One	

13. Discontinues subtest correctly — Yes   No
14. Removes puzzle pieces from child's view once subtest is completed — Yes   No

Scoring Guidelines

15. Scores items correctly — Yes   No

Record Form

16. Records completion time correctly — Yes   No
17. Records correct number of junctures in Number of Correct Junctures column correctly — Yes   No
18. Circles 0, 1, 2, 3, 4, or 5 in Score column correctly — Yes   No
19. Notes additional points correctly — Yes   No
20. Adds points correctly — Yes   No
21. Enters Total Raw Score in shaded box correctly — Yes   No

Comments

_____

_____

_____

Picture Naming

(See pp. 478–479 in text for detailed information.)

Background Considerations

1. Reads items verbatim — Yes   No
2. Reads items clearly — Yes   No
3. Positions Stimulus Book 2 correctly — Yes   No
4. Turns pages of Stimulus Book 2 correctly — Yes   No
5. For item 1, gives child correct answer, if needed — Yes   No
6. For items 2 to 30, does not tell child correct answers — Yes   No
7. Points to pictures correctly — Yes   No
8. Queries correctly — Yes   No

Starting Considerations

9. Starts with appropriate item — Yes   No

Reverse Sequence

10. Administers items in reverse sequence correctly — Yes   No

Discontinue Considerations

11. Counts items administered in reverse sequence toward discontinue criterion — Yes   No
12. Discontinues subtest correctly — Yes   No
13. Removes Stimulus Book 2 from child's view once subtest is completed — Yes   No

Scoring Guidelines

14. Scores items correctly — Yes   No

Record Form

15. Records child's responses verbatim — Yes   No

(*Continued*)

Table B-20 (*Continued*)

Picture Naming (*Continued*)	Circle One	
16. Circles 0 or 1 in Score column correctly	Yes	No
17. Notes additional points correctly	Yes	No
18. Adds points correctly	Yes	No
19. Enters Total Raw Score in shaded box correctly	Yes	No

Comments

_____

_____

_____

Front Page of Record Form

1. Enters child's full name, sex, grade, school, parent's/guardian's full name, place of testing, and examiner's full name correctly — Yes No

Calculation of Child's Age

2. Records date of testing correctly (Y, M, D) — Yes No
3. Records child's date of birth correctly (Y, M, D) — Yes No
4. Computes child's age at testing correctly (Y, M, D) — Yes No

Total Raw Score to Scaled Score Conversion

5. For each subtest administered, transfers Total Raw Score to front of Record Form correctly — Yes No
6. Enters correct scaled score in appropriate unshaded box — Yes No
7. For Verbal subtests, sums two or three scaled scores correctly and enters sum in appropriate shaded box — Yes No
8. For Performance subtests, sums two or three scaled scores correctly and enters sum in appropriate shaded box — Yes No
9. For Processing Speed subtests, sums two scaled scores correctly and enters sum in appropriate shaded box — Yes No
10. For Full Scale IQ, sums four or seven scaled scores correctly and enters sum in appropriate shaded box — Yes No
11. For General Language Composite, sums two scaled scores correctly and enters sum in appropriate shaded box — Yes No

Sum of Scaled Scores to Composite Score Conversions

12. Transfers sums of scaled scores to appropriate shaded boxes — Yes No
13. Enters correct Verbal IQ — Yes No
14. Enters correct Performance IQ — Yes No
15. Enters correct Processing Speed Quotient — Yes No
16. Enters correct Full Scale IQ — Yes No
17. Enters correct General Language Composite — Yes No
18. Enters correct Verbal IQ percentile rank — Yes No
19. Enters correct Performance IQ percentile rank — Yes No

Front Page of Record Form (*Continued*)	Circle One	
20. Enters correct Processing Speed Quotient percentile rank	Yes	No
21. Enters correct Full Scale IQ percentile rank	Yes	No
22. Enters correct General Language Composite percentile rank	Yes	No
23. Enters selected confidence interval	Yes	No
24. Enters correct Verbal IQ confidence interval	Yes	No
25. Enters correct Performance IQ confidence interval	Yes	No
26. Enters correct Processing Speed Quotient confidence interval	Yes	No
27. Enters correct Full Scale IQ confidence interval	Yes	No
28. Enters correct General Language Composite confidence interval	Yes	No

Subtest Scaled Score Profile

29. Completes Subtest Scaled Score Profile correctly (optional) — Yes No

Composite Score Profile

30. Completes Composite Score Profile correctly (optional) — Yes No
31. Notes on Record Form order of administering subtests, if different from standard order — Yes No

Comments

_____

_____

_____

Discrepancy Analysis Page

Discrepancy Comparisons

1. Enters scaled scores in Scaled Score 1 and Scaled Score 2 columns correctly — Yes No
2. Calculates difference scores correctly — Yes No
3. Enters critical values correctly — Yes No
4. Enters significant difference (Y or N) correctly — Yes No
5. Enters base rate in standardization sample correctly — Yes No
6. Checks one of two basis-for-comparison boxes — Yes No
7. Checks one of two basis-for-statistical-significance boxes — Yes No

Determining Strengths and Weaknesses

8. Enters subtest scaled scores correctly — Yes No
9. Enters mean scaled scores correctly — Yes No
10. Calculates differences from mean scaled scores correctly — Yes No
11. Enters critical values correctly — Yes No
12. Enters strengths or weaknesses (S or W) correctly, if needed — Yes No
13. Enters base rate in standardization sample for strengths and weaknesses, if needed — Yes No
14. Checks one of two basis-for-comparison boxes — Yes No

(Continued)

Table B-20 (*Continued*)

Discrepancy Analysis Page (*Continued*)	Circle One	
15. Checks one of two basis-for-statistical-significance boxes	Yes	No
16. Enters sums of scaled scores for 7 subtests, 3 Verbal subtests, and 3 Performance subtests (ages 4-0 to 7-3) or sum of scaled scores for 4 subtests (ages 2-6 to 3-11) correctly	Yes	No
17. Enters mean scores for 7 subtests, 3 Verbal subtests, and 3 Performance subtests (ages 4-0 to 7-3) or sum of scaled scores for 4 subtests (ages 2-6 to 3-11) correctly	Yes	No

General Evaluation

	Circle One	
1. Maintains rapport throughout testing	Yes	No
2. Is alert to child's moods	Yes	No
3. Does not become impatient or frustrated with child	Yes	No
4. Does not badger child	Yes	No
5. Handles behavior problems correctly	Yes	No
6. Makes accommodations for any physical impairments child has that may affect assessment (e.g., hearing or visual loss)	Yes	No
7. Does not take break in middle of a subtest	Yes	No
8. Allows child to walk around room, if needed	Yes	No
9. Encourages child to perform a task, if needed	Yes	No
10. Praises child's effort	Yes	No
11. Does not say "Good" or "Right" after a correct response	Yes	No
12. Shows empathy if child is concerned about poor performance	Yes	No

Administering Test Items

	Circle One	
13. Administers test in professional, unhurried manner	Yes	No
14. Speaks clearly throughout testing	Yes	No
15. Is well organized and has all needed materials nearby	Yes	No
16. Administers subtests in order noted on page 22 of Administration Manual, altering order based on clinical need	Yes	No
17. Maintains steady pace	Yes	No
18. Makes a smooth transition from one subtest to the next	Yes	No
19. Repeats directions on request when appropriate	Yes	No
20. Repeats items when appropriate	Yes	No
21. Uses good judgment in deciding how much time to give child to solve each item on untimed subtests	Yes	No
22. Begins timing correctly	Yes	No
23. Adheres to time limits	Yes	No
24. Stops timing when child has obviously finished	Yes	No
25. Stops timing when time limit is reached	Yes	No
26. Does not stop timing prematurely	Yes	No
27. Places test materials not currently in use out of child's sight	Yes	No

General Evaluation (*Continued*)	Circle One	
28. Clears table of unessential materials	Yes	No
29. Positions Record Form so that child cannot see correct answers	Yes	No
30. Positions Administration Manual so that child cannot see correct answers	Yes	No
31. Makes appropriate eye contact with child	Yes	No
32. Reads directions exactly as written in Administration Manual	Yes	No
33. Reads items exactly as written in Administration Manual	Yes	No
34. Takes short break, as needed, at end of a subtest	Yes	No
35. Does not give additional items for practice	Yes	No
36. Does not ask leading questions	Yes	No
37. Does not spell words on any subtest	Yes	No
38. Does not define words	Yes	No
39. Does not use Vocabulary words in a sentence	Yes	No
40. Queries correctly	Yes	No
41. Records Q for queried responses	Yes	No
42. Prompts correctly	Yes	No
43. Records P for prompted responses	Yes	No
44. Gives second trials correctly	Yes	No
45. Follows start item with appropriate item	Yes	No
46. Administers reverse sequence correctly	Yes	No
47. Shows child how to solve problems when appropriate	Yes	No
48. Permits child to use scrap paper to write on, if appropriate	Yes	No
49. Conducts testing-of-limits after all subtests have been administered, if desired	Yes	No
50. Makes every effort to administer entire test in one session	Yes	No

Scoring Test Items

	Circle One	
51. Scores each item after child answers	Yes	No
52. Gives credit for correct responses given at any time during test, when appropriate	Yes	No
53. Does not give credit for correct answers given after time limit	Yes	No
54. Makes entry in Record Form for every item administered	Yes	No
55. Awards full credit for all items preceding first two items with perfect scores, regardless of child's performance on preceding items, by putting slash mark in Score column through the possible scores for the item preceding the two items with perfect scores and writing the numerals for these points	Yes	No
56. Does not give credit for any items beyond last score of 0 required for discontinue criterion, regardless of child's performance on these items if they have been administered	Yes	No
57. Does not count a supplemental subtest in computing Full Scale IQ, unless it is substituted for one of the core subtests	Yes	No

(*Continued*)

Table B-20 (*Continued*)

General Evaluation (*Continued*)	Circle One
58. Does not count an optional subtest in computing Full Scale IQ	Yes No
59. Uses good judgment overall in scoring responses	Yes No
60. Rechecks scoring after test is administered	Yes No

Completing Record Form

61. Records any deviation from procedure on Record Form	Yes No
62. Completes Front Page of Record Form correctly	Yes No
63. Completes Discrepancy Analysis Page of Record Form correctly	Yes No

Qualitative Feedback

_____

_____

_____

Overall Strengths

_____

_____

_____

Areas Needing Improvement

_____

_____

_____

Other Comments

_____

_____

_____

Overall Evaluation

Circle one: Excellent   Good   Average   Below Average   Poor

Table C-1
Confidence Intervals for WAIS–III Scales and Index Scores Based on Obtained Score Only

Age group	Scale	Confidence level				
		68%	85%	90%	95%	99%
16–17	Verbal Scale IQ	±3	±5	±5	±6	±8
	Performance Scale IQ	±5	±6	±7	±8	±11
	Full Scale IQ	±3	±4	±5	±6	±7
	Verbal Comprehension	±4	±6	±6	±8	±10
	Perceptual Organization	±5	±6	±7	±8	±11
	Working Memory	±4	±6	±7	±8	±11
	Processing Speed	±6	±8	±10	±11	±15
18–19	Verbal Scale IQ	±3	±4	±5	±5	±7
	Performance Scale IQ	±5	±6	±7	±9	±11
	Full Scale IQ	±3	±4	±4	±5	±7
	Verbal Comprehension	±4	±5	±6	±7	±9
	Perceptual Organization	±5	±7	±8	±9	±12
	Working Memory	±4	±5	±6	±7	±9
	Processing Speed	±6	±8	±10	±11	±15
20–24	Verbal Scale IQ	±3	±4	±5	±6	±7
	Performance Scale IQ	±4	±6	±7	±8	±10
	Full Scale IQ	±3	±4	±4	±5	±7
	Verbal Comprehension	±4	±5	±6	±7	±9
	Perceptual Organization	±4	±6	±7	±8	±10
	Working Memory	±4	±6	±7	±8	±11
	Processing Speed	±6	±9	±10	±11	±15
25–29	Verbal Scale IQ	±3	±4	±5	±5	±7
	Performance Scale IQ	±4	±5	±6	±7	±9
	Full Scale IQ	±3	±4	±4	±5	±6
	Verbal Comprehension	±4	±5	±6	±6	±8
	Perceptual Organization	±4	±5	±6	±7	±9
	Working Memory	±4	±6	±7	±8	±11
	Processing Speed	±6	±8	±9	±11	±15
30–34	Verbal Scale IQ	±3	±4	±5	±5	±7
	Performance Scale IQ	±4	±6	±7	±8	±11
	Full Scale IQ	±3	±4	±4	±5	±6
	Verbal Comprehension	±3	±5	±6	±6	±8
	Perceptual Organization	±5	±6	±6	±7	±9
	Working Memory	±4	±6	±7	±8	±11
	Processing Speed	±5	±8	±9	±11	±15
35–44	Verbal Scale IQ	±3	±4	±5	±5	±7
	Performance Scale IQ	±4	±6	±6	±7	±10
	Full Scale IQ	±3	±4	±4	±5	±6
	Verbal Comprehension	±4	±5	±5	±6	±8
	Perceptual Organization	±4	±6	±7	±8	±10
	Working Memory	±4	±6	±7	±8	±10
	Processing Speed	±5	±8	±9	±10	±13
45–54	Verbal Scale IQ	±3	±4	±5	±5	±7
	Performance Scale IQ	±4	±6	±6	±7	±10
	Full Scale IQ	±3	±4	±4	±5	±6
	Verbal Comprehension	±4	±5	±5	±6	±8
	Perceptual Organization	±4	±6	±7	±8	±11
	Working Memory	±4	±6	±7	±7	±10
	Processing Speed	±5	±8	±9	±10	±13

(Continued)

Table C-1 (*Continued*)

Age group	Scale	Confidence level				
		68%	85%	90%	95%	99%
55–64	Verbal Scale IQ	±3	±4	±4	±5	±7
	Performance Scale IQ	±4	±5	±6	±7	±9
	Full Scale IQ	±3	±3	±4	±5	±6
	Verbal Comprehension	±3	±4	±5	±6	±8
	Perceptual Organization	±4	±5	±6	±7	±9
	Working Memory	±4	±6	±7	±8	±10
	Processing Speed	±5	±7	±8	±10	±13
65–69	Verbal Scale IQ	±3	±4	±4	±5	±6
	Performance Scale IQ	±4	±5	±5	±6	±8
	Full Scale IQ	±2	±3	±4	±4	±5
	Verbal Comprehension	±3	±4	±5	±6	±7
	Perceptual Organization	±4	±5	±6	±7	±9
	Working Memory	±4	±6	±7	±8	±10
	Processing Speed	±5	±7	±8	±10	±13
70–74	Verbal Scale IQ	±3	±4	±5	±5	±7
	Performance Scale IQ	±4	±5	±6	±7	±9
	Full Scale IQ	±3	±4	±4	±5	±6
	Verbal Comprehension	±4	±5	±6	±7	±9
	Perceptual Organization	±4	±6	±7	±8	±10
	Working Memory	±4	±6	±6	±7	±10
	Processing Speed	±5	±8	±9	±10	±13
75–79	Verbal Scale IQ	±3	±4	±5	±6	±7
	Performance Scale IQ	±5	±6	±7	±8	±11
	Full Scale IQ	±3	±4	±5	±5	±7
	Verbal Comprehension	±3	±5	±5	±6	±8
	Perceptual Organization	±5	±7	±8	±9	±12
	Working Memory	±5	±7	±8	±9	±12
	Processing Speed	±6	±8	±9	±10	±14
80–84	Verbal Scale IQ	±3	±4	±5	±5	±7
	Performance Scale IQ	±4	±6	±6	±8	±10
	Full Scale IQ	±3	±4	±4	±5	±6
	Verbal Comprehension	±3	±4	±5	±6	±8
	Perceptual Organization	±5	±6	±7	±9	±11
	Working Memory	±4	±6	±7	±8	±10
	Processing Speed	±6	±8	±9	±10	±14
85–89	Verbal Scale IQ	±4	±5	±6	±6	±8
	Performance Scale IQ	±4	±6	±7	±8	±10
	Full Scale IQ	±3	±4	±5	±6	±7
	Verbal Comprehension	±3	±5	±5	±6	±8
	Perceptual Organization	±5	±7	±8	±10	±13
	Working Memory	±5	±7	±8	±9	±12
	Processing Speed	±6	±8	±9	±10	±13
Average	Verbal Scale IQ	±3	±4	±5	±5	±7
	Performance Scale IQ	±4	±6	±7	±8	±10
	Full Scale IQ	±3	±4	±4	±5	±6
	Verbal Comprehension	±4	±5	±5	±6	±8
	Perceptual Organization	±4	±6	±7	±8	±11
	Working Memory	±4	±6	±7	±8	±10
	Processing Speed	±6	±8	±9	±11	±14

Note. See Table A-1 for an explanation of the method used to obtain confidence intervals. Confidence intervals in this table were obtained by using the appropriate SEM located in Table 3.4 (p. 54) in the *WAIS–III—WMS–III Technical Manual.*

Table C-2
Significant Differences Between WAIS–III Scaled Scores, IQs, and Indexes at Ages 16 to 17, at Ages 18 to 19, and for the Average of the 13 Age Groups (.05/.01 significance levels)

Ages 16–17

Subtest	V	S	A	DS	I	C	LN	PC	CD	BD	MR	PA	SS	OA	VSIQ	PSIQ	VCSS	POSS	WMSS	PSSS
V	—	4	3	3	3	3	4	4	4	3	3	4	4	4	—	—	—	—	—	—
S	5	—	4	4	4	4	4	4	4	4	4	5	4	4	—	—	—	—	—	—
A	4	5	—	3	3	4	4	4	4	3	3	4	4	4	—	—	—	—	—	—
DS	4	5	4	—	3	3	4	4	4	3	3	4	4	4	—	—	—	—	—	—
I	4	5	4	4	—	4	4	4	4	3	3	4	4	4	—	—	—	—	—	—
C	4	5	5	4	5	—	4	4	4	4	4	4	4	4	—	—	—	—	—	—
LN	5	6	5	5	5	5	—	4	4	4	4	5	5	5	—	—	—	—	—	—
PC	5	5	5	5	5	5	5	—	4	4	4	5	4	4	—	—	—	—	—	—
CD	5	5	5	5	5	5	6	5	—	4	4	5	4	4	—	—	—	—	—	—
BD	4	5	4	4	4	5	5	5	5	—	3	4	4	4	—	—	—	—	—	—
MR	4	5	4	4	4	5	5	5	5	4	—	4	4	4	—	—	—	—	—	—
PA	5	6	6	5	5	6	6	6	6	6	6	—	5	5	—	—	—	—	—	—
SS	5	6	5	5	5	6	6	6	6	5	5	6	—	5	—	—	—	—	—	—
OA	5	6	5	5	5	6	6	6	6	5	5	6	6	—	—	—	—	—	—	—
VSIQ	—	—	—	—	—	—	—	—	—	—	—	—	—	—	—	10	—	—	—	—
PSIQ	—	—	—	—	—	—	—	—	—	—	—	—	—	—	13	—	—	—	—	—
VCSS	—	—	—	—	—	—	—	—	—	—	—	—	—	—	—	—	—	11	11	13
POSS	—	—	—	—	—	—	—	—	—	—	—	—	—	—	—	—	14	—	12	14
WMSS	—	—	—	—	—	—	—	—	—	—	—	—	—	—	—	—	14	15	—	14
PSSS	—	—	—	—	—	—	—	—	—	—	—	—	—	—	—	—	18	18	18	—

Ages 18–19

Subtest	V	S	A	DS	I	C	LN	PC	CD	BD	MR	PA	SS	OA	VSIQ	PSIQ	VCSS	POSS	WMSS	PSSS
V	—	3	3	3	3	3	3	4	3	3	3	4	4	4	—	—	—	—	—	—
S	4	—	4	3	3	4	4	4	4	4	3	4	4	4	—	—	—	—	—	—
A	4	5	—	3	3	3	3	4	4	3	3	4	4	4	—	—	—	—	—	—
DS	4	4	4	—	3	3	3	4	4	3	3	4	4	4	—	—	—	—	—	—
I	4	4	4	4	—	3	3	4	4	3	3	4	4	4	—	—	—	—	—	—
C	4	5	4	4	4	—	3	4	4	3	3	4	4	4	—	—	—	—	—	—
LN	4	5	4	4	4	4	—	4	4	3	3	4	4	4	—	—	—	—	—	—
PC	5	5	5	5	5	5	5	—	4	4	4	5	5	5	—	—	—	—	—	—
CD	4	5	5	5	5	5	5	6	—	4	4	5	4	5	—	—	—	—	—	—
BD	4	5	4	4	4	4	4	5	5	—	3	4	4	4	—	—	—	—	—	—
MR	4	4	4	4	4	4	4	5	5	4	—	4	4	4	—	—	—	—	—	—
PA	5	6	5	5	5	6	5	6	6	5	5	—	5	5	—	—	—	—	—	—
SS	5	5	5	8	5	5	5	6	6	5	5	6	—	5	—	—	—	—	—	—
OA	5	6	6	5	5	6	6	6	6	6	5	6	6	—	—	—	—	—	—	—
VSIQ	—	—	—	—	—	—	—	—	—	—	—	—	—	—	—	10	—	—	—	—
PSIQ	—	—	—	—	—	—	—	—	—	—	—	—	—	—	13	—	—	—	—	—
VCSS	—	—	—	—	—	—	—	—	—	—	—	—	—	—	—	—	—	11	9	13
POSS	—	—	—	—	—	—	—	—	—	—	—	—	—	—	—	—	14	—	11	14
WMSS	—	—	—	—	—	—	—	—	—	—	—	—	—	—	—	—	12	15	—	13
PSSS	—	—	—	—	—	—	—	—	—	—	—	—	—	—	—	—	17	19	17	—

(Continued)

Table C-2 (Continued)

Average of 13 age groups

Subtest	V	S	A	DS	I	C	LN	PC	CD	BD	MR	PA	SS	OA	VSIQ	PSIQ	VCSS	POSS	WMSS	PSSS
V	—	3	3	3	3	3	3	3	3	3	3	4	4	4	—	—	—	—	—	—
S	4	—	3	3	3	4	4	4	4	4	3	4	4	4	—	—	—	—	—	—
A	4	4	—	3	3	4	4	4	4	4	3	4	4	4	—	—	—	—	—	—
DS	4	4	4	—	3	3	4	4	3	3	3	4	4	4	—	—	—	—	—	—
I	4	4	4	4	—	3	4	4	3	3	3	4	4	4	—	—	—	—	—	—
C	4	5	5	4	4	—	4	4	4	4	4	4	4	5	—	—	—	—	—	—
LN	4	5	5	5	5	5	—	4	4	4	4	4	4	5	—	—	—	—	—	—
PC	4	5	5	5	4	5	5	—	4	4	4	4	4	5	—	—	—	—	—	—
CD	4	5	5	4	4	5	5	5	—	4	3	4	4	4	—	—	—	—	—	—
BD	4	5	4	4	4	5	5	5	5	—	3	4	4	4	—	—	—	—	—	—
MR	4	4	4	4	4	4	5	5	4	4	—	4	4	4	—	—	—	—	—	—
PA	5	5	5	5	5	6	6	6	5	5	5	—	5	5	—	—	—	—	—	—
SS	5	5	5	5	5	5	5	5	5	5	5	6	—	5	—	—	—	—	—	—
OA	5	6	6	5	5	6	6	6	6	6	5	6	6	—	—	—	—	—	—	—
VSIQ	—	—	—	—	—	—	—	—	—	—	—	—	—	—	—	9	—	—	—	—
PSIQ	—	—	—	—	—	—	—	—	—	—	—	—	—	—	12	—	—	—	—	—
VCSS	—	—	—	—	—	—	—	—	—	—	—	—	—	—	—	—	—	10	10	12
POSS	—	—	—	—	—	—	—	—	—	—	—	—	—	—	—	—	13	—	11	13
WMSS	—	—	—	—	—	—	—	—	—	—	—	—	—	—	—	—	13	15	—	13
PSSS	—	—	—	—	—	—	—	—	—	—	—	—	—	—	—	—	16	17	17	—

Note. Abbreviations: V = Vocabulary, S = Similarities, A = Arithmetic, DS = Digit Span, I = Information, C = Comprehension, LN = Letter–Number Sequencing, PC = Picture Completion, CD = Digit Symbol—Coding, BD = Block Design, MR = Matrix Reasoning, PA = Picture Arrangement, SS = Symbol Search, OA = Object Assembly; VSIQ = Verbal Scale IQ; PSIQ = Performance Scale IQ; VCSS = Verbal Comprehension Standard Score; POSS = Perceptual Organization Standard Score; WMSS = Working Memory Standard Score; PSSS = Processing Speed Standard Score.

The factor scores are composed of the following subtests: Verbal Comprehension: Vocabulary, Similarities, Information; Perceptual Organization: Picture Completion, Block Design, Matrix Reasoning; Working Memory: Arithmetic, Digit Span, Letter–Number Sequencing; Processing Speed: Digit Symbol—Coding, Symbol Search.

Sample reading: A difference of 4 points between scaled scores on Vocabulary and Similarities is significant at the .05 level; a difference of 5 points is significant at the .01 level. The first small box shows that a 10-point difference between the Verbal Scale IQ and the Performance Scale IQ is needed at the .05 level, and a 13-point difference is needed at the .01 level. The second small box shows that a difference of 11 points is needed between the Verbal Comprehension Standard Score and the Perceptual Organization Standard Score at the .05 level, and a difference of 14 points is needed at the .01 level. The other comparisons are read in a similar manner.

The values in this table for the subtest comparisons are overly liberal when more than one comparison is made for a subtest. They are more accurate when a priori planned comparisons are made, such as Information vs. Comprehension or Digit Span vs. Arithmetic.

See Chapter 11, Exhibit 11-1 for an explanation of the method used to arrive at the magnitudes of differences.

See Table D-11 in Appendix D for the procedure used to obtain the reliability coefficients for the Indexes (or short forms).

A. B. Silverstein (personal communication, February 1990) suggests that the following formula be used to obtain a value for the significant difference (at the .05 level) that must exist between the highest and lowest subtest scores on a profile before individual subtest comparisons can be made:

$$D = q \sqrt{\frac{\sum \text{SEM}^2}{k}}$$

where

D = significant difference
q = critical value of the Studentized range statistic
SEM = standard error of measurement of a particular subtest
k = number of subtests

For the WAIS–III, the q value is 4.55 at the .05 level for $k = 11$ (11 subtests) and ∞ degrees of freedom. The sum of the SEM^2 for the 11 subtests is .62 + 1.25 + 1.10 + .88 + .83 + 1.46 + 1.56 + 1.42 + 1.30 + .94 + 2.34 = 13.70. Thus,

$$D = 4.55 \times \sqrt{\frac{13.70}{11}} = 4.55 \times \sqrt{1.25} = 4.55 \times 1.116 = 5.08$$

Thus, a difference of 6 points between the highest and lowest subtest scaled scores represents a significant difference at the .05 level.

Table C-3
Estimates of Probability of Obtaining Designated Differences Between Individual WAIS–III Verbal and Performance IQs by Chance

Probability of obtaining given or greater discrepancy by chance	Age group													
	16–17	18–19	20–24	25–29	30–34	35–44	45–54	55–64	65–69	70–74	75–79	80–84	85–89	Av.[a]
.50	3.31	3.21	3.10	2.82	3.12	2.89	2.90	2.70	2.48	2.84	3.22	2.96	3.24	2.99
.25	5.69	5.51	5.32	4.85	5.36	4.96	4.97	4.63	4.26	4.88	5.52	5.07	5.57	5.14
.20	6.33	6.13	5.92	5.40	5.97	5.53	5.53	5.15	4.74	5.43	6.14	5.65	6.20	5.72
.10	8.16	7.90	7.63	6.95	7.69	7.12	7.13	6.64	6.11	7.00	7.92	7.28	7.99	7.37
.05	9.70	9.39	9.06	8.26	9.14	8.46	8.47	7.89	7.26	8.32	9.41	8.65	9.49	8.76
.02	11.53	11.16	10.77	9.82	10.86	10.06	10.07	9.38	8.63	9.89	11.18	10.28	11.28	10.41
.01	12.76	12.35	11.93	10.88	12.03	11.14	11.15	10.39	9.56	10.95	12.38	11.38	12.49	11.53
.001	16.28	15.75	15.21	13.87	15.34	14.20	14.22	13.25	12.19	13.96	15.79	14.51	15.93	14.70

Note. To use this table, find the column appropriate to the individual's age. Locate the discrepancy that is *just less* than the discrepancy obtained by the individual. The entry in the first column in that same row gives the probability of obtaining the given (or a greater) discrepancy by chance. For example, the probability that a 16-year-old individual obtained a Verbal-Performance discrepancy of 12 by chance is estimated to be less than 2%. This table is two-tailed. See Exhibit 11-1 in Chapter 11 for an explanation of the method used to arrive at magnitudes of differences.
[a]Av. = Average of 13 age groups.

Table C-4
Frequencies (cumulative percentages) of Differences Between WAIS–III Verbal Scale and Performance Scale IQs and Between Indexes in the Standardization Group When V > P, VC > PO, VC > WM, PO > PS, VC > PS, PO > WM, and WM > PS

Amount of discrepancy	Scales/Indexes						
	Verbal > Performance (VIQ > PIQ)	Verbal Comprehension > Perceptual Organization (VCI > POI)	Verbal Comprehension > Working Memory (VCI > WMI)	Perceptual Organization > Processing Speed (POI > PSI)	Verbal Comprehension > Processing Speed (VCI > PSI)	Perceptual Organization > Working Memory (POI > WMI)	Working Memory > Processing Speed (WMI > PSI)
≥ 40	0.0	0.1	0.4	0.3	0.5	0.1	0.4
39	0.1	0.1	0.4	0.4	0.6	0.2	0.5
38	0.1	0.2	0.4	0.5	0.6	0.2	0.6
37	0.2	0.2	0.4	0.5	0.6	0.2	0.8
36	0.2	0.2	0.4	0.5	0.7	0.3	1.0
35	0.2	0.3	0.4	0.7	0.9	0.3	1.0
34	0.2	0.4	0.6	0.8	1.0	0.4	1.2
33	0.4	0.5	0.6	0.9	1.3	0.7	1.4
32	0.4	0.7	0.7	1.3	1.5	0.9	1.8
31	0.5	1.0	0.8	1.3	1.8	1.1	2.1
30	0.5	1.0	1.0	1.9	2.1	1.4	2.4
29	0.6	1.1	1.2	2.2	2.3	1.5	2.5
28	0.7	1.5	1.8	2.4	2.7	1.9	3.0
27	1.1	1.8	2.2	3.0	3.4	2.2	3.9
26	1.3	2.0	2.4	3.4	4.2	2.7	4.2
25	1.7	2.7	3.1	4.0	4.6	3.2	4.6
24	2.1	3.1	3.3	4.4	5.2	3.8	5.3
23	2.6	4.1	4.2	5.3	6.2	4.2	5.9
22	3.1	4.5	4.8	6.5	7.0	4.6	7.0
21	3.4	5.4	5.6	7.1	8.4	5.7	7.4
20	4.1	5.8	6.2	8.1	9.2	6.0	8.4
19	4.8	7.3	7.4	9.2	10.8	7.8	9.0
18	5.6	8.0	8.6	10.3	11.7	7.8	10.6
17	6.5	9.3	10.3	11.5	13.4	9.2	11.3
16	7.8	10.0	11.7	12.4	14.7	9.7	13.4
15	8.7	11.2	13.7	14.2	16.2	12.4	14.9
14	9.9	12.5	14.6	15.4	17.8	13.4	15.8
13	11.8	14.8	16.6	16.8	19.6	14.2	18.6
12	13.6	16.6	19.0	18.7	21.6	16.2	20.2
11	16.0	18.6	21.1	20.2	23.5	19.4	22.2
10	18.2	21.4	23.4	23.1	26.2	21.4	24.0
9	20.5	23.8	25.1	24.7	27.9	23.8	26.8
8	23.1	26.5	28.3	28.0	30.0	26.6	29.3
7	26.2	29.5	30.2	30.8	32.8	29.8	31.5
6	29.5	32.2	32.9	33.5	35.0	31.7	34.5
5	32.6	35.4	35.8	36.2	38.0	34.7	37.0
4	35.9	38.5	40.3	38.8	40.9	37.8	39.8
3	39.9	41.5	44.9	41.8	43.5	41.8	43.2
2	43.4	46.5	48.2	44.9	46.6	45.0	45.1
1	47.5	49.5	52.2	47.7	49.2	48.5	48.2
0	—	—	—	—	—	—	—
Mdn	7.0	8.0	9.0	8.0	10.0	8.0	9.0

Source: Reprinted and adapted with permission of the authors, The Psychological Corporation, and the publisher of the journal, Swets and Zeitlinger, from D. S. Tulsky, E. L. Rolfhus, and J. J. Zhu (2000), "Two-Tailed versus One-Tailed Base Rates of Discrepancy Scores in the WAIS–III," *The Clinical Neuropsychologist, 14,* 451–460. *Wechsler Adult Intelligence Scale: Third Edition.* Copyright © 1997 by The Psychological Corporation, a Harcourt Assessment Company. Reproduced by permission. All rights reserved. "Wechsler Adult Intelligence Scale" and "WAIS" are trademarks of The Psychological Corporation registered in the United States and/or other jurisdictions.

Table C-5
Frequencies (cumulative percentages) of Differences Between WAIS–III Verbal Scale and Performance Scale IQs and Between Indexes in the Standardization Group When P > V, PO > VC, WM > VC, PS > PO, PS > VC, WM > PO, and PS > WM

Amount of discrepancy	Scales/Indexes						
	Performance > Verbal (PIQ > VIQ)	Perceptual Organization > Verbal Comprehension (POI > VCI)	Working Memory > Verbal Comprehension (WMI > VCI)	Processing Speed > Perceptual Organization (PSI > POI)	Processing Speed > Verbal Comprehension (PSI > VCI)	Working Memory > Perceptual Organization (WMI > POI)	Processing Speed > Working Memory (PSI > WMI)
≥ 40	0.0	0.2	0.1	0.3	0.3	0.2	0.4
39	0.1	0.2	0.1	0.3	0.4	0.2	0.4
38	0.1	0.2	0.1	0.4	0.5	0.2	0.4
37	0.1	0.2	0.5	0.5	0.8	0.6	0.5
36	0.1	0.2	0.5	0.7	1.0	0.7	0.7
35	0.1	0.2	0.5	0.7	1.2	0.7	0.9
34	0.1	0.4	0.5	0.9	1.6	0.7	1.0
33	0.2	0.5	0.6	1.1	1.6	0.9	1.2
32	0.2	0.7	1.0	1.3	1.8	1.0	1.4
31	0.2	0.9	1.2	1.5	2.4	1.2	1.4
30	0.2	1.1	1.3	1.8	2.7	1.4	2.1
29	0.3	1.3	1.4	2.1	3.0	2.0	2.2
28	0.5	1.5	1.4	2.5	3.3	2.7	3.0
27	0.5	2.0	1.6	2.7	3.6	3.0	3.4
26	0.7	2.2	1.9	3.4	4.2	3.1	4.1
25	0.9	2.7	2.2	3.8	4.8	3.8	5.2
24	1.0	2.9	2.8	4.3	5.9	4.3	5.8
23	1.5	3.8	3.1	5.3	6.5	4.7	6.3
22	1.8	4.3	4.0	6.0	7.5	5.2	7.1
21	2.5	5.1	4.6	6.7	8.2	5.8	8.0
20	3.2	6.0	6.0	8.1	9.5	7.0	8.8
19	4.1	6.9	7.0	9.2	10.5	7.7	9.9
18	5.1	8.4	8.0	10.1	11.5	8.4	10.9
17	6.2	9.5	9.5	11.6	13.2	9.6	11.8
16	7.8	10.7	10.8	12.4	14.2	10.9	13.4
15	8.9	11.8	11.8	14.5	16.2	12.0	15.4
14	10.5	13.0	13.5	16.2	17.5	14.2	16.8
13	12.0	15.4	15.0	18.0	19.8	15.4	19.5
12	14.2	16.4	16.6	19.9	21.9	17.9	21.0
11	16.4	19.2	17.8	21.8	23.8	19.5	22.8
10	19.1	20.7	21.4	23.9	26.7	22.7	23.8
9	22.3	23.6	22.6	26.0	28.1	24.1	28.2
8	24.9	26.2	26.6	28.2	30.6	27.3	31.2
7	27.5	28.7	27.3	30.9	32.8	28.5	33.0
6	30.9	31.4	32.2	34.2	35.0	32.4	35.6
5	33.8	33.7	34.1	36.7	38.0	35.0	37.6
4	37.4	37.8	37.4	39.6	39.5	39.5	41.2
3	41.2	39.8	39.2	42.9	42.5	41.8	43.6
2	44.9	43.9	41.4	46.7	46.2	45.9	47.3
1	49.0	45.8	45.4	48.9	48.1	48.6	49.2
0	—	—	—	—	—	—	—
Mdn	7.0	8.0	8.0	9.0	10.0	8.0	9.0

Table C-6
Differences Required for Significance When Each WAIS–III Subtest Scaled Score Is Compared to the Mean Subtest Scaled Score for Any Individual

	Average of all age groups											
	Mean of 2 subtests		Mean of 3 subtests[a]		Mean of 3 subtests		Mean of 5 subtests		Mean of 6 subtests[b]		Mean of 6 subtests	
Subtest	.05	.01	.05	.01	.05	.01	.05	.01	.05	.01	.05	.01
Vocabulary	—	—	1.70	2.09	—	—	—	—	2.02	2.41	—	—
Similarities	—	—	2.03	2.48	—	—	—	—	2.65	3.15	—	—
Arithmetic	—	—	—	—	2.11	2.58	—	—	2.51	2.99	—	—
Digit Span	—	—	—	—	2.00	2.46	—	—	2.30	2.74	—	—
Information	—	—	1.82	2.23	—	—	—	—	2.24	2.67	—	—
Comprehension	—	—	—	—	—	—	—	—	2.83	3.36	—	—
Letter–Number Seq.	—	—	—	—	2.36	2.89	—	—	—	—	—	—
Picture Completion	—	—	2.32	2.85	—	—	2.87	3.44	3.02	3.59	3.04	3.62
Digit Symbol—Coding	2.08	2.61	—	—	—	—	2.77	3.32	2.91	3.46	2.93	3.48
Block Design	—	—	2.21	2.71	—	—	2.68	3.21	2.81	3.34	2.83	3.37
Matrix Reasoning	—	—	2.05	2.51	—	—	2.40	2.88	2.50	2.97	2.52	3.00
Picture Arrangement	—	—	—	—	—	—	3.37	4.04	3.57	4.24	3.59	4.27
Symbol Search	2.08	2.61	—	—	—	—	—	—	3.37	4.01	—	—
Object Assembly	—	—	—	—	—	—	—	—	—	—	3.85	4.58
	Mean of 7 subtests[c]		Mean of 11 subtests		Mean of 11 subtests		Mean of 11 subtests		Mean of 11 subtests		Mean of 12 subtests	
Subtest	.05	.01	.05	.01	.05	.01	.05	.01	.05	.01	.05	.01
Vocabulary	2.09	2.48	2.24	2.62	2.26	2.64	2.25	2.63	2.26	2.65	2.27	2.64
Similarities	2.76	3.28	3.03	3.54	3.04	3.55	3.04	3.55	3.05	3.56	3.08	3.59
Arithmetic	2.66	3.11	2.86	3.35	2.87	3.36	2.87	3.35	2.88	3.36	2.91	3.38
Digit Span	2.39	2.84	2.60	3.04	—	—	2.61	3.05	—	—	2.64	3.07
Information	2.33	2.72	2.53	2.95	2.54	2.96	2.53	2.96	2.54	2.97	2.56	2.98
Comprehension	2.95	3.50	3.25	3.80	3.26	3.81	3.26	3.81	3.27	3.82	3.31	3.85
Letter–Number Seq.	3.15	3.72	—	—	3.48	4.07	—	—	3.49	4.08	3.53	4.11
Picture Completion	3.15	3.73	3.25	3.92	3.36	3.93	3.36	3.92	3.36	3.93	3.41	3.96
Digit Symbol—Coding	3.02	3.59	3.20	3.74	3.21	3.75	—	—	—	—	3.26	3.79
Block Design	2.92	3.47	3.08	3.60	3.09	3.61	3.09	3.61	3.10	3.62	3.13	3.64
Matrix Reasoning	2.59	3.07	2.67	3.12	2.68	3.13	2.68	3.13	2.69	3.14	2.71	3.15
Picture Arrangement	3.73	4.43	4.05	4.73	4.05	4.74	4.05	4.73	4.06	4.74	4.12	4.79
Symbol Search	3.52	4.17	—	—	—	—	2.80	4.44	3.81	4.45	—	—
Object Assembly	4.01	4.75	—	—	—	—	—	—	—	—	—	—

(Continued)

Table C-6 (*Continued*)

	Average of all age groups											
	Mean of 12 subtests		Mean of 12 subtests		Mean of 13 subtests		Mean of 13 subtests		Mean of 13 subtests		Mean of 14 subtests	
Subtest	.05	.01	.05	.01	.05	.01	.05	.01	.05	.01	.05	.01
Vocabulary	2.28	2.65	2.29	2.66	2.30	2.67	2.30	2.68	2.31	2.68	2.33	2.69
Similarities	3.08	3.59	3.09	3.60	3.12	3.63	3.12	3.63	3.13	3.64	3.17	3.66
Arithmetic	2.91	3.39	2.92	3.39	2.94	3.42	2.95	3.43	2.95	3.43	2.99	3.45
Digit Span	2.64	3.07	2.65	3.08	2.67	3.10	2.67	3.11	2.68	3.11	2.71	3.13
Information	2.57	2.99	2.57	3.00	2.59	3.01	2.60	3.02	2.60	3.02	2.63	3.04
Comprehension	3.31	3.85	3.32	3.86	3.35	3.89	3.35	3.90	3.36	3.90	3.40	3.93
Letter–Number Seq.	—	—	—	—	3.58	4.16	3.58	4.17	—	—	3.64	4.20
Picture Completion	3.41	3.97	3.42	3.98	3.45	4.01	3.46	4.02	3.46	4.02	3.51	4.05
Digit Symbol—Coding	3.26	3.79	3.27	3.80	3.30	3.83	3.30	3.84	3.30	3.84	3.35	3.87
Block Design	3.13	3.65	3.14	3.65	3.17	3.69	3.18	3.69	3.18	3.69	3.22	3.72
Matrix Reasoning	2.71	3.16	2.72	3.17	2.74	3.19	2.75	3.19	2.75	3.20	2.78	3.21
Picture Arrangement	4.12	4.79	4.12	4.80	4.17	4.85	4.18	4.86	4.18	4.86	4.24	4.89
Symbol Search	3.86	4.50	—	—	3.91	4.55	—	—	3.92	4.56	3.98	4.59
Object Assembly	—	—	4.46	5.19	—	—	4.51	5.25	4.52	5.25	4.58	5.29

Note. This table shows the minimum deviations from an individual's average subtest scaled score that are significant at the .05 and .01 levels.

The following formula, obtained from Davis (1959), was used to compute the deviations from average that are significant at the desired significance level:

$$D = \text{CR} \times \text{SEM}_{((T/m)-Z_I)}$$

where

D = deviation from average
CR = critical ratio desired
$\text{SEM}_{((T/m)-Z_I)}$ = standard error of measurement of the difference between an average subtest scaled score and any one of the subtest scaled scores that entered into the average

The standard error of measurement can be obtained from the following formula:

$$\text{SEM}_{((T/m)-Z_I)} = \sqrt{\frac{\text{SEM}_T^2}{m^2} + \left(\frac{m-2}{m}\right)\text{SEM}_{Z_I}^2}$$

where

SEM_T^2 = sum of the squared standard errors of measurement of the m subtests
m = number of subtests included in the average
T/m = average of the subtest scaled scores
$\text{SEM}_{Z_I}^2$ = squared standard error of measurement of any one of the subtest scaled scores

The critical ratios used were based on the Bonferroni inequality, which controls the family-wise error rate at .05 (or .01) by setting the error rate per comparison at .05/m (or .01/m). The critical ratios at the .05 level are 2.39 for 3 subtests, 2.50 for 4 subtests, 2.58 for 5 subtests, 2.81 for 10 subtests, 2.84 for 11 subtests, 2.87 for 12 subtests, 2.89 for 13 subtests, and 2.91 for 14 subtests. The critical ratios at the .01 level are 2.93 for 3 subtests, 3.02 for 4 subtests, 3.10 for 5 subtests, 3.30 for 10 subtests, 3.32 for 11 subtests, 3.35 for 12 subtests, 3.36 for 13 subtests, and 3.38 for 14 subtests. For 6 and 7 subtests, the Bonferroni inequality critical ratios would be 2.64 and 2.69, respectively, at the .05 level and 3.14 and 3.19, respectively, at the .01 level.

The following example illustrates the procedure. We will determine the minimum deviation required for a 16-year-old individual's score on the WAIS–III Vocabulary subtest to be significantly different from his or her average score on the three Verbal Comprehension subtests (Vocabulary, Similarities, and Information) at the 95% level of confidence. We calculate SEM_T^2 by first squaring the appropriate average standard error of measurement for each of the three subtests and then summing the squares:

$$\text{SEM}_T^2 = (.62)^2 + (1.25)^2 + (1.10)^2 = 2.97$$

We determine $\text{SEM}_{Z_I}^2$ by squaring the average standard error of measurement of the subtest of interest, the Vocabulary subtest:

$$\text{SEM}_{Z_I}^2 = (.79)^2 = .62$$

The number of subtests, m, equals 3. Substituting these values into the formula yields the following:

$$\text{SEM}_{((T/m)-Z_I)} = \sqrt{\frac{2.97}{(3)^2} + \left(\frac{3-2}{3}\right).62} = .537$$

The value, .537, is then multiplied by the appropriate z value for the 95% confidence level to obtain the minimum significant

(*Continued*)

Table C-6 (*Continued*)

deviation (*D*). Using the Bonferroni correction (.05/3 = .0167), we have a *z* value of 2.39.

$$D = 2.39 \times .537 = 1.28$$

The Bonferonni correction was not applied to the two-subtest mean comparisons.

[a]In this column, the entries for Vocabulary, Similarities, and Information are compared to the mean of these three subtests. Similarly, the entries for Picture Completion, Block Design, and Matrix Reasoning are compared to the mean of these three subtests.

[b]In this column, the entries for Vocabulary, Similarities, Arithmetic, Digit Span, Information, and Comprehension are compared to the mean of these six subtests. Similarly, the entries for Picture Completion, Digit Symbol—Coding, Block Design, Matrix Reasoning, Picture Arrangement, and Symbol Search are compared to the mean of these six subtests.

[c]In this column, the entries for Vocabulary, Similarities, Arithmetic, Digit Span, Information, Comprehension, and Letter–Number Sequencing are compared to the mean of these seven subtests. Similarly, the entries for Picture Completion, Digit Symbol—Coding, Block Design, Matrix Reasoning, Picture Arrangement, Symbol Search, and Object Assembly are compared to the mean of these seven subtests.

Table C-7
Cumulative Frequencies of Differences from the Mean of Six WAIS–III Verbal Subtests When Letter–Number Sequencing Replaces Digit Span

Subtest	Cumulative percentage				
	25%	10%	5%	2%	1%
Vocabulary	1.60	2.30	2.73	3.25	3.58
Similarities	1.82	2.62	3.11	3.70	4.08
Arithmetic	2.10	3.01	3.57	4.25	4.69
Information	1.73	2.49	2.96	3.51	3.88
Comprehension	1.86	2.66	3.16	3.76	4.15
Letter–Number Seq.	2.53	3.62	4.31	5.12	5.65

Source: Adapted with permission of the publisher from S. G. LoBello, A. P. Thompson, and V. Evani, Supplementary WAIS–III Tables for Determining Subtest Strengths and Weaknesses, *Journal of Psychoeducational Assessment, 16,* Table 3, page 198. Copyright © 1998 by The Psychoeducational Corporation.

Table C-9
Cumulative Frequencies of Differences from the Mean of Five WAIS–III Performance Subtests When Symbol Search Replaces Digit Symbol—Coding

Subtest	Cumulative percentage				
	25%	10%	5%	2%	1%
Picture Completion	2.21	3.17	3.77	4.48	4.94
Block Design	2.03	2.91	3.46	4.11	4.54
Matrix Reasoning	2.12	3.04	3.62	4.30	4.74
Picture Arrangement	2.26	3.25	3.86	4.59	5.06
Symbol Search	2.24	3.22	3.82	4.54	5.01

Source: Adapted with permission of the publisher from S. G. LoBello, A. P. Thompson, and V. Evani, Supplementary WAIS–III Tables for Determining Subtest Strengths and Weaknesses, *Journal of Psychoeducational Assessment, 16,* Table 2, page 198. Copyright © 1998 by The Psychoeducational Corporation.

Table C-8
Cumulative Frequencies of Differences from the Mean of Five WAIS–III Performance Subtests Plus Symbol Search

Subtest	Cumulative percentage				
	25%	10%	5%	2%	1%
Picture Completion	2.30	3.31	3.93	4.67	5.15
Digit Symbol—Coding	2.43	3.49	4.14	4.92	5.43
Block Design	2.14	3.08	3.65	4.34	4.80
Matrix Reasoning	2.23	3.19	3.79	4.51	4.97
Picture Arrangement	2.36	3.39	4.03	4.79	5.28
Symbol Search	2.10	3.01	3.57	4.25	4.69

Source: Adapted with permission of the publisher from S. G. LoBello, A. P. Thompson, and V. Evani, Supplementary WAIS–III Tables for Determining Subtest Strengths and Weaknesses, *Journal of Psychoeducational Assessment, 16,* Table 1, page 198. Copyright © 1998 by The Psychoeducational Corporation.

Table C-10
Cumulative Frequencies of Differences from the Mean of 11 WAIS–III Subtests Plus Letter–Number Sequencing

Subtest	Cumulative percentage				
	25%	10%	5%	2%	1%
Vocabulary	1.64	2.77	3.31	3.93	4.36
Similarities	1.75	2.95	3.53	4.19	4.64
Arithmetic	1.83	3.10	3.70	4.40	4.87
Digit Span	2.29	3.87	4.62	5.50	6.09
Information	1.74	2.95	3.52	4.18	4.63
Comprehension	1.81	3.06	3.66	4.35	4.81
Letter–Numbering Seq.	2.08	3.53	4.21	5.01	5.55
Picture Completion	2.17	3.68	4.39	5.22	5.78
Digit Symbol—Coding	2.32	3.93	4.69	5.58	6.18
Block Design	2.01	3.40	4.07	4.83	5.35
Matrix Reasoning	1.93	3.26	3.89	4.63	5.12
Picture Arrangement	2.10	3.54	4.23	5.03	5.57

Note. The information in this table was obtained by use of Silverstein's (1984) formula, which is shown in the Note to Table A-6 in Appendix A.

Table C-11
Cumulative Frequencies of Differences from the Mean of the Standard 11 WAIS–III Subtests When Letter–Number Sequencing Replaces Digit Span

Subtest	25%	10%	5%	2%	1%
	Cumulative percentage				
Vocabulary	1.61	2.73	3.26	3.87	4.29
Similarities	1.71	2.89	3.45	4.11	4.55
Arithmetic	1.86	3.14	3.75	4.46	4.94
Information	1.70	2.88	3.44	4.09	4.53
Comprehension	1.78	3.00	3.59	4.26	4.72
Letter–Numbering Seq.	2.14	3.63	4.33	5.15	5.70
Picture Completion	2.14	3.63	4.33	5.15	5.70
Digit Symbol—Coding	2.33	3.93	4.70	5.59	6.19
Block Design	1.99	3.36	4.02	4.78	5.29
Matrix Reasoning	1.92	3.24	3.87	4.61	5.10
Picture Arrangement	2.07	3.50	4.18	4.97	5.50

Note. The information in this table was obtained by use of Silverstein's (1984) formula, which is shown in the Note to Table A-6 in Appendix A.

Table C-12
Cumulative Frequencies of Differences from the Mean of the Standard 11 WAIS–III Subtests When Symbol Search Replaces Digit Symbol—Coding

Subtest	25%	10%	5%	2%	1%
	Cumulative percentage				
Vocabulary	1.62	2.74	3.28	3.90	4.32
Similarities	1.71	2.89	3.45	4.10	4.54
Arithmetic	1.84	3.11	3.71	4.41	4.89
Digit Span	2.35	3.97	4.75	5.64	6.25
Information	1.71	2.89	3.45	4.10	4.54
Comprehension	1.77	3.00	3.58	4.26	4.72
Picture Completion	2.15	3.64	4.35	5.17	5.73
Block Design	1.97	3.34	3.99	4.74	5.25
Matrix Reasoning	1.91	3.23	3.86	4.59	5.08
Picture Arrangement	2.07	3.49	4.17	4.96	5.49
Symbol Search	2.08	3.52	4.21	5.01	5.54

Note. The information in this table was obtained by use of Silverstein's (1984) formula, which is shown in the Note to Table A-6 in Appendix A.

Table C-13
Estimates of the Probability of Obtaining Designated Differences Between Individual WAIS–III Indexes by Chance

Probability of obtaining given or greater discrepancy by chance	Verbal Comprehension Index vs. Perceptual Organization Index	Verbal Comprehension Index vs. Processing Speed Index	Verbal Comprehension Index vs. Working Memory Index	Perceptual Organization Index vs. Processing Speed Index	Perceptual Organization Index vs. Working Memory Index	Processing Speed Index vs. Working Memory Index
.50	3.33	3.99	3.27	4.34	3.69	4.29
.25	5.71	6.84	5.61	7.45	6.34	7.37
.20	6.36	7.61	6.25	8.29	7.05	8.20
.10	8.19	9.81	8.05	10.68	9.09	10.57
.05	9.73	11.66	9.56	12.69	10.80	12.56
.02	11.57	13.86	11.37	15.09	12.84	14.93
.01	12.81	15.35	12.59	16.70	14.21	16.53
.001	16.34	19.57	16.05	21.30	18.12	21.08

Note. The values in this table are based on the total group. Locate the discrepancy that is *just less* than the discrepancy obtained by the individual. The entry in the first column in that same row gives the probability of obtaining the given (or a greater) discrepancy by chance. For example, the probability that an individual obtained a Verbal Comprehension Index–Perceptual Organization Index discrepancy of 10 by chance is estimated to be 5%. This table is two-tailed. See Exhibit 11-1 in Chapter 11 for an explanation of the method used to arrive at the magnitudes of the differences.

Table C-14
Cumulative Frequencies of Differences from the Mean of WAIS–III Subtests on Verbal Comprehension, Perceptual Organization, Working Memory, and Processing Speed Indexes

Subtest	Cumulative percentage				
	25%	10%	5%	2%	1%
Verbal Comprehension					
Vocabulary	1.50	2.15	2.56	3.04	3.36
Information	1.48	2.12	2.51	2.99	3.31
Similarities	1.30	1.87	2.22	2.64	2.92
Perceptual Organization					
Picture Completion	2.06	2.95	3.50	4.17	4.61
Block Design	1.81	2.60	3.09	3.67	4.06
Matrix Reasoning	1.90	2.72	3.23	3.84	4.26
Working Memory					
Arithmetic	1.95	2.79	3.32	3.94	4.37
Digit Span	1.85	2.64	3.14	3.73	4.13
Letter–Number Seq.	1.90	2.73	3.24	3.85	4.27
Processing Speed					
Digit Symbol—Coding	1.44	2.07	2.46	2.92	3.24
Symbol Search	1.44	2.07	2.46	2.92	3.24

Note. The information in this table was obtained by use of Silverstein's (1984) formula, which is shown in the Note to Table A-6 in Appendix A.

Table C-15
Reliability and Validity Coefficients of Proposed WAIS–III Short Forms

Two subtests

Short form		r_{tt}	r
V	MR	.945	.881
V	BD	.930	.876
V	A	.941	.875
I	MR[a]	.938	.867
I	BD	.922	.865
S	A	.917	.863
S	MR	.922	.861
C	MR	.914	.856
V	I	.955	.853
V	S	.940	.853
I	PC[a]	.911	.836
A	MR[a]	.930	.830
A	PC[a]	.896	.829
I	CD[a]	.909	.824
BD	MR[b]	.925	.790
PC	MR[a,b]	.909	.787
PC	BD[b]	.899	.780
CD	MR[b]	.907	.774
PC	CD[a,b]	.881	.733
DS	LN[c]	.911	.729
CD	SS[d]	.882	.727
I	S	.932	.852
BD	CD	.894	.763
I	A	.936	.850

Three subtests

Short form			r_{tt}	r
V	I	BD	.954	.906
V	A	PC	.939	.906
V	A	MR	.955	.905
V	A	BD	.947	.905
V	I	MR	.961	.905
V	A	PA	.927	.904
V	S	MR	.954	.902
S	I	MR	.950	.900
V	S	BD	.947	.899
V	C	MR	.950	.899
A	I	MR[a]	.952	.891
A	I	PC[a]	.936	.891
I	PC	MR[a]	.939	.887
I	CD	MR[a]	.938	.886
CD	BD	MR[b]	.931	.834
PC	BD	MR[b]	.934	.832
PC	CD	MR[b]	.922	.830
PC	CD	BD[b]	.917	.810
I	S	DS	.945	.882
V	S	I[e]	.960	.871
A	DS	LN[f]	.936	.820

Four subtests

Short form				r_{tt}	r
V	I	BD	MR	.963	.922
V	A	PC	MR	.955	.921
V	S	A	MR	.962	.920
V	A	BD	PA	.942	.920
V	S	A	BD	.957	.919
V	S	A	PC	.953	.919
V	A	I	BD	.962	.919
V	I	PC	MR	.959	.918
V	DS	I	BD	.950	.918
V	S	A	PA	.946	.912
A	I	PC	MR[a]	.953	.911
DS	I	PC	MR[a]	.950	.905
A	I	CD	MR[a]	.953	.904
A	I	PC	CD[a]	.942	.900
PC	CD	BD	MR[b]	.941	.855
I	A	DS	S	.957	.899
I	S	CD	LN	.941	.918
MR	PC	CD	SS	.933	.865
I	A	PC	BD	.948	.907
S	A	CD	LN	.938	.912

Five subtests

Short form					r_{tt}	r
V	A	I	PC	MR	.965	.934
V	S	A	PC	MR	.962	.935
V	A	C	PC	MR	.961	.933
V	S	A	BD	PA	.954	.933
V	DS	I	BD	MR	.967	.933
V	A	I	PC	BD	.962	.932
V	DS	I	PC	MR	.964	.932
V	I	CD	BD	MR	.963	.932
V	A	C	BD	PA	.953	.932
V	A	I	BD	PA	.958	.932
A	I	PC	CD	MR[a]	.955	.921
A	DS	I	PC	MR[a]	.960	.920
DS	I	PC	CD	MR[a]	.953	.915
A	DS	I	PC	CD[a]	.960	.909

Note. Abbreviations: V = Vocabulary, S = Similarities, A = Arithmetic, DS = Digit Span, I = Information, C = Comprehension, LN = Letter–Number Sequencing, PC = Picture Completion, CD = Digit Symbol—Coding, BD = Block Design, MR = Matrix Reasoning, PA = Picture Arrangement, SS = Symbol Search.

The first 10 combinations in each list represent the best ones based on validity. See Table D-11 in Appendix D for formulas used to obtain reliability and validity coefficients.

[a]This combination is useful for a rapid screening.
[b]This combination is useful for individuals who are hearing impaired.
[c]This combination provides an estimate of the Working Memory Index score.
[d]This combination provides an estimate of the Processing Speed Index score.
[e]This combination represents the subtests in the Verbal Comprehension Index.
[f]This combination represents the subtests in the Working Memory Index.

Table C-16
Reliable and Unusual Scaled-Score Ranges for Selected WAIS–III Subtest Combinations

Short form			Reliable scaled score range	Unusual scaled-score range
Two subtests				
I	CD		3	6
BD	CD		4	6
A	PC		4	6
PC	CD		4	6
CD	MR		4	6
I	PC		4	6
I	BD		3	6
MR	PC		4	6
V	BD		3	5
C	MR		4	5
PC	BD		4	5
I	MR		3	5
S	MR		3	5
V	MR		3	5
S	A		4	5
DS	LN		4	5
A	MR		3	5
V	A		3	5
BD	MR		3	5
I	A		3	5
CD	SS		4	5
I	S		4	4
V	I		3	4
V	S		3	4
Three subtests				
PC	CD	MR	4	6
I	CD	MR	4	6
PC	CD	BD	4	6
CD	BD	MR	4	6
I	PC	MR	4	6
V	A	PC	4	6
A	I	PC	4	6
I	S	DS	3	6
PC	BD	MR	4	6
V	A	BD	3	5
V	A	PA	4	6
A	DS	LN	4	5
V	A	MR	3	5
A	I	MR	3	5
V	I	BD	3	5
S	I	MR	3	5
V	S	BD	3	5
V	C	MR	3	5

Short form				Reliable scaled score range	Unusual scaled-score range
Three subtests (*Continued*)					
V	I	MR		3	5
V	S	MR		3	5
V	S	I		3	4
Four subtests					
DS	I	PC	MR	4	6
A	I	PC	CD	4	6
PC	CD	BD	MR	4	6
A	S	CD	LN	4	6
MR	PC	CD	SS	4	6
V	DS	I	BD	3	6
A	I	CD	MR	4	6
I	A	PC	BD	4	6
V	A	PC	MR	4	6
A	I	PC	MR	4	6
V	A	BD	PA	4	6
I	A	DS	S	4	6
V	I	PC	MR	4	6
V	S	A	PC	4	6
V	I	BD	MR	3	6
V	S	A	PA	4	6
V	S	A	BD	4	5
V	A	I	BD	3	5
V	S	A	MR	3	5

Short form					Reliable scaled score range	Unusual scaled-score range
Five subtests						
DS	I	PC	CD	MR	4	7
A	DS	I	PC	CD	4	6
A	I	PC	CD	MR	4	6
A	DS	I	PC	MR	4	6
V	DS	I	PC	MR	4	6
V	I	CD	BD	MR	4	6
V	DS	I	BD	MR	3	6
V	A	C	C	MR	4	6
V	A	I	PC	BD	4	6
V	A	C	BD	PA	4	6
V	S	A	PC	MR	4	6
V	A	I	PC	MR	4	6
V	S	A	BD	PA	4	6
V	A	I	BD	PA	4	6

Short form						Reliable scaled score range	Unusual scaled-score range
Six or seven subtests							
V	S	I	PC	BD	MR	4	6
I	A	DS	S	PC	BD	CD	4	6
I	A	DS	S	PC	MR	CD	4	6

Note. See Table A-8 for the formulas.

Table C-17
Estimated WAIS–III Full Scale IQs for Sum of Scaled Scores for 10 Best 2-Subtest Short Forms and Other Combinations

Sum of scaled scores	Combination													
	C2	C3	C4	C5	C6	C7	C8	C9	C10	C11	C12	C13	C14	C15
2	46	47	48	48	48	49	49	49	49	50	50	50	51	52
3	49	50	51	51	51	51	52	52	52	52	53	53	54	55
4	52	53	54	54	54	54	54	55	55	55	56	56	57	57
5	55	56	56	57	57	57	57	58	58	58	58	59	59	60
6	58	59	59	60	60	60	60	60	61	61	61	61	62	63
7	61	62	62	62	63	63	63	63	63	64	64	64	65	65
8	64	65	65	65	66	66	66	66	66	66	67	67	67	68
9	67	68	68	68	68	69	69	69	69	69	70	70	70	71
10	70	71	71	71	71	71	72	72	72	72	72	72	73	73
11	73	74	74	74	74	74	74	75	75	75	75	75	76	76
12	76	77	77	77	77	77	77	77	77	78	78	78	78	79
13	79	80	80	80	80	80	80	80	80	80	81	81	81	81
14	82	82	83	83	83	83	83	83	83	83	83	83	84	84
15	85	85	85	86	86	86	86	86	86	86	86	86	86	87
16	88	88	88	88	89	89	89	89	89	89	89	89	89	89
17	91	91	91	91	91	91	91	92	92	92	92	92	92	92
18	84	94	94	94	94	94	94	94	94	94	94	94	95	95
19	97	97	97	97	97	97	97	97	97	97	97	97	97	97
20	100	100	100	100	100	100	100	100	100	100	100	100	100	100
21	103	103	103	103	103	103	103	103	103	103	103	103	103	103
22	106	106	106	106	106	106	106	106	106	106	106	106	105	105
23	109	109	109	109	109	109	109	108	108	108	108	108	108	108
24	112	112	112	112	111	111	111	111	111	111	111	111	111	111
25	115	115	115	114	114	114	114	114	114	114	114	114	114	113
26	118	118	117	117	117	117	117	117	117	117	117	117	116	116
27	121	120	120	120	120	120	120	120	120	120	119	119	119	119
28	124	123	123	123	123	123	123	123	123	122	122	122	122	121
29	127	126	126	126	126	126	126	125	125	125	125	125	124	124
30	130	129	129	129	129	129	128	128	128	128	128	128	127	127
31	133	132	132	132	132	131	131	131	131	131	130	130	130	129
32	136	135	135	135	134	134	134	134	134	134	133	133	133	132
33	139	138	138	138	137	137	137	137	137	136	136	136	135	135
34	142	141	141	140	140	140	140	140	139	139	139	139	138	137
35	145	144	144	143	143	143	143	142	142	142	142	141	141	140
36	148	147	146	146	146	146	146	145	145	145	144	144	143	143
37	151	150	149	149	149	149	148	148	148	148	147	147	146	145
38	154	153	152	152	152	151	151	151	151	150	150	150	149	148

Note. The subtest combinations are as follows:

C2 = I + CD[a]
    BD + CD[b]
    A + PC[a]
    PC + CD[a,b]
    CD + MR[b]

C3 = I + PC[a]
C4 = I + BD[c]
    MR + PC[a,b]

C5 = V + BD[c]
C6 = C + MR[c]
    PC + BD[b]
C7 = I + MR[a,c]

C8 = S + MR[c]
    V + MR[c]
C9 = S + A[c]
    DS + LN[d]

C10 = A + MR[e]
C11 = V + A[c]
    BD + MR[b]
C12 = I + A

C13 = CD + SS[e]
C14 = I + S[a]
C15 = V + I[c]
    V + S[c]

Abbreviations: V = Vocabulary, S = Similarities, A = Arithmetic, DS = Digit Span, I = Information, C = Comprehension, LN = Letter–Number Sequencing, PC = Picture Completion, CD = Digit Symbol—Coding, BD = Block Design, MR = Matrix Reasoning, PA = Picture Arrangement, SS = Symbol Search.

    Reliability and validity coefficients associated with each short-form combination are shown in Table C-15. See Table D-11 in Appendix D for an explanation of the procedure used to obtain the estimated IQs.

[a]This combination is useful for a rapid screening.
[b]This combination is useful for individuals who are hearing impaired.
[c]This combination is one of the 10 best 2-subtest short forms.
[d]This combination provides an estimate of the Working Memory factor.
[e]This combination provides an estimate of the Processing Speed factor.

Table C-18
Estimated WAIS–III Full Scale IQs for Sum of Scaled Scores for 10 Best 3-Subtest Short Forms and Other Combinations

Sum of scaled scores	Combination																
	C2	C3	C4	C5	C6	C7	C8	C9	C10	C11	C12	C13	C14	C15	C16	C17	C18
3	43	43	43	44	45	45	45	46	47	47	47	47	47	48	48	48	51
4	45	45	45	46	47	47	47	48	49	49	49	49	49	49	50	50	52
5	47	47	47	48	49	49	49	50	51	51	51	51	51	51	52	52	54
6	49	49	49	50	51	51	51	52	53	53	53	53	53	53	54	54	56
7	51	51	52	52	53	53	53	54	55	55	55	55	55	55	56	56	58
8	53	54	54	54	55	55	55	56	57	57	57	57	57	57	57	57	60
9	55	56	56	56	57	57	57	58	59	59	59	59	59	59	59	59	62
10	58	58	58	59	59	59	59	60	61	61	61	61	61	61	61	61	63
11	60	60	60	61	61	61	61	62	63	63	63	63	63	63	63	63	65
12	62	62	62	63	63	63	63	64	65	65	65	65	65	65	65	65	67
13	64	64	64	65	65	65	65	66	67	67	67	67	67	67	67	67	69
14	66	66	66	67	67	67	67	68	68	69	69	69	69	69	69	69	71
15	68	68	68	69	69	69	69	70	70	71	71	71	71	71	71	71	73
16	70	70	71	71	71	71	71	72	72	73	73	73	73	73	73	73	74
17	72	73	73	73	73	73	73	74	74	74	75	75	75	75	75	75	76
18	75	75	75	75	75	75	76	76	76	76	76	77	77	77	77	77	78
19	77	77	77	77	77	78	78	78	78	78	78	78	79	79	79	79	80
20	79	79	79	79	79	80	80	80	80	80	80	80	80	81	81	81	82
21	81	81	81	81	82	82	82	82	82	82	82	82	82	83	83	83	84
22	83	83	83	83	84	84	84	84	84	84	84	84	84	84	85	85	85
23	85	85	85	85	86	86	86	86	86	86	86	86	86	86	86	86	87
24	87	87	87	88	88	88	88	88	88	88	88	88	88	88	88	88	89
25	89	89	89	90	90	90	90	90	90	90	90	90	90	90	90	90	91
26	92	92	92	92	92	92	92	92	92	92	92	92	92	92	92	92	93
27	94	94	94	94	94	94	94	94	94	94	94	94	94	94	94	94	95
28	96	96	96	96	96	96	96	96	96	96	96	96	96	96	96	96	96
29	98	98	98	98	98	98	98	98	98	98	98	98	98	98	98	98	98
30	100	100	100	100	100	100	100	100	100	100	100	100	100	100	100	100	100
31	102	102	102	102	102	102	102	102	102	102	102	102	102	102	102	102	102
32	104	104	104	104	104	104	104	104	104	104	104	104	104	104	104	104	104
33	106	106	106	106	106	106	106	106	106	106	106	106	106	106	106	106	105
34	108	108	108	108	108	108	108	108	108	108	108	108	108	108	108	108	107
35	111	111	111	110	110	110	110	110	110	110	110	110	110	110	110	110	109
36	113	113	113	112	112	112	112	112	112	112	112	112	112	112	112	112	111
37	115	115	115	115	114	114	114	114	114	114	114	114	114	114	114	114	113
38	117	117	117	117	116	116	116	116	116	116	116	116	116	116	115	115	115
39	119	119	119	119	118	118	118	118	118	118	118	118	118	118	117	117	116
40	121	121	121	121	121	120	120	120	120	120	120	120	120	119	119	119	118
41	123	123	123	123	123	122	122	122	122	122	122	122	121	121	121	121	120
42	125	125	125	125	125	125	124	124	124	124	124	123	123	123	123	123	122
43	128	127	127	127	127	127	127	126	126	126	125	125	125	125	125	125	124
44	130	130	129	129	129	129	129	128	128	127	127	127	127	127	127	127	126
45	132	132	132	131	131	131	131	130	130	129	129	129	129	129	129	129	127
46	134	134	134	133	133	133	133	132	132	131	131	131	131	131	131	131	129
47	136	136	136	135	135	135	135	134	133	133	133	133	133	133	133	133	131
48	138	138	138	137	137	137	137	136	135	135	135	135	135	135	135	135	133
49	140	140	140	139	139	139	139	138	137	137	137	137	137	137	137	137	135

(Continued)

Table C-18 (*Continued*)

Sum of scaled scores	Combination																
	C2	C3	C4	C5	C6	C7	C8	C9	C10	C11	C12	C13	C14	C15	C16	C17	C18
50	142	142	142	141	141	141	141	140	139	139	139	139	139	139	139	139	137
51	145	144	144	144	143	143	143	142	141	141	141	141	141	141	141	141	138
52	147	146	146	146	145	145	145	144	143	143	143	143	143	143	143	143	140
53	149	149	148	148	147	147	147	146	145	145	145	145	145	145	144	144	142
54	151	151	151	150	149	149	149	148	147	147	147	147	147	147	146	146	144
55	153	153	153	152	151	151	151	150	149	149	149	149	149	149	148	148	146
56	155	155	155	154	153	153	153	152	151	151	151	151	151	151	150	150	148
57	157	157	157	156	155	155	155	154	153	153	153	153	153	152	152	152	149

Note. The subtest combinations are as follows:

C2 = PC + CD + MR[a]
C3 = I + CD + MR[b]
C4 = PC + CD + BD[a]
C5 = CD + BD + MR[a]
C6 = I + PC + MR[b]
    V + A + PC[c]
C7 = A + I + PC[b]
C8 = I + S + DS
C9 = PC + BD + MR[b]
    V + A + BD[c]
    V + A + PA[c]
    A + DS + LN[d]

C10 = V + A + MR[c]
C11 = A + I + MR[b]
C12 = V + I + BD[c]
C13 = S + I + MR[c]
C14 = V + S + BD[c]
C15 = V + C + MR[c]
C16 = V + I + MR[c]
C17 = V + S + MR[c]
C18 = V + S + I[e]

Abbreviations: V = Vocabulary, S = Similarities, A = Arithmetic, DS = Digit Span, I = Information, C = Comprehension, LN = Letter–Number Sequencing, PC = Picture Completion, CD = Digit Symbol—Coding, BD = Block Design, MR = Matrix Reasoning, PA = Picture Arrangement, SS = Symbol Search.

Reliability and validity coefficients associated with each short-form combination are shown in Table C-15. See Table D-11 in Appendix D for an explanation of the procedure used to obtain the estimated IQs.

[a]This combination is useful for a rapid screening.
[b]This combination is useful for individuals who are hearing impaired. It also represents the subtests in the Perceptual Organization Index.
[c]This combination is one of the 10 best 3-subtest short forms.
[d]This combination represents the subtests in the Working Memory Index.
[e]This combination represents the subtests in the Verbal Comprehension Index.

Table C-19
Estimated WAIS–III Full Scale IQs for Sum of Scaled Scores for 10 Best 4-Subtest Short Forms and Other Combinations

Sum of scaled scores	Combination															
	C2	C3	C4	C5	C6	C7	C8	C9	C10	C11	C12	C13	C14	C15	C16	C17
4	41	41	42	42	42	43	43	43	44	44	44	44	45	45	46	46
5	42	43	44	44	44	44	45	45	45	45	46	46	46	47	47	48
6	44	44	45	45	46	46	46	47	47	47	47	48	48	48	49	49
7	46	46	47	47	47	48	48	48	48	48	49	49	49	50	50	51
8	47	48	48	49	49	49	50	50	50	50	50	51	51	51	52	52
9	49	49	50	50	50	51	51	51	51	51	52	52	52	53	53	54
10	50	51	52	52	52	52	53	53	53	53	54	54	54	54	55	55
11	52	53	53	53	54	54	54	54	55	55	55	55	55	56	56	57
12	54	54	55	55	55	56	56	56	56	56	57	57	57	57	58	58
13	55	56	56	57	57	57	57	58	58	58	58	58	58	59	59	60
14	57	58	58	58	58	59	59	59	59	59	60	60	60	61	61	61
15	59	59	60	60	60	60	61	61	61	61	61	61	62	62	62	63
16	60	61	61	61	62	62	62	62	62	62	63	63	63	64	64	64
17	62	62	63	63	63	63	64	64	64	64	64	65	65	65	65	66
18	64	64	64	65	65	65	65	65	65	66	66	66	66	67	67	67
19	65	66	66	66	66	67	67	67	67	67	68	68	68	68	68	69
20	67	67	68	68	68	68	68	69	69	69	69	69	69	70	70	70
21	69	69	69	69	70	70	70	70	70	70	71	71	71	71	71	72
22	70	71	71	71	71	71	72	72	72	72	72	72	72	73	73	73
23	72	72	73	73	73	73	73	73	73	73	74	74	74	74	74	75
24	74	74	74	74	74	75	75	75	75	75	75	75	75	76	76	76
25	75	76	76	76	76	76	76	76	76	77	77	77	77	77	77	78
26	77	77	77	78	78	78	78	78	78	78	78	78	78	79	79	79
27	79	79	79	79	79	79	80	80	80	80	80	80	80	80	80	81
28	80	80	81	81	81	81	81	81	81	81	81	81	82	82	82	82
29	82	82	82	82	82	83	83	83	83	83	83	83	83	83	83	84
30	83	84	84	84	84	84	84	84	84	84	85	85	85	85	85	85
31	85	85	85	86	86	86	86	86	86	86	86	86	86	86	86	87
32	87	87	87	87	87	87	87	87	87	87	88	88	88	88	88	88
33	88	89	89	89	89	89	89	89	89	89	89	89	89	89	89	90
34	90	90	90	90	90	90	91	91	91	91	91	91	91	91	91	91
35	92	92	92	92	92	92	92	92	92	92	92	92	92	92	92	93
36	93	93	94	94	94	94	94	94	94	94	94	94	94	94	94	94
37	95	95	95	95	95	95	95	95	95	95	95	95	95	95	95	96
38	97	97	97	97	97	97	97	97	97	97	97	97	97	97	97	97
39	98	98	98	98	98	98	98	98	98	98	98	98	98	98	98	99
40	100	100	100	100	100	100	100	100	100	100	100	100	100	100	100	100
41	102	102	102	102	102	102	102	102	102	102	102	102	102	102	102	101
42	103	103	103	103	103	103	103	103	103	103	103	103	103	103	103	103
43	105	105	105	105	105	105	105	105	105	105	105	105	105	105	105	104
44	107	107	106	106	106	106	106	106	106	106	106	106	106	106	106	106
45	108	108	108	108	108	108	108	108	108	108	108	108	108	108	108	107
46	110	110	110	110	110	110	109	109	109	109	109	109	109	109	109	109
47	112	111	111	111	111	111	111	111	111	111	111	111	111	111	111	110
48	113	113	113	113	113	113	113	113	113	113	112	112	112	112	112	112
49	115	115	115	114	114	114	114	114	114	114	114	114	114	114	114	113

(Continued)

Table C-19 (*Continued*)

Sum of scaled scores	Combination															
	C2	C3	C4	C5	C6	C7	C8	C9	C10	C11	C12	C13	C14	C15	C16	C17
50	117	116	116	116	116	116	116	116	116	116	115	115	115	115	115	115
51	118	118	118	118	118	117	117	117	117	117	117	117	117	117	117	116
52	120	120	119	119	119	119	119	119	119	119	119	119	118	118	118	118
53	121	121	121	121	121	121	120	120	120	120	120	120	120	120	120	119
54	123	123	123	122	122	122	122	122	122	122	122	122	122	121	123	121
55	125	124	124	124	124	124	124	124	124	123	123	123	123	123	124	122
56	126	126	126	126	126	125	125	125	125	125	125	125	125	124	126	124
57	128	128	127	127	127	127	127	127	127	127	126	126	126	126	127	125
58	130	129	129	129	129	129	128	128	128	128	128	128	128	127	129	127
59	131	131	131	131	130	130	130	130	130	130	129	129	129	129	130	128
60	133	133	132	132	132	132	132	131	131	131	131	131	131	130	132	130
61	135	134	134	134	134	133	133	133	133	133	132	132	132	132	133	131
62	136	136	136	135	135	135	135	135	135	134	134	134	134	133	135	133
63	138	138	137	137	137	137	136	136	136	136	136	135	135	135	136	134
64	140	139	139	139	138	138	138	138	138	138	137	137	137	136	138	136
65	141	141	140	140	140	140	139	139	139	139	139	139	138	138	139	137
66	143	142	142	142	142	141	141	141	141	141	140	140	140	139	141	139
67	145	144	144	143	143	143	143	142	142	142	142	142	142	141	142	140
68	146	146	145	145	145	144	144	144	144	144	143	143	143	143	144	142
69	148	147	147	147	146	146	146	146	145	145	145	145	145	144	145	143
70	150	149	148	148	148	148	147	147	147	147	146	146	146	146	147	145
71	151	151	150	150	150	149	149	149	149	149	148	148	148	147	148	146
72	153	152	152	151	151	151	150	150	150	150	150	149	149	149	150	148
73	154	154	153	153	153	152	152	152	152	152	151	151	151	150	151	149
74	156	156	155	155	154	154	154	153	153	153	153	152	152	152	153	151
75	158	157	156	156	156	156	155	155	155	155	154	154	154	153	154	152
76	159	159	158	158	158	157	157	157	156	156	156	156	155	155	156	154

Note. The subtest combinations are as follows:

C2 = DS + I + PC + MR[a]

C3 = A + I + PC + CD[a]

C4 = PC + CD + BD + MR[b]

C5 = A + S + CD + LN

C6 = MR + PC + CD + SS

C7 = V + DS + I + BD[c]

    A + I + CD + MR[a]

C8 = I + A + PC + BD

C9 = V + A + PC + MR[c]

C10 = A + I + PC + MR[a]

C11 = V + A + BD + PA[c]

C12 = I + A + DS + S

C13 = V + I + PC + MR[c]

C14 = V + S + A + PC[c]

C15 = V + I + BD + MR[c]

    V + S + A + PA[c]

C16 = V + S + A + BD[c]

    V + A + I + BD[c]

C17 = V + S + A + MR[c]

Abbreviations: V = Vocabulary, S = Similarities, A = Arithmetic, DS = Digit Span, I = Information, C = Comprehension, LN = Letter–Number Sequencing, PC = Picture Completion, CD = Digit Symbol—Coding, BD = Block Design, MR = Matrix Reasoning, PA = Picture Arrangement, SS = Symbol Search.

Reliability and validity coefficients associated with each short-form combination are shown in Table C-15. See Table D-11 in Appendix D for an explanation of the procedure used to obtain the estimated IQs.

[a]This combination is useful for a rapid screening.

[b]This combination is useful for individuals who are hearing impaired.

[c]This combination is one of the 10 best 4-subtest short forms.

Table C-20
Estimated WAIS–III Full Scale IQs for Sum of Scaled Scores for 10 Best 5-Subtest Short Forms and Other Combinations

Sum of scaled scores	Combination										
	C2	C3	C4	C5	C6	C7	C8	C9	C10	C11	C12
5	38	39	41	41	41	42	43	43	43	44	44
6	40	40	42	42	43	43	45	45	45	45	45
7	41	42	43	43	44	45	46	46	46	46	46
8	42	43	45	45	45	46	47	47	47	47	48
9	44	44	46	46	46	47	48	48	48	49	49
10	45	46	47	47	48	49	50	50	50	50	50
11	46	47	49	49	49	50	51	51	51	51	51
12	48	48	50	50	50	51	52	52	52	52	53
13	49	50	51	51	52	52	53	53	54	54	54
14	51	51	52	53	53	54	55	55	55	55	55
15	52	52	54	54	54	55	56	56	56	56	56
16	53	54	55	55	56	56	57	57	57	57	58
17	55	55	56	57	57	58	58	59	59	59	59
18	56	57	58	58	58	59	60	60	60	60	60
19	57	58	59	59	59	60	61	61	61	61	61
20	59	59	60	61	61	61	62	62	62	62	63
21	60	61	62	62	62	63	63	64	64	64	64
22	62	62	63	63	63	64	65	65	65	65	65
23	63	63	64	64	65	65	66	66	66	66	66
24	64	65	66	66	66	67	67	67	67	67	68
25	66	66	67	67	67	68	68	69	69	69	69
26	67	67	68	68	69	69	70	70	70	70	70
27	68	69	70	70	70	70	71	71	71	71	71
28	70	70	71	71	71	72	72	72	72	72	73
29	71	71	72	72	73	73	74	74	74	74	74
30	73	73	74	74	74	74	75	75	75	75	75
31	74	74	75	75	75	76	76	76	76	76	76
32	75	76	76	76	76	77	77	77	77	77	78
33	77	77	78	78	78	78	79	79	79	79	79
34	78	78	79	79	79	79	80	80	80	80	80
35	79	80	80	80	80	81	81	81	81	81	81
36	81	81	82	82	82	82	82	82	82	82	83
37	82	82	83	83	83	83	84	84	84	84	84
38	84	84	84	84	84	85	85	85	85	85	85
39	85	85	85	86	86	86	86	86	86	86	86
40	86	86	87	87	87	87	87	87	87	87	88
41	88	88	88	88	88	88	89	89	89	89	89
42	89	89	89	89	90	90	90	90	90	90	90
43	90	90	91	91	91	91	91	91	91	91	91
44	92	92	92	92	92	92	92	92	92	92	93
45	93	93	93	93	93	94	94	94	94	94	94
46	95	95	95	95	95	95	95	95	95	95	95
47	96	96	96	96	96	96	96	96	96	96	96
48	97	97	97	97	97	97	97	97	97	97	98
49	99	99	99	99	99	99	99	99	99	99	99
50	100	100	100	100	100	100	100	100	100	100	100
51	101	101	101	101	101	101	101	101	101	101	101
52	103	103	103	103	103	103	103	103	103	103	102
53	104	104	104	104	104	104	104	104	104	104	104
54	105	105	105	105	105	105	105	105	105	105	105

(Continued)

Table C-20 (*Continued*)

Sum of scaled scores	Combination										
	C2	C3	C4	C5	C6	C7	C8	C9	C10	C11	C12
55	107	107	107	107	107	106	106	106	106	106	106
56	108	108	108	108	108	108	108	108	108	108	107
57	110	110	109	109	109	109	109	109	109	109	109
58	111	111	111	111	110	110	110	110	110	110	110
59	112	112	112	112	112	112	111	111	111	111	111
60	114	114	113	113	113	113	113	113	113	113	112
61	115	115	115	114	114	114	114	114	114	114	114
62	116	116	116	116	116	115	115	115	115	115	115
63	118	118	117	117	117	117	116	116	116	116	116
64	119	119	118	118	118	118	118	118	118	118	117
65	121	120	120	120	120	119	119	119	119	119	119
66	122	122	121	121	121	121	120	120	120	120	120
67	123	123	122	122	122	122	121	121	121	121	121
68	125	124	124	124	124	123	123	123	123	123	122
69	126	126	125	125	125	124	124	124	124	124	124
70	127	127	126	126	126	126	125	125	125	125	125
71	129	129	128	128	127	127	126	126	126	126	126
72	130	130	129	129	129	128	128	128	128	128	127
73	132	131	130	130	130	130	129	129	129	129	129
74	133	133	132	132	131	131	130	130	130	130	130
75	134	134	133	133	133	132	132	131	131	131	131
76	136	135	134	134	134	133	133	133	133	133	132
77	137	137	136	136	135	135	134	134	134	134	134
78	138	138	137	137	137	136	135	135	135	135	135
79	140	139	138	138	138	137	137	136	136	136	136
80	141	141	140	139	139	139	138	138	138	138	137
81	143	142	141	141	141	140	139	139	139	139	139
82	144	143	142	142	142	141	140	140	140	140	140
83	145	145	144	143	143	142	142	141	141	141	141
84	147	146	145	145	144	144	143	143	143	143	142
85	148	148	146	146	146	145	144	144	144	144	144
86	149	149	148	147	147	146	145	145	145	145	145
87	151	150	149	149	148	148	147	147	146	146	146
88	152	152	150	150	150	149	148	148	148	148	147
89	154	153	151	151	151	150	149	149	149	149	149
90	155	154	153	153	152	151	150	150	150	150	150
91	156	156	154	154	154	153	152	152	152	151	151
92	158	157	155	155	155	154	153	153	153	153	152
93	159	158	157	157	156	155	154	154	154	154	154
94	160	160	158	158	157	157	155	155	155	155	155

Note. The subtest combinations are as follows:
C2 = DS + I + PC + CD + MR[a]
C3 = A + DS + I + PC + CD[a]
C4 = A + I + PC + CD + MR[a]
C5 = A + DS + I + PC + MR[a]
C6 = V + DS + I + PC + MR[b]
C7 = V + I + CD + BD + MR[b]
　　 V + DS + I + BD + MR[b]
C8 = V + A + C + PC + MR[b]
　　 V + A + I + PC + BD[b]
C9 = V + A + C + BD + PA[b]
C10 = V + S + A + PC + MR[b]
C11 = V + A + I + PC + MR[b]
　　 V + S + A + BD + PA[b]
C12 = V + A + I + BD + PA[b]

Abbreviations: V = Vocabulary, S = Similarities, A = Arithmetic, DS = Digit Span, I = Information, C = Comprehension, LN = Letter–Number Sequencing, PC = Picture Completion, CD = Digit Symbol—Coding, BD = Block Design, MR = Matrix Reasoning, PA = Picture Arrangement, SS = Symbol Search.

Reliability and validity coefficients associated with each short-form combination are shown in Table C-15. See Table D-11 in Appendix D for an explanation of the procedure used to obtain the estimated IQs.

[a]This combination is useful for a rapid screening.
[b]This combination is one of the 10 best 5-subtest short forms.

Table C-21
Estimated WAIS–III Full Scale IQs for Sum of Scaled Scores for One 6-Subtest Short Form and Two 7-Subtest Short Forms

Sum of scaled scores	Combination			Sum of scaled scores	Combination			Sum of scaled scores	Combination			Sum of scaled scores	Combination		
	C2	C3	C4		C2	C3	C4		C2	C3	C4		C2	C3	C4
6	43	—	—	41	80	72	72	76	117	106	106	111	154	140	140
7	44	39	39	42	81	73	73	77	118	107	107	112	155	141	141
8	45	40	40	43	82	74	74	78	119	108	108	113	156	142	142
9	46	41	41	44	83	75	75	79	120	109	109	114	157	143	143
10	48	42	42	45	84	76	76	80	121	110	110	115	158	144	144
11	49	42	43	46	85	77	77	81	122	111	111	116		145	145
12	50	43	44	47	86	78	78	82	123	112	112	117		146	146
13	51	44	45	48	87	79	79	83	124	113	113	118		147	147
14	52	45	46	49	88	80	80	84	125	114	114	119		148	148
15	53	46	47	50	90	81	81	85	126	115	115	120		149	149
16	54	47	48	51	91	81	82	86	127	116	116	121		150	149
17	55	48	49	52	92	82	83	87	128	117	116	122		151	150
18	56	49	50	53	93	83	84	88	129	118	117	123		152	151
19	57	50	51	54	94	84	84	89	130	119	118	124		153	152
20	58	51	51	55	95	85	85	90	131	119	119	125		154	153
21	59	52	52	56	96	86	86	91	133	120	120	126		155	154
22	60	53	53	57	97	87	87	92	134	121	121	127		156	155
23	61	54	54	58	98	88	88	93	135	122	122	128		157	156
24	62	55	55	59	99	89	89	94	136	123	123	129		158	157
25	63	56	56	60	100	90	90	95	137	124	124	130		158	158
26	64	57	57	61	101	91	91	96	138	125	125	131		159	159
27	65	58	58	62	102	92	92	97	139	126	126	132		160	160
28	66	59	59	63	103	93	93	98	140	127	127	133		161	161
29	67	60	60	64	104	94	94	99	141	128	128				
30	69	61	61	65	105	95	95	100	142	129	129				
31	70	62	62	66	106	96	96	101	143	130	130				
32	71	63	63	67	107	97	97	102	144	131	131				
33	72	64	64	68	108	98	98	103	145	132	132				
34	73	65	65	69	109	99	99	104	146	133	133				
35	74	66	66	70	110	100	100	105	147	134	134				
36	75	67	67	71	112	101	101	106	148	135	135				
37	76	68	68	72	113	102	102	107	149	136	136				
38	77	69	69	73	114	103	103	108	150	137	137				
39	78	70	70	74	115	104	104	109	151	138	138				
40	79	71	71	75	116	105	105	110	152	139	139				

Note. The subtest combinations are as follows:

C2 = V + S + I + PC + BD + MR[a]
C3 = I + A + DS + S + PC + BD + CD[b]
C4 = I + A + DS + S + PC + MR + CD[c]

Abbreviations: V = Vocabulary, S = Similarities, A = Arithmetic, DS = Digit Span, I = Information, PC = Picture Completion, CD = Digit Symbol—Coding, BD = Block Design, MR = Matrix Reasoning.

See Table D-11 in Appendix D for an explanation of the procedure used to obtain the estimated IQs.
[a]The reliability and validity of this combination are r_{xx} = .966 and r = .946, respectively.
[b]The reliability and validity of this combination are r_{xx} = .965 and r = .942, respectively.
[c]The reliability and validity of this combination are r_{xx} = .967 and r = .944, respectively.

Table C-22
Administrative Checklist for the WAIS–III

ADMINISTRATIVE CHECKLIST FOR THE WAIS–III

Name of examiner: _____   Date: _____

Name of individual: _____   Name of observer: _____

(Note: If an item is not applicable, mark NA to the left of the number.)

Before Beginning   Circle One

1. Room is well lit   Yes   No
2. Furniture is comfortable and size is appropri-
    ate for individual   Yes   No
3. Room is free of distractions   Yes   No
4. Positions individual correctly   Yes   No
5. Sits directly across from individual   Yes   No
6. Establishes rapport   Yes   No
7. Tells individual that breaks are OK and to let
    examiner know when he or she needs a break   Yes   No
8. Does not prolong getting-acquainted period   Yes   No
9. Avoids use of term *intelligence* when
    introducing test   Yes   No
10. Responds truthfully to any questions indi-
    vidual has about purpose of testing   Yes   No
11. Keeps test materials in order   Yes   No
12. Keeps test kit out of individual's view   Yes   No
13. Begins test when rapport has been established   Yes   No
14. Positions Record Form and Administration
    Manual so that individual cannot read ques-
    tions or answers   Yes   No
15. Introduces test by reading directions in
    Administration Manual verbatim   Yes   No

Comments

_____

_____

_____

Picture Completion
(See pp. 520–521 in text for detailed information.)

Background Considerations

1. Reads directions verbatim   Yes   No
2. Reads directions clearly   Yes   No
3. Reads items verbatim   Yes   No
4. Reads items clearly   Yes   No
5. Repeats directions correctly   Yes   No
6. Places Stimulus Booklet properly   Yes   No
7. Opens Stimulus Booklet correctly   Yes   No
8. Allows 20 seconds for each item   Yes   No
9. Shortens or eliminates directions correctly   Yes   No
10. Begins timing correctly   Yes   No
11. Stops timing correctly   Yes   No
12. For items 6 and 7, gives correct answers, if
    needed   Yes   No

Picture Completion (*Continued*)   Circle One

13. For items 8 to 25, does not give individual
    correct answers   Yes   No
14. Prompts or queries specific responses only
    once during subtest   Yes   No
15. Queries ambiguous or incomplete responses
    correctly   Yes   No

Starting Considerations

16. Starts with appropriate item   Yes   No

Reverse Sequence

17. Administers items in reverse sequence
    correctly   Yes   No

Discontinue Considerations

18. Counts items administered in reverse
    sequence toward discontinue criterion   Yes   No
19. Discontinues subtest correctly   Yes   No
20. Removes Stimulus Booklet from individual's
    view once subtest is completed   Yes   No

Scoring Guidelines

21. Scores items correctly   Yes   No

Record Form

22. Records individual's responses in Response
    column correctly   Yes   No
23. Records PC for correct pointing responses   Yes   No
24. Records PX for incorrect pointing responses   Yes   No
25. Enters score in Score column correctly   Yes   No
26. Notes additional points correctly   Yes   No
27. Adds points correctly   Yes   No
28. Enters Total Raw Score in shaded box
    correctly   Yes   No

Comments

_____

_____

_____

Vocabulary
(See pp. 522–523 in text for detailed information.)

Background Considerations

1. Reads directions verbatim   Yes   No
2. Reads directions clearly   Yes   No

(Continued)

Table C-22 (Continued)

Vocabulary (Continued)	Circle One	
3. Shortens directions correctly	Yes	No
4. Places Stimulus Booklet properly and points to appropriate word correctly	Yes	No
5. Pronounces words clearly and correctly	Yes	No
6. Repeats directions correctly	Yes	No
7. Repeats items correctly	Yes	No
8. In cases of suspected hearing deficit, queries appropriately	Yes	No
9. Queries correctly when individual gives multiple responses of varying quality	Yes	No
10. Grants additional time appropriately	Yes	No
11. Queries unclear or vague responses correctly	Yes	No

Starting Considerations

	Circle One	
12. Starts with appropriate item	Yes	No

Reverse Sequence

	Circle One	
13. Administers items in reverse sequence correctly	Yes	No

Discontinue Considerations

	Circle One	
14. Counts items administered in reverse sequence toward discontinue criterion	Yes	No
15. Discontinues subtest correctly	Yes	No
16. Removes Stimulus Booklet from individual's view once subtest is completed	Yes	No

Scoring Guidelines

	Circle One	
17. Scores responses correctly	Yes	No

Record Form

	Circle One	
18. Records individual's responses correctly	Yes	No
19. Enters score in Score column correctly	Yes	No
20. Notes additional points correctly	Yes	No
21. Adds points correctly	Yes	No
22. Enters Total Raw Score in shaded box correctly	Yes	No

Comments

_____

_____

_____

Digit Symbol—Coding
(See pp. 526–527 in text for detailed information.)

Background Considerations

	Circle One	
1. Provides smooth working surface	Yes	No
2. Reads directions verbatim	Yes	No
3. Reads directions clearly	Yes	No
4. Repeats directions correctly	Yes	No
5. Points to key while reading directions	Yes	No
6. Waits until individual understands task before proceeding with items	Yes	No
7. Uses stopwatch	Yes	No
8. Places stopwatch correctly	Yes	No

Digit Symbol—Coding (Continued)	Circle One	
9. Times correctly	Yes	No
10. Notes individual's handedness on Record Form	Yes	No
11. Positions Response Booklet properly for left-handed individual	Yes	No
12. Demonstrates sample correctly	Yes	No
13. Gives individual number 2 pencil without eraser	Yes	No
14. Does not provide or allow individual to use eraser	Yes	No
15. Corrects individual's mistakes correctly	Yes	No
16. Does not start the subtest until individual understands task	Yes	No
17. Gives appropriate responses to inquiries and appropriate prompts	Yes	No
18. Counts time for prompts as part of 120-second time limit	Yes	No
19. Allows spontaneous corrections, unless corrections impede performance	Yes	No

Starting Considerations

	Circle One	
20. Starts with appropriate item	Yes	No

Discontinue Considerations

	Circle One	
21. Discontinues subtest correctly	Yes	No
22. Stops timing if individual finishes before 120 seconds	Yes	No
23. Says "Stop" after 120 seconds and discontinues subtest	Yes	No
24. Closes Response Booklet and removes it from individual's view once subtest is completed	Yes	No
25. If Digit Symbol—Incidental Learning will be administered and individual has not completed four rows within 120 seconds, allows additional time	Yes	No

Scoring Guidelines

	Circle One	
26. Scores subtest correctly	Yes	No

Record Form

	Circle One	
27. Records completion time correctly	Yes	No
28. Enters Total Raw Score in shaded box correctly	Yes	No

Comments

_____

_____

_____

Similarities
(See pp. 529–530 in text for detailed information.)

Background Considerations

	Circle One	
1. Reads directions verbatim	Yes	No
2. Reads directions clearly	Yes	No

(Continued)

Table C-22 (*Continued*)

Similarities (*Continued*)	Circle One	
3. Reads items verbatim	Yes	No
4. Reads items clearly	Yes	No
5. Repeats directions correctly	Yes	No
6. Repeats items correctly	Yes	No
7. Queries correctly	Yes	No
8. Grants additional time appropriately	Yes	No

Starting Considerations

9. Starts with appropriate item	Yes	No

Reverse Sequence

10. Administers items in reverse sequence correctly	Yes	No

Discontinue Considerations

11. Counts items administered in reverse sequence toward discontinue criterion	Yes	No
12. Discontinues subtest correctly	Yes	No

Scoring Guidelines

13. Scores responses correctly	Yes	No

Record Form

14. Records individual's responses correctly	Yes	No
15. Enters score in Score column correctly	Yes	No
16. Notes additional points correctly	Yes	No
17. Adds points correctly	Yes	No
18. Enters Total Raw Score in shaded box correctly	Yes	No

Comments

_____

_____

_____

Block Design

(See pp. 532–534 in text for detailed information.)

Background Considerations

1. Clears table	Yes	No
2. Seats individual directly in front of table	Yes	No
3. Reads directions verbatim	Yes	No
4. Reads directions clearly	Yes	No
5. Uses stopwatch	Yes	No
6. Places stopwatch correctly	Yes	No
7. Repeats directions correctly	Yes	No
8. Shows different sides of block correctly while reading directions	Yes	No
9. Gives individual number of blocks needed for each item	Yes	No
10. Disassembles models correctly	Yes	No
11. Places intact model or Stimulus Booklet and blocks properly	Yes	No
12. Turns pages of Stimulus Booklet correctly	Yes	No
13. Uses blocks and/or pictures as models correctly	Yes	No

Block Design (*Continued*)	Circle One	
14. Leaves model intact for items 1 to 5	Yes	No
15. Scrambles blocks between designs	Yes	No
16. Removes all unnecessary blocks from individual's view	Yes	No
17. Does not permit individual to rotate Stimulus Booklet	Yes	No
18. Times correctly	Yes	No
19. Constructs designs for items 1 and 2 correctly	Yes	No
20. Constructs designs for items 3 to 5 correctly	Yes	No
21. If individual rotates or reverses a design, gives appropriate instruction one time only	Yes	No
22. Administers trials correctly	Yes	No

Starting Considerations

23. Starts with appropriate item	Yes	No

Reverse Sequence

24. Administers items in reverse sequence correctly	Yes	No

Discontinue Considerations

25. Counts items administered in reverse sequence toward discontinue criterion	Yes	No
26. Discontinues subtest correctly	Yes	No
27. Removes Stimulus Booklet and blocks from individual's view once subtest is completed	Yes	No

Scoring Guidelines

28. Scores items correctly	Yes	No

Record Form

29. Records completion time in Completion Time in Seconds column correctly	Yes	No
30. Notes or sketches incorrect designs in Incorrect Design column correctly	Yes	No
31. Notes rotations and the amount of rotation in Incorrect Design column correctly	Yes	No
32. Circles Y or N in Correct Design column correctly	Yes	No
33. Circles appropriate number in Score column	Yes	No
34. Notes additional points correctly	Yes	No
35. Enters Total Raw Score in shaded box correctly	Yes	No

Comments

_____

_____

_____

Arithmetic

(See pp. 536–537 in text for detailed information.)

Background Considerations

1. Reads directions verbatim	Yes	No
2. Reads directions clearly	Yes	No
3. Repeats directions correctly	Yes	No

Table C-22 (*Continued*)

Arithmetic (*Continued*)	Circle One	
4. Repeats items correctly	Yes	No
5. Times correctly	Yes	No
6. Does not allow individual to use pencil and paper	Yes	No
7. Allows individual to use finger to "write" on table	Yes	No
8. When it is not clear which of two responses is final choice, gives appropriate prompt	Yes	No

Starting Considerations

9. Starts with appropriate item	Yes	No

Reverse Sequence

10. Administers items in reverse sequence correctly	Yes	No

Discontinue Considerations

11. Counts items administered in reverse sequence toward discontinue criterion	Yes	No
12. Discontinues subtest correctly	Yes	No

Scoring Guidelines

13. Scores items correctly	Yes	No

Record Form

14. Records individual's responses in Response column correctly	Yes	No
15. Records completion time in Completion Time in Seconds column correctly	Yes	No
16. For items 1 to 18, enters score in Score column correctly	Yes	No
17. For item 19, circles 0, 1, or 2 in Score column correctly	Yes	No
18. For item 20, circles 0, 1, or 2 in Score column correctly	Yes	No
19. Notes additional points correctly	Yes	No
20. Adds points correctly	Yes	No
21. Enters Total Raw Score in shaded box correctly	Yes	No

Comments

_____

_____

_____

Matrix Reasoning
(See pp. 538–539 in text for detailed information.)

Background Considerations

1. Reads directions verbatim	Yes	No
2. Reads directions clearly	Yes	No
3. Places Stimulus Booklet properly	Yes	No
4. Clarifies directions correctly	Yes	No
5. If individual fails any sample, demonstrates correct way to solve problem	Yes	No
6. Repeats directions correctly	Yes	No
7. Gives appropriate prompts	Yes	No

Matrix Reasoning (*Continued*)	Circle One	
8. Provides feedback only on three samples	Yes	No
9. Grants additional time appropriately	Yes	No

Starting Considerations

10. Starts with appropriate item	Yes	No

Reverse Sequence

11. Administers items in reverse sequence correctly	Yes	No

Discontinue Considerations

12. Counts items administered in reverse sequence toward discontinue criterion	Yes	No
13. Discontinues subtest correctly	Yes	No
14. Removes Stimulus Booklet from individual's view once subtest is completed	Yes	No

Scoring Guidelines

15. Scores items correctly	Yes	No

Record Form

16. Circles response number or DK correctly	Yes	No
17. Enters score in Score column correctly	Yes	No
18. Notes additional points correctly	Yes	No
19. Adds points correctly	Yes	No
20. Enters Total Raw Score in shaded box correctly	Yes	No

Comments

_____

_____

_____

Digit Span
(See pp. 540–541 in text for detailed information.)

Background Considerations

1. Reads directions verbatim	Yes	No
2. Reads directions clearly	Yes	No
3. Repeats directions correctly	Yes	No
4. Shields digits in Record Form and Administration Manual from individual's view	Yes	No
5. Reads digits clearly, at rate of one digit per second and without chunking, and drops voice slightly on last digit	Yes	No
6. Administers items correctly	Yes	No
7. Administers sample on Digits Backward correctly	Yes	No
8. Does not repeat trials	Yes	No

Starting Considerations

9. Starts with appropriate item	Yes	No

Discontinue Considerations

10. Discontinues subtest correctly	Yes	No

Scoring Guidelines

11. Scores items correctly	Yes	No

(*Continued*)

Table C-22 (*Continued*)

Digit Span (*Continued*)	Circle One	

Record Form

12. Records individual's responses correctly	Yes	No
13. Enters score in Item Score column correctly	Yes	No
14. Enters Digits Forward Total Score and Digits Backward Total Score correctly	Yes	No
15. Sums Digits Forward and Digits Backward Total Scores and enters the sum in shaded box correctly	Yes	No

Comments

_____

_____

_____

Information

(See p. 543 in text for detailed information.)

Background Considerations

1. Reads directions verbatim	Yes	No
2. Reads directions clearly	Yes	No
3. Reads items verbatim	Yes	No
4. Reads items clearly	Yes	No
5. Repeats items correctly	Yes	No
6. Repeats directions correctly	Yes	No
7. Queries correctly	Yes	No
8. For items 6 and 21, gives prompts correctly	Yes	No

Starting Considerations

9. Starts with appropriate item	Yes	No

Reverse Sequence

10. Administers items in reverse sequence correctly	Yes	No

Discontinue Considerations

11. Counts items administered in reverse sequence toward discontinue criterion	Yes	No
12. Discontinues subtest correctly	Yes	No

Scoring Guidelines

13. Scores items correctly	Yes	No

Record Form

14. Records individual's responses correctly	Yes	No
15. Enters score in Score column correctly	Yes	No
16. Notes additional points correctly	Yes	No
17. Adds points correctly	Yes	No
18. Enters Total Raw Score in shaded box correctly	Yes	No

Comments

_____

_____

_____

Picture Arrangement	Circle One	

(See p. 545 in text for detailed information.)

Background Considerations

1. Clears table	Yes	No
2. Seats individual directly in front of table	Yes	No
3. Reads directions verbatim	Yes	No
4. Reads directions clearly	Yes	No
5. Uses stopwatch	Yes	No
6. Places stopwatch correctly	Yes	No
7. Places cards correctly	Yes	No
8. Times correctly	Yes	No
9. If individual places cards from right to left, asks where story begins	Yes	No
10. Records individual's card sequences correctly	Yes	No
11. If individual fails both trials of item 1, proceeds to item 2	Yes	No

Starting Considerations

12. Starts with appropriate item	Yes	No

Discontinue Considerations

13. Discontinues subtest correctly	Yes	No

Scoring Guidelines

14. Scores items correctly	Yes	No

Record Form

15. Records individual's arrangements in Response Order column correctly	Yes	No
16. Records completion time in Completion Time in Seconds column correctly	Yes	No
17. For items 1, 5, 6, 7, 8, and 9, circles 0, 1, or 2 in Score column correctly	Yes	No
18. For items 2, 3, 4, 10, and 11, circles 0 or 2 in Score column correctly	Yes	No
19. Enters Total Raw Score in shaded box correctly	Yes	No

Comments

_____

_____

_____

Comprehension

(See pp. 547–548 in text for detailed information.)

Background Considerations

1. Reads directions verbatim	Yes	No
2. Reads directions clearly	Yes	No
3. Reads items verbatim	Yes	No
4. Reads items clearly	Yes	No
5. Repeats questions correctly	Yes	No
6. Repeats items correctly	Yes	No
7. If individual is hesitant, gives appropriate prompts	Yes	No
8. Queries correctly	Yes	No

(*Continued*)

Table C-22 (*Continued*)

Comprehension (*Continued*)	Circle One	
9. For five items noted by an asterisk, prompts individual for a second response when initial response reflects only one correct general concept	Yes	No
10. Grants additional time appropriately	Yes	No

Starting Considerations

11. Starts with appropriate item	Yes	No

Reverse Sequence

12. Administers items in reverse sequence correctly	Yes	No

Discontinue Considerations

13. Counts items administered in reverse sequence toward discontinue criterion	Yes	No
14. Discontinues subtest correctly	Yes	No

Scoring Guidelines

15. Scores items correctly	Yes	No

Record Form

16. Records responses in Response column correctly	Yes	No
17. Enters score in Score column correctly	Yes	No
18. Notes additional points correctly	Yes	No
19. Adds points correctly	Yes	No
20. Enters Total Raw Score in shaded box correctly	Yes	No

Comments

_____

_____

_____

Symbol Search
(See pp. 549–550 in text for detailed information.)

Background Considerations

1. Provides smooth working surface	Yes	No
2. Reads directions verbatim	Yes	No
3. Reads directions clearly	Yes	No
4. Repeats directions correctly	Yes	No
5. Uses stopwatch	Yes	No
6. Places stopwatch correctly	Yes	No
7. Times correctly	Yes	No
8. Gives individual number 2 pencil without eraser	Yes	No
9. Shows individual Response Booklet	Yes	No
10. Points to target symbols and array for samples while reading directions	Yes	No
11. For samples, draws diagonal line through correct box (YES or NO)	Yes	No
12. For practice items, points to target symbol and array and gives appropriate directions	Yes	No
13. Gives appropriate feedback	Yes	No

Symbol Search (*Continued*)	Circle One	
14. If individual makes an error on practice items, follows correct procedure	Yes	No
15. Explains directions using practice items, if needed	Yes	No
16. Does not proceed to test items unless individual understands task	Yes	No
17. Opens Response Booklet to page 1	Yes	No
18. Reads directions verbatim, briefly shows third and fourth pages of Response Booklet, and folds pages so that only page 1 shows	Yes	No
19. Before saying "Go," gives further explanations, if necessary	Yes	No
20. Begins timing correctly	Yes	No
21. If necessary, says, "Do the items in order"	Yes	No

Starting Considerations

22. Starts with appropriate item	Yes	No

Discontinue Considerations

23. Discontinues subtest correctly	Yes	No
24. Stops timing if individual finishes before 120 seconds	Yes	No
25. Says "Stop" after 120 seconds and discontinues subtest	Yes	No
26. Closes Response Booklet and removes it from individual's view once subtest is completed	Yes	No

Scoring Guidelines

27. Scores subtest correctly	Yes	No

Response Booklet

28. Enters identifying data on Response Booklet and circles individual's handedness	Yes	No

Record Form

29. Records completion time in Completion Time in Seconds column correctly	Yes	No
30. Enters total number of correct items in Number Correct box correctly	Yes	No
31. Enters total number of incorrect items in Number Incorrect box correctly	Yes	No
32. Subtracts number incorrect from number correct and enters score in Total Raw Score box correctly	Yes	No

Comments

_____

_____

_____

Letter–Number Sequencing
(See pp. 551–552 in text for detailed information.)

Background Considerations

1. Reads directions verbatim	Yes	No
2. Reads directions clearly	Yes	No

(*Continued*)

Table C-22 (*Continued*)

Letter–Number Sequencing (*Continued*)	Circle One
3. Repeats directions correctly	Yes No
4. Shields digits and letters in Administration Manual and on Record Form from individual's view	Yes No
5. Reads digits and letters clearly, at rate of one digit or letter per second and without chunking	Yes No
6. Drops voice slightly on last digit or letter in sequence	Yes No
7. If individual fails a practice item, repeats directions as necessary	Yes No
8. Administers all practice items	Yes No
9. If individual fails all practice items, continues with subtest	Yes No
10. Administers all three trials of each item	Yes No
11. Pauses after each sequence to allow individual to respond	Yes No
12. Does not repeat any digits or letters during subtest proper	Yes No
13. If asked to repeat a trial of an item, gives appropriate response	Yes No
14. Says nothing if individual makes a mistake on items 1 to 7	Yes No

Starting Considerations

15. Starts with appropriate item	Yes No

Discontinue Considerations

16. Discontinues subtest correctly	Yes No

Scoring Guidelines

17. Scores items correctly	Yes No

Record Form

18. Records responses of each trial in Item/Response column correctly	Yes No
19. Enters score in Trial Score column correctly	Yes No
20. Enters score in Item Score column correctly	Yes No
21. Enters Total Raw Score in shaded box correctly	Yes No

Comments

_____

_____

_____

Object Assembly
(See pp. 553–554 in text for detailed information.)

Background Considerations

1. Clears table	Yes No
2. Reads directions verbatim	Yes No
3. Reads directions clearly	Yes No
4. Uses stopwatch	Yes No
5. Places stopwatch correctly	Yes No
6. Lays out pieces for each item correctly	Yes No
7. Times correctly	Yes No

Object Assembly (*Continued*)	Circle One
8. Shields pictures of correctly assembled objects in Administration Manual from individual's view	Yes No
9. If individual turns over a piece, turns it right side up correctly	Yes No
10. Does not tell names of objects	Yes No
11. If individual fails item 1, gives help correctly	Yes No

Starting Considerations

12. Starts with appropriate item	Yes No

Discontinue Considerations

13. Discontinues subtest correctly	Yes No
14. Removes puzzle pieces from individual's view once each item is completed	Yes No

Scoring Guidelines

15. Scores items correctly	Yes No

Record Form

16. Records completion time in Completion Time in Seconds column correctly	Yes No
17. Records correct number of junctures in Number of Correct Junctures column correctly	Yes No
18. Circles 0 in Score column correctly, as appropriate	Yes No
19. Scores partially correct items correctly and circles resulting score in Score column correctly	Yes No
20. For correctly completed items, circles appropriate number in Score column correctly	Yes No
21. Enters Total Raw Score in shaded box correctly	Yes No

Comments

_____

_____

_____

Record Form

1. Enters individual's full name and age, examiner's full name, and date of testing correctly	Yes No
2. Records any deviation from procedure on Record Form	Yes No
3. Completes Profile Page correctly	Yes No
4. Completes Score Conversion Page correctly	Yes No
5. Completes Discrepancy Analysis Page correctly	Yes No
6. Completes Demographic Page correctly	Yes No

General Evaluation

Rapport

1. Maintains rapport throughout testing	Yes No
2. Is alert to individual's moods	Yes No

(*Continued*)

Table C-22 (*Continued*)

General Evaluation (*Continued*)	Circle One	
3. Does not become impatient or frustrated with individual	Yes	No
4. Does not badger individual	Yes	No
5. Handles behavior problems correctly	Yes	No
6. Makes accommodations for any physical impairments individual has that may affect assessment (e.g., hearing or visual loss)	Yes	No
7. Does not take break in middle of a subtest	Yes	No
8. Allows individual to walk around room, if needed	Yes	No
9. Encourages individual to perform a task, if needed	Yes	No
10. Praises individual's effort	Yes	No
11. Does not say "Good" or "Right" after a correct response	Yes	No
12. Shows empathy if individual is concerned about poor performance	Yes	No

Administering Test Items

13. Administers test in professional, unhurried manner	Yes	No
14. Speaks clearly throughout testing	Yes	No
15. Is well organized and has all needed materials nearby	Yes	No
16. Administers subtests in order noted on page 37 of Administration Manual, altering order based on clinical need	Yes	No
17. Maintains steady pace	Yes	No
18. Makes a smooth transition from one subtest to the next	Yes	No
19. Repeats directions on request when appropriate	Yes	No
20. Repeats items when appropriate	Yes	No
21. Uses good judgment in deciding how much time to give individual to solve each item on untimed subtests	Yes	No
22. Begins timing correctly	Yes	No
23. Adheres to time limits	Yes	No
24. Stops timing when individual has obviously finished	Yes	No
25. Stops timing when time limit is reached	Yes	No
26. Does not stop timing prematurely	Yes	No
27. Places test materials not currently in use out of individual's sight	Yes	No
28. Clears table of unessential materials	Yes	No
29. Positions Record Form so that individual cannot see correct answers	Yes	No
30. Positions Administration Manual so that individual cannot see correct answers	Yes	No
31. Makes appropriate eye contact with individual	Yes	No
32. Reads directions exactly as written in Administration Manual	Yes	No
33. Reads items exactly as written in Administration Manual	Yes	No

General Evaluation (*Continued*)	Circle One	
34. Takes short break, as needed, at end of a subtest	Yes	No
35. Does not give additional items for practice	Yes	No
36. Does not ask leading questions	Yes	No
37. Does not spell words on any subtest	Yes	No
38. Does not define words	Yes	No
39. Does not use Vocabulary words in a sentence	Yes	No
40. Queries correctly	Yes	No
41. Records Q for queried responses	Yes	No
42. Prompts correctly	Yes	No
43. Records P for prompted responses	Yes	No
44. Gives second trials correctly	Yes	No
45. Follows start item with appropriate item	Yes	No
46. Administers reverse sequence correctly	Yes	No
47. Shows individual how to solve problems when appropriate	Yes	No
48. Permits individual to use scrap paper to write on, if appropriate	Yes	No
49. Conducts testing-of-limits after all subtests have been administered, if desired	Yes	No
50. Makes every effort to administer entire test in one session	Yes	No

Scoring Test Items

51. Scores each item after individual answers	Yes	No
52. Gives credit for correct responses given at any time during test, when appropriate	Yes	No
53. Does not give credit for correct answers given after time limit	Yes	No
54. Makes entry in Record Form for every item administered	Yes	No
55. Awards full credit for all items preceding first two items with perfect scores, regardless of individual's performance on preceding items, by putting slash mark in Score column through the possible scores for the item preceding the two items with perfect scores and writing the numerals for these points	Yes	No
56. Does not give credit for any items beyond last score of 0 required for discontinue criterion, regardless of individual's performance on these items if they have been administered	Yes	No
57. Does not count a supplemental subtest in computing Full Scale IQ, unless it is substituted for one of the 10 core subtests	Yes	No
58. Uses good judgment overall in scoring responses	Yes	No
59. Rechecks scoring after test is administered	Yes	No

Qualitative Feedback

_____

_____

_____

Table C-22 (*Continued*)

Overall Strengths

_____

_____

_____

Areas Needing Improvement

_____

_____

_____

Other Comments

_____

_____

_____

Overall Evaluation

Circle One: Excellent   Good   Average   Below Average   Poor

APPENDIX D

TABLES FOR THE WECHSLER TESTS

Table D-1
Percentile Ranks and Suggested Qualitative Descriptions for Scaled Scores on the Wechsler Tests

Scaled score	Percentile rank	Three-category qualitative descriptions	Five-category qualitative descriptions
19	99		Exceptional strength or Very well developed or Superior or Excellent
18	99		
17	99		
16	98	Strength or Above average	
15	95		Strength or Well developed or Above average or Good
14	91		
13	84		
12	75		Average
11	63		
10	50	Average	
9	37		
8	25		
7	16		Weakness or Poorly developed or Below average or Poor
6	9		
5	5	Weakness or Below average	
4	2		Exceptional weakness or Very poorly developed or Far below average or Very poor
3	1		
2	1		
1	1		

Table D-2
Confidence Intervals Based on Estimated True Scores for Tests with $M = 100$, $SD = 15$, and Reliabilities Ranging from $r_{xx} = .81$ to $r_{xx} = .98$

The letters in the following charts indicate the section of the table to consult in order to obtain confidence intervals based on estimated true scores for the Wechsler scales, the Stanford Binet 5, and other tests. See the Note on page 154 for instructions on how to compute the intervals.

WISC–IV

Examinee's age	Verbal Comprehension Index	Perceptual Reasoning Index	Working Memory Index	Processing Speed Index	Full Scale IQ
6	K	K	L	C	P
7	L	L	J	A	P
8	L	M	K	H	P
9	N	M	L	I	P
10	N	M	L	J	P
11	M	M	L	J	P
12	O	M	M	I	P
13	N	M	K	I	P
14	O	L	M	I	P
15	O	L	L	J	P
16	O	K	M	I	P
Average	N	L	L	H	P

WPPSI–III

Examinee's age	Verbal IQ	Performance IQ	Processing Speed Quotient	Full Scale IQ
2½	O	I	—	O
3	O	I	—	O
3½	O	K	—	P
Average	O	J	—	O
4	O	K	L	P
4½	O	N	K	Q
5	P	N	L	Q
5½	O	N	G	Q
6	N	N	G	P
7	O	O	F	Q
Average	O	M	I	P

(Continued)

Table D-2 (*Continued*)

WAIS–III

Examinee's age	Verbal Scale IQ	Performance Scale IQ	Full Scale IQ
16–17	P	M	Q
18–19	Q	M	Q
20–24	Q	M	R
25–29	Q	O	R
30–34	Q	M	R
35–44	Q	N	R
45–54	Q	N	R
55–64	R	O	R
65–69	R	P	R
70–74	Q	O	R
75–79	Q	M	Q
80–84	Q	N	R
85–89	P	N	Q
Average	Q	N	R

SB5

Examinee's age	Nonverbal IQ	Verbal IQ	Full Scale IQ
2	O	O	Q
3	P	P	R
4	O	P	Q
5	O	P	R
6	N	P	Q
7	N	O	Q
8	N	Q	R
9	O	P	R
10	N	O	Q
11	N	N	Q
12	N	N	Q
13	M	O	Q
14	O	P	R
15	P	P	R
16	P	P	R
17–20	P	P	R
21–29	P	P	R
30–39	O	P	R
40–49	Q	Q	R
50–59	Q	Q	R
60–69	Q	P	R
70–79	Q	Q	R
80+	P	Q	R
Average	O	P	R

(*Continued*)

Table D-2 (*Continued*)

A. $r_{xx} = .81$
WISC–IV: Processing Speed Index, Age 7

68%			85%			90%			95%			99%		
IQ	L	U	IQ	L	U	IQ	L	U	IQ	L	U	IQ	L	U
40–41	6	17	40–41	4	19	40	3	20	40–41	1	22	40–41	−2	25
42–43	6	16	42	3	19	41–43	2	20	42	1	21	42	−3	25
44–46	5	16	43–46	3	18	44–46	2	19	43–46	0	21	43–46	−3	24
47–48	5	15	47–48	2	18	47–48	1	19	47	0	20	47–48	−4	24
49–51	4	15	49–51	2	17	49–51	1	18	48–52	−1	20	49–51	−4	23
52–53	4	14	52–53	1	17	52–53	0	18	53	−1	19	52–53	−5	23
54–56	3	14	54–57	1	16	54–56	0	17	54–57	−2	19	54–57	−5	22
57–58	3	13	58	0	16	57–59	−1	17	58	−2	18	58	−6	22
59–62	2	13	59–62	0	15	60–61	−1	16	59–62	−3	18	59–62	−6	21
63–64	2	12	63	−1	15	62–64	−2	16	63	−3	17	63–64	−7	21
65–67	1	12	64–67	−1	14	65–67	−2	15	64–67	−4	17	65–67	−7	20
68–69	1	11	68–69	−2	14	68–69	−3	15	68–69	−4	16	68–69	−8	20
70–72	0	11	70–73	−2	13	70–72	−3	14	70–73	−5	16	70–72	−8	19
73–74	0	10	74	−3	13	73–74	−4	14	74	−5	15	73–74	−9	19
75–77	−1	10	75–78	−3	12	75–77	−4	13	75–78	−6	15	75–78	−9	18
78–80	−1	9	79	−4	12	78–80	−5	13	79	−6	14	79	−10	18
81–83	−2	9	80–83	−4	11	81–82	−5	12	80–83	−7	14	80–83	−10	17
84–85	−2	8	84	−5	11	83–85	−6	12	84	−7	13	84–85	−11	17
86–88	−3	8	85–88	−5	10	86–88	−6	11	85–88	−8	13	86–88	−11	16
89–90	−3	7	89–90	−6	10	89–90	−7	11	89–90	−8	12	89–90	−12	16
91–93	−4	7	91–94	−6	9	91–93	−7	10	91–94	−9	12	91–93	−12	15
94–95	−4	6	95	−7	9	94–96	−8	10	95	−9	11	94–95	−13	15
96–98	−5	6	96–99	−7	8	97–98	−8	9	96–99	−10	11	96–99	−13	14
99–101	−5	5	100	−8	8	99–101	−9	9	100	−10	10	100	−14	14
102–104	−6	5	101–104	−8	7	102–103	−9	8	101–104	−11	10	101–104	−14	13
105–106	−6	4	105	−9	7	104–106	−10	8	105	−11	9	105–106	−15	13
107–109	−7	4	106–109	−9	6	107–109	−10	7	106–109	−12	9	107–109	−15	12
110–111	−7	3	110–111	−10	6	110–111	−11	7	110–111	−12	8	110–111	−16	12
112–114	−8	3	112–115	−10	5	112–114	−11	6	112–115	−13	8	112–114	−16	11
115–116	−8	2	116	−11	5	115–117	−12	6	116	−13	7	115–116	−17	11
117–119	−9	2	117–120	−11	4	118–119	−12	5	117–120	−14	7	117–120	−17	10
120–122	−9	1	121	−12	4	120–122	−13	5	121	−14	6	121	−18	10
123–125	−10	1	122–125	−12	3	123–125	−13	4	122–125	−15	6	122–125	−18	9
126–127	−10	0	126	−13	3	126–127	−14	4	126	−15	5	126–127	−19	9
128–130	−11	0	127–130	−13	2	128–130	−14	3	127–130	−16	5	128–130	−19	8
131–132	−11	−1	131–132	−14	2	131–132	−15	3	131–132	−16	4	131–132	−20	8
133–135	−12	−1	133–136	−14	1	133–135	−15	2	133–136	−17	4	133–135	−20	7
136–137	−12	−2	137	−15	1	136–138	−16	2	137	−17	3	136–137	−21	7
138–141	−13	−2	138–141	−15	0	139–140	−16	1	138–141	−18	3	138–141	−21	6
142–143	−13	−3	142	−16	0	141–143	−17	1	142	−18	2	142	−22	6
144–146	−14	−3	143–146	−16	−1	144–146	−17	0	143–146	−19	2	143–146	−22	5
147–148	−14	−4	147–148	−17	−1	147–148	−18	0	147	−19	1	147–148	−23	5
149–151	−15	−4	149–151	−17	−2	149–151	−18	−1	148–152	−20	1	149–151	−23	4
152–153	−15	−5	152–153	−18	−2	152–153	−19	−1	153	−20	0	152–153	−24	4
154–156	−16	−5	154–157	−18	−3	154–156	−19	−2	154–157	−21	0	154–157	−24	3
157–158	−16	−6	158	−19	−3	157–159	−20	−2	158	−21	−1	158	−25	3
159–160	−17	−6	159–160	−19	−4	160	−20	−3	159–160	−22	−1	159–160	−25	2

(*Continued*)

Table D-2 (Continued)

B. $r_{xx} = .82$

68%			85%			90%			95%			99%		
IQ	L	U	IQ	L	U	IQ	L	U	IQ	L	U	IQ	L	U
40	6	16	40–44	3	18	40–43	2	19	40	1	21	40–44	−3	24
41–42	5	16	45–49	2	17	44–45	1	19	41–42	0	21	45–49	−4	23
43–46	5	15	50	1	17	46–49	1	18	43–45	0	20	50	−4	22
47–48	4	15	51–55	1	16	50	0	18	46–48	−1	20	51–55	−5	22
49–51	4	14	56–61	0	15	51–54	0	17	49–51	−1	19	56–60	−6	21
52–53	3	14	62–66	−1	14	55–56	−1	17	52–54	−2	19	61	−6	20
54–57	3	13	67–72	−2	13	57–60	−1	16	55–57	−2	18	62–66	−7	20
58–59	2	13	73–77	−3	12	61	−2	16	58–59	−3	18	67–71	−8	19
60–62	2	12	78–83	−4	11	62–66	−2	15	60–62	−3	17	72	−8	18
63–65	1	12	84–88	−5	10	67	−3	15	63–65	−4	17	73–77	−9	18
66–68	1	11	89–94	−6	9	68–71	−3	14	66–68	−4	16	78	−9	17
69–70	0	11	95–99	−7	8	72	−4	14	69–70	−5	16	79–83	−10	17
71–73	0	10	100	−8	8	73–77	−4	13	71–73	−5	15	84–88	−11	16
74–76	−1	10	101–105	−8	7	78	−5	13	74–76	−6	15	89	−11	15
77–79	−1	9	106–111	−9	6	79–82	−5	12	77–79	−6	14	90–94	−12	15
80–81	−2	9	112–116	−10	5	83	−6	12	80–81	−7	14	95–99	−13	14
82–84	−2	8	117–122	−11	4	84–88	−6	11	82–84	−7	13	100	−13	13
85–87	−3	8	123–127	−12	3	89	−7	11	85–87	−8	13	101–105	−14	13
88–90	−3	7	128–133	−13	2	90–93	−7	10	88–90	−8	12	106–110	−15	12
91–92	−4	7	134–138	−14	1	94–95	−8	10	91–92	−9	12	111	−15	11
93–96	−4	6	139–144	−15	0	96–99	−8	9	93–95	−9	11	112–116	−16	11
97–98	−5	6	145–149	−16	−1	100	−9	9	96–98	−10	11	117–121	−17	10
99–101	−5	5	150	−17	−1	101–104	−9	8	99–101	−10	10	122	−17	9
102–103	−6	5	151–155	−17	−2	105–106	−10	8	102–104	−11	10	123–127	−18	9
104–107	−6	4	156–160	−18	−3	107–110	−10	7	105–107	−11	9	128	−18	8
108–109	−7	4				111	−11	7	108–109	−12	9	129–133	−19	8
110–112	−7	3				112–116	−11	6	110–112	−12	8	134–138	−20	7
113–115	−8	3				117	−12	6	113–115	−13	8	139	−20	6
116–118	−8	2				118–121	−12	5	116–118	−13	7	140–144	−21	6
119–120	−9	2				122	−13	5	119–120	−14	7	145–149	−22	5
121–123	−9	1				123–127	−13	4	121–123	−14	6	150	−22	4
124–126	−10	1				128	−14	4	124–126	−15	6	151–155	−23	4
127–129	−10	0				129–132	−14	3	127–129	−15	5	156–160	−24	3
130–131	−11	0				133	−15	3	130–131	−16	5			
132–134	−11	−1				134–138	−15	2	132–134	−16	4			
135–137	−12	−1				139	−16	2	135–137	−17	4			
138–140	−12	−2				140–143	−16	1	138–140	−17	3			
141–142	−13	−2				144–145	−17	1	141–142	−18	3			
143–146	−13	−3				146–149	−18	0	143–145	−18	2			
147–148	−14	−3				150	−18	0	146–148	−19	2			
149–151	−14	−4				151–154	−18	−1	149–151	−19	1			
152–153	−15	−4				155–156	−19	−1	152–154	−20	1			
154–157	−15	−5				157–160	−19	−2	155–157	−20	0			
158–159	−16	−5							158–159	−21	0			
160	−16	−6							160	−21	−1			

(Continued)

Table D-2 (*Continued*)

C. r_{xx} = .83
WISC–IV: Processing Speed Index, Age 6

68%			85%			90%			95%			99%		
IQ	L	U	IQ	L	U	IQ	L	U	IQ	L	U	IQ	L	U
40–43	5	15	40	3	18	40	2	19	40–43	0	20	40–42	–3	23
44	4	15	41	3	17	41	2	18	44	–1	20	43–45	–4	23
45–49	4	14	42–46	2	17	42–46	1	18	45–49	–1	19	46–48	–4	22
50	3	14	47	2	16	47	1	17	50	–2	19	49–51	–5	22
51–55	3	13	48–52	1	16	48–52	0	17	51–55	–2	18	52–54	–5	21
56	2	13	53	1	15	53	0	16	56	–3	18	55–57	–6	21
57–61	1	12	54–58	0	15	54–58	–1	16	57–61	–3	17	58–60	–6	20
62	1	12	59	0	14	59	–1	15	62	–4	17	61–63	–7	20
63–66	0	11	60–64	–1	14	60–64	–2	15	63–67	–4	16	64–66	–7	19
67–68	0	11	65	–1	13	65–70	–3	14	68–73	–5	15	67–69	–8	19
69–72	–1	10	66–69	–2	13	71–76	–4	13	74–79	–6	14	70–72	–8	18
73–74	–1	10	70–71	–2	12	77–82	–5	12	80–84	–7	13	73–74	–9	18
75–78	–2	9	72–75	–3	12	83–88	–6	11	85	–8	13	75–78	–9	17
79–80	–2	9	76–77	–3	11	89–93	–7	10	86–90	–8	12	79–80	–10	17
81–84	–3	8	78–81	–4	11	94	–7	9	91	–9	12	81–83	–10	16
85–86	–3	8	82–83	–4	10	95–99	–8	9	92–96	–9	11	84–86	–11	16
87–90	–4	7	84–87	–5	10	100	–8	8	97	–10	11	87–89	–11	15
91	–4	7	88	–5	9	101–105	–9	8	98–102	–10	10	90–92	–12	15
92–96	–5	6	89–93	–6	9	106	–9	7	103	–11	10	93–95	–12	14
97	–5	6	94	–6	8	107–111	–10	7	104–108	–11	9	96–98	–13	14
98–102	–6	5	95–99	–7	8	112–117	–11	6	109	–12	9	99–101	–13	13
103	–6	5	100	–7	7	118–123	–12	5	110–114	–12	8	102–104	–14	13
104–108	–7	4	101–105	–8	7	124–129	–13	4	115	–13	8	105–107	–14	12
109	–7	4	106	–8	7	130–135	–14	3	116–120	–13	7	108–110	–15	12
110–113	–8	3	107–111	–9	6	136–140	–15	2	121–126	–14	6	111–113	–15	11
114–115	–8	3	112	–9	6	141	–15	1	127–132	–15	5	114–116	–16	11
116–119	–9	2	113–116	–10	5	142–146	–16	1	133–137	–16	4	117–119	–16	10
120–121	–9	2	117–118	–10	5	147	–16	0	138	–17	4	120–121	–17	10
122–125	–9	1	119–122	–11	4	148–152	–17	0	139–143	–17	3	122–125	–17	9
126–127	–10	1	123–124	–11	4	153	–17	–1	144	–18	3	126–127	–18	9
128–131	–10	0	125–128	–12	3	154–158	–18	–1	145–149	–18	2	128–130	–18	8
132–133	–11	0	129–130	–12	3	159	–18	–2	150	–19	2	131–133	–19	8
134–137	–11	–1	131–134	–13	2	160	–19	–2	151–155	–19	1	134–136	–19	7
138	–12	–1	135	–13	2				156	–20	1	137–139	–20	7
139–143	–12	–2	136–140	–14	1				157–160	–20	0	140–142	–20	6
144	–13	–2	141	–14	1							143–145	–21	6
145–149	–13	–3	142–146	–15	0							146–148	–21	5
150	–14	–3	147	–15	0							149–151	–22	5
151–155	–14	–4	148–152	–16	–1							152–154	–22	4
156	–15	–4	153	–16	–1							155–157	–23	4
157–160	–15	–5	154–158	–17	–2							158–160	–23	3
			159	–17	–2									
			160	–18	–3									

(*Continued*)

Table D-2 (*Continued*)

D. r_{xx} = .84

68%			85%			90%			95%			99%		
IQ	L	U	IQ	L	U	IQ	L	U	IQ	L	U	IQ	L	U
40	5	15	40–42	2	17	40–42	1	18	40–41	0	19	40	–3	23
41–46	4	14	43–45	2	16	43–44	1	17	42–46	–1	19	41–46	–4	22
47	3	14	46–48	1	16	45–48	0	17	47	–1	18	47–53	–5	21
48–52	3	13	49–51	1	15	49–51	0	16	48–52	–2	18	54–59	–6	20
53	2	13	52–54	0	15	52–55	–1	16	53	–2	17	60–65	–7	19
54–59	2	12	55–57	0	14	56–57	–1	15	54–58	–3	17	66–71	–8	18
60–65	1	11	58–60	–1	14	58–61	–2	15	59–60	–3	16	72–78	–9	17
66–71	0	10	61–64	–1	13	62–63	–2	14	61–64	–4	16	79–84	–10	16
72	–1	10	65–67	–2	13	64–67	–3	14	65–66	–4	15	85–90	–11	15
73–77	–1	9	68–70	–2	12	68–69	–3	13	67–71	–5	15	91–96	–12	14
78	–2	9	71–73	–3	12	70–73	–4	13	72	–5	14	97–103	–13	13
79–84	–2	8	74–76	–3	11	74–76	–4	12	73–77	–6	14	104–109	–14	12
85–90	–3	7	77–79	–4	11	77–80	–5	12	78	–6	13	110–115	–15	11
91–96	–4	6	80–82	–4	10	81–82	–5	11	79–83	–7	13	116–121	–16	10
97	–5	6	83–85	–5	10	83–86	–6	11	84–85	–7	12	122–128	–17	9
98–102	–5	5	86–89	–5	9	87–88	–6	10	86–89	–8	12	129–134	–18	8
103	–6	5	90–92	–6	9	89–92	–7	10	90–91	–8	11	135–140	–19	7
104–109	–6	4	93–95	–6	8	93–94	–7	9	92–96	–9	11	141–146	–20	6
110–115	–7	3	96–98	–7	8	95–98	–8	9	97	–9	10	147–153	–21	5
116–121	–8	2	99–101	–7	7	99–101	–8	8	98–102	–10	10	154–159	–22	4
122	–9	2	102–104	–8	7	102–105	–9	8	103	–10	9	160	–23	3
123–127	–10	1	105–107	–8	6	106–107	–9	7	104–108	–11	9			
128	–10	1	108–110	–9	6	108–111	–10	7	109–110	–11	8			
129–134	–11	0	111–114	–9	5	112–113	–10	6	111–114	–12	8			
135–140	–11	–1	115–117	–10	5	114–117	–11	6	115–116	–12	7			
141–146	–12	–2	118–120	–10	4	118–119	–11	5	117–121	–13	7			
147	–13	–2	121–123	–11	4	120–123	–12	5	122	–13	6			
148–152	–13	–3	124–126	–11	3	124–126	–12	4	123–127	–14	6			
153	–14	–3	127–129	–12	3	127–130	–13	4	128	–14	5			
154–159	–14	–4	130–132	–12	2	131–132	–13	3	129–133	–15	5			
160	–15	–5	133–135	–13	2	133–136	–14	3	134–135	–15	4			
			136–139	–13	1	137–138	–14	2	136–139	–16	4			
			140–142	–14	1	139–142	–15	2	140–141	–16	3			
			143–145	–14	0	143–144	–15	1	142–146	–17	3			
			146–148	–15	0	145–148	–16	1	147	–17	2			
			149–151	–15	–1	149–151	–16	0	148–152	–18	2			
			152–154	–16	–1	152–155	–17	0	153	–18	1			
			155–157	–16	–2	156–157	–17	–1	154–158	–19	1			
			158–160	–17	–2	158–160	–18	–1	159–160	–19	0			

(*Continued*)

Table D-2 (*Continued*)

E. $r_{xx} = .85$

68%			85%			90%			95%			99%		
IQ	L	U	IQ	L	U	IQ	L	U	IQ	L	U	IQ	L	U
40–42	4	14	40–42	2	16	40–42	1	17	40–41	−1	19	40–41	−4	22
43	4	13	43–44	1	16	43–44	0	17	42–45	−1	18	42–45	−4	21
44–49	3	13	45–49	1	15	45–49	0	16	46–47	−2	18	46–48	−5	21
50	3	12	50	0	15	50	−1	16	48–52	−2	17	49–51	−5	20
51–56	2	12	51–55	0	14	51–55	−1	15	53–54	−3	17	52–54	−6	20
57	2	11	56–57	−1	14	56–57	−2	15	55–58	−3	16	55–58	−6	19
58–62	1	11	58–62	−1	13	58–62	−2	14	59–61	−4	16	59–61	−7	19
63	1	10	63–64	−2	13	63–64	−3	14	62–65	−4	15	62–65	−7	18
64–69	0	10	65–69	−2	12	65–69	−3	13	66–67	−5	15	66–68	−8	18
70	0	9	70	−3	12	70	−4	13	68–72	−5	14	69–71	−8	17
71–76	−1	9	71–75	−3	11	71–75	−4	12	73–74	−6	14	72–74	−9	17
77	−1	8	76–77	−4	11	76–77	−5	12	75–78	−6	13	75–78	−9	16
78–82	−2	8	78–82	−4	10	78–82	−5	11	79–81	−7	13	79–81	−10	16
83	−2	7	83–84	−5	10	83–84	−6	11	82–85	−7	12	82–85	−10	15
84–89	−3	7	85–89	−5	9	85–89	−6	10	86–87	−8	12	86–88	−11	15
90	−3	6	90	−6	9	90	−7	10	88–92	−8	11	89–91	−11	14
91–96	−4	6	91–95	−6	8	91–95	−7	9	93–94	−9	11	92–94	−12	14
97	−4	5	96–97	−7	8	96–97	−8	9	95–98	−9	10	95–98	−12	13
98–102	−5	5	98–102	−7	7	98–102	−8	8	99–101	−10	10	99–101	−13	13
103	−5	4	103–104	−8	7	103–104	−9	8	102–105	−10	9	102–105	−13	12
104–109	−6	4	105–109	−8	6	105–109	−9	7	106–107	−11	9	106–108	−14	12
110	−6	3	110	−9	6	110	−10	7	108–112	−11	8	109–111	−14	11
111–116	−7	3	111–115	−9	5	111–115	−10	6	113–114	−12	8	112–114	−15	11
117	−7	2	116–117	−10	5	116–117	−11	6	115–118	−12	7	115–118	−15	10
118–122	−8	2	118–122	−10	4	118–122	−11	5	119–121	−13	7	119–121	−16	10
123	−8	1	123–124	−11	4	123–124	−12	5	122–125	−13	6	122–125	−16	9
124–129	−9	1	125–129	−11	3	125–129	−12	4	126–127	−14	6	126–128	−17	9
130	−9	0	130	−12	3	130	−13	4	128–132	−14	5	129–131	−17	8
131–136	−10	0	131–135	−12	2	131–135	−13	3	133–134	−15	5	132–134	−18	8
137	−10	−1	136–137	−13	2	136–137	−14	3	135–138	−15	4	135–138	−18	7
138–142	−11	−1	138–142	−13	1	138–142	−14	2	139–141	−16	4	139–141	−19	7
143	−11	−2	143–144	−14	1	143–144	−15	2	142–145	−16	3	142–145	−19	6
144–149	−12	−2	145–149	−14	0	145–149	−15	1	146–147	−17	3	146–148	−20	6
150	−12	−3	150	−15	0	150	−16	1	148–152	−17	2	149–151	−20	5
151–156	−13	−3	151–155	−15	−1	151–155	−16	0	153–154	−18	2	152–154	−21	5
157	−13	−4	156–157	−16	−1	156–157	−17	0	155–158	−18	1	155–158	−21	4
158–160	−14	−4	158–160	−16	−2	158–160	−17	−1	159–160	−19	1	159–160	−22	4

(*Continued*)

Table D-2 (*Continued*)

F. r_{xx} = .86
WPPSI–III: Processing Speed Quotient, Age 7

68%			85%			90%			95%			99%		
IQ	L	U	IQ	L	U	IQ	L	U	IQ	L	U	IQ	L	U
40	4	13	40–46	1	15	40–46	0	16	40–42	−1	18	40–42	−4	21
41–45	3	13	47–53	0	14	47–53	−1	15	43	−1	17	43	−4	20
46–47	3	12	54–60	−1	13	54–60	−2	14	44–49	−2	17	44–49	−5	20
48–52	2	12	61	−1	12	61–67	−3	13	50	−2	16	50	−5	19
53–54	2	11	62–67	−2	12	68	−3	12	51–56	−3	16	51–56	−6	19
55–59	1	11	68	−2	11	69–74	−4	12	57	−3	15	57	−6	18
60–61	1	10	69–74	−3	11	75	−4	11	58–64	−4	15	58–63	−7	18
62–66	0	10	75	−3	10	76–81	−5	11	65–71	−5	14	64	−7	17
67–69	0	9	76–81	−4	10	82	−5	10	72–78	−6	13	65–71	−8	17
70–73	−1	9	82	−4	9	83–89	−6	10	79–85	−7	12	72–78	−9	16
74–76	−1	8	83–88	−5	9	90–96	−7	9	86–92	−8	11	79–85	−10	15
77–80	−2	8	89	−5	8	97–103	−8	8	93	−8	10	86	−10	14
81–83	−2	7	90–96	−6	8	104–110	−9	7	94–99	−9	10	87–92	−11	14
84–88	−3	7	97–103	−7	7	111–117	−10	6	100	−9	9	93	−11	13
89–90	−3	6	104–110	−8	6	118	−10	5	101–106	−10	9	94–99	−12	13
91–95	−4	6	111	−8	5	119–124	−11	5	107	−10	8	100	−12	12
96–97	−4	5	112–117	−9	5	125	−11	4	108–114	−11	8	101–106	−13	12
98–102	−5	5	118	−9	4	126–131	−12	4	115–121	−12	7	107	−13	11
103–104	−5	4	119–124	−10	4	132	−12	3	122–128	−13	6	108–113	−14	11
105–109	−6	4	125	−10	3	133–139	−13	3	129–135	−14	5	114	−14	10
110–111	−6	3	126–131	−11	3	140–146	−14	2	136–142	−15	4	115–121	−15	10
112–116	−7	3	132	−11	2	147–153	−15	1	143	−15	3	122–128	−16	9
117–119	−7	2	133–138	−12	2	154–160	−16	0	144–149	−16	3	129–135	−17	8
120–123	−8	2	139	−12	1				150	−16	2	136	−17	7
124–126	−8	1	140–146	−13	1				151–156	−17	2	137–142	−18	7
127–130	−9	1	147–153	−14	0				157	−17	1	143	−18	6
131–133	−9	0	154–160	−15	−1				158–160	−18	1	144–149	−19	6
134–138	−10	0										150	−19	5
139–140	−10	−1										151–156	−20	5
141–145	−11	−1										157	−20	4
146–147	−11	−2										158–160	−21	4
148–152	−12	−2												
153–154	−12	−3												
155–159	−13	−3												
160	−13	−4												

(*Continued*)

Table D-2 (*Continued*)

G. r_{xx} = .87
WPPSI–III: Processing Speed Quotient, Ages 5½ and 6

68%			85%			90%			95%			99%		
IQ	*L*	*U*	*IQ*	*L*	*U*	*IQ*	*L*	*U*	*IQ*	*L*	*U*	*IQ*	*L*	*U*
40	3	13	40	1	15	40	0	16	40	−1	17	40–41	−4	20
41–44	3	12	41–44	1	14	41–44	0	15	41–44	−2	17	42–43	−5	20
45–47	2	12	45–48	0	14	45–48	−1	15	45–48	−2	16	44–48	−5	19
48–52	2	11	49–51	0	13	49–51	−1	14	49–51	−3	16	49–51	−6	19
53–55	1	11	52–55	−1	13	52–55	−2	14	52–55	−3	15	52–56	−6	18
56–59	1	10	56–59	−1	12	56–59	−2	13	56–59	−4	15	57–58	−7	18
60–63	0	10	60–63	−2	12	60–63	−3	13	60–63	−4	14	59–64	−7	17
64–67	0	9	64–67	−2	11	64–67	−3	12	64–67	−5	14	65–66	−8	17
68–70	−1	9	68–71	−3	11	68–71	−4	12	68–71	−5	13	67–72	−8	16
71–75	−1	8	72–74	−3	10	72–74	−4	11	72–74	−6	13	73–74	−9	16
76–78	−2	8	75–79	−4	10	75–78	−5	11	75–79	−6	12	75–79	−9	15
79–83	−2	7	80–82	−4	9	79–82	−5	10	80–82	−7	12	80–81	−10	15
84–86	−3	7	83–86	−5	9	83–86	−6	10	83–86	−7	11	82–87	−10	14
87–90	−3	6	87–90	−5	8	87–90	−6	9	87–90	−8	11	88–89	−11	14
91–93	−4	6	91–94	−6	8	91–94	−7	9	91–94	−8	10	90–95	−11	13
94–98	−4	5	95–97	−6	7	95–97	−7	8	95–97	−9	10	96–97	−12	13
99–101	−5	5	98–102	−7	7	98–102	−8	8	98–102	−9	9	98–102	−12	12
102–106	−5	4	103–105	−7	6	103–105	−8	7	103–105	−10	9	103–104	−13	12
107–109	−6	4	106–109	−8	6	106–109	−9	7	106–109	−10	8	105–110	−13	11
110–113	−6	3	110–113	−8	5	110–113	−9	6	110–113	−11	8	111–112	−14	11
114–116	−7	3	114–117	−9	5	114–117	−10	6	114–117	−11	7	113–118	−14	10
117–121	−7	2	118–120	−9	4	118–121	−10	5	118–120	−12	7	119–120	−15	10
122–124	−8	2	121–125	−10	4	122–125	−11	5	121–125	−12	6	121–125	−15	9
125–129	−8	1	126–128	−10	3	126–128	−11	4	126–128	−13	6	126–127	−16	9
130–132	−9	1	129–132	−11	3	129–132	−12	4	129–132	−13	5	128–133	−16	8
133–136	−9	0	133–136	−11	2	133–136	−12	3	133–136	−14	5	134–135	−17	8
137–140	−10	0	137–140	−12	2	137–140	−13	3	137–140	−14	4	136–141	−17	7
141–144	−10	−1	141–144	−12	1	141–144	−13	2	141–144	−15	4	142–143	−18	7
145–147	−11	−1	145–148	−13	1	145–148	−14	2	145–148	−15	3	144–148	−18	6
148–152	−11	−2	149–151	−13	0	149–151	−14	1	149–151	−16	3	149–151	−19	6
153–155	−12	−2	152–155	−14	0	152–155	−15	1	152–155	−16	2	152–156	−19	5
156–159	−12	−3	156–159	−14	−1	156–159	−15	0	156–159	−17	2	157–158	−20	5
160	−13	−3	160	−15	−1	160	−16	0	160	−17	1	159–160	−20	4

(Continued)

Table D-2 (*Continued*)

H. r_{xx} = .88
WISC–IV: Processing Speed Index, Age 8 and Average

68%			85%			90%			95%			99%		
IQ	*L*	*U*	*IQ*	*L*	*U*	*IQ*	*L*	*U*	*IQ*	*L*	*U*	*IQ*	*L*	*U*
40–41	3	12	40	1	14	40–41	0	15	40–45	–2	16	40–44	–5	19
42	2	12	41–42	0	14	42	–1	15	46	–2	15	45–47	–5	18
43–49	2	11	43–49	0	13	43–49	–1	14	47–53	–3	15	48–52	–6	18
50	1	11	50	–1	13	50	–2	14	54	–3	14	53–55	–6	17
51–57	1	10	51–57	–1	12	51–57	–2	13	55–62	–4	14	56–60	–7	17
58	0	10	58–59	–2	12	58	–3	13	63–70	–5	13	61–64	–7	16
59–66	0	9	60–65	–2	11	59–66	–3	12	71	–5	12	65–69	–8	16
67	–1	9	66–67	–3	11	67	–4	12	72–78	–6	12	70–72	–8	15
68–74	–1	8	68–74	–3	10	68–74	–4	11	79	–6	11	73–77	–9	15
75	–2	8	75	–4	10	75	–5	11	80–87	–7	11	78–80	–9	14
76–82	–2	7	76–82	–4	9	76–82	–5	10	88–95	–8	10	81–85	–10	14
83	–3	7	83–84	–5	9	83	–6	10	96	–8	9	86–89	–10	13
84–91	–3	6	85–90	–5	8	84–91	–6	9	97–103	–9	9	90–94	–11	13
92	–4	6	91–92	–6	8	92	–7	9	104	–9	8	95–97	–11	12
93–99	–4	5	93–99	–6	7	93–99	–7	8	105–112	–10	8	98–102	–12	12
100	–5	5	100	–7	7	100	–8	8	113–120	–11	7	103–105	–12	11
101–107	–5	4	101–107	–7	6	101–107	–8	7	121	–11	6	106–110	–13	11
108	–6	4	108–109	–8	6	108	–9	7	122–128	–12	6	111–114	–13	10
109–116	–6	3	110–115	–8	5	109–116	–9	6	129	–12	5	115–119	–14	10
117	–7	3	116–117	–9	5	117	–10	6	130–137	–13	5	120–122	–14	9
118–124	–7	2	118–124	–9	4	118–124	–10	5	138–145	–14	4	123–127	–15	9
125	–8	2	125	–10	4	125	–11	5	146	–14	3	128–130	–15	8
126–132	–8	1	126–132	–10	3	126–132	–11	4	147–153	–15	3	131–135	–16	8
133	–9	1	133–134	–11	3	133	–12	4	154	–15	2	136–139	–16	7
134–141	–9	0	135–140	–11	2	134–141	–12	3	155–160	–16	2	140–144	–17	7
142	–10	0	141–142	–12	2	142	–13	3				145–147	–17	6
143–149	–10	–1	143–149	–12	1	143–149	–13	2				148–152	–18	6
150	–11	–1	150	–13	1	150	–14	2				153–155	–18	5
151–157	–11	–2	151–157	–13	0	151–157	–14	1				156–160	–19	5
158	–12	–2	158–159	–14	0	158	–15	1						
159–160	–12	–3	160	–14	–1	159–160	–15	0						

(*Continued*)

Table D-2 (*Continued*)

I. $r_{xx} = .89$
WISC–IV: Processing Speed Index, Ages 9, 12, 13, 14, and 16
WPPSI–III: Performance IQ, Ages 2½ and 3
WPPSI–III: Processing Speed Quotient, Average for Ages 4–7¼

68%			85%			90%			95%			99%		
IQ	L	U	IQ	L	U	IQ	L	U	IQ	L	U	IQ	L	U
40–44	2	11	40–44	0	13	40–43	−1	14	40–43	−2	15	40–44	−5	18
45–46	2	10	45–46	0	12	44–47	−1	13	44–47	−3	15	45–46	−5	17
47–53	1	10	47–53	−1	12	48–52	−2	13	48–52	−3	14	47–53	−6	17
54–55	1	9	54–55	−1	11	53–56	−2	12	53–56	−4	14	54–55	−6	16
56–62	0	9	56–62	−2	11	57–61	−3	12	57–62	−4	13	56–62	−7	16
63–64	0	8	63–64	−2	10	62–65	−3	11	63–65	−5	13	63–64	−7	15
65–72	−1	8	65–71	−3	10	66–70	−4	11	66–71	−5	12	65–72	−8	15
73	−1	7	72–73	−3	9	71–74	−4	10	72–74	−6	12	73	−8	14
74–81	−2	7	74–80	−4	9	75–80	−5	10	75–80	−6	11	74–81	−9	14
82	−2	6	81–82	−4	8	81–83	−5	9	81–83	−7	11	82	−9	13
83–90	−3	6	83–89	−5	8	84–89	−6	9	84–89	−7	10	83–90	−10	13
91	−3	5	90–92	−5	7	90–92	−6	8	90–92	−8	10	91	−10	12
92–99	−4	5	93–98	−6	7	93–98	−7	8	93–98	−8	9	92–99	−11	12
100	−4	4	99–101	−6	6	99–101	−7	7	99–101	−9	9	100	−11	11
101–108	−5	4	102–107	−7	6	102–107	−8	7	102–107	−9	8	101–108	−12	11
109	−5	3	108–110	−7	5	108–110	−8	6	108–110	−10	8	109	−12	10
110–117	−6	3	111–117	−8	5	111–116	−9	6	111–116	−10	7	110–117	−13	10
118	−6	2	118–119	−8	4	117–119	−9	5	117–119	−11	7	118	−13	9
119–126	−7	2	120–126	−9	4	120–125	−10	5	120–125	−11	6	119–126	−14	9
127	−7	1	127–128	−9	3	126–129	−10	4	126–128	−12	6	127	−14	8
128–135	−8	1	129–135	−10	3	130–134	−11	4	129–134	−12	5	128–135	−15	8
136–137	−8	0	136–137	−10	2	135–138	−11	3	135–137	−13	5	136–137	−15	7
138–144	−9	0	138–144	−11	2	139–143	−12	3	138–143	−13	4	138–144	−16	7
145–146	−9	−1	145–146	−11	1	144–147	−12	2	144–147	−14	4	145–146	−16	6
147–153	−10	−1	147–153	−12	1	148–152	−13	2	148–152	−14	3	147–153	−17	6
154–155	−10	−2	154–155	−12	0	153–156	−13	1	153–156	−15	3	154–155	−17	5
156–160	−11	−2	156–160	−13	0	157–160	−14	1	157–160	−15	2	156–160	−18	5

(*Continued*)

Table D-2 (*Continued*)

J. r_{xx} = .90
WISC–IV: Working Memory Index, Age 7
WISC–IV: Processing Speed Index, Ages 10, 11, 15
WPPSI–III: Performance IQ, Average for Ages $2^1/_2$–$3^{11}/_{12}$

| | 68% | | | 85% | | | 90% | | | 95% | | | 99% | |
IQ	L	U	IQ	L	U	IQ	L	U	IQ	L	U	IQ	L	U
40–42	2	10	40–43	0	12	40–44	−1	13	40–41	−2	14	40–44	−5	17
43–47	1	10	44–46	−1	12	45	−2	13	42–48	−3	14	45	−6	17
48–52	1	9	47–53	−1	11	46–54	−2	12	49–51	−3	13	46–54	−6	16
53–57	0	9	54–56	−2	11	55	−3	12	52–58	−4	13	55	−7	16
58–62	0	8	57–63	−2	10	56–64	−3	11	59–61	−4	12	56–64	−7	15
63–67	−1	8	64–66	−3	10	65	−4	11	62–68	−5	12	65	−8	15
68–72	−1	7	67–73	−3	9	66–74	−4	10	69–71	−5	11	66–74	−8	14
73–77	−2	7	74–76	−4	9	75	−5	10	72–78	−6	11	75	−9	14
78–82	−2	6	77–83	−4	8	76–84	−5	9	79–81	−6	10	76–84	−9	13
83–87	−3	6	84–86	−5	8	85	−6	9	82–88	−7	10	85	−10	13
88–92	−3	5	87–93	−5	7	86–94	−6	8	89–91	−7	9	86–94	−10	12
93–97	−4	5	94–96	−6	7	95	−7	8	92–98	−8	9	95	−11	12
98–102	−4	4	97–103	−6	6	96–104	−7	7	99–101	−8	8	96–104	−11	11
103–107	−5	4	104–106	−7	6	105	−8	7	102–108	−9	8	105	−12	11
108–112	−5	3	107–113	−7	5	106–114	−8	6	109–111	−9	7	106–114	−12	10
113–117	−6	3	114–116	−8	5	115	−9	6	112–118	−10	7	115	−13	10
118–122	−6	2	117–123	−8	4	116–124	−9	5	119–121	−10	6	116–124	−13	9
123–127	−7	2	124–126	−9	4	125	−10	5	122–128	−11	6	125	−14	9
128–132	−7	1	127–133	−9	3	126–134	−10	4	129–131	−11	5	126–134	−14	8
133–137	−8	1	134–136	−10	3	135	−11	4	132–138	−12	5	135	−15	8
138–142	−8	0	137–143	−10	2	136–144	−11	3	139–141	−12	4	136–144	−15	7
143–147	−9	0	144–146	−11	2	145	−12	3	142–148	−13	4	145	−16	7
148–152	−9	−1	147–153	−11	1	146–154	−12	2	149–151	−13	3	146–154	−16	6
153–157	−10	−1	154–156	−12	1	155	−13	2	152–158	−14	3	155	−17	6
158–160	−10	−2	157–160	−12	0	156–160	−13	1	159–160	−14	2	156–160	−17	5

(*Continued*)

Table D-2 (*Continued*)

K. r_{xx} = .91
WISC–IV: Verbal Comprehension Index, Age 6
WISC–IV: Perceptual Reasoning Index, Ages 6 and 16
WISC–IV: Working Memory Index, Ages 8 and 13
WPPSI–III: Performance IQ, Ages 3½ and 4
WPPSI–III: Processing Speed Quotient, Age 4½

68%			*85%*			*90%*			*95%*			*99%*		
IQ	*L*	*U*	*IQ*	*L*	*U*	*IQ*	*L*	*U*	*IQ*	*L*	*U*	*IQ*	*L*	*U*
40–48	1	9	40	0	11	40–41	−1	12	40–49	−3	13	40–43	−5	16
49–51	0	9	41–48	−1	11	42–47	−2	12	50	−4	13	44–45	−6	16
52–60	0	8	49–51	−1	10	48–52	−2	11	51–60	−4	12	46–54	−6	15
61–62	−1	8	52–59	−2	10	53–58	−3	11	61	−5	12	55–56	−7	15
63–71	−1	7	60–62	−2	9	59–63	−3	10	62–71	−5	11	57–65	−7	14
72–73	−2	7	63–71	−3	9	64–69	−4	10	72	−6	11	66–67	−8	14
74–82	−2	6	72–73	−3	8	70–74	−4	9	73–83	−6	10	68–77	−8	13
83–84	−3	6	74–82	−4	8	75–80	−5	9	84–94	−7	9	78	−9	13
85–93	−3	5	83–84	−4	7	81–86	−5	8	95–105	−8	8	79–88	−9	12
94–95	−4	5	85–93	−5	7	87–91	−6	8	106–116	−9	7	89	−10	12
96–104	−4	4	94–95	−5	6	92–97	−6	7	117–127	−10	6	90–99	−10	11
105–106	−5	4	96–104	−6	6	98–102	−7	7	128	−11	6	100	−11	11
107–115	−5	3	105–106	−6	5	103–108	−7	6	129–138	−11	5	101–110	−11	10
116–117	−6	3	107–115	−7	5	109–113	−8	6	139	−12	5	111	−12	10
118–126	−6	2	116–117	−7	4	114–119	−8	5	140–149	−12	4	112–121	−12	9
127–128	−7	2	118–126	−8	4	120–125	−9	5	150	−13	4	122	−13	9
129–137	−7	1	127–128	−8	3	126–130	−9	4	151–160	−13	3	123–132	−13	8
138–139	−8	1	129–137	−9	3	131–136	−10	4				133–134	−14	8
140–148	−8	0	138–140	−9	2	137–141	−10	3				135–143	−14	7
149–151	−9	0	141–148	−10	2	142–147	−11	3				144–145	−15	7
152–160	−9	−1	149–151	−10	1	148–152	−11	2				146–154	−15	6
			152–159	−11	1	153–158	−12	2				155–156	−16	6
			160	−11	0	159–160	−12	1				157–160	−16	5

(Continued)

Table D-2 (*Continued*)

L. $r_{xx} = .92$
WISC–IV: Verbal Comprehension Index, Ages 7 and 8
WISC–IV: Perceptual Reasoning Index, Ages 7, 14, 15, and Average
WISC–IV: Working Memory Index, Ages 6, 9, 10, 11, 15, and Average
WPPSI–III: Processing Speed Quotient, Ages 4 and 5

68%			85%			90%			95%			99%		
IQ	L	U	IQ	L	U	IQ	L	U	IQ	L	U	IQ	L	U
40–42	1	9	40–48	−1	10	40–49	−2	11	40–48	−3	12	40–42	−5	15
43–44	1	8	49–51	−2	10	50	−2	10	49–51	−4	12	43–44	−6	15
45–55	0	8	52–60	−2	9	51–61	−3	10	52–60	−4	11	45–55	−6	14
56–57	0	7	61–64	−3	9	62–63	−3	9	61–64	−5	11	56–57	−7	14
58–67	−1	7	65–73	−3	8	64–74	−4	9	65–73	−5	10	58–67	−7	13
68–69	−1	6	74–76	−4	8	75	−4	8	74–76	−6	10	68–69	−8	13
70–80	−2	6	77–85	−4	7	76–86	−5	8	77–85	−6	9	70–80	−8	12
81–82	−2	5	86–89	−5	7	87–88	−5	7	86–89	−7	9	81–82	−9	12
83–92	−3	5	90–98	−5	6	89–99	−6	7	90–98	−7	8	83–92	−9	11
93–94	−3	4	99–101	−6	6	100	−6	6	99–101	−8	8	93–94	−10	11
95–105	−4	4	102–110	−6	5	101–111	−7	6	102–110	−8	7	95–105	−10	10
106–107	−4	3	111–114	−7	5	112–113	−7	5	111–114	−9	7	106–107	−11	10
108–117	−5	3	115–123	−7	4	114–124	−8	5	115–123	−9	6	108–117	−11	9
118–119	−5	2	124–126	−8	4	125	−8	4	124–126	−10	6	118–119	−12	9
120–130	−6	2	127–135	−8	3	126–136	−9	4	127–135	−10	5	120–130	−12	8
131–132	−6	1	136–139	−9	3	137–138	−9	3	136–139	−11	5	131–132	−13	8
133–142	−7	1	140–148	−9	2	139–149	−10	3	140–148	−11	4	133–142	−13	7
143–144	−7	0	149–151	−10	2	150	−10	2	149–151	−12	4	143–144	−14	7
145–155	−8	0	152–160	−10	1	151–160	−11	2	152–160	−12	3	145–155	−14	6
156–157	−8	−1										156–157	−15	6
158–160	−9	−1										158–160	−15	5

(Continued)

Table D-2 (*Continued*)

M. r_{xx} = .93
WISC–IV: Verbal Comprehension Index, Age 11
WISC–IV: Perceptual Reasoning Index, Ages 8, 9, 10, 11, 12, and 13
WISC–IV: Working Memory Index, Ages 12, 14, and 16
WPPSI–III: Performance IQ, Average for Ages 4–7¼
WAIS–III: Performance Scale IQ, Ages 16–17, 18–19, 20–24, 30–34, and 75–79
SB5: Nonverbal IQ, Age 13

68%			85%			90%			95%			99%		
IQ	L	U	IQ	L	U	IQ	L	U	IQ	L	U	IQ	L	U
40	1	8	40	−1	10	40–48	−2	10	40–46	−3	11	40–42	−5	14
41–45	0	8	41–45	−1	9	49–51	−3	10	47–53	−4	11	43	−6	14
46–54	0	7	46–54	−2	9	52–63	−3	9	54–60	−4	10	44–56	−6	13
55–59	−1	7	55–59	−2	8	64–65	−4	9	61–67	−5	10	57	−7	13
60–68	−1	6	60–68	−3	8	66–77	−4	8	68–75	−5	9	58–71	−7	12
69–74	−2	6	69–74	−3	7	78–79	−5	8	76–81	−6	9	72–85	−8	11
75–82	−2	5	75–83	−4	7	80–91	−5	7	82–89	−6	8	86	−9	11
83–88	−3	5	84–88	−4	6	92–94	−6	7	90–96	−7	8	87–99	−9	10
89–97	−3	4	89–97	−5	6	95–105	−6	6	97–103	−7	7	100	−10	10
98–102	−4	4	98–102	−5	5	106–108	−7	6	104–110	−8	7	101–113	−10	9
103–111	−4	3	103–111	−6	5	109–120	−7	5	111–118	−8	6	114	−11	9
112–117	−5	3	112–116	−6	4	121–122	−8	5	119–124	−9	6	115–128	−11	8
118–125	−5	2	117–125	−7	4	123–134	−8	4	125–132	−9	5	129–142	−12	7
126–131	−6	2	126–131	−7	3	135–136	−9	4	133–139	−10	5	143	−13	7
132–140	−6	1	132–140	−8	3	137–148	−9	3	140–146	−10	4	144–156	−13	6
141–145	−7	1	141–145	−8	2	149–151	−10	3	147–153	−11	4	157	−14	6
146–154	−7	0	146–154	−9	2	152–160	−10	2	154–160	−11	3	158–160	−14	5
155–159	−8	0	155–159	−9	1									
160	−8	−1	160	−10	1									

(Continued)

Table D-2 (*Continued*)

N. r_{xx} = .94
WISC–IV: Verbal Comprehension Index, Ages 9, 10, 13, and Average
WPPSI–III: Verbal IQ, Age 6
WPPSI–III: Performance IQ, Ages 4½, 5, 5½, and 6
WAIS–III: Performance Scale IQ, Ages 35–44, 45–54, 80–84, 85–89, and Average
SB5: Nonverbal IQ, Ages 6, 7, 8, 10, 11, and 12
SB5: Verbal IQ, Ages 11 and 12

68%			85%			90%			95%			99%		
IQ	L	U	IQ	L	U	IQ	L	U	IQ	L	U	IQ	L	U
40–49	0	7	40–41	−1	9	40–46	−2	9	40–45	−3	10	40	−5	13
50	0	6	42	−1	8	47–53	−3	9	46–54	−4	10	41–43	−5	12
51–65	−1	6	43–57	−2	8	54–63	−3	8	55–62	−4	9	44–56	−6	12
66–67	−1	5	58	−2	7	64–69	−4	8	63–71	−5	9	57–59	−6	11
68–82	−2	5	59–74	−3	7	70–80	−4	7	72–78	−5	8	60–73	−7	11
83–84	−2	4	75	−3	6	81–86	−5	7	79–87	−6	8	74–76	−7	10
85–99	−3	4	76–91	−4	6	87–96	−5	6	88–95	−6	7	77–90	−8	10
100	−3	3	92	−4	5	97–103	−6	6	96–104	−7	7	91–93	−8	9
101–115	−4	3	93–107	−5	5	104–113	−6	5	105–112	−7	6	94–106	−9	9
116–117	−4	2	108	−5	4	114–119	−7	5	113–121	−8	6	107–109	−9	8
118–132	−5	2	109–124	−6	4	120–130	−7	4	122–128	−8	5	110–123	−10	8
133–134	−5	1	125	−6	3	131–136	−8	4	129–137	−9	5	124–126	−10	7
135–149	−6	1	126–141	−7	3	137–146	−8	3	138–145	−9	4	127–140	−11	7
150	−6	0	142	−7	2	147–153	−9	3	146–154	−10	4	141–143	−11	6
151–160	−7	0	143–157	−8	2	154–160	−9	2	155–160	−10	3	144–156	−12	6
			158	−8	1							157–159	−12	5
			159–160	−9	1							160	−13	5

(Continued)

Table D-2 (*Continued*)

O. $r_{xx} = .95$
WISC–IV: Verbal Comprehension Index, Ages 12, 14, 15, and 16
WPPSI–III: Verbal IQ, Ages 2½, 3, 3½, Average for Ages 2¹/₂–3¹¹/₁₂ , 4, 4½, 5½, 7, and Average for Ages 4–7¼
WPPSI–III: Performance IQ, Age 7
WPPSI–III: Full Scale IQ, Ages 2½, 3, and Average for Ages 2¹/₂–3¹¹/₁₂
WAIS–III: Performance Scale IQ, Ages 25–29, 55–64, and 70–74
SB5: Nonverbal IQ, Ages 2, 4, 5, 9, 14, 30–39, and Average
SB5: Verbal IQ, Ages 2, 7, 10, and 13

68%			85%			90%			95%			99%		
IQ	L	U	IQ	L	U	IQ	L	U	IQ	L	U	IQ	L	U
40–46	0	6	40–41	−2	8	40–44	−2	8	40–45	−3	9	40–45	−5	11
47–53	−1	6	42–58	−2	7	45–55	−3	8	46–54	−4	9	46–54	−6	11
54–66	−1	5	59–61	−3	7	56–64	−3	7	55–65	−4	8	55–65	−6	10
67–73	−2	5	62–78	−3	6	65–75	−4	7	66–74	−5	8	66–74	−7	10
74–86	−2	4	79–81	−4	6	76–84	−4	6	75–85	−5	7	75–85	−7	9
87–93	−3	4	82–98	−4	5	85–95	−5	6	86–94	−6	7	86–94	−8	9
94–106	−3	3	99–101	−5	5	96–104	−5	5	95–105	−6	6	95–105	−8	8
107–113	−4	3	102–118	−5	4	105–115	−6	5	106–114	−7	6	106–114	−9	8
114–126	−4	2	119–121	−6	4	116–124	−6	4	115–125	−7	5	115–125	−9	7
127–133	−5	2	122–138	−6	3	125–135	−7	4	126–134	−8	5	126–134	−10	7
134–146	−5	1	139–141	−7	3	136–144	−7	3	135–145	−8	4	135–145	−10	6
147–153	−6	1	142–158	−7	2	145–155	−8	3	146–154	−9	4	146–154	−11	6
154–160	−6	0	159–160	−8	2	156–160	−8	2	155–160	−9	3	155–160	−11	5

P. $r_{xx} = .96$
WISC–IV: Full Scale IQ, Ages 6, 7, 8, 9, 10, 11, 12, 13, 14, 15, 16, and Average
WPPSI–III: Verbal IQ, Age 5
WPPSI–III: Full Scale IQ, Ages 3½, 4, 6, and Average for Ages 4–7¼
WAIS–III: Verbal Scale IQ, Ages 16–17 and 85–89
WAIS–III: Performance Scale IQ, Ages 65–69
SB5: Nonverbal IQ, Ages 3, 15, 16, 17–20, 21–29, and 80+
SB5: Verbal IQ, Ages 3, 4, 5, 6, 9, 14, 15, 16, 17–20, 21–29, 30–39, 60–69, and Average

68%			85%			90%			95%			99%		
IQ	L	U	IQ	L	U	IQ	L	U	IQ	L	U	IQ	L	U
40	0	5	40–41	−2	7	40–43	−2	7	40–46	−3	8	40–48	−5	10
41–59	−1	5	42–58	−2	6	44–56	−3	7	47–53	−4	8	49–51	−5	9
60–65	−1	4	59–66	−3	6	57–68	−3	6	54–71	−4	7	52–73	−6	9
66–84	−2	4	67–83	−3	5	69–81	−4	6	72–78	−5	7	74–76	−6	8
85–90	−2	3	84–91	−4	5	82–93	−4	5	79–96	−5	6	77–98	−7	8
91–109	−3	3	92–108	−4	4	94–106	−5	5	97–103	−6	6	99–101	−7	7
110–115	−3	2	109–116	−5	4	107–116	−5	4	104–121	−6	5	102–123	−8	7
116–134	−4	2	117–133	−5	3	117–131	−6	4	122–128	−7	5	124–126	−8	6
135–140	−4	1	134–141	−6	3	132–143	−6	3	129–146	−7	4	127–148	−9	6
141–159	−5	1	142–158	−6	2	144–156	−7	3	147–153	−8	4	149–151	−9	5
160	−5	0	159–160	−7	2	157–160	−7	2	154–160	−8	3	152–160	−10	5

(Continued)

Table D-2 (*Continued*)

Q. $r_{xx} = .97$
WPPSI–III: Full Scale IQ, Ages 4½, 5, 5½, and 7
WAIS–III: Full Scale IQ, Ages 16–17, 18–19, 75–79, and 85–89
WAIS–III: Verbal Scale IQ, Ages 18–19, 20–24, 25–29, 30–34, 45–54, 70–74, 75–79, and Average
SB5: Full Scale IQ, Ages 2, 4, 6, 7, 10, 11, 12, and 13
SB5: Verbal IQ, Ages 8, 40–49, 50–59, 70–79, and 80+
SB5: Nonverbal IQ, Ages 40–49, 50–59, 60–69, and 70–79

68%			85%			90%			95%			99%		
IQ	L	U	IQ	L	U	IQ	L	U	IQ	L	U	IQ	L	U
40–65	−1	4	40–62	−2	5	40–44	−2	6	40–47	−3	7	40–66	−5	8
66–67	−2	4	63–70	−3	5	45–55	−3	6	48–52	−3	6	67–99	−6	7
68–99	−2	3	71–95	−3	4	56–78	−3	5	53–81	−4	6	100	−7	7
100	−3	3	96–104	−4	4	79–88	−4	5	82–85	−4	5	101–133	−7	6
101–132	−3	2	105–129	−4	3	89–111	−4	4	86–114	−5	5	134–160	−8	5
133–134	−4	2	130–137	−5	3	112–121	−5	4	115–118	−5	4			
135–160	−4	1	138–160	−5	2	122–144	−5	3	119–147	−6	4			
						145–155	−6	3	148–152	−6	3			
						156–160	−6	2	153–160	−7	3			

R. $r_{xx} = .98$
WAIS–III: Verbal Scale IQ, Ages 55–64 and 65–69
WAIS–III: Full Scale IQ, Ages 20–24, 25–29, 30–34, 35–44, 45–54, 55–64, 65–69, 70–74, 80–84, and Average
SB5: Full Scale IQ, Ages 3, 8, 9, 14, 15, 16, 17–20, 21–29, 30–39, 40–49, 50–59, 60–69, 70–79, 80+, and Average

68%			85%			90%			95%			99%		
IQ	L	U	IQ	L	U	IQ	L	U	IQ	L	U	IQ	L	U
40–71	−1	3	40–74	−2	4	40–46	−2	5	40–71	−3	5	40–43	−4	7
72–78	−2	3	75	−2	3	47–53	−2	4	72–78	−4	5	44–56	−4	6
79–121	−2	2	76–124	−3	3	54–96	−3	4	79–121	−4	4	57–93	−5	6
122–128	−3	2	125	−3	2	97–103	−3	3	122–128	−5	4	94–106	−5	5
129–160	−3	1	126–160	−4	2	104–146	−4	3	129–160	−5	3	107–143	−6	5
						147–153	−4	2				144–156	−6	4
						154–160	−5	2				157–160	−7	4

Note. To compute the confidence interval for an obtained IQ, first find L and U for that IQ and the desired confidence level. Then subtract L from the obtained IQ to find the lower limit and add U to the obtained IQ to find the upper limit. For example, for a 7-year-old, the confidence interval at the 95% confidence level for an obtained IQ of 40 on the WISC–IV Processing Speed Index (see Section A) is 39 to 62 (40 − 1 = 39; 40 + 22 = 62). For a 7-year-old, the confidence interval at the 95% confidence level for an obtained IQ of 160 on the WISC–IV Processing Speed Index (see Section A) is 138 to 161 (160 − 22 = 138; 160 + 1 = 161). Note that the scores in the IQ column can also refer to Indexes.

The values of L and U in the various sections of this table can be used for any test with the specified reliability coefficient and a standard score distribution with $M = 100$ and $SD = 15$.

See Chapter 4, pages 113–114, for an explanation of how the values were computed.

Table D-3
Interpretive Rationales, Implications of High and Low Scores, and Instructional Implications for Wechsler Subtests

Ability	Background factors	Possible implications of high scores	Possible implications of low scores	Instructional implications
Arithmetic (AR)				
Quantitative knowledge (Gq) Short-term memory (Gsm) Fluid reasoning ability (Gf) Mathematical achievement (A3) Working memory (MW) Quantitative reasoning (RQ) Long-term memory Numerical reasoning ability Mental computation Application of basic arithmetical processes Concentration Attention Mental alertness Auditory sequential processing	Opportunity to acquire fundamental arithmetical processes Quality of early education and general education Auditory acuity Ability to self-monitor	Good working memory Good ability in mental arithmetic Good ability to apply reasoning skills to solve mathematical problems Good ability to apply arithmetical skills in personal and social problem-solving situations Good concentration Good attention Good short-term memory Good ability to convert word problems into mathematical calculations Good ability to engage in complex thought patterns (mainly for upper-level items) Good interest in school achievement	Poor working memory Poor ability in mental arithmetic Poor ability to apply reasoning skills to solve mathematical problems Poor ability to apply arithmetical skills in personal and social problem-solving situations Poor concentration Poor attention Poor short-term memory Poor ability to convert word problems into mathematical calculations Poor ability to engage in complex thought patterns (mainly for upper-level items) Lack of interest in school achievement	Develop arithmetical skills Develop concentration skills Use concrete objects to introduce concepts Drill in basic skills Provide interesting "real" problems to solve Use exercises involving analyzing arithmetical word problems Increase attention span
Block Design (BD)				
Visual processing (Gv) Visualization (VZ) Spatial relations (SR) Visual-perceptual reasoning Visual-perceptual organization Visual-motor coordination Spatial perception Abstract conceptualizing ability Analysis and synthesis Speed of mental and visual-motor processing Nonverbal reasoning Planning ability Concentration Fine-motor coordination Visual-perceptual discrimination	Rate of motor activity Color vision Ability to work under time pressure Visual acuity Trial-and-error learning Motivation and persistence	Good visual-perceptual reasoning Good visual-perceptual organization Good visual-spatial construction ability Good visual-motor-spatial integration Good conceptualizing, analyzing, and synthesizing ability Good speed and accuracy Good nonverbal reasoning ability Good trial-and-error methods Good vision Good hand-eye coordination Good attention to detail Good motivation and persistence	Poor visual-perceptual reasoning Poor visual-perceptual organization Poor visual-spatial construction ability Poor visual-motor-spatial integration Poor conceptualizing, analyzing, and synthesizing ability Poor speed and accuracy Poor nonverbal reasoning ability Poor trial-and-error methods Poor vision Poor hand-eye coordination Poor attention to detail Poor motivation and persistence	Use puzzles, blocks, Legos, spatial-visual tasks, perceptual tasks involving breaking down an object and building it up again, and art work with geometric forms and flannel board Focus on part-whole relationships and working with a model Focus on activities involving recognition of visual details

(Continued)

Table D-3 (Continued)

Ability	Background factors	Possible implications of high scores	Possible implications of low scores	Instructional implications
Cancellation (CA)				
Processing speed (Gs) Perceptual speed (P) Rate of test taking (R9) Visual-motor coordination or dexterity Visual processing Speed of visual processing Speed of mental operation Scanning ability Psychomotor speed Short-term visual memory Visual recall Attention Concentration Fine-motor coordination Visual-perceptual recognition Visual-perceptual discrimination	Rate of motor activity Motivation and persistence Visual acuity Ability to work under time pressure	Good processing speed Good perceptual scanning ability Good perceptual recognition ability Good vision Good attention and concentration Good short-term memory Good ability to work under time pressure Good motivation and persistence	Poor processing speed Poor perceptual scanning ability Poor perceptual recognition ability Poor vision Poor attention and concentration Poor short-term memory Poor ability to work under time pressure Poor motivation and persistence	Use scanning exercises, such as looking at two or more objects and deciding if they are the same or different Increase attention span Reinforce persistence Increase motivation Reduce stress of working under time pressure
Coding (CD)				
Processing speed (Gs) Rate of test taking (R9) Visual-motor coordination or dexterity Speed of mental operation Scanning ability Psychomotor speed Visual short-term memory Visual recall Attention Concentration Visual-perceptual symbol-associative skills Visual processing Fine-motor coordination Numerical recognition Visual-perceptual discrimination	Rate of motor activity Motivation and persistence Visual acuity Ability to work under time pressure	Good processing speed Good visual sequential processing ability Good visual-motor dexterity Good vision Good attention and concentration Good ability to learn new material associatively and reproduce it quickly and accurately Good scanning ability Good motivation and persistence Good pencil control Good ability to work under time pressure	Poor processing speed Poor visual sequential processing ability Poor visual-motor dexterity Poor vision Poor attention and concentration Poor ability to learn new material associatively and reproduce it quickly and accurately Poor scanning ability Poor motivation and persistence Poor pencil control Poor ability to work under time pressure	Use visual-motor learning exercises, such as developing a code for matching geometric figures and numbers, learning Morse Code, and working on tracing activities Improve scanning techniques aimed at identifying things that go together Reinforce persistence Reduce stress of working under time pressure Increase attention span Increase motivation

(Continued)

Table D-3 (*Continued*)				
Ability	*Background factors*	*Possible implications of high scores*	*Possible implications of low scores*	*Instructional implications*
Comprehension (CO)				
Crystallized knowledge (Gc) Language development (LD) General (verbal) information (K0) Verbal comprehension Social judgment Common sense Logical reasoning Application of practical reasoning and judgment in social situations Knowledge of conventional standards of behavior (fund of information) Reasoning Ability to evaluate past experience Moral and ethical judgment Long-term memory Receptive and expressive language	Cultural opportunities Quality of early education and general education Development of conscience or moral sense Awareness of environment	Good verbal comprehension Good social judgment Good common sense Good knowledge of rules of conventional behavior Good ability to organize knowledge Good ability to verbalize Social maturity Wide range of experience	Poor verbal comprehension Poor social judgment Poor common sense Poor knowledge of rules of conventional behavior Poor ability to organize knowledge Poor ability to verbalize Social immaturity Limited range of experience	Help child understand social mores, customs, and societal activities, such as how other children react to things, how the government works, and how banks operate Discuss the actions of others to help child develop an awareness of social relationships and others' expectations Encourage child to consider others' points of view Role-play situations, such as reporting fires, calling police, and calling the plumber
Digit Span (DS)				
Auditory short-term memory (Gsm) Working memory (MW) Memory span (MS) Rote learning Immediate auditory memory Concentration Auditory sequential processing Numerical ability	Auditory acuity Ability to self-monitor Ability to use encoding strategies Ability to use rehearsal strategies	Good auditory sequential processing Good auditory short-term memory Good rote memory Good immediate recall Good attention and concentration Good encoding ability Good rehearsal strategies Good ability to self-monitor	Poor auditory sequential processing Poor auditory short-term memory Poor rote memory Poor immediate recall Poor attention and concentration Poor encoding ability Poor rehearsal strategies Poor ability to self-monitor	Emphasize listening skills by using sequencing activities, reading a short story and asking the child to recall details, and seeing whether the child can follow directions Develop visualization skills Use short and simple directions and repeat when necessary Use other memory exercises and memory games Decrease anxiety

(*Continued*)

Table D-3 (Continued)

Ability	Background factors	Possible implications of high scores	Possible implications of low scores	Instructional implications
Information (IN)				
Crystallized knowledge (Gc) General (verbal) information (K0) Verbal comprehension Range of factual knowledge Long-term memory Receptive and expressive language	Richness of early environment Quality of early education and general education Cultural opportunities Interests and reading patterns Alertness to environment Intellectual curiosity and drive	Good range of factual knowledge Good knowledge of the culture Good long-term memory Enriched background Alertness and interest in the environment Intellectual ambitiousness Intellectual curiosity Urge to collect knowledge	Poor range of factual knowledge Poor knowledge of the culture Poor long-term memory Limited background Limited alertness and interest in the environment Limited intellectual ambitiousness Limited intellectual curiosity Limited urge to collect knowledge	Stress factual material by having child read newspaper articles, watch television news broadcasts or listen to radio news broadcasts, discuss current events, and do memory exercises Use other enrichment activities, including activities centering on national holidays, science and social studies projects, and projects involving animals and their function in society
Letter–Number Sequencing (LN)				
Auditory short-term memory (Gsm) Working memory (MW) Memory span (MS) Rote memory Immediate auditory memory Attention Concentration Auditory sequential processing Numerical ability	Auditory acuity Ability to self-monitor Ability to use encoding strategies Ability to use rehearsal strategies	Good auditory sequential processing Good auditory short-term memory Good rote memory Good attention and concentration Good encoding ability Good rehearsal strategies Good ability to self-monitor	Poor auditory sequential processing Poor auditory short-term memory Poor rote memory Poor attention and concentration Poor encoding ability Poor rehearsal strategies Poor ability to self-monitor	Emphasize listening skills by using sequencing activities, reading a short story and asking the child to recall details, and seeing whether the child can follow directions Develop visualization skills Use short and simple directions and repeat when necessary Use other memory exercises and memory games

(Continued)

Table D-3 (*Continued*)

Ability	Background factors	Possible implications of high scores	Possible implications of low scores	Instructional implications
Matrix Reasoning (MR)				
Fluid reasoning ability (Gf) Visual processing (Gv) Induction (I) Visualization (VZ) Visual-perceptual analogic reasoning Visual-perceptual organization Reasoning ability Classification ability Ability to form analogies Attention to detail Concentration Spatial ability Visual-perceptual discrimination	Motivation and persistence Ability to work toward a goal Ability to use trial and error Visual acuity	Good visual-perceptual reasoning Good visual-perceptual organization Good reasoning ability Good attention to detail Good concentration Good vision Good motivation and persistence	Poor visual-perceptual reasoning Poor visual-perceptual organization Poor reasoning ability Poor attention to detail Poor concentration Poor vision Poor motivation and persistence	Use puzzles, blocks, Legos, spatial-visual tasks, perceptual tasks involving breaking down an object and building it up again, and art work with geometric forms and flannel board Focus on part-whole relationships Use sequencing tasks
Object Assembly (OA)				
Visual processing (Gv) Spatial relations (SR) Closure speed (CS) Visual-perceptual organization Visual-perceptual discrimination Visual-motor coordination Ability to synthesize concrete parts into meaningful wholes Speed of mental processing Fine-motor coordination Nonverbal reasoning Perception of meaningful stimuli Analysis and synthesis Psychomotor speed	Rate of motor activity Familiarity with figures and puzzles Motivation and persistence Experience with part-whole relationships Ability to work toward an unknown goal Ability to work under time pressure Trial-and-error learning Visual acuity	Good visual-perceptual organization Good visual-motor coordination Good ability to visualize a whole from its parts Good trial-and-error ability Experience in assembling puzzles Good motivation and persistence Good ability to work under time pressure	Poor visual-perceptual organization Poor visual-motor coordination Poor ability to visualize a whole from its parts Poor trial-and-error ability Limited experience in assembling puzzles Poor motivation and persistence Poor ability to work under time pressure	Develop perceptual and psychomotor skills through guided practice in assembling parts into familiar configurations Encourage trial-and-error activities Reinforce persistence Work with puzzles and activities centering on recognition of missing body parts Employ construction, cutting, and pasting activities Focus on interpretation of wholes from minimal cues

(*Continued*)

Table D-3 (Continued)

Ability	Background factors	Possible implications of high scores	Possible implications of low scores	Instructional implications
Picture Arrangement (PA)				
Visual processing (Gv) Crystallized knowledge (Gc) General (verbal) information (K0) Visualization (VZ) Visual-perceptual organization Planning ability Interpretation of social situations Nonverbal reasoning ability Attention to details Alertness Common sense Anticipation of consequences	Cultural opportunities Ability to work under time pressure Ability to infer cause-and-effect relationships Visual acuity	Good visual-perceptual organization Good planning ability Good ability to interpret social situations Good nonverbal reasoning ability Good ability to attend to detail Good ability to synthesize parts into intelligible wholes Good ability to work under time pressure	Poor visual-perceptual organization Poor planning ability Poor ability to interpret social situations Poor nonverbal reasoning ability Poor ability to attend to detail Poor ability to synthesize parts into intelligible wholes Poor ability to work under time pressure	Focus on cause-and-effect relationships, logical sequential presentations, and part-whole relationships Use story completion exercises Discuss alternative behaviors and endings in stories and events
Picture Completion (PCm)				
Crystallized knowledge (Gc) Visual processing (Gv) Flexibility of closure (CF) General (verbal) information (K0) Visual-perceptual organization Visual discrimination Visual-perceptual discrimination Visual long-term memory Ability to differentiate essential from nonessential details Identification of familiar objects (visual recognition) Concentration on visually perceived material Alertness to detail Reasoning Speed of mental processing Scanning ability Attention Nonverbal reasoning Spatial perception Perception of meaningful stimuli Receptive and expressive language	Cultural opportunities Alertness to environment Quality of early education and general education Ability to work under time pressure Visual acuity Willingness to guess when uncertain	Good visual-perceptual reasoning Good perception and concentration Good alertness to details Good ability to differentiate between essential and nonessential details Good vision	Poor visual-perceptual reasoning Poor perception and concentration Poor alertness to details Poor ability to differentiate between essential and nonessential details Poor vision Preoccupation with irrelevant details Anxiety Negativism	Focus on visual learning techniques stressing individual parts that make up the whole Use perceptual activities that focus on recognizing objects, describing objects, and paying attention to details (e.g., maps and art work) Improve scanning techniques aimed at identifying missing elements in pictures

(Continued)

Table D-3 (*Continued*)				
Ability	Background factors	Possible implications of high scores	Possible implications of low scores	Instructional implications
Picture Concepts (PCn)				
Fluid reasoning ability (Gf) Crystallized knowledge (Gc) Induction (I) Lexical knowledge (VL) Visual-perceptual recognition processing Visual-perceptual reasoning Conceptual thinking Language ability Ability to separate essential from nonessential details Nonverbal reasoning Visual-perceptual organization Visual-perceptual discrimination Visual processing Perception of meaningful stimuli Reasoning	Cultural opportunities Interests and reading patterns Intellectual curiosity Quality of early education and general education Visual acuity	Good visual-perceptual reasoning Good conceptual thinking Good ability to use logical and abstract thinking Good ability to discriminate fundamental from superficial relationships Good ability to select appropriate relationships between two objects or concepts Good vision	Poor visual-perceptual reasoning Poor conceptual thinking Poor ability to use logical and abstract thinking Poor ability to discriminate fundamental from superficial relationships Poor ability to select appropriate relationships between two objects or concepts Poor vision	Focus on describing the parts of objects Focus on recognizing differences and similarities in shapes, textures, and daily surroundings Use exercises involving classification and making generalizations
Picture Naming (PN)				
Crystallized knowledge (Gc) Language development (LD) Lexical knowledge (VL) Word knowledge Verbal comprehension Acquired knowledge Fund of information Long-term memory Perception of meaningful stimuli Visual memory Visual processing Visual-perceptual discrimination Receptive and expressive language	Cultural opportunities Interests and reading patterns Richness of early environment Quality of early education and general education Visual acuity	Good word knowledge Good verbal comprehension Good verbal skills and language development Enriched background Good early education and general education Good ability to conceptualize Good long-term memory Intellectual striving	Poor word knowledge Poor verbal comprehension Poor verbal skills and language development Limited background Limited early education and general education Poor ability to conceptualize Poor long-term memory Limited intellectual striving English as a second language	Develop working vocabulary Encourage child to discuss experiences, ask questions, and make a dictionary Use other verbal enrichment exercises, including Scrabble, analogy, and other word games

(*Continued*)

Table D-3 (*Continued*)

Ability	Background factors	Possible implications of high scores	Possible implications of low scores	Instructional implications
Receptive Vocabulary (RV)				
Crystallized knowledge (Gc) Language development (LD) Lexical knowledge (VL) Word knowledge Verbal comprehension Fund of information Long-term memory Perception of meaningful stimuli Visual memory Visual processing Visual-perceptual discrimination Receptive and expressive language	Cultural opportunities Interests and reading patterns Richness of early environment Quality of early education and general education Intellectual curiosity Visual acuity	Good word knowledge Good verbal comprehension Good verbal skills and language development Enriched background Good early education and general education Good ability to conceptualize Intellectual striving	Poor word knowledge Poor verbal comprehension Poor verbal skills and language development Limited background Limited early education and general education Poor ability to conceptualize Limited intellectual striving English as a second language	Develop working vocabulary Encourage child to discuss experiences, ask questions, and make a dictionary Use other verbal enrichment exercises, including Scrabble, analogy, and other word games
Similarities (SI)				
Crystallized knowledge (Gc) Language development (LD) Lexical knowledge (VL) Verbal concept formation Verbal comprehension Abstract thinking ability Reasoning ability Capacity for associative thinking Ability to separate essential from nonessential details Long-term memory Vocabulary Receptive and expressive language	Quality of early education and general education Cultural opportunities Richness of early environment Interests and reading patterns	Good verbal comprehension Good conceptual thinking Good ability to see relationships Good ability to use logical and abstract thinking Good ability to discriminate fundamental from superficial relationships Good ability to conceptualize and verbalize appropriate relationships between two objects or concepts Flexibility of thought processes	Poor verbal comprehension Poor conceptual thinking Poor ability to see relationships Poor ability to use logical and abstract thinking Poor ability to discriminate fundamental from superficial relationships Poor ability to conceptualize and verbalize appropriate relationships between two objects or concepts Rigidity of thought processes	Focus on recognizing differences and similarities in shapes, textures, and daily surroundings Provide activities involving sorting objects or pictures Stress language development, synonyms and antonyms, and exercises involving abstract words, classifications, and generalizations

(Continued)

Table D-3 (*Continued*)

Ability	Background factors	Possible implications of high scores	Possible implications of low scores	Instructional implications
Symbol Search (SS)				
Processing speed (Gs) Perceptual speed (P) Rate of test taking (R9) Visual-perceptual discrimination Speed of mental processing Scanning ability Psychomotor speed Attention Concentration Visual short-term memory Fine-motor coordination	Rate of motor activity Motivation and persistence Ability to work under time pressure Visual acuity	Good processing speed Good visual-perceptual discrimination Good attention and concentration Good visual short-term memory Good vision Good motivation and persistence Good ability to work under time pressure	Poor processing speed Poor visual-perceptual discrimination Poor attention and concentration Poor visual short-term memory Poor vision Poor motivation and persistence Poor ability to work under time pressure	Use scanning exercises, such as looking at two or more objects and deciding if they are the same or different Reinforce persistence Reduce stress of working under time pressure Increase attention span Increase motivation
Vocabulary (VC)				
Crystallized knowledge (Gc) Language development (LD) Lexical knowledge (VL) Verbal comprehension Vocabulary Word knowledge Fund of information Richness of ideas Long-term memory Verbal fluency Conceptual thinking Receptive and expressive language	Cultural opportunities Interests and reading patterns Richness of early environment Quality of early education and general education Intellectual curiosity	Good word knowledge Good verbal comprehension Good verbal skills Good language development Good ability to conceptualize Good intellectual striving Enriched background Good early education and general education Good encouragement of verbal communication in family	Poor word knowledge Poor verbal comprehension Poor verbal skills Poor language development Poor ability to conceptualize Limited intellectual striving Limited background Limited early education and general education Limited encouragement of verbal communication in family English as a second language	Develop working vocabulary Encourage child to discuss experiences, ask questions, and make cards containing vocabulary words and definitions Use other verbal enrichment exercises, including Scrabble, analogy, and other word games Encourage child to write about his or her activities and to keep a diary

(Continued)

Table D-3 (Continued)

Ability	Background factors	Possible implications of high scores	Possible implicationsof low scores	Instructional implications
Word Reasoning (WR)				
Crystallized knowledge (Gc)	Cultural opportunities	Good verbal comprehension	Poor verbal comprehension	Focus on reasoning tasks
Fluid reasoning ability (Gf)	Interests and reading patterns	Good analogic reasoning ability	Poor analogic reasoning ability	Develop understanding
Language development (LD)	Quality of early education and general	Good integration and synthesizing ability	Poor integration and synthesizing ability	of how to use information in a
Lexical knowledge (VL)	education	Good ability to generate alternative concepts	Poor ability to generate alternative concepts	logical manner
Induction (I)	Intellectual curiosity	Good ability to see relationships	Poor ability to see relationships	Use guessing games such as "20
Verbal comprehension		Good long-term memory	Poor long-term memory	Questions"
Verbal reasoning		Good vocabulary	Poor vocabulary	
Analogic reasoning		Good attention	Poor attention	
Capacity for associative thinking				
Integration and synthesizing ability				
Ability to generate alternative concepts				
Long-term memory				
Attention				
Conceptual thinking				
Short-term memory				
Vocabulary				
Receptive and expressive language				

Note. Abbreviations for the broad and narrow abilities in the Cattell-Horn-Carroll (CHC) model are shown within the parentheses. Table D-4 defines the CHC broad and narrow abilities associated with the Wechsler subtests, and Table D-5 shows the CHC broad and narrow abilities associated with the Wechsler subtests, Indexes, and Full Scale in grid form.

Crystallized knowledge is also referred to as crystallized intelligence or crystallized ability. Fluid reasoning ability is also referred to as fluid ability, fluid reasoning, or fluid intelligence.

Select the appropriate implication(s) based on the entire test protocol and background information.

Source: The CHC broad and narrow abilities adapted, in part, from Flanagan, McGrew, and Ortiz (2000) and Horn (1987, 1998).

Table D-4
Definitions of Broad and Narrow Abilities in the Cattell-Horn-Carroll (CHC) Model Associated with Wechsler Subtests

Broad and narrow abilities	Subtests
Crystallized Knowledge (Gc): The ability to use the knowledge base accumulated over time in the process of acculturation.	Comprehension, Information, Picture Arrangement, Picture Completion, Picture Concepts, Picture Naming, Receptive Vocabulary, Similarities, Vocabulary, Word Reasoning
General (verbal) Information (K0): The ability to use a range of general knowledge.	Comprehension, Information, Picture Arrangement, Picture Completion
Language Development (LD): The ability to understand spoken native language.	Comprehension, Picture Naming, Receptive Vocabulary, Similarities, Vocabulary, Word Reasoning
Lexical Knowledge (VL): The ability to use and understand words.	Picture Concepts, Picture Naming, Receptive Vocabulary, Similarities, Vocabulary, Word Reasoning
Fluid Reasoning Ability (Gf): The ability to solve relatively novel tasks by forming and recognizing concepts, identifying and perceiving relationships, drawing inferences, and reorganizing and transforming information.	Arithmetic, Matrix Reasoning, Picture Concepts, Word Reasoning
Induction (I): The ability to draw conclusions from known facts or principles.	Matrix Reasoning, Picture Concepts, Word Reasoning
Quantitative Reasoning (RQ): The ability to reason inductively and deductively using mathematical concepts.	Arithmetic
Quantitative Knowledge (Gq): The ability to use acquired mathematical knowledge.	Arithmetic
Mathematical Achievement (A3): The ability to demonstrate mathematical ability on an achievement test.	Arithmetic
Processing Speed (Gs): The ability to perform relatively easy and over-learned cognitive tasks quickly and efficiently using sustained attention and concentration.	Cancellation, Coding, Symbol Search
Perceptual Speed (P): The ability to distinguish similar visual patterns and to find instances of a particular pattern under high-speed conditions.	Cancellation, Symbol Search
Rate of Test Taking (R9): The ability to perform relatively simple tasks quickly.	Cancellation, Coding, Symbol Search
Short-Term Memory (Gsm): The ability to hold information in immediate memory and then use it within a few seconds.	Arithmetic, Digit Span, Letter–Number Sequencing
Memory Span (MS): The ability to recall a series of arbitrary elements (letters, numbers) after a few seconds.	Digit Span (primarily Digit Span Forward), Letter–Number Sequencing
Working Memory (MW): The ability to perform cognitive operations on information stored in short-term memory.	Arithmetic, Digit Span (primarily Digit Span Backward), Letter–Number Sequencing
Visual Processing (Gv): The ability to solve simple and complex visual problems.	Block Design, Matrix Reasoning, Object Assembly, Picture Arrangement, Picture Completion
Closure Speed (CS): The ability to rapidly organize separate visual stimuli into a meaningful whole.	Object Assembly
Flexibility of Closure (CF): The ability to identify a particular figure in a complex visual array.	Picture Completion
Spatial Relations (SR): The ability to solve problems involving spatial relations.	Block Design, Object Assembly
Visualization (VZ): The ability to mentally manipulate objects or visual patterns.	Block Design, Matrix Reasoning, Picture Arrangement

Note. Crystallized knowledge is also referred to as crystallized intelligence or crystallized ability. Fluid reasoning ability is also referred to as fluid ability, fluid reasoning, or fluid intelligence.

Source: Adapted, in part, from Flanagan, McGrew, and Ortiz (2000) and Horn (1987, 1998).

Table D-5
Broad and Narrow Abilities in the Cattell-Horn-Carroll (CHC) Model Associated with Wechsler Subtests, Indexes, and Full Scale IQs

CHC broad and narrow abilities	Arithmetic	Block Design	Cancellation	Coding	Comprehension	Digit Span	Information	Letter–Number Sequencing	Matrix Reasoning	Object Assembly	Picture Arrangement	Picture Completion
Crystallized Knowledge (Gc)					■		■				■	■
General Information (K0)					■		■				■	■
Language Development (LD)					■							
Lexical Knowledge (VL)												
Fluid Reasoning Ability (Gf)	■								■			
Induction (I)									■			
Quantitative Reasoning (RQ)	■											
Quantitative Knowledge (Gq)	■											
Mathematical Achievement (A3)	■											
Processing Speed (Gs)			■	■								
Perceptual Speed (P)			■									
Rate of Test Taking (R9)			■	■								
Short-Term Memory (Gsm)	■					■		■				
Memory Span (MS)						■		■				
Working Memory (MW)	■					■		■				
Visual Processing (Gv)		■							■	■	■	■
Closure Speed (CS)										■		
Flexibility of Closure (CF)												■
Spatial Relations (SR)		■								■		
Visualization (VZ)		■							■		■	

(*Continued*)

Table D-5 (*Continued*)

Picture Concepts	Picture Naming	Receptive Vocabulary	Similarities	Symbol Search	Vocabulary	Word Reasoning	Verbal Comprehension Index[a]	Perceptual Reasoning Index[b]	Working Memory Index	Processing Speed Index	Full Scale IQ[c]	CHC broad and narrow abilities
■	■	■	■		■	■	■				■	**Crystallized Knowledge (Gc)**
							■				■	General Information (K0)
	■	■	■		■	■	■				■	Language Development (LD)
■	■	■	■		■	■	■				■	Lexical Knowledge (VL)
■						■	■	■			■	**Fluid Reasoning Ability (Gf)**
■						■		■			■	Induction (I)
											■	Quantitative Reasoning (RQ)
											■	**Quantitative Knowledge (Gq)**
											■	Mathematical Achievement (A3)
				■						■	■	**Processing Speed (Gs)**
				■						■	■	Perceptual Speed (P)
				■						■	■	Rate of Test Taking (R9)
									■		■	**Short-Term Memory (Gsm)**
									■		■	Memory Span (MS)
									■		■	Working Memory (MW)
								■			■	**Visual Processing (Gv)**
											■	Closure Speed (CS)
											■	Flexibility of Closure (CF)
								■			■	Spatial Relations (SR)
								■			■	Visualization (VZ)

Note. Processing Speed Index is referred to as Processing Speed Quotient on the WPPSI–III. Crystallized knowledge is also referred to as crystallized intelligence or crystallized ability. Fluid reasoning ability is also referred to as fluid ability, fluid reasoning, or fluid intelligence.

[a]Also referred to as Verbal Composite in some Wechsler scales.
[b]Also referred to as Performance Composite in some Wechsler scales.
[c]The CHC broad and narrow abilities listed for the Full Scale only pertain if the subtest with this ability is part of the Full Scale.

Table D-6
Interpretive Rationales, Implications of High and Low Scores, and Instructional Implications for Wechsler Composites and Scales

Ability	Background factors	Possible implications of high scores	Possible implications of low scores	Instructional implications
Full Scale Composite				
Crystallized knowledge (Gc) Fluid reasoning ability (Gf) Quantitative knowledge (Gq) Processing speed (Gs) Short-term memory (Gsm) Visual processing (Gv) General intelligence Scholastic aptitude Academic aptitude Readiness to master a school curriculum Verbal skills Nonverbal skills Retrieval of material from long-term memory Attention Concentration	Cultural opportunities Quality of early education and general education Ability to self-monitor Ability to process visual information Ability to process verbal information Auditory and visual short-term memory Auditory and visual acuity Ability to work under time pressure Motivation and persistence	Good general intelligence Good scholastic aptitude Good verbal and nonverbal skills Good readiness to master school curriculum	Poor general intelligence Poor scholastic aptitude Poor verbal and nonverbal skills Poor readiness to master school curriculum	Focus on language development activities Focus on visual learning activities Use spatial-visual activities Develop concept formation skills Reinforce persistence and motivation Reduce stress
Verbal Comprehension Composite/Verbal Scale				
Crystallized knowledge (Gc) Fluid reasoning ability (Gf) Language development (LD) Lexical knowledge (VL) General information (K0) Verbal comprehension Application of verbal skills and information to solve new problems Verbal ability Ability to process verbal information Ability to think with words Auditory-vocal processing Retrieval of material from long-term memory Attention	Richness of early environment Quality of early education and general education Cultural opportunities Interests and reading patterns	Good verbal comprehension Good language development Good scholastic aptitude Good knowledge of the cultural milieu Good concept formation Good readiness to master school curriculum	Poor verbal comprehension Poor language development Poor scholastic aptitude Poor knowledge of the cultural milieu Poor concept formation Poor readiness to master school curriculum	Stress language development activities Use verbal enrichment activities Focus on current events Use exercises involving concept formation

(Continued)

Table D-6 (*Continued*)

Ability	Background factors	Possible implications of high scores	Possible implications of low scores	Instructional implications
Perceptual Reasoning Composite/Performance Scale				
Fluid reasoning ability (Gf) Induction (I) Visual processing (Gv) Spatial relations (SR) Visualization (VZ) Visual-perceptual reasoning Visual-perceptual organization Ability to think in visual images and manipulate them with fluency and relative speed Ability to interpret or organize visually perceived material quickly Nonverbal reasoning Visual-perceptual discrimination Ability to form relatively abstract concepts and relationships without the use of words Immediate problem-solving ability Attention Concentration	Motivation and persistence Ability to use trial and error Alertness Cultural opportunities Interests Visual acuity	Good visual-perceptual reasoning Good visual-perceptual organization Good alertness to detail Good nonverbal reasoning ability Good motivation and persistence Good ability to work quickly and efficiently Good spatial ability	Poor visual-perceptual reasoning Poor visual-perceptual organization Poor alertness to detail Poor nonverbal reasoning ability Poor motivation and persistence Poor ability to work quickly and efficiently Poor spatial ability	Focus on visual learning activities Focus on part-whole relationships Use spatial-visual tasks Encourage trial-and-error activities Reinforce persistence Focus on visual planning activities
Working Memory Composite				
Auditory short-term memory (Gsm) Working memory (MW) Memory span (MS) Rote memory Immediate auditory memory Attention Concentration Numerical ability	Ability to receive stimuli Ability to self-monitor Auditory acuity and discrimination Ability to use encoding strategies Ability to use rehearsal strategies	Good auditory short-term memory Good working memory Good rote memory Good ability to sustain attention and concentrate Good encoding ability Good rehearsal strategies Good ability to self-monitor	Poor auditory short-term memory Poor working memory Poor rote memory Poor ability to sustain attention and concentrate Poor encoding ability Poor rehearsal strategies Poor ability to self-monitor	Develop short-term auditory memory skills Emphasize listening skills Develop attention skills Develop concentration skills Develop visualization skills Focus on small, meaningful units of instruction Develop basic arithmetical skills Reduce stress

(*Continued*)

Table D-6 (Continued)

Ability	Background factors	Possible implications of high scores	Possible implications of low scores	Instructional implications
Processing Speed Composite				
Processing speed (Gs) Perceptual speed (P) Rate of test taking (R9) Visual-motor coordination and dexterity Speed of mental operation Scanning ability Psychomotor speed Attention Concentration Short-term visual memory Fine-motor coordination Visual-perceptual discrimination	Rate of motor activity Motivation and persistence Visual acuity Ability to work under time pressure	Good processing speed Good visual-perceptual speed Good attention and concentration Good visual short-term memory Good sustained energy or persistence Good visual-perceptual scanning ability Good visual processing Good motivation and persistence Good ability to work under time pressure Good visual-perceptual discrimination ability	Poor processing speed Poor visual-perceptual speed Poor attention and concentration Poor visual short-term memory Poor sustained energy or persistence Poor visual-perceptual scanning ability Poor visual processing Poor motivation and persistence Poor ability to work under time pressure Poor visual-perceptual discrimination ability	Develop visual-motor skills Develop concentration skills Focus on learning codes Focus on selecting numbers that match Improve scanning techniques

Note. Abbreviations for the broad and narrow abilities in the Cattell-Horn-Carroll (CHC) model are shown within the parentheses. Table D-4 defines the CHC broad and narrow abilities associated with the Wechsler subtests, Indexes, and Full Scale, and Table D-5 shows the CHC broad and narrow abilities associated with the Wechsler subtests in grid form.

Crystallized knowledge is also referred to as crystallized intelligence or crystallized ability. Fluid reasoning ability is also referred to as fluid ability, fluid reasoning, or fluid intelligence.

Source: The CHC broad and narrow abilities adapted, in part, from Flanagan, McGrew, and Ortiz (2000) and Horn (1987, 1998).

Table D-7
Suggested Remediation Activities for Wechsler Composites

Composite	CHC ability	Instructional implications
Verbal Comprehension or Verbal Scale	Crystallized knowledge (Gc) Fluid reasoning ability (Gf) Language development (LD) Lexical knowledge (VL) General information (K0)	Have children • review basic concepts, such as days of the week, months, time, distances, and directions • report major current events by referring to pictures and articles from magazines and newspapers • use a dictionary • learn new words • repeat simple stories in their own words • explain how story characters are feeling and thinking • participate in show-and-tell activities • make scrapbooks of classifications such as animals, vehicles, or utensils • find similarities among dissimilar objects • sort words by categories
Perceptual Reasoning or Performance Scale	Fluid reasoning ability (Gf) Visual processing (Gv) Spatial relations (SR) Visualization (VZ) Induction (I)	Have children • identify common objects and discuss details • sort pictures by categories • play guessing games involving description of a person, place, or thing • match letters, shapes, and numbers • complete jigsaw puzzles • play with Tinkertoys • play with blocks • make pegboard designs • solve mazes • describe details in pictures • arrange pictures on cards in a meaningful sequence
Working Memory	Auditory short-term memory (Gsm) Memory span (MS) Working memory (MW)	Have children • learn their own telephone numbers and addresses, days of the week, months of the year, and other important information • play spelling games • play memory games • do mathematical word problems • play listening games such as follow the leader
Processing Speed	Processing speed (Gs) Perceptual speed (P) Rate of test taking (R9)	Have children • do paper-folding activities • do finger-painting activities • do dot-to-dot exercises • cut things out with scissors • string beads in patterns • follow a moving object with their eyes • trace items such as their own hands, geometric forms, and letters • make large circles and lines on a chalkboard • copy from patterns • draw pictures from memory • visually scan pictures or objects

Note. Abbreviations for the broad and narrow abilities in the Cattell-Horn-Carroll (CHC) model are shown within the parentheses. Table D-4 defines the CHC broad and narrow abilities associated with the Wechsler subtests, and Table D-5 shows the CHC broad and narrow abilities associated with the Wechsler subtests, Indexes, and Full Scale in grid form.

Crystallized knowledge is also referred to as crystallized intelligence or crystallized ability. Fluid reasoning ability is also referred to as fluid ability, fluid reasoning, or fluid intelligence.
Source: The CHC broad and narrow abilities adapted, in part, from Flanagan, McGrew, and Ortiz (2000) and Horn (1987, 1998).

Table D-8
Reporting on Wechsler Composites and Subtests

Following are summaries of the essential features of the WISC–IV, WPPSI–III, and WAIS–III Composites, scales, and subtests. You can use this material in discussing assessment results with parents and referral sources and in writing your report.

COMPOSITES

Full Scale Composite

The Full Scale IQ is a general estimate of a child's current level of cognitive ability. It includes measures of verbal comprehension, perceptual reasoning, working memory, and processing speed. Of the various measures in the test, the Full Scale IQ is usually the most reliable and valid estimate of the child's general intelligence, scholastic aptitude, and readiness to master a school curriculum. Factors that may be related to an examinee's score include cultural opportunities, quality of early education and general education, ability to self-monitor, ability to process visual information, ability to process verbal information, auditory and visual short-term memory, auditory and visual acuity, ability to work under time pressure, and motivation and persistence.

Verbal Comprehension Composite or Verbal Scale

The Verbal Comprehension Composite or Verbal Scale measures verbal comprehension and other verbal skills. These skills include ability to apply verbal skills and information to the solution of new problems, ability to process verbal information, and ability to think with words. Factors that may be related to an examinee's score include richness of early environment, quality of early education and general education, cultural opportunities, and interests and reading patterns.

Perceptual Reasoning Composite or Performance Scale

The Perceptual Reasoning Composite or Performance Scale measures nonverbal reasoning skills. These skills include ability to think in visual images and to manipulate them with fluency, ability to interpret or organize visually perceived material quickly, attention, and concentration. Factors that may be related to an examinee's score include motivation and persistence, ability to use trial and error, alertness, cultural opportunities, interests, and visual acuity.

Working Memory Composite

The Working Memory Composite measures working memory. These skills include auditory short-term memory, ability to sustain attention, and numerical ability. Factors that may be related to an examinee's score include ability to self-monitor, auditory acuity and discrimination, ability to use encoding strategies, and ability to use rehearsal strategies.

Processing Speed Composite

The Processing Speed Composite measures processing speed skills. These skills include visual-perceptual discrimination, visual-motor coordination and dexterity, and speed of mental operation. Factors that may be related to an examinee's score include rate of motor activity, motivation and persistence, visual acuity, and ability to work under time pressure.

SUBTESTS

Arithmetic

The Arithmetic subtest measures facility in mental arithmetic. The examinee is asked to solve several types of arithmetic problems involving addition, subtraction, multiplication, division, and problem-solving strategies. The subtest provides valuable information about an examinee's numerical reasoning ability, concentration, attention, auditory short-term memory, and long-term memory. Factors that may be related to an examinee's score include opportunity to acquire fundamental arithmetical processes, quality of early education and general education, auditory acuity, and ability to self-monitor.

Block Design

The Block Design subtest measures spatial visualization and nonverbal reasoning ability. The examinee is asked to use blocks to assemble a design identical to one made by the examiner or one pictured on a card. The subtest provides valuable information about an examinee's (a) ability to analyze and synthesize visual-spatial material and (b) visual-motor coordination. Factors that may be related to an examinee's score include rate of motor activity, color vision, ability to work under time pressure, visual acuity, trial-and-error learning, and motivation and persistence.

Cancellation

The Cancellation subtest measures visual alertness and visual scanning ability. The examinee is asked to mark only pictures of animals on pages with pictures of both animals and objects. The subtest provides valuable information about an examinee's perceptual discrimination, speed and accuracy, attention, concentration, and vigilance. Factors that may be related to an examinee's score include rate of motor activity, motivation and persistence, visual acuity, and ability to work under time pressure.

Coding

The Coding subtest measures processing speed. The examinee is asked to look at a key in which symbols are matched with other symbols. Below the key are rectangles, each with a symbol in the upper part and a blank space in the lower part. In the blank space, the examinee must draw the symbol that matches the one above, according to the key. The subtest provides valuable information about psychomotor speed, visual-motor coordination or dexterity, scanning ability, attention, and concentration. Factors that may be related to an examinee's score include rate of motor activity, motivation and persistence, visual acuity, and ability to work under time pressure.

Comprehension

The Comprehension subtest measures social judgment and common sense. The examinee is asked to answer questions about various situations that, in part, involve interpersonal relations and social mores. The subtest provides valuable information about an examinee's knowledge of conventional

(Continued)

standards of behavior. Factors that may be related to an examinee's score include cultural opportunities, quality of early education and general education, development of conscience or moral sense, and awareness of the environment.

Digit Span

The Digit Span subtest measures auditory short-term memory. The examinee is asked to repeat series of digits given orally by the examiner and then to repeat different series of digits in reverse order. The subtest provides valuable information about an examinee's auditory short-term memory, attention, and concentration. Factors that may be related to an examinee's score include auditory acuity, ability to self-monitor, ability to use encoding strategies, and ability to use rehearsal strategies.

Information

The Information subtest measures general knowledge. The examinee is asked to answer questions on a range of topics. The subtest provides valuable information about an examinee's range of factual knowledge and long-term memory. Factors that may be related to an examinee's score include richness of early environment, quality of early education and general education, cultural opportunities, interests and reading patterns, alertness to environment, and intellectual curiosity and drive.

Letter–Number Sequencing

The Letter–Number Sequencing subtest measures auditory short-term memory, including ability to attend and concentrate. The examinee is asked to repeat, in ascending and alphabetic order, a series of numbers and letters presented orally. The subtest provides valuable information about an examinee's concentration, attention, and mental manipulation. Factors that may be related to an examinee's score include auditory acuity, ability to self-monitor, ability to use encoding strategies, and ability to use rehearsal strategies.

Matrix Reasoning

The Matrix Reasoning subtest measures nonverbal problem-solving ability. The examinee is asked to look at an incomplete matrix and to choose from five options the one that best completes the matrix. The subtest provides valuable information about an examinee's inductive reasoning, visual processing, and problem-solving abilities. Factors that may be related to an examinee's score include motivation and persistence, ability to work toward a goal, ability to use trial and error, and visual acuity.

Object Assembly

The Object Assembly subtest measures visual processing. The examinee is asked to assemble puzzle pieces into a meaningful whole. The subtest provides valuable information about an examinee's spatial abilities, understanding of part-to-whole relationships, nonverbal reasoning, and trial-and-error learning. Factors that may be related to an examinee's score include rate of motor activity, familiarity with figures and puzzles, motivation and persistence, experience with part-whole relationships, ability to work toward an unknown goal, ability to work under time pressure, and visual acuity.

Picture Arrangement

The Picture Arrangement subtest measures visual-perceptual organization. The examinee is asked to rearrange pictures so that they form a logical sequence. The subtest provides valuable information about an examinee's planning ability, ability to interpret social situations, and nonverbal reasoning ability. Factors that may be related to an examinee's score include cultural opportunities, ability to work under time pressure, ability to infer cause-and-effect relationships, and visual acuity.

Picture Completion

The Picture Completion subtest measures visual-perceptual reasoning. The examinee is asked to indicate the single most important part missing in pictures of people and ordinary objects. The subtest provides valuable information about an examinee's ability to concentrate on visually perceived material and alertness to details. Factors that may be related to an examinee's score include cultural opportunities, alertness to environment, quality of early education and general education, ability to work under time pressure, visual acuity, and willingness to guess when uncertain.

Picture Concepts

The Picture Concepts subtest measures abstract, categorical reasoning based on perceptual recognition processes. The examinee is asked to look at an array of pictures and determine what two pictures have a common characteristic. The subtest provides valuable information about an examinee's categorical nonverbal reasoning ability. Factors that may be related to an examinee's score include cultural opportunities, interests and reading patterns, intellectual curiosity, quality of early education and general education, and visual acuity.

Picture Naming

The Picture Naming subtest measures expressive word knowledge. The examinee is asked to name items presented in pictures. The subtest provides valuable information about an examinee's language development, fund of information, and visual memory. Factors that may be related to an examinee's score include cultural opportunities, interests and reading patterns, richness of early environment, quality of early education and general education, and visual acuity.

Receptive Vocabulary

The Receptive Vocabulary subtest measures receptive word knowledge. The examinee is asked to select the one picture that best matches a word given by the examiner. The subtest provides valuable information about an examinee's verbal skills, language development, and long-term memory. Factors that may be related to an examinee's score include cultural opportunities, interests and reading patterns, richness of early environment, quality of early education and general education, intellectual curiosity, and visual acuity.

Similarities

The Similarities subtest measures the ability to perceive and verbalize appropriate relationships between two objects or concepts. The examinee is asked to state how two things are

(*Continued*)

alike. A response indicating an abstract classification receives more credit than a response indicating a concrete classification. The subtest provides valuable information about an examinee's verbal concept formation and long-term memory. Factors that may be related to an examinee's score include quality of early education and general education, cultural opportunities, richness of early environment, and interests and reading patterns.

Symbol Search

The Symbol Search subtest measures visual discrimination and visual-perceptual scanning ability. The examinee is first asked to look at one or two target symbols and then indicate whether the symbol or symbols are also in another group of symbols. The subtest provides valuable information about an examinee's perceptual discrimination, speed and accuracy, attention, concentration, and visual short-term memory. Factors that may be related to an examinee's score include rate of motor activity, motivation and persistence, ability to work under time pressure, and visual acuity.

Vocabulary

The Vocabulary subtest measures word knowledge. The examinee is asked to define individual words of increasing difficulty.

The subtest provides valuable information about an examinee's verbal skills, language development, and long-term memory. Factors that may be related to an examinee's score include cultural opportunities, interests and reading patterns, richness of early environment, quality of early education and general education, and intellectual curiosity.

Word Reasoning

The Word Reasoning subtest measures verbal reasoning. The examinee is given a series of clues about an object or concept and asked to identify the object or concept. The subtest provides valuable information about an examinee's verbal comprehension, general reasoning abilities, and ability to analyze and integrate different types of information. Factors that may be related to an examinee's score include cultural opportunities, interests and reading patterns, quality of early education and general education, and intellectual curiosity.

Administer the Wechsler Scales to examinees with hearing impairments in their native language or preferred mode of communication, such as American Sign Language. If this is not possible, use the modified instructions below for selected Wechsler subtests, recognizing that modifications introduce an unknown source of error. On the Record Form, write the word "Estimate" next to any subtest scores, Indexes, or IQs obtained using modified procedures.

For examinees with hearing impairments who can read, prepare an instruction sheet for each subtest, as described below. It is important that examinees look at you when you are giving instructions in American Sign Language or pantomime and that they look at the models that you construct, the Response Booklet, the instruction sheet, or any similar materials when instructed to do so. Thus, you should not speak, nod, or gesture when examinees are looking at materials.

To communicate to examinees the need to work quickly, you should try to convey a sense of urgency with your body language when you give instructions in American Sign Language or another mode of communication. Also, be sure that examinees see the stopwatch. Consider fingerspelling or signing the word *fast* if the examinee knows either of these methods. (You sign the word *fast* by making a fist with your thumb tucked under your forefinger and then quickly lowering the fist and snapping out the thumb as if shooting a marble.)

BLOCK DESIGN

Additional Materials
Prepare a different instruction sheet for each version of the Block Design subtest, containing the information printed in color (a) on pages 65 to 68 of the WISC–IV Administration Manual, (b) on pages 59 to 67 of the WPPSI–III Administration Manual, or (c) on pages 116 to 122 of the WAIS–III Administration Manual.

Procedure
If the examinee can read, give him or her the instruction sheet. Then, whether or not the examinee can read, motion for him or her to assemble the design. Point to the examinee, point to the blocks, and point to the model or the card with the design. Follow the instructions for the Block Design subtest in the WISC–IV Administration Manual, in the WPPSI–III Administration Manual, or in the WAIS–III Administration Manual.

CANCELLATION

Additional Materials
Prepare an instruction sheet for the WISC–IV Cancellation subtest, containing the information printed in color on pages 173 and 174 of the WISC–IV Administration Manual.

Procedure
If the examinee can read, give him or her the instruction sheet. Then, whether or not the examinee can read, demonstrate the sample item. Open Response Booklet 2 to the first page. Show the first page to the examinee. Move your finger in a sweeping motion, from the examinee's left to right, across the first row of animals (the row below the word *Animals*). Then go to the second row. Point to each object individually. As you point to each object, let the examinee look at it. Making sure that you catch the examinee's eye, shake your head "no" for pictures that are not animals and nod your head "yes" for pictures of animals, and then draw a line through each animal. Motion to the examinee to do the same on the practice items: Move your finger in a sweeping motion across the practice items. Give the examinee a red pencil; point to the car, then to the umbrella, and then to the baby chick; and draw a line through the baby chick. Then point to the other items and motion for the examinee to proceed.

CODING or DIGIT SYMBOL–CODING

Additional Materials
Prepare a different instruction sheet for each version of the Coding subtest, containing the information printed in color (a) on pages 97 and 98 of the WISC–IV Administration Manual for Coding A, (b) on pages 98 and 99 of the WISC–IV Administration Manual for Coding B, (c) on pages 125 and 126 of the WPPSI–III Administration Manual, or (d) on pages 93 to 95 of the WAIS–III Administration Manual.

For WISC–IV Coding A (for examinees ages 6 to 7 years) and for the WPPSI–III, photocopy item CD-1 and paste it on a sheet of 8½" × 11" paper. For WISC–IV Coding B (for examinees ages 8 to 16 years) and for the WAIS–III, photocopy item CD-2 and paste it on a sheet of 8½" × 11" paper. Items CD-1 and CD-2 consist of a key and two practice trials.

Procedure for WISC–IV Coding A (Examinees Ages 6 to 7) and for WPPSI–III Coding
Show the examinee item CD-1. Point to the key (the geometric shapes with symbols inside). Then go to trial 1 (the first row), which contains six practice items. Point to the first empty geometric shape in trial 1. Draw the symbol inside the triangle. Follow the same procedure for the second and third geometric

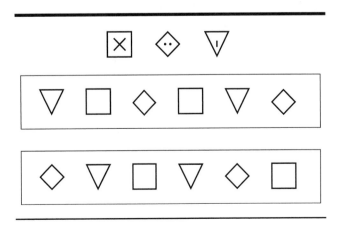

Item CD-1. Practice items for WISC–IV Coding A and for WPPSI–III Coding for examinees who are hearing impaired.

(Continued)

Table D-9 (*Continued*)

10	11	12
0	X	—

11	10	12	10	12	11

11	10	12	11	12	10

Item CD-2. Practice items for WISC–IV Coding B and for WAIS–III Digit Symbol–Coding for examinees who are hearing impaired.

shapes. Then point to the examinee and motion for him or her to complete the remaining three shapes. For trial 2 (the second row), follow the same procedure as for trial 1: Demonstrate to the examinee how to complete the first three shapes, and have the examinee complete the last three shapes.

If the examinee can read, give him or her the instruction sheet. Then, whether or not the examinee can read, for the WISC–IV, take out Response Booklet 1 and open it to Coding A. For the WPPSI–III, take out the Response Booklet and open it to Coding. Point to the examinee, point to the sample box, and motion for the examinee to begin. After the sample items have been completed, point to the examinee, point to the first box of the subtest proper, and then with a sweeping motion indicate that the examinee should begin the task. Follow the instructions in the WISC–IV Administration Manual or in the WPPSI–III Administration Manual for the Coding subtest. It is important to communicate the need for speed on Coding A.

Procedure for WISC–IV Coding B (Examinees Ages 8 to 16) and for WAIS–III Digit Symbol–Coding

Show the examinee item CD-2. Point to the key (the boxes that have a number in the upper half and a symbol in the lower half). Then go to trial 1 (the first row), which contains six practice items. Draw the appropriate symbol in the first empty box, under the number 11. Follow the same procedure for the second and third boxes. Then point to the examinee and motion for her or him to complete the remaining three boxes. For trial 2 (the second row), follow the same procedure as for trial 1: Demonstrate how to complete the first three boxes, and have the examinee complete the last three boxes.

If the examinee can read, give him or her the instruction sheet. Then, whether or not the examinee can read, for the WISC–IV, open Response Booklet 1 to Coding B. For the WAIS–III, open the Response Booklet to the Digit Symbol–Coding

page. Point to the examinee, point to the sample box, and motion for the examinee to begin. After the sample items have been completed, point to the examinee, point to the first box of the subtest proper, and then with a sweeping motion indicate that the examinee should begin. Follow the instructions in the WISC–IV Administration Manual for the Coding subtest or in the WAIS–III Administration Manual for the Digit Symbol–Coding subtest. It is important to communicate the need for speed on Coding B and on Digit Symbol–Coding.

MATRIX REASONING

Additional Materials

Prepare a different instruction sheet for each version of the Matrix Reasoning subtest, containing the information printed in

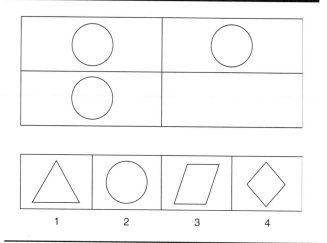

Item MR-1. Practice item for WISC–IV and WAIS–III Matrix Reasoning for examinees who are hearing impaired.

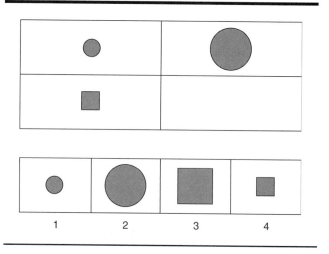

Item MR-2. Practice item for WISC–IV and WAIS–III Matrix Reasoning for examinees who are hearing impaired.

(*Continued*)

Table D-9 (*Continued*)

color (a) on pages 132 to 133 of the WISC–IV Administration Manual, (b) on pages 82 and 83 of the WPPSI–III Administration Manual, or (c) on pages 130 and 131 of the WAIS–III Administration Manual.

Photocopy items MR-1 and MR-2 and paste each one on a 3" × 5" card.

Procedure

Show the examinee item MR-1. Point to each box containing a circle (i.e., upper right, upper left, lower left). Next, point to the four choices below the boxes by moving your finger in a sweeping motion, from the examinee's left to right. Then point to the blank box. Point to the four choices again in a sweeping motion. Then stop at the circle (2), and make sure you catch the examinee's eye before nodding your head "yes."

Show the examinee item MR-2. Point to each box containing a figure (i.e., upper right, upper left, lower left). Then point to the four choices below the boxes by moving your finger in a sweeping motion, from the examinee's left to right. Then point to the blank box. Motion for the examinee to begin. If the examinee points to the correct choice (3), nod your head "yes." If the examinee points to an incorrect choice, shake your head "no," point to the correct choice, and nod your head "yes."

If the examinee can read, give him or her the instruction sheet. Then, whether or not the examinee can read, open the Stimulus Book to the Matrix Reasoning subtest. Point to the examinee, point to the first sample item, and motion for the examinee to begin. After the sample items have been completed, point to the examinee, point to the start-point item of the subtest proper, and then with a sweeping motion indicate that the examinee should begin the task. Follow the instructions in the WISC–IV Administration Manual, in the WPPSI–III Administration Manual, or in the WAIS–III Administration Manual for the Matrix Reasoning subtest.

OBJECT ASSEMBLY

Additional Materials

Prepare a different instruction sheet for each version of the Object Assembly subtest, containing the information printed in color on pages 205 to 207 of the WPPSI–III Administration Manual or on pages 173 to 174 of the WAIS–III Administration Manual.

Before you begin the assessment, select a picture of an automobile from a magazine.

Procedure

Show the examinee the picture from the magazine. Then cut the picture into three pieces. Place the three pieces in a random arrangement on the table. Then put the pieces together. Present the pieces to the examinee in a random arrangement. Motion to indicate that the examinee should put the pieces together.

If the examinee can read, give him or her the instruction sheet. Then, whether or not the examinee can read, place the first item before the examinee. Point to the examinee, point to the puzzle pieces, and motion to indicate that the examinee should put the pieces together. Follow the instructions in the WPPSI–III Administration Manual or in the WAIS–III Administration Manual for the Object Assembly subtest.

PICTURE ARRANGEMENT

Additional Materials

Prepare an instruction sheet for the WAIS–III Picture Arrangement subtest, containing the information printed in color on pages 143 and 144 of the WAIS–III Administration Manual. Prepare two practice items, items PA-1 and PA-2, on three unlined white 3" × 5" cards.

1. *Item PA-1.* Print the number 1 on one card, the number 2 on another card, and the number 3 on a third card. On the back of each card, print the word NUMBERS and the number that you put on the front of the card.
2. *Item PA-2.* Print the letter A on one card, the letter B on another card, and the letter C on a third card. On the back of each card, print the word LETTERS and the letter that you put on the front of the card.

Procedure

Position the cards in item PA-1 (NUMBERS) in the order 2, 3, 1 from the examinee's left to right. Then arrange the cards in correct numerical sequence. Allow the examinee to view the arrangement for 10 seconds. Rearrange the cards in the original order. By pointing to the examinee and the cards with a general sweeping motion, indicate to the examinee to arrange the cards. If the examinee does not respond or arrange the cards correctly, arrange the cards in the correct sequence. Then rearrange the cards in the original order and again motion to the examinee to arrange the cards. Follow the same procedure for item PA-2 (LETTERS).

If the examinee can read, give him or her the instruction sheet. Then, whether or not the examinee can read, follow the instructions in the WAIS–III Administration Manual for the Picture Arrangement subtest.

PICTURE COMPLETION

Additional Materials

Prepare a different instruction sheet for each version of the Picture Completion subtest, containing the information printed in color (a) on pages 164 to 166 of the WISC–IV Administration Manual, (b) on pages 150 to 152 of the WPPSI–III Administration Manual, or (c) on pages 64 and 65 of the WAIS–III Administration Manual.

Photocopy items PCm-1, PCm-2, and PCm-3. For each item, cut the photocopy on the dotted line to separate the two pictures, and then paste one on each side of a 3" × 5" card. For item PCm-1, the picture of a bird missing a wing will be on one side of the card and the picture of the complete bird on the other side. For item PCm-2, the picture of a bow and arrow missing part of the arrow will be on one side of the card and the picture of the complete bow and arrow on the other side. For item PCm-3, the picture of a pair of scissors missing part of the handle will be on one side of the card and the picture of the complete pair of scissors on the other side.

Procedure

First show the examinee the side of item PCm-1 with the picture of the complete bird. Then turn the card over and show the

(*Continued*)

Table D-9 (*Continued*)

Item PCm-1. Practice item for WISC–IV, WPPSI–III, and WAIS–IV Picture Completion for examinees who are hearing impaired.

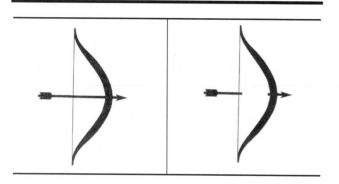

Item PCm-2. Practice item for WISC–IV, WPPSI–III, and WAIS–IV Picture Completion for examinees who are hearing impaired.

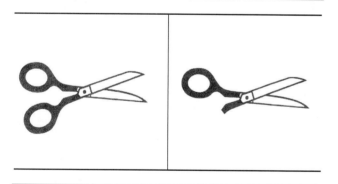

Item PCm-3. Practice item for WISC–IV, WPPSI–III, and WAIS–IV Picture Completion for examinees who are hearing impaired.

picture of the bird with the missing wing. Point to the space where the wing should be.

Show the examinee the side of item PCm-2 with the picture of the complete bow and arrow. Then turn the card over and

show the picture of the bow and arrow with a part of the arrow missing. Point to the space where part of the arrow is missing.

Show the examinee the side of item PCm-3 with the picture of the scissors with part of the handle missing. Motion for the examinee to point. If the examinee points to the space where part of the handle is missing, nod your head to indicate "yes." If the examinee points to a part of the picture where nothing is missing or does not point, point to the space where part of the handle is missing. Then turn the card over and show the examinee the picture of the complete pair of scissors. Present the sample item from the Picture Completion subtest in the Stimulus Book.

If the examinee can read, give him or her the instruction sheet. Then, whether or not the examinee can read, follow the instructions in the WISC–IV Administration Manual, in the WPPSI–III Administration Manual, or in the WAIS–III Administration Manual for the Picture Completion subtest.

PICTURE CONCEPTS

Additional Materials
Prepare a different instruction sheet for each version of the Picture Concepts subtest, containing the information printed in color on pages 91 and 92 of the WISC–IV Administration Manual or on pages 108 and 109 of the WPPSI–III Administration Manual.

Photocopy items PCn-1, PCn-2, and PCn-3 and paste each one on a 3" × 5" card.

Procedure
Show the examinee item PCn-1. Move your finger in a sweeping motion, from the examinee's left to right, across the top row and

Item PCn-1. Practice item for WISC–IV and WPPSI–III Picture Concepts for examinees who are hearing impaired.

(Continued)

Table D-9 (*Continued*)

Item PCn-2. Practice item for WISC–IV and WPPSI–III Picture Concepts for examinees who are hearing impaired.

Item PCn-3. Practice item for WISC–IV and WPPSI–III Picture Concepts for examinees who are hearing impaired.

then across the bottom row. Next point to the strawberry in the top row and then make a sweeping motion across the bottom row. Point to the giraffe in the bottom row. Shake your head from side to side to indicate "no." Point to the airplane in the bottom row and shake your head from side to side to indicate "no." Point to the deer in the top row. Then point to the giraffe in the bottom row and nod your head to indicate "yes."

Show the examinee item PCn-2. Move your finger in a sweeping motion, from the examinee's left to right, across the top row and then across the bottom row. Motion for the examinee to begin. If the examinee points to the two correct choices (car and truck), nod your head to indicate "yes." If the examinee points to two incorrect choices, shake your head to indicate "no." Then point to the car and truck and nod your head to indicate "yes."

If the examinee can read, give him or her the instruction sheet. Then, whether or not the examinee can read, follow the instructions in the WPPSI–III Administration Manual or in the WISC–IV Administration Manual for the Picture Concepts sub-test. If the examinee reaches item 13 on the WISC–IV or item 27 on the WPPSI–III, show the examinee item PCn-3 before you administer that item. Move your finger in a sweeping motion, from the examinee's left to right, across the top row of the sample, then across the middle row, and then across the bottom row. Let the examinee study the pictures. Next point to the guitar in the first row, then to the saxophone in the second row, and then to the trumpet in the third row. Making sure that you catch the examinee's eye, nod your head "yes" as you point to the designated picture in each row. Then continue to administer the subtest beginning with item 13 for the WISC–IV or item 27 for the WPPSI–III.

SYMBOL SEARCH

Additional Materials

Prepare a different instruction sheet for each version of the Symbol Search subtest, containing the information printed in color (a) on pages 145 to 147 of the WISC–IV Administration Manual for Symbol Search A, (b) on pages 147 to 149 of the WISC–IV Administration Manual for Symbol Search B, (c) on pages 114 to 115 of the WPPSI–III Administration Manual, or (d) on pages 166 to 168 of the WAIS–III Administration Manual.

Procedure for WISC–IV Symbol Search A (Examinees Ages 6 to 7)

The following instructions cover the sample items, practice items, and subtest items.

Sample items. Open Response Booklet 1 to Symbol Search A on page 3. Move your finger in a sweeping motion, from the examinee's left to right, across the entire row of the first sample item. Then point to the single target symbol in the first column. Next point to the first symbol in the search group. Then, making sure that you catch the examinee's eye, shake your head "no" to indicate that the first search symbol does not match the target symbol.

Repeat this procedure two more times for the first sample item. Point to the single target symbol and then to the second search symbol. Shake your head "no." Again point to the single target symbol and then to the third search symbol. This time, nod your head "yes" to indicate that the search symbol matches the target symbol. With a number 2 pencil, draw a diagonal line

(Continued)

Table D-9 (*Continued*)

through the YES box. Be sure that the examinee is looking at the Response Booklet or at you at the appropriate times.

For the second sample item, generally follow the same procedure. However, for this item, shake your head "no" for each search symbol. After you point to the third search symbol, draw a diagonal line through the NO box.

Practice items. Give the examinee a number 2 pencil without an eraser. Point to the first row of the practice items and move your finger in a sweeping motion, from the examinee's left to right, along the entire row. Nod your head to indicate to the examinee to begin. If the examinee draws a diagonal line through the YES box, nod your head to indicate "good" and go to the second practice item.

If the examinee draws a diagonal line through the NO box on the first practice item, correct him or her. Point to the target symbol and then to the second search symbol. Nod your head to indicate "yes." Then draw a diagonal line through the YES box. Do not point to the third symbol.

Point to the second practice item and, by nodding your head, encourage the examinee to answer it. If the examinee draws a diagonal line through the NO box, nod your head to indicate "good" and proceed to the regular subtest items (see below).

If the examinee draws a diagonal line through the YES box, correct him or her. Point to the target symbol and to each of the three search symbols in turn, shaking your head each time to indicate "no." Then draw a diagonal line through the NO box.

Do not go on to the regular subtest items until the examinee understands the task. You may have to erase your marks and the examinee's marks and have the examinee do the sample items and/or practice items again.

Subtest items. When the examinee understands the task, open Response Booklet 1 to page 4 and fold the page over. If the examinee can read, give him or her the instruction sheet; after the examinee has read the instructions, point to the first row to indicate that he or she should begin the task.

If the examinee cannot read, run your finger down the entire page 4. Then turn to page 5, and again run your finger down the entire page. Then turn to page 6, and again run your finger down the entire page. After showing the examinee the three pages of items, turn back to page 3. Point to the pencil and then to the first row, run your finger down the page, and then nod your head to indicate to the examinee to begin. It is important to communicate the need for speed on Symbol Search A.

If the examinee ceases to work after completing the first row, direct his or her attention to the second row (by pointing to the entire second row with a sweeping motion) and encourage him or her to continue. If the examinee stops at the end of page 3, turn to page 4 and encourage him or her to continue. If the examinee stops at the end of page 4, turn to page 5 and encourage him or her to continue. Allow 120 seconds.

Procedure for WISC–IV Symbol Search B (Examinees Ages 8 to 16)
The following instructions cover the sample items, practice items, and subtest items.

Sample items. Open Response Booklet 1 to page 7. Move your finger in a sweeping motion, from the examinee's left to right, across the entire row of the first sample item in Part B. Then point to the two target symbols in the first column. Next point to the first symbol in the search group. Then, making sure that you catch the examinee's eye, nod your head "yes" to indicate that the first search symbol matches the target symbol. With a number 2 pencil, draw a diagonal line through the YES box. Go to the second sample item without pointing to the remaining symbols in the first sample item.

For the second sample item, point to the two target symbols and then to the first search symbol. Shake your head "no" to indicate that the search symbol does not match either of the target symbols. Repeat this procedure four more times. In each case, point to the two target symbols and then to the search symbol. Shake your head "no" each time. After pointing to the last search symbol, draw a diagonal line through the NO box. Make sure that the examinee is looking at the Response Booklet or at you at the appropriate times.

Practice items. Give the examinee a number 2 pencil without an eraser. Point to the first row of the practice items and move your finger in a sweeping motion, from the examinee's left to right, along the entire row. Nod your head to indicate to the examinee to begin. If the examinee draws a diagonal line through the YES box, nod your head to indicate "good" and go to the second practice item.

If the examinee draws a diagonal line through the NO box on the first practice item, correct him or her. Point to the two target symbols and then to the second search symbol. Nod your head to indicate "yes." Then draw a diagonal line through the YES box. Do not point to the other three symbols.

Point to the second practice item and, by nodding your head, encourage the examinee to do it. If the examinee draws a diagonal line through the NO box, nod your head to indicate "good" and proceed to the regular subtest items (see below).

If the examinee draws a diagonal line through the YES box, correct him or her. Point to the two target symbols and to each of the five search symbols in turn, shaking your head each time to indicate "no." Then draw a diagonal line through the NO box.

Do not go on to the regular subtest items until the examinee understands the task. You may have to erase your marks and the examinee's marks and have the examinee do the sample items and/or practice items again. It is important to communicate the need for speed on Symbol Search B.

Subtest items. When the examinee understands the task, open Response Booklet 1 to page 8 and fold the page over. If the examinee can read, show him or her the second instruction sheet; after the examinee has read the instructions, point to the first row to indicate that he or she should begin the task.

If the examinee cannot read, run your finger down the entire page 8. Then turn to page 9, and again run your finger down the entire page. Follow the same procedure for pages 10 and 11. After showing the examinee the four pages of items, turn back to page 8. Point to the pencil and then to the first row, run your

(*Continued*)

Table D-9 (*Continued*)

finger down the page, and then nod your head to indicate to the examinee to begin.

If the examinee ceases to work after completing the first row, direct his or her attention to the second row (by pointing to the entire second row with a sweeping motion) and encourage him or her to continue. If the examinee stops at the end of page 8, turn to page 9. If the examinee stops at the end of page 9, turn to page 10. If the examinee stops at the end of page 10, turn to page 11. Allow 120 seconds.

Procedure for WPPSI–III Symbol Search

The following instructions cover the Symbol Search sample items, practice items, and subtest items.

Sample items. Open the Response Booklet to page 1. Move your finger in a sweeping motion, from the examinee's left to right, across the entire row of the first sample item. Then point to the single target symbol in the first column. Next point to the first symbol in the search group. Then, making sure that you catch the examinee's eye, shake your head "no" to indicate that the first search symbol does not match the target symbol.

Point to the single target symbol and then to the second search symbol. This time, nod your head "yes" to indicate that the search symbol matches the target symbol. With a number 2 pencil, draw a diagonal line through the matching symbol.

Point to the single target symbol and then to the third search symbol. Shake your head "no" to indicate that the third search symbol does not match the target symbol.

Repeat this procedure one more time. Point to the single target symbol and then to the fourth search symbol. Shake your head "no."

For the second sample item, generally follow the same procedure. However, for this item, shake your head "no" for each search symbol. After pointing to the third search symbol, draw a diagonal line through the question mark. Be sure that the examinee is looking at the Response Booklet or at you at the appropriate times.

Practice items. Give the examinee a number 2 pencil without an eraser. Point to the first row of the practice items and move your finger in a sweeping motion, from the examinee's left to right, along the entire row. Nod your head to indicate to the examinee to begin. If the examinee draws a diagonal line through the second search symbol, nod your head to indicate "good" and go to the second practice item.

If the examinee draws a diagonal line through the question mark on the first practice item, correct him or her. Point to the target symbol and then to the second search symbol. Nod your head to indicate "yes." Then draw a diagonal line through the second search symbol.

Point to the second practice item and, by nodding your head, encourage the examinee to do it. If the examinee draws a diagonal line through the question mark, nod your head to indicate "good" and proceed to the third practice item.

If the examinee draws a diagonal line through a nonmatching symbol, correct him or her. Point to the target symbol and to each of the three search symbols in turn, shaking your head

each time to indicate "no." Then draw a diagonal line through the question mark.

Follow the same procedure for the third and fourth practice items.

Do not go on to the regular subtest items until the examinee understands the task. You may have to erase your marks and the examinee's marks and have the examinee do the sample items and/or practice items again. It is important to communicate the need for speed on Symbol Search.

Subtest items. When the examinee understands the task, open Response Booklet 1 to page 2 and fold the page over. If the examinee can read, give him or her the instruction sheet; after the examinee has read the instructions, point to the first row to indicate that the examinee should begin the task.

If the examinee cannot read, run your finger down the entire page 2. Then turn to page 3, and again run your finger down the entire page. Then turn to page 4, and again run your finger down the entire page. Do the same for pages 5 and 6. After showing the examinee the five pages of items, turn back to page 2. Point to the pencil and then to the first row, run your finger down the page, and then nod your head to indicate to the examinee to begin.

If the examinee ceases to work after completing the first row, direct his or her attention to the second row (by pointing to the entire second row with a sweeping motion) and encourage him or her to continue. If the examinee stops at the end of page 2, turn to page 3 and encourage him or her to continue. If the examinee stops at the end of page 3, turn to page 4 and encourage him or her to continue. Follow the same procedure for pages 4 and 5. Allow 120 seconds.

Procedure for WAIS–III Symbol Search

The following instructions cover the sample items, practice items, and subtest items.

Sample items. Open the Response Booklet to the Symbol Search opening page. Move your finger in a sweeping motion, from the examinee's left to right, across the entire row of the first sample item. Then point to the two target symbols in the first column. Next point to the first symbol in the search group. Then, making sure that you catch the examinee's eye, nod your head "yes" to indicate that the first search symbol matches the target symbol. With a number 2 pencil, draw a diagonal line through the YES box. Go to the second sample item without pointing to the remaining symbols in the first sample item.

For the second sample item, point to the two target symbols in the first column. Next point to the first symbol in the search group. Then, making sure that you catch the examinee's eye, shake your head "no" to indicate that the second search symbol does not match the target symbol. Next point to the second symbol in the search group and nod your head "yes" to indicate that the second search symbol matches the target symbol. With a number 2 pencil, draw a diagonal line through the YES box. Go to the third sample item without pointing to the remaining symbols in the second sample item.

For the third sample item, point to the two target symbols and then to the first search symbol. Shake your head "no" to indicate

(*Continued*)

Table D-9 (*Continued*)

that the search symbol does not match either of the target symbols. Repeat this procedure four more times. In each case, point to the two target symbols and then to the search symbol. Shake your head "no" each time. After pointing to the last search symbol, draw a diagonal line through the NO box. Be sure that the examinee is looking at the Response Booklet or at you at the appropriate times.

Practice items. Give the examinee a number 2 pencil without an eraser. Point to the first row of the practice items and move your finger in a sweeping motion, from the examinee's left to right, along the entire row. Nod your head to indicate to the examinee to begin. If the examinee draws a diagonal line through the YES box, nod your head to indicate "good" and go to the second practice item.

If the examinee marks NO on the first practice item, correct him or her. Point to the two target symbols and then to the second search symbol. Nod your head to indicate "yes." Then draw a diagonal line through the YES box. Do not point to the remaining three symbols.

Point to the second practice item and, by nodding your head, encourage the examinee to do it. If the examinee marks NO, nod your head to indicate "good" and go to the third practice item.

If the examinee marks YES, correct him or her. Point to the two target symbols and to each of the five search symbols in turn, shaking your head each time to indicate "no." Then draw a diagonal line through the NO box.

Point to the third practice item and, by nodding your head, encourage the examinee to do it. If the examinee marks NO, nod your head to indicate "good" and proceed to the regular subtest items (see below).

If the examinee marks YES, correct him or her. Point to the two target symbols and to each of the five search symbols in turn, shaking your head each time to indicate "no." Then draw a diagonal line through the NO box.

Do not go on to the regular subtest items until the examinee understands the task. You may have to erase your marks and the examinee's marks and have the examinee do the sample items and/or practice items again. It is important to communicate the need for speed on Symbol Search.

Subtest items. When the examinee understands the task, open the Response Booklet to page 1 and fold the page over. If the examinee can read, give him or her the instruction sheet; after the examinee has read the instructions, point to the first row to indicate that the examinee should begin the task.

If the examinee cannot read, run your finger down the entire page 1. Then turn to page 2, and again run your finger down the entire page. Then turn to page 3, and again run your finger down the entire page. Then turn to page 4, and again run your finger down the entire page. After showing the examinee the four pages of items, turn back to page 1. Point to the pencil and then to the first row, run your finger down the page, and then nod your head to indicate to the examinee to begin.

If the examinee ceases to work after completing the first row, direct his or her attention to the second row (by pointing to the entire second row with a sweeping motion) and encourage him or her to continue. If the examinee stops at the end of page 1, turn to page 2. If the examinee stops at the end of page 2, turn to page 3. If the examinee stops at the end of page 3, turn to page 4. Allow 120 seconds.

Table D-10
Physical Abilities Necessary for the Wechsler Subtests or Their Adaptation

Subtest	Physical ability required
Arithmetic	For items 1–5 on the WISC–IV, individual must be able to see; adaptation is not feasible if individual is blind or more than mildly vision-impaired. For items 6–34 on the WISC–IV and all items on the WAIS–III, if individual cannot see or individual cannot hear, the subtest is adaptable. Individual who is able to read can be shown the questions. If individual cannot read, he or she must be able to hear. If individual can neither read nor hear, the subtest should not be administered. If individual cannot speak, the subtest is adaptable. Individuals need not have use of arms/hands, but those who are able to can write their answers.
Block Design	Individual must be able to see; adaptation is not feasible if individual is blind or more than mildly vision-impaired. If individual cannot hear, the subtest is adaptable. Individual need not be able to speak. Use of arms/hands is required; adaptation is not feasible if this function is absent or more than mildly impaired.
Cancellation	Individual must be able to see; adaptation is not feasible if individual is blind or more than mildly vision-impaired. If individual cannot hear, the subtest is adaptable. Individuals who are able to speak can say their answers; those who are able to can point to their answers; and those who are able to can write their answers.
Coding	Individual must be able to see; adaptation is not feasible if individual is blind or more than mildly vision-impaired. If individual cannot hear, the subtest is adaptable. Individual need not be able to speak. Use of arms/hands is required; adaptation is not feasible if this function is absent or more than mildly impaired.
Comprehension	If individual cannot see or individual cannot hear, the subtest is adaptable. Individual who is able to read can be shown the questions. If individual cannot read, he or she must be able to hear. If individual can neither read nor hear, the subtest should not be administered. If individual cannot speak, the subtest is adaptable. Individuals need not have use of arms/hands, but those who are able to can write their answers.
Digit Span	Individual need not be able to see. Individual must be able to hear; adaptation is not feasible if individual is deaf or more than mildly hearing-impaired. If individual cannot speak, the subtest is adaptable. Individuals need not have use of arms/hands, but those who are able to can write their answers.
Information	If individual cannot see or individual cannot hear, the subtest is adaptable. Individual who is able to read can be shown the questions. If individual cannot read, he or she must be able to hear. If individual can neither read nor hear, the subtest should not be administered. If individual cannot speak, the subtest is adaptable. Individuals need not have use of arms/hands, but those who are able to can write their answers.
Letter–Number Sequencing	Individual need not be able to see. Individual must be able to hear; adaptation is not feasible if individual is deaf or more than mildly hearing-impaired. If individual cannot speak, the subtest is adaptable. Individuals need not have use of arms/hands, but those who are able to can write their answers.
Matrix Reasoning	Individual must be able to see; adaptation is not feasible if individual is blind or more than mildly vision-impaired. If individual cannot hear, the subtest is adaptable. Individuals who are able to speak can say their answers; those who are able to can point to their answers; and those who are able to can write their answers.
Object Assembly	Individual must be able to see; adaptation is not feasible if individual is blind or more than mildly vision-impaired. If individual cannot hear, the subtest is adaptable. Individual need not be able to speak. Use of arms/hands is required; adaptation is not feasible if this function is absent or more than mildly impaired.
Picture Arrangement	Individual must be able to see; adaptation is not feasible if individual is blind or more than mildly vision-impaired. If individual cannot hear, the subtest is adaptable. Individual need not be able to speak. If individual does not have use of arms/hands, adaptation is feasible.

(Continued)

Table D-10 (*Continued*)

Subtest	Physical ability required
Picture Completion	Individual must be able to see; adaptation is not feasible if individual is blind or more than mildly vision-impaired. If individual cannot hear, the subtest is adaptable. Individuals who are able to speak can say their answers; those who are able to can point to their answers; and those who are able to can write their answers.
Picture Concepts	Individual must be able to see; adaptation is not feasible if individual is blind or more than mildly vision-impaired. If individual cannot hear, the subtest is adaptable. Individuals who are able to speak can say their answers; those who are able to can point to their answers; and those who are able to can write their answers.
Picture Naming	Individual must be able to see; adaptation is not feasible if individual is blind or more than mildly vision-impaired. If individual cannot hear and speak, the subtest is adaptable. Individuals need not have use of arms/hands, but those who are able to can write their answers.
Receptive Vocabulary	Individual must be able to see; adaptation is not feasible if individual is blind or more than mildly vision-impaired. If individual cannot hear, the subtest is adaptable. Individuals who are able to speak can say their answers; those who are able to can point to their answers; and those who are able to can write their answers.
Similarities	If individual cannot see or individual cannot hear, the subtest is adaptable. Individual who is able to read can be shown the questions. If individual cannot read, he or she must be able to hear. If individual can neither read nor hear, the subtest should not be administered. If individual cannot speak, the subtest is adaptable. Individuals need not have use of arms/hands, but those who are able to can write their answers.
Symbol Search	Individual must be able to see; adaptation is not feasible if individual is blind or more than mildly vision-impaired. If individual cannot hear, the subtest is adaptable. Individuals who are able to speak can say their answers; those who are able to can point to their answers; and those who are able to can write their answers.
Vocabulary	If individual cannot see or individual cannot hear, the subtest is adaptable. Individual who is able to read can be shown the questions. If individual cannot read, he or she must be able to hear. If individual can neither read nor hear, the subtest should not be administered. If individual cannot speak, the subtest is adaptable. Individuals need not have use of arms/hands, but those who are able to can write their answers.
Word Reasoning	If individual cannot see or individual cannot hear, the subtest is adaptable. Individual who is able to read can be shown the questions. If individual cannot read, he or she must be able to hear. If individual can neither read nor hear, the subtest should not be administered. If individual cannot speak, the subtest is adaptable. Individuals need not have use of arms/hands, but those who are able to can write their answers.

Table D-11
Tellegen and Briggs Procedure for Obtaining Full Scale IQs, Plus Reliability and Validity Coefficients, for Wechsler Short Forms

Computing the Full Scale IQ of a Short Form

The following formula is used to compute the Full Scale IQ for a short form:

$$\text{Full Scale IQ} = \left(\frac{15}{S_c}\right)(X_c - M_c) + 100$$

where $S_c = S_s\sqrt{n + 2\Sigma r_{jk}}$ (standard deviation of composite score)

X_c = composite score (sum of subtest scaled scores in the short form)

M_c = normative mean, which is equal to $10n$

S_s = subtest standard deviation, which is equal to 3

n = number of component subtests

Σr_{jk} = sum of the correlations between component subtests

This equation considers the number of subtests in the short form, the correlations between the subtests, and the total scaled-score points obtained on the short form.

A more straightforward formula for obtaining the Full Scale IQ is as follows:

$$\text{Full Scale IQ} = (\text{composite score} \times a) + b$$

where $a = \dfrac{15}{S_c}$

$b = \dfrac{100 - n(150)}{S_c}$

Table D-12 can be used to obtain the appropriate a and b constants. In using Table D-12, first select the heading corresponding to the number of subtests in the short form. The first column under each heading is Σr_{jk}. This term represents the sum of the correlations between the subtests making up the composite score. To obtain Σr_{jk}, use the WISC–IV correlation table for the group closest in age to the examinee (Tables A.1– A.11 on pages 112–122 of the WISC–IV Technical Manual). With two subtests in the short form, only one correlation is needed. With three subtests in the short form, three correlations are summed (1 with 2, 1 with 3, and 2 with 3). With four subtests in the short form, six correlations are summed (1 with 2, 1 with 3, 1 with 4, 2 with 3, 2 with 4, and 3 with 4). With five subtests in the short form, 10 correlations are summed (1 with 2, 1 with 3, 1 with 4, 1 with 5, 2 with 3, 2 with 4, 2 with 5, 3 with 4, 3 with 5, and 4 with 5). After calculating Σr_{jk}, you obtain the values for the two constants by looking under the appropriate headings.

The procedure used to obtain the Full Scale IQ can be summarized as follows:

1. Sum the scaled scores of the subtests in the short form to obtain the composite score.
2. Sum the correlations between the subtests to obtain Σr_{jk}.
3. Using Σr_{jk}, find the appropriate a and b constants in Table D-12.
4. Using the composite score and the a and b constants, compute the Full Scale IQ.

Example: A three-subtest short form composed of the Block Design, Vocabulary, and Letter–Number Sequencing subtests is administered to a 6-year-old child. The child obtains scaled scores of 7, 12, and 13 on the three subtests. The four steps are as follows:

1. The three scaled scores are summed to yield a composite score of 32.
2. The correlations between the subtests are obtained from Table A.1 (page 112) of the WISC–IV Technical Manual: Block Design and Vocabulary, .37; Block Design and Letter–Number Sequencing, .26; Vocabulary and Letter–Number Sequencing, .35. These are summed to yield Σr_{jk} = .98.
3. The appropriate row in Table D-12 is the fifth row under the heading "3 Subtests." The values for the constants a and b are 2.2 and 34, respectively.
4. These values are substituted into the formula for the Full Scale IQ:

$$
\begin{aligned}
\text{Full Scale IQ} &= (\text{composite score} \times a) + b \\
&= (32 \times 2.2) + 34 \\
&= 70.4 + 34 \\
&= 104
\end{aligned}
$$

Computing the Reliability Coefficient of a Short Form

The following formula is used to obtain the reliability of a short form:

$$r_{ss} = \frac{\Sigma r_{ii} + 2\Sigma r_{ij}}{k + \Sigma 2 r_{ij}}$$

where r_{ss} = reliability of the short form

r_{ii} = reliability of subtest i

r_{ij} = correlation between any subtests i and j

k = number of component subtests

Example: The reliability of the two-subtest combination of Block Design and Vocabulary (for the overall average) is calculated in the following way, given that r_{ii} is .86 for Block Design, r_{ii} is .89 for Vocabulary, and r_{ij} is .48 for Block Design and Vocabulary:

$$r_{ss} = \frac{1.75 + .96}{2 + .96} = \frac{2.71}{2.96} = .92$$

Computing the Validity Coefficient of a Short Form

The following formula is used to obtain the validity of a short form:

$$r'_{pw} = \frac{\Sigma\Sigma r_{jl}}{\sqrt{k + 2\Sigma r_{ij}}\ \sqrt{t + 2\Sigma r_{lm}}}$$

where r'_{pw} = modified coefficient of correlation between the composite part and the composite whole

r_{jl} = correlation between any subtest j included in the part and any subtest l included in the whole, where any included correlation between a subtest and itself is represented by its reliability coefficient

r_{ij} = correlation between subtests i and j

r_{lm} = correlation between subtests l and m

k = number of component subtests

t = number of subtests included in the whole

(Continued)

Table D-11 (*Continued*)

To obtain $\Sigma\Sigma r_{jl}$, total the following three sums: (a) the sum of the reliabilities of the component subtests, (b) twice the sum of the intercorrelations among the component subtests ($2\Sigma r_{ij}$), and (c) the sum of the intercorrelations between any component subtest and any noncomponent core subtest.

Example: The validity of the two-subtest combination of Vocabulary and Block Design is calculated in the following way,

given that r_{ii} is .86 for Block Design, r_{ii} is .89 for Vocabulary, and r_{ij} is .48 for Block Design and Vocabulary:

$$r'_{pw} = \frac{1.75 + .96 + 7.28}{\sqrt{2 + 2(.48)}\ \sqrt{10 + 2(18.67)}}$$

$$= \frac{9.99}{(1.72)(6.88)} = \frac{9.99}{11.83} = .84$$

Source: Adapted from Tellegen and Briggs (1967).

Table D-12
Constants for Converting Wechsler Composite Scores into Intelligence Quotients

2 Subtests			3 Subtests			4 Subtests			5 Subtests		
Σr_{jk}	a	b	Σr_{jk}	a	b	Σr_{jk}	a	b	Σr_{jk}	a	b
.78–.92	2.6	48	2.16–2.58	1.8	46	3.95–4.85	1.4	44	6.96–8.83	1.1	45
.66–.77	2.7	46	1.79–2.15	1.9	43	3.21–3.94	1.5	40	5.50–6.95	1.2	40
.54–.65	2.8	44	1.48–1.78	2.0	40	2.60–3.20	1.6	36	4.36–5.49	1.3	35
.44–.53	2.9	42	1.21–1.47	2.1	37	2.09–2.59	1.7	32	3.45–4.35	1.4	30
.35–.43	3.0	40	.97–1.20	2.2	34	1.66–2.08	1.8	28	2.71–3.44	1.5	25
.26–.34	3.1	38	.77– .96	2.3	31	1.29–1.65	1.9	24	2.10–2.70	1.6	20
.19–.25	3.2	36	.59– .76	2.4	28	.98–1.28	2.0	20	1.59–2.09	1.7	15

Source: Reprinted by permission of the publisher and authors from A. Tellegen and P. F. Briggs, "Old Wine in New Skins: Grouping Wechsler Subtests into New Scales," *Journal of Consulting Psychology,* 1967, *31,* p. 504. Copyright 1967 by American Psychological Association.

APPENDIX E

TABLES FOR THE SB5

Table E-1
Interpretive Rationales, Implications of High and Low Scores, and Instructional Implications for SB5 Subtests

Ability	Background factors	Possible implications of high scores	Possible implications of low scores	Instructional implications
Nonverbal Fluid Reasoning (NFR)				
Fluid reasoning ability (Gf)	Motivation and persistence	Good nonverbal reasoning ability	Poor nonverbal reasoning ability	Use puzzles, blocks, Legos, spatial-visual tasks, perceptual tasks involving breaking down an object and building it up again, and art work with geometric forms and flannel board
Induction (I)	Ability to work toward a goal	Good ability to draw conclusions from known facts or principles	Poor ability to draw conclusions from known facts or principles	
General sequential reasoning (RG)	Visual acuity			
Deductive reasoning	Trial-and-error learning	Good visualization ability	Poor visualization ability	
Visualization		Good cognitive flexibility	Poor cognitive flexibility	Focus on part-whole relationships
Cognitive flexibility		Good concentration	Poor concentration	Use sequencing tasks
Concentration		Good trial-and-error methods	Poor trial-and-error methods	
Nonverbal Knowledge (NKN)				
Crystallized knowledge (Gc)	Quality of early education and general education	Good general information	Poor general information	Focus on visual learning techniques stressing individual parts that make up the whole
General information (K0)	Cultural opportunities	Good listening ability	Poor listening ability	
Oral production and fluency (OP)	Trial-and-error learning	Good verbal fluency	Poor verbal fluency	
Verbal comprehension		Good verbal comprehension	Poor verbal comprehension	Use perceptual activities that focus on recognizing objects, describing objects, and paying attention to details (e.g., maps and art work)
Scanning ability		Good scanning ability	Poor scanning ability	
Fund of general information		Good fund of general information	Poor fund of general information	
Synthesis of information		Good synthesis of information	Poor synthesis of information	
Cognitive flexibility		Good cognitive flexibility	Poor cognitive flexibility	Improve scanning techniques aimed at identifying missing elements in pictures
		Good trial-and-error methods	Poor trial-and-error methods	
Nonverbal Quantitative Reasoning (NQR)				
Quantitative reasoning (RQ)	Opportunity to acquire fundamental arithmetical processes	Good quantitative reasoning	Poor quantitative reasoning	Develop arithmetical skills
Mathematical knowledge (KM)	Quality of early education and general education	Good mathematical knowledge	Poor mathematical knowledge	Develop concentration skills
Quantitative knowledge (Gq)	Visual acuity	Good ability to think logically	Poor ability to think logically	Use concrete objects to introduce concepts
Logical thinking		Good visual discrimination strategies	Poor visual discrimination strategies	Drill in basic skills
Visual discrimination strategies		Good synthesis of information	Poor synthesis of information	Provide interesting "real" problems to solve
Synthesis of information		Good cognitive flexibility	Poor cognitive flexibility	Use exercises involving analyzing arithmetical word problems
Cognitive flexibility		Good scanning ability	Poor scanning ability	
Scanning ability		Good attention	Poor attention	
Attention		Good concentration	Poor concentration	Increase attention span
Concentration				

(Continued)

Table E-1 (Continued)

Ability	Background factors	Possible implications of high scores	Possible implications of low scores	Instructional implications
Nonverbal Visual-Spatial Processing (NVS)				
Visual processing (Gv) Spatial relations (SR) Closure speed (CS) Visualization (VZ) Perceptual reasoning Spatial reasoning Visual discrimination Planning Problem solving Cognitive flexibility Speed of movement Scanning ability Attention Concentration	Motivation and persistence Alertness Interests Eye-hand coordination Visual acuity Color vision Trial-and-error learning	Good visual-spatial ability Good perceptual reasoning Good visualization ability Good spatial reasoning Good visual discrimination Good planning ability Good problem solving ability Good cognitive flexibility Good speed of movement Good scanning ability Good attention Good concentration Good trial-and-error methods	Poor visual-spatial ability Poor perceptual reasoning Poor visualization ability Poor spatial reasoning Poor visual discrimination Poor planning ability Poor problem-solving ability Poor cognitive flexibility Poor speed of movement Poor scanning ability Poor attention Poor concentration Poor trial-and-error methods	Focus on visual learning Teach part-whole relationships Use spatial-visual tasks Reinforce persistence Supplement visual materials with verbal explanations
Nonverbal Working Memory (NWM)				
Short-term memory (Gsm) Working memory (MW) Memory span (MS) Visual memory (MV) Serial perceptual integration (PI) Short-term visual memory Attention Concentration	Ability to use visual encoding strategies Auditory acuity Ability to use rehearsal strategies	Good short-term visual memory Good working memory Good attention Good concentration	Poor short-term visual memory Poor working memory Poor attention Poor concentration	Develop short-term memory skills Develop attention skills Develop concentration skills Develop visualization skills Focus on small, meaningful units of instruction Decrease anxiety

(Continued)

Table E-1 (*Continued*)

Ability	Background factors	Possible implications of high scores	Possible implications of low scores	Instructional implications
Verbal Fluid Reasoning (VFR)				
Fluid reasoning ability (Gf) Induction (I) General sequential reasoning (RG) Oral production and fluency (OP) Visual processing (Gv) Visual memory (MV) Visualization Fund of general information Conceptual thinking Synthesis of information Cognitive flexibility Attention Concentration	Cultural opportunities Quality of early education and general education Trial-and-error learning	Good verbal reasoning ability Good ability to draw conclusions from known facts or principles Good sequential reasoning Good verbal fluency Good visual memory Good visualization Good fund of general information Good conceptual thinking Good ability to synthesize information Good cognitive flexibility Good attention Good concentration Good trial-and-error methods	Poor verbal reasoning ability Poor ability to draw conclusions from known facts or principles Poor sequential reasoning Poor verbal fluency Poor visual memory Poor visualization Poor fund of general information Poor conceptual thinking Poor ability to synthesize information Poor cognitive flexibility Poor attention Poor concentration Poor trial-and-error methods	Emphasize how things are organized Focus on visual learning techniques, stressing cause-and-effect relationships Stress language development, synonyms and antonyms, and exercises involving abstract words, classifications, and generalizations
Verbal Knowledge (VKN)				
Crystallized knowledge (Gc) Lexical knowledge (VL) Fund of information Conceptual thinking Verbal fluency Synthesis of information Attention Concentration	Cultural opportunities Interests and reading patterns Richness of early environment Quality of early education and general education Intellectual curiosity	Good general information Good verbal comprehension Good fund of information Good conceptual thinking Good verbal fluency Good ability to synthesize information Good attention Good concentration	Poor general information Poor verbal comprehension Poor fund of information Poor conceptual thinking Poor verbal fluency Poor ability to synthesize information Poor attention Poor concentration	Develop working vocabulary Encourage child to discuss experiences, ask questions, and make cards containing vocabulary words and definitions Use other verbal enrichment exercises, including Scrabble, analogy, and other word games Encourage child to write about his or her activities and to keep a diary

(Continued)

Table E-1 (*Continued*)

Ability	Background factors	Possible implications of high scores	Possible implications of low scores	Instructional implications
Verbal Quantitative Reasoning (VQR)				
Fluid reasoning ability (Gf) Quantitative reasoning (RQ) Quantitative knowledge (Gq) Mathematical knowledge (KM) Rehearsal strategies Conceptual thinking Synthesis of information Cognitive flexibility Attention Concentration	Opportunity to acquire fundamental arithmetical processes Quality of early education and general education Visual acuity Trial-and-error learning	Good quantitative reasoning Good quantitative knowledge Good mathematical knowledge Good rehearsal strategies Good conceptual thinking Good synthesis of information Good cognitive flexibility Good attention Good concentration Good trial-and-error methods	Poor quantitative reasoning Poor quantitative knowledge Poor mathematical knowledge Poor rehearsal strategies Poor conceptual thinking Poor synthesis of information Poor cognitive flexibility Poor attention Poor concentration Poor trial-and-error methods	Develop arithmetical skills Develop concentration skills Use concrete objects to introduce concepts Drill in basic skills Provide interesting "real" problems to solve Use exercises involving analyzing arithmetical word problems Increase attention span
Verbal Visual-Spatial Processing (VVS)				
Visual processing (Gv) Visualization (VZ) Verbal fluency Spatial ability Planning ability Attention Concentration	Motivation and persistence Alertness Interests Eye-hand coordination Visual acuity	Good visual processing Good visualization Good verbal fluency Good spatial ability Good planning ability Good attention Good concentration	Poor visual processing Poor visualization Poor verbal fluency Poor spatial ability Poor planning ability Poor attention Poor concentration	Focus on visual learning Teach part-whole relationships Use spatial-visual tasks Reinforce persistence Supplement visual materials with verbal explanations
Verbal Working Memory (VWM)				
Short-term memory (Gsm) Memory span (MS) Working memory (MW) Language development (LD) Attention Concentration	Auditory acuity Ability to self-monitor Ability to use encoding strategies Ability to use rehearsal strategies	Good short-term memory Good memory span Good working memory Good language development Good attention Good concentration	Poor short-term memory Poor memory span Poor working memory Poor language development Poor attention Poor concentration	Emphasize listening skills by using sequencing activities, reading a short story and asking the child to recall details, and seeing whether the child can follow directions Use short and simple directions and repeat when necessary Use other memory exercises and memory games Decrease anxiety

Source: Adapted, in part, from Roid (2003).

Table E-2

Definitions of Broad and Narrow Abilities in the Cattell-Horn-Carroll (CHC) Model Associated with SB5 Subtests

Broad and narrow abilities	Subtests
Crystallized Knowledge (Gc): The ability to use the knowledge base accumulated over time in the process of acculturation.	Nonverbal Knowledge, Verbal Knowledge
General (verbal) Information (K0): The ability to use a range of general knowledge.	Nonverbal Knowledge
Language Development (LD): The ability to understand spoken native language.	Verbal Working Memory
Lexical Knowledge (VL): The ability to use and understand words.	Verbal Knowledge
Listening Ability (LS): The ability to listen and comprehend oral communications.	Nonverbal Knowledge
Oral Production and Fluency (OP): The ability to produce a story or verbal description clearly and fluently.	Verbal Fluid Reasoning
Fluid Reasoning Ability (Gf): The ability to solve relatively novel tasks by forming and recognizing concepts, identifying and perceiving relationships, drawing inferences, and reorganizing and transforming information.	Nonverbal Fluid Reasoning, Verbal Fluid Reasoning, Verbal Quantitative Reasoning
General Sequential Reasoning (RG): The ability to reach a logical conclusion based on the information provided.	Nonverbal Fluid Reasoning, Verbal Fluid Reasoning
Induction (I): The ability to draw conclusions from known facts or principles.	Nonverbal Fluid Reasoning, Verbal Fluid Reasoning
Quantitative Reasoning (RQ): The ability to reason inductively and deductively using mathematical concepts.	Nonverbal Quantitative Reasoning, Verbal Quantitative Reasoning
Quantitative Knowledge (Gq): The ability to use acquired mathematical knowledge.	Nonverbal Quantitative Reasoning, Verbal Quantitative Reasoning
Mathematical Knowledge (KM): The ability to use mathematical concepts and methods to solve mathematical problems.	Nonverbal Quantitative Reasoning, Verbal Quantitative Reasoning
Short-Term Memory (Gsm): The ability to hold information in immediate memory and then use it within a few seconds.	Nonverbal Working Memory, Verbal Working Memory
Memory Span (MS): The ability to recall a series of arbitrary elements (letters, numbers) after a few seconds.	Nonverbal Working Memory, Verbal Working Memory
Working Memory (MW): The ability to perform cognitive operations on information stored in short-term memory.	Nonverbal Working Memory, Verbal Working Memory
Visual Processing (Gv): The ability to solve simple and complex visual problems.	Nonverbal Visual-Spatial Processing, Verbal Fluid Reasoning, Verbal Visual-Spatial Processing
Spatial Relations (SR): The ability to solve problems involving spatial relations.	Nonverbal Visual-Spatial Processing
Closure Speed (CS): The ability to rapidly organize separate visual stimuli into a meaningful whole.	Nonverbal Visual-Spatial Processing
Visualization (VZ): The ability to mentally manipulate objects or visual patterns.	Nonverbal Visual-Spatial Processing, Verbal Visual-Spatial Processing
Visual Memory (MV): The ability to store a mental representation of a visual stimulus and then recognize or recall it later.	Nonverbal Working Memory, Verbal Fluid Reasoning
Serial Perceptual Integration (PI): The ability to identify a visual pattern when parts of the pattern are presented rapidly and serially.	Nonverbal Working Memory

Note. Crystallized knowledge is also referred to as crystallized intelligence or crystallized ability. Fluid reasoning ability is also referred to as fluid ability, fluid reasoning, or fluid intelligence.

Source: Adapted, in part, from Flanagan, McGrew, and Ortiz (2000); Horn (1987, 1998); and Roid (2003).

Table E-3
Broad and Narrow Abilities in the Cattell-Horn-Carroll (CHC) Model Associated with SB5 Subtests

CHC broad and narrow abilities	Nonverbal Fluid Reasoning	Nonverbal Knowledge	Nonverbal Quantitative Reasoning	Nonverbal Visual-Spatial Processing	Nonverbal Working Memory	Verbal Fluid Reasoning	Verbal Knowledge	Verbal Quantitative Reasoning	Verbal Visual-Spatial Processing	Verbal Working Memory
Crystallized Knowledge (Gc)		■					■			
General Information (K0)		■								
Language Development (LD)										■
Lexical Knowledge (VL)							■			
Listening Ability (LS)							■			
Oral Production and Fluency (OP)						■				
Fluid Reasoning Ability (Gf)	■					■		■		
General Sequential Reasoning (RG)	■					■				
Induction (I)	■					■				
Quantitative Reasoning (RQ)			■					■		
Quantitative Knowledge (Gq)			■					■		
Mathematical Knowledge (KM)			■					■		
Short-Term Memory (Gsm)					■					■
Memory Span (MS)					■					■
Working Memory (MW)					■					■
Visual Processing (Gv)				■		■			■	
Spatial Relations (SR)				■						
Closure Speed (CS)				■						
Visualization (VZ)				■					■	
Visual Memory (MV)					■	■				
Serial Perceptual Integration (PI)					■					

Source: Adapted from Roid (2003).

Table E-4
Broad and Narrow Abilities in the Cattell-Horn-Carroll (CHC) Model Associated with SB5 Factors

CHC broad and narrow abilities	Fluid Reasoning	Knowledge	Quantitative Reasoning	Visual-Spatial Processing	Working Memory
Crystallized Knowledge (Gc)	■	■			
General Information (K0)		■			
Language Development (LD)					■
Lexical Knowledge (VL)		■			
Listening Ability (LS)		■			
Oral Production and Fluency (OP)	■	■			
Fluid Reasoning Ability (Gf)	■		■		
Induction (I)	■				
General Sequential Reasoning (RG)	■				
Quantitative Reasoning (RQ)			■		
Quantitative Knowledge (Gq)			■		
Mathematical Knowledge (KM)			■		
Short-Term Memory (Gsm)					■
Memory Span (MS)					■
Working Memory (MW)					■
Visual Processing (Gv)	■			■	
Closure Speed (CS)				■	
Spatial Relations (SR)				■	
Visualization (VZ)				■	
Visual Memory (MV)					■
Serial Perceptual Integration (PI)					■

Source: Adapted from Roid (2003).

Table E-5
Administrative Checklist for the SB5

ADMINISTRATIVE CHECKLIST FOR THE SB5

Name of examiner: _____

Date: _____

Name of individual: _____

Name of observer: _____

(Note: If an item is not applicable, mark NA to the left of the number.)

Before Beginning   Circle One

1. Room is well lit   Yes   No
2. Furniture is comfortable and size is
   appropriate for individual   Yes   No
3. Room is free of distractions   Yes   No
4. Asks parent, if present, to remain in back-
   ground and observe quietly   Yes   No
5. Positions individual correctly   Yes   No
6. Sits directly across from individual   Yes   No
7. Establishes rapport   Yes   No
8. Tells individual that breaks are OK and asks
   individual to let examiner know when he or
   she needs a break   Yes   No
9. Does not prolong getting-acquainted period   Yes   No
10. Does not overstimulate individual or entertain
    individual excessively before starting test   Yes   No
11. Avoids use of term *intelligence* when
    introducing test   Yes   No
12. Responds truthfully to any questions
    individual has about purpose of testing   Yes   No
13. Keeps test materials in order   Yes   No
14. Keeps test kit out of individual's view   Yes   No
15. Begins test after establishing rapport   Yes   No
16. Positions Record Form and Item Books so
    that individual cannot read questions or
    answers   Yes   No
17. Introduces test by reading directions in Item
    Book 1 verbatim   Yes   No

Comments

_____

_____

_____

Nonverbal Fluid Reasoning
(See pp. 581–582 in text for detailed information.)

Background Considerations

1. Reads directions verbatim   Yes   No
2. Reads directions clearly   Yes   No
3. Shields Record Form from individual   Yes   No
4. Leaves Item Book 1 on table and turns over
   pages one at a time   Yes   No
5. For items 1 to 8, places layout card correctly   Yes   No

Nonverbal Fluid Reasoning (*Continued*)   Circle One

6. For items 1, 5, 9, and 14, gives appropriate
   feedback   Yes   No
7. Times correctly   Yes   No

Starting Considerations

8. Starts with appropriate item   Yes   No

Reverse Rule for Start Points Only

9. Administers items in reverse sequence
   correctly   Yes   No

Discontinue Considerations

10. Discontinues subtest correctly   Yes   No

Scoring Guidelines

11. Scores items correctly   Yes   No

Record Form

12. Circles response letter correctly   Yes   No
13. Circles 0 or 1 in Score column correctly   Yes   No
14. Records number of Base Points in
    appropriate box correctly   Yes   No
15. Records number of Earned Points in
    appropriate box correctly   Yes   No
16. Adds base points and earned points and
    enters total score in Raw Score box correctly   Yes   No

Comments

_____

_____

Nonverbal Knowledge
(See p. 583 in text for detailed information.)

Background Considerations

1. Reads directions verbatim   Yes   No
2. Reads directions clearly   Yes   No
3. Uses stopwatch   Yes   No
4. Places stopwatch correctly   Yes   No
5. For item 1 in Levels 2 to 5, gives appropriate
   feedback   Yes   No
6. For all items in Level 3, gives appropriate
   prompt   Yes   No

(Continued)

Table E-5 (*Continued*)		

Nonverbal Knowledge (*Continued*) — Circle One

7. For items 1 to 6 in Levels 4 to 6, gives appropriate prompt — Yes No
8. For items in Levels 4 to 6, queries appropriately — Yes No

Starting Considerations

9. Starts with appropriate item — Yes No

Basal Rule

10. For Levels 3 and 4, follows basal rule correctly — Yes No
11. For Level 5, follows basal rule correctly — Yes No

Discontinue Considerations

12. Discontinues subtest correctly — Yes No

Scoring Guidelines

13. Scores items correctly — Yes No

Record Form

14. For each item administered, circles 0 or 1 in Score column correctly — Yes No
15. For Levels 4 to 6, records individual's responses correctly — Yes No
16. For each level administered, adds points and enters score in Raw Score box correctly — Yes No

Comments

_____

_____

_____

Nonverbal Quantitative Reasoning
(See pp. 584–585 in text for detailed information.)

Background Considerations

1. Reads directions verbatim — Yes No
2. Reads directions clearly — Yes No
3. Uses stopwatch — Yes No
4. Places stopwatch correctly — Yes No
5. For items 1 and 2 in Level 2, places counting rods correctly — Yes No
6. For item 1 in Levels 2 to 5, gives feedback appropriately — Yes No
7. For items 3 and 4 in Level 3, uses layout card correctly — Yes No
8. For oral responses, prompts correctly — Yes No
9. For item 1 in Level 4, follows procedure for counting rods — Yes No
10. For items in Levels 5 and 6, provides paper and pencil — Yes No
11. For all items in Level 6 and for oral responses that are not one of the options, prompts correctly — Yes No
12. Times correctly — Yes No

Nonverbal Quantitative Reasoning (*Continued*) — Circle One

Starting Considerations

13. Starts with appropriate item — Yes No

Basal Rule

14. For Levels 3 and 4, follows basal rule correctly — Yes No
15. For Level 5, follows basal rule correctly — Yes No

Discontinue Considerations

16. Discontinues subtest correctly — Yes No

Scoring Guidelines

17. Scores items correctly — Yes No

Record Form

18. For each item administered, circles 0 or 1 in Score column correctly — Yes No
19. For each level administered, adds points correctly and enters score in Raw Score box correctly — Yes No

Comments

_____

_____

_____

Nonverbal Visual-Spatial Processing
(See pp. 586–587 in text for detailed information.)

Background Considerations

1. Clears table — Yes No
2. Seats individual directly in front of table — Yes No
3. Reads directions verbatim — Yes No
4. Reads directions clearly — Yes No
5. Uses stopwatch — Yes No
6. Places stopwatch correctly — Yes No
7. For Levels 1 and 2, places form board correctly — Yes No
8. For item 4 in Level 1, turns form board correctly — Yes No
9. For item 6 in Level 2, turns form board correctly — Yes No
10. For Levels 3 to 6, shields Record Form — Yes No
11. For items in Levels 3 to 6, places pieces correctly — Yes No
12. After item 1 in Level 3 is completed, adds additional pieces correctly — Yes No
13. Administers sample item correctly — Yes No
14. Times correctly in Levels 3 to 6 — Yes No

Starting Considerations

15. Starts with appropriate item — Yes No

Basal Rule

16. For Levels 2 to 4, follows basal rule correctly — Yes No

(*Continued*)

Table E-5 (*Continued*)

Nonverbal Visual-Spatial Processing (*Continued*)	Circle One	
17. For Level 5, follows basal rule correctly	Yes	No
Discontinue Considerations		
18. Discontinues subtest correctly	Yes	No
Scoring Guidelines		
19. Scores subtest correctly	Yes	No
Record Form		
20. For each item administered, circles appropriate number in Score column correctly	Yes	No
21. For each level administered, adds points correctly and enters score in Raw Score box correctly	Yes	No

Comments

_____

_____

_____

Nonverbal Working Memory
(See pp. 588–589 in text for detailed information.)

Background Considerations		
1. Clears table	Yes	No
2. For items 3 and 4 in Level 1, uses layout card correctly	Yes	No
3. Follows directions when placing pieces under cup	Yes	No
4. For Levels 2 to 6, orients layout card correctly	Yes	No
5. Taps correctly	Yes	No
6. Repeats sample items correctly	Yes	No
7. Gives feedback on sample items in Levels 2 to 5 correctly	Yes	No
8. Does not repeat tapping items	Yes	No
9. Places required number of blocks in front of individual	Yes	No
10. For sample item 2 in Level 3, speaks slowly and clearly	Yes	No
11. For items in Levels 3 to 6, repeats prompt appropriately	Yes	No
Starting Considerations		
12. Starts with appropriate item	Yes	No
Basal Rule		
13. For Levels 2 to 4, follows basal rule correctly	Yes	No
14. For Level 5, follows basal rule correctly	Yes	No
Discontinue Considerations		
15. Discontinues subtest correctly	Yes	No
Scoring Guidelines		
16. Scores items correctly	Yes	No

Nonverbal Working Memory (*Continued*)	Circle One	
Record Form		
17. For each sample item administered, circles F or P correctly	Yes	No
18. For each item administered, circles 0 or 1 in Score column correctly	Yes	No
19. For each level administered, adds points and enters score in Raw Score box correctly	Yes	No

Comments

_____

_____

_____

Verbal Fluid Reasoning
(See pp. 589–590 in text for detailed information.)

Background Considerations		
1. Reads directions verbatim	Yes	No
2. Reads directions clearly	Yes	No
3. Leaves Item Book 3 on table and turns pages one at a time	Yes	No
4. For Levels 2 and 4, gives appropriate feedback for item 1	Yes	No
5. For Level 2, queries appropriately	Yes	No
6. For Level 3, uses stopwatch	Yes	No
7. Places stopwatch correctly	Yes	No
8. For Level 3, places sorting chips correctly	Yes	No
9. For Level 3, removes chips correctly	Yes	No
10. For Level 3, gives prompts correctly	Yes	No
11. For Level 4, gives feedback on item 1 correctly	Yes	No
12. For Levels 5 and 6, points correctly	Yes	No
Starting Considerations		
13. Starts with appropriate item	Yes	No
Basal Rule		
14. For Levels 3 and 4, follows basal rule correctly	Yes	No
15. For Level 5, follows basal rule correctly	Yes	No
Discontinue Considerations		
16. Discontinues subtest correctly	Yes	No
Scoring Guidelines		
17. Scores items correctly	Yes	No
Record Form		
18. For Levels 2, 4, 5, and 6, records individual's answers in Record Individual's Response column correctly	Yes	No
19. For each item administered in Levels 2, 4, 5, and 6, circles 0, 1, or 2 in Score column correctly	Yes	No

(*Continued*)

Table E-5 (*Continued*)

Verbal Fluid Reasoning (*Continued*)	Circle One	
20. For Levels 2, 4, 5, and 6, adds points and enters score in Raw Score boxes correctly	Yes	No
21. For Level 3, records individual's responses correctly	Yes	No
22. For Level 3, determines number of points earned correctly	Yes	No
23. For Level 3, enters score in Raw Score box correctly	Yes	No

Comments

_____

_____

_____

Verbal Knowledge

(See pp. 591–592 in text for detailed information.)

Background Considerations	Circle One	
1. Reads directions verbatim	Yes	No
2. Reads directions clearly	Yes	No
3. For item 1, points correctly	Yes	No
4. For items 1, 2, 4, 6, 10, and 15, gives correct answer appropriately	Yes	No
5. For items 15 to 44, queries appropriately	Yes	No

Starting Considerations
6. Starts with appropriate item	Yes	No

Reverse Rule for Start Points Only
7. Administers items in reverse sequence correctly	Yes	No

Scoring Guidelines
8. Scores items correctly	Yes	No

Discontinue Considerations
9. Discontinues subtest correctly	Yes	No

Record Form
10. For items 1 to 14, circles correct answers correctly	Yes	No
11. For items 15 to 44, records individual's response verbatim in Record Individual's Response column correctly	Yes	No
12. Circles appropriate number in Score column correctly	Yes	No
13. Records number of Base Points in appropriate box correctly	Yes	No
14. Records number of Earned Points in appropriate box correctly	Yes	No
15. Adds base points and earned points and enters total score in Raw Score box correctly	Yes	No

Comments

_____

_____

_____

Verbal Quantitative Reasoning

(See p. 593 in text for detailed information.)

Background Considerations	Circle One	
1. Reads directions verbatim	Yes	No
2. Reads directions clearly	Yes	No
3. For item 1 in Levels 2 to 5, gives appropriate feedback	Yes	No
4. For item 1 in Level 2, does not use fingers, blocks, or toys to elicit response	Yes	No
5. For items in Level 3, allows individual to "write" on table or gesture with fingers	Yes	No
6. For items 2 and 3 in Level 4, allows individual to take block structure apart to count segments	Yes	No
7. For item 4 in Level 3, uses alternative wording to rephrase problem if needed	Yes	No
8. For items in Levels 5 and 6, provides paper and pencil	Yes	No
9. For Levels 5 and 6, has individual look at problems while examiner reads them aloud	Yes	No
10. Times correctly	Yes	No

Starting Considerations
11. Starts with appropriate item	Yes	No

Basal Rule
12. For Levels 3 and 4, follows basal rule correctly	Yes	No
13. For Level 5, follows basal rule correctly	Yes	No

Discontinue Considerations
14. Discontinues subtest correctly	Yes	No

Scoring Guidelines
15. Scores items correctly	Yes	No

Record Form
16. For each item administered, circles 0 or 1 in Score column correctly	Yes	No
17. For each level administered, adds points and enters score in Raw Score box correctly	Yes	No

Comments

_____

_____

_____

Verbal Visual-Spatial Processing

(See pp. 594–595 in text for detailed information.)

Background Considerations	Circle One	
1. Clears table	Yes	No
2. For item 1 in Levels 2 to 5, gives appropriate feedback	Yes	No
3. For items 3 to 6 in Level 2 and for items 1 to 6 in Level 4, positions Item Book 3 correctly	Yes	No
4. For item 1 in Level 3, queries appropriately	Yes	No

Table E-5 (*Continued*)

Verbal Visual-Spatial Processing (*Continued*)	Circle One	
5. For item 6 in Level 3, queries appropriately	Yes	No
6. For items 4, 5, and 6 in Level 5 and for all items in Level 6, repeats items correctly	Yes	No
7. For items 1 to 3 in Level 5, gives prompt correctly	Yes	No

Starting Considerations

8. Starts with appropriate item	Yes	No

Basal Rule

9. For Levels 3 and 4, follows basal rule correctly	Yes	No
10. For Level 5, follows basal rule correctly	Yes	No

Discontinue Considerations

11. Discontinues subtest correctly	Yes	No

Scoring Guidelines

12. Scores items correctly	Yes	No

Record Form

13. For each item administered, circles 0, 1, or 2 in Score column correctly	Yes	No
14. For each level administered, adds points correctly and enters score in Raw Score box correctly	Yes	No

Comments

_____

_____

_____

Verbal Working Memory

(See p. 596 in text for detailed information.)

Background Considerations

1. Places Item Book 3 correctly	Yes	No
2. Reads each sentence or phrase clearly and at an even rate	Yes	No
3. For Levels 2 and 3, drops voice at end of each sentence	Yes	No
4. Does not repeat any items	Yes	No
5. For sample items in Levels 2 to 5, gives feedback correctly	Yes	No
6. Permits individual to vocally rehearse during item presentation	Yes	No
7. Gives individual time to answer questions, but does not pause between items	Yes	No
8. For Levels 4 to 6, accepts answers to questions in any form	Yes	No

Starting Considerations

9. Starts with appropriate item	Yes	No

Basal Rule

10. For Levels 3 and 4, follows basal rule correctly	Yes	No
11. For Level 5, follows basal rule correctly	Yes	No

Verbal Working Memory (*Continued*)	Circle One	

Discontinue Considerations

12. Discontinues subtest correctly	Yes	No

Scoring Guidelines

13. Scores subtest correctly	Yes	No

Record Form

14. For each item administered, circles 0 or 1 in Score column correctly	Yes	No
15. For each sample item administered at Levels 4 and 5, circles F or P correctly	Yes	No
16. For each level administered, adds points and enters score in Raw Score box correctly	Yes	No
17. Records appropriately	Yes	No

Comments

_____

_____

_____

Front Page of Record Form

1. Enters information on top of page correctly	Yes	No
2. Records date of testing correctly (Y, M, D)	Yes	No
3. Records individual's date of birth correctly (Y, M, D)	Yes	No
4. Computes individual's age at testing correctly (Y, M, D)	Yes	No
5. Enters Nonverbal Domain raw scores correctly	Yes	No
6. Enters Verbal Domain raw scores correctly	Yes	No
7. Enters sum of scaled scores, standard score, percentile rank, and confidence interval correctly for each IQ and Index	Yes	No
8. Completes Subtest Profile—Scaled Scores correctly	Yes	No
9. Completes Composite Profile—Scaled Scores correctly	Yes	No

General Evaluation

Rapport

1. Maintains rapport throughout testing	Yes	No
2. Is alert to individual's moods	Yes	No
3. Does not become impatient or frustrated with individual	Yes	No
4. Does not badger individual	Yes	No
5. Handles behavior problems correctly	Yes	No
6. Makes accommodations for any physical impairments individual has that may affect assessment (e.g., hearing or visual loss)	Yes	No
7. Does not take break in middle of a subtest	Yes	No
8. Allows individual to walk around room, if needed	Yes	No
9. Encourages individual to perform a task, if needed	Yes	No
10. Praises individual's effort	Yes	No

(*Continued*)

Table E-5 (Continued)

General Evaluation (Continued)	Circle One	
11. Does not say "Good" or "Right" after a correct response	Yes	No
12. Shows empathy if individual is concerned about poor performance	Yes	No

Administering Test Items

13. Administers test in professional, unhurried manner	Yes	No
14. Speaks clearly throughout testing	Yes	No
15. Is well organized and has all needed materials nearby	Yes	No
16. Administers subtests in appropriate order	Yes	No
17. Maintains steady pace	Yes	No
18. Makes a smooth transition from one subtest to the next	Yes	No
19. Repeats directions on request when appropriate	Yes	No
20. Repeats items when appropriate	Yes	No
21. Uses good judgment in deciding how much time to give individual to solve each item on untimed subtests	Yes	No
22. Begins timing correctly	Yes	No
23. Adheres to time limits	Yes	No
24. Stops timing when individual has obviously finished	Yes	No
25. Stops timing when time limit is reached	Yes	No
26. Does not stop timing prematurely	Yes	No
27. Places test materials not currently in use out of individual's sight	Yes	No
28. Clears table of unessential materials	Yes	No
29. Positions Record Form so that individual cannot see correct answers	Yes	No
30. Positions Item Books so that individual cannot see correct answers	Yes	No
31. Makes appropriate eye contact with individual	Yes	No
32. Reads directions exactly as written in Item Books	Yes	No
33. Reads items exactly as written in Item Books	Yes	Np
34. Takes short break, as needed, at end of a subtest	Yes	No
35. Does not give additional items for practice	Yes	No
36. Does not ask leading questions	Yes	No
37. Does not spell words on any subtest	Yes	No
38. Does not define words	Yes	No
39. Does not use Vocabulary words in a sentence	Yes	No
40. Queries correctly	Yes	No
41. Records Q for queried responses	Yes	No
42. Prompts correctly	Yes	No
43. Records P for prompted responses	Yes	No
44. Gives second trials correctly	Yes	No
45. Follows start item with appropriate item	Yes	No
46. Administers reverse sequence correctly	Yes	No

General Evaluation (Continued)	Circle One	
47. Shows individual how to solve problems when appropriate	Yes	No
48. Conducts testing-of-limits after all subtests have been administered, if desired	Yes	No
49. Makes every effort to administer entire test in one session	Yes	No

Scoring Test Items

50. Scores each item after individual answers	Yes	No
51. Gives credit for correct responses given at any time during test, when appropriate	Yes	No
52. Does not give credit for correct answers given after time limit	Yes	No
53. Makes entry in Record Form for every item administered	Yes	No
54. Awards full credit for items not administered, as appropriate	Yes	No
55. Uses good judgment overall in scoring responses	Yes	No
56. Rechecks scoring after test is administered	Yes	No

Completing Record Form

57. Records any deviation from procedure on Record Form	Yes	No
58. Completes Front Page of Record Form correctly	Yes	No
59. Completes page 2 of Record Form (if desired) correctly	Yes	No

Qualitative Feedback

_____

_____

_____

Overall Strengths

_____

_____

_____

Areas Needing Improvement

_____

_____

_____

Other Comments

_____

_____

_____

Overall Evaluation

Circle One: Excellent Good Average Below Average Poor

APPENDIX F

TABLES FOR THE DAS–II

Table F-1
Interpretive Rationales, Implications of High and Low Scores, and Instructional Implications for DAS–II Subtests

Ability	Background factors	Possible implications of high scores	Possible implications of low scores	Instructional implications
Copying (Copy)				
Visual processing (Gv) Visualization (VZ) Perceptual discrimination Fine-motor coordination Spatial perception Pencil control	Motor ability Visual acuity Experience with paper and pencil	Good perceptual discrimination Good fine-motor coordination Good perception of spatial orientation Good integration of perceptual and motor processes Good pencil control	Poor perceptual discrimination Poor fine-motor coordination Poor perception of spatial orientation Poor integration of perceptual and motor processes Poor pencil control	Use pencils and crayons to develop fine-motor skills Use tracing activities with a variety of shapes and designs Teach proper pencil grasp and pressure
Early Number Concepts (ENC)				
Crystallized knowledge (Gc) Fluid reasoning ability (Gf) General (verbal) information (K0) Language development (LD) Piagetian reasoning (RP) Knowledge of quantitative, prenumerical, and numerical concepts Verbal comprehension Knowledge of basic language concepts Visual perception and analysis	Cultural opportunities Experience in using language to express number or quantity Intellectual curiosity Quality of early education and general education Visual acuity Fund of information	Good nonverbal reasoning ability Good knowledge of quantitative, prenumerical, and numerical concepts Good verbal comprehension Good knowledge of basic language concepts Good visual perception and analysis	Poor nonverbal reasoning ability Poor knowledge of quantitative, prenumerical, and numerical concepts Poor verbal comprehension Poor knowledge of basic language concepts Poor visual perception and analysis	Provide instruction and practice with counting, sorting, adding, and subtracting Focus on recognizing and describing differences and similarities in sizes, shapes, textures, and objects in surroundings Use exercises involving classifications and generalizations
Matching Letter-Like Forms (MLLF)				
Visual processing (Gv) Visualization (VZ) Visual-perceptual discrimination ability Perception and discrimination of spatial orientation of letter-like figures Scanning strategies	Cultural opportunities Experience in visual matching activities Familiarity with figures and puzzles Ability to follow verbal instructions and visual cues Visual acuity	Good visual-spatial ability Good visual-perceptual discrimination ability Good perception and discrimination of spatial orientation of letter-like figures Good scanning strategies Good ability to follow verbal instructions and visual cues	Poor visual-spatial ability Poor visual-perceptual discrimination ability Poor perception and discrimination of spatial orientation of letter-like figures Poor scanning strategies Poor ability to follow verbal instructions and visual cues	Focus on matching objects Work with geometric forms

(Continued)

Table F-1 (*Continued*)				
Ability	*Background factors*	*Possible implications of high scores*	*Possible implications of low scores*	*Instructional implications*
Matrices (Mat)				
Fluid reasoning ability (Gf) Induction (I) Visual-perceptual analogic reasoning Visual-perceptual organization Visual-perceptual discrimination	Motivation and persistence Ability to work toward a goal Ability to use trial and error Visual acuity	Good nonverbal reasoning ability Good ability to draw conclusions from known facts or principles Good visual-perceptual analogic reasoning Good visual-perceptual organization Good visual-perceptual discrimination	Poor nonverbal reasoning ability Poor ability to draw conclusions from known facts or principles Poor visual-perceptual analogic reasoning Poor visual-perceptual organization Poor visual-perceptual discrimination	Use puzzles, blocks, Legos, spatial-visual tasks, perceptual tasks involving breaking down an object and building it up again, and art work with geometric forms and flannel board Focus on part-whole relationships Use sequencing tasks
Naming Vocabulary (NVoc)				
Crystallized knowledge (Gc) Lexical knowledge (VL) Expressive language ability Word knowledge Fund of information Long-term memory Perception of meaningful stimuli	Cultural opportunities Interests and reading patterns Intellectual curiosity Richness of early environment Quality of early education and general education Visual acuity	Good expressive language Good word knowledge Good fund of information Good long-term memory Good perception of meaningful stimuli	Poor expressive language Poor word knowledge Poor fund of information Poor long-term memory Poor perception of meaningful stimuli	Develop working vocabulary Encourage child to discuss experiences, ask questions, and make a dictionary Use other verbal enrichment exercises, including Scrabble, analogy, and other word games
Pattern Construction (PCon)				
Fluid reasoning ability (Gf) Visual processing (Gv) Spatial relations (SR) Visual-motor coordination Analysis and synthesis Attention Concentration	Color vision Ability to work under time pressure Visual acuity Trial-and-error learning Motivation and persistence	Good nonverbal reasoning ability Good visual-spatial ability Good spatial relations Good visual-motor coordination Good analysis and synthesis Good attention Good concentration	Poor nonverbal reasoning ability Poor visual-spatial ability Poor spatial relations Poor visual-motor coordination Poor analysis and synthesis Poor attention Poor concentration	Use puzzles, blocks, Legos, spatial-visual tasks, perceptual tasks involving breaking down an object and building it up again, and art work with geometric forms and flannel board Focus on part-whole relationships and working with a model or a key Focus on activities involving recognition of visual details

(*Continued*)

Ability	Background factors	Possible implications of high scores	Possible implications of low scores	Instructional implications
Phonological Processing (PhP)				
Auditory processing (Ga) Phonetic coding (PC) Oral language development Phonological awareness Ability to manipulate sounds within words Attention Concentration	Cultural opportunities Exposure to word and sound games at home and in school Experience in being read to during the preschool years Quality of early education and general education Auditory acuity	Good oral language development Good phonological awareness Good ability to manipulate sounds within words Good attention Good concentration	Poor oral language development Poor phonological awareness Poor ability to manipulate sounds within words Poor attention Poor concentration	Focus on rhyming activities Focus on identifying pictures of items whose names begin with the same sound Focus on combining smaller phonological units into spoken words Focus on breaking whole words into smaller chunks
Picture Similarities (PSim)				
Fluid reasoning ability (Gf) Induction (I) Visual-perceptual reasoning Conceptual thinking Visual-perceptual discrimination Visual processing Fund of information	Cultural opportunities Interests and reading patterns Intellectual curiosity Quality of early education and general education Visual acuity	Good nonverbal reasoning ability Good ability to draw conclusions from known facts or principles Good visual-perceptual reasoning Good conceptual thinking Good visual-perceptual discrimination Good visual processing Good fund of information	Poor nonverbal reasoning ability Poor ability to draw conclusions from known facts or principles Poor visual-perceptual reasoning Poor conceptual thinking Poor visual-perceptual discrimination Poor visual processing Poor fund of information	Use activities involving sorting objects and pictures Use exercises involving classification and generalization Focus on recognizing differences and similarities in shapes, textures, and daily surroundings
Rapid Naming (RNam)				
Processing speed (Gs) Perceptual speed: Complex (Pc) Speed with which words are identified and retrieved from long-term memory Fluency of speech Integration of visual and verbal processing Attention Concentration	Color vision Ability to work under time pressure Visual acuity Motivation and persistence	Good processing speed Good perceptual speed Good ability to quickly retrieve words from long-term memory Good fluency of speech Good integration of visual and verbal processing Good attention Good concentration	Poor processing speed Poor perceptual speed Poor ability to quickly retrieve words from long-term memory Poor fluency of speech Poor integration of visual and verbal processing Poor attention Poor concentration	Emphasize scanning activities Emphasize language activities Develop attention and concentration skills

(*Continued*)

Ability	Background factors	Possible implications of high scores	Possible implications of low scores	Instructional implications
Recall of Designs (RDes)				
Visual processing (Gv) Visual Memory (MV) Short-term visual recall Spatial perception Fine-motor coordination	Motor ability Visual acuity Experience with paper and pencil	Good short-term visual recall Good perception of spatial orientation Good fine-motor coordination Good integration of perceptual and motor processes	Poor short-term visual recall Poor perception of spatial orientation Poor fine-motor coordination Poor integration of perceptual and motor processes	Use memory exercises and memory games Develop visualization skills Use pencils and crayons to develop fine-motor skills Use tracing activities with a variety of shapes and designs Teach proper pencil grasp and pressure
Recall of Digits Backward (DigB)				
Short-term memory (Gsm) Working memory (MW) Strategies for transforming digit sequences Attention Concentration	Auditory acuity Ability to self-monitor Ability to use encoding strategies Ability to use rehearsal strategies	Good short-term memory Good working memory Use of strategies for transforming digit sequences Good attention Good concentration Good auditory sequential processing	Poor short-term memory Poor working memory Little use of strategies for transforming digit sequences Poor attention Poor concentration Poor auditory sequential processing	Emphasize listening skills by using sequencing activities, reading a short story and asking the child to recall details, and seeing whether the child can follow directions Develop visualization skills Use short and simple directions and repeat when necessary Use other memory exercises and memory games Decrease anxiety
Recall of Digits Forward (DigF)				
Short-term memory (Gsm) Memory span (MS) Short-term auditory memory Oral recall of sequences of numbers Attention Concentration	Auditory acuity Ability to self-monitor Ability to use encoding strategies Ability to use rehearsal strategies	Good short-term auditory memory Good memory span Good recall of sequences of numbers presented orally Good attention Good concentration	Poor short-term auditory memory Poor memory span Poor recall of sequences of numbers presented orally Poor attention Poor concentration	Emphasize listening skills by using sequencing activities, reading a short story and asking the child to recall details, and seeing whether the child can follow directions Develop visualization skills Use short and simple directions and repeat when necessary Use other memory exercises and memory games Decrease anxiety

(Continued)

Ability	Background factors	Possible implications of high scores	Possible implications of low scores	Instructional implications
Recall of Objects–Immediate (RObI) and Recall of Objects–Delayed (RObD)				
Long-term retrieval (Glr) Free-recall memory (M6) Short-term visual-verbal memory (Recall of Objects–Immediate) Intermediate-term visual-verbal memory (Recall of Objects–Delayed) Integration of visual and verbal processing Verbal encoding ability Attention Concentration	Visual acuity Ability to self-monitor Ability to use encoding strategies Ability to use rehearsal and retrieval strategies	Good short-term visual-verbal memory (Recall of Objects–Immediate) Good intermediate-term visual-verbal memory (Recall of Objects–Delayed) Good integration of visual and verbal processing Good verbal encoding ability Good rehearsal and retrieval strategies Good attention Good concentration	Poor short-term visual-verbal memory (Recall of Objects–Immediate) Poor intermediate-term visual-verbal memory (Recall of Objects–Delayed) Poor integration of visual and verbal processing Poor verbal encoding ability Poor rehearsal and retrieval strategies Poor attention Poor concentration	Emphasize listening skills by using sequencing activities, reading a short story and asking the child to recall details, and seeing whether the child can follow directions Develop visualization skills Use short and simple directions and repeat when necessary Use other memory exercises and memory games
Recall of Sequential Order (SeqO)				
Short-term memory (Gsm) Working memory (MW) Strategies for transforming word sequences Attention Concentration	Auditory acuity Ability to self-monitor Ability to use encoding strategies Ability to use rehearsal strategies	Good short-term memory Good working memory Use of strategies for transforming word sequences Good attention Good concentration	Poor short-term memory Poor working memory Little use of strategies for transforming word sequences Poor attention Poor concentration	Emphasize listening skills by using sequencing activities, reading a short story and asking the child to recall details, and seeing whether the child can follow directions Develop visualization skills Use short and simple directions and repeat when necessary Use other memory exercises and memory games
Recognition of Pictures (RPic)				
Visual processing (Gv) Visual memory (MV) Short-term visual memory Recognition memory for pictures Visual imagery Memory for detail Memory for orientation Verbal mediation strategies Attention Concentration	Ability to receive visual stimuli Visual acuity Ability to self-monitor Ability to use encoding strategies Ability to use rehearsal strategies	Good visual-spatial ability Good short-term visual memory Good recognition memory for pictures Good visual imagery Good memory for detail Good memory for orientation Use of verbal mediation strategies Good attention Good concentration	Poor visual-spatial ability Poor short-term visual memory Poor recognition memory for pictures Poor visual imagery Poor memory for detail Poor memory for orientation Little use of verbal mediation strategies Poor attention Poor concentration	Use memory exercises and memory games Develop visualization skills Decrease anxiety Add verbal explanations when presenting material visually

(Continued)

Ability	Background factors	Possible implications of high scores	Possible implications of low scores	Instructional implications
Sequential and Quantitative Reasoning (SQR)				
Fluid reasoning ability (Gf) Induction (I) Quantitative reasoning (RQ; in Set B) Ability to perceive sequential patterns or relationships Analytical reasoning ability Ability to formulate and test hypotheses Integration of visual with verbal information processing strategies Long-term memory (in Set B)	Opportunity to acquire fundamental arithmetical processes Quality of early education and general education Visual acuity	Good nonverbal reasoning ability Good ability to draw conclusions from known facts or principles Good quantitative reasoning (in Set B) Good ability to perceive sequential patterns or relationships Good analytical reasoning ability Good ability to formulate and test hypotheses Good integration of visual with verbal information processing strategies Good long-term memory (in Set B)	Poor nonverbal reasoning ability Poor ability to draw conclusions from known facts or principles Poor quantitative reasoning (in Set B) Poor ability to perceive sequential patterns or relationships Poor analytical reasoning ability Poor ability to formulate and test hypotheses Poor integration of visual with verbal information processing strategies Poor long-term memory (in Set B)	Develop arithmetical skills Develop concentration skills Use concrete objects to introduce concepts Drill in basic skills Provide interesting "real" problems to solve Use exercises involving analyzing arithmetical word problems Increase attention span
Speed of Information Processing (SIP)				
Processing speed (Gs) Perceptual speed: scanning (Ps) Ability to make quantitative comparisons rapidly Ability to use sequential strategies for making comparisons Understanding of ordinal-number concepts Short-term numerical memory Attention Concentration	Rate of motor activity Motivation and persistence Visual acuity Ability to work under time pressure Ability to self-monitor	Good speed in performing simple mental operations Good ability to work fast under time pressure Good ability to make quantitative comparisons rapidly Good ability to use sequential strategies for making comparisons Good understanding of ordinal-number concepts Good short-term numerical memory Good attention Good concentration	Poor speed in performing simple mental operations Poor ability to work fast under time pressure Poor ability to make quantitative comparisons rapidly Poor ability to use sequential strategies for making comparisons Poor understanding of ordinal-number concepts Poor short-term numerical memory Poor attention Poor concentration	Use scanning exercises, such as looking at two or more objects and deciding if they are the same or different Increase attention span Reinforce persistence Increase motivation Reduce stress of working under time pressure

(*Continued*)

Table F-1 (*Continued*)

Ability	Background factors	Possible implications of high scores	Possible implications of low scores	Instructional implications
Verbal Comprehension (VCom)				
Crystallized knowledge (Gc) Listening ability (LS) Receptive language Understanding of verbal instructions Short-term memory Word knowledge Verbal comprehension Fund of information Perception of meaningful stimuli Visual-spatial ability Visual-perceptual discrimination	Cultural opportunities Richness of early environment Quality of early education and general education Intellectual curiosity Visual acuity	Good receptive language Good understanding of verbal instructions Good short-term memory Good word knowledge Good verbal comprehension Good fund of information Good perception of meaningful stimuli Good visual-spatial ability Good visual-perceptual discrimination	Poor receptive language Poor understanding of verbal instructions Poor short-term memory Poor word knowledge Poor verbal comprehension Poor fund of information Poor perception of meaningful stimuli Poor visual-spatial ability Poor visual-perceptual discrimination	Develop working vocabulary Encourage child to discuss experiences and ask questions
Verbal Similarities (VSim)				
Crystallized knowledge (Gc) Language development (LD) Verbal inductive reasoning ability Word knowledge Fund of information Abstract thinking ability Ability to distinguish essential from nonessential details	Quality of early education and general education Cultural opportunities Richness of early environment Interests and reading patterns	Good verbal inductive reasoning ability Good word knowledge Good fund of information Good abstract thinking ability Good ability to distinguish essential from nonessential details	Poor verbal inductive reasoning ability Poor word knowledge Poor fund of information Poor abstract thinking ability Poor ability to distinguish essential from nonessential details	Focus on recognizing differences and similarities in shapes, textures, and daily surroundings Provide activities involving sorting objects or pictures Stress language development, synonyms and antonyms, and exercises involving abstract words, classifications, and generalizations

(*Continued*)

Table F-1 (*Continued*)

Ability	Background factors	Possible implications of high scores	Possible implications of low scores	Instructional implications
Word Definitions (WDef)				
Crystallized knowledge (Gc) Language development (LD) Lexical knowledge (VL) Word knowledge Receptive and expressive language Fund of information Verbal conceptualization Abstract thinking Long-term information retrieval	Cultural opportunities Interests and reading patterns Richness of early environment Quality of early education and general education Intellectual curiosity	Good word knowledge Good receptive and expressive language Good fund of information Good verbal conceptualization Good abstract thinking Good long-term information retrieval	Poor word knowledge Poor receptive and expressive language Poor fund of information Poor verbal conceptualization Poor abstract thinking Poor long-term information retrieval	Develop working vocabulary Encourage child to discuss experiences, ask questions, and make cards containing vocabulary words and definitions Use other verbal enrichment exercises, including Scrabble, analogy, and other word games Encourage child to write about his or her activities and to keep a diary

Note. Abbreviations for the broad and narrow abilities in the Cattell-Horn-Carroll (CHC) model are shown within the parentheses. Table F-2 defines the CHC broad and narrow abilities associated with the DAS–II subtests, and Tables F-3 and F-4 show, in grid form, the CHC broad and narrow abilities associated with the DAS–II core subtests and diagnostic subtests, respectively.

Crystallized knowledge is also referred to as crystallized intelligence or crystallized ability. Fluid reasoning ability is also referred to as fluid ability, fluid reasoning, or fluid intelligence.

Select the appropriate implication(s) based on the entire test protocol and background information.

Source: Adapted from Elliott (2007).

Table F-2

Definitions of Broad and Narrow Abilities in the Cattell-Horn-Carroll (CHC) Model Associated with DAS–II Subtests

Broad and narrow abilities	Subtests
Crystallized Knowledge (Gc): The ability to use the knowledge base accumulated over time in the process of acculturation.	Naming Vocabulary, Verbal Comprehension, Verbal Similarities, Word Definitions, Early Number Concepts
General Information (K0): The ability to use a range of general knowledge.	Early Number Concepts
Language Development (LD): The ability to understand spoken native language.	Early Number Concepts, Verbal Similarities, Word Definitions
Lexical Knowledge (VL): The ability to use and understand words.	Naming Vocabulary, Word Definitions
Listening Ability (LS): The ability to listen and comprehend oral communications.	Verbal Comprehension
Fluid Reasoning Ability (Gf): The ability to solve relatively novel tasks by forming and recognizing concepts, identifying and perceiving relationships, drawing inferences, and reorganizing and transforming information.	Matrices, Pattern Construction, Picture Similarities, Sequential and Quantitative Reasoning, Early Number Concepts
Induction (I): The ability to draw conclusions from known facts or principles.	Matrices, Picture Similarities, Sequential and Quantitative Reasoning
Quantitative Reasoning (RQ): The ability to reason inductively and deductively using mathematical concepts.	Sequential and Quantitative Reasoning (in Set B)
Piagetian Reasoning (RP): The ability to use seriation, conservation, classification, and other logical thinking processes as defined by Piaget's developmental theory.	Early Number Concepts
Processing Speed (Gs): The ability to perform relatively easy and over-learned cognitive tasks quickly and efficiently using sustained attention and concentration.	Rapid Naming, Speed of Information Processing
Perceptual Speed: Complex (Pc): The ability to identify complex visual stimuli rapidly.	Rapid Naming
Perceptual Speed: Scanning (Ps): The ability to process visual information rapidly.	Speed of Information Processing
Short-Term Memory (Gsm): The ability to hold information in immediate memory and then use it within a few seconds.	Recall of Digits Backward, Recall of Digits Forward, Recall of Sequential Order
Memory Span (MS): The ability to recall a series of arbitrary elements (letters, numbers) after a few seconds.	Recall of Digits Forward
Working Memory (MW): The ability to perform cognitive operations on information stored in short-term memory.	Recall of Digits Backward, Recall of Sequential Order
Long-Term Retrieval (Glr): The ability to store information in long-term memory and fluently retrieve it.	Recall of Objects
Free Recall Memory (M6): The ability to recall items in any order after a large collection of items has been presented.	Recall of Objects
Visual Processing (Gv): The ability to solve simple and complex visual problems.	Copying, Pattern Construction, Recall of Designs, Matching Letter-Like Forms, Recognition of Pictures
Spatial Relations (SR): The ability to solve problems involving spatial relations.	Pattern Construction
Visualization (VZ): The ability to mentally manipulate objects or visual patterns.	Copying, Matching Letter-Like Forms
Visual Memory (MV): The ability to store a mental representation of a visual stimulus and then recognize or recall it later.	Recall of Designs, Recognition of Pictures

(Continued)

Table F-2 (*Continued*)

Broad and narrow abilities	Subtests
Auditory Processing (Ga): The ability to perceive, analyze, and synthesize patterns in auditory stimuli and to discriminate subtle nuances in patterns of sound and speech even when presented under distorted conditions.	Phonological Processing
Phonetic Coding (PC): The ability to process speech sounds, including identifying, isolating, blending, and rhyming sounds.	Phonological Processing

Note. Crystallized knowledge is also referred to as crystallized intelligence or crystallized ability. Fluid reasoning ability is also referred to as fluid ability, fluid reasoning, or fluid intelligence.

Source: Adapted from Elliott (2007) and Flanagan, McGrew, and Ortiz (2000).

Table F-3
Broad and Narrow Abilities in the Cattell-Horn-Carroll (CHC) Model Associated with DAS–II Core Subtests

CHC broad and narrow abilities	Copying	Matrices	Naming Vocabulary	Pattern Construction	Picture Similarities	Recall of Designs	Sequential and Quantitative Reasoning	Verbal Comprehension	Verbal Similarities	Word Definitions
Crystallized Knowledge (Gc)			■					■	■	■
Language Development (LD)									■	■
Lexical Knowledge (VL)			■							■
Listening Ability (LS)								■		
Fluid Reasoning Ability (Gf)		■		■	■		■			
Induction (I)		■			■		■			
Quantitative Reasoning (RQ)							■[a]			
Visual Processing (Gv)	■			■		■				
Spatial Relations (SR)				■						
Visualization (VZ)	■									
Visual Memory (MV)						■				

Note. Crystallized knowledge is also referred to as crystallized intelligence or crystallized ability. Fluid reasoning ability is also referred to as fluid ability, fluid reasoning, or fluid intelligence.

[a] In Set B.
Source: Adapted from Elliott (2007).

Table F-4
Broad and Narrow Abilities in the Cattell-Horn-Carroll (CHC) Model Associated with DAS–II Diagnostic Subtests

CHC broad and narrow abilities	Early Number Concepts	Matching Letter-Like Forms	Phonological Processing	Rapid Naming	Recall of Digits Backward	Recall of Digits Forward	Recall of Objects	Recall of Sequential Order	Recognition of Pictures	Speed of Information Processing
Crystallized Knowledge (Gc)	■									
General (verbal) Information (K0)	■									
Language Development (LD)	■									
Fluid Reasoning Ability (Gf)	■									
Piagetian Reasoning (RP)	■									
Processing Speed (Gs)				■						■
Perceptual Speed: Complex (Pc)				■						
Perceptual Speed: Scanning (Ps)										■
Short-Term Memory (Gsm)					■	■		■		
Memory Span (MS)						■				
Working Memory (MW)					■			■		
Long Term Retrieval (Glr)							■			
Free-Recall Memory (M6)							■			
Visual Processing (Gv)		■							■	
Visualization (VZ)		■								
Visual Memory (MV)									■	
Auditory Processing (Ga)			■							
Phonetic Coding (PC)			■							

Note. Crystallized knowledge is also referred to as crystallized intelligence or crystallized ability. Fluid reasoning ability is also referred to as fluid ability, fluid reasoning, or fluid intelligence.

Source: Adapted from Elliott (2007).

Table F-5
Interpretive Rationales, Implications of High and Low Scores, and Instructional Implications for DAS–II Clusters and Composites

Ability	Background factors	Possible implications of high scores	Possible implications of low scores	Instructional implications
Verbal Ability				
Crystallized knowledge (Gc) Verbal skills Verbal concepts and knowledge Language comprehension Language expression Level of vocabulary development General knowledge base	Richness of early environment Quality of early education and general education Cultural opportunities Interests and reading patterns	Good verbal skills Good verbal concepts and knowledge Good language comprehension Good language expression Good level of vocabulary development Good general knowledge base	Poor verbal skills Poor verbal concepts and knowledge Poor language comprehension Poor language expression Poor level of vocabulary development Poor general knowledge base	Stress language development activities Use verbal enrichment activities Teach current events Use exercises involving concept formation
Nonverbal Ability and Nonverbal Reasoning Ability				
Fluid reasoning ability (Gf) Visual processing (Gv; for ages 2-6 to 3-5) Inductive reasoning Analytical reasoning ability Perception of visual detail Understanding of simple verbal instructions and visual cues	Richness of early environment Visual acuity	Good nonverbal reasoning ability Good visual-spatial ability (ages 2-6 to 3-5) Good ability to draw conclusions from known facts or principles Good analytical reasoning ability Good perception of visual detail Good understanding of simple verbal instructions and visual cues	Poor nonverbal reasoning ability Poor visual-spatial ability (ages 2-6 to 3-5) Poor ability to draw conclusions from known facts or principles Poor analytical reasoning ability Poor perception of visual detail Poor understanding of simple verbal instructions and visual cues	Focus on visual learning and planning activities Teach part-whole relationships Use spatial-visual tasks Encourage trial-and-error activities Reinforce persistence
Spatial Ability				
Visual processing (Gv) Perceptual reasoning Visual-spatial analysis and synthesis ability Ability in spatial imagery and visualization Perception of spatial orientation Visual-spatial matching ability Attention to visual detail	Motivation and persistence Alertness Interests Eye-hand coordination Visual acuity	Good visual-spatial ability Good perceptual reasoning Good visual-spatial analysis and synthesis Good spatial imagery and visualization ability Good perception of spatial orientation Good visual-spatial matching ability Good attention to visual detail	Poor visual-spatial ability Poor perceptual reasoning Poor visual-spatial analysis and synthesis Poor spatial imagery and visualization ability Poor perception of spatial orientation Poor visual-spatial matching ability Poor attention to visual detail	Focus on visual learning and planning activities Teach part-whole relationships Use spatial-visual tasks Encourage trial-and-error activities Reinforce persistence Supplement visual materials with verbal explanations

(Continued)

Table F-5 (*Continued*)

Ability	Background factors	Possible implications of high scores	Possible implications of low scores	Instructional implications
School Readiness				
Skills underlying literacy and numeracy Language and conceptual ability Ability to match objects Auditory and visual discrimination ability Phonological processing	Richness of early environment Quality of early education and general education	Good development of skills underlying literacy and numeracy Good language and conceptual ability Good ability to match objects Good auditory and visual discrimination ability Good phonological processing	Poor development of skills underlying literacy and numeracy Poor language and conceptual ability Poor ability to match objects Poor auditory and visual discrimination ability Poor phonological processing	Emphasize early reading Emphasize early numerical skills Emphasize listening skills Develop attention skills Focus on small, meaningful units of instruction Teach phonological skills
Working Memory				
Working memory (MW) Short-term auditory memory Strategies for transferring word sequences Attention Concentration	Auditory acuity and discrimination Ability to use encoding strategies Ability to use rehearsal strategies Ability to delay responding until appropriate	Good working memory Good short-term auditory memory Use of strategies for transferring word sequences Good attention Good concentration	Poor working memory Poor short-term auditory memory Little use of strategies for transferring word sequences Poor attention Poor concentration	Develop short-term auditory memory skills Emphasize listening skills Develop attention skills Develop concentration skills Develop visualization skills Focus on small, meaningful units of instruction Develop basic arithmetical skills Reduce stress
Processing Speed				
Processing speed (Gs) Ability to work fast under time pressure Ability to integrate visual and verbal processing Scanning ability Attention Concentration	Rate of motor activity Motivation and persistence Visual acuity Ability to delay responding until appropriate	Good processing speed Good ability to work fast under time pressure Good ability to integrate visual and verbal processing Good scanning ability Good attention Good concentration	Poor processing speed Poor ability to work fast under time pressure Poor ability to integrate visual and verbal processing Poor scanning ability Poor attention Poor concentration	Develop visual-motor skills Develop concentration skills Focus on learning codes, such as using symbols to represent letters or numbers Focus on recognizing similarities among objects Improve scanning techniques

(*Continued*)

Table F-5 (*Continued*)

Ability	Background factors	Possible implications of high scores	Possible implications of low scores	Instructional implications
General Conceptual Ability				
Crystallized knowledge (Gc) Fluid reasoning ability (Gf) Visual processing (Gv) General intelligence Scholastic aptitude Academic aptitude Readiness to master a school curriculum Verbal skills Nonverbal skills Retrieval of material from long-term memory Attention Concentration	Cultural opportunities Quality of early education and general education Ability to self-monitor Ability to process visual information Ability to process verbal information Auditory and visual short-term memory Auditory and visual acuity Ability to work under time pressure Motivation and persistence	Good general intelligence Good scholastic aptitude Good verbal and nonverbal skills Readiness to master school curriculum	Poor general intelligence Poor scholastic aptitude Poor verbal and nonverbal skills Lack of readiness to master school curriculum	Focus on language development activities Focus on visual learning and planning activities Use spatial-visual activities Develop concept-formation skills Reinforce persistence and motivation Reduce stress
Special Nonverbal Composite				
Fluid reasoning ability (Gf) Visual processing (Gv) Spatial relations (SR) Induction (I) Fine-motor coordination Perceptual discrimination Integration of perceptual and motor processes	Motivation and persistence Visual acuity Rate of motor activity Eye-hand coordination Ability to work under time pressure Trial-and-error learning	Good nonverbal reasoning ability Good visual-spatial ability Good spatial relations Good ability to draw conclusions from known facts or principles Good fine-motor coordination Good perceptual discrimination Good integration of perceptual and motor processes	Poor nonverbal reasoning ability Poor visual-spatial ability Poor spatial relations Poor ability to draw conclusions from known facts or principles Poor fine-motor coordination Poor perceptual discrimination Poor integration of perceptual and motor processes	Focus on visual learning and planning activities Teach part-whole relationships Use spatial-visual tasks Encourage trial-and-error activities Reinforce persistence

Note. Abbreviations for the broad and narrow abilities in the Cattell-Horn-Carroll (CHC) model are shown within the parentheses. Table F-2 defines the CHC broad and narrow abilities associated with the DAS–II subtests, and Tables F-3 and F-4 show, in grid form, the CHC broad and narrow abilities associated with the DAS–II core subtests and diagnostic subtests, respectively.

Crystallized knowledge is also referred to as crystallized intelligence or crystallized ability. Fluid reasoning ability is also referred to as fluid ability, fluid reasoning, or fluid intelligence.
Source: Adapted from Elliott (2007).

Table F-6
Administrative Checklist for the DAS–II

ADMINISTRATIVE CHECKLIST FOR THE DAS–II

Name of examiner: _____   Date: _____

Name of child: _____   Name of observer: _____

(Note: The subtests below are presented in alphabetical order, which is not the order in which they are administered. If an item is not applicable, mark NA to the left of the number.)

Before Beginning   Circle One

1. Room is well lit — Yes No
2. Furniture is comfortable and size is appropriate for child — Yes No
3. Room is free of distractions — Yes No
4. Asks parent, if present, to remain in background and observe quietly — Yes No
5. Positions child correctly — Yes No
6. Sits directly across from child — Yes No
7. Establishes rapport — Yes No
8. Tells child that breaks are OK and asks child to let examiner know when he or she needs a break — Yes No
9. Does not prolong getting-acquainted period — Yes No
10. Does not overstimulate child or entertain child excessively before starting test — Yes No
11. Avoids use of term *intelligence* when introducing test — Yes No
12. Responds truthfully to any questions child has about purpose of testing — Yes No
13. Keeps test materials in order — Yes No
14. Keeps test kit out of child's view — Yes No
15. Begins test after establishing rapport — Yes No
16. Positions Record Form so that child cannot read questions or answers — Yes No
17. Introduces test by reading directions in Administration Manual verbatim — Yes No

Comments

_____

_____

_____

Copying
(See pp. 626–627 in text for detailed information.)

Background Considerations

1. Reads directions verbatim — Yes No
2. Reads directions clearly — Yes No
3. Gives child appropriate pencil — Yes No
4. Gives child appropriate sheet of paper — Yes No
5. For item 1, demonstrates task correctly — Yes No
6. Removes drawing correctly and gives child appropriate blank sheet of paper — Yes No

Copying (*Continued*)   Circle One

7. For item 2, demonstrates task correctly — Yes No
8. For items 3 to 20, presents item in Stimulus Book 1 correctly — Yes No
9. Omits instructions appropriately — Yes No
10. Writes *Top* on paper as needed — Yes No
11. Allows child to erase — Yes No
12. Allows child to make second attempt — Yes No
13. Gives child a new blank sheet of paper as needed — Yes No
14. Makes appropriate notes on new sheet of paper — Yes No
15. After subtest is completed, clips or staples various sheets of paper together — Yes No

Starting Considerations

16. Starts with appropriate item — Yes No

Decision Points

17. Follows decision-point rules correctly — Yes No

Alternative Stop Point

18. Follows alternative stop-point rules correctly — Yes No

Scoring Guidelines

19. Assigns tentative score for each item in P/F column of Record Form — Yes No
20. Scores items correctly — Yes No

Record Form

21. Circles appropriate number in Score column correctly — Yes No
22. Adds points correctly — Yes No
23. Enters Raw Score in appropriate box correctly — Yes No
24. Enters numbers in Item Set Administered boxes correctly — Yes No
25. Enters Ability Score in appropriate box correctly — Yes No

Comments

_____

_____

_____

(*Continued*)

Table F-6 (*Continued*)

Early Number Concepts	Circle One	
(See p. 628 in text for detailed information.)		

Background Considerations

1.	Reads directions verbatim	Yes	No
2.	Reads directions clearly	Yes	No
3.	Clears table	Yes	No
4.	Lines up green squares correctly	Yes	No
5.	Holds out hand correctly and gives appropriate instructions	Yes	No
6.	For teaching items, follows guidelines correctly	Yes	No
7.	Administers second trial of item 3 appropriately	Yes	No
8.	Removes green squares correctly	Yes	No
9.	For item 4, places Stimulus Book 2 properly	Yes	No
10.	Positions Stimulus Book 2 correctly	Yes	No
11.	Repeats directions correctly	Yes	No
12.	For items 14, 17, 31, 32, and 33, gives appropriate prompt	Yes	No
13.	For items 24 and 26, gives appropriate prompt	Yes	No
14.	If child gives two responses to an item, gives appropriate prompt	Yes	No

Starting Considerations

15.	Starts with appropriate item	Yes	No

Decision Points

16.	Follows decision-point rules correctly	Yes	No

Alternative Stop Point

17.	Follows alternative stop-point rules correctly	Yes	No

Scoring Guidelines

18.	Scores items 1 and 2 and items 4 to 33 correctly	Yes	No
19.	Scores item 3 correctly	Yes	No
20.	Gives credit for correct nonverbal responses	Yes	No

Record Form

21.	Records child's response correctly	Yes	No
22.	For item 3, circles highest number that child says on "Recite" line	Yes	No
23.	For item 3, circles highest number that child points to on "Points with reciting" line correctly	Yes	No
24.	Enters 0 or 1 in Score column for all items, except item 3, correctly	Yes	No
25.	Enters 0, 1, 2, or 3 in each of two Score column boxes for item 3 correctly	Yes	No
26.	Adds points correctly	Yes	No
27.	Enters Raw Score in appropriate box correctly	Yes	No
28.	Enters numbers in Item Set Administered boxes correctly	Yes	No
29.	Enters Ability Score in appropriate box correctly	Yes	No

Early Number Concepts (*Continued*)	Circle One	

Comments

_____

_____

_____

Matching Letter-Like Forms

(See p. 629 in text for detailed information.)

Background Considerations

1.	Reads directions verbatim	Yes	No
2.	Reads directions clearly	Yes	No
3.	Positions Stimulus Book 2 correctly	Yes	No
4.	For teaching items and Sample A, follows guidelines correctly	Yes	No

Starting Consideration

5.	Starts with appropriate item	Yes	No

Decision Points

6.	Follows decision-point rules correctly	Yes	No

Alternative Stop Points

7.	Follows alternative stop-point rules correctly	Yes	No

Scoring Guidelines

8.	Scores items correctly	Yes	No

Record Form

9.	Circles number in Response column correctly	Yes	No
10.	Enters 0 or 1 in Score column correctly	Yes	No
11.	Adds points correctly	Yes	No
12.	Enters Raw Score in appropriate box correctly	Yes	No
13.	Enters numbers in Item Set Administered boxes correctly	Yes	No
14.	Enters Ability Score in appropriate box correctly	Yes	No

Comments

_____

_____

_____

Matrices

(See pp. 630–631 in text for detailed information.)

Background Considerations

1.	Reads directions verbatim	Yes	No
2.	Reads directions clearly	Yes	No
3.	Points to appropriate parts of each matrix as directions are given	Yes	No
4.	Positions Stimulus Book 3 correctly	Yes	No
5.	If child does not point to a response, gives appropriate prompt	Yes	No
6.	Repeats directions correctly	Yes	No

(*Continued*)

Table F-6 (*Continued*)

Matrices (*Continued*)	Circle One	
7. For teaching items, follows guidelines correctly	Yes	No
8. For Sample D, gives teaching instructions correctly	Yes	No
9. Removes Stimulus Book 3 correctly	Yes	No

Starting Considerations

10. Starts with appropriate item	Yes	No

Decision Points

11. Follows decision-point rules correctly	Yes	No

Alternative Stop Points

12. Follows alternative stop-point rules correctly	Yes	No

Scoring Guidelines

13. Scores items correctly	Yes	No

Record Form

14. Circles number in Response column correctly	Yes	No
15. Enters 0 or 1 in Score column correctly	Yes	No
16. Adds points correctly	Yes	No
17. Enters Raw Score in appropriate box correctly	Yes	No
18. Enters numbers in Item Set Administered boxes correctly	Yes	No
19. Enters Ability Score in appropriate box correctly	Yes	No

Comments

_____

_____

_____

Naming Vocabulary
(See p. 632 in text for detailed information.)

Background Considerations

1. Reads directions verbatim	Yes	No
2. Reads directions clearly	Yes	No
3. Positions Stimulus Book 3 correctly	Yes	No
4. For each item, points to object and says, "What is this?"	Yes	No
5. If child does not respond, gives appropriate prompt	Yes	No
6. Repeats directions correctly	Yes	No
7. If child does not respond or gives an ambiguous or questionable response, gives appropriate prompt	Yes	No
8. For teaching items, follows guidelines correctly	Yes	No

Starting Considerations

9. Starts with appropriate item	Yes	No

Decision Points

10. Follows decision-point rules correctly	Yes	No

Naming Vocabulary (*Continued*)	Circle One	
Alternative Stop Points		
11. Follows alternative stop-point rules correctly	Yes	No

Scoring Guidelines

12. Scores items correctly	Yes	No

Record Form

13. Records responses verbatim in Response column correctly	Yes	No
14. Enters 0 or 1 in Score column correctly	Yes	No
15. Adds points correctly	Yes	No
16. Enters Raw Score in appropriate box correctly	Yes	No
17. Enters numbers in Item Set Administered boxes correctly	Yes	No
18. Enters Ability Score in appropriate box correctly	Yes	No

Comments

_____

_____

_____

Pattern Construction
(See pp. 633–634 in text for detailed information.)

Background Considerations

1. Clears table	Yes	No
2. Reads directions verbatim	Yes	No
3. Reads directions clearly	Yes	No
4. Uses stopwatch	Yes	No
5. Places stopwatch correctly	Yes	No
6. Clarifies directions correctly	Yes	No
7. For Set B, shows foam squares correctly	Yes	No
8. For Set C, shows plastic blocks correctly	Yes	No
9. For each item, gives child correct number of blocks or squares	Yes	No
10. For each item, uses a model, a picture, or a demonstration appropriately	Yes	No
11. Places intact model or Stimulus Book and blocks properly	Yes	No
12. Turns pages of Stimulus Book correctly	Yes	No
13. For items using a model, leaves model intact appropriately	Yes	No
14. Disassembles models correctly	Yes	No
15. On Set C, if child attempts to duplicate sides of model, gives appropriate caution	Yes	No
16. Mixes up squares or blocks between designs correctly	Yes	No
17. Removes all unnecessary squares or blocks from child's view correctly	Yes	No
18. Times correctly	Yes	No
19. Administers items 36 to 38 only as part of alternative scoring procedure	Yes	No

(*Continued*)

Table F-6 (*Continued*)

Pattern Construction (*Continued*)	Circle One	

Starting Considerations

20. Starts with appropriate item — Yes   No

Decision Points

21. Follows decision-point rules correctly — Yes   No
22. Does not count scores on sample items when applying decision-point rules — Yes   No

Alternative Stop Points

23. Follows alternative stop-point rules correctly — Yes   No

Scoring Guidelines

24. Scores items correctly — Yes   No

Record Form

25. For each item in Sets B and C, records completion time in Time column correctly — Yes   No
26. For correct constructions on items 14 to 35, circles time range in Score for Response Time columns correctly — Yes   No
27. If child's construction is wrong, sketches construction in blank squares in Incorrect column correctly — Yes   No
28. Enters P or F in the P/F column correctly — Yes   No
29. Enters appropriate number in Score column correctly — Yes   No
30. Adds points correctly — Yes   No
31. Enters Raw Score in appropriate box correctly — Yes   No
32. Enters numbers in Item Set Administered boxes correctly — Yes   No
33. Enters Ability Score in appropriate box correctly — Yes   No
34. For Alternative Procedure, circles appropriate score correctly — Yes   No

Comments

_____

_____

Phonological Processing
(See pp. 635–636 in text for detailed information.)

Background Considerations

1. Reads directions verbatim — Yes   No
2. Reads directions clearly — Yes   No
3. Studied Phonological Processing CD before administration — Yes   No
4. Follows guidelines on page 269 of Administration Manual — Yes   No
5. Repeats instructions and sample items correctly — Yes   No
6. Administers teaching items correctly — Yes   No

Starting Considerations

7. Starts with appropriate item — Yes   No

Phonological Processing (*Continued*)	Circle One	

Discontinue Considerations

8. Discontinues subtest correctly — Yes   No

Scoring Guidelines

9. Scores items correctly — Yes   No

Record Form

10. Records child's responses verbatim in Response Column — Yes   No
11. Writes 0 or 1 in Score column correctly — Yes   No
12. Adds points correctly — Yes   No
13. Enters Raw Scores for Tasks 1 to 4 in appropriate boxes correctly — Yes   No
14. Enters Ability Scores for Tasks 1 to 4 in appropriate boxes correctly — Yes   No
15. Enters Standard Errors for Tasks 1 to 4 in appropriate boxes correctly — Yes   No
16. Finds the Difference Between Ability Scores for Task Pairs Required for Statistical Significance correctly — Yes   No
17. Completes Ability Score Comparisons boxes correctly — Yes   No
18. Computes the Phonological Processing Subtest Score correctly — Yes   No
19. Enters Total Raw Score in appropriate box correctly — Yes   No
20. Enters Phonological Processing Ability Score in appropriate box correctly — Yes   No

Comments

_____

_____

Picture Similarities
(See p. 637 in text for detailed information.)

Background Considerations

1. Reads directions verbatim — Yes   No
2. Reads directions clearly — Yes   No
3. Places Stimulus Book 3 properly — Yes   No
4. Arranges deck of picture cards correctly — Yes   No
5. Administers each item correctly — Yes   No
6. If child's picture placement is not clear, queries appropriately — Yes   No
7. If child becomes concerned about card's orientation, gives appropriate instruction — Yes   No
8. Repeats directions correctly — Yes   No
9. For teaching items, follows guidelines correctly — Yes   No

Starting Considerations

10. Starts with appropriate item — Yes   No

Decision Points

11. Follows decision-point rules correctly — Yes   No

(*Continued*)

Table F-6 (*Continued*)

Picture Similarities (*Continued*)	Circle One	

Alternative Stop Points

12. Follows alternative stop-point rules correctly — Yes   No

Scoring Guidelines

13. Scores items correctly — Yes   No

Record Form

14. Circles number of child's response in Response column correctly — Yes   No
15. Enters 0 or 1 in Score column correctly — Yes   No
16. Adds points correctly — Yes   No
17. Enters Raw Score in appropriate box correctly — Yes   No
18. Enters numbers in Item Set Administered boxes correctly — Yes   No
19. Enters Ability Score in appropriate box correctly — Yes   No

Comments

_____

_____

_____

Rapid Naming

(See p. 638 in text for detailed information.)

Background Considerations

1. Reads directions verbatim — Yes   No
2. Reads directions clearly — Yes   No
3. Places Stimulus Book 4 properly — Yes   No
4. Times items accurately — Yes   No
5. For sample items, follows guidelines correctly — Yes   No
6. Administers each item correctly — Yes   No
7. Repeats directions correctly — Yes   No
8. If child has difficulty understanding task, gives prompts appropriately — Yes   No

Starting Considerations

9. Starts with appropriate item — Yes   No

Discontinue Considerations

10. Discontinues subtest correctly — Yes   No

Scoring Guidelines

11. Follows scoring guidelines — Yes   No

Record Form

12. Follows recording guidelines — Yes   No
13. Draws a slash through any color or picture the child skips — Yes   No
14. Circles each color or picture named incorrectly — Yes   No
15. Records any word substitutions verbatim — Yes   No
16. Records "SC" above color or picture when child corrects response — Yes   No

Rapid Naming (*Continued*)	Circle One	

17. Records an "X" next to last color or picture that child names at the end of time limit — Yes   No
18. Records Completion Time in seconds in appropriate box correctly — Yes   No
19. Records Number Correct for each item in appropriate box correctly — Yes   No
20. Enters Color Naming, Picture Naming, and Color-Picture Converted Raw Scores in appropriate boxes correctly — Yes   No
21. Completes Simple Naming boxes correctly — Yes   No
22. Completes Complex Naming boxes correctly — Yes   No
23. Enters Difference Between Ability Scores for Simple versus Complex Naming Required for Statistical Significance in appropriate boxes correctly — Yes   No
24. Completes Rapid Naming Subtest Score boxes correctly — Yes   No
25. Enters Total Converted Raw Score in appropriate box correctly — Yes   No
26. Enters Rapid Naming Ability Score in appropriate box correctly — Yes   No

Comments

_____

_____

_____

Recall of Designs

(See pp. 639–640 in text for detailed information.)

Background Considerations

1. Reads directions verbatim — Yes   No
2. Reads directions clearly — Yes   No
3. Gives child appropriate pencil — Yes   No
4. Gives child appropriate blank sheet of paper — Yes   No
5. Opens Stimulus Book 1 correctly — Yes   No
6. Exposes each item correctly — Yes   No
7. If child wants to draw before 5-second presentation is over, follows correct procedure — Yes   No
8. Allows child to make tracing movements above sheet of paper — Yes   No
9. After child completes a drawing, follows appropriate procedure — Yes   No
10. For Samples A, B, and C, follows guidelines correctly — Yes   No
11. After child learns task, omits instructions — Yes   No
12. If child rotates sheet of paper, writes word *Top* on it — Yes   No
13. Allows child to erase — Yes   No
14. Allows child to make a second attempt — Yes   No
15. If child makes a second attempt, gives child a new blank sheet of paper — Yes   No
16. For second attempts, marks new blank sheet of paper appropriately — Yes   No

(*Continued*)

Table F-6 (*Continued*)

Recall of Designs (*Continued*)	Circle One	
17. After subtest is completed, clips or staples various sheets of paper together	Yes	No
Starting Considerations		
18. Starts with appropriate item	Yes	No
Decision Points		
19. Follows decision-point rules correctly	Yes	No
Alternative Stop Points		
20. Follows alternative stop-point rules correctly	Yes	No
Scoring Guidelines		
21. Assigns tentative scores in P/F column in Record Form correctly	Yes	No
22. After administering battery, scores items correctly	Yes	No
Record Form		
23. Circles item scores correctly	Yes	No
24. Adds points correctly	Yes	No
25. Enters Raw Score in appropriate box correctly	Yes	No
26. Enters numbers in Item Set Administered boxes correctly	Yes	No
27. Enters Ability Score in appropriate box correctly	Yes	No

Comments

_____

_____

_____

Recall of Digits Backward
(See pp. 641–642 in text for detailed information.)

Background Considerations		
1. Reads directions verbatim	Yes	No
2. Reads directions clearly	Yes	No
3. For Sample A, follows guidelines correctly	Yes	No
4. If child asks for repetition of a digit or a sequence, responds correctly	Yes	No
5. Administers items 1 to 30 correctly	Yes	No
6. Reads numbers in an even tone at a rate of two digits per second	Yes	No
7. If child repeats digits in a different way, gives credit and prompts appropriately	Yes	No
8. Follows Administration Manual guidelines on establishing basal and ceiling levels	Yes	No
Starting Considerations		
9. Starts with appropriate item	Yes	No
Discontinue Considerations		
10. Discontinues subtest correctly	Yes	No

Recall of Digits Backward (*Continued*)	Circle One	
Scoring Guidelines		
11. Scores items correctly	Yes	No
Record Form		
12. Records responses verbatim in Response column	Yes	No
13. Enters 0 or 1 in Score column correctly	Yes	No
14. Adds points correctly	Yes	No
15. Enters Number Correct in appropriate box correctly	Yes	No
16. Enters Ability Score in appropriate box correctly	Yes	No

Comments

_____

_____

_____

Recall of Digits Forward
(See p. 643 in text for detailed information.)

Background Considerations		
1. Reads directions verbatim	Yes	No
2. Reads directions clearly	Yes	No
3. Before administering item 1, instructs child to wait until all numbers are said	Yes	No
4. If child asks for repetition of sequence, responds correctly	Yes	No
5. Reads numbers in an even tone at a rate of two digits per second	Yes	No
6. If child repeats digits in a different way, gives credit and prompts appropriately	Yes	No
7. Follows Administration Manual guidelines on establishing basal and ceiling levels	Yes	No
Starting Considerations		
8. Starts with appropriate item	Yes	No
Discontinue Considerations		
9. Discontinues subtest correctly	Yes	No
Scoring Guidelines		
10. Scores items correctly	Yes	No
Record Form		
11. Records responses verbatim in Response column	Yes	No
12. Enters 0 or 1 in Score column correctly	Yes	No
13. Adds points correctly	Yes	No
14. Enters Number Correct in appropriate box correctly	Yes	No
15. Enters Ability Score in appropriate box correctly	Yes	No

(*Continued*)

Table F-6 (*Continued*)

Recall of Digits Forward (*Continued*)	Circle One	

Comments

_____

_____

_____

_____

Recall of Objects
(See pp. 644–645 in text for detailed information.)

Background Considerations

1.	Reads directions verbatim	Yes	No
2.	Reads directions clearly	Yes	No
3.	Names objects at a rate of about one per second	Yes	No
4.	Points to each object while naming it	Yes	No
5.	If child spontaneously begins to name objects, allows child to do so, but continues to name them	Yes	No
6.	After naming objects, continues to expose card until time limit is up	Yes	No
7.	If child asks for name of object during Trial 1, tells child name of object	Yes	No
8.	Does not name objects during Trials 2 and 3	Yes	No
9.	Times correctly	Yes	No
10.	If child recalls all 20 objects in both Trials 1 and 2, does not administer Trial 3	Yes	No
11.	For each trial, encourages child to name as many objects as possible	Yes	No
12.	For Trials 2 and 3, if child does not name any objects that were named in first trial, questions appropriately	Yes	No
13.	Does not tell child there will be a Delayed Trial	Yes	No
14.	Administers Delayed Trial within 30 minutes	Yes	No

Starting Considerations

15.	Starts with appropriate item	Yes	No

Scoring Guidelines

16.	Scores items correctly	Yes	No

Record Form: Recall of Objects–Immediate

17.	Enters time in Time Test Ended box correctly	Yes	No
18.	When child correctly recalls an object, places a checkmark in appropriate place in Response column	Yes	No
19.	Enters 0 in Score column for each object not recalled correctly	Yes	No
20.	Enters 1 in Score column for each object recalled correctly	Yes	No
21.	Adds points correctly	Yes	No
22.	Enters Raw Score for each trial in appropriate box correctly	Yes	No
23.	Enters Immediate Raw Score in appropriate box correctly	Yes	No

Recall of Objects (*Continued*)	Circle One	

Record Form: Recall of Objects–Delayed

24.	Enters time Recall of Objects–Delayed part started in Time Delayed Trial Started box correctly	Yes	No
25.	When child recalls an object, places a checkmark in appropriate place in Response column	Yes	No
26.	Enters 0 in Score column for each object not recalled correctly	Yes	No
27.	Enters 1 in Score column for each object recalled correctly	Yes	No
28.	Adds points correctly	Yes	No
29.	Enters Delayed Raw Score in appropriate box correctly	Yes	No
30.	Enters *T* Score for Delayed Trial in appropriate oval correctly	Yes	No
31.	Enters Immediate Raw Score in appropriate box correctly	Yes	No
32.	Enters Ability Score for Immediate Trials in appropriate oval correctly	Yes	No

Comments

_____

_____

_____

Recall of Sequential Order
(See pp. 646–647 in text for detailed information.)

Background Considerations

1.	Reads directions verbatim	Yes	No
2.	Reads directions clearly	Yes	No
3.	Places Stimulus Book 2 properly and opens it to appropriate page	Yes	No
4.	For sample items, follows guidelines correctly	Yes	No
5.	If child fails Samples A, B, and C, discontinues subtest	Yes	No
6.	If child passes Samples A, B, and C, administers Sample D	Yes	No
7.	If child fails Samples D and E, discontinues subtest	Yes	No
8.	For Samples D and E and for items 1 to 12, turns to stimulus picture in Stimulus Book 2 and keeps it in front of child	Yes	No
9.	Does not allow child to touch picture	Yes	No
10.	For items 13 to 32, removes stimulus picture from child's view and reads items correctly	Yes	No
11.	Administers Sample F before item 21	Yes	No
12.	For teaching items, follows guidelines correctly	Yes	No
13.	If necessary, prompts child to listen carefully	Yes	No
14.	Reads words in an even tone at a rate of one word per second	Yes	No

(*Continued*)

Table F-6 (*Continued*)

Recall of Sequential Order (*Continued*)	Circle One	
15. Does not repeat word sequences	Yes	No
16. If child asks for a repetition of a word sequence, responds appropriately	Yes	No
17. Follows Administration Manual guidelines on establishing basal and ceiling levels	Yes	No

Starting Considerations
18. Starts with appropriate item	Yes	No

Decision Points
19. Follows decision-point rules correctly	Yes	No

Discontinue Considerations
20. Discontinues subtest correctly	Yes	No

Scoring Guidelines
21. Scores items correctly	Yes	No

Record Form
22. For Samples A, B, and C, circles P or F in Response column correctly	Yes	No
23. Does not score Samples D and E	Yes	No
24. Records child's responses verbatim in Response column	Yes	No
25. Enters 0 or 1 in Score column correctly	Yes	No
26. Adds points correctly	Yes	No
27. Enters Number Correct in appropriate box correctly	Yes	No
28. Enters Ability Score in appropriate box correctly	Yes	No

Comments

_____

_____

_____

Recognition of Pictures

(See pp. 648–649 in text for detailed information.)

Background Considerations
1. Reads directions verbatim	Yes	No
2. Reads directions clearly	Yes	No
3. Shows child Sample A for 2 seconds	Yes	No
4. Shows child Sample B and items 1 to 20 for 5 seconds each	Yes	No
5. For Sample A, shows child picture as directions are read	Yes	No
6. For Sample B and for items 1 to 20, gives first sentence of directions before showing child a picture	Yes	No
7. Does not name any objects in picture	Yes	No
8. Uses stopwatch	Yes	No
9. Places stopwatch correctly	Yes	No
10. For Sample B, starts stopwatch before giving instructions	Yes	No

Recognition of Pictures (*Continued*)	Circle One	
11. Looks at each picture for the 5-second exposure period while it is being shown to child	Yes	No
12. Positions Stimulus Book 4 correctly	Yes	No
13. For sample items, follows guidelines correctly	Yes	No
14. If child points to only one object when two or more objects are shown, gives appropriate prompts	Yes	No
15. If child points to all objects in turn, gives appropriate prompts	Yes	No
16. If child does not point to any object, gives appropriate prompts	Yes	No

Starting Considerations
17. Starts with appropriate item	Yes	No

Decision Points
18. Follows decision-point rules correctly	Yes	No

Alternative Stop Point
19. Follows alternative stop-point rules correctly	Yes	No

Scoring Guidelines
20. Scores items correctly	Yes	No

Record Form
21. Selects Child's View column or Opposite View column and draws a line through column not used	Yes	No
22. Circles child's responses correctly	Yes	No
23. Enters 0 or 1 in Score column correctly	Yes	No
24. Adds points correctly	Yes	No
25. Enters Raw Score in appropriate box correctly	Yes	No
26. Enters numbers in Item Set Administered boxes correctly	Yes	No
27. Enters Ability Score in appropriate box	Yes	No

Comments

_____

_____

_____

Sequential and Quantitative Reasoning

(See pp. 649–650 in text for detailed information.)

Background Considerations
1. Reads directions verbatim	Yes	No
2. Reads directions clearly	Yes	No
3. For Set A, opens Stimulus Book 4 to item 1 and gives directions correctly	Yes	No
4. For Set A, if child does not point to his or her choice, gives prompts correctly	Yes	No
5. For Set B, opens Stimulus Book 1 to Sample A and gives directions correctly	Yes	No

(Continued)

Table F-6 (*Continued*)

Sequential and Quantitative Reasoning (*Continued*)	Circle One	
6. Repeats directions correctly	Yes	No
7. Permits child to write answers to items in Set B, but does not permit child to use a pencil and paper to make calculations	Yes	No
8. For teaching items, follows guidelines correctly	Yes	No
9. For sample items, follows guidelines correctly	Yes	No

Starting Considerations

10. Starts with appropriate item	Yes	No

Decision Points

11. Follows decision-point rules correctly	Yes	No

Alternative Stop Point

12. Follows alternative stop-point rules correctly	Yes	No

Scoring Guidelines

13. Scores items correctly	Yes	No

Record Form

14. For Set A, circles number that corresponds to figure chosen by child	Yes	No
15. For Set B, records child's responses verbatim in Response column	Yes	No
16. Enters 0 or 1 in Score column correctly	Yes	No
17. Enters Raw Score in appropriate box correctly	Yes	No
18. Enters numbers in Item Set Administered boxes correctly	Yes	No
19. Enters Ability Score in appropriate box correctly	Yes	No

Comments

_____

_____

_____

Speed of Information Processing

(See pp. 651–652 in text for detailed information.)

Background Considerations

1. Reads directions verbatim	Yes	No
2. Reads directions clearly	Yes	No
3. Gives child a pencil without an eraser	Yes	No
4. Does not provide an eraser or allow child to use one	Yes	No
5. Places Response Booklet A properly	Yes	No
6. Places Response Booklets B and C properly	Yes	No
7. Folds back page of Response Booklet so that only Sample A is showing	Yes	No
8. Tells child to point to first sample item and not use a pencil	Yes	No
9. For sample items, follows guidelines correctly	Yes	No
10. For all items, follows guidelines correctly	Yes	No

Speed of Information Processing (*Continued*)	Circle One	
11. Encourages child to work quickly, if necessary	Yes	No
12. Turns pages of Response Booklet for child	Yes	No
13. Times items correctly	Yes	No
14. If child makes unnecessarily long lines or complex drawings, follows guidelines correctly	Yes	No
15. If child asks whether speed or accuracy is more important, follows guidelines correctly	Yes	No
16. If child does not understand expression "the biggest number," follows guidelines correctly	Yes	No
17. Checks each page after child finishes and corrects child's errors	Yes	No

Starting Considerations

18. Starts with appropriate item	Yes	No

Decision Points

19. Follows decision-point rules correctly	Yes	No

Alternative Stop Point

20. Follows alternative stop-point rules correctly	Yes	No

Scoring Guidelines

21. Sums scores on six scored items to obtain total raw score correctly	Yes	No
22. If an item has three or more uncorrected errors, gives a score of 0	Yes	No
23. If an item has two or fewer uncorrected errors, gives a score of 0 to 6 based on completion time	Yes	No

Record Form

24. Records completion time in seconds for each item in Time column correctly	Yes	No
25. Records number of uncorrected errors for each item in Errors column correctly	Yes	No
26. Circles appropriate time band	Yes	No
27. Enters score in Score column correctly	Yes	No
28. Sums scores for appropriate item set and enters sum in Raw Score box correctly	Yes	No
29. Transfers Raw Score from item set to Raw Score box correctly	Yes	No
30. Enters numbers in Item Set Administered boxes correctly	Yes	No
31. Enters Ability Score in appropriate box correctly	Yes	No

Comments

_____

_____

_____

(*Continued*)

Table F-6 (*Continued*)

Verbal Comprehension
(See p. 653 in text for detailed information.)

Circle One

Background Considerations

1. Reads directions verbatim	Yes	No
2. Reads directions clearly	Yes	No
3. Makes sure child is paying attention before presenting an item	Yes	No
4. Reads all items in an engaging manner	Yes	No
5. Positions Stimulus Book 3 correctly	Yes	No
6. For items that begin with instruction "Give me," holds out hand so that child can place object in it	Yes	No
7. If child asks if objects can be taken out of tray or be stood up, responds appropriately	Yes	No
8. Names objects in Inset Tray before administering items 13 to 23	Yes	No
9. Does not administer items 37 to 42 unless child passes two Chips Pretest items	Yes	No
10. Repeats directions correctly	Yes	No
11. Does not repeat instructions after child fails an item	Yes	No
12. After finishing with a picture or an object, removes it from table	Yes	No

Starting Considerations

13. Starts with appropriate item	Yes	No

Decision Points

14. Follows decision-point rules correctly	Yes	No

Alternative Stop Point

15. Follows alternative stop-point rules correctly	Yes	No

Scoring Guidelines

16. Scores items correctly	Yes	No
17. Gives credit for self-corrections	Yes	No

Record Form

18. Circles response number in Response column for items 24 to 36 correctly	Yes	No
19. Enters 0 or 1 in Score column correctly	Yes	No
20. Circles P or F in Score column for two Chips Pretest items correctly	Yes	No
21. Adds points correctly	Yes	No
22. Enters Raw Score in appropriate box correctly	Yes	No
23. Enters numbers in Item Set Administered boxes correctly	Yes	No
24. Enters Ability Score in appropriate box correctly	Yes	No

Comments

_____

_____

_____

Verbal Similarities
(See p. 654 in text for detailed information.)

Circle One

Background Considerations

1. Reads directions verbatim	Yes	No
2. Reads directions clearly	Yes	No
3. Questions appropriately	Yes	No
4. For teaching items, follows guidelines correctly	Yes	No
5. Repeats each item correctly	Yes	No
6. Once child understands task, says three stimulus words	Yes	No

Starting Considerations

7. Starts with appropriate item	Yes	No

Decision Points

8. Follows decision-point rules correctly	Yes	No

Alternative Stop Point

9. Follows alternative stop-point rules correctly	Yes	No

Scoring Guidelines

10. Scores items correctly	Yes	No

Record Form

11. Records responses verbatim in Response column	Yes	No
12. For items 1 to 26 and for items 30, 31, and 33, circles 0 or 1 correctly	Yes	No
13. For items 27, 28, 29, and 32, circles 0, 1, or 2 correctly	Yes	No
14. Adds points correctly	Yes	No
15. Enters Raw Score in appropriate box correctly	Yes	No
16. Enters numbers in Item Set Administered boxes correctly	Yes	No
17. Enters Ability Score in appropriate box correctly	Yes	No

Comments

_____

_____

_____

Word Definitions
(See pp. 655–656 in text for detailed information.)

Background Considerations

1. Reads directions verbatim	Yes	No
2. Reads directions clearly	Yes	No
3. Introduces task correctly	Yes	No
4. Presents each item correctly	Yes	No
5. If child does not recognize a word, repeats word, spells it aloud, or writes it on paper	Yes	No
6. Repeats target word correctly	Yes	No

(*Continued*)

Table F-6 (*Continued*)

Word Definitions (*Continued*)	Circle One	
7. For teaching items, follows guidelines correctly	Yes	No
8. Questions all responses indicated by a Q in Administration Manual	Yes	No
9. For items 4, 5, 7, 10, 17, 20, and 23, prompts appropriately	Yes	No

Starting Considerations

10. Starts with appropriate item	Yes	No

Decision Points

11. Follows decision-point rules correctly	Yes	No

Alternative Stop Point

12. Follows alternative stop-point rules correctly	Yes	No

Scoring Guidelines

13. Assigns tentative score for each item	Yes	No
14. Uses general scoring guidelines correctly to assign tentative scores	Yes	No
15. Scores items correctly	Yes	No

Record Form

16. Records responses verbatim in Response column	Yes	No
17. Enters 0 or 1 in Score column correctly	Yes	No
18. Adds points correctly	Yes	No
19. Enters Raw Score in appropriate box correctly	Yes	No
20. Enters numbers in Item Set Administered boxes correctly	Yes	No
21. Enters Ability Score in appropriate box correctly	Yes	No

Comments

_____

_____

_____

Front Page of Record Form

1. Enters child's full name, age, and examiner's full name correctly	Yes	No
2. Records date of testing correctly (Y, M, D)	Yes	No
3. Records child's date of birth correctly (Y, M, D)	Yes	No
4. Computes child's age at testing correctly (Y, M)	Yes	No

Summary Page

1. Completes top of page correctly	Yes	No
2. Completes Core Subtest *T* Scores section correctly	Yes	No
3. Completes Cluster/Composite Scores section correctly	Yes	No
4. Completes Diagnostic Subtest *T* Scores section correctly	Yes	No

Normative Score Profile Page	Circle One	
1. Completes Core Cluster Profile section correctly	Yes	No
2. Completes Core Subtest Profile section correctly	Yes	No
3. Completes Mean Core *T* Score section correctly for upper part of page	Yes	No
4. Completes Diagnostic Cluster Profile section correctly	Yes	No
5. Completes Diagnostic Subtest Profile section correctly	Yes	No
6. Completes Mean Core *T* Score section correctly for lower part of page	Yes	No

Behavioral Observations Page

1. Completes each part of page correctly	Yes	No

Optional Core Analysis Page

1. Completes each part of page correctly	Yes	No

Optional Diagnostic Analysis Page

1. Completes each part of page correctly	Yes	No

General Evaluation

Rapport

1. Maintains rapport throughout testing	Yes	No
2. Is alert to child's moods	Yes	No
3. Does not become impatient or frustrated with child	Yes	No
4. Does not badger child	Yes	No
5. Handles behavior problems correctly	Yes	No
6. Makes accommodations for any physical impairments child has that may affect assessment (e.g., hearing or visual loss)	Yes	No
7. Does not take break in middle of a subtest	Yes	No
8. Allows child to walk around room, if needed	Yes	No
9. Encourages child to perform a task, if needed	Yes	No
10. Praises child's effort	Yes	No
11. Does not say "Good" or "Right" after a correct response	Yes	No
12. Shows empathy if child is concerned about poor performance	Yes	No

Administering Test Items

13. Administers test in professional, unhurried manner	Yes	No
14. Speaks clearly throughout testing	Yes	No
15. Is well organized and has all needed materials nearby	Yes	No
16. Administers subtests in appropriate order	Yes	No
17. Maintains steady pace	Yes	No
18. Makes a smooth transition from one subtest to the next	Yes	No
19. Repeats directions on request when appropriate	Yes	No
20. Repeats items when appropriate	Yes	No

(*Continued*)

Table F-6 (*Continued*)

General Evaluation (*Continued*)	Circle One	
21. Uses good judgment in deciding how much time to give child to solve each item on untimed subtests	Yes	No
22. Begins timing correctly	Yes	No
23. Adheres to time limits	Yes	No
24. Stops timing when child has obviously finished	Yes	No
25. Stops timing when time limit is reached	Yes	No
26. Does not stop timing prematurely	Yes	No
27. Places test materials not currently in use out of child's sight	Yes	No
28. Clears table of unessential materials	Yes	No
29. Positions Record Form so that child cannot see correct answers	Yes	No
30. Positions Administration Manual so that child cannot see correct answers	Yes	No
31. Makes appropriate eye contact with child	Yes	No
32. Reads directions exactly as written in Administration Manual	Yes	No
33. Reads items exactly as written in Administration Manual	Yes	No
34. Takes short break, as needed, at end of a subtest	Yes	No
35. Does not give additional items for practice	Yes	No
36. Does not ask leading questions	Yes	No
37. Does not spell words on any subtest	Yes	No
38. Does not define words	Yes	No
39. Does not use Vocabulary words in a sentence	Yes	No
40. Queries correctly	Yes	No
41. Records "Q" for queried responses	Yes	No
42. Prompts correctly	Yes	No
43. Records "P" for prompted responses	Yes	No
44. Gives second trials correctly	Yes	No
45. Follows start item with appropriate item	Yes	No
46. Administers reverse sequence correctly	Yes	No
47. Shows child how to solve problems when appropriate	Yes	No
48. Conducts testing-of-limits after all subtests have been administered, if desired	Yes	No
49. Makes every effort to administer entire test in one session	Yes	No

Scoring Test Items

50. Scores each item after child answers	Yes	No

General Evaluation (*Continued*)	Circle One	
51. Gives credit for correct responses given at any time during test, when appropriate	Yes	No
52. Does not give credit for correct answers given after time limit	Yes	No
53. Makes entry in Record Form for every item administered	Yes	No
54. Uses good judgment overall in scoring responses	Yes	No
55. Rechecks scoring after test is administered	Yes	No

Completing Record Form

56. Records any deviation from procedure on Record Form	Yes	No
57. Completes Front Page of Record Form correctly	Yes	No
58. Completes Analysis Page of Record Form correctly	Yes	No

Qualitative Feedback

_____
_____
_____

Overall Strengths

_____
_____
_____

Areas Needing Improvement

_____
_____
_____

Other Comments

_____
_____
_____

Overall Evaluation

Circle One: Excellent   Good   Average   Below Average   Poor

From *Assessment of Children: Cognitive Foundations (Fifth Edition)* by Jerome M. Sattler. Copyright 2008 by Jerome M. Sattler, Publisher, Inc. Permission to photocopy this table is granted to purchasers of this book for personal use only (see copyright page for details).

APPENDIX G

MISCELLANEOUS TABLES

Table G-1
Indicators of Psychological or Physical Difficulties

INDICATORS OF PSYCHOLOGICAL OR PHYSICAL DIFFICULTIES

Name: _____   Date: _____

Sex: _____   Grade: _____   School: _____

Birthdate: _____   Teacher: _____

Directions: Place a check mark in the box next to each appropriate item. (See Table G-2 for an explanation of the terms.)

Appearance
- ☐ 1. Atypical posture
- ☐ 2. Bad breath
- ☐ 3. Bizarre hair style
- ☐ 4. Body odor
- ☐ 5. Body piercing
- ☐ 6. Disheveled
- ☐ 7. Emaciated
- ☐ 8. Excessively thin
- ☐ 9. Inappropriate facial expressions
- ☐ 10. Inflamed eyes
- ☐ 11. Multiple tattoos
- ☐ 12. Outlandish dress
- ☐ 13. Obese
- ☐ 14. Poor teeth
- ☐ 15. Provocative dress
- ☐ 16. Rigid posture
- ☐ 17. Scars
- ☐ 18. Slumped posture
- ☐ 19. Soiled clothes
- ☐ 20. Watery eyes
- ☐ Other: _____

Attitude Toward Examiner
- ☐ 1. Avoids eye contact
- ☐ 2. Avoids talking
- ☐ 3. Clinging
- ☐ 4. Defensive
- ☐ 5. Demanding
- ☐ 6. Domineering
- ☐ 7. Evasive
- ☐ 8. Excessively dependent
- ☐ 9. Hostile
- ☐ 10. Indifferent
- ☐ 11. Ingratiating
- ☐ 12. Overcompliant
- ☐ 13. Provocative
- ☐ 14. Seductive
- ☐ 15. Suspicious
- ☐ 16. Unfriendly
- ☐ 17. Withdrawn
- ☐ Other: _____

Motor Behavior
- ☐ 1. Absence seizure
- ☐ 2. Apraxia
- ☐ 3. Astereognosis
- ☐ 4. Ataxia
- ☐ 5. Athetosis
- ☐ 6. Body asymmetries
- ☐ 7. Dyspraxia
- ☐ 8. Echopraxia
- ☐ 9. Extremely limited use of gestures
- ☐ 10. Extremely relaxed posture
- ☐ 11. Facial apraxia
- ☐ 12. Fine-motor coordination difficulties
- ☐ 13. Grand mal seizure
- ☐ 14. Graphesthesia
- ☐ 15. Gross excitement
- ☐ 16. Gross-motor coordination difficulties
- ☐ 17. Hemiplegia
- ☐ 18. Hyperactivity
- ☐ 19. Hypoactivity
- ☐ 20. Involuntary body movements
- ☐ 21. Mixed laterality
- ☐ 22. Motor difficulties
- ☐ 23. Motor retardation
- ☐ 24. Muscle tone difficulties
- ☐ 25. Nervous habits
- ☐ 26. Odd mannerisms
- ☐ 27. Restlessness or fidgetiness
- ☐ 28. Spastic contractions
- ☐ 29. Spastic gait
- ☐ 30. Squirming
- ☐ 31. Tense musculature
- ☐ Other: _____

Affect
- ☐ 1. Agitated affect
- ☐ 2. Angry affect
- ☐ 3. Anxious affect
- ☐ 4. Apathetic affect
- ☐ 5. Blunted affect
- ☐ 6. Depressed affect
- ☐ 7. Flat affect
- ☐ 8. Hypomanic affect
- ☐ 9. Incongruous affect
- ☐ 10. Irritable affect
- ☐ 11. Labile affect
- ☐ 12. Panicked affect
- ☐ 13. Perplexed affect
- ☐ 14. Restricted affect
- ☐ 15. Silly affect
- ☐ 16. Tense affect

- ☐ Other: _____

Vocal Production
- ☐ 1. Disfluency
- ☐ 2. Distractible speech
- ☐ 3. Dysarthria
- ☐ 4. Dysphonia
- ☐ 5. Dysprosody
- ☐ 6. Loud voice
- ☐ 7. Low voice
- ☐ 8. No speech or delayed speech
- ☐ 9. Rapid speech
- ☐ 10. Slow speech
- ☐ 11. Stutters
- ☐ 12. Unintelligible speech
- ☐ Other: _____

Language and Thought
- ☐ 1. Agnosia
- ☐ 2. Agrammatism
- ☐ 3. Alexia
- ☐ 4. Amnesia
- ☐ 5. Anomia
- ☐ 6. Anterograde amnesia
- ☐ 7. Aphasia
- ☐ 8. Aphonia
- ☐ 9. Apraxia
- ☐ 10. Asymbolia
- ☐ 11. Auditory agnosia
- ☐ 12. Auditory aphasia
- ☐ 13. Automatic speaking
- ☐ 14. Autotopagnosia
- ☐ 15. Blocking
- ☐ 16. Circumlocution
- ☐ 17. Circumstantiality
- ☐ 18. Clang association
- ☐ 19. Concrete thinking
- ☐ 20. Confabulation
- ☐ 21. Confusion
- ☐ 22. Constructional apraxia
- ☐ 23. Deja vu
- ☐ 24. Delusion
- ☐ 25. Denial
- ☐ 26. Depersonalization
- ☐ 27. Derailment
- ☐ 28. Derealization
- ☐ 29. Disorientation

(Continued)

Table G-1 (*Continued*)

Language and Thought (*Continued*)

- ☐ 30. Distortion of ideas
- ☐ 31. Distractible speech
- ☐ 32. Dysgraphia
- ☐ 33. Dyslexia
- ☐ 34. Echolalia
- ☐ 35. Embarrassing speech
- ☐ 36. Expressive aphasia
- ☐ 37. Expressive difficulties
- ☐ 38. Finger agnosia
- ☐ 39. Flight of ideas
- ☐ 40. Global aphasia
- ☐ 41. Hallucination
- ☐ 42. Homicidal ideation
- ☐ 43. Ideas of reference
- ☐ 44. Ideational agnosia
- ☐ 45. Ideational apraxia
- ☐ 46. Ideomotor apraxia
- ☐ 47. Illogicality
- ☐ 48. Illusions
- ☐ 49. Inappropriate grammar
- ☐ 50. Inconsistencies and gaps
- ☐ 51. Irrelevant language
- ☐ 52. Jamais vu
- ☐ 53. Lateral confusion
- ☐ 54. Letter reversal
- ☐ 55. Limited content
- ☐ 56. Loose association
- ☐ 57. Loss of train of thought
- ☐ 58. Malingering
- ☐ 59. Minimal insight
- ☐ 60. Mixed type of aphasia
- ☐ 61. Monomania
- ☐ 62. Multiple personality
- ☐ 63. Neologisms
- ☐ 64. Nonfluent aphasia
- ☐ 65. Paragrammatism
- ☐ 66. Paramnesia
- ☐ 67. Paraphasia
- ☐ 68. Perseveration
- ☐ 69. Phobias
- ☐ 70. Phonemic paraphasia
- ☐ 71. Poverty of speech
- ☐ 72. Poverty of thought
- ☐ 73. Prolongations of sounds
- ☐ 74. Pronoun reversal
- ☐ 75. Prosopagnosia
- ☐ 76. Rambling
- ☐ 77. Receptive aphasia
- ☐ 78. Repetitions
- ☐ 79. Ruminations
- ☐ 80. Self-reference
- ☐ 81. Somatic concerns
- ☐ 82. Stilted speech
- ☐ 83. Suicidal ideation
- ☐ 84. Tactile agnosia
- ☐ 85. Tangentiality
- ☐ 86. Telegraphic speech
- ☐ 87. Underproductive responses
- ☐ 88. Visual agnosia
- ☐ 89. Visual-spatial agnosia
- ☐ 90. Word approximations
- ☐ 91. Word salad
- ☐ Other: _____

Behavior and Attention

- ☐ 1. Attention difficulties
- ☐ 2. Automatism
- ☐ 3. Blank spells
- ☐ 4. Carelessness
- ☐ 5. Catalepsy
- ☐ 6. Compulsive rituals
- ☐ 7. Concentration difficulties
- ☐ 8. Disorganized behavior
- ☐ 9. Distractibility
- ☐ 10. Grimacing
- ☐ 11. Hearing difficulties
- ☐ 12. Hemianopsia
- ☐ 13. Immaturity
- ☐ 14. Impulsivity
- ☐ 15. Inappropriate behavior
- ☐ 16. Limited frustration tolerance
- ☐ 17. Limited stamina
- ☐ 18. Obsessive behavior
- ☐ 19. Perfectionism
- ☐ 20. Preoccupation with irrelevant details
- ☐ 21. Resistance to clarifying answers
- ☐ 22. Rigidity
- ☐ 23. Self-mutilation
- ☐ 24. Shifting difficulties
- ☐ 25. Slow reaction time
- ☐ 26. Staring
- ☐ 27. Temper tantrums
- ☐ 28. Unaware of failure
- ☐ 29. Unaware of time limits
- ☐ 30. Visual difficulties
- ☐ 31. Withdrawn behavior
- ☐ Other: _____

Table G-2
Explanation of Indicators of Psychological or Physical Difficulties from Table G-1

Attitude Toward Examiner

1. *Avoids eye contact*—Does not look at examiner; lowers eyes; closes eyes at times
2. *Avoids talking*—Is reluctant to speak; does not speak unless strongly encouraged to do so
3. *Clinging*—Clings to examiner; seeks physical contact; demands constant attention and direction
4. *Defensive*—Tries to protect self against criticism or exposure of shortcomings
5. *Demanding*—Demands examiner's attention; wants an immediate response to every request
6. *Domineering*—Tells examiner what to do and how to do it
7. *Evasive*—Is intentionally vague, ambiguous, or equivocal
8. *Excessively dependent*—Constantly asks for reassurance and feedback
9. *Hostile*—Is disrespectful, belligerent, or quarrelsome
10. *Indifferent*—Is apathetic; has no particular interest or concern
11. *Ingratiating*—Is calculatedly pleasing or agreeable
12. *Overcompliant*—Is passive; fails to assert self
13. *Provocative*—Deliberately attempts to anger examiner
14. *Seductive*—Behaves enticingly
15. *Suspicious*—Is wary, guarded, or distrustful of examiner
16. *Unfriendly*—Refuses to cooperate; makes guarded, evasive replies; remains silent; is manipulative or defiant
17. *Withdrawn*—Is preoccupied; avoids eye contact with examiner; acts aloof or distant; responds mechanically

Motor Behavior

1. *Absence seizure*—Has brief episodes of staring into space; jerks and twitches muscles (formerly referred to as *petit mal seizure*)
2. *Apraxia*—Is unable to perform purposeful movements, despite having no paralysis or sensory disturbance
3. *Astereognosis*—Is unable to identify objects by touch
4. *Ataxia*—Displays jerky patterns of movement; has a lurching walk
5. *Athetosis*—Displays slow, recurring, writhing movements of arms and legs; makes facial grimaces
6. *Body asymmetries*—Displays drooping of one side of the face, weakness in one arm, or other body asymmetries
7. *Dyspraxia*—Displays uncoordinated movements
8. *Echopraxia*—Imitates others' movements and gestures
9. *Extremely limited use of gestures*—Fails to use gestures as would normally be expected, given his or her cultural background
10. *Extremely relaxed posture*—Slouches or acts inappropriately relaxed
11. *Facial apraxia*—Is unable to execute facial movements on command (e.g., whistling, puckering lips, or sticking out tongue) but can do so spontaneously
12. *Fine-motor coordination difficulties*—Is unable to do precise fine-motor movements, such as those required for writing and drawing
13. *Grand mal seizure*—Has violent convulsions marked by muscle spasm and loss of consciousness

14. *Graphesthesia*—Is unable to recognize numbers, words, or symbols traced or written on her or his skin
15. *Gross excitement*—Throws things; runs; jumps around; waves arms wildly; shouts; screams
16. *Gross-motor coordination difficulties*—Displays awkward, stiff, or clumsy gross-motor movements; stumbles
17. *Hemiplegia*—Has paralysis on one side of the body
18. *Hyperactivity*—Is excessively active
19. *Hypoactivity*—Is lethargic or sleepy; moves little
20. *Involuntary body movements*—Displays *at-rest tremors* (tremors that appear when one is still), *choreiform movements* (jerky involuntary movements or spasms of short duration), *tics* (involuntary movements, usually of eyes, lips, or cheeks), *dyskinesias* (defects in voluntary movement), *dystonias* (disordered muscle tone and posture), or *intention tremors* (tremors that appear when one is asked to perform an action)
21. *Mixed laterality*—Tends to shift between dominance of left and right sides of the body when performing a particular action
22. *Motor difficulties*—Displays *akathisia* (motor restlessness indicated by muscular quivering and inability to sit still), *akinesia* (lowered level of muscle activity), *athetoid movements* (slow, recurring, writhing movements of arms and legs), or *deviant locomotion* (walking on toes, twirling, or running in small circles)
23. *Motor retardation*—Sits unusually still; is sluggish; has slow, feeble, or labored movements; walks slowly; performs movements after a delay
24. *Muscle tone difficulties*—Displays *atonia* (no muscle tone), *flaccidity* (slumps, lets arms dangle limply, has slack facial muscles), or *hypotonia* (low muscle tone)
25. *Nervous habits*—Taps or "drums" with hands or feet; grinds teeth; sucks tongue; bites lips, nails, hands, or cuticles; sucks body parts (fingers, hair, etc.); picks skin, scabs, or nose; twists hair
26. *Odd mannerisms*—Exhibits odd, stylized movements, postures, or actions (e.g., maintains uncomfortable or inappropriate postures of trunk or extremities, flaps or oscillates hands, wiggles fingers or positions them bizarrely); makes bizarre facial movements; engages in complex, usually idiosyncratic motor rituals; performs compulsive rituals (e.g., touching and counting things, folding arms in order to avoid germs); darts and lunges peculiarly; sits in one peculiar position for a long time; rocks; sways; bangs head; rolls head; engages in repetitive jumping; rubs hand round and round on head; nods head constantly
27. *Restlessness or fidgetiness*—Paces up and down; makes frequent unnecessary movements
28. *Spastic contractions*—Has sudden, violent, involuntary contractions of a muscle or a group of muscles
29. *Spastic gait*—Walks with a choppy and stiff gait
30. *Squirming*—Wriggles or shifts restlessly in chair
31. *Tense musculature*—Holds body taut or rigid; clenches jaw; grips arms of chair; has trembling hands

(Continued)

Table G-2 (*Continued*)

Affect

1. *Agitated affect*—Is unsettled, restless, and distressed
2. *Angry affect*—Is angry, hostile, antagonistic, touchy, or violent; erupts easily; throws things or threatens to throw things
3. *Anxious affect*—Is fearful, apprehensive, overconcerned, tense, or worried; speaks in a frightened tone of voice; has tremor; has sweaty palms
4. *Apathetic affect*—Is indifferent; has almost no interest in anything
5. *Blunted affect*—Has restricted range and intensity of emotional expression; has expressionless face and voice; has limited emotional responses to distressing topics
6. *Depressed affect*—Appears sad; has mournful facial expression; breaks into tears; speaks in a monotone; frequently sighs deeply; voice chokes on distressing topics
7. *Flat affect*—Displays almost no emotion
8. *Hypomanic affect*—Has an elevated mood, irritability, racing thoughts, grandiose thinking, and pressured speech
9. *Incongruous affect*—Displays affect not in keeping with content of his or her verbal communication
10. *Irritable affect*—Is easily annoyed, bad tempered, or crabby
11. *Labile affect*—Has rapid shifts from one emotion to another
12. *Panicked affect*—Displays a sudden, overpowering terror; is greatly agitated; is extremely fearful
13. *Perplexed affect*—Looks puzzled; cannot explain or understand experiences
14. *Restricted affect*—Shows limited variability of emotion
15. *Silly affect*—Engages in excessive clowning; is giddy or facetious; makes jokes or flippant remarks
16. *Tense affect*—Is edgy, fidgety, jittery, or jumpy

Vocal Production

1. *Disfluency*—Does not use complete words or phrases
2. *Distractible speech*—Changes the subject in the middle of a sentence in response to a stimulus (e.g., "I graduated from high school and . . . where did you get that picture?")
3. *Dysarthria*—Has a motor speech disorder characterized by poor articulation and poor control of tongue, throat, or lips
4. *Dysphonia*—Has speaking difficulty because of hoarseness or other phonation problems
5. *Dysprosody*—Uses question-like (rising) inflection when speaking; chants; uses sing-song inflection; has monotonic speech; exhibits other manneristic changes in pitch, intonation, stress, phrasing, or rhythm
6. *Loud voice*—Is boisterous; shouts; sings loudly; shrieks; squeals
7. *Low voice*—Has a weak, soft, whispering, monotonous, or almost inaudible voice
8. *No speech or delayed speech*—Has no speech or a delay of more than 1 year in the appearance of individual speech sounds
9. *Rapid speech*—Speaks very quickly
10. *Slow speech*—Leaves long pauses between words
11. *Stutters*—Has difficulty speaking; prolongs sounds
12. *Unintelligible speech*—Has slurred, mumbled, or heavily accented speech

Language and Thought

1. *Agnosia*—Cannot recognize, interpret, or comprehend the meaning of sensory stimuli, despite having no perceptual disability
2. *Agrammatism*—Has difficulty following grammatical rules while speaking, including rules governing word use, verb tense, and subject-verb agreement (e.g., says "Ah . . . Tuesday . . . ah, mom and Jim Rudy [referring to himself] . . . hospital")
3. *Alexia*—Is unable to read, despite adequate vision and intelligence
4. *Amnesia*—Has partial or total loss of memory for past experiences
5. *Anomia*—Has difficulty finding the right word when speaking (e.g., says "He, uh, just hurried along" for "He ran"; says "the thing you put in your mouth" for "the spoon")
6. *Anterograde amnesia*—Is unable to remember events that occurred after the onset of amnesia
7. *Aphasia*—Has difficulty comprehending spoken or written language or articulating ideas (formerly referred to as *dysphasia*)
8. *Aphonia*— Cannot speak
9. *Apraxia*—Is unable to perform purposeful movements, despite having no paralysis or sensory disturbance
10. *Asymbolia*—Is unable to comprehend the significance of signs or symbols
11. *Auditory agnosia*—Is unable to identify sounds
12. *Auditory aphasia*—Is unable to comprehend spoken language
13. *Automatic speaking*—Speaks without voluntary control
14. *Autotopagnosia*—Is unable to identify his or her own body parts
15. *Blocking*—Is unable to complete a train of thought; suddenly stops speaking
16. *Circumlocution*—Uses unnecessary words and indirect language; main point is never lost but rather accompanied by much nonessential information (e.g., the question "How do you tell time?" elicits "I wear it right here," pointing to his or her wrist)
17. *Circumstantiality*—Has unnecessary digressions in speech, eventually reaching the main thought; is excessively long-winded; speech is filled with tedious details and parenthetical remarks
18. *Clang association*—Uses words based on their sounds rather than on their meaning (e.g., "I want to say the play of the day, ray, stay, may I pay?")
19. *Concrete thinking*—Is unable to think in abstract terms; gives over-literal interpretations of events; talks only about specific ideas or things
20. *Confabulation*—Gives false and irrelevant information
21. *Confusion*—Is unable to make sense of the environment
22. *Constructional apraxia*—Is unable to construct objects
23. *Deja vu*—Expresses his or her sense that an event has already been experienced
24. *Delusion*—Has false beliefs
25. *Denial*—Is unable to acknowledge unpleasant or traumatic experiences

(*Continued*)

Table G-2 (Continued)

26. *Depersonalization*—Expresses feelings of being detached, unreal, and physically altered (e.g., describes out-of-body experiences, fears that body parts have been altered, feels cut off from other people)

27. *Derailment*—Displays loose or oblique associations related to the topic under discussion; makes illogical connections in speech (e.g., "Last week when I was at the lake, you know, the new movie, boy, it sure is hot near the refrigerator")

28. *Derealization*—Expresses feelings that the surroundings are unreal

29. *Disorientation*—Is confused as to time, place, or person

30. *Distortion of ideas*—Uses hyperbole or exaggeration; misrepresents facts

31. *Distractible speech*—Changes the subject when a nearby stimulus gains his or her attention

32. *Dysgraphia*—Has difficulty expressing ideas in writing

33. *Dyslexia*—Is unable to read either silently or aloud

34. *Echolalia*—Echoes others' words either immediately or after a delay (e.g., the question "How are you today?" elicits "Are you today?")

35. *Embarrassing speech*—Says things that make others uncomfortable

36. *Expressive aphasia*—Has difficulty speaking, writing, or using signs

37. *Expressive difficulties*—Has difficulty coming up with the right word; has halting speech

38. *Finger agnosia*—Is unable to identify the individual fingers of her or his hands or the hands of others

39. *Flight of ideas*—Shifts rapidly from topic to topic when speaking

40. *Global aphasia*—Can neither express nor understand speech and other forms of communication (also called *total aphasia*)

41. *Hallucination*—Sees things in the absence of a physical external stimulus

42. *Homicidal ideation*—Talks about the possibility of killing someone

43. *Ideas of reference*—Believes that other people's statements or actions have special reference to him or her when they do not

44. *Ideational agnosia*—Is unable to state the function or purpose of an object when shown it

45. *Ideational apraxia*—Is unable to execute a series of acts, even though she or he can perform each step correctly

46. *Ideomotor apraxia*—Is unable to carry out an action on verbal command, even though he or she can perform the action automatically and despite having intact comprehension

47. *Illogicality*—Reaches illogical conclusions; uses non sequiturs; makes faulty inductive inferences

48. *Illusions*—Has erroneous perceptions of reality

49. *Inappropriate grammar*—Uses poor grammar

50. *Inconsistencies and gaps*—Has incomplete speech

51. *Irrelevant language*—Uses language unrelated to the matter being considered

52. *Jamais vu*—Has the impression of being unfamiliar with a person or situation that is very familiar

53. *Lateral confusion*—Is unable to distinguish left from right

54. *Letter reversal*—Reverses letters when reading

55. *Limited content*—Is unable to recognize when answers are correct or incorrect

56. *Loose association*—Says things that are either only distantly related or completely unrelated to one another

57. *Loss of train of thought*—Fails to follow a chain of thought through to its natural conclusion

58. *Malingering*—Fabricates or grossly exaggerates physical or psychological symptoms

59. *Minimal insight*—Displays limited understanding of her or his problems

60. *Mixed type of aphasia*—Has impaired expressive and receptive language

61. *Monomania*—Is intensely preoccupied with a single idea or subject

62. *Multiple personality*—Displays two or more distinct personalities (also called *dissociative disorder*)

63. *Neologisms*—Makes up nonsensical and unrecognizable words (e.g., says *plint* for *door*)

64. *Nonfluent aphasia*—Has better auditory comprehension than verbal expression

65. *Paragrammatism*—Uses verbs, clauses, or prepositional phrases incorrectly

66. *Paramnesia*—Recollects events that never occurred

67. *Paraphasia*—Substitutes incorrect words for intended words (e.g., says "The flower is up the garden" for "The flower is in the garden")

68. *Perseveration*—Has difficulty shifting from one strategy or procedure to another or repeatedly says the same sound, word, or phrase

69. *Phobias*—Has persistent fears of situations, objects, activities, or persons

70. *Phonemic paraphasia*—Substitutes one sound for another, primarily as a result of a breakdown in the retrieval of phonological word patterns (e.g., *pike* for *pipe*, *amihal* for *animal*)

71. *Poverty of speech*—Gives brief, concrete, and unelaborated replies to questions; is reluctant to give unprompted additional information

72. *Poverty of thought*—Speech is vague, empty, or stereotyped or contains multiple repetitions

73. *Prolongations of sounds*—Draws out sounds

74. *Pronoun reversal*—Reverses pronouns (e.g., refers to self as "you" and to other people as "I")

75. *Prosopagnosia*—Is unable to recognize familiar faces

76. *Rambling*—Digresses when speaking; has unrelated thoughts; talks aimlessly

77. *Receptive aphasia*—Is unable to understand spoken or written language, even though auditory and visual senses are intact (also referred to as *fluent aphasia*)

78. *Repetitions*—Repeats ideas or words

79. *Ruminations*—Has persistent and recurrent worries

80. *Self-reference*—Refers the subject under discussion back to self, even when someone else is talking (e.g., the question "How is your mother doing?" elicits "I did not sleep well last night")

(*Continued*)

Table G-2 (Continued)

81. *Somatic concerns*—Has concerns about his or her body
82. *Stilted speech*—Uses pompous, distant, overpolite, or formal speech (e.g., "The attorney comported himself indecorously")
83. *Suicidal ideation*—Has thoughts about killing self; is preoccupied with death and dying; appears to be preparing for death (e.g., giving away possessions, making funeral arrangements)
84. *Tactile agnosia*—Is unable to identify familiar objects placed in his or her hand without looking
85. *Tangentiality*—Replies to questions in an oblique or irrelevant way; constantly digresses to irrelevant topics and fails to arrive at main point (e.g., the question "What is your occupation?" elicits "Well, there are many jobs out there and I can do things like my father. You know, fix things.")
86. *Telegraphic speech*—Omits connectives, prepositions, modifiers, and refinements of language when speaking (e.g., says "Mother, father . . . making dogs" for "A mother and father are fixing hotdogs")
87. *Underproductive responses*—Does not answer questions fully; gives monosyllabic answers; has to be pressured for an answer
88. *Visual agnosia*—Is unable to recognize familiar objects by sight
89. *Visual-spatial agnosia*—Is unable to understand spatial details (e.g., follow directions, understand the floor plan of a house)
90. *Word approximations*—Uses words in new and unconventional ways; develops new words (e.g., says "His boss was a seeover" for "His boss was an overseer")
91. *Word salad*— Has incomprehensible speech in which real words are strung together in gibberish (e.g., the question "What should you do when it is cold outside?" elicits "Well, the new blue moon, silly will, come to me, let's read") (also referred to as *jargon aphasia*)

Behavior and Attention
1. *Attention difficulties*—Is unable to focus on a task
2. *Automatism*—Performs actions without conscious awareness
3. *Blank spells*—Has abrupt interruptions of attention lasting a few seconds or longer
4. *Carelessness*—Is indifferent to his or her performance; does not give sufficient attention to his or her work during the evaluation
5. *Catalepsy*—Has a sudden episode of muscle weakness triggered by strong emotions
6. *Compulsive rituals*—Displays rituals (e.g., checks work repeatedly, touches desk three times before beginning a task)
7. *Concentration difficulties*—Is unable to bring together thought processes or focus on a task for an extended time
8. *Disorganized behavior*—Is unable to solve tasks in an organized manner

9. *Distractibility*—Is unable to maintain attention when extraneous stimuli are present
10. *Grimacing*—Has expressions of pain, contempt, or disgust
11. *Hearing difficulties*—Does not respond to directions; leans forward to hear speaker; makes mistakes in carrying out spoken instructions
12. *Hemianopsia*—Is unable to see one half of the visual field
13. *Immaturity*—Acts younger than his or her age
14. *Impulsivity*—Acts quickly without thinking
15. *Inappropriate behavior*—Engages in peculiar or inappropriate behavior (e.g., passively lets objects fall out of his or her hand; flicks fingers at objects; feels, strokes, rubs, or scratches objects; is preoccupied with trivial specks, breaks, points, and the like in objects; uses objects ritualistically or in a bizarre, idiosyncratic manner; spins objects; remains preoccupied with the same object or activity; ignores objects; holds an object without paying attention to it; mouths or sucks objects; taps; stares at objects or at nothing in particular; engages in repetitive banging; cries inappropriately; is excessively slow or excessively quick in responding)
16. *Limited frustration tolerance*—Gives up easily when faced with difficult questions; fails to try; breaks into tears at times
17. *Limited stamina*—Has no energy
18. *Obsessive behavior*—Has unwanted ideas or impulses (e.g., persistent fears that he or she may be harmed, unreasonable fear of becoming contaminated)
19. *Perfectionism*—Attends to every possible detail; is self-critical even when answers are correct
20. *Preoccupation with irrelevant* details—Is preoccupied with details not relevant to the situation
21. *Resistance to clarifying answers*—Fails to elaborate on an answer when asked to do so
22. *Rigidity*—Is unyielding in a point of view even when it is no longer appropriate to maintain it
23. *Self-mutilation*—Deliberately inflicts harm on his or her body (e.g., bites, scratches, hits self, bangs head)
24. *Shifting difficulties*—Is unable to move easily from one task to another
25. *Slow reaction time*—Responds to questions slowly; has difficulty solving tasks quickly
26. *Staring*—Stares at examiner; fixates on a picture in the office
27. *Temper tantrums*—Acts out frustrations (e.g., screams, kicks, has fits of anger)
28. *Unaware of failure*—Does not seem to realize when items have been failed
29. *Unaware of time limits*—Does not seem to realize when time limits have been reached
30. *Visual difficulties*—Is unable to see objects clearly; squints or frowns when looking at something; has jerky eye movements
31. *Withdrawn behavior*—Is preoccupied; avoids eye contact; is aloof

Note. Table G-1 provides a checklist for the terms covered in this table.

Table G-3
Recording Form for NICHD Classroom Observation System

RECORDING FORM FOR NICHD CLASSROOM OBSERVATION SYSTEM

Teacher's Name: _____   Observer's Name: _____

Grade: _____   School: _____   Date: _____

	Scale							
	1	2	3	4	5	6	7	
	Low			Mid			High	

Children's Classroom Scale Codes		Circle one					
1. Positive Affect	1	2	3	4	5	6	7
2. Self-Reliance	1	2	3	4	5	6	7
3. Social/Cooperative Behavior with Peers	1	2	3	4	5	6	7
4. Attention	1	2	3	4	5	6	7
5. Disruptive Behavior	1	2	3	4	5	6	7
6. Activity Level	1	2	3	4	5	6	7
7. Child-Teacher Relationship	1	2	3	4	5	6	7

Teacher's Classroom Scale Codes		Circle one					
1. Richness of Instructional Methods	1	2	3	4	5	6	7
2. Over-Control	1	2	3	4	5	6	7
3. Chaos	1	2	3	4	5	6	7
4. Detachment	1	2	3	4	5	6	7
5. Positive Climate	1	2	3	4	5	6	7
6. Negative Climate	1	2	3	4	5	6	7
7. Productive Use of Instructional Time	1	2	3	4	5	6	7
8. Teacher Sensitivity	1	2	3	4	5	6	7
9. Evaluative Feedback	1	2	3	4	5	6	7

Source: Adapted from Chapters 53 and 73 of the NICHD Study of Early Child Care and Youth Development (2000a, 2000b). From *Assessment of Children: Cognitive Foundations (Fifth Edition)* by Jerome M. Sattler. Copyright 2008 by Jerome M. Sattler, Publisher, Inc. Permission to photocopy this appendix table is granted to purchasers of this book for personal use only (see copyright page for details).

Table G-4
NICHD Classroom Observation System

CHILDREN'S CLASSROOM SCALE CODES

Positive Affect

High on positive affect. Children smile, laugh, speak in a positive tone of voice, express enthusiasm, clap, and/or cheer.

Low on positive affect. Children display no indications of happiness or contentment. They are disengaged, glum, bored, detached, subdued, and/or low key; show limited facial expression; and/or show flat affect.

Self-Reliance

High on self-reliance. Children take responsibility for materials, actions, and activities and/or show initiative, leadership, or willingness to take risks. Children persist in difficult situations, tolerate frustration, need little direction from teacher or other adults, and appear to use knowledge of routines and class structure to plan ahead and complete required work.

Low on self-reliance. Children lack confidence and seek adult assistance before attempting a challenging task. They are passive and unmotivated, do not initiate actions until told what to do, do not assert themselves with peers, and retreat if rebuffed by peers.

Social/Cooperative Behavior with Peers

High on social/cooperative behavior with peers. Children seek out peer contact, acknowledge peers or respond to peer initiations, and generally work and play agreeably with peers. They easily and frequently join group activities, initiate conversation and social interaction, appear to enjoy the company of other children, and engage in cooperative play.

Low on social/cooperative behavior with peers. Children are withdrawn or disengaged from others despite opportunities to interact with peers. They either show little interest in engaging with peers or engage peers negatively (e.g., they do not accommodate to the wishes of others and try to impose their own agenda without compromise). They are stubborn and bossy, obstruct the play of others, try to dominate and control a group learning activity, and/or inappropriately call attention to themselves during a group activity.

Attention

High on attention. Children have sustained, focused attention to ongoing activities when in a group or when doing individual seatwork. They focus intently on each activity, ignore or dismiss intrusions from others, remain on task, and are "tuned in" to teacher's expectations.

Low on attention. Children have difficulty attending to and becoming involved in classroom activities and assigned work. They are easily distracted by anything else that is going on around them or create their own diversions (e.g., fidgeting or playing with objects such as pencils or clothes). They seem to flit from one inappropriate activity to another, to be aimless, and/or to daydream.

Disruptive Behavior

High on disruptive behavior. Children openly violate accepted classroom rules. They annoy others or call attention to themselves by calling out inappropriately, making odd noises, talking or singing, laughing inappropriately, tapping pencils, clowning around, and/or making faces. They interfere with lessons, talk back to teacher, talk to peers inappropriately, pass notes to other children, and/or are noncompliant in other ways.

Low on disruptive behavior. Children cooperate with teacher and peers, follow classroom rules, and generally are compliant. If they are inattentive or off-task, they remain quiet, do not call attention to themselves, and do not disturb others.

Activity Level

High on activity level. Children are very active, restless, or fidgety. They frequently move in their seats to look around at others, engage in gross body and/or limb movements (e.g., sustained and intense leg-swinging), rock back and forth, or even get up out of their seats when they are expected to remain seated.

Low on activity level. Children are noticeably low key, passive, inactive, and generally still during teacher-directed activities or seatwork.

Child-Teacher Relationship

High on child-teacher relationship. Children respond positively to teacher's initiation of an activity (e.g., attend to teacher's suggestions or demonstrations of an activity, cooperate, willingly comply with teacher, and respond enthusiastically and respectfully to teacher), initiate positive contact with teacher (e.g., share experiences or information), look at teacher and attend to teacher's communications, and express affection toward teacher.

Low on child-teacher relationship. Children actively reject teacher; defy teacher's requests; ignore teacher; misbehave; speak to teacher in a harsh, whining, or petulant tone of voice; make demands on teacher; make critical statements about teacher; and/or argue with teacher.

TEACHER'S CLASSROOM SCALE CODES

Richness of Instructional Methods

High on richness of instructional methods. Teacher uses a variety of intellectually engaging strategies to present lessons and to promote children's thinking and understanding of higher levels of complexity, integration, and meaning. Teacher poses problems or points out discrepancies, asks thought-provoking questions, adds complexity to tasks, and engages in reciprocal discussion with children and takes their ideas seriously. Teacher models, demonstrates, explains, and provides information, coaching, and direct instruction. Teacher encourages high levels of thinking skills (e.g., analyzing, synthesizing, evaluating, originating) and problem-solving approaches (e.g., comparing and contrasting, hypothesizing, predicting, making inferences, seeing connections, using multiple steps to reach solutions).

(Continued)

Low on richness of instructional methods. Teacher presents subjects in a very basic format. Teacher uses worksheets that elicit only short answers and do not require problem-solving skills, asks class to follow along in the textbook, or presents lectures without discussion. Teacher takes a facts-only approach and does not expand on topics through the use of experimentation, analysis, or synthesis. Teacher uses activities that require memory and recall or repetition of information and seems to want only brief answers without elaboration. There is no true discourse or instructional conversation between children and teacher, and none of the activities involve the use of higher-level thinking strategies.

Over-Control

High on over-control. Teacher rigidly structures the classroom and follows an agenda that does not consider children's needs and interests. Teacher insists that children stay in their seats for extended periods of time, that they remain involved in the activities on the teacher's agenda, and that they be quiet in class. Teacher does most of the talking. Children do not appear to behave spontaneously and are not given any choices.

Low on over-control. Teacher demonstrates respect for children's autonomy and responsibility. Children are given a role and voice in various activities and are usually active participants in activities.

Chaos

High on chaos. Teacher permits a high level of disruption, goofing off, rude behavior, aggression, and inattention. Children may be out of control during lessons, transition periods, or free time and may appear not to know where they are supposed to be or what they are supposed to be doing. Teacher allows situations to get out of hand before intervening, and situations requiring discipline are dealt with arbitrarily or half-heartedly.

Low on chaos. Teacher is organized, has clear expectations, follows through on communications with children, allows few interruptions, and encourages children to be attentive. The tone of the classroom is respectful and can be light-hearted even when loud.

Detachment

High on detachment. Teacher appears to lack emotional involvement with children and/or to lack awareness of children's need for appropriate interactions with activities, materials, or peers. Teacher fails to use disciplinary techniques or to give children feedback in situations that clearly warrant action (e.g., fails to act when peer conflicts escalate or when children require additional assistance or structure). Teacher fails to monitor the appropriateness of children's behavior. Teacher is rarely involved with children in activities or conversation, permits children to have long stretches of unoccupied time, and/or allows children to wander without directing them to an activity. Teacher conveys nonverbally that children are not to bother teacher. Teacher places much emphasis on activities involving the layout of the classroom or paperwork (e.g., decorating bulletin boards, recording grades) or on interactions with other adults (e.g., talking to the classroom aide or to other teachers in the hall).

Low on detachment. Teacher is highly involved with children and acknowledges their bids for attention in a timely fashion. Teacher gives children ample opportunity to try to solve problems by themselves, but steps in as necessary to prevent too much frustration or disappointment. During individual seatwork, teacher actively monitors children's progress.

Positive Climate

High on positive climate. Teacher maintains a safe and respectful environment. Teacher and other adults in the classroom speak to children in respectful and pleasant tones. Teacher encourages children to speak to each other respectfully, listen attentively to others, wait patiently in line, help other children negotiate transitions in the classroom or from the classroom to some other place, and disagree respectfully with others' ideas. Teacher gives children positive emotional support and feedback and posts rules of behavior.

Low on positive climate. Teacher maintains a bland and unchallenging climate in the classroom. Teacher presents lessons unenthusiastically, speaks in a monotone, and does not engage the children in the lesson. Children appear disengaged, withdrawn, or fearful and behave disrespectfully to each other. Teacher shows little concern for safety in the classroom (e.g., fails to control roughhousing or to monitor children's use of potentially dangerous tools such as scissors). Teacher and children are sarcastic and critical of others. Teacher does little, if anything, to counteract problems and may even add to the problems by uneven enforcement of rules of behavior.

Negative Climate

High on negative climate. Teacher expresses anger or hostility toward children, appears to regard children negatively, expresses disapproval of children, criticizes children, and appears annoyed with children. Teacher is irritable, appears to ignore children's feelings and agendas, and uses punitive controls (e.g., shames or humiliates children, uses threats of personal injury or withholding of privileges). Teacher uses harsh tones when speaking to children. Teacher uses sarcasm, shows body tension, speaks with a negative tone of voice, and/or displays tense facial muscles and strained expressions.

Low on negative climate. Teacher does not express anger or hostility toward children, does not regard children negatively, does not express disapproval, does not criticize children, and/or does not show annoyance with children. Teacher seems relaxed, displays concern for children's feelings and agendas, uses positive reinforcement (e.g., praises children, gives rewards, acknowledges their contributions), and does not use threats of personal injury or withholding of privileges. Teacher does not use sarcasm, does not show body tension, and/or does not display tense facial muscles or strained expressions.

(*Continued*)

Table G-4 (*Continued*)

Productive Use of Instructional Time

High on productive use of instructional time. Teacher manages time and activities to ensure productivity, engagement, and efficient use of instructional time. Routines seem to be understood and are automatized by everyone in the class in order to minimize the loss of instructional time. Teacher begins lessons promptly and uses efficient transitions within and between lessons. The pacing and level of the activities allows all children to be productively involved.

Low on productive use of instructional time. Teacher spends a lot of time without purpose. Children mill around waiting for—or even ignoring—directions from teacher on what to do next. Teacher allows interruptions to cut into time available for instruction. Instructional time is also lost to transitions, which may be chaotic. The daily routine appears to be awkward and unplanned.

Teacher Sensitivity

High on teacher sensitivity. Teacher demonstrates child-centered behavior and appears to be aware of each child's needs, moods, interests, and capabilities and to use this awareness to guide activities with each child. Teacher offers a mix of support and independence so that children can experience mastery, success, and pride and develop effective skills. Teacher is neither over-controlling nor detached. When conflicts arise, teacher first allows children to try to resolve their own conflicts and intervenes only when necessary. Teacher responds quickly, clearly, and firmly to behaviors that pose a danger to a single child or to all children. When children violate rules or display discourteous behavior, teacher explains why the behaviors are inappropriate.

Low on teacher sensitivity. Teacher appears unresponsive to the content of children's talk or to their activities and does not acknowledge children's affect. Teacher does not facilitate children's learning and play. Teacher does not time activities to reflect children's interests or change the pace when children appear bored, overexcited, or tired. Teacher does not express positive affect with children, does not provide an appropriate range and variety of activities, and does not discipline children in a manner that matches violations. Teacher does not explain the rationale for disciplinary procedures and/or is not flexible in handling compliance and autonomy issues.

Evaluative Feedback

High on evaluative feedback. Teacher provides frequent and high-quality feedback to children when they make a response, answer a question, or hand in a paper. The feedback is designed to help children consolidate, reinforce, and deepen their knowledge. Teacher and children frequently interact to exchange information.

Low on evaluative feedback. Teacher gives feedback that is perfunctory, occasional, and lacking depth and information.

Source: Adapted from Chapters 53 and 73 of the NICHD Study of Early Child Care and Youth Development (2000a, 2000b).

Table G-5
Norms for the Coloured Progressive Matrices

Total score	5½ (5.03 to 5.08)	6 (5.09 to 6.02)	6½ (6.03 to 6.08)	7 (6.09 to 7.02)	7½ (7.03 to 7.08)	8 (7.09 to 8.02)	8½ (8.03 to 8.08)	9 (8.09 to 9.02)	9½ (9.03 to 9.08)	10 (9.09 to 10.02)	10½ (10.03 to 10.08)	11 (10.09 to 11.02)	11½ (11.03 to 11.09)
										Age (in years)			
35							99	97	95	95	94	94	88
34						98	97	95	93	93	90	89	75
33					98	96	95	93	90	89	83	77	65
32				99	96	94	93	90	85	78	75	64	57
31				97	94	92	90	85	76	65	66	56	50
30			99	95	92	90	85	76	67	60	57	50	44
29			97	93	90	86	76	67	60	55	50	44	39
28			95	91	87	81	68	60	55	50	44	39	34
27		98	93	90	83	75	63	55	50	45	40	34	29
26		96	92	87	79	69	58	50	45	40	35	30	25
25	98	94	90	84	75	64	54	45	39	35	30	25	21
24	96	92	87	80	70	59	50	39	34	30	25	21	17
23	94	90	84	75	65	54	45	34	30	25	21	17	14
22	93	87	80	70	60	50	41	29	25	21	17	14	12
21	90	83	75	65	55	45	36	25	21	17	14	12	10
20	87	79	70	60	50	41	30	21	17	14	12	10	8
19	83	75	65	55	45	36	24	17	14	12	10	8	6
18	79	70	60	50	41	31	20	14	12	10	8	6	5
17	75	66	55	45	37	25	15	12	10	8	6	5	4
16	70	61	50	39	31	18	12	10	8	6	5	4	2
15	66	56	44	33	24	13	10	8	6	5	4	2	
14	62	50	36	24	16	10	8	6	5	4	2		
13	56	39	25	15	10	7	6	5	4	2			
12	48	26	15	10	7	5	5	4	2				
11	31	17	10	7	5	3	4	2					
10	16	10	7	5	3	1	2						
9	10	6	5	3	1								
8	6	3	3	1									
7	2	1											
6	1												

Note. These are smoothed norms for U.S. children.

Source: Reprinted with permission of the authors and publisher from J. C. Raven and B. Summers, *Manual for Raven's Progressive Matrices and Vocabulary Scales—Research Supplement No. 3,* 1986, p. 36. London: H. K. Lewis & Co.

Table G-6
Norms for the Standard Progressive Matrices

Age (in years)

Total score	6½ (6.03 to 6.08)	7 (6.09 to 7.02)	7½ (7.03 to 7.08)	8 (7.09 to 8.02)	8½ (8.03 to 8.08)	9 (8.09 to 9.02)	9½ (9.03 to 9.08)	10 (9.09 to 10.02)	10½ (10.03 to 10.08)	11 (10.09 to 11.02)	11½ (11.03 to 11.08)	12 (11.09 to 12.02)	12½ (12.03 to 12.08)	13 (12.09 to 13.02)	13½ (13.03 to 13.08)	14 (13.09 to 14.02)	14½ (14.03 to 14.08)	15 (14.09 to 15.02)	15½ (15.03 to 15.08)	16 (15.09 to 16.02)	16½ (16.03 to 16.08)
59																				99	99
58																		99	99	97	98
57																99	99	97	97	95	95
56															99	98	97	95	94	93	90
55														99	98	96	95	93	92	90	85
54													99	97	96	94	93	92	90	87	80
53												99	97	95	94	92	92	90	86	82	75
52											99	98	96	94	92	90	90	87	81	75	70
51										99	97	96	94	92	90	86	87	82	75	69	65
50									99	98	95	94	92	90	86	81	82	74	68	64	59
49								99	97	96	94	92	90	86	81	75	75	67	63	59	54
48							99	97	96	94	92	90	86	81	75	70	68	62	58	54	50
47							98	96	94	92	90	86	81	75	70	65	63	57	54	50	46
46						99	97	94	92	90	86	81	75	70	65	61	58	53	50	47	43
45						98	96	92	90	86	81	75	70	65	61	57	54	50	46	43	39
44					99	96	94	90	87	81	75	70	65	61	57	53	50	46	42	39	35
43					98	95	92	87	83	75	70	65	61	57	53	50	46	42	39	36	31
42				99	97	94	90	83	79	70	65	61	57	53	50	46	42	39	35	31	25
41				98	95	92	87	79	75	65	61	57	53	50	46	42	38	35	31	25	18
40				97	94	90	83	75	70	61	57	53	50	46	43	38	34	31	24	18	15
39			99	96	92	87	79	70	64	57	53	50	46	43	38	34	29	24	18	15	13
38			98	94	90	83	75	66	59	53	50	46	42	39	34	30	24	17	15	13	11
37			97	92	87	79	70	61	54	50	46	42	38	35	30	24	19	14	12	12	10
36		99	95	90	83	75	66	57	50	46	42	38	34	31	24	19	16	13	11	10	9
35		97	93	87	79	70	61	53	46	42	37	34	30	24	19	16	13	11	10	9	8
34	99	96	91	84	75	67	57	50	43	39	33	30	25	18	16	13	11	10	9	8	7
33	98	95	89	81	71	63	53	46	40	35	29	25	20	15	13	11	10	9	8	7	6
32	97	94	87	78	68	60	50	43	37	32	25	20	16	12	11	10	9	8	7	6	6
31	96	91	85	75	65	56	46	40	34	28	21	16	14	11	10	9	8	7	6	6	5
30	95	89	82	72	61	53	43	37	31	25	18	14	12	10	9	8	7	6	6	5	4

(Continued)

Table G-6 (Continued)

Total score	Age (in years)																				
	6½ (6.03 to 6.08)	7 (6.09 to 7.02)	7½ (7.03 to 7.08)	8 (7.09 to 8.02)	8½ (8.03 to 8.08)	9 (8.09 to 9.02)	9½ (9.03 to 9.08)	10 (9.09 to 10.02)	10½ (10.03 to 10.08)	11 (10.09 to 11.02)	11½ (11.03 to 11.08)	12 (11.09 to 12.02)	12½ (12.03 to 12.08)	13 (12.09 to 13.02)	13½ (13.03 to 13.08)	14 (13.09 to 14.02)	14½ (14.03 to 14.08)	15 (14.09 to 15.02)	15½ (15.03 to 15.08)	16 (15.09 to 16.02)	16½ (16.03 to 16.08)
29	93	87	78	69	58	50	40	34	28	22	15	12	11	9	8	7	6	5	5	4	2
28	91	85	75	65	56	47	37	31	25	19	14	11	10	8	7	6	5	4	4	3	1
27	89	82	71	62	53	44	34	28	22	16	12	10	9	7	6	5	4	3	2	1	
26	87	78	68	59	50	41	31	25	19	14	11	9	8	6	5	4	3	2	1		
25	85	75	65	56	47	38	28	22	17	13	10	8	7	6	4	3	2	1			
24	83	72	62	53	44	35	25	19	15	11	9	7	6	5	3	2	1				
23	81	69	59	50	42	32	22	17	13	10	8	6	6	4	2	1					
22	78	66	56	47	39	29	19	15	11	9	7	6	5	3	1						
21	75	63	53	44	36	25	17	13	10	8	6	5	4	2							
20	72	60	50	41	32	20	15	11	8	7	6	4	3	1							
19	69	57	46	38	29	17	13	10	7	6	5	3	2								
18	66	53	43	34	25	14	11	8	6	5	4	2	1								
17	62	49	39	30	20	11	10	7	5	4	3	1									
16	59	45	35	24	15	10	8	6	4	3	2										
15	55	40	30	18	13	8	7	5	3	2	1										
14	49	33	24	13	10	7	6	4	2	1											
13	39	25	18	10	8	6	5	3	1												
12	26	18	13	8	6	5	4	2													
11	18	13	10	6	5	4	3	1													
10	14	10	7	5	4	3	2														
9	10	7	5	4	3	2	1														
8	7	5	4	3	2	1															
7	5	4	3	2	1																
6	4	3	2	1																	
5	3	2	1																		
4	2	1																			
3	1																				

Note. These are smoothed norms for U.S. children.

Source: Reprinted with permission of the authors and publisher from J. C. Raven and B. Summers, *Manual for Raven's Progressive Matrices and Vocabulary Scales—Research Supplement No. 3*, 1986, p. 15. London: H. K. Lewis & Co.

Table G-7
Checklist for Assessing Student's Multiple Intelligences

CHECKLIST FOR ASSESSING STUDENT'S MULTIPLE INTELLIGENCES

Name of student: _____   Date: _____

Name of rater: _____   Teacher's name: _____

Directions:
Check each item that applies.

Linguistic Intelligence

_____   Writes better than average for age

_____   Spins tall tales or tells jokes and stories

_____   Has a good memory for names, places, dates, or trivia

_____   Enjoys word games

_____   Enjoys reading books

_____   Spells words accurately (or, if in preschool, developmental spelling is advanced for age)

_____   Appreciates nonsense rhymes, puns, tongue twisters, etc.

_____   Enjoys listening to the spoken word (stories, commentary on radio, talking books, etc.)

_____   Has a good vocabulary for age

_____   Communicates with others using good verbal skills

Other linguistic strengths: _____

_____

Logical-Mathematical Intelligence

_____   Asks a lot of questions about how things work

_____   Computes arithmetic problems in his or her head quickly (or, if in preschool, understanding of math concepts is advanced for age)

_____   Enjoys math class (or, if in preschool, enjoys counting and using numbers)

_____   Finds math computer games interesting (or, if not exposed to computers, enjoys other math or counting games)

_____   Enjoys playing chess, checkers, or other strategy games (or, if in preschool, enjoys board games requiring counting squares)

_____   Enjoys working on logic puzzles or brainteasers (or, if in preschool, enjoys hearing logical nonsense such as in Alice's Adventures in Wonderland)

_____   Enjoys putting things in categories or hierarchies

_____   Likes to experiment in a way that shows higher order cognitive thinking processes

_____   Thinks on a more abstract or conceptual level than peers

_____   Has a good sense of cause-and-effect relationships for age

Other logical-mathematical strengths: _____

_____

Spatial Intelligence

_____   Good at visualizing objects

_____   Gets more out of pictures than words while reading

_____   Reads maps, charts, and diagrams more easily than text (or, if in preschool, enjoys looking at such materials more than looking at text)

_____   Daydreams more than peers

_____   Enjoys art activities

_____   Draws figures that are advanced for age

_____   Likes to view movies, slides, or other visual presentations

_____   Enjoys doing puzzles, mazes, "Where's Waldo?" or similar visual activities

_____   Builds interesting three-dimensional constructions for age (e.g., Lego buildings)

_____   Doodles on workbooks, worksheets, or other materials

Other spatial strengths: _____

_____

Bodily-Kinesthetic Intelligence

_____   Excels in one or more sports (or, if in preschool, shows physical prowess advanced for age)

_____   Learns best by physically doing something, rather than by reading or hearing about it

_____   Moves, twitches, taps, or fidgets while seated for a long time

_____   Cleverly mimics other people's gestures or mannerisms

_____   Loves to take things apart and put them back together again

_____   Likes to handle and manually investigate objects

_____   Enjoys running, jumping, wrestling, and other physical activities

_____   Shows skill in a craft (e.g., woodworking, sewing, mechanics) or exhibits good fine-motor coordination in other ways

_____   Has a dramatic way of expressing herself or himself

_____   Enjoys working with clay or other tactile experiences (e.g., fingerpainting)

Other bodily-kinesthetic strengths: _____

_____

(Continued)

Table G-7 (*Continued*)

Musical Intelligence

_____ Notices when music sounds off-key or disturbing in some other way

_____ Remembers melodies of songs

_____ Has a good singing voice

_____ Plays a musical instrument or sings in a choir or other group (or, if in preschool, enjoys playing percussion instruments and/or singing in a group)

_____ Unconsciously hums to himself or herself

_____ Taps rhythmically on the table or desk as he or she works

_____ Is sensitive to environmental noises (e.g., rain on the roof)

_____ Responds favorably when music is played

_____ Sings songs that he or she has learned outside of the classroom

Other musical strengths: _____

_____

Interpersonal Intelligence

_____ Enjoys socializing with peers

_____ Seems to be a natural leader

_____ Gives advice to friends who have problems

_____ Seems to be "street-smart"

_____ Belongs to clubs, committees, or other organizations (or, if in preschool, seems to be part of a regular social group)

_____ Enjoys informally teaching other children

_____ Likes to play games with other children

_____ Has two or more close friends

_____ Has a good sense of empathy or concern for others

_____ Others seek out his or her company

Other interpersonal strengths: _____

_____

Intrapersonal Intelligence

_____ Displays a sense of independence or a strong will

_____ Has a realistic sense of his or her strengths and weaknesses

_____ Does well when left alone to play or study

_____ "Marches to the beat of a different drummer"—his or her style of living and learning is unique

_____ Has an interest or hobby that he or she doesn't talk much about

_____ Has a good sense of self-direction

_____ Prefers working alone to working with others

_____ Accurately expresses how he or she is feeling

_____ Is able to learn from his or her failures and successes in life

_____ Has high self-esteem

Other intrapersonal strengths: _____

_____

Naturalistic Intelligence

_____ Enjoys being outdoors

_____ Notices things in the environment that others often miss

_____ Knows the names of different types of birds, trees, and plants

_____ Is keenly aware of his or her surroundings and of changes in the environment

_____ Enjoys collecting natural objects, such as bugs, flowers, or rocks

_____ Likes to observe natural phenomena like the moon, stars, and tides

_____ Keeps detailed records of his or her observations of nature

_____ Uses scientific equipment for observing nature

_____ Enjoys subjects and stories dealing with animals or natural phenomena

_____ Likes animals or plants

Other naturalistic strengths: _____

_____

Source: Reprinted, with changes in notation and additions, with permission of the publisher from T. Armstrong, *Multiple Intelligences in the Classroom,* copyright 1994 by Association for Supervision and Curriculum Development, pp. 29–31.

APPENDIX H

IDEA 2004, SECTION 504, AND ADA

Co-authored with Guy McBride

This appendix supplements the overview presented in Chapter 3 of three federal laws relating to the assessment of children: the Individuals with Disabilities Education Improvement Act (IDEA 2004), Section 504 of the Rehabilitation Act, and the Americans with Disabilities Act (ADA). IDEA 2004 is covered in the greatest detail because it provides the most extensive guidelines for the assessment of children with disabilities. We encourage you to review the overview of the three laws presented in Chapter 3 before reading this appendix.

In addition to becoming familiar with IDEA 2004, Section 504, and the ADA, you will also need to become familiar with your state's regulations regarding educational services for children with disabilities. Not only may states award additional rights not prescribed in IDEA 2004; they also are responsible for establishing eligibility criteria under IDEA for each disability category. *Note that nothing in this appendix is intended as a legal guide to the three laws.*

INDIVIDUALS WITH DISABILITIES EDUCATION IMPROVEMENT ACT (IDEA 2004)

In 1975, the U.S. Congress passed Public Law 94-142, the Education for all Handicapped Children Act. Congress designed the law to ensure the right to a free and appropriate public education for all children with disabilities. Before the law was passed, "more than half of the children with disabilities in the United States did not receive appropriate educational services, and a million children with disabilities were excluded entirely from the public school system" (*Federal Register,* March 12, 1999, p. 12414).

In 1990, Congress updated Public Law 94-142 and changed its name to Individuals with Disabilities Education Act (IDEA; Public Law 101-476). In 1997, IDEA was reauthorized and amended (Public Law 105-17); it was then re-

ferred to as IDEA '97. In 2004, Congress again reauthorized IDEA (Public Law 108-446) and changed its name slightly to Individuals with Disabilities Education Improvement Act (referred to as IDEA 2004 or IDEIA 2004).

IDEA 2004 has several purposes:

- To ensure that all children with disabilities have access to a free and appropriate public education that emphasizes special education and related services designed to meet their unique needs and to prepare them for further education, employment, and independent living
- To ensure that the rights of children with disabilities and their parents are protected
- To assist states, localities, educational service agencies, and federal agencies in helping to provide for the education of children with disabilities
- To assist states in the implementation of a statewide, comprehensive, coordinated, multidisciplinary, interagency system of early intervention services for infants and toddlers with disabilities and their families
- To facilitate the coordination of payment for early intervention services from federal, state, local, and private sources (including public and private insurance coverage)
- To enhance states' capacity to provide quality early intervention services and expand and improve existing early intervention services being provided to infants and toddlers with disabilities and their families
- To encourage states to expand opportunities for children under 3 years of age who would be at risk of substantial developmental delay if they did not receive early intervention services
- To ensure that educators and parents have the necessary tools to improve educational results for children with disabilities by supporting system improvements; coordinated research and preparation of personnel; coordinated technical assistance, dissemination, and support; and development of technology and media services

- To assess and ensure the effectiveness of efforts to educate children with disabilities

IDEA 2004 includes provisions for services to infants and toddlers who have disabilities because Congress declared that there is an urgent and substantial need for the nation to do the following:

- Enhance the development of infants and toddlers with disabilities, minimize their potential for developmental delay, and recognize the significant brain development that occurs during a child's first three years of life
- Reduce educational costs to society and the nation's schools by minimizing the need for special education and related services once children with disabilities reach school age
- Maximize the potential for individuals with disabilities to live independently in society
- Enhance the capacity of families to meet the special needs of their infants and toddlers with disabilities
- Enhance the capacity of state and local agencies and service providers to identify, evaluate, and meet the needs of all children, particularly minority, low-income, inner-city, and rural children and infants and toddlers in foster care

Copyright © 1999 by John P. Wood. Reprinted with permission.

Free Appropriate Public Education

A major focus of IDEA 2004 is to make available a free appropriate public education to all children between the ages of 3 and 21 years. This includes both children with disabilities who have been suspended or expelled from school and children with disabilities who need special education and related services even though they have not failed or been retained in a course or grade. The determination of whether a child is eligible for services must be made on an individual basis by the group within the child's local educational agency responsible for making eligibility determinations.

Each state must ensure that a free appropriate public education is available to each eligible child beginning no later than the child's third birthday, by which time an individualized education program (IEP) for the child or an individualized family service plan (IFSP) must be in effect. If a child's third birthday occurs during the summer, the child's IEP team determines when the child will begin to receive services under the IEP or the IFSP.

IDEA 2004 and the Courts

IDEA 2004 is a complex law covering a myriad of issues pertaining to the education of children with disabilities. The law has been the subject of much litigation since its inception. Its sheer volume—as well as the hundreds of issues it addresses—leaves IDEA 2004 open to different interpretations. Courts have become involved in interpreting and implementing the provisions of IDEA 2004 because the law permits a party adversely affected by an administrative de-

cision to obtain a judicial review. IDEA 2004 gives courts broad discretion to grant appropriate relief to the party who prevails at a hearing.

Evolving case law is expanding our understanding of the requirements of IDEA 2004. IDEA 2004 does not specify the particular level of educational benefit that must be provided through an IEP, only that services must be appropriate for each child with a disability. According to the U.S. Supreme Court, the educational placement chosen for a child need not be the best possible one, maximize the potential of the child, or cause the child to achieve outstanding results in school (*Board of Education v. Rowley,* 1982).

IDEA says that a child is entitled to nonmedical-related services if such services are needed in order for the child to receive a free and appropriate education. At first, courts disagreed as to how "medical service" was to be defined. But in 1999, the U.S. Supreme Court, in *Cedar Rapids Community School District v. Garret F.,* ruled that if a service did not have to be provided by a doctor and was needed in order for a child to receive a free and appropriate education, the child was entitled to that service, no matter what the cost.

No case is a "sure win," either for parents or for state or local educational agencies, as statutes and case decisions are interpreted differently by different judges, attorneys, and educators in different parts of the country. The saying "There are two sides to every argument" has particular significance with regard to educational litigation. One Circuit Court of Appeals may issue a ruling that is in direct conflict with that of another Circuit Court of Appeals. One judge will uphold a certain legal principle, and another judge will do the opposite.

Even within the same Circuit Court of Appeals, two seemingly similar cases may have different outcomes. One case may be decided based on a child's educational progress and the other based on the procedures followed by the school in providing services to the child.

Decisions from a U.S. District Court may be appealed to a U.S. Circuit Court of Appeals; rulings from a U.S. Circuit Court of Appeals may be appealed to the U.S. Supreme Court. The Supreme Court usually hears cases only when two or more circuit courts have ruled differently or when a compelling public policy question is at issue. Rulings from the Supreme Court and the Circuit Court of Appeals for your state are binding on lower courts of your state. Rulings from other courts, including other Circuit Courts of Appeals, may influence courts in your jurisdiction, but they do not carry the same weight as the rulings of your own Circuit Court of Appeals.

Full and Appropriate Individual Initial Evaluation

Each child being considered for special education and related services must receive a full and appropriate individual initial evaluation. The assessment must be administered in the form most likely to yield accurate information about what the child knows and what he or she can do academically, developmentally, and functionally. IDEA 2004 specifies that the following criteria must be applied to any evaluation procedures used to determine whether a child has a disability and what the child's educational needs are. These criteria, although open to interpretation, provide excellent guidelines for any type of assessment.

1. *Multiple assessment tools and strategies.* A variety of assessment tools and strategies must be used to gather relevant information, including requesting information from the parent.

2. *Multiple types of information.* Functional, developmental, and academic information should be obtained about the child. The information gathered should be helpful in determining whether the child has a disability and in developing the content of the child's IEP.

3. *Multiple criteria.* No single procedure should be used as the sole criterion to determine whether a child has a disability or to develop an appropriate educational program for the child.

4. *Technically sound instruments.* Only technically sound instruments should be used to assess the relative contributions of cognitive, behavioral, physical, and developmental factors. Thus, any instruments used for the identification of children must be reliable and valid and used for their intended purposes.

5. *Nondiscriminatory assessment procedures.* The assessment must be nondiscriminatory—that is, without racial or cultural bias. The assessment instruments must be administered in the child's native language—that is, the language normally used by the child in the home or learning environment. For a child who is deaf or blind or for a child who has no written language, "native language" refers to the mode of communication normally used by the child, such as sign language, Braille, or oral communication. Assessment instruments used with a child with limited English proficiency must measure the extent to which the child has a disability and needs special education, not the extent of the child's English language proficiency.

6. *Trained and knowledgeable personnel.* All evaluations must be conducted by trained and knowledgeable personnel, in accordance with the instructions provided by the publisher of the assessment materials.

7. *Consideration of sensory, manual, and speaking skills.* Examiners must ensure that the results of an assessment of a child with impaired sensory, manual, or speaking skills accurately reflect the child's aptitude or achievement level (or whatever other factors the tests purport to measure), rather than the child's impaired sensory, manual, or speaking skills (unless those skills are the factors that the tests purport to measure).

8. *Comprehensive coverage.* Evaluation materials should assess specific areas of educational ability and not merely provide a single general intelligence quotient. The child should be assessed in all areas related to the suspected disability, including, if appropriate, health, vision, hearing, social and emotional status, general intelligence, academic performance, communicative status, and motor abilities. The evaluation must be sufficiently comprehensive to identify all of the child's special education and related services needs, whether or not these needs and services are commonly linked to the child's disability category.

As part of the initial evaluation and/or any reevaluation, a group consisting of the IEP team and other qualified professionals, as appropriate, must review (a) existing evaluation data on the child, including evaluations and information provided by the child's parents, (b) current classroom-based, local, or state assessments, (c) classroom-based observations, and (d) observations by teachers and related services providers. On the basis of the review and input from the child's parents, the group identifies what additional data, if any, are needed to determine whether the child has a disability and what the child's educational needs are. The group may conduct its review without a meeting. However, if any of the above-mentioned data have not been collected, the public agency must obtain the data by administering the appropriate assessments and other evaluation measures.

In the case of reevaluations, the group must consider (a) whether the child continues to have a disability, (b) the child's educational needs, (c) the child's present levels of academic achievement and related developmental needs, (d) whether the child needs special education and related services, and (e) whether any additions or modifications to the special education and related services are needed to enable the child to meet the measurable annual goals set out in the child's IEP and to participate, as appropriate, in the general education curriculum.

In addition to the general evaluation procedures discussed above, IDEA 2004 specifies the procedures that psychologists must use to identify children with specific learning disabilities (see Exhibit H-1). The use of a process based on "the child's response to scientific, research-based intervention," described in Exhibit H-1 as a possible way of establishing a diagnosis of learning disability, has become known as *response to intervention* or *RTI*. The RTI model is a multi-tiered approach in which services and interventions are provided to students at increasing levels of intensity, based on progress monitoring and data analysis. Although the instruction and interventions encompassed within the RTI model may involve different levels of intensity and individualization, they are usually considered to fall within three broad classes, or tiers. Tier 1 (or primary) interventions consist of a general education program based on evidence-based practices. Tier 2 (or secondary) interventions are more intensive and relatively short-term. Tier 3 (or tertiary) interventions are long-term and may lead to special education services.

The term *scientifically based research* is defined the same way in IDEA 2004 as it is in section 9101(37) of the Elementary and Secondary Education Act of 1965 (ESEA) and in the *Federal Register* (August 14, 2006, p. 46576): research that involves the application of rigorous, systematic, and objective procedures to obtain reliable and valid knowledge relevant to education activities and programs. Scientifically based research includes research that

- Employs systematic, empirical methods that draw on observation or experiment
- Involves rigorous data analyses that are adequate to test the stated hypotheses and justify the general conclusions drawn
- Relies on measurements or observational methods that provide reliable and valid data across evaluators and observers, across multiple measurements and observations, and across studies by the same or different investigators
- Uses experimental or quasi-experimental designs in which individuals, entities, programs, or activities are assigned to different conditions and with appropriate controls to evaluate the effects of the condition of interest, with a preference for random-assignment experiments, or other designs to the extent that those designs contain within-condition or across-condition controls
- Ensures that experimental studies are presented in sufficient detail and clarity to allow for replication or, at a minimum, offer the opportunity to build systematically on their findings
- Has been accepted by a peer-reviewed journal or approved by a panel of independent experts through a comparably rigorous, objective, and scientific review

The local educational agency must determine whether a child has a disability within 60 days of receiving parental consent for the evaluation or within the time frame established by the state. The time frame can be altered if the child changes schools or if the parents repeatedly fail or refuse to produce the child for an evaluation. In the former case, the two schools must coordinate the assessment so that it is completed expeditiously. The time frame for evaluating a child with a specific learning disability can also be altered if a child's parents and a group of qualified professionals agree in writing that additional time is needed.

At the completion of the evaluation, a group consisting of qualified professionals and the parent of the child meet to determine whether the child is eligible for services under IDEA 2004. The group must ensure that all relevant information—including aptitude and achievement tests, parent input, teacher recommendations, and information about the child's physical condition, social or cultural background, and adaptive behavior—is well documented and carefully considered. A child is not considered eligible if the determining factor is lack of appropriate instruction in reading or math or limited English proficiency. The parent must be given a copy of the evaluation report and documentation of determination of eligibility at no cost.

Before determining that a child formerly judged to be eligible no longer has the disability, the local educational agency must evaluate the child. However, evaluation is not required if the child is graduating from secondary school with a regular diploma or if the child has reached the age at which he or she is no longer eligible for a free and appropriate education under state law. In these cases, the local educational agency must provide the child with a summary of his or her academic achievement and functional performance, including recommendations on how he or she might be assisted in meeting any postsecondary educational goals.

The screening of a child by a teacher or specialist to determine appropriate instructional strategies for curriculum implementation is not considered to be an evaluation for eligibility for special education and related services.

Individualized Education Program (IEP)

Children with disabilities who are eligible for special education and related services must have an individualized education program (IEP), and this IEP must be reviewed at least annually. An IEP is an important document, because it spells out the needs of the child with a disability and how the public agency will satisfy these needs. Professionals who work with children with disabilities all know the axiom "The IEP determines placement." Its contents can be a source of contention between the parents and the public agency and may be challenged in a due process hearing or in court. Each word in the term *individualized education program* was carefully chosen: *individualized* because the document focuses on the unique needs of a specific child, *education* because it is directed toward learning activities, and *program* because it provides specific and clearly formulated annual goals and objectives and the means of reaching those goals and objectives.

Exhibit H-1
Procedures Outlined in IDEA 2004 for Identifying Children with Specific Learning Disabilities

Sec. 300.307 Specific Learning Disabilities

(a) *General.* A State must adopt criteria for determining whether a child has a specific learning disability that is consistent with the specifications provided in the law. In addition, the criteria adopted by the State—

(1) Must not require the use of a severe discrepancy between intellectual ability and achievement for determining whether a child has a specific learning disability;

(2) Must permit the use of a process based on the child's response to scientific, research-based intervention; and

(3) May permit the use of other alternative research-based procedures for determining whether a child has a specific learning disability;

(b) *Consistency with State criteria.* A public agency must use the State criteria adopted pursuant to paragraph (a) of this section in determining whether a child has a specific learning disability. Note that a public agency includes the state educational agency (SEA), local educational agency (LEA), educational service agency (ESA), and nonprofit public charter schools.

Sec. 300.308 Additional Group Members

The determination of whether a child suspected of having a specific learning disability is a child with a disability . . . must be made by the child's parents and a team of qualified professionals, which must include—

(a)(1) The child's regular teacher; or

(2) If the child does not have a regular teacher, a regular classroom teacher qualified to teach a child of his or her age; or

(3) For a child of less than school age, an individual qualified by the SEA to teach a child of his or her age; and

(b) At least one person qualified to conduct individual diagnostic examinations of children, such as a school psychologist, speech-language pathologist, or remedial reading teacher.

Sec. 300.309 Determining the Existence of a Specific Learning Disability

(a) The group of qualified professionals and the parent may determine that a child has a specific learning disability [see Table 2-1, p. 24 in text, for the IDEA definition of specific learning disability] if—

(1) The child does not achieve adequately for the child's age or meet State-approved grade-level standards in one or more of the following areas, when provided with learning experiences and instruction appropriate for the child's age or State-approved grade-level standards:

(i) Oral expression.

(ii) Listening comprehension.

(iii) Written expression.

(iv) Basic reading skill.

(v) Reading fluency skills.

(vi) Reading comprehension.

(vii) Mathematics calculation.

(viii) Mathematics problem solving.

(2)(i) The child does not make sufficient progress to meet age or State-approved grade-level standards in one or more of the areas identified in the above paragraph when using a pro-

cess based on the child's response to scientific, research-based intervention; or

(ii) The child exhibits a pattern of strengths and weaknesses in performance, achievement, or both, relative to age, State-approved grade-level standards, or intellectual development, that is determined by the group to be relevant to the identification of a specific learning disability, using appropriate assessments, and

(3) The group determines that its findings are not primarily the result of—

(i) A visual, hearing, or motor disability;

(ii) Mental retardation;

(iii) Emotional disturbance;

(iv) Cultural factors;

(v) Environmental or economic disadvantage; or

(vi) Limited English proficiency.

(b) To ensure that underachievement in a child suspected of having a specific learning disability is not due to lack of appropriate instruction in reading or math, the group must consider—

(1) Data that demonstrate that prior to, or as a part of, the referral process, the child was provided appropriate instruction in regular education settings, delivered by qualified personnel; and

(2) Data-based documentation of repeated assessments of achievement at reasonable intervals, reflecting formal assessment of student progress during instruction, which was provided to the child's parents.

(c) The public agency must promptly request parental consent to evaluate the child to determine if the child needs special education and related services, and must adhere to the appropriate time frames, unless extended by mutual written agreement of the child's parents and a group of qualified professionals—

(1) If, prior to a referral, a child has not made adequate progress after an appropriate period of time when provided instruction; and

(2) Whenever a child is referred for an evaluation.

Sec. 300.310 Observation

(a) The public agency must ensure that the child is observed in the child's learning environment (including the regular classroom setting) to document the child's academic performance and behavior in the areas of difficulty.

(b) The group, in determining whether a child has a specific learning disability, must decide to—

(1) Use information from an observation in routine classroom instruction and monitoring of the child's performance that was done before the child was referred for an evaluation; or

(2) Have at least one member of the group conduct an observation of the child's academic performance in the regular classroom after the child has been referred for an evaluation and parental consent is obtained.

(c) In the case of a child of less than school age or out of school, a group member must observe the child in an environment appropriate for a child of that age.

(Continued)

Exhibit H-1 (*Continued*)

Sec. 300.311 Specific Documentation for the Eligibility Determination

(a) For a child suspected of having a specific learning disability, the documentation of the determination of eligibility must contain a statement of—

(1) Whether the child has a specific learning disability;

(2) The basis for making the determination, including an assurance that the determination has been made in accordance with law;

(3) The relevant behavior, if any, noted during the observation of the child and the relationship of that behavior to the child's academic functioning;

(4) The educationally relevant medical findings, if any;

(5) Whether—

(i) The child does not achieve adequately for the child's age or to meet State-approved grade-level standards; and

(ii)(A) The child does not make sufficient progress to meet age or State-approved grade-level standards; or

(B) The child exhibits a pattern of strengths and weaknesses in performance, achievement, or both, relative to age, State-approved grade level standards or intellectual development;

(6) The determination of the group concerning the effects of a visual, hearing, or motor disability; mental retardation; emotional disturbance; cultural factors; environmental or economic disadvantage; or limited English proficiency on the child's achievement level; and

(7) If the child has participated in a process that assesses the child's response to scientific, research-based intervention—

(i) The instructional strategies used and the student-centered data collected; and

(ii) The documentation that the child's parents were notified about—

(A) The State's policies regarding the amount and nature of student performance data that would be collected and the general education services that would be provided;

(B) Strategies for increasing the child's rate of learning; and

(C) The parents' right to request an evaluation.

(b) Each group member must certify in writing whether the report reflects the member's conclusion. If it does not reflect the member's conclusion, the group member must submit a separate statement presenting the member's conclusions.

Source: Adapted from the *Federal Register,* 2006, pp. 46786–46787.

An IEP must be written and must include the following:

1. *Present levels of performance.* The IEP must describe the child's present levels of academic achievement and functional performance, including how the child's disability affects his or her involvement and progress in the general education curriculum (or, for preschool children, his or her participation in appropriate activities).

2. *Measurable annual goals, including both academic and functional goals.* The goals outlined in the IEP must be designed to enable the child to be involved in and make progress in the general education curriculum. In addition, the goals must meet any other educational needs that result from the child's disability.

Here are some examples of statements of annual goals:

- The child will demonstrate mastery of third-grade reading with 90% accuracy as measured by third-grade reading tests.
- The child will spell at a level that is 90% of that expected for her age group.
- The child will write a five-sentence paragraph with appropriate punctuation and grammar with 90% accuracy.
- The child will control aggressive behavior toward other children by walking away from potential confrontations 100% of the time and by practicing suitable replacement behaviors, such as running around the track, hitting a punching bag, or writing about angry feelings in a journal.

For children with disabilities who take alternative assessments aligned with alternative achievement standards, the IEP must include a statement describing benchmarks or short-term objectives. The following are examples:

- The child will learn to read three passages from the XYZ Reader by three weeks after the tutorial sessions begin.
- The child will learn 10 spelling words from the required list of spelling words one week after the tutorial sessions begin.

3. *Means of measuring and reporting progress.* The IEP must include a statement about how the child's progress toward meeting the annual goals will be measured and when periodic reports about the child's progress will be provided.

4. *Services needed by the child.* The IEP must include a statement (based on peer-reviewed research, to the extent practical) of the appropriate special education and related services (including supplementary aids and services) to be provided for the child. A statement is also needed about any program modifications or supports that will be provided to school personnel to enable the child to attain annual goals, be involved in and make progress in the general education curriculum, take part in extracurricular and other nonacademic activities, and participate in various activities with other children with or without disabilities.

5. *Extent of nonparticipation.* The IEP must explain the extent, if any, to which the child will not participate with children without disabilities in the regular class and in various other activities.

6. *Accommodations.* The IEP must describe any accommodations needed to measure the child's academic achievement and functional performance on statewide and districtwide

assessments. If the IEP team determines that the child must take an alternative assessment instead of a regular statewide or districtwide assessment of student achievement, the IEP must state why the child cannot participate in the regular assessment and which particular alternative assessment is appropriate for the child.

Following are some accommodations that might be considered under IDEA 2004 (as well as Section 504 and regulations on statewide testing) to allow students with disabilities to take tests.

- *Flexible scheduling:* extending the time permitted to complete the test, allowing breaks as needed, and administering the test over two or more sessions or days
- *Flexible setting:* administering the test individually or in small groups or in classrooms specially designed to reduce distractions or to accommodate special needs through lighting, sound systems, or adaptive furniture
- *Revised test format:* using Braille editions or large-print editions, increasing the space between test items, reducing the number of test items per page, increasing the size of answer bubbles on the answer sheet, arranging multiple-choice items in vertical format with answer bubbles to the right of response choices, presenting reading passages with one complete sentence per line, and including on the answer sheet visual cues (e.g., arrows, stop signs) that relate to the test directions
- *Revised test directions:* simplifying language in the directions, providing additional examples, providing cues (e.g., arrows) on answer forms, and highlighting verbs in instructions
- *Use of aids for test items and responses:* allowing use of such devices as a visual magnification device, auditory amplification device, auditory tape of test items, mask to maintain place, tape recorder, typewriter, word processor, pointer, communication board, or adaptive writing instrument and allowing signing or oral presentation for all directions and for items other than reading items
- *Use of an aide to help children:* having an aide read directions, repeat oral comprehension items, read or sign test items, provide cues to maintain on-task behavior, and record answers given by the child

7. *Projected schedule for services.* The IEP must give a projected date for the beginning of the services and modifications being provided for the child, as well as the anticipated frequency, location, and duration of those services and modifications.

8. *Transition services.* The first IEP to be in effect after the child turns 16 years of age (or younger, if determined appropriate by the IEP team) must state the transition services (including courses of study) needed by the child, and this statement must be updated annually thereafter. The IEP must include appropriate measurable postsecondary goals based on age-appropriate transition assessments related to training,

education, employment, and, where appropriate, independent living skills.

Transition services are a coordinated set of activities that are part of a results-oriented process intended to facilitate the movement of a child with a disability from school to post-school activities (postsecondary education, vocational education, employment, independent living, and/or community participation). Transition services are based on the individual child's needs, strengths, preferences, and interests. Transition services may include instruction, functional vocational evaluation, special education services, or related services.

9. *Transfer rights.* The first IEP to be in effect after the child turns 16 years of age (or younger, if determined appropriate by the IEP team) must indicate that the child has been informed of the rights, if any, that will transfer to him or her when he or she reaches the age of majority under state law.

IEP team.   The IEP team is composed of the following individuals:

- The child's parents. According to the *Federal Register* (August 14, 2006), a parent is "(a) a biological or adoptive parent of a child; (b) a foster parent, unless state law, regulations, or contractual obligations with a state or local entity prohibit a foster parent from acting as a parent; (c) a guardian generally authorized to act as the child's parent, or authorized to make educational decisions for the child (but not the state if the child is a ward of the state); (d) an individual acting in the place of a biological or adoptive parent (including a grandparent, stepparent, or other relative) with whom the child lives, or an individual who is legally responsible for the child's welfare; (e) a surrogate parent who has been appointed in accordance with other provisions of the law" (p. 46760, with changes in notation).
- At least one of the child's regular education teachers, if the child is or may be participating in regular education
- At least one of the child's special education teachers (or, where appropriate, one special education provider)
- A representative of the public agency who is qualified to provide or supervise the provision of instruction specially designed to meet the unique needs of children with disabilities, is knowledgeable about the general education curriculum, and is knowledgeable about the resources of the public agency (one of the other members of the IEP team can also serve as the public agency representative)
- An individual who can interpret the instructional implications of the evaluation results (this individual can be one of the members of the IEP team noted above)
- Other individuals who have knowledge or special expertise regarding the child, including related services personnel, at the discretion of the parent or the public agency
- The child with a disability, whenever appropriate
- A representative of any participating agency that is likely to be responsible for providing or paying for transition services, where appropriate (and only with the consent of the parents or of a child who has reached the age of majority)

Participation in IEP meeting. IDEA 2004 requires that the public agency ensure that one or both of the parents of a child with a disability are present at each IEP team meeting or are afforded the opportunity to participate. The public agency must notify the parents about the meeting early enough to ensure that they have an opportunity to attend. The meeting must be at a mutually agreed on time and place.

If neither parent can attend an IEP team meeting, the public agency must use other methods to ensure parent participation, such as video conferencing or individual telephone calls. A meeting may be conducted without a parent in attendance if the public agency is unable to convince the parents that they should attend. In this case, the public agency must keep a record of its attempts to arrange a mutually agreeable time and place for the meeting (e.g., detailed records of telephone calls made or attempted and the results of those calls, copies of correspondence sent to the parents and any responses received, and records of visits made to the parents' home or place of employment and the results of those visits).

To ensure that parents understand the proceedings of the IEP team meeting, the public agency must arrange for an interpreter for parents who are deaf or hard of hearing or whose native language is not English. The public agency must give the parents a copy of the child's IEP at no cost to the parents. (However, if the parents bring an attorney to the IEP meeting, the parents will not be reimbursed for the attorney's fees unless the meeting is convened as a result of an administrative proceeding or a judicial action or for mediation.)

The public agency must invite the child with a disability to attend the team meeting if the team will be considering postsecondary goals for the child and the transition services needed to assist the child in reaching those goals. If the child does not attend the IEP team meeting, the public agency must take other steps to ensure that the child's preferences and interests are considered by the IEP team.

An IEP meeting serves in part as an opportunity for communication between the parents and school personnel. Such meetings enable the various parties to jointly decide on the child's needs, what services will be provided to meet those needs, and what the anticipated outcomes may be. Furthermore, the meeting allows for resolution of any differences between the parents and school personnel concerning the special educational needs of the child with a disability. During an IEP meeting, some parents may prefer to receive information passively, rather than contribute actively. By encouraging parents to share their perceptions about their child's needs (and their own needs related to helping the child excel in school), you may enable them to take a more active role in the meeting.

When IEPs must be in effect. IEPs must be in effect at the beginning of each school year. The public agency must ensure that a meeting to develop an IEP is conducted within 30 days of the determination that a child needs special education and related services. As soon as possible following development of the IEP, special education and related services must be made available to the child in accordance with the IEP. The public agency must ensure that the child's IEP is ac-

cessible to each regular education teacher, special education teacher, and related services provider, as well as any other service provider who is responsible for its implementation. Each teacher and provider of services should be informed of his or her specific responsibilities related to implementing the child's IEP and the specific accommodations, modifications, and supports that must be provided for the child in accordance with the IEP.

IEP or IFSP for children ages 3 to 5. In the case of a child age 3 to 5 years with a disability (or, at the discretion of the state educational agency, a 2-year-old child with a disability who will turn 3 years of age during the school year), the IEP team must consider creating an IFSP (see the discussion of IDEA 2004 Part C later in this appendix). The IFSP may serve as the child's IEP, if this is consistent with state policy and agreed to by the public agency and the child's parents. The public agency must provide the child's parents with a detailed explanation of the differences between an IFSP and an IEP and obtain the parents' written informed consent if they choose the IFSP over an IEP.

IEPs for children who transfer within a state or from another state. When a child with a disability who has an IEP transfers to a new public agency in the same or another state and enrolls in a new school, the new public agency (in consultation with the parents) must provide the child with services comparable to those described in the child's IEP from the previous public agency. These services must be provided until the new public agency either adopts the child's IEP from the previous public agency or develops, adopts, and implements a new IEP that meets the child's current needs.

IDEA 2004 notes that "to facilitate the transition for a child who transfers within a State or from another State, the new public agency in which the child enrolls must take reasonable steps to promptly obtain the child's records, including the IEP and supporting documents and any other records relating to the provision of special education or related services to the child, from the previous public agency in which the child was enrolled. The previous public agency in which the child was enrolled must take reasonable steps to promptly respond to the request from the new public agency" (*Federal Register,* August 14, 2006, pp. 46789–46790, with changes in notation).

Changing the IEP. Changes may be made to a child's IEP after an annual IEP meeting without convening another IEP meeting. The child's parents and the local educational agency may instead agree to develop a written document that amends or modifies the child's current IEP.

Multi-year IEP. States may give parents and the local educational agency the opportunity to develop a comprehensive multi-year IEP, with a term not to exceed 3 years. This term must coincide with a transition for the child from preschool to elementary school, from elementary school to middle or junior high school, from middle or junior high school to secondary school, or from secondary school to postsecondary activities.

"Oscar, I do not consider 'beating some sense into their stubborn little heads' an acceptable behavioral objective."

Courtesy of Phi Delta Kappan and the artist, Bardulf Ueland.

Least Restrictive Environment

The public agency must ensure that, to the maximum extent appropriate, children with disabilities who are in public or private institutions or other care facilities are educated with children without disabilities. Children with disabilities should be removed from the regular educational environment and placed in special classes or separate schooling only if the nature or severity of their disability prevents them from being educated in regular classes with the use of supplementary aids and services.

The public agency must ensure that a continuum of alternative placements is available to meet the needs of children with disabilities, including instruction in regular classes, special classes, special schools, homes, and hospitals and institutions. In addition, the public agency must make provision for supplementary services (such as resource room or itinerant instruction) to be provided in conjunction with regular class placement.

The educational placement decision should be made by a group composed of the parents and other persons who are knowledgeable about the child. This group must consider the meaning of any evaluation data and the placement options. The child should be placed as close as possible geographically to his or her home and in a school that he or she would attend if not disabled, unless the child's IEP requires some other arrangement. The placement must be determined at least annually and must be based on the child's IEP. In selecting the least restrictive environment, the group must consider any potential harmful effects of the placement on the child or on the quality of services that he or she needs. A child with a disability should not be removed from an age-appropriate regular classroom solely because modifications to the general education curriculum are needed. A child with a disability should have the opportunity to participate with nondisabled children in extracurricular activities, to the maximum extent appropriate, and to have available supplementary aids and services to help him or her participate in these activities.

A vigorous debate continues about the value of inclusion and the degree to which children with disabilities should be included in the regular classroom. Let's look at the arguments for and against educating children with disabilities with children without disabilities in the least restrictive environment. The term *full inclusion* refers to placing children with disabilities in regular education classes full time and providing them with all needed services in that setting, whereas the term *mainstreaming* refers to the placement of special education students in one or more regular education classes for part of the day.

ARGUMENTS FOR FULL INCLUSION

- May increase the academic achievement of children with disabilities
- May increase social benefits for children with disabilities, such as by enhancing self-esteem, improving social skills, and encouraging greater independence
- May better prepare children with disabilities for careers and for participation in society
- May help children without disabilities better understand children with disabilities
- May reduce the stigma associated with disabilities

ARGUMENTS AGAINST FULL INCLUSION

- May place an inappropriate burden on general education teachers who are not trained to work with children with disabilities
- May require an excessive amount of teacher time and energy
- May cause children with disabilities to be rejected by children without disabilities
- May diminish the intensity of services provided to or even deny services to children with disabilities
- May make it difficult for local educational agencies to hire teachers who can provide the classroom structure and specialized curriculum needed by children with disabilities

Courts use various criteria in determining whether a school district has violated the least restrictive environment mandate in IDEA 2004 (*L.B., & J.B. v. Nebo School District*, 2004). These criteria may include the following:

- Whether education could be achieved satisfactorily in a regular classroom with the use of supplemental aids and services
- Whether the school district took appropriate steps to accommodate the child in a regular classroom, including considering a continuum of placement and support services
- Whether the academic benefits the child would receive in a regular classroom compare favorably with those he or she receives in a special education classroom

- Whether the child's overall experience in regular education, including nonacademic benefits, would compare favorably with that received in special education
- Whether the presence of the child with a disability in the regular classroom would affect the classroom
- Whether the costs of full inclusion (including the cost of supplementary aides and services necessary to maintain the child in a regular classroom) would be reasonable when compared to the cost of placing the child in a more restrictive setting
- Whether the services that make placement in a segregated facility superior could feasibly be provided in a nonsegregated setting

Note that no single factor is controlling. Courts are likely to acknowledge the fiscal reality that school districts with limited resources must balance the needs of each child with a disability against the needs of other children in the district. Regardless of the merits of full inclusion, IDEA 2004 requires, as noted above, that a continuum of alternative placements be available to meet the needs of children with disabilities.

Procedural Safeguards

The procedural safeguards in IDEA 2004 are designed to ensure that (a) the rights of children with disabilities and their parents are protected, (b) children with disabilities and their parents are provided with the information they need to make informed decisions about the child's educational opportunities, and (c) procedures and mechanisms are in place to resolve disagreements between parents and school districts. Each public agency must adhere to the procedural safeguards established by IDEA 2004. Let's look at some of the major procedural safeguards covered in IDEA 2004. (The rights of a parent to participate in IEP meetings were discussed earlier.)

Opportunity to examine records and participate in meetings.
The parents of a child with a disability must be informed that they have the right to inspect and review all their child's educational records and to participate in meetings about the identification, evaluation, and educational placement of their child. (Informal conversations or preparatory activities engaged in by public agency personnel are not considered meetings.)

Parent involvement in placement decisions.
A parent of a child with a disability must be given the opportunity to be a member of any group that makes decisions about the educational placement of his or her child. If a parent cannot attend meetings, the public agency must use other methods to ensure the parent's participation, such as individual telephone calls, conference calls, or video conferences. If the public agency cannot obtain the parent's participation in the decision, the group can make a placement decision without the involvement of a parent. In such cases, the public agency must keep records of its attempts to contact a parent.

General right to an independent evaluation.
The parents of a child with a disability have the right to an independent educational evaluation of their child.

Each public agency must provide to parents, upon request for an independent educational evaluation, information about where an independent educational evaluation may be obtained, and the agency criteria applicable for an independent educational evaluation. An *independent educational evaluation* means an evaluation conducted by a qualified examiner who is not employed by the public agency responsible for the education of the child in question, and *at public expense* means that the public agency either pays for the full cost of the evaluation or ensures that the evaluation is otherwise provided at no cost to the parent.

A parent has the right to an independent educational evaluation at public expense if the parent disagrees with an evaluation obtained by the public agency. If a parent requests an independent educational evaluation at public expense, the public agency must, without unnecessary delay, either file a due process complaint to request a hearing to show that its evaluation is appropriate or ensure that an independent educational evaluation is provided at public expense, unless the agency demonstrates in a hearing that the evaluation obtained by the parent did not meet agency criteria.

If the public agency files a due process complaint notice to request a hearing and the final decision is that the agency's evaluation is appropriate, the parent still has the right to an independent educational evaluation, but not at public expense. If a parent requests an independent educational evaluation, the public agency may ask for the parent's reason why he or she objects to the public agency's evaluation. However, the public agency may not require the parent to provide an explanation and may not unreasonably delay either providing the independent educational evaluation at public expense or filing a due process complaint to request a due process hearing to defend the public evaluation. A parent is entitled to only one independent educational evaluation at public expense each time the public agency conducts an evaluation with which the parent disagrees. (*Federal Register,* August 14, 2006, pp. 46791–46792, with changes in notation)

An independent educational evaluation obtained by parents, whether at public or private expense, must, if it meets agency criteria, be considered by the public agency in any decision made with respect to the provision of a free and appropriate public education to the child. Any party may present an independent educational evaluation as evidence at a hearing on a due process complaint. Independent educational evaluations conducted at public expense must meet the same standards as those used by the public agency to the extent that the standards are consistent with the parents' right to an independent educational evaluation. Finally, "If a hearing officer requests an independent educational evaluation as part of a hearing on a due process complaint, the cost of the evaluation must be at public expense" (*Federal Register,* August 14, 2006, p. 46792).

Prior notice to the parents.
The public agency must give written notice to the parents of a child with a disability a reasonable amount of time before it initiates or changes (or refuses to initiate or change) the identification, evaluation, or educational placement of the child. The notice must include

- A description of the action proposed or refused by the agency
- An explanation of why the agency proposes or refuses to take the action
- A description of each evaluation procedure, assessment, record, and report the agency used as a basis for its decision
- A statement that the parents of a child with a disability have protection under the procedural safeguards of the law and a description of how a copy of the procedural safeguards can be obtained
- Sources for parents to contact to obtain assistance in understanding these provisions of the law
- A description of other options that the IEP team considered and the reasons why those options were rejected
- A description of other factors relevant to the agency's proposal

In addition, "the notice must be written in language understandable to the general public and provided in the native language of the parent or other mode of communication used by the parent, unless it is clearly not feasible to do so. If the native language or other mode of communication of the parent is not a written language, the public agency must take steps to ensure that (a) the notice is translated orally or by other means to the parent in his or her native language or other mode of communication, (b) the parent understands the content of the notice, and (c) there is written evidence that the requirements of IDEA 2004 have been met" (*Federal Register,* August 14, 2006, p. 46792, with changes in notation).

Procedural safeguards notice.
The public agency must give the parents of a child with a disability a copy of the IDEA 2004 procedural safeguards once per school year. However, a copy also must be given to the parents (a) upon initial referral or a parent request for evaluation, (b) upon receipt of a complaint filed with the state, (c) upon receipt of the first due process complaint in a school year, (d) in accordance with the discipline procedures of IDEA 2004, and (e) upon request by a parent. A public agency that has a Web site should place a current copy of the procedural safeguards notice on its site.

The procedural safeguards notice must include a full explanation of all of the procedural safeguards available under IDEA 2004. The notice must meet all of the requirements described in the section above, "Prior notice to the parents." A parent of a child with a disability may elect to receive notices by email, if the public agency makes that option available.

Due process complaint.
A parent or a public agency may file a due process complaint on any matter relating to the identification, evaluation, or educational placement of a child with a disability or the provision of a free and appropriate public education to the child. No more than 2 years may have passed since the alleged violation occurred or since the parent or public agency knew or should have known about it. (States also may have explicit time limits for filing due process complaints.) The public agency must inform the parent of any free or low-cost legal and other relevant services available in the area if the parent requests this information or when the parent or the agency files a due process complaint, and each state educational agency must have model forms to assist parents and public agencies in filing due process complaints.

The party filing a due process complaint must forward a copy of the due process complaint to the state educational agency. The due process complaint must include (a) the name of the child, address of residence (or available contact information for a homeless child), and the name of the school the child is attending, (b) a description of the child's problem and the matters under contention, and (c) a proposed resolution of the problem to the extent known and available to the party at the time of the complaint.

A hearing cannot be scheduled until a due process complaint has been filed. Either party can contest the sufficiency of the complaint within 15 days of receipt. The hearing officer has 5 days to determine whether the due process complaint is satisfactory and to notify the parties of his or her determination. "A party may amend its due process complaint only if the other party consents in writing to the amendment and is given the opportunity to resolve the due process complaint through a meeting . . ." (*Federal Register,* August 14, 2006, p. 46793).

The party receiving a due process complaint must, within 10 days of receiving it, send to the other party a response that addresses the issues raised in the complaint. If the local educational agency has not sent prior written notice regarding the decision at issue in the due process complaint, it must do so within 10 days.

Resolution process.
Within 15 days of receiving notice of the parent's due process complaint and prior to the initiation of a due process hearing, the local educational agency must convene a meeting with the parent. The meeting must be attended by the member or members of the IEP team who have specific knowledge of the facts cited in the due process complaint and a representative of the public agency who has decision-making authority on behalf of that agency. However, the local educational agency cannot have an attorney present unless the parent is accompanied by an attorney. The purpose of the meeting is for representatives of the public agency and the parent of the child with a disability to discuss the due process complaint so that it can be resolved.

The meeting need not be held if the parent and the local educational agency agree in writing to waive the meeting or to use mediation. "If the local educational agency has not resolved the due process complaint to the satisfaction of the parent within 30 days of the receipt of the complaint, the due process hearing may occur" (*Federal Register,* August 14, 2006, p. 46794, with changes in notation). An agreement reached as a result of a resolution session may be voided by either party within three business days; after that, the agreement becomes a contractual agreement, enforceable by a state or federal court.

Mediation. Each public agency must establish and implement procedures that will allow parties who make claims under IDEA 2004 to resolve disputes through a mediation process. The mediation process must be voluntary, cannot be used to deny or delay a parent's right to a hearing on a due process complaint or to deny any other rights afforded under IDEA 2004, and must be conducted by a trained, qualified, and impartial mediator.

For situations in which mediation is not chosen, a public agency may establish procedures to offer to the parents and schools an opportunity to meet with a qualified disinterested party (e.g., someone associated with a dispute-resolution entity, a parent training and information center, or a community parent resource center) at a time and location convenient to the parents. This party would explain the benefits of, and encourage the use of, the mediation process to the parents.

Each state is required to maintain a list of qualified mediators knowledgeable about special education laws and regulations. A mediator cannot be an employee of the state educational agency or the local educational agency that is involved in the education or care of the child and must not have a personal or professional interest that conflicts with his or her objectivity. The state educational agency must select mediators on a random, rotational, or other impartial basis and bear the cost of the mediation process. Mediation sessions must be scheduled in a timely manner and must be held in a location convenient to the parties to the dispute. Legally binding agreements must be signed when the parties resolve a dispute through mediation. Discussions that occur during the mediation process are confidential.

Due process hearing. At a due process hearing, the parents and the school both present evidence by calling witnesses and submitting reports and evaluations that support their positions. An impartial hearing officer is hired by the local educational agency or state to conduct the hearing. A hearing officer cannot be an employee of the state educational agency or the local educational agency that is involved in the education or care of the child and must not have a personal or professional interest that conflicts with his or her objectivity in the hearing. In addition, a hearing officer must possess the knowledge and the ability to (a) understand the provisions of IDEA 2004, federal and state regulations pertaining to IDEA 2004, and legal interpretations of IDEA 2004 by federal and state courts, (b) conduct hearings in accordance with standard legal practice, and (c) render and write decisions in accordance with standard legal practice.

Hearing rights. The party requesting the due process hearing may not raise issues at the hearing that were not raised in the due process complaint unless the other party agrees. Both the parents and the local educational agency have the right to have the child who is the subject of the hearing present and to have the hearing open to the public. In addition, either party may be accompanied and advised by an attorney and by individuals with relevant knowledge or training. Either party may

present evidence and confront, cross examine, and compel the attendance of witnesses. Finally, both parties are entitled to a written or, at the option of the parents, electronic verbatim record of the hearing, the facts, and the decision. The record of the hearing and the findings of fact and decisions about the hearing must be provided at no cost to parents. The U.S. Supreme Court ruled that in due process hearings that challenge an IEP, the burden of proof is on the party seeking relief, which usually is the parents (*Schaffer v. Weast,* 2005).

A hearing officer must make his or her decision on substantive grounds based on a determination of whether the child received a free and appropriate education. In matters alleging a procedural violation, a hearing officer may find that a child did not receive a free and appropriate education only if the procedural inadequacies (a) impeded the child's right to a free and appropriate public education, (b) significantly impeded the parents' opportunity to participate in the decision-making process regarding the provision of a free and appropriate public education, or (c) caused a deprivation of educational benefit.

Finality of decision, appeal, and impartial review. Any party involved in a due process hearing may appeal the decision. If there is an appeal, the state educational agency must conduct an impartial review of the findings and the decision that has been appealed. The official conducting the review must (a) examine the entire hearing record, (b) ensure that the procedures at the hearing were consistent with the requirements of due process, (c) seek additional evidence if necessary, (d) afford the parties an opportunity for oral or written argument or both, at the discretion of the reviewing official, (e) make an independent decision on completion of the review, and (f) give all parties a written or, at the option of the parents, electronic record of findings of fact and decisions.

The state educational agency, after deleting any personally identifiable information, must transmit the findings and decisions of the due process hearing review to the relevant state advisory panel and make those findings and decisions available to the public. The decision made by the reviewing official is final unless a party brings a civil action.

Child's status during proceedings. The child's status during any proceeding depends on several factors. If the child is enrolled in a public school, he or she must remain in his or her current educational placement unless the state or local educational agency and the child's parents agree otherwise. If the complaint involves an application for initial admission to a public school, the child, with the consent of the parents, must be placed in the public school until all proceedings have been completed. If the complaint involves an application for initial services for a child who is transitioning from infant services to preschool services because he or she has turned 3 years of age, the public agency is not required to continue to provide services. Finally, if the child was found eligible for special education and related services and the parent consented to the initial provision of special education and related services, the public agency must provide those special education and related services that are not in dispute between the parent and the public agency.

Surrogate parents.   Public agencies must ensure that a child's rights are protected when (a) he or she does not have a parent (see the definition of *parent* earlier in this appendix under "IEP team"), (b) the public agency, after reasonable efforts, cannot locate a parent, (c) the child is a ward of the state, or (d) the child is an unaccompanied homeless youth. When a public agency determines that a child needs a surrogate parent, it must assign an individual to act as a surrogate. In the case of a child who is a ward of the state, the surrogate parent may be appointed by the judge overseeing the child's case.

Transfer of parental rights at age of majority.   A state may provide that, when a child with a disability (other than a child with a disability who has been determined to be incompetent under state law) reaches the age of majority under state law that applies to all children, the public agency must provide a notice to both the child and the parents that the rights given to the parents under the law transfer to any child who is attending school or is incarcerated in an adult or juvenile state or local correctional institution.

Discipline Procedures

Children with disabilities who violate a code of student conduct may be removed from their current placement and placed in an appropriate interim alternative educational or other setting or suspended for not more than 10 consecutive school days, as long as such dispositions also apply to children without disabilities. Additional removals of not more than 10 consecutive school days may be imposed in the same school year for separate incidents of misconduct, as long as those removals do not form a pattern that constitutes a change of placement. Once a child with a disability has been removed from his or her current placement for more than 10 consecutive school days in the same school year, the public agency must provide services for the child during any subsequent days of removal.

If the behavior that gave rise to the violation of the school code is determined *not* to be a manifestation of the child's disability and the disciplinary removals would exceed 10 consecutive school days, school personnel may apply the same disciplinary procedures to children with disabilities as they would to children without disabilities. However, a child with a disability who is removed from his or her current placement must continue to receive educational services in order to enable him or her to continue to participate in the general education curriculum and progress toward meeting the goals set out in the child's IEP. The child must also receive, as appropriate, a functional behavioral assessment, behavioral intervention services, and modifications designed to address the behavior violation so that it does not recur. The

services required may be provided in an interim alternative educational setting.

The local educational agency must notify the parents when their child with a disability has been removed from his or her class because of a violation of a code of student conduct and must provide the parents with a procedural safeguards notice (described earlier in this appendix). The IEP team determines the child's interim alternative educational setting for services.

Within 10 school days of any decision to remove a child with a disability from his or her placement because of a violation of a code of student conduct, the local educational agency, the parent, and relevant members of the child's IEP team must review all relevant information in the child's file, including the child's IEP, any teacher observations, and any relevant information provided by the parents, to determine whether the conduct in question (a) was caused by or had a direct and substantial relationship to the child's disability or (b) was the direct result of the local educational agency's failure to implement the IEP.

If the local educational agency, the parent, and the relevant members of the child's IEP team determine that the child's conduct was a manifestation of his or her disability, the IEP team must conduct a functional behavioral assessment (unless one was previously performed) and implement a behavioral intervention plan for the child. If the child already has a behavioral intervention plan, the IEP team must review the plan and modify it, as necessary, to address the behavior. If the local educational agency, the parent, and members of the child's IEP team determine that the child's behavior was the direct result of the local educational agency's failure to implement the child's IEP, the local educational agency must take immediate steps to remedy the deficiencies.

In most cases, the child should be returned to the placement from which he or she was removed, unless the parent and the local educational agency agree to a change of placement as part of the modification of the behavioral intervention plan. School personnel may remove a child to an interim alternative educational setting for not more than 45 school days, whether or not the behavior is determined to be a manifestation of the child's disability, for the following reasons:

- *If the child carries a weapon to school or possesses a weapon on school premises or at a school function under the jurisdiction of a state or local educational agency*
- *If the child knowingly possesses or uses illegal drugs or sells or solicits the sale of a controlled substance while on school premises or at a school function under the jurisdiction of a state or local educational agency*
- *If the child inflicts serious bodily injury on another person while on school premises or at a school function under the jurisdiction of a state or local educational agency*

A change of placement is considered to have occurred if a child with a disability is removed from his or her current placement for more than 10 consecutive school days or if the child has been subject to a series of removals that total more than 10 school days and that exhibit a pattern—for example,

Don't go! I'm sure Billy's page 3 of the Behavior Management Plan within his third Comprehensive Individual Assessment's Individual Education Plan is here somewhere.

Courtesy of Daniel Miller.

the behavior that led to the removal was substantially similar in each case or the removals were in close succession.

Appeal. If the parents of a child with a disability disagree with a decision regarding placement or with a decision that the child's violation was not a manifestation of his or her disability, they may file an appeal. Similarly, the local educational agency may request a hearing if it believes that maintaining the child's current placement is substantially likely to result in injury to the child or others. The appeal is heard by a hearing officer, who makes a decision based on the merits of the case. If the hearing officer decides that the child's removal was a violation of the law or that the child's behavior was a manifestation of his or her disability, the hearing officer can order the child to be returned to the placement from which he or she was removed. If the hearing officer determines that maintaining the child's current placement is substantially likely to result in injury to the child or to others, the hearing officer may order a change of placement of the child to an appropriate interim alternative educational setting for not more than 45 school days.

The state or local educational agency is responsible for arranging an expedited due process hearing regarding disciplinary removal. Unless the parents and the local educational agency agree in writing to waive the resolution meeting or to use the mediation process, a resolution meeting must occur within 7 days of receiving notice of the due process complaint. And unless the matter has been resolved to the satisfaction of both parties within 15 days of the receipt of the due process complaint, the due process hearing must be held. The hearing must occur within 20 school days of the date the complaint requesting the hearing was filed, and the hearing officer must make a determination within 10 school days after the hearing.

Protection for children not determined eligible for special education and related services. A child who

has not been determined to be eligible for special education and related services and who has engaged in behavior that has violated a code of student conduct may assert any of the protections provided to children with disabilities if the public agency had knowledge, before the behavior that precipitated the disciplinary action occurred, that the child has a disability. A public agency is deemed to have knowledge that a child has a disability if any of the following occurred:

1. The child's parent expressed concern in writing to an appropriate party (e.g., a supervisor or an administrator of the appropriate local educational agency or the child's teacher) that the child was in need of special education and related services.
2. The child's parent requested an evaluation of the child.
3. The child's teacher or other personnel of the local educational agency expressed specific concerns about the child's pattern of behavior directly to an appropriate party, such as the director of special education of the agency or other supervisory personnel of the agency.

A public agency is deemed *not* to have knowledge that a child has a disability if any of the following occurred:

1. The child's parent did not allow the child to be evaluated.
2. The child's parent refused services for the child.
3. The child was evaluated and determined not to have a disability.

If a public agency does not have knowledge that a child has a disability, the child may be subjected to the disciplinary measures applied to children without disabilities who engage in comparable behaviors, which can include suspension or expulsion without educational services. If a request is made for an evaluation of the child during the period in which the child is subjected to disciplinary measures, the evaluation must be conducted in an expedited manner. Until the evaluation is completed, the child must remain in the educational placement determined by school authorities.

Referral to and action by law enforcement and judicial authorities. Nothing in IDEA prohibits an agency from reporting a crime committed by a child with a disability to appropriate authorities or prevents state law enforcement and judicial authorities from exercising their responsibilities and enforcing federal and state laws regarding any crimes committed by a child with a disability. An agency reporting a crime committed by a child with a disability must ensure that copies of the child's special education and disciplinary records are transmitted to the appropriate authorities to whom the agency reports the crime (to the extent that transmission is permitted by the Family Educational Rights and Privacy Act; see Chapter 3 in the text).

Reviews

IDEA 2004 requires that parents of children with disabilities be notified (through report cards or other means) at least

SCHOOLIES © 1999 by John P. Wood

Here's your new student and a stack of blank incident report forms.

- Are the goals and objectives of the IEP being achieved? For example, has the child's reading (or mathematics, written expression, etc.) level improved?
- What progress is the child making toward achieving the objectives of the regular curriculum?
- If improvement has occurred, what has been most helpful?
- If improvement has not occurred, what factors might account for the lack of improvement (e.g., ineffective instruction, sporadic provision of services, absences from school, failure to do homework)?
- Is the child still eligible for special education services? If so, what is his or her disability?
- Are any previously identified problem areas (e.g., weaknesses in phonological awareness, verbal memory, executive functions) still problems?
- Are any new problems apparent? If so, what are they?
- How does the child's identified condition affect his or her performance in class?
- Are changes needed in instructional strategies, educational placement, services provided, or home schooling? If so, what changes are needed?
- Would the use of assistive technology (e.g., word processor, calculator, text reading program) improve the child's learning and academic performance?
- Would additional accommodations or modifications (e.g., extended testing time, use of large print materials) help the child improve academically?
- If accommodations or modifications have been used, which ones are no longer appropriate?
- What strategies are appropriate to assist the child in transitioning from special education to regular education?
- Should an alternative plan be developed for the child if he or she is no longer eligible for special education? If so, what accommodations or modifications are needed in the general education setting? How should progress in regular education be monitored?

as often as parents of children who are not disabled about how the children are progressing in meeting their annual goals and objectives. Reviews have several functions. They help to determine whether a child continues to be eligible for special education services (i.e., whether the child continues to have a disability), to evaluate the child's progress, to identify any problems with the child's IEP and to determine the reasons for those problems, to identify new areas for instruction, to determine whether any further information is needed about the child's present levels of performance and educational needs, to develop new intervention plans to meet new needs that have been identified, and to provide feedback to those responsible for developing and implementing the plan.

A child's IEP must be reviewed at least once a year—generally on the anniversary of the child's original placement—to determine whether its stated goals and objectives are being achieved and whether revisions are needed. A review of the IEP will be needed sooner if the child transfers to another school district or there is a change in placement.

Reevaluations

The school must reevaluate a child with a disability if conditions warrant or if the child's parents or teacher requests a reevaluation, but at least once every 3 years unless the parent and the public agency agree that a reevaluation is not necessary. Typical questions addressed by a reevaluation include the following:

The assessment principles that apply to the initial evaluation also apply to a reevaluation. To conduct the reevaluation, you will need to (a) review existing evaluation data, including results from teacher-made and statewide tests, (b) obtain information about the child's functioning from the teacher and parents, (c) observe the child in various settings, and (d) determine what additional information is needed and then obtain this information.

Formal psychological testing may not be needed for reevaluations if you have sufficient information to make the appropriate decisions and recommendations without additional testing. Generally, if the IEP team agrees that the present placement is appropriate, extensive reevaluation is not needed. Formal psychological testing, however, remains a useful part of a reevaluation when (a) you suspect additional disabling conditions, (b) the child's level of functioning has changed markedly, (c) there are gaps in the previous assessment, (d) the child's parents or guardians have requested formal testing to evaluate their child's progress (note that the school is not required to perform an evaluation if the parents request aptitude testing), or (e) the child is transferred out of special education and administering standardized tests would be helpful in documenting the child's progress.

Parents are an integral part of the reevaluation process. The local educational agency must notify parents that their child needs to be reevaluated and inform them of their right to request standardized instruments or other assessments at the time of reevaluation. Parents must be told about the procedures that will be used in the reevaluation, and the local educational agency must obtain written consent from the parents for additional assessments. However, as noted previously, the local educational agency can perform a reevaluation without parental approval if it has taken reasonable steps to obtain parental consent and the parents failed to respond to the request.

Services for Children at Private Schools

Local educational agencies are responsible for identifying and evaluating children with disabilities who have been enrolled in private schools by their parents and determining whether they are in need of special education and related services. The responsibility for serving private school children rests with the district in which the school is located, not the district in which the child resides.

The local educational agency is required to perform the following duties in connection with these evaluations:

1. Develop a service plan comparable to an IEP for any children with disabilities enrolled in private schools who are designated to receive services. The local educational agency must ensure that a representative from the private school participates, if possible, at each service plan meeting. If the representative cannot attend, the local educational agency should use other methods to ensure participation, including individual or conference telephone calls. The agency must permit private schools to offer to children with disabilities a different amount of services than is offered to children in public schools. Parentally placed private school children with disabilities do not have an individual right to receive some or all of the special education and related services that they would receive if enrolled in a public school. It is the local educational agency that makes the final decision with respect to the services to be provided to eligible parentally placed private school children with disabilities.
2. Assure that the services provided to children with disabilities in private schools are given "by personnel meeting the same standards as personnel providing services in the public schools, except that private elementary school and secondary school teachers who are providing equitable services to parentally placed private school children with disabilities do not have to meet the highly qualified special education teacher requirements that public school teachers need to meet" (*Federal Register,* August 14, 2006, p. 46768, with changes in notation). Note that private school teachers hired by or under contract with the local educational agencies do not qualify for this exemption.

3. Provide a written summary of the number of private school children evaluated, found eligible, and served.
4. Consult with private school representatives during the design and development of special education services and obtain written affirmation of their participation in the consultation.
5. Provide a private school with a written explanation when it disagrees with the school regarding the provision of services.

The local educational agency may provide services on the premises of private schools, including religious schools, as long as the services are provided in a manner that does not violate the establishment clause of the first amendment to the U.S. Constitution and is consistent with the applicable state constitution and laws. Federal funds, in an amount proportional to those allocated for all disabled children in the school district, may be spent on services for children with disabilities at private schools.

The law gives private schools the right to complain to the state educational agency if they believe that a consultation was less than meaningful or timely. Appeals can also be filed with the U.S. Secretary of Education.

Services for Children at Charter Schools

Children with disabilities attending charter schools that are public schools in the local educational agency district must be served by the local educational agency in the same manner as children with disabilities in other schools. For example, the local educational agency must provide similar supplementary and related services on site at the charter school and must provide funding for these services. If the public charter school is a local educational agency, it is responsible for ensuring that the requirements of the law are met, unless state law assigns that responsibility to some other entity.

Records of Migratory Children with Disabilities

The local educational agency must cooperate with federal and state governments to ensure the linkage of records pertaining to migratory children with disabilities so that health and educational information about these children can be exchanged electronically.

Statewide Assessments

IDEA 2004 requires that all children in special education participate in statewide and districtwide assessments of achievement. A child's IEP should provide guidance about what accommodations are needed to help the child with a disability take group-administered tests or alternative assessments. If the IEP team determines that a child cannot participate in group testing, it must explain why and then use an alternative assessment based on state-approved guidelines.

For children unable to participate in a statewide or districtwide assessment program, states must provide alternative assessments. These may include observation of the child's learning environment (sometimes called *ecological assessment*), use of curriculum-based measurement, and analysis of the child's work products (sometimes referred to as *authentic assessment* or *portfolio assessment*). IDEA 2004 requires that state educational agencies develop guidelines for alternative assessments and provide reports to the public about the number (but not the names) of children with disabilities participating in regular assessments and in alternative assessments.

If an IEP team recommends exemption from statewide or districtwide testing, the parents must be informed of the reason an exception was recommended and how their child will be assessed. Exemption from statewide assessment may result in a child's being denied the right to receive a diploma because he or she failed to demonstrate competency. Parents should be informed of the long-term implications of an exemption decision.

Disproportionality and Overidentification

Each state must have in effect policies and procedures designed to prevent the inappropriate overidentification or disproportionate representation by race and ethnicity of children with disabilities. States are required to report to the federal government information about disproportionality, including the ethnicity and race of the children receiving services under IDEA 2004; the placement of the children in particular educational settings; and the incidence, duration, and type of disciplinary actions, including suspensions and expulsions. If a local educational agency finds significant disproportionality, it is required to provide comprehensive and coordinated early intervention services to children in the local educational area, particularly children in those groups that were significantly overidentified. The local educational agency must make public any revisions of policies, practices, and procedures related to the disproportionality.

IDEA 2004 Part C: Infants and Toddlers with Disabilities

A section of IDEA 2004 referred to as Part C requires states to adopt a policy providing services to all infants and toddlers who have disabilities, including those who are at home, and services for their families (*Federal Register,* December 3, 2004). IDEA 2004 defines an infant or toddler with a disability as an individual under 3 years of age who needs early intervention services because he or she (a) is experiencing developmental delays, as measured by appropriate diagnostic instruments and procedures, in cognitive development, physical development, communication development, social or emotional development, and/or adaptive development or (b) has a diagnosed physical or mental condition that has a high probability of resulting in developmental delay. At a state's discretion, services may be provided to infants and toddlers who are at risk of having substantial developmental delays without early intervention services.

Early intervention services. Under Part C, states are encouraged to provide early intervention services under public supervision and at no cost, except where federal or state law provides for a system of payments by families, including a schedule of sliding fees. At the discretion of the states, early intervention services may include family training, counseling, and home visits; special instruction; speech-language pathology and audiology services, including sign language and cued language services; occupational therapy; physical therapy; psychological services; medical services for diagnostic or evaluation purposes only; early identification, screening, and assessment services; health services necessary to enable the infant or toddler to benefit from the other early intervention services; social work services; vision services; assistive technology devices and assistive technology services; coordination of all of the above services; and transportation to enable an infant or toddler and his or her family to receive the above services.

The services should be provided by qualified personnel, including special educators, speech-language pathologists and audiologists, occupational therapists, physical therapists, psychologists, social workers, nurses, registered dietitians, family therapists, vision specialists (including ophthalmologists and optometrists), orientation and mobility specialists, and pediatricians and other physicians. The services, to the maximum extent appropriate, must be provided in natural environments, including the child's home and the community settings in which children without disabilities participate. Finally, the services must be provided in conformity with an individualized family service plan (IFSP).

Individualized Family Service Plan (IFSP). Once a child has been identified, an individualized family service plan (IFSP) must be developed by the staff and parents. The IFSP must include the following:

- The infant's or toddler's present levels of physical development, cognitive development, communication development, social or emotional development, and adaptive development, based on objective criteria
- The family's resources, priorities, and concerns related to enhancing the development of the infant or toddler with a disability
- The measurable results or outcomes expected to be achieved by the infant or toddler and the family, including the criteria, procedures, and timelines to be used to determine progress toward achieving the results or outcomes
- A description of specific early intervention services (based on peer-reviewed research, to the extent practicable) needed to meet the unique needs of the infant or toddler and the family, including the frequency, intensity, and method of delivering services

- The natural environments in which early intervention services will be provided and a justification, if necessary, for not providing services in a natural environment
- The projected dates of initiation of services and the anticipated length, duration, and frequency of the services
- The identification of the service coordinator who will be responsible for the implementation of the plan and for coordinating with other agencies and persons and providing transition services
- The steps to be taken to support the transition of the toddler with a disability to preschool or other appropriate services

The IFSP must be reevaluated once a year and reviewed with the family at 6-month intervals or more often, depending on the needs of the infant or toddler and family. The IFSP must be developed within a reasonable time after the assessment is completed. However, with the parents' consent, early intervention services may commence prior to the completion of the assessment. The content of the IFSP must be explained to the parents and their informed written consent obtained prior to the initiation of services. Only the services consented to by the parents can be provided; if the parents do not give their approval to a particular early intervention service, it must not be provided.

Procedural safeguards.

Following are the major procedural safeguards provided by Part C, to protect the basic rights of the children and families involved in an early intervention program:

- Complaints by parents must be resolved in a timely manner, and services must continue during the resolution process, unless the parents and the state agency agree otherwise.
- The confidentiality of personally identifiable information must be maintained.
- Parents have the right to accept or decline any or all services.
- Parents have the right to examine records relating to assessment, screening, eligibility determination, and implementation of the IFSP.
- Procedures designed to protect the rights of the infant or toddler must be implemented whenever the parents of the infant or toddler are not known or cannot be found or the infant or toddler is a ward of the state.
- Parents must receive prior written notice of any activity related to intervention (including a change in services, evaluation, placement, or provision of appropriate early intervention services to the child).

Flexibility in serving children from 3 years of age until entrance into elementary school.

A state may develop a policy under which parents of children with disabilities who have received services under Part C may continue early intervention services for their children until the children enter or are eligible to enter kindergarten. If a state develops such a policy, the state must then ensure that the parents are given an annual notice containing (a) a description of parental rights and (b) an explanation of the differences between the services offered under Part C and Part B of the law. (Part C provides for IFSPs; Part B provides for IEPs.) The explanation should include the types of services offered under each part of the law, the locations where the services are provided, applicable procedural safeguards, and possible costs. Early intervention services that continue during the preschool period must include an educational component that promotes school readiness and incorporates preliteracy, language, and numeracy skills. In addition, the state policy should not affect the right of any child to receive a free appropriate public education under Part B of the law. All early intervention services outlined in the child's IFSP will continue while any determination of eligibility for continued services is being made. For early intervention services to continue, the parents of infants or toddlers with disabilities must give their informed written consent before their children reach 3 years of age.

Overall guidelines for states.

IDEA 2004 requires that each state perform the following actions (along with other actions) to carry out the provisions of Part C of the law:

- Formulate a rigorous definition of the term *developmental delay* in order to appropriately identify infants and toddlers with disabilities who are in need of services.
- Develop a policy to ensure that appropriate early intervention services are based on scientifically based research, to the extent practicable. The services should be available to all infants and toddlers with disabilities and their families, including Indian infants and toddlers with disabilities and their families residing on reservations and infants and toddlers with disabilities and their families who are homeless.
- Perform a timely, comprehensive, multidisciplinary evaluation of the functioning of each infant or toddler in the state who has a disability, and identify the needs of each infant's or toddler's family in order to help the family assist in the development of the infant or toddler.
- Develop a procedure for creating an IFSP for each infant or toddler with a disability who resides in the state.
- Develop a comprehensive child-find system (i.e., a system designed to identify, locate, and evaluate all children with disabilities who are in need of early intervention or special education services), with appropriate timelines for making referrals.
- Produce a public awareness program focusing on early identification of infants and toddlers with disabilities. The program should provide information to hospitals and physicians about how they can help parents of premature infants and infants with other physical risk factors associated with learning or developmental complications, and about the availability of early intervention services.
- Produce a central directory that includes information on early intervention services, resources, experts available in the state, and research and demonstration projects being conducted in the state.

- Develop a system for training primary referral sources about the basic components of early intervention services available in the state.
- Develop policies and procedures to ensure that personnel who provide early intervention services, including paraprofessionals and assistants, are appropriately prepared and trained. The personnel development plan should address recruitment and retention of providers, as well as certification, licensing, registration, or other comparable requirements. The plan should also promote the training of personnel to coordinate transition services for infants and toddlers and to work in rural or inner-city areas.

Reports to the Public

Reports made available to the public by state and local educational agencies must include information about the following: (a) the number of children with disabilities provided accommodations in order to participate in regular assessments, (b) the number of children with disabilities participating in alternative assessments, and (c) how the performance of children with disabilities on regular assessments and on alternative assessments compares with the achievement of all children, including children with disabilities, on those assessments (if the number of children with disabilities participating in those assessments is sufficient to yield statistically reliable information and if reporting that information will not reveal personally identifiable information about an individual child).

SECTION 504 OF THE REHABILITATION ACT OF 1973 (SECTION 504)

Section 504 of the Rehabilitation Act of 1973 (Public Law 93-112) was designed to protect individuals with disabilities from discrimination in any setting provided by an entity receiving financial assistance from the federal government. A person is considered to be disabled under Section 504 if he or she (a) has a physical or mental impairment that substantially limits one or more major life activities, (b) has a record of such an impairment, or (c) is regarded as having such an impairment. The impairment must have a material effect on the person's ability to perform a major life activity.

Physical or mental impairment refers to (a) any physiological disorder or condition, cosmetic disfigurement, or anatomical loss affecting one or more of the following body systems: neurological, musculoskeletal, special sense organs, respiratory (including speech organs), cardiovascular, reproductive, digestive, genitourinary, hemic and lymphatic skin, or endocrine or (b) any mental or psychological disorder such as mental retardation, organic brain syndrome, emotional or mental illness, or specific learning disability. *Major life activities* refer to functions such as caring for one's self, performing manual tasks, walking, seeing, hearing, speaking, breathing, learning, and working.

According to Section 504, an individual is qualified for services provided at a public preschool, elementary or secondary school, or adult education facility if he or she is of an age at which persons without disabilities are provided such services, is of an age at which it is mandatory under state law to provide such services to persons with disabilities, or is a person for whom a state is required to provide a free appropriate public education under the Individuals with Disabilities Education Improvement Act. (Section 504 uses the term a "qualified handicapped person" to designate a person eligible to receive services.)

Responsibilities of Schools

Under Section 504, schools must carry out the following responsibilities:

- Identify and locate annually all unserved children with disabilities.
- Provide to each child with a disability, regardless of the nature or severity of the disability, a free appropriate public education that is comparable to the education provided to children without disabilities.
- Ensure that each child with a disability is educated with children without disabilities to the maximum extent appropriate.
- Establish nondiscriminatory evaluation and placement procedures.
- Provide appropriate accommodations within the regular education program, such as giving preferential seating, adjusting the length of time allowed to complete an assignment, allowing tape recording of lectures, allowing children to dictate answers, allowing more time to take tests, providing an interpreter or reader, using behavioral management techniques, and providing a structured learning environment.
- Establish procedural safeguards to enable parents and guardians to participate meaningfully in decisions regarding the evaluation and placement of their children, including allowing parents and guardians to examine relevant records, request an impartial hearing and be represented by counsel at the hearing, and request a review of the hearing decision.
- Ensure that children with disabilities have an equal opportunity to participate in nonacademic and extracurricular services and activities such as counseling, physical education, recreational activities, athletics, transportation, health services, special interest groups or clubs sponsored by the school, and child employment.
- Ensure that all programs and activities are readily accessible to children with disabilities. (Buildings built before June 3, 1977 do not have to be structurally modified, whereas those built after that date do have to be accessible.)
- Notify college applicants and other interested parties that the college offers auxiliary aids and services and can make needed academic adjustments.

- Provide college applicants and other interested parties with the name of the person designated to coordinate the college's efforts to carry out the requirements of Section 504.

Note that it is the child's responsibility to make his or her disabling condition known to a college (e.g., to the Section 504 Coordinator, to an appropriate dean, to a faculty advisor, to each professor on an individual basis) and to request academic adjustments.

Following are some examples of reasonable accommodation plans:

- Allowing a child with a long-term debilitating medical problem, such as cancer, to have a class schedule that allows for rest and recuperation following chemotherapy
- Allowing a child with a chronic medical problem, such as kidney or liver disease, to have a special parking space, extra time between classes, or other privileges that help to conserve the child's energy for academic pursuits
- Allowing a child with diabetes to leave the classroom to check his or her blood sugar level as needed
- Allowing a child with a seizure disorder to leave the classroom in case of a seizure and giving the child a place to sleep afterwards, if needed. Accommodations may also be needed if stressful activities such as lengthy academic testing or competitive athletic endeavors trigger seizures.
- Allowing a child with Tourette Syndrome to leave the classroom when stressed and return when he or she regains composure
- Allowing a child with arthritis who has persistent pain, tenderness, or swelling in one or more joints to have a modified physical education program
- Allowing an emotionally or mentally ill child to have an adjusted class schedule that includes time for regular counseling or therapy
- Allowing a high school student with a conduct disorder to go to the next class 5 minutes early in order to avoid confrontation with other children when the halls are crowded

Section 504 and the Courts

Two examples of the kinds of cases heard by federal appeals courts under Section 504 are *DeBord v. Board of Education of the Ferguson-Florissant School District* (1997) and *Todd v. Elkins School District* (1998).

Kelly DeBord was prescribed a dosage of Ritalin that exceeded the recommended dosage in the *Physician's Desk Reference* (PDR). The school nurse refused to administer the prescribed dosage because the school had a policy of following the recommendations contained in the PDR. The school offered several accommodations to allow Kelly's parents to administer the drug, but the parents sought relief from the courts. The appeals court ruled that the school had the right to establish guidelines for the administration of drugs. Schools that have objective standards for implementing services do not have to modify those standards if they believe that there is potential liability in following the modified procedure. Courts look favorably on standards applied equally to all children.

Jacob Todd was a fourth-grade special education student with muscular dystrophy. While he was being pushed in a wheelchair—unbuckled—to the playground by a fellow student, he fell from the wheelchair and sustained a broken leg. Jacob's IEP did not provide for an adult aide, although one was available to assist him if needed; instead, the school district had Jacob's peers transport him to recess at times in order to minimize his isolation and encourage relationships with other children. Jacob's parents asked for damages, claiming that school officials had violated Jacob's rights under Section 504. The parents claimed that the school was indifferent to and had intentionally disregarded their son's safety and had denied him the right to participate in various programs. An appeals court affirmed the district court's ruling that the school district did not discriminate against Jacob. The school district's policy did not markedly depart from accepted professional judgment, practice, or standards. Furthermore, the school district did not show bad faith or gross misjudgment.

Other court decisions relevant to Section 504 include the ruling that parents cannot repackage a claim that could have been brought under IDEA 2004 and bring it under Section 504 or other statutes instead (*W.B. v. Matula,* 1995). Also, there is general judicial agreement that money damages are available when school districts intentionally violate Section 504 by showing bad faith or gross misjudgment (*Hoekstra v. Independent School District,* 1996; *Whitehead v. School Board of Hillsborough County,* 1996).

Comparison of Section 504 and IDEA 2004

Let's look at some of the similarities and differences between Section 504 and IDEA 2004.

SIMILARITIES

- Both laws require schools to provide a free and appropriate education for every child with a disability.
- Both laws embrace the concept that a child with a disability is entitled to equal opportunities to engage in both nonacademic and academic activities.
- Both laws require that children with disabilities be educated in the least restrictive environment.
- Both laws acknowledge that children with disabilities are entitled to special education and related services (including but not limited to speech therapy, occupational therapy, physical therapy, psychological counseling, and medical diagnostic services) and accommodations not available to regular education students if these services and accommodations are needed for them to receive a free and appropriate public education.
- Both laws allow children with disabilities to be disciplined for up to 10 days in the same manner as other children.

- Both laws allow local educational agencies to take disciplinary action when children with disabilities illegally use drugs or alcohol at school.
- Both laws require parental consent to conduct initial evaluations.
- Both laws require the use of a variety of assessment tools, careful documentation of the information obtained in assessments, and a knowledgeable team to make placement decisions.
- Both laws provide procedural safeguards, including hearings before a hearing officer.

DIFFERENCES

- IDEA 2004 is a partially funded federal statute whose purpose is to provide financial aid to states in their efforts to ensure adequate and appropriate educational services for children with disabilities, whereas Section 504 is an unfunded federal civil rights law designed to protect the rights of individuals with disabilities in programs and activities that receive federal funds from the Department of Education.
- The Office of Special Education in the Department of Education enforces IDEA 2004, whereas the Office of Civil Rights in the Department of Education enforces Section 504.
- Under IDEA 2004, parents must be invited to meetings at which decisions are to be made about their child's special education, whereas under Section 504, local educational agencies may provide such invitations but are not required to do so.
- All children covered by IDEA 2004 are also covered by Section 504, but not all children covered by Section 504 are covered by IDEA 2004. For example, children with attention-deficit/hyperactivity disorder who require specially designed instruction (special education) to receive a free and appropriate public education would be eligible for protection under both IDEA 2004 and Section 504, whereas children with attention-deficit/hyperactivity disorder who need related services or accommodations but not special education in order to receive a free and appropriate public education would be entitled to protection only under Section 504.
- IDEA 2004 requires that each identified child have an IEP, whereas Section 504 does not require a written plan or a written consent from the parent, although most local educational agencies draw up a written agreement (e.g., a "504 Plan") to document that they have met their obligations.
- IDEA 2004 has a provision for keeping a child in his or her current educational placement when the school and parents are in disagreement over the child's services (popularly known as "stay put"), whereas Section 504 does not have such a provision.
- IDEA 2004 provides protection for suspended or expelled children not yet identified as disabled if the local educational agency knew or should have known that they were children with disabilities, whereas Section 504 does not have such a provision.
- IDEA 2004 provides continuing educational services to children with disabilities who are expelled, whether or not their behavior was a manifestation of their disabilities, whereas Section 504 does not require services if children who are not disabled do not receive such services when they are expelled. However, under Section 504, if the behavior leading up to the expulsion was a manifestation of the child's disability, he or she could not be expelled.
- IDEA 2004 requires parents to try to find an administrative remedy before going to federal district court, whereas Section 504 allows parents to go directly to federal court.
- IDEA 2004 requires that a reevaluation be completed at least every 3 years, unless the local educational agency and parents agree in writing that it is not necessary, whereas Section 504 requires periodic reevaluations but does not specify a time interval.
- IDEA 2004 allows parents to obtain an independent educational evaluation at public expense if they disagree with the local educational agency's evaluation, whereas Section 504 does not have such a provision.

AMERICANS WITH DISABILITIES ACT (ADA)

The Americans with Disabilities Act (ADA) of 1990 (Public Law 101-336) provides protection from discrimination for individuals with disabilities in all settings, regardless of whether federal funds are involved. For example, the law gives people with disabilities the right to compete fairly for jobs, to stay in whatever hotel they choose, to patronize any establishment open to the public, and to use public transportation. The law also requires that reasonable accommodations be made for individuals with disabilities in school and work settings.

In an assessment setting, children with disabilities need to feel comfortable and secure and be able to participate to the fullest extent of their capabilities. In order to obtain a valid estimate of their abilities, be prepared to make any needed accommodations (such as removing from the setting obstacles that impede them from taking examinations and providing qualified readers or interpreters—accommodations discussed in more detail earlier in the appendix). You must be sure that the assessment results accurately reflect their individual skills and aptitudes rather than their impaired sensory, manual, or speaking skills, except where such skills are the factors that the assessment purports to evaluate.

The U.S. Supreme Court interpreted the ADA in three rulings handed down in 1999. In each case, by a 7-to-2 vote, the Supreme Court ruled that people with physical impairments who can function normally when they wear their glasses or take their medicine generally cannot be considered disabled and therefore do not come under the protection of the ADA

(*Albertsons v. Kirkingburg,* 1999; *Murphy v. UPS,* 1999; *Sutton v. United Airlines,* 1999). The justices said that the law was not designed to protect individuals with treatable impairments such as poor eyesight, hypertension, or diabetes.

RECOMMENDED INTERNET RESOURCES FOR IDEA 2004, SECTION 504, AND THE ADA

The following Web sites are useful resources for obtaining more information about IDEA 2004, Section 504, the ADA, and related topics.

- http://a257.g.akamaitech.net/7/257/2422/01jan20061800/edocket.access.gpo.gov/2006/pdf/06–6656.pdf: This is the link to the *Federal Register,* August 14, 2006, for the final rule on 34 CFR Parts 300 and 301, Assistance to States for the Education of Children with Disabilities and Preschool Grants for Children with Disabilities.
- http://nichcy.org/reauth/PL108–446.pdf: This is the link to the *Federal Register,* Dec. 3, 2004, for the regulations on Part C of IDEA 2004, pp. 2744–2763.
- http://idea.ed.gov/explore/home: This is the Web site of OSEP's Office of Special Education Programs.
- http://www.pattan.k12.pa.us/regsforms/Osep.aspx: This is the search engine for OSEP's policy letters.
- http://www.nichcy.org/index.html: This the Web site of the National Dissemination Center for Children with Disabilities, an organization that is funded by OSEP's Office of Special Education Programs and serves as a central source of information on various topics related to IDEA 2004, the No Child Left Behind Act as it relates to children with disabilities, and obtaining research-based information on effective educational practices.
- http://www.ed.gov/policy/rights/reg/ocr/edlite-34cfr104.html: This a link to Section 504 regulations.
- http://www.ed.gov/about/offices/list/ocr/504faq.html: This is an OCR policy statement clarifying their interpretation of several policy issues regarding Section 504.
- http://www.ed.gov/about/offices/list/ocr/docs/edlite-FAPE504.html: This is an OCR policy statement regarding the rights of children in public school settings.
- http://www.ed.gov/about/offices/list/ocr/docs/placpub.html: This is a brief but authoritative overview of public school children's rights under Section 504.
- http://www.ed.gov/policy/rights/reg/ocr/edlite-28cfr35.html: This is a link to ADA regulations.

COMMENT ON IDEA 2004, SECTION 504, AND THE ADA

Interpretations of IDEA 2004, Section 504, and the ADA involve complex judgments on the part of (a) educators and professionals working in schools, (b) administrative hearing officers at both the local and the state level, (c) judges in U.S. District Courts and U.S. Circuit Courts of Appeals, and (d) U.S. Supreme Court justices. It is admirable that our nation wants to provide a free and appropriate public education to all children. But what is not admirable is the amount of litigation associated with IDEA 2004. *Decisions about educational methodology are best left to experts—namely, educators—and not judges or attorneys.* Obviously, there are legitimate reasons for parents to bring a lawsuit against a school district when their child is denied the right to needed services. But it is not right for parents to use the law to challenge a valid diagnostic assessment and/or placement decision in order to pursue a hidden agenda. Members of the judiciary are not acquainted with curriculum standards, teaching methods, children with disabilities, or educational interventions. They have not taught in the classroom or worked with children with special needs, their parents, or administrators. For these and other reasons, members of the judiciary must listen to teachers and understand that teachers are in the best position to judge how children should be taught and what is needed in the classroom. Of course, it is important that school officials understand and follow the laws related to education of all children, including those with disabilities and those who are from different ethnic and cultural groups.

When school districts fail to use appropriate educational practices and children fail to learn, however, the door is left open for courts to dictate educational practice. Courts are more likely to rule in favor of schools that (a) can show that a child progressed in their program, (b) have expert witnesses testify in support of their program, (c) used methods that are current and accepted in the field, and (d) can supply evidence that they have provided both teacher and parent training, where needed.

It is critical that schools keep accurate records of all meetings, as well as copies of consent forms, IEPs, IFSPs, and anything else related to a child's assessment and intervention plans. Courts may scrutinize the child's entire school record. They will look carefully at the IEP or the IFSP to determine whether the provisions listed in the plan were carried out and whether the goals and objectives relate to the child's disability. Failure to develop appropriate plans can be just as damaging as failure to carry out the plans properly.

Congress included procedural safeguards in IDEA 2004 in an attempt to promote fair classification. School placement decisions are important to children and families, and they should not be undertaken lightly or arbitrarily. Congress wanted to hold schools accountable for the accuracy of their classifications and for the appropriateness of their programs. School personnel are obliged to specify the basis for their classifications of children and to demonstrate that programs are likely to benefit them.

Courts need to consider that the diagnostic process involves both art and science—that is, both subjective and objective processes. For example, in *Muller v. Committee on*

Special Education of the East Islip Union Free School District (1998), the school psychologist employed by the school district arrived at a "conduct disorder" diagnosis, whereas the psychologist working for a private residential facility arrived at a diagnosis of "seriously emotionally disturbed." The former diagnosis meant that the child was not eligible for special education services, whereas the latter diagnosis meant that the child might be eligible for these services. If the child was deemed eligible for services, the private residential facility could receive payment from the school district. In such cases, on what basis can a court determine which diagnosis is correct? In cases where a school's evaluation is in dispute, we believe that the procedure that is fair to all parties is for the school to have the child tested by a neutral third party with expertise in the area of disability. Following this procedure might prevent litigation. If both sides approve the evaluator, one significant area of contention is bypassed. For example, a child might be tested at a local college or university training center. In high-stakes litigation (i.e., most litigation), schools must consider bringing in neutral outside experts.

Parents and children should never be coerced or intimidated into accepting a school's placement decision and an IEP or IFSP. The IEP team or the IFSP team must take care to express decisions about eligibility, placement, program goals, and the review process in clear, understandable, and jargon-free language. Even so, some parents will have difficulty comprehending their child's IEP or IFSP and educational program. Schools should do their best to help these parents gain the necessary understanding.

Following the letter of the law may not be enough to avoid litigation. Rather, there must be an effort by schools to work cooperatively with parents, to ensure that the parents' position is given credence, and to recognize that the education of children with disabilities sometimes involves trial and error. Having the parents "on board" is the best and safest way to proceed. Parents are less likely to hire an attorney when they understand how the school arrived at the recommendations and when they believe that their concerns are being addressed. For example, it may be prudent for a school to grant the wish of parents who want their child to attend general education classes for 80% of the day rather than 50% of the day, as preferred by the school. What evidence is there that the child's education will be more significantly enhanced by a 50/50 split than by an 80/20 split? If there is such evidence, it behooves the school to present it to the parents in a comprehensible way.

Interpretation of IDEA 2004 and Section 504, as well as the role of the ADA in special education disputes, is still evolving and changing. The unpredictable nature of court rulings should make both parents and schools want to avoid litigation. Even in situations where the law might not require

School psychologist on the way to work

Courtesy of Daniel Miller.

a school system to provide services, spending a little extra money to assist a child may be a wiser decision than giving money to attorneys just to prove a point. And once litigation begins, there is no certainty that the school will receive a favorable decision.

An ambiguous component of IDEA 2004 is its call for assessment procedures to be selected and administered so as not to be racially or culturally discriminatory. The law does not clearly define what such procedures might be; in fact, the law does not specify any acceptable or unacceptable assessment procedures. Similarly, in the definition of a disability in Section 504, the phrase "substantially limits one or more major life activities" is a term of art rather than of science, because there is no statistical way of quantifying "substantially limits."

It is to be hoped that in the future the courts will recognize their limitations and defer to the judgment of specialists in education when it comes to educational matters. Until that happens, all professionals who work in schools with children who may have disabilities need to be aware of IDEA 2004, Section 504, and the ADA and of how these laws are interpreted by the courts. All such professionals need to follow the provisions of these laws as carefully as possible and take precautions to avoid costly litigation. The ultimate measure of the usefulness of these laws is the quality of the education received by each child (and adult) with a disability, how the education is used to benefit the child and society, and how society integrates individuals with disabilities into the mainstream of daily living.

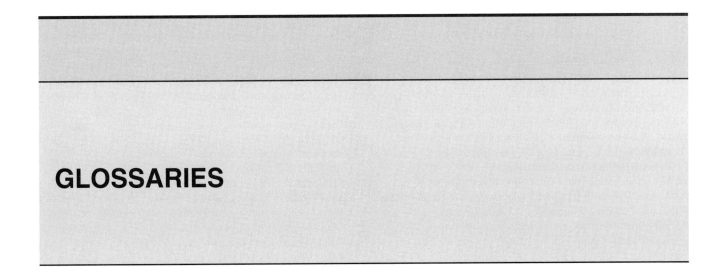

GLOSSARIES

AAC. Augmentative and alternative communication.
AADB. American Association of the Deaf-Blind.
AAMR. American Association on Mental Retardation.
ABA. Applied behavioral analysis; American Bar Association.
ABDC. Association of Birth Defect Children.
ACCH. Association for the Care of Children's Health.
ACF. Administration on Children and Families.
ACYF. Administration on Children, Youth, and Families.
ADA. Americans with Disabilities Act; average daily attendance.
ADC. Adult disabled children.
ADHD. Attention-deficit/hyperactivity disorder.
ADL. Activities of daily living.
AE. Age equivalent.
AEP. Alternative education placement.
AFB. American Federation of the Blind.
AFDC. Aid to Families with Dependent Children.
AG. Annual goal.
AGA. Appropriate for gestational age.
AHA. American Hospital Association.
AIT. Auditory integration training.
ALJ. Administrative law judge.
AMA. American Medical Association.
AMI. Alliance for the Mentally Ill.
APA. American Psychological Association; American Psychiatric Association.
APD. Auditory processing disorder.
APE. Adaptive physical education.
APWA. American Public Welfare Association.
ARC. Association for Retarded Citizens.
ARD. Admission, review, and dismissal process.
AS. Asperger's syndrome.
ASA. Autism Society of America.
ASL. American Sign Language.
AT. Assistive technology.
AU. Autistic.

BD. Behavior disorder.
BIA. Bureau of Indian Affairs.
BIP. Behavioral intervention plan.
BL. Blind.
BP. Bi-polar.
BVI. Blind and visually impaired.

CA. Chronological age.
CAPD. Central auditory processing disorder.
CARF. Commission on the Accreditation of Rehabilitation Facilities.
CASA. Court-appointed special advocate.
CD. Conduct disorder.
CDB. Childhood disability benefit.
CDC. Centers for Disease Control and Prevention.
CDF. Children's Defense Fund.
CEC. Council for Exceptional Children.
CFR. Code of Federal Regulations.
CHADD. Children with Attention Deficit Disorder.
CHINS. Child in need of supervision.

CHIPS. Child in need of protection or services.
CMS. Children's medical services.
CNS. Central nervous system.
COBRA. Consolidated Omnibus Budget Reconciliation Act.
COHI. Crippled and other health impaired.
CPS. Child Protective Services.
CRS. Children's rehabilitative services.
CSHN. Children with special health needs.
CSN. Children with special needs.
CWLA. Child Welfare League of America.

D&E. Diagnosis and evaluation.
DB. Deaf/blind (also abbreviated D/BL).
DCP. Disabled Children's Program.
DD. Developmental disabilities.
DE. Department of Education.
DEC. Developmental evaluation clinic.
DF. Deaf.
DH. Developmentally handicapped.
D/HH. Deaf/hard of hearing.
DHHS. Department of Health and Human Services.
DHR. Department of Human Resources.
DIS. Designated instructional services.
DMH. Department of Mental Health.
DMR. Department of Mental Retardation.
DoDDS. Department of Defense Dependent Schools.
DOE. Department of Education.
DSA. Down Syndrome Association.
DSM–IV–TR. *Diagnostic and Statistical Manual of Mental Disorders (Fourth Edition)–Text Revision.*
DVR. Department of Vocational Rehabilitation.
Dx. Diagnosis.

ECI. Early childhood initiative.
ECSE. Early childhood special education.
ED. Department of Education; emotionally disturbed.
EDGAR. Education Department General Administrative Regulations.
EFA. Epilepsy Foundation of America.
EH. Emotionally handicapped.
EHA. Education for the Handicapped Act.
EI. Early intervention.
ELL. English language learner.
EMH. Educable mentally handicapped.
EPSDT. Medicaid Early Periodic Screening, Diagnosis and Treatment Program.
ERIC. Educational Resources Information Center.
ESA. Educational service agency.
ESEA. Elementary and Secondary Education Act.
ESL. English as a second language.
ESOL. English as a second or other language.
ESY. Extended school year.

FAE. Fetal alcohol effects.
FAPE. Free appropriate public education.
FAS. Fetal alcohol syndrome.

FBA. Functional behavioral assessment.
FC. Facilitated communication.
FEOG. Full educational opportunity goal.
FERPA. Family Educational Rights and Privacy Act (also known as the Buckley Amendment).
FMLA. Family Medical Leave Act.
FOIA. Freedom of Information Act.
FPCO. Family Policy Compliance Office.
FR. Federal Register.
FSA. Family Support Act.
FTE. Full-time equivalent.
FTT. Failure to thrive.

GAL. Guardian ad litem.
GE. Grade equivalent.
GED. General Educational Development Diploma.
GEPA. General Education Provisions Act.
GT. Gifted/talented.

HB. House bill.
HCFA. Health Care Financing Administration.
HCY. Healthy Children and Youth Program.
HFA. High functioning autism.
HH. Hearing handicapped.
HHS. Department of Health and Human Services.
HI. Hearing impaired.
HMO. Health Maintenance Organization.
HO. Hearing officer.
HOH. Hard of hearing.
HRO. Hearing review officer.
HT. Home teaching.

I&R. Information and referral.
IAES. Interim alternative educational setting.
IASA. Improving America's Schools Act.
ICF/MR. Intermediate care facility for the mentally retarded.
ICRC. Infant care review committee.
ICWA. Indian Child Welfare Act.
IDEA. Individuals with Disabilities Education Act.
IDEIA. Individuals with Disabilities Education Improvement Act.
IDELR. Individuals with Disabilities Education Law Reporter.
IDT. Interdisciplinary team.
IEE. Independent educational evaluation.
IEP. Individualized Education Program.
IEU. Intermediate educational unit.
IFSP. Individualized Family Service Plan.
ILC. Independent Living Center.
IRC. Instructional Resource Center.
ISP. Individualized service plan.
ITP. Individualized treatment plan; individual transition plan.
IWEN. Individual with exceptional needs.

LAS. Language and speech program.
LBW. Low birthweight.
LD. Learning disability.
LDA. Learning Disabilities Association.
LEA. Local educational agency.
LEP. Limited English proficiency.
LFA. Low-functioning autism.
LLD. Language-based learning disability.

LoF. Letter of Finding issued by the Office for Civil Rights.
LRE. Least restrictive environment.

MA. Mental age.
MBD. Minimum brain dysfunction.
MCH. Maternal and child health.
M-D. Manic depression.
MDD. Major depressive disorder.
MDE. Multidisciplinary evaluation.
MDT. Multidisciplinary team.
MH. Multiple handicapped.
MHA. Mental Health Association.
MHLP. Mental Health Law Project.
MI. Mentally ill.
MPD. Multiple personality disorder.
MR. Mental retardation.
MR/DD. Mental retardation and developmental disabilities.
MRRC. Mental Retardation Research Center.

NAMI. National Association for the Mentally Ill.
NASDSE. National Association of State Directors of Special Education.
NASP. National Association of School Psychologists.
NBD. Neurobiological disorders.
NCCA. National Center for Child Advocacy.
NCCAN. National Center on Child Abuse and Neglect.
NCES. National Center for Education Statistics.
NCLB. No Child Left Behind Act of 2001.
NCLD. National Center for Learning Disabilities.
NH. Nonhandicapped.
NIC. National Information Clearinghouse for Infants with Disabilities and Life-Threatening Conditions.
NICHCY. National Information Center for Children and Youth with Disabilities.
NIH. National Institutes of Health.
NLD. Nonverbal learning disability.
NOS. Not otherwise specified.
NPND. National Parent Network on Disability.
NPRM. Notice of proposed rulemaking.
NVLD. Nonverbal learning disability.

OCD. Obsessive-compulsive disorder.
OCR. Office of Civil Rights.
ODD. Oppositional-defiant disorder.
OH. Orthopedically handicapped.
OHDS. Office of Human Development Services.
OHI. Other health impairment.
OMB. Office of Management and Budget.
OMRDD. Office of Mental Retardation and Developmental Disabilities.
ORT-OHI. Orthopedically handicapped and other health impaired.
OSC. Order to show cause.
OSEP. Office of Special Education Programs.
OSERS. Office of Special Education and Rehabilitative Services.
OT. Occupational therapist.

P&A. Protection and advocacy.
PASS. Plan for achieving self-support.
PBIS. Positive behavioral interventions and supports.
PCA. Personal care assistant.

PDD. Pervasive developmental disorder.
PDDNOS. Pervasive developmental disorder not otherwise specified.
PE. Physical education.
PH. Physically handicapped.
PI. Physically impaired.
PINS. Person in need of supervision.
PL. Public law.
PLAAFP. Present levels of academic achievement and functional performance.
PLEP. Present levels of educational performance.
PLOP. Present levels of performance.
PMH. Profoundly mentally handicapped.
PMR. Profoundly mentally retarded.
POHI. Physically or otherwise health impaired.
PPRA. Protection of Pupil Rights Amendment.
PS. Partially sighted.
PSM. Problem solving model.
PT. Physical therapy.
PTA. Posttraumatic amnesia.
PTI. Parent Training and Information center.
PTSD. Posttraumatic stress disorder.

REI. Regular education initiative.
RRC. Regional resource center.
RSP. Resource specialist program.
RSPT. Resource specialist program teacher.
RST. Resource specialist teacher.
RT. Recreational therapy.
RTI. Response to intervention.

SB. Senate bill.
SCAN. Suspected child abuse and neglect.
SDC. Special day class.
SDD. Severe developmental disabilities.
SEA. State educational agency.
Sec (§). Section.
SED. Seriously emotionally disturbed.
SGA. Small for gestational age.
SH. Severely handicapped.
SIB. Self-injurious behavior.

SID. Sensory integration dysfunction.
SLD. Specific learning disability.
SLP. Speech-language pathologist.
SNF. Skilled nursing facility.
SP. Speech impaired.
SPED. Special education.
SPEDLAW. Special Education Law.
SQ. Social quotient.
SSA. Social Security Administration.
SSDI. Social Security Disability Income.
SSI. Supplemental Security Income.
STD. Sexually transmitted disease.
SWD. Students with disabilities.

TA. Technical assistance.
TANF. Temporary Aid to Needy Families Law.
TAPP. Technical Assistance to Parents Program.
TASH. The Association for Persons with Severe Handicaps.
TBI. Traumatic brain injury.
TDD. Telecommunication device for the deaf.
TEACCH. Treatment and Education of Autistic and related Communication-handicapped Children.
TMH. Trainable mentally handicapped.
TMR. Trainable mentally retarded.
TPR. Termination of parental rights.
TRO. Temporary restraining order.
TT. Text telephone.
TTD. Teletypewriting device.
TTY. Teletypewriter.

UCPA. United Cerebral Palsy Association.
USC. United States Code.

VH. Visually handicapped.
VI. Visually impaired.
VLBW. Very low birthweight.
VR. Vocational rehabilitation.

WIC. Women, Infants, and Children Program.
WPN. Written prior notice.

Abandonment. The failure or refusal of a parent, caregiver, or legal guardian to support his or her child physically, emotionally, or financially. An abandoned child is one who is left without provision for reasonable and necessary care or supervision or whose parent has failed to maintain a reasonable degree of interest, concern, or responsibility for his or her welfare.

Accessory. A person who contributes to or aids in the commission of a crime, either before or after it is committed.

Accomplice. A person who knowingly assists the primary perpetrator in a crime.

Acquittal. The finding in a criminal case that a defendant is not guilty of the crime with which he or she has been charged.

Action. A lawsuit brought by one or more individuals seeking redress for or prevention of a wrong or protection of a right.

Adjudicated father. A male determined by the court to be a child's father, usually through a court action and genetic testing. See also *Paternity.*

Adjudication. A decision made by a court or administrative agency with respect to a case.

Adjudication hearing. A trial in juvenile court to determine whether allegations are true and whether they indicate a need for the court to intervene.

Admissible evidence. Evidence determined by a court to satisfy rules and laws about what a judge or jury may take into consideration.

Admission. A voluntary statement that something is true.

Admonition. Advice, instruction, or caution by a judge to jury members about what is and is not admissible, about their duties or conduct, or about alternative verdicts; a warning by a judge to a defendant or convicted felon of the consequences of future misconduct; a caution or reprimand of an attorney by a judge.

Adversarial system. A trial process whereby a judge or jury listens to the plaintiff and the defendant (or their attorneys) argue their cases and then decides which side has proven its claim.

Adversary parties. Individuals or groups in litigation whose interests are opposed to each other.

Adverse witness. A witness for the opposing party.

Advocate. An individual who is not an attorney but who assists individuals in their dealings with other entities—for example, helping parents negotiate with the school district regarding a child's special education program.

Affidavit. A written statement of facts that is formally confirmed by oath or by affirmation.

Affirm. To confirm a judgment. In affirming, an appellate court says that the decision of the trial court is correct.

Aggravating circumstance. A factor that tends to increase the sentence given a defendant.

ALI rule. A rule, proposed by the American Law Institute Model Penal Code and widely adopted in the United States, stating that a person is not responsible for criminal conduct if, at the time of the crime, as a result of mental disease or defect, the person lacked substantial capacity to appreciate the criminality (wrongfulness) of the act or to conform his or her conduct to the requirements of the law.

Allegation. A charge or complaint that is to be judged true or false at a hearing or trial.

Amicus curiae. "Friend of the court"; a person or organization that has an interest in a lawsuit and is granted permission to appear in court, file briefs, and present oral arguments, even though this person or organization is not party to the action.

Answer. The defendant's response to a plaintiff's allegations.

Appeal. A procedure in which a party seeks to reverse or modify a judgment or final order of a lower court or administrative agency, usually on the grounds that the lower court misinterpreted or misapplied the law, rather than on the grounds that it made an incorrect finding of fact.

Appeals court. A court that hears an appeal after a trial court has made a judgment.

Appellant. The party who initiates an appeal to a higher court.

Appellee. The party in a lawsuit against whom an appeal is made.

Appointed counsel. An attorney appointed by a court to render legal assistance to a person unable, for any of various reasons, to obtain counsel.

Arraignment. The process of bringing persons accused of crimes before a court to be advised of the charges against them and of their rights and, in certain cases, to give them an opportunity to state their answers to the charges (to plead guilty or not guilty); also known as *first appearance* or *initial appearance.*

Arrest. The process of taking a person into custody. Peace officers must have probable cause to arrest individuals.

Attorney-client privilege. A legal doctrine that permits a person to refuse to disclose, and to prevent others from disclosing, communications between the person and his or her attorney (or the attorney's agent) that are made during the course of their professional relationship.

Bail. The security, usually money, given to the court in exchange for the release of an arrested person. Designed to ensure that the person will appear in court on a specified date, bail is generally provided by a bail bondsperson, who thereby becomes responsible for the released person's return.

Bailiff. A court official who keeps order in a courtroom.

Bench trial. A trial with no jury, in which the judge renders the final verdict.

Beyond a reasonable doubt. See *Proof beyond a reasonable doubt.*

Bifurcated. Divided into two parts or sections. A hearing held in two parts, with separate issues decided at each hearing, is called a bifurcated hearing.

Bind over. To find that there is the probable cause needed to initiate grand jury or trial proceedings.

Brief. A written argument filed in court by an attorney.

Burden of proof. The standard a party has to meet to demonstrate to the court that the weight of the evidence in a legal action favors his or her side, position, or argument. See *Clear and convincing evidence, Preponderance of evidence, Proof beyond a reasonable doubt.*

Case law. Law established by previous cases decided by courts rather than by statute.

Cert. denied. The expression used by a superior court—usually the United States Supreme Court—to indicate that the court has declined to review a lower court's decision.

Certiorari. A discretionary writ giving a superior court the right to review the decision of a lower court.

Child in need of supervision (CHINS). A juvenile who has committed a delinquent act and has been found by a children's court judge to require further court supervision, often through probation or transfer of custody to a relative or public or private welfare agency for a period usually not to exceed one year; known as *person in need of supervision (PINS)* or *minor in need of supervision (MINS)* in some states.

Child neglect. See *Neglect.*

Child Protective Services (CPS). Public social services agency designated, in most states, to receive and investigate reports of child maltreatment and to provide rehabilitation services to children and families experiencing child maltreatment problems.

Circuit Court of Appeals. The intermediate appeals court in the federal system.

Circumstantial evidence. Fact from which a conclusion can reasonably be inferred. For example, a parent's possession of a broken appliance cord may be circumstantial evidence connecting the parent to the infliction of wounds on a child's body.

Civil action. See *Civil proceeding.*

Civil complaint. A legal document submitted to the court by the plaintiffs, in which they inform the court and the defendants that they are bringing a lawsuit and set out the reasons they are suing and the relief they want.

Civil proceeding. Any legal action other than a criminal prosecution; also known as *civil action.* Parties bringing a civil proceeding need not meet the standard of providing proof beyond a reasonable doubt, as is required in criminal proceedings; the standard is a preponderance of evidence. Juvenile and family court cases are considered civil proceedings.

Civil rights. Rights guaranteed to all citizens by the U.S. Constitution and relevant acts of Congress.

Class action. A lawsuit filed by one or a few people on behalf of a larger number of persons with a grievance against the same party.

Clear and convincing evidence. Evidence sufficient to persuade a judge or jury that the allegations against a defendant are very likely true. This is the intermediate burden of proof—more than a preponderance of evidence, but less than proof beyond a reasonable doubt.

Closing argument. An attorney's final statement to the court, summing up the case and the points proven, as well as those points not proven by opposing counsel; also known as a *final argument.*

Commission, act of. Willful or volitional act.

Commitment. In juvenile law, a court order placing a delinquent, neglected, dependent, or uncared-for child in a mental health facility or correctional facility.

Common law. Body of law based on judicial decision, precedents, customs, and usages.

Commutation. A reduction in punishment—as, for example, from a death sentence to life imprisonment.

Compensatory damages. Remuneration awarded to a party to compensate for an actual loss suffered, such as medical expenses.

Competency. The capacity to perform a given function with a degree of rationality, the requisite degree depending on the function to be performed.

Complainant. The party who initiates the complaint in an action; also known as the *plaintiff* or the *petitioner.*

Conciliation court. A civil court, found in many states, that helps resolve marital disputes and provides counseling services for couples considering divorce.

Confession. An admission of guilt by a person who committed a criminal act.

Confidential communication. A statement made under circumstances indicating that the speaker intended the statement only for the person addressed. If a communication is made in the presence of a third party whose presence is not reasonably necessary for the communication, it is not confidential. See also *Privileged communication.*

Confidentiality. Ethical obligation of a professional not to reveal, without specific consent, information obtained through professional contact with a client. It protects the client from unauthorized disclosure of information given in confidence to a professional. Confidentiality must be broken when the client threatens another person, talks about abusing children or about having been abused, or says he or she wants to harm himself or herself. See also *Tarasoff v. Regents of University of California.*

Consent decree. An agreement reached out of court by the parties to a lawsuit and then formally approved by the court.

Contempt. An act calculated to inhibit, hinder, or affront the court in the administration of justice; obstruction of the court's work. Disobedience of a judge's order is one type of contempt.

Continuance. A court order that postpones legal action, such as a court hearing, until a later time.

Contract action. A lawsuit based on the breach of an oral or written contract.

Court-appointed special advocate (CASA). An individual (usually a volunteer) whose responsibility is to ensure that the needs and best interests of a child are fully protected in judicial proceedings. See also *Guardian ad litem.*

Court diversion. An order by the court that a youth who has come before the court must make restitution, engage in community service, or complete a designated court-sponsored or -approved program.

Credibility. The degree to which a person appears to be worthy of belief; a quality of witnesses that makes their testimony believable.

Criminal complaint. A legal document that initiates a criminal proceeding; a written statement by the investigating officer(s) outlining the facts in a particular criminal violation and charging a suspect with the crime.

Cross examination. Questioning of an opposing party's witness who has already been questioned through direct examination by that party's attorney.

Custodial confinement. Placement in a secure facility, ordered by a court for the rehabilitation of a juvenile delinquent.

Custodial parent. Parent who has the physical control, care, and custody of a minor child.

Custody. The right to care for and control a child; the duty to provide food, clothing, shelter, ordinary medical care, education, and discipline for a child.

Custody evaluation. An investigative procedure in which facts about a family are gathered and analyzed for the purpose of making a recommendation to the court regarding child custody and/or visitation. A custody evaluation may be initiated by order of the court or by stipulation of the parties involved, pursuant to local court rules.

Custody hearing. A legal process, usually in family or juvenile court, to determine who will be awarded legal or physical custody of a minor. A custody hearing may involve one parent against the other, a parent against a third party, or a parent against a social services agency seeking protective custody in juvenile court.

Damages. Monetary compensation awarded by a court in a civil action to an individual who has been injured through the wrongful conduct of another party.

Daubert v. Merrell Dow Pharmaceuticals (509 U.S. 579, 1993). A case in which the U.S. Supreme Court set a two-pronged test for the admissibility of expert witnesses' testimony during legal proceedings: Federal trial judges must evaluate expert witnesses to determine whether their testimony is both *relevant* and *reliable.*

Declaration of parentage. A judicial decision stating who the parents of a child are.

Declaratory judgment. A statement in which a judge establishes the involved parties' rights or expresses an opinion on a legal question without ordering that anything be done.

De facto. "In fact"; a phrase used to describe a past action or a state of affairs that must be accepted for all practical purposes but is not necessarily legal or legitimate.

Default. Failure to meet a deadline or put in an appearance, causing a defendant to lose the legal right to challenge.

Defendant. A person against whom civil or criminal action is brought.

De jure. "In law"; a phrase used in contrast to *de facto.*

De minimus. "Insignificant"; a phrase used to designate a matter not sufficiently important to be dealt with judicially.

Dependency/neglect petition. A request on the part of Child Protective Services, filed by the county or district attorney, to remove a child from an allegedly abusive home for a period longer than the initial 48-hour emergency period.

Dependent child. A child who is homeless, destitute, or without proper care or support through no fault of his or her parent, guardian, or custodian; who lacks proper care or support because of the mental or physical condition of his or her parent, guardian, or custodian; or whose condition or environment warrants the state to assume guardianship in the child's interest.

Deposition. The questioning of a party or witness, under oath, outside of the courtroom by an attorney; also, the answers given in response to the questions. A deposition is usually taken in the office of an attorney representing one of the litigants.

Detention center. A place where a juvenile is held in custody while awaiting an adjudication hearing, disposition, or commitment placement. Placement in a detention center may also be used as "timeout" in domestic violence cases and for post-adjudicatory punishment.

Detention hearing. In juvenile court, the bail hearing.

Direct evidence. Information offered by witnesses who testify about their own knowledge of the facts.

Direct examination. Initial courtroom questioning of a witness testifying on behalf of the party who called the witness to the stand. This questioning is usually done by the attorney of the party who called the witness.

Discovery. Pretrial procedures that enable the parties involved in a court proceeding to find out about the evidence supporting the positions taken by the other parties, including facts that those parties believe support their positions.

Discretionary filing to try a minor as an adult. A request, filed by a state, to criminally prosecute a juvenile of 14 years of age or older in adult court for a serious, violent, or chronic offense.

Dismissal. An order by a judge dismissing a case. Cases can be dismissed with or without prejudice. Cases dismissed with prejudice cannot be filed again. Cases dismissed without prejudice can be filed again if certain circumstances change—for example, if additional evidence is obtained.

Disposition. The court's final determination of the outcome of a lawsuit or criminal charge. In child protection matters, the disposition is the order of a court, issued at a hearing, stating whether a minor already found to be delinquent or in need of protection or services should remain in or return to the parental home, be under a particular type of supervision, or be placed out of home (and, if so, in what kind of setting).

Divided custody. See *Joint custody.*

Due process of law. A person's right to be treated with fairness in legal proceedings. This right includes the right to adequate advance notice of a hearing, the right to notice of allegations of misconduct, the right to the assistance of an attorney, the right to confront and cross examine witnesses, and the right to refuse to give self-incriminating testimony. In public education, due process of law encompasses the educational rights of students under relevant local, state, and federal law.

Durham rule. A principle of criminal law stating that, in order for an insanity defense to be valid, the accused person must have been suffering from a defective mental condition at the time of the alleged offense and the alleged offense must have been caused by the defective mental condition. See also *Irresistible impulse rule* and *M'Naghton rule.*

Educational neglect. Failing to provide for a child's educational needs by not enrolling the child in school or tolerating truancy.

Emancipated minor. A minor who, as a result of exhibiting adequate control over his or her life, is found by a court to no longer require the care or custody of his or her parents or guardians and is thus accorded the rights of an adult.

Emancipation. An action by a court that grants independence to a minor who has not yet reached the age of majority defined by that state (usually 16 or 18 years). Several states do not grant emancipation.

Emergency custody. See *Protective custody.*

Emergency hearing. In juvenile and family court, a hearing held to determine the need for emergency protection of a child who may have been a victim of maltreatment.

Emotional abuse. A form of child maltreatment in which parents or other persons repeatedly convey to the child that he or she is worthless, unwanted, or of value only in meeting another's needs; also known as *emotional/psychological maltreatment* or *psychological abuse.* The abuse may include serious threats of physical or psychological violence.

Emotional neglect. See *Neglect.*

Enjoin. To issue a court order commanding a person to perform or abstain from performing a specified act.

Equal protection of the law. The constitutional guarantee that no person or class of persons shall be denied the legal protection that is enjoyed by other persons or other classes in like circumstances.

Evidence. Any sort of proof submitted to a court in support of an allegation or argument. See also *Circumstantial evidence, Direct evidence, Hearsay, Physical evidence.*

Evidentiary standards. Guidelines used to determine whether evidence was legally collected, whether it is factual, and whether it legally proves or is relevant to the case being heard. See also *Clear and convincing evidence, Preponderance of evidence, Proof beyond a reasonable doubt.*

Exculpatory. Clearing or tending to clear someone of guilt; excusing.

Exhibit. An item, produced during a trial or hearing, that is related to the case before the court and that, upon acceptance by the court, is marked for identification and made a part of the case.

Ex parte. "Involving only one party." An *ex parte* judicial proceeding is one brought by one party, without notice to or opportunity for challenge by the opposing party, in order to protect rights that could not otherwise be adequately protected. The judge's decision in such a proceeding will usually be subject to review at a subsequent proceeding, in which the opposing party will have the opportunity to participate.

Expert witness. An individual who, by reason of education or specialized experience, possesses extensive knowledge of a subject and is therefore determined by a court to be qualified to give an opinion in that subject area. Expert witnesses assist the jury in understanding complicated and technical subjects not within the realm of the average lay person.

Expunge. To delete from a court record. Expungement may be ordered by the court after a specified number of years or when a juvenile, parent, or defendant applies for expungement and shows that his or her conduct has improved. Expungement may also apply to removal of an unverified report of abuse or neglect that has been made to a central registry.

Ex rel. "On behalf of"; a term used in the title of a case when one party is bringing an action on behalf of another party.

Family court. A civil court, found in some states, that combines the functions of domestic relations, juvenile, and probate courts.

Family law. Field of law involving family issues, such as divorce, paternity, guardianship, dependency, adoption, and domestic violence.

Family preservation/reunification. The philosophical principle, established in law and policy and followed by social service agencies, that children should remain in their own families if their safety can be ensured.

Felony. A serious crime for which the punishment may be lengthy imprisonment and/or a significant fine.

Fifth Amendment to the U.S. Constitution. Amendment providing that no person will be compelled to present self-incriminating testimony, required to answer for crimes without an indictment or grand jury decision, tried twice for the same crime, or deprived of life, liberty, or property without due process of law.

Final argument. See *Closing argument.*

Finding. Determination of fact by a court, based on the evidence presented.

Forensic. Relating to courts of law. Forensic psychology refers to psychological methods or knowledge applied to resolve legal disputes. A forensic evaluation is a medical or psychological evaluation that interprets or establishes the facts in a civil or criminal case.

Forensic interview. An interview used to gather information from a possible victim, defendant, witness, or offender for the purpose of informing the court.

Frye standard. A standard regarding the admissibility of procedures, principles, or techniques presented by expert witnesses during legal proceedings, set in *Frye v. United States* (293 F. 1013 DC Cir 1923) by the District of Columbia Circuit Court: Trial judges must decide whether the evidence presented to the court is "generally accepted" by a meaningful segment of the relevant scientific community.

Gault decision. The ruling by the U.S. Supreme Court in *In re Gault* (387 U.S. 1, 1967) that juveniles are entitled to the same due process rights as adults.

Guardian ad litem (GAL). "Guardian at law"; an attorney, mental health professional, or (in some states) lay person, appointed by the court, who represents a child's best interests in juvenile or family court. In a civil legal proceeding, this person may perform a variety of roles on behalf of the child who is legally incapable of doing so on his or her own, including acting as an independent investigator, advocate, advisor, and guardian for the child. See also *Court-appointed special advocate.*

Guardianship. Legal responsibility of a person to provide for the protection, care, and management of a person considered unable to take care of his or her own affairs.

Habeas corpus. "[We command that] you have the body." A writ of habeus corpus requires that a person be brought before a court or a judge. It usually alleges that the person is illegally imprisoned.

Hearing. A judicial or legal examination of issues of law and fact disputed between parties; a formal proceeding at which evidence is taken for the purpose of determining an issue of fact and reaching a decision on the basis of that evidence.

Hearsay. Statements by someone who is not in court and therefore not subject to cross examination; second-hand evidence. Such evidence is usually excluded because it is considered unreliable and because the person making the original statement cannot be cross examined.

Hostile witness. A witness who is subject to cross examination by the party who called him or her because he or she antagonized that party during direct examination.

Hypothetical question. A question based on assumed facts, often asked of an expert witness to elicit an opinion.

Immunity from prosecution. Exemption from legal prosecution provided to certain individuals or categories of individuals. For example, a person who reports child abuse or neglect is immune from civil lawsuits and criminal prosecution as long as the report is made in good faith.

Impeachment. Calling into question a witness's truthfulness or credibility.

In camera. "In chambers"; taking place in a judge's chambers or another location where the public is not allowed to be present.

Incest. Sexual relations between persons who are closely related by blood and who are forbidden by law to marry. The most common form of incest is between fathers and daughters.

Indeterminate sentence. A prison term, imposed on a defendant convicted of a crime, that is stated in terms of a range of time, such as "5 to 10 years," rather than a specific period of time or a release date.

Indictment. A report of a grand jury charging an adult with criminal conduct. The process of indictment by a grand jury bypasses the filing of a criminal complaint and the holding of a preliminary hearing, so prosecution begins immediately.

Informed consent. Consent to a treatment that is based on adequate knowledge about the risks and benefits of the treatment, is voluntary, and is given while the individual is competent to make a decision.

Infra. "Later."

Injunction. A court order to act or abstain from a specific act.

Injunctive relief. A court-ordered remedy forbidding or requiring some action by the defendant.

In loco parentis. "In the place of a parent." A guardian or other nonparental custodian or authority acts *in loco parentis.*

In re. "In the matter of"; a term often used in the title of a court case.

Intake hearing. In juvenile court, a preliminary hearing to determine the appropriate disposition of a case in which a child is charged with a status offense (an action that is an offense only when performed by a minor). Dispositions range from diversion from the juvenile court system to adjudication (trial).

Inter alia. "Among other things"; a term used to make clear that an issue is only one of several involved.

Interlocutory. Temporary; provisional; not final.

Interrogation. An emphatic investigative interview, often with the goal of obtaining a confession from a person believed to have committed a crime.

Interrogatories. Written questions in a civil action that must be responded to with a truthful answer or with an explanation of why they cannot be answered.

Interstate compact re children. Agreement among a number of states governing interstate placement of children, defining state financial and supervisory responsibilities, and guaranteeing certain constitutional protections for children.

Investigation. A process of close examination or systematic inquiry.

Investigative interview. In child maltreatment, an interview designed to obtain information about possible maltreatment. It is perhaps the most stringent type of interview with a child and may play an important role in the criminal indictment of another individual.

Involuntary client. A person who has been referred for services, often through court order, but who has not asked for help.

Involuntary placement. Court-ordered assignment of custody to an agency for placement of a child, often against the parents' wishes, after a formal court proceeding; the taking of emergency or protective custody of a child, against the parents' wishes, preceding a custody hearing.

Irreparable harm. Any damage or wrong, resulting from a violation of a legal right, for which monetary damages would be inadequate compensation. The threat of irreparable harm may require some form of intervention, such as an injunction.

Irresistible impulse rule. A legal standard for insanity in some states, stating that even if a person knew that the act he or she was committing was wrong, the person cannot be held criminally responsible if he or she was driven by an irresistible impulse to perform the act or had a diminished capacity to resist performing the act.

Joint custody. A custodial arrangement in which both parents share the rights and responsibilities to make decisions regarding the health, education, and welfare of a child. See also *Joint physical custody.*

Joint physical custody. A custodial arrangement in which a child spends significant periods of time with each parent.

Judgment. An order by a court after a verdict has been reached; a judicial decision.

Jurisdiction. The realm in which a particular court has the power and authority to hear and determine cases, usually defined in terms of certain categories of persons or allegations.

Jury. A group of adult citizens who serve as fact finders, judging the truth of allegations made in a legal proceeding.

Juvenile. In a majority of states, a youth under the age of 18 years; a minor.

Juvenile court. A court with jurisdiction over minors. A juvenile court usually handles cases involving suspected delinquency, suspected child maltreatment, and termination of parental rights.

Juvenile court judge. The presiding officer in a juvenile court.

Juvenile delinquent. A minor who has been determined by a court to have violated a federal, state, or local criminal law.

Leading case. Precedent often cited as an authoritative or controlling guide in subsequent cases.

Leading question. A question that leads a witness toward a conclusion that supports the argument of the attorney asking the question. Leading questions are usually prohibited during direct examination.

Least restrictive alternative. The concept that, when the government is authorized to infringe on individual liberty, it must do so in the least drastic manner possible.

Litigation. The process that follows the filing of a lawsuit in court. Litigation includes such proceedings as the review of evidence, hearings before a judge, and the trial itself.

Malfeasance. Commission of an act in violation of legal duty. For example, a mental health professional who breaches confidentiality commits an act of malfeasance. See also *Nonfeasance.*

Malingering. Conscious fabrication or gross exaggeration of physical or psychological symptoms in pursuit of a recognizable goal.

Mandamus. "We command." A writ of mandamus is an order from a superior court to a lower court or other body commanding that a specified act be done.

Mandated reporters. In child maltreatment, persons legally required to report suspected cases of child maltreatment to the mandated agency. Mandated reporters are usually professionals (such as physicians, nurses, school personnel, social workers, psychologists, and clergy) or their delegates who have frequent contact with children and families.

Material. A legal term meaning relevant.

Mediation. A voluntary dispute resolution process involving intermediaries.

Minor in need of supervision (MINS). See *Child in need of supervision.*

Miranda warning. Warning given by police to advise suspects of their rights: "You have the right to remain silent. Anything you say may be used as evidence against you. You have the right to consult with an attorney and to have an attorney present during questioning. If you cannot afford an attorney, one will be appointed for you prior to any questioning, if you desire." A suspect's statement or confession is usually inadmissible as evidence in court proceedings if the suspect was not informed of these rights before the confession was made. The name "Miranda" comes from the U.S. Supreme Court case of *Miranda* *v. Arizona* (384 U.S. 436), in which the Court established the four-part warning.

Misdemeanor. A relatively minor offense punishable by a small fine or a short jail sentence.

Mistrial. A trial that is declared invalid, usually because of procedural errors.

Mitigating circumstance. A factor that tends to reduce the severity of the sentence given a defendant.

M'Naghton rule. The legal standard for insanity in many states, stating that someone who is guilty of committing a crime cannot be held criminally responsible if, at the time the crime is committed, he or she suffered from a disease of the mind that prevented him or her from knowing right from wrong.

Modification. Changing of a prior order of a court.

Motion. An application made to a court for an order or ruling.

Multidisciplinary team. A group of individuals from various disciplines who work together at all levels; also known as a *transdisciplinary team.*

Negligence. Failure to use the degree of care and skill that a prudent person would use in the same circumstances.

Neglect. Failure of a parent or caregiver to provide for a child's basic needs and a proper level of care with respect to food, shelter, hygiene, medical attention, and/or supervision. *Emotional neglect* refers to passive or passive-aggressive inattention to a child's emotional needs, nurturing, and/or emotional well-being. *Physical neglect* refers to failure to provide for a child's basic survival needs, such as food, clothing, shelter, and/or supervision, such that the child's health or safety is threatened.

Nolo contendre. "I will not contest it." A plea of *nolo contendre* in a criminal action has the same legal effect as a plea of guilty relative to the proceeding at hand. However, a *nolo* plea cannot be used against the defendant in a later civil suit regarding the same issues.

Nonfeasance. Failure to complete an act that is part of a legal duty. A mental health professional who fails to act to protect a third party from imminent danger from a patient may be guilty of nonfeasance in some states.

Nonoffending parent. A parent of an abused child who is not involved in the abusive act.

Objection. Contention by a party to a court proceeding that a question asked by the opposing attorney is improper.

Objection overruled. The expression used by a judge to signify that an objection is without legal basis.

Objection sustained. The expression used by a judge to indicate that an objection was appropriate and that the judge has ruled in favor of the party making the objection.

Omission, act of. In child maltreatment, failure of a parent or caregiver to provide for a child's physical and/or emotional well-being, due to unwillingness or inability.

Omnibus hearing. A hearing held in criminal court to resolve certain issues before trial (such as whether evidence is admissible) so as to ensure a fair and expeditious trial and avoid a multiplicity of court appearances.

Opening statement. An argument made by an attorney at the start of a trial or at the beginning of his or her presentation in court, summarizing what he or she plans to prove and the evidence to be presented.

Opinion. A formal written decision by a judge or court, containing the legal principles and rationale behind the ruling.

Order to show cause (OSC). An order to appear in court and present reasons why a particular action should not be taken. If the party receiving the order fails to appear or to give sufficient reasons why the court should desist, the court will take the action in question.

Out-of-home care. Child care, foster care, or residential care provided to children who are separated from their families, usually under the jurisdiction of juvenile or family court.

Parens patriae. "Parent of the country." A state's authority to act on behalf of persons who cannot act in their own interests, such as minors, persons who are incompetent as a result of mental illness, and some developmentally disabled persons.

Party. Any person involved in a lawsuit—the person who filed the suit or the person against whom the suit was filed.

Paternity. Being the father of a child. The law presumes that a man is a child's father under specified circumstances. See also *Adjudicated father.*

Pedophile. An adult who prefers to obtain sexual gratification through contact with children.

Pedophilia. Sexual behavior by an adult directed toward a prepubescent child.

Peremptory challenge. The right of an attorney, during jury selection, to remove a prospective juror from consideration without stating a valid reason. Each side can exercise a limited number of peremptory challenges.

Perjury. Lying under oath. Being convicted of perjury, which is a felony, can deprive a citizen of the right to vote, hold office, and hold a professional license.

Petition. A formal written application to a court for judicial action on a matter, stating allegations that, if true, form the basis for court intervention.

Petitioner. See *Complainant.*

Physical abuse. Physical harm inflicted on a child intentionally by his or her parents or caregiver.

Physical custody. A person's right to have a child reside with him or her and to make the day-to-day decisions regarding the child's care.

Physical evidence. Any tangible piece of proof, such as a document, an x-ray, a photograph, or a weapon used to inflict an injury. See also *Exhibit.*

Physical indicators of child maltreatment. Broken bones, burns, rashes, bites, and other signs suggestive of physical injuries or neglect.

Physical neglect. See *Neglect.*

Plaintiff. The party bringing a lawsuit.

Plea bargaining. In criminal cases, negotiation between a prosecutor (on behalf of the state) and a defendant of a mutually agreed-on disposition of the case, which is then submitted to the court for approval.

Pleadings. Statements, in logical and legal form, of each side of a case.

Precedent. Prior court decisions invoked in analyzing similar legal problems subsequently.

Preponderance of evidence. Evidence sufficient to persuade a judge or jury that it is more likely true than not true that the facts necessary to prove the plaintiff's case are as alleged by the plaintiff. This is the level of proof required to prevail in most civil cases.

Presentence investigation report. A document that details the subject's prior legal entanglements and other relevant factors and recommends a particular disposition or sentence. Such a report is prepared by a probation officer for the court's consideration at the time of disposition or sentencing in a case.

Presumption. An assumption of fact based on another fact or group of facts. A presumption is either conclusive (not subject to opposition) or rebuttable (capable of being rebutted by presentation of contrary proof).

Pretrial diversion. A decision of a district or county attorney's office not to file charges in a criminal case even though the charges would likely be provable. The decision is usually made on the condition that the defendant agree to participate in rehabilitative services.

Prima facie. "On the first appearance"; a term used to describe a fact presumed to be true unless it is disapproved.

Privileged communication. A disclosure made by a client to a professional, such as a psychologist, social worker, marriage and family counselor, attorney, clergyperson, psychiatrist, or other physician, that cannot be revealed during legal proceedings without the client's informed consent. See also *Confidentiality*.

Probable cause. Reasonable grounds, based on solid evidence, for the belief that an accused person should be subject to arrest or to the issuance of a warrant.

Probation. A sentencing alternative in which a convicted criminal defendant or a juvenile found to be delinquent is allowed to remain at liberty, generally under the supervision of a probation officer and under the threat of imprisonment if he or she fails to meet certain conditions.

Pro bono. "For the public good"; a term used to describe attorneys' or other professionals' services rendered at no charge.

Proceeding. Events comprising the process by which administrative or judicial action is initiated and resolved.

Proof beyond a reasonable doubt. Evidence that does not leave any significant doubt in the judge's or jury's mind as to the guilt of the accused. The judge or jury must be fully satisfied that the evidence is factual and that the facts proven establish guilt. This is the most stringent standard, which must be met in criminal cases to prove that the alleged offender violated the law.

Pro se. "For self"; a term used to describe representing oneself without assistance of legal counsel.

Prosecutor. Attorney for the local, state, or federal government in a criminal case.

Protection order. A court order generally issued in an emergency to protect a child from someone who might harm him or her.

Protective custody. Detainment of a child on an emergency basis until a written detention request can be filed; also known as *emergency custody*.

Psychological abuse. See *Emotional abuse*.

Psychological autopsy. A profile developed after an individual's death, from a retrospective analysis of the individual's writings and interviews with family members and friends.

Quash. To annul; to suppress—as, for example, a subpoena.

Quid pro quo. "Something for something." A *quid pro quo* exists when parties to a contract or agreement exchange something for something else.

Reasonable cause. Plausible suspicion that a crime is being committed or is being planned. This is a much lower standard than probable cause, the standard used in criminal matters. See also *Probable cause*.

Reasonable doubt. Doubt that would occur to a reasonable or prudent person. A judge or jury that has reasonable doubt must acquit a defendant.

Reasonable efforts. Plausible attempts by Child Protective Services or a similar agency to keep a family together or, if a child has already been removed, to reunite the family.

Reasonable medical judgment. A determination made by a prudent physician who is knowledgeable about the cause of an illness and its possible treatments.

Rebuttal. Refuting of statements made and evidence introduced; the stage of a trial during which such refuting is appropriate.

Recidivism. Repetition of a criminal act by the same offender.

Recommendation conference. A hearing at which a judge and attorneys review the recommendations of a custody evaluator and try to reach a settlement.

Records. Any written documents, audio or video recordings, or other tangible items that contain information related to a lawsuit.

Recross examination. Questioning of a witness by the party who previously cross examined the same witness.

Redirect examination. Questioning of a witness by the party who previously questioned the witness on direct examination.

Refreshing recollection. See *Refreshing the memory*.

Refreshing the memory. Reading documents in order to remember details related to one's testimony; also known as *refreshing recollection*.

Regulations. Rules of law created by government agencies (as opposed to statutes passed by state or federal legislatures).

Relevancy. The degree to which evidence addresses the issue before a court. Evidence not relevant to the issue before the court is usually not admissible.

Relief. A remedy requested by a plaintiff for some legal wrong. Relief is granted by a court or jury against a defendant. Examples include monetary damage, performance of a contractual obligation, a temporary restraining order, and a preliminary injunction.

Remand. An order from an appellate court sending a lawsuit back to a lower court with specific instructions on how to handle it.

Reporting laws. In cases of child maltreatment, laws that require specified categories of persons, such as professionals involved with children, to notify public authorities of cases of suspected child maltreatment. All 50 states have reporting laws.

Res ipsa loquitur. "The thing speaks for itself"; a legal doctrine, applicable to negligence law, under which no proof is needed other than the incident itself.

Respondent. The person who answers a petition.

Restraining order. A court order prohibiting a party from committing particular acts, either until a hearing can be held (temporary) or for a specific period of time.

Reversal. An appellate court's decision that the judgment of a lower court or other body should be set aside, vacated, or changed.

Review hearing. A hearing held in juvenile or family court (usually every 6 months) to reexamine earlier dispositions and determine whether to keep a child in out-of-home care and/or maintain the court's jurisdiction over the child.

Risk assessment. A process for determining whether a child is in danger of maltreatment and needs to be removed from the home or needs protective services. Risk assessment is usually done by Child Protective Services workers or law enforcement personnel.

Sanctions. Penalties imposed by a judge on witnesses who ignore a judge's orders to participate in the proceedings in an appropriate manner as dictated by law. Sanctions may include incarceration or a fine.

Sealing. In juvenile or criminal court practice, closing court records to inspection by all but the subject of the records.

Search warrant. A written order by a magistrate or a judge giving authorization to search a specific premise for specific items.

Sentencing. The last stage of criminal prosecution, in which a convicted defendant is imprisoned, fined, ordered to pay restitution, or granted a conditional release from custody. Sentencing is the equivalent of disposition in a juvenile case.

Settlement. Determination of a disputed matter by agreement of all parties. Settlement sometimes requires approval by the court, resulting in a court order outlining the parties' agreement.

Sexual abuse. Contacts or interactions between a child and an adult in which the adult uses the child for sexual stimulation and has power or control over the victim.

Sexual assault. Forcible sexual actions committed against a person's will; criminal sexual conduct.

Sexual exploitation. Involvement of children and adolescents in sexual activities that they do not usually fully comprehend, to which they are unable to give informed consent, and that violate social taboos.

Show cause. See *Order to show cause.*

Situational child abuse and neglect. A form of child maltreatment caused by problems over which the parents have little control, such as limited or no income.

Sodomy. Anal or oral intercourse between people or any sexual relations between a human being and an animal, punishable as a criminal offense.

Split custody. A custodial arrangement in which each parent has physical custody of at least one child of the marriage and specific visitation rights with the other child or children.

Standard of proof. See *Burden of proof.*

Stare decisis. "Let the decision stand"; the policy of the courts of following legal precedent.

Status offense. An action that is a crime only if the perpetrator is a minor. Examples are consumption of alcohol by a minor, underage driving, underage sexual activity, truancy, incorrigibility, and delinquency.

Statute. Law established by a legislature.

Statute of limitation. Time limit within which a lawsuit must be commenced.

Statutory laws. Written laws enacted by legislative bodies.

Statutory right. A right based on a statute passed by a unit of federal, state, or local government.

Stay. To stop, hold, or restrain; to suspend a case or part of it.

Stipulate. To agree.

Stipulation. A statement, either oral or written, that establishes certain facts agreed on by all parties in a court case.

Subpoena. A court order requiring a person to appear at a certain time to give testimony in a specified case. Failure to obey a subpoena may subject the person to contempt proceedings.

Subpoena duces tecum. "Under penalty you shall bring with you"; a court order requiring a person to bring specified records in her or his control or possession to the court.

Substantiated. Determined to be supported by credible evidence; also known as *founded.* An allegation of abuse or neglect may or may not be substantiated.

Substantive right. A right usually granted by statutes and constitutions.

Summary judgment. A decision made by a trial court based on written documentation submitted before any trial occurs. Summary judgments may be granted only when a case involves no genuine issues of material fact.

Summons. A document issued by a court clerk and usually delivered by a process server or law enforcement officer, notifying a person of the filing of a lawsuit against him or her and of the deadline for answering the suit.

Supervised visitation. An arrangement under which a court allows a parent to visit a child only in the presence of a designated third person.

Supra. "Before."

Tarasoff v. Regents of University of California [17 Cal.3d 425, 551 P.2d 334, 131 Cal. Rptr. 14 (1976)]. A landmark California case holding that a therapist is responsible for taking steps, such as warning others, to prevent his or her patient from harming another person.

Temporary restraining order (TRO). An emergency remedy of brief duration, issued by a court under exceptional circumstances, to protect a potential victim from the alleged behavior of another person until a hearing can be held on the matter.

Termination of parental rights. A formal judicial proceeding that permanently or indefinitely severs legal rights and responsibilities for a child. The parent's rights are no longer legally recognized, and the state assumes legal responsibility for the care and welfare of the child.

Testimony. Statements made by a witness, usually under oath in court. See also *Expert witness.*

Tort. Any legally recognized private injury or wrong, other than one that is litigated as a breach of contract.

Transcript. A verbatim copy of the record of a trial or hearing.

Transfer hearing. A hearing to decide whether a juvenile should be tried in an adult court; also called a *waiver hearing.*

Trial. A judicial examination and determination of issues of law and fact disputed by parties to a lawsuit.

Trial court. A local court that initially hears all cases in dispute. If an attorney or party believes that a trial court judge has exceeded judicial authority or inappropriately applied the law, an appeal can be made to an appeals court.

Undue influence. Any wrongful insistence, maneuvering, or threats used by one person to overpower another's free will and coerce him or her to perform acts against his or her own wishes.

Unsubstantiated. Determined not to be supported by credible evidence; also known as *unfounded.* In child maltreatment, any report of suspected abuse or neglect that the mandated agency is unable to confirm on investigation is deemed unsubstantiated.

Vacate. To rescind a decree or judgment.

Venue. The particular district, county, or state where a case may be heard and decided.

Verbatim. "Word for word; in the same words." The statements of sex offenders, sexual abuse victims, and principal parties must be recorded verbatim in order to avoid misunderstandings caused by interpretations that change the facts.

Verdict. A decision by a judge or jury in favor of one side or the other in a case.

Verification of maltreatment. A finding that maltreatment occurred, following an investigation of a suspected case by mandated agency workers or law enforcement officers.

Voir dire. "To speak the truth"; the procedure whereby attorneys question prospective jurors to determine their biases, competencies, and interests; the procedure whereby the court or attorneys question witnesses regarding their interests and qualifications before they give testimony.

Volitional insanity defense. See *Irresistible impulse rule.*

Voluntary placement. The voluntary relinquishing of custody of a child by a parent without a formal court proceeding.

Waiver. An intentional and voluntary relinquishment of a known right.

Wanton. With reckless disregard for consequences and the safety and welfare of others; malicious or immoral; undisciplined, unruly, or unjustified.

Ward of the court. A person (such as a minor child or someone who is psychotic) who, by reason of incapacity, is under protection of a court, either directly or through a court-appointed guardian.

Warrant. A document issued by a judge, authorizing a peace officer to arrest or detain a person or search a place and seize specified items.

Witness. A person whose declaration under oath is received as evidence. See also *Expert witness.*

Writ. A court order requiring performance of a specified act.

Ability testing. The use of a standardized test to evaluate an individual's current performance in a defined domain of cognitive, psychomotor, or physical functioning.

Accommodations. Modifications in the way assessments are designed or administered, to permit their use with students with disabilities.

Achievement test. A test that measures educationally relevant skills or knowledge in a subject such as reading, writing, or mathematics.

Adaptive testing. A sequential form of individual testing in which successive test items are chosen based both on their psychometric properties and content and on the individual's responses to previous items.

Age-equivalent score. A score reflecting the age group in the standardization sample that obtained the same average raw score (also known as *test age* or *age equivalent*). Thus, if individuals 10 years, 6 months of age have an average raw score of 17 on a test, a person with a raw score of 17 is said to have an age-equivalent score of 10-6.

Age norm. A value representing the average performance of individuals in an age group.

Age-scale format. A test design in which norms (expressed in units of years and months) are used to evaluate an individual's performance and scores are expressed in units of age.

Alternate forms. Two (or more) forms of a test with different items that are considered interchangeable in that they measure the same constructs, are intended for the same purposes, and are administered using the same directions.

Alternate forms reliability. The degree to which two (or more) forms of a test, designed to meet the same item specifications, have similar means and variances and are correlated (also referred to as *parallel forms reliability* or *equivalent forms reliability*).

Alternative assessment. Assessment based on an examination of an individual's performance, through such means as journals, portfolios, demonstrations, and investigations (also referred to as *authentic assessment* or *performance assessment*). Alternative assessment requires individuals to actively accomplish tasks, bringing to bear prior knowledge, recent learning, and relevant skills to solve problems.

Aptitude test. A standardized measure of an individual's ability to profit from further training or experience in an occupation or skill.

Arithmetic mean. A measure of the average or central tendency of a group of scores, computed by dividing the sum of the scores by the number of scores.

Assessment. Any systematic method of obtaining evidence from tests, examinations, questionnaires, surveys, and other sources in order to draw inferences about characteristics of people or groups.

Attenuation. A decrease in the magnitude of the correlation between two measures, such as a test and a criterion measure, caused by unreliability in the measures.

Authentic assessment. See *Alternative assessment.*

Average. A statistic that indicates the central tendency or most typical score of a group of scores. Most often, average refers to the arithmetic mean, which is the sum of a set of scores divided by the number of scores in the set.

Basal level. The level on an ability test at which an individual passes all (or most) items.

Base rate. The rate at which a condition exists in the population prior to any treatment.

Battery. A group of tests administered to an individual or group.

Benchmark. A standard (or specific level of performance) against which an individual's performance is measured.

Bias. Any one of several factors that lead to inaccurate scores.

Biased sample. A sample that gives a distorted picture of a group.

Bimodal distribution. A frequency distribution with two modes reflecting equal or nearly equal frequencies.

Biserial correlation coefficient (r_b). A correlation coefficient that measures the relationship between a dichotomous variable (i.e., one that has only two possible values, such as 1 or 0) and a continuous variable (i.e., one that has an infinite number of possible values, such as 51, 52, 53, . . .).

Bivariate analysis. Statistical analysis of the relationship between two variables.

Breadth. The comprehensiveness of the content of a measure.

Ceiling. The highest score attainable on a test. A test with a low ceiling does not have a sufficient number of difficult items.

Classical test theory. The view that an individual's observed score on a test is the sum of a true score component plus an independent measurement error component.

Closed-ended question. A question that requires an individual to choose one of several possible responses given by the examiner or interviewer.

Coefficient alpha (α). An internal consistency reliability coefficient based on the number of parts into which a test is partitioned (e.g., items, subtests, or raters), the interrelationships of the parts, and the total test score variance (also called *Cronbach's coefficient alpha* or, for dichotomous items, *KR-20*).

Coefficient of determination (r^2). The square of the correlation coefficient showing the strength of association between two variables. It indicates the amount of the variance in one variable that can be predicted or explained by the other variable.

Coefficient of equivalence. The type of reliability coefficient obtained when parallel forms of the same test are administered to the same individuals.

Coefficient of stability. See *Test-retest reliability coefficient.*

Cohen's *d*. A measure of effect size, computed by obtaining the difference between two means divided by the standard deviation. See also *Effect size.*

Cohort. Any group of people with a common classification or characteristic.

Common factor. In factor analysis, a factor on which two or more variables load.

Common variance. Variation shared between two or more tests.

Communality (h^2). The proportion of a variable's variability accounted for by common variance; reliability minus specificity.

Composite score. A score calculated by combining two or more scores.

Concurrent validity. The degree to which results of a test correlate with those of other similar tests taken at the same time.

Confidence interval. A band or range of scores around an individual's obtained score that likely includes the individual's true score.

Confidence level. A statistical "degree of certainty" (e.g., 68, 95, or 99 percent) indicating the probability that an obtained value represents the population (or true) value.

Confirmatory factor analysis. A factor analysis performed for the purpose of confirming an established theory.

Confounding variable. An extraneous variable that was not controlled for, causing a particular "confounded" result to be observed. For example, if investigators found a positive relationship between children's weight and a country's gross domestic product over time and concluded that a higher gross domestic product caused weight gain in children, they would be ignoring the confounding variable of time, which is the real cause of both gains in weight and gains in gross domestic product.

Construct. The complex idea or concept, synthesized from simpler ideas, that a test is designed to measure.

Construct domain. The set of interrelated attributes (e.g., behaviors, attitudes, values) included in a construct.

Construct validity. The degree to which a test measures a specified psychological construct or trait.

Content analysis. A systematic, objective, and quantitative method of studying and analyzing a test's content or an individual's communication, in order to measure the frequency with which certain terms, ideas, or emotions are expressed.

Content domain. The set of behaviors, knowledge, skills, abilities, attitudes, and/or other characteristics measured by a test.

Content validity. The degree to which a test measures what it is supposed to measure.

Continuous variables. Variables (e.g., temperature, age, height) characterized by an infinite number of possible values.

Control group. A group of participants in an experiment that is comparable to the experimental group, except that it is not given the treatment or otherwise exposed to the independent variable.

Convergent validity. The degree to which measures of the same domain in different formats correlate positively.

Correction for attenuation. A correction that results in an estimate of what the correlation between two variables would be if both variables were perfectly reliable.

Correlation coefficient (*r*). An index of the strength and direction of the relationship between two variables.

Criterion. A standard against which a test may be validated.

Criterion-referenced test. A test designed to measure how well a learner has mastered a specific skill.

Criterion-related validity. The degree to which test scores and some type of criterion or outcome (such as ratings, classifications, or other test scores) correlate positively.

Cronbach's coefficient alpha. See *Coefficient alpha*.

Cross-validation. Assessment of the validity of a model by applying it to new data.

Curvilinear relationship. A relationship between two variables that can be portrayed better by a curve than by a straight line.

Cut-off score. A point on a scale at or above which scores are interpreted differently than they are below that point.

Database. A collection of data.

Data matrix. A rectangular arrangement of raw data on *n* cases over *m* variables. Most commonly, rows are used for the cases and columns for the variables.

Dependent variable. A measure of behavior that the experimenter observes but does not manipulate or control.

Derived score. A score resulting from the conversion of a raw score to a percentile rank, standard score, or other type of score.

Descriptive statistics. Statistics that summarize data obtained about a sample of individuals.

Deviation from the mean. The distance of a single score from the mean of the distribution from which the score was derived.

Deviation score. The difference between the mean of a distribution and an individual score in that distribution. Deviation scores are always found by subtracting the mean from the score; a positive value indicates a score above the mean, and a negative value indicates a score below the mean.

Diagnostic test. An achievement test composed of items in a number of subject areas and designed to diagnose an individual's relative strengths and weaknesses in those areas.

Dichotomous variable. A variable that can have only one of two values.

Difference score. The difference between a score on a test and a score on another administration of the same test or an equivalent test.

Differential item functioning (DIF). A statistical procedure that reveals whether test items function differently in different groups.

Differential validity. The degree to which a test predicts one criterion better than another criterion.

Difficulty index. The proportion or percentage of individuals passing a given test item. The larger the index, the easier the item is.

Discrete variables. Variables (e.g., gender, color, number of children in a family) characterized by separate, indivisible categories, with no intermediate values.

Discriminant validity. The extent to which measures of performance in different domains do not correlate with each other.

Discrimination index. An index that indicates how well an item discriminates between low and high scores on some criterion.

Dispersion. The variability of scores in a set or distribution of scores.

Distracter. An answer to a multiple-choice test item that is not the correct answer.

Distribution. A tabulation of scores that shows the frequency of each score.

Divergent validity. See *Discriminant validity*.

Documentation. The body of literature (test manuals, manual supplements, research reports, user's guides, etc.) made available by publishers and test authors to support test use.

Domain-referenced test. A test designed to measure a well-defined set of tasks or a body of knowledge.

Domain sampling. The process of selecting test items to represent a specified domain of performance.

Double-barreled question. A question that combines two or more issues.

Ecological validity. The extent to which assessment findings generalize to behaviors that occur in natural settings.

Effect size. A statistical index often based on standard deviation units, independent of sample size; often used to evaluate the strength of a relationship between variables in a study.

Eigenvalue. The variance in a set of variables explained by a factor or component; the sum of squared values in the column of a factor matrix, denoted by λ (lambda).

Empirical keying. Using empirical relationships between individual test items and the criterion of interest as the basis for test scoring. Items are weighted according to an external criterion, such as responses of people who belong to a certain group.

Equity. Freedom from bias or favoritism.

Equivalent forms reliability. See *Alternate forms reliability*.

Error of measurement. The difference between an observed score and the corresponding true score.

Error score. The score associated with the unreliability of a test.

Error variance. The proportion of variance attributable to random error, such as sampling error or experimental error. In factor analysis, error variance is assumed to be independent of common variance; it is a component of a variable's unique variance.

Examiner reliability. See *Interrater reliability.*

Exploratory factor analysis. Factor analysis used to explore the underlying structure of a collection of variables, when there are no a priori hypotheses about the factor structure.

Extrapolation. The process of extending norms to scores not actually obtained by the standardization sample.

Face validity. The extent to which test items appear to measure what the test is supposed to measure.

Factor. In factor analysis, a statistically derived, hypothetical dimension that accounts for part of the intercorrelation among tests.

Factor analysis. A statistical technique used to explain the pattern of intercorrelations among a set of variables by deriving the smallest number of meaningful variables or factors.

Factor loadings. The factor pattern coefficients or structure coefficients in a factor analysis.

Factor matrix. A matrix of coefficients in which the factors are presented in the columns and the variables are presented in the rows.

Factor scores. Linear combinations of variables that represent factors.

Fairness. The extent to which the items on a test are a representative sample of what individuals have been exposed to.

First unrotated factor. In factor analysis, a general factor on which most variables have high loadings.

Five percent level. A statistical level indicating that the obtained results would be expected to occur 5 percent of the time or less by chance alone. It is a common threshold for statistical significance.

Floor. The lowest score attainable on a test.

Frequency distribution. The frequencies of occurrence of a set of scores, arranged from lowest to highest.

Functional equivalence. The degree to which a test translated into another language measures the same functions as the original test.

g. General intelligence.

Gaussian distribution. See *Normal distribution.*

General factor. A factor on which all the variables in a factor analysis load.

Grade-equivalent score. A score reflecting the grade at which students in the standardization sample obtained the same average raw score. Thus, if students at the middle of the 6th grade have an average raw score of 21 on a test, a person with a raw score of 21 is said to have a grade-equivalent score of 6.5.

Grade norm. A value representing the average performance of students in a given grade.

Group factor. In factor analysis, a factor present in more than one test in a set of tests but not present in all tests. Examples of group factors are verbal abilities, spatial abilities, memory abilities, and visual-motor abilities.

Group test. A test that may be administered to a number of individuals simultaneously.

High-stakes test. A test whose results have important, direct consequences for individuals, programs, or institutions involved in the testing.

Independent variable. A variable manipulated by the experimenter.

Individual test. A test that is administered to one individual at a time.

Inferential statistics. Statistics that permit one to make inferences about a population based on a sample of the population.

Informal test. A nonstandardized test designed to provide information about an individual's level of ability.

Internal consistency reliability. The degree to which the scores from a single test administration are consistent in their measurement.

Interpolation. The process of estimating a value between two given values or points.

Interrater reliability. The degree to which raters agree (also referred to as *examiner reliability* or *scorer reliability*).

Interval measurement scale. A scale that has equal intervals and an arbitrary zero point and that classifies and orders.

Inventory. A questionnaire designed to obtain information about one or more specific areas of interest.

Ipsative method. Comparison of an individual's responses on an assessment measure to other responses of that individual, rather than to the responses of other individuals.

Item. An individual question in a test.

Item analysis. A general term for procedures designed to assess the usefulness of test items. See also *Difficulty index, Discrimination index.*

Item characteristic curve (ICC). A line representing the relationship between the probability of passing an item and an individual's position on the construct being measured.

Item difficulty. See *Difficulty index.*

Item discrimination. See *Discrimination index.*

Item gradient. The ratio of raw score to standard score; the number of raw-score points required to earn one standard-score point.

Item pool. The aggregate of items from which test items are selected during test development.

Item response theory (IRT). A theory that provides useful information about the relationships between the attribute being measured and test responses through the use of three parameters: item discrimination, item difficulty, and a "guessing" parameter, which corresponds to the probability that a correct response will occur by chance (also known as the *latent trait model*).

Kuder-Richardson formula 20 (KR-20). A formula for estimating the internal consistency reliability of a test based on a single administration of the test. See *Coefficient alpha.*

Latent trait model. See *Item response theory.*

Latent variable. A theoretical variable hypothesized to influence a number of observed variables.

Leading question. A question that suggests a certain answer.

Likert scale. A scale designed to measure attitudes, usually with five or seven points (e.g., from "strongly agree" to "strongly disagree").

Linear equation. An equation describing a relationship between two variables that can be represented on a graph by a straight line.

Linear relationship. A relationship between two variables that can be represented on a graph by a straight line.

Loadings. See *Factor loadings*.

Local norms. Norms based on a local school or school system and used in place of or in addition to national norms.

Longitudinal study. A study in which data on the same group of individuals are collected repeatedly over a period of time.

Main diagonal. The elements in a square matrix running in a diagonal line from the upper left to the lower right corner. Communality estimates are inserted in the main diagonal of a correlation matrix when a factor analysis is performed. When a principal component analysis is performed, the main diagonal of the correlation matrix will contain 1s.

Mastery test. A test designed to indicate whether an individual has mastered some domain, knowledge, or skill.

Mean. See *Arithmetic mean*.

Measurement error variance. That portion of the observed score variance attributable to one or more sources of measurement error.

Measure of central tendency. A single score that in some way best describes the scores in a data set (e.g., the mean, the median, the mode).

Median. The middle point in a set of scores arranged in order of magnitude.

Meta-analysis. A procedure in which rigorous research techniques (including quantitative methods) are used to summarize a body of similar studies for the purpose of integrating their findings.

Midpoint of an interval. The value located halfway between the upper and lower limits of an interval.

Mode. The score that occurs most frequently in a set of scores.

Moderator variables. Variables, such as sex, age, race, social class, and personality characteristics, that affect the relationship (correlation) between two other variables.

Multi-factor test. An instrument that measures two or more constructs that are less than perfectly correlated.

Multiple-choice test. A test in which several possible answers are given and individuals select one.

Multiple correlation coefficient (*R*). A measure of the overall degree of relationship between several predictor variables and a single criterion variable. The coefficient may range from 0.00 to +1.00.

Multiple regression. A statistical technique that allows one to make predictions about performance on one variable or measure (called the *criterion variable*) based on performance on two or more other variables (called the *predictor variables*).

National norms. Norms based on a national sample.

Naturalistic observation. Observation conducted in a real-world setting such as a playground, classroom, job site, or home.

Negative correlation. A relationship in which scores on two variables move in opposite directions.

Nominal measurement scale. A scale consisting of a set of categories that do not have a sequential order and that are each identified by a name, number, or letter. The names, numbers, or letters are merely labels or classifications and usually represent mutually exclusive categories, which cannot be arranged in a meaningful order.

Normal curve. The bell-shaped curve that results when a normal frequency distribution is graphed.

Normal curve equivalents (NCEs). Standard scores with a mean of 50 and a standard deviation of approximately 21.

Normal distribution. A distribution of scores that forms a bell-shaped curve (also called a *Gaussian distribution*).

Normalized scores. Scores that have been transformed to approximate a normal distribution.

Norm-referenced measurement. A type of measurement in which an individual's performance is compared with the performance of a specific group of individuals, referred to as a *norm group* or a *standardization sample*.

Norms. The scores of a sample of individuals that provide the standards for interpreting test scores.

Objective test. A test that can be scored objectively because there is a definitive correct answer to each question.

Oblique factors. In factor analysis, correlated factors.

Oblique rotation. In factor analysis, a rotation in which the factor axes are allowed to form acute or obtuse angles so that the factors can be correlated and a second- or third-order factor extracted.

Obtained score. See *Raw score*.

Odd-even reliability. The correlation between scores on the odd-numbered items and the even-numbered items on a test, corrected by the Spearman-Brown reliability formula. See also *Split-half reliability*.

One percent level. A statistical level indicating that the obtained results would be expected to occur 1 percent of the time or less by chance alone.

Open-ended question. A question that allows individuals to respond in their own words.

Ordinal measurement scale. A scale that ranks or orders—for example, into first, second, etc.

Orthogonal factors. In factor analysis, uncorrelated factors.

Orthogonal rotation. In factor analysis, a rotation that maintains the independence of factors—the axes are at right angles and the factors are therefore uncorrelated.

Outlier. A number that deviates extremely from the other numbers in a distribution; an atypical number.

Parallel forms reliability. See *Alternate forms reliability*.

Partial correlation. The correlation between two variables when the influence of a third variable is removed.

Pearson product-moment correlation coefficient. The correlation coefficient suitable for continuous variables.

Percentage agreement. The percentage of items on which two or more raters give the identical rating to the behavior or criterion being judged.

Percentile. See *Percentile rank*.

Percentile band. A range of percentile ranks, each with a certain probability of containing an individual's true score on a test.

Percentile norms. Norms expressed in terms of the percentile standings of individuals on a test.

Percentile rank. A point in a distribution at or below which the scores of a given percentage of individuals fall.

Performance assessment. See *Alternative assessment*.

Performance test. A test composed of nonverbal items.

Personal documents. Anything written, photographed, or recorded by an individual.

Phi coefficient. A correlation coefficient suitable for two dichotomous variables.

Pilot test. A preliminary test administered to a representative sample of individuals to determine the test's properties.

Point-biserial coefficient. A correlation coefficient suitable for one dichotomous variable and one continuous variable.

Point-scale format. A test design in which each item is assigned a point value and the individual's performance is rated on the basis of the total number of points earned.

Population. A complete group or set of cases.

Portfolio assessment. An assessment of a collection of a student's work (usually classroom work).

Positive correlation. A relationship in which scores on two variables move in the same direction.

Power test. A test with ample time limits (as opposed to one that requires speed).

Practice effects. Effects, seen on retest, that are associated with having had previous experience taking the test.

Precision of measurement. A general term for a measure's reliability or its sensitivity to measurement error.

Predictive power. A special type of predictive validity that assesses the accuracy of decisions made on the basis of a given measure.

Predictive validity. The extent to which results from a test correlate with a criterion measure taken at a later time.

Premorbid level. The level at which a trait or an ability was present before an injury, disease, or disability.

Principal axes or factors. In factor analysis, the main factors obtained.

Principal components analysis (PCA). A method of factoring aimed at determining the set of factors that can account for all common and unique variance in a set of variables, without estimating communalities.

Principal factor analysis (PFA). A method of factoring aimed at determining the smallest set of factors that can account for the common variance in a set of variables, taking into account prior communality estimates.

Product-moment correlation coefficient. An index of the relationship between two variables.

Psychological assessment. The process of administering a psychological test, evaluating and integrating test results and collateral information, and writing a report.

Psychological testing. Any procedure that involves the use of tests or inventories to assess particular psychological constructs in an individual.

Psychometrics. The branch of psychology that deals with the design, administration, and interpretation of quantitative tests that measure psychological variables such as intelligence, aptitude, and personality traits.

Quartile. A percentile that is an even multiple of 25. The 25th percentile is the first quartile, the 50th percentile is the second quartile (as well as the median), and the 75th percentile is the third quartile.

Random error. Any unsystematic error; a quantity (often observed indirectly) that appears to have no relationship to any other variable.

Random sample. A sample in which every person in the sample had an equal chance of being selected for the sample.

Range. The difference between the highest and lowest scores in a distribution.

Rank-order correlation (ρ). A correlation suitable for ranked data (also referred to as *Spearman's rho*).

Rasch scaling. An item scaling method in which the probability of a correct response is assumed to depend on two independently estimated parameters: the extent to which the item elicits the latent trait and the degree to which the individual possesses the latent trait.

Rating scale. A scale used by a rater to estimate the magnitude of a trait or quality being rated.

Ratio IQ. An intelligence quotient obtained by dividing the mental age obtained on an intelligence test by the individual's chronological age and multiplying by 100.

Ratio measurement scale. A scale with a true zero point, equal intervals between adjacent units, and equality of ratios.

Raw score. The unconverted score on a test (e.g., the number of correct answers or the number of correct answers minus incorrect answers).

Reactivity. An alteration in performance that occurs when people are aware of participating in a study or of being observed.

Readiness test. A test that measures the extent to which an individual possesses the skills and knowledge necessary to learn a complex subject, such as reading or writing.

Reading age. A score that indicates an individual's reading ability in terms of the age of the group in the standardization sample at that level.

Recognition item. A test item that requires recognizing the correct answer in a list of possible answers.

Reference group. The norm group that serves as the comparison group for computing standard scores, percentile ranks, or related statistics.

Regression effect. Tendency for a retest score to be closer to the mean than the initial test score (also referred to as *regression artifact, regression to the mean,* or *statistical regression*).

Regression equation. An equation for predicting a score on one variable, given a score on another variable.

Reliability. The degree to which a test is consistent in its measurements. See also *Alternate forms reliability, Internal consistency reliability, Split-half reliability.*

Reliability coefficient. An index from .00 to 1.00 that expresses the degree of consistency in the measurement of test scores.

Representative sample. A group drawn from a population and considered sufficiently representative of that population that conclusions based on the group also will be valid for the population.

Response bias. See *Response set.*

Response set. The tendency to respond to test items in a specific way, regardless of the content of the items (also referred to as *response bias*). Examples are agreeing with items regardless of content and endorsing items because it is socially desirable to do so. Response sets tend to distort the validity of a measure.

Restriction of range. Reduction in the observed score variance of a sample.

Rotation of factors. In factor analysis, a transformation of the principal factors or components in order to approximate a simple structure.

Rotation of figures. Changing the orientation of figures such as designs or letters.

Sample. A subset of the population.

Sampling. The process of drawing a sample from a population.

Scale. A system for assigning values or scores to some measurable trait or characteristic.

Scaled score. A type of standard score earned on subtests within an ability test. Subtests typically have scaled scores with $M = 10$ and $SD = 3$.

Score. Any specific number resulting from the assessment of an individual.

Scorer reliability. See *Interrater reliability.*

Screening test. A test used to quickly and efficiently identify individuals who meet a certain criterion level.

Semi-interquartile range (Q). Half the distance between the first and third quartiles in a frequency distribution.

Significance. The likelihood that a result did not occur by chance or as a result of random factors alone.

Simple structure. In factor analysis, the set of factors, arrived at through rotation, that produces the simplest solution.

Skewness. The degree of asymmetry of a frequency distribution.

Social desirability response set. The tendency for an individual to provide answers that are socially desirable.

Spearman-Brown formula. See *Split-half reliability.*

Spearman's rho. See *Rank-order correlation.*

Special ability tests. Tests that measure special abilities, such as mechanical, clerical, musical, or artistic ability.

Specific factor. A factor on which only one variable loads.

Specificity. The proportion of a variable's variability accounted for by specific variance rather than measurement error or common factors.

Specific variance. Variance associated with a specific test, in contrast to the variance the test has in common with other tests; in factor analysis, the component of unique variance that is reliable but not explained by common factors.

Specimen set. A sample set of testing materials available from a commercial test publisher.

Split-half reliability. An internal consistency coefficient obtained by using half the items on a test to yield one score and the other half of the items to yield a second, independent score and then adjusting for length using the Spearman-Brown formula.

Spread. See *Dispersion.*

Stability coefficient. See *Test-retest reliability coefficient.*

Standard deviation. A measure of how much scores vary, or deviate, from the mean.

Standard error of estimate. A measure in a regression equation of the accuracy of an individual's predicted score.

Standard error of measurement. An estimate of the amount of error associated with an obtained score.

Standardization. Administering a test to a large, representative sample of people under standard conditions for the purpose of determining test norms.

Standardization sample. See *Norm-referenced measurement.*

Standardized test. A test, administered under standard conditions, that has norms and reliability and validity data.

Standard score. A raw score that has been transformed so that it has a predetermined mean and standard deviation. Standard scores express an individual's distance from the mean in terms of the standard deviation of the distribution. T scores, IQs, z scores, and stanines are all standard scores.

Stanine. A standard score on a scale consisting of the scores 1 through 9, with a mean of 5 and a standard deviation of 2.

Statistic. Any value that represents the end result of statistical manipulation of other values.

Statistical inference. The process of making use of information from a sample to draw conclusions or inferences about the population from which the sample was taken.

Statistical significance. See *Significance.*

Sten score. A linearly transformed standard score on a scale consisting of the scores 0 through 9, with a mean of 5.5 and a standard deviation of 2.

Stratified sample. A sample in which cases are selected so that they closely match the population in terms of some specified characteristics such as geographical region, community size, grade, age, sex, or ethnicity.

Systematic error. A component of a score not related to test performance.

Test age. See *Age-equivalent score.*

Test of significance. A statistical procedure that determines whether variations observed under various treatment conditions are due to changes in conditions or to chance fluctuations.

Test-retest reliability coefficient. A reliability coefficient obtained by administering the same test a second time to the same group after a time interval and correlating the two sets of scores (also called *coefficient of stability*).

Tetrachoric correlation. The correlation between two dichotomized measures. Computation is based on the assumption that the underlying variables are continuous and normally distributed.

Thurstone scale. An attitude scale consisting of several statements, each representing a different degree of favorableness or unfavorableness toward a topic, arranged to form a continuum with equally spaced levels.

Traits. Distinguishable, relatively enduring ways in which one individual differs from another.

True score. The hypothetical score that measures an individual's true knowledge of the test material. In test theory, an individual's true score on a test is the mean of the distribution of scores that would result if the individual took the test an infinite number of times.

True variance. That part of the difference in test scores that is due to true differences in the characteristics under consideration.

T score. A standard score with a mean of 50 and a standard deviation of 10.

Uniqueness. The proportion of a variable's variability that is not shared with a factor structure; 1 minus communality.

Unique variance. In factor analysis, the proportion of variance in a variable not explained by common factors. Unique variance is composed of specific variance and error variance.

Validation. The process of gathering evidence that supports inferences made on the basis of test scores.

Validity. The extent to which a test measures what it is intended to measure and, therefore, is appropriately used to make inferences.

Variability. The amount of dispersion in a set of scores.

Variable. A condition or characteristic that can take on different values or categories.

Variance. A measure of the amount of variability of scores around the mean—the greater the variability, the greater the variance.

Varimax rotation. In factor analysis, the orthogonal rotation that maximizes the variance of the squared elements in the columns of a factor matrix. Varimax is the most common rotational criterion. It produces factors that have the minimum correlation with one another.

Verbal test. A test in which the ability to understand and use words plays a crucial role in determining performance.

Weighted scoring. A method of scoring a test in which the number of points awarded for a correct response is not the same for all items on the test.

z score. A standard score with a mean of 0 and a standard deviation of 1.

REFERENCES

Albertsons v. Kirkingburg, 119 S. Ct. 2162 (1999), LEXIS 4369.

Armstrong, T. (1994). *Multiple intelligences in the classroom.* Alexandria, VA: Association for Supervision and Curriculum Development.

Board of Education v. Rowley, 458 U.S. 176 (1982), LEXIS 10.

Cedar Rapids Community School District v. Garret F., 119 S. Ct. 992 (1999), LEXIS 1709.

Davis, F. B. (1959). Interpretation of differences among averages and individual test scores. *Journal of Educational Psychology, 50,* 162–170.

DeBord v. Board of Education of the Ferguson-Florissant School District, 126 F.3d 1102 (8th Cir. 1997), LEXIS 27851.

Elliott, C. D. (2007). *Differential Ability Scales–Second Edition: Introductory and technical handbook.* San Antonio: Harcourt Assessment.

Federal Register. (1999, March 12). *Part II. Department of Education: 34 CFR Parts 300 and 303, Assistance to states for the education of children with disabilities and the early intervention program for infants and toddlers with disabilities; Final regulations.* Retrieved May 15, 1999, from http://frwebgate.access.gpo.gov/cgi-bin/getdoc.cgi?dbname=1999_register&docid=page+12405–12454.pdf

Federal Register. (2004, December 3). *Part C–Infants and toddlers with disabilities.* Retrieved November 12, 2006, from http://nichcy.org/reauth/PL108–446.pdf

Federal Register. (2006, August 14). *Part II. Department of Education: 34 CFR Parts 300 and 301, Assistance to states for the education of children with disabilities and preschool grants for children with disabilities; Final rule.* Retrieved September 20, 2006, from http://edocket.access.gpo.gov/2006/pdf/06–6656.pdf

Flanagan, D. P., McGrew, K. S., & Ortiz, S. O. (2000). *The Wechsler Intelligence Scales and Gf-Gc theory: A contemporary approach to interpretation.* Boston: Allyn & Bacon.

Hoekstra v. Independent School District, 103 F.3d 624 (8th Cir. 1996), LEXIS 33334.

Horn, J. L. (1987). A context for understanding information processing studies of human abilities. In P. A. Vernon (Ed.), *Speed of information-processing and intelligence* (pp. 201–238). Norwood, NJ: Ablex.

Horn, J. L. (1998). A basis for research on age differences in cognitive capabilities. In J. J. McArdle & R. W. Woodcock (Eds.), *Human cognitive abilities in theory and practice* (pp. 57–87). Mahwah, NJ: Erlbaum.

Keith, T. Z., Fine, J. G., Taub, G. E., Reynolds, M. R., & Kranzler, J. H. (2006). Higher order, multisample, confirmatory factor analysis of the Wechsler Intelligence Scale for Children–Fourth Edition: What does it measure? *School Psychology Review, 35,* 108–127.

L.B. & J.B. v. Nebo School District, 41 IDELR 206 (10th Cir. 2004).

LoBello, S. G., Thompson, A. P., & Evani, V. (1998). Supplementary WAIS–III tables for determining subtest strengths and weaknesses. *Journal of Psychoeducational Assessment, 16,* 196–200.

Muller v. Committee on Special Education of the East Islip Union Free School District, 145 F.3d 95 (2nd Cir. 1998), LEXIS 10313.

Murphy v. UPS, 119 S. Ct. 1331 (1999), LEXIS 2238.

NICHD Study of Early Child Care and Youth Development. (2000a). *Chapter 53: Third grade classroom observation: Qualitative.* Retrieved December 10, 2006, from http://secc.rti.org/display.cfm?t=m&i=Chapter_53_6

NICHD Study of Early Child Care and Youth Development. (2000b). *Chapter 73: Fifth grade classroom observation: Qualitative.* Retrieved December 10, 2006, from http://secc.rti.org/display.cfm?t=m&i=Chapter_73_6

Raven, J. C., & Summers, B. (1986). *Manual for Raven's Progressive Matrices and Vocabulary Scales–Research supplement no. 3.* London: Lewis.

Roid, G. H. (2003). *Stanford-Binet Intelligence Scales, Fifth Edition: Interpretive manual.* Itasca, IL: Riverside Publishing.

Saklofske, D. H., Prifitera, A., Weiss, L. G., Rolfhus, E., & Zhu, J. (2005). Clinical interpretation of the WISC–IV FSIQ and GAI. In A. Prifitera, D. H. Saklofske, & L. G. Weiss (Eds.), *WISC–IV clinical use and interpretation* (pp. 33–65). Burlington, MA: Elsevier Academic Press.

Schaffer v. Weast, 546 U.S. 49 (2005) 377 F.3d 449.

Silverstein, A. B. (1984). Pattern analysis: The question of abnormality. *Journal of Consulting and Clinical Psychology, 52,* 936–939.

Silverstein, A. B. (1989). Reliability and abnormality of scaled-score ranges. *Journal of Clinical Psychology, 45,* 926–929.

Sutton v. United Airlines, 119 S. Ct. 2139 (1999), LEXIS 4371.

Tellegen, A., & Briggs, P. F. (1967). Old wine in new skins: Grouping Wechsler subtests into new scales. *Journal of Consulting Psychology, 31,* 499–506.

Todd v. Elkins School District No. 10, 149 F.3d 1188 (8th Cir. 1998), LEXIS 22489.

Tulsky, D. S., Rolfhus, E. L., & Zhu, J. (2000). Two-tailed versus one-tailed base rates of discrepancy scores in the WAIS–III. *Clinical Neuropsychologist, 14,* 451–460.

W.B. v. Matula, 67 F.3d 484 (3rd Cir. 1995), LEXIS 28925.

Whitehead v. School Board of Hillsborough County, 918 F. Supp. 1515 (1996).